CAMBRIDGE STUDIES IN AMERICAN LITERATURE AND CULTURE

Penelope's Web

CAMBRIDGE STUDIES IN AMERICAN LITERATURE AND CULTURE

Editor
Albert Gelpi, Stanford University

Advisory Board

Nina Baym, University of Illinois, Champaign-Urbana
Sacvan Bercovitch, Harvard University
David Levin, University of Virginia
Joel Porte, Cornell University
Eric Sundquist, University of California, Berkeley
Tony Tanner, Cambridge University
Mike Weaver, Oxford University

Selected books in the series
Charles Altieri, *Painterly Abstraction in Modernist American Poetry*
Douglas Anderson, *A House Undivided*
Sacvan Bercovitch and Myra Jehlen (eds.), *Ideology and Classic American Literature**
Michael Davidson, *The San Francisco Renaissance*
George Dekker, *The American Historical Romance**
Stephen Fredman, *Poets' Prose*
Albert Gelpi (ed.), *Wallace Stevens**
Richard Godden, *Fictions of Capital*
Russell Goodman, *American Philosophy and the Romantic Tradition*
Richard Gray, *Writing the South**
Ezra Greenspan, *Walt Whitman and the American Reader*
Alfred Habegger, *Henry James and the "Woman Business"*
David Halliburton, *The Color of the Sky*
Susan K. Harris, *19th Century American Women's Novels*
Robert Lawson-Peebles, *Landscape and Written Expression in Revolutionary America*
Robert S. Levine, *Conspiracy and Romance*
John Limon, *The Place of Fiction in the Time of Science*
Susan Manning, *The Puritan-Provincial Vision*
John McWilliams, *The American Epic*
David Miller, *Dark Eden*
Michael Oriard, *Sporting with the Gods*
Tim Redman, *Ezra Pound and Italian Fascism*
Eric Sigg, *The American T.S. Eliot*
Brook Thomas, *Cross Examinations of Law and Literature**
David Wyatt, *The Fall into Eden*

See the back for a complete list of books in the series
*Published in hardback and paperback.

Penelope's Web

Gender, Modernity, H.D.'s Fiction

SUSAN STANFORD FRIEDMAN
University of Wisconsin at Madison

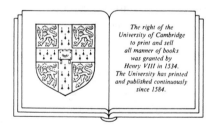

The right of the
University of Cambridge
to print and sell
all manner of books
was granted by
Henry VIII in 1534.
The University has printed
and published continuously
since 1584.

CAMBRIDGE UNIVERSITY PRESS

CAMBRIDGE

NEW YORK   PORT CHESTER   MELBOURNE   SYDNEY

Published by the Press Syndicate of the University of Cambridge
The Pitt Building, Trumpington Street, Cambridge CB2 IRP
40 West 20th Street, New York, NY 10011, USA
10 Stamford Road, Oakleigh, Melbourne 3166, Australia

© Cambridge University Press 1990

First published 1990

Printed in the United States of America

Library of Congress Cataloging-in-Publication Data
Friedman, Susan Stanford.
Penelope's web : gender, modernity, H.D. 's fiction / Susan
Stanford Friedman.
p.   cm. – (Cambridge studies in American literature and
culture)
Includes bibliographical references.
ISBN 0-521-25579-1
1. H.D. (Hilda Doolittle), 1886–1961 – Criticism and
interpretation.   2. Women and literature – United States–
History – 20th century.   3. Modernism (Literature) – United States.
4. Sex role in literature.   I. Title.   II. Series.
PS3507.0726Z65   1990
811'.52 – dc20   90–33126
                                                               CIP

British Library Cataloguing in Publication Data
Friedman, Susan Stanford
Penelope's web : gender, modernity, H.D.'s fiction. –
(Cambridge studies in American literature and culture)
1. English literature. American writers. H. D. Hilda
Doolittle 1886–1961
I. Title
818.5209

ISBN 0-521-25579-1 hardback

For
Edward Friedman,
my companion in this flame

I have tried to write of these experiences. In fact, it is the fear of losing them, forgetting them, or just giving them up as neurotic fantasies, residue of the war, confinement and the epidemic, that drives me on to begin again and again a fresh outline of the "novel." It is obviously Penelope's web that I am weaving.

H.D., *Advent*

Contents

Preface

Penelope's Web examines the weave of H.D.'s modernity as it is patterned
by gender, genre, and history in the discourse of her prose. In recent
years, H.D. has been read increasingly as a poet whose innovative lyrics
and magisterial epics contribute significantly to the remapping of modernism, of women's place within its theory and practice, and of a wom-
en's poetic tradition. H.D., however, worked as hard and consistently
at her prose as she did her poetry and produced an impressive oeuvre in
a variety of genres – novels, novellas, short stories, essays, and memoirs.
She saw only a fraction of this prose in print during her lifetime, most
of it privately printed and distributed mainly to friends and an avant-
garde network. This prose, much of it now published, was essential to
the development of her poetry. Moreover, many of the texts stand on
their own as brilliantly innovative and deserve to be read in the context
of the experimental writing of modernists like Virginia Woolf, James
Joyce, Gertrude Stein, and Dorothy Richardson.

    Penelope's Web offers such a reading, examining both the scope of
H.D.'s prose oeuvre and its specific achievement in a number of texts.
The book argues that H.D.'s poetic and prose texts exist in symbiotic
relationship, each constituted as distinct discourses that are nonetheless
necessary to each other. H.D.'s prose developed as a personal, narrative
discourse in opposition to the impersonal discourse of her early lyrics.
Impelled by the catastrophic events of history to reconstruct a shattered
self as a woman/writer, her fiction and personal essays were more directly
about gender, as well as a performance of it, than her early poetry.
Consequently, the prose was more experimental, more disruptive, more
distinctly feminized – in short, more disturbing – in its linguistic excesses,
its bisexual desire. So personal and radical was this prose in its critique
of culture that H.D. suppressed much of it, keeping it in a kind of limbo,
as work prepared for publication, but screened from the public eye. It
remained a kind of silent speech that represented her particular negoti-

ation as a woman writer in the male world of letters. Largely veiled, H.D.'s prose constituted a difference that made a difference to her subsequent poetic development, and that makes a difference to the tradition of women's prose and to the way we read women and modernity.

As such, H.D.'s prose anticipates much post-structuralist theory of the feminine, which in turn provides compelling interpretive tools for reading her texts, especially the work of Julia Kristeva, Hélène Cixous, and Luce Irigaray. However, *Penelope's Web* resists a reading of H.D.'s prose as illustrative praxis for the proof of post-structuralist theory. It argues instead for the double reference in H.D.'s writing: its simultaneous gestures toward "the real" of history (both personal and societal) and toward the intertextual mosaic of various literary languages. Although much of *Penelope's Web* was written before I read Nancy K. Miller's essay "Arachnology," the book is an attempt to perform what she calls an arachnological "reading for the signature." It sets out to locate and interpret the historical and material conditions that mark H.D.'s texts with the story of their production. It proposes as an inseparable part of that reference the narrative of H.D.'s self-conscious reading and rescripting of the cultural and literary texts in which she and other modernists were enmeshed. It assumes, in other words, that H.D., along with many other women writers, asserted an agency and identity made in and through language, one that she constituted in opposition to an ideology that would deny her the status of subject.

Penelope's Web has been a long time in the making. It reflects an expansion in my own education necessitated not only by the difference of H.D.'s prose, but also by the dramatic changes resulting from the introduction of post-structuralist theory into literary studies. In particular, contemporary theories of narrative and lyric, the self or subject, desire and gender, transference and resistance, autobiography, and (inter)textuality inform its feminist inquiry into the production, discourse, and reception of H.D.'s prose. This book does not, however, represent a conversion narrative, but rather reveals a dialogic play in its methodologies that refers back to my own alternating excitement with and resistance to post-structuralism, particularly post-structuralist feminism. The book reflects in many ways a self-conscious negotiation between post-structuralist and non-post-structuralist feminist discourses, between materialist and linguistic interpretive strategies. On the one hand, it owes a great deal to the rich insights about textuality, language, and desire that have been developed by post-structuralist theory. On the other hand, it reflects a strong suspicion of post-structuralism's tendency to stake its claim to radical critique solely on the terrain of the linguistic. However textualized, the historical and the political retain for me their existence in "the real," in the "experience" of writers who act, who make things happen through their writing, who have a reason to write beyond the pleasure of the play of empty signifiers.

The shape of *Penelope's Web* emerges out of the autobiographical project of H.D.'s prose discourse. The Introduction places H.D.'s prose oeuvre within the complex terrain of modernity, both as she herself formulated a modernist poetics and politics in texts like *Notes on Thought and Vision* and *Borderline,* and as we can interpret its Penelopean production, configuration, and reception. Chapter 1 examines the genesis and shape of H.D.'s prose discourse – its relation to her noms de plume; its origin, in the midst of World War I, in flight from the impersonal, timeless discourse of her imagist lyrics; its autobiographical telos; its poststructuralist stylistics. Chapters 2 through 5 present readings of the textualized selves H.D. constructed as she reflected on her various pasts in her prose fictions and memoirs. They follow the life cycle of created selves rather than the chronology of composition – beginning with her self-portrait of the young poet living in her parents' home and ending with the self she (re)made in the midst of the Battle of Britain by circling back to her beginnings in Bethlehem. Chapter 2 examines her portrait of artistic origins in *HER* as the formation and deformation of "H.D. Imagiste" within a bisexual economy of desire acted out before the flight to Europe in 1911. Chapter 3 reads the Madrigal cycle of novels about the young lover/wife/mother/poet caught in the grip of World War I. It treats *Paint It To-Day, Asphodel,* and *Bid Me To Live (A Madrigal)* as distinct layers in a composite "text" that is structured like a psyche, interpretable through the lens of psychoanalytic concepts such as the censor, the dream-work, transference, and working through. Chapter 4 charts the postwar borderline selves that H.D. constructed in her history novels and the Dijon fiction that ghosted for her life in the 1920s and early 1930s. It reads texts like *Palimpsest, Hedylus, Narthex, Kora and Ka,* and *Nights* as reconstructions of the increasingly split and bisexual self in exile from the maternal body. Chapter 5 looks at the death and rebirth of the self as narrated in her memoirs of analysis in the 1930s and World War II. Using psychoanalytic concepts of transference, resistance, and working through, it reads *Tribute to Freud, Advent, The Gift,* and H.D.'s letters to Winifred Bryher from Vienna as a palimpsest made up of distinct but interpenetrating layers that enact a "writing cure" that mirrors the scene of analysis. The Coda returns to the issue of difference by suggesting briefly the tracings of the same in the oppositional, yet symbiotic and ultimately intermingling, discourses of H.D.'s poetic and prose discourses. Throughout *Penelope's Web,* I have drawn heavily from the H.D. Papers, most of which are located at the Beinecke Rare Book and

Manuscript Library, Yale University. In quoting from her unpublished writings, I have retained her idiosyncratic spelling and corrected a few obvious typos with bracketed additions or silently deleted extra letters.

Complementing the text of *Penelope's Web* is a series of collages inspired by those in H.D.'s Scrapbook, a forty-page photo album kept up over a period of years from the 1920s until the mid-1930s. Encased in an elegantly tooled leather cover, the Scrapbook was probably collaboratively made by H.D., Bryher, Perdita, and Kenneth Macpherson. It includes a number of elaborately arranged collages and snapshots of people and images that meant a great deal to H.D. and her immediate family. The collages in *Penelope's Web*, some of which include images cut from the Scrapbook collages, are visual and narrative arrangements whose self-evident construction draws attention to the compositional nature of H.D.'s autobiographical, experimental writing. They honor the presence of collage in modernism itself, as well as in the traditional femmage of women's scrapbooks and needlework, from which so many of the innovations of modernism sprung. As palimpsests themselves, they are visual commentaries on key layers in *Penelope's Web*, strata that include, first, H.D. and those with whom she was most intimate from youth until the early 1940s; second, H.D.'s fictionalized constructions of her self and her companions; and third, the interpretations I offer of those texts in *Penelope's Web*.

Other illustrations for *Penelope's Web* include four reproductions of typescript and manuscript pages from *HER* and *Tribute to Freud*, chosen to reflect the processes of self-construction and self-censorship. Finally, the cover image was selected from Boccaccio's *De Claris Mulieribus* (1355–9) for its resonance with the title and argument of *Penelope's Web*. Boccaccio's idealization of "noble women," both historical and mythical whom he held up as models for contemporary women, is part of a pervasively androcentric perspective, which in turn inspired Christine de Pisan's *Book of the City of Ladies* (1405), a visionary vindication of women's nature and achievement. My use of Boccaccio's image is an appropriation made in the spirit of Christine de Pisan's *Book*.

Penelope's Web is a different book from its older companion, *Psyche Reborn: The Emergence of H.D.*, which appeared in 1981 and came out of my own formation as a feminist scholar in the 1970s. Reflecting its emergence in the 1980s, *Penelope's Web* owes as much to feminism as the earlier volume, but a feminism that has changed as it has become intellectually more complex, woven into multiplying discourses of the academy. If anything, my sense of commitment and participation in a collaborative deformation and reformation of knowledge with other feminists has intensified in the past decade. I felt quite lonely at times, in writing *Psyche Reborn,* needing to prove to everyone that H.D. was worth reading, intensely aware of my vulnerability as a feminist critic working at the margins of intellectual "respectability." In writing *Penelope's Web,* I have instead been overwhelmed at the wealth and richness and diversity of feminisms; I have recognized as well that the very success of feminist criticism has been complicated by its dialogic engagement with other discourses and by the politics of its position in the academy.

In particular, this book has been deeply influenced by an immediate audience of H.D. scholars from whose work I have learned a great deal. Rachel Blau DuPlessis, both in her friendship and her work, has been a brilliant teacher and probing listener, as well as partner, in the work on H.D. that we have done together. Albert Gelpi, Alicia Ostriker, and Adalaide Morris have offered striking commentaries on the book that have both sustained and enlightened me. In addition to these, a number of others have published valuable studies of one or another of H.D.'s prose texts – especially Deborah Kelly Kloepfer, Cassandra Laity, Diana Collecott, Jeanne Kerblat-Houghton, John Walsh, Perdita Schaffner, Linda Wagner-Martin, and Joseph Milicia. I am indebted to their readings as I have formulated my own. The biographies of H.D. by Barbara Guest and Janice S. Robinson have pushed me to sharpen my own interpretations of the vast archival material. Louis H. Silverstein, the brilliant cataloguer of the H.D. Papers at Beinecke Library, has been a constant resource who has helped me locate obscure manuscript material and make my biographical summaries more accurate. Robert Spoo was a great help in tracking the early publications of Frances Gregg. I have benefited greatly from the work of Eileen Gregory, whose leadership as the founding editor of the *H.D. Newsletter* has helped to create a community of readers, many others of whom have taught me much about reading H.D.

The University of Wisconsin at Madison has been a lively site for intellectual and personal growth. Judith Walzer Leavitt, Linda Gordon, Nellie Y. McKay, Ruth Bleier, Allen Hunter, Elaine Marks, and Lewis Leavitt have been particularly sustaining presences whose encouragements and challenges are woven deeply into the fabric of *Penelope's Web.* My husband, Edward Friedman, has provided the example in his own work of steadfast intellectual integrity and a probing originality always ahead of its time and far from the safer conventionalities of various prevailing bandwagons. My daughters Ruth Jennifer Friedman and Joanna Stanford Friedman have broadened my horizons as a mother as they have grown their separate ways into young women, thereby providing me with an experiential base out of which to generate the book's examination of mother–daughter psychodynamics. My colleagues in the English Department's Draft Group offered critically important reactions to and suggestions for Chapter 1: I am especially indebted to Cyrena N.

Pondrom, Jay Clayton, Jeffrey Steele, Leah Marcus, Tilottama Rajan, Eric Rothstein, William L. Andrews, Phillip Herring, Carol Pasternak, Betsy Draine, Michael Hinden, Thomas H. Schaub, and Gordon Hutner. As a distant but "honorary" member of the Draft Group, Robert Caserio provided me with a rigorous critique of Chapter 1. Various research assistants who have helped me track down resources in the library for this and other related projects include Elizabeth T. Black, Biddy Martin, Kathy Cummings, Elizabeth A. Hirsch, Wendy McGown, Thomas Jackson, and Aswhin Bhouraskar. Their creative diligence has been invaluable. Beyond my Madison network has been a community of friends whose ideas have challenged my own to emerge, whose conversations and letters have been much-needed support. I am particularly grateful to Margaret Homans, Jane Marcus, Carolyn Heilbrun, Celeste Schenck, Marilyn Brownstein, Joseph Boone, Christine Froula, Shari Benstock, Martha Nell Smith, Louis L. Martz, and Susan Howe.

Grants from the National Endowment for the Humanities, the American Psychoanalytic Association, and the Graduate School of the University of Wisconsin at Madison have greatly facilitated my research. Moreover, my exchanges with the Wisconsin Psychoanalytic Study Group and the Chicago Institute for Psychoanalysis greatly influenced my consideration of the psychodynamics of the analytic scene. I am, in particular, indebted to Joseph G. Kepecs, Mark Trewartha, Brooks Brenneis, Thomas Ewens, George H. Pollock, and George Moraitis. I am grateful as well for all the help I received at Beinecke – especially from the curators, David Schoonover and Patricia Willis, and from the library's staff, particularly Louis Silverstein, Steve Jones, and Aldo Cupo. For much-needed encouragement and advice for my collages and illustrations, I must thank Laurie Beth Clark, Lewis Leavitt, Judith Walzer Leavitt, Bacia Edelman, Melanie Herzog, and Rachel Blau DuPlessis. H.D.'s friends, Silvia Dobson and Erich Heydt, have been an invaluable source of insight and encouragement.

Perdita Schaffner has been a stunningly wise and kind literary executor of H.D.'s estate – ever willing to provide help and encouragement, ever generous in her written and oral remembrances of things past, reconciled enough to its difficulties to let a hundred flowers of opinion bloom in the community of scholars rushing to write about her mother.

Madison, Wisconsin
July 1989

Acknowledgments

Quotations from the following sources are used by permission of New Directions Publishing Corp.: *The Collected Poems, 1912–1944* (copyright 1925 by Hilda Doolittle; copyright © 1944, 1945, 1959, 1969 by Norman Holmes Pearson; copyright © 1982 by the Estate of Hilda Doolittle; copyright © 1975, 1983 by Perdita Schaffner); *End to Torment* (copyright © 1979 by New Directions Library Publishing Corp.); *The Gift* (copyright © 1959, 1982 by the Estate of Hilda Doolittle); *Helen in Egypt* (copyright © 1961 by Norman Holmes Pearson); *HERmione* (copyright © 1981 by the Estate of Hilda Doolittle); *Hermetic Definition* (copyright © 1958, 1959, 1961, 1969, 1972 by Norman Holmes Pearson); *Nights* (copyright © 1986 by Perdita Schaffner); *Tribute to Freud* (copyright © 1956, 1974 by Norman Holmes Pearson).

Quotations from the following sources are used by permission of New Directions Publishing Corp., agents for Perdita Schaffner: *Bid Me to Live (A Madrigal)* (copyright © 1960 by Norman Holmes Pearson); *Hedylus* (copyright © 1925, 1980 by the Estate of Hilda Doolittle); *Hippolytus Temporizes* (copyright © 1925 by Hilda Aldington; copyright © 1985 by Perdita Schaffner).

All previously unpublished material is copyright © 1990 by Perdita Schaffner and used by permission of New Directions Publishing Corp., agents and the Collection of American Literature, Beinecke Rare Book and Manuscript Library, Yale University. All out-of-print material is used by permission of New Directions Publishing Corp., agents for Perdita Schaffner. Permission to quote from Perdita Schaffner's introductions to H.D.'s *Bid Me to Live (A Madrigal)*, *The Hedgehog*, and *Hedylus* is granted by Perdita Schaffner and New Directions Publishing Corp. Quotations from "Hilda's Book" by Ezra Pound (copyright © 1979 by the Trustees of the Ezra Pound Literary Property Trust) are used by permission of New Directions Publishing Corp.

Quotations from *Asphodel* (copyright © forthcoming by Perdita Schaffner) are used by permission of New Directions Publishing Corp., agents and Duke University Press, publisher. Quotations from *Notes on Thought and Vision* (copyright © 1982 by the Estate of Hilda Doolittle) are reprinted by permission of City Lights Books. Quotations from *Paint*

It To-Day (copyright © forthcoming by Perdita Schaffner) are reprinted by permission of New York University Press.

Quotations from the unpublished correspondence and notes in the H.D. Papers (H.D.'s letters to Havelock Ellis, Viola Jordan, Robert McAlmon, George Plank, Ezra Pound, Kenneth Macpherson, Winifred Bryher, and Norman Holmes Peason; letters to H.D. from Bryher, Robert Herring, Marianne Moore, Norman Holmes Pearson, and Edith Sitwell; Pearson's notes for an H.D. biography) are used by permission of Perdita Schaffner and the Collection of American Literature, Beinecke Rare Book and Manuscript Library, Yale University. Quotations from H.D.'s letters to John Cournos and Houghton Mifflin are used courtesy of Perdita Schaffner and the Houghton Library, Harvard University. Quotations from H.D.'s letters to Marianne Moore are used courtesy of Perdita Schaffner and the Rosenbach Foundation, Philadelphia, PA. Quotations from H.D.'s letters to Richard Aldington are used courtesy of Perdita Schaffner and the Morris Library, University of Southern Illinois. Quotation from H.D.'s letter to Conrad Aiken is used courtesy of Perdita Schaffner and the Huntington Library, Los Angeles, CA.

Photographs for the collages (of H.D., Bryher, Macpherson, Perdita, the Wolle and Doolittle families, Aldington, Cournos, and Brigit Patmore) and the facsimile reproductions of manuscript pages from *HER* and *Tribute to Freud* are used with permission granted courtesy of New Directions Publishing Corp., Perdita Schaffner, and the Yale Collection of American Literature, Beinecke Rare Book and Manuscript Library, Yale University. Photographs of Ezra Pound are used courtesy of Vanni Scheiwiller and Alvin Langdon Coburn. Photographs of Frances Gregg are used courtesy of Oliver Wilkinson. The photo of Warrington Crescent, London, is used courtesy of Bison Books Limited. The photo "After the Somme" is used courtesy of Lyn Mcdonald. The photo of D. H. Lawrence is used courtesy of Edward Westen. One photo of Bryher is used courtesy of Carl Van Vechten. One photo of Kenneth Macpherson is used courtesy of Kar-Seymour. One photo of H.D. is used by permission of the Man Ray Estate. The etching of Sigmund Freud and the photo of his books is used courtesy of Ferdinand Schmutzer, Ernst Freud, Lucie Freud, and Ilse Grubrich-Simitis. The photo of Freud's statue of Athena is used courtesy of the Freud Museum, London.

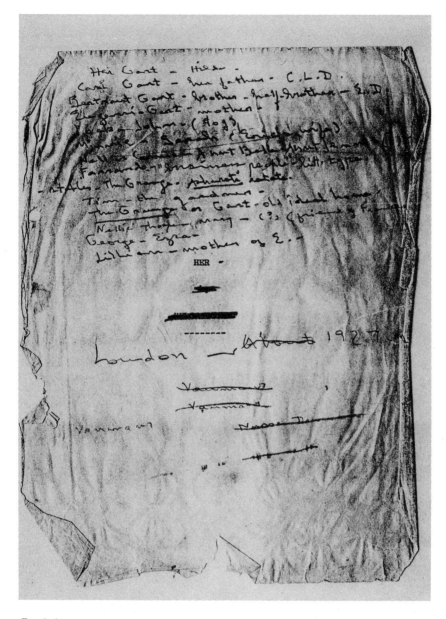

Frontispiece:
Dramatis Personae – Title Page of *HER*, with Pen Name Helga Doorn Crossed Out and "Actors" Penciled In

Introduction: The Double Weave of H.D.'s Prose Modernism

Penelope: The place of space, stasis, the chaste. The figure of home, the (loyal) body as home, the place of start and finish, the womb/tomb. Unnarratable, the space out of which narrative time emerges, to which it returns. The dutiful daughter-in-law whose weaving and unweaving of the father-in-law's shroud protects the husband's honor. The figure of Not-Helen, the wife as ever-there, never-lost (never-here/ever-lost) maternal body, the origin and end of adventure. A figment of fantasy. Of (men's) modernity.

For. Penelope is a weaver. She too is a trickster, *fabric*/ator, spinner of artifice. She too has a story to tell, woven into a weave of wiles. For her, home is not unnarratable, but the time and space of the going and coming of men – the absent husband, the growing son, the pressing suitors, the dying father-in-law. The loom (womb/tomb) is the scene of motion, constant; the site of production, the place of making, unmaking, and remaking the already narrated. Women's work, the space of women's repetitive time. A web of wiles, a ruse that conceals what it reveals in the discourse of (women's) modernity.

I. PENELOPE'S NOVEL MODERNITY

"It must be Penelope's web I'm weaving," H.D. wrote about "the novel" she was perpetually doing and undoing, the story of her woman/poethood in the modern world split open by war (*Advent* 153). This "novel" – not a single, but rather a composite, palimpsestic text – stands at the borderline between two Penelopes: Penelope as the nostalgic sign of WOMAN in the discourse of (masculine) modernity – the ever-faithful mother/wife lost to the new world of the modern; and Penelope as the weaver, a figure of agency, however circumscribed by the social order, in the production of her own survival. Ever aware of her position in men's texts as signifier of the desired, H.D.-as-Penelope wove herself into the design as another kind of signifi-er, that is, as *the one who signifies,*

I

who signs her own desire within and against an economy that would deny her that agency.[1]

To read the woven discourses of the two Penelopes in H.D.'s "novel," we must untangle the dialectical interplay between what Alice A. Jardine has called "gynesis" and what Nancy K. Miller has termed "arachnology." As gynesis, Penelope represents "the putting into discourse of 'woman' as that *process* diagnosed in France as intrinsic to the condition of modernity; indeed, the valorization of the feminine, woman . . . as somehow intrinsic to new and necessary modes of thinking, writing, speaking" (*Gynesis* 25). Within this linguistic economy of desire, Penelope is "the master narratives' own 'nonknowledge,' what has eluded them": "this other-than-themselves [that] is almost always a 'space' of some kind . . . coded as *feminine, as woman*" (25). Penelope, within Jardine's framework, is the written, not the writer; she represents the elusive, ever-deferred and deferring signifier that makes (male) texts possible and that gives modernity its special cachet.[2] As arachnology, Penelope is a woven text marked by "the grossly material, the sometimes brutal⁻ traces of the culture of gender; the inscriptions of its political structures" (*Subject* 84). A woman's text, within Miller's perspective, contains the marks of its "signature," the gendered subjectivity that wove it and the "political structures" of the historical moment that conditioned it. Reading woman's texts requires an "overreading," "which reads *against* the weave of indifferentiation to discover the embodiment in writing of a gendered subjectivity" (80). H.D.'s Penelope exercises her agency as weaver/writer within and against a tradition of letters in which she has been fixed as sign. It was for H.D., in the words of Rachel Blau DuPlessis, "the career of that struggle": "It was the struggle not to be reduced, to be neither muse nor poetess" ("Family" 145). "H.D., always," DuPlessis continued in *The Career of That Struggle*, "posited a speaking Otherness, not a silent one" (38).

The (en)gendering of modernism is a story with a number of intersecting narrative threads. Jardine theorized that (male) modernity posits WOMAN as signifier of its characteristic "epistemological crisis" of the subject, signification, language, and writing. Within this perspective, the feminine *(en)gendered* modernity. WOMAN, or the desire for her, fueled the process of modernist representation and marked its avant-garde forms. By itself, however, this gendered modernism leaves out the story of women-as-writers in its production. It leaves out, to echo Miller, the agency of women who wove their female signatures and the "political structures" of production into their modernist webs. Modernism was thus doubly and differently gendered: first, by the *absence* of the elusive WOMAN whose trace nonetheless governed the signifying process; and second, by the active *presence* of women as innovative and important figures in the formation of modernist poetics and practice. The interplay between the two generates the question of gender difference in the male- and female-authored texts of modernism. How do the writings of men and women in the modernist period resonate and dissonate? Where do they converge and diverge? Traditional histories of modernism – such canon-forming texts as Hugh Kenner's *The Pound Era* or, more recently, Frederick Karl's *Modern and Modernism* – narrate the story of modernism as if women existed primarily as mothers, wives, and lovers of men who were the significant agents of literary history. Revisionist examinations of modernism – such as DuPlessis's *Writing beyond the Ending: Narrative Strategies of Twentieth-Century Women Writers,* Sandra M. Gilbert's and Susan Gubar's three-volume *No Man's Land: The Place of the Woman Writer in the Twentieth Century,* or Bonnie Kime Scott's *The Gender of Modernism* – insert women as writers into literary history, an addition that ultimately transforms the terrain of modernism in its male as well as its female forms.[3]

Gendering modernism – reading gender in modernism – needs to weave together these different strands of how it was (en)gendered. The tendency in male modernism to fix women in the silent space of the feminine meant that many female modernists had to release themselves from this linguistic trap as the (pre)condition of their speech. Unweaving their textualization as WOMAN was inseparable from (re)weaving the story of their own subjectivity. Reading the gender in women's texts, consequently, often means reading intertextually, seeing what Roland Barthes called, in "The Death of the Author," "the multidimensional space in which a variety of writings... blend and clash" (*Image* 146). Barthes, as Miller pointed out, regarded intertextual space as "anonymous," a "tissue" of "quotation" without "filiation" or origin in "authors" (*Subject* 79–81).[4] But Miller's insistence on a "political intertextuality" provides us with a model for intertextual reading that does not erase the historical writer and the conditions of her writing (*Subject* 111). Reading the gendered strands of women's modernist texts means reading both with and against the grain of male texts. As DuPlessis defined the overdetermined intertextuality of women's reading/writing in "Language Acquisition," an essay on H.D.'s modernity:

> If a woman reads as she has been read, she will be limited.
>
> Reading the sign of the woman, reading signs generated around women, reading the presence of the sign, woman, in culture, means reading a situation of being read. A woman writer is never just written, she is read, as a woman. So, as a woman, she needs to originate her own reading. Her own methods. (267)

The story of filiation, however, is a multilayered set of relations, with same-sex as well as opposite-sex precursors, peers, and newcomers, as Gilbert and Gubar pointed out in *The War of the Words,* volume 1 of *No Man's Land.*[5] Myra Jehlen's advocacy of a feminist reading strategy that focuses entirely on the no man's land, the borderline of difference between men's and women's writing, excludes the equally significant intertextual dialogue among female texts in the production of a gendered modernism ("Archimedes"). Like many women modernists, H.D. engaged dramatically with the representations of WOMAN in the texts of the male modernists with whom she felt a particular affinity, writers such as Ezra Pound, D. H. Lawrence, Sigmund Freud, T. S. Eliot, James Joyce, and William Carlos Williams. But she also felt and inscribed an affiliation with many of the women who were caught in the same framework, modernists like Gertrude Stein, Virginia Woolf, Djuna Barnes, Marianne Moore, Dorothy Richardson, and May Sinclair. Male writers may have experienced themselves as individuals in the modernist period, but women writers have seldom had the luxury of forgetting their gender in a world of letters that fetishized or forgot them for it. Consequently, reading the gender of modernism, as Shari Benstock has pointed out in *Women of the Left Bank,* requires uncovering the forgotten network of relations among women and learning to hear the intertextual blend and clash on the borders between them.

H.D.'s prose occupies a different place from her poetry in the multiple weavings of gender in the (en)gendering of modernism. It is that difference, as it was formulated and performed in her prose texts, that is the main subject of this book. H.D. was, during her lifetime, and is today mainly identified as a poet. Her fictional self-portraits were always of poets: Ray Bart in *Palimpsest* and *Narthex;* Her Gart in *HER;* Hedylus in *Hedylus;* Julia Ashton in *Bid Me to Live (A Madrigal).* But her first publications were prose – short story sketches written some time after 1907 and published in newspapers between 1910 and 1913.[6] During the period when she was establishing herself as an imagist poet, from 1913 until 1916, she probably wrote little or no prose. But, for the rest of her life, she wrote prose – fiction, essays, memoirs, and journals – with as much passion and persistence as she did poetry. Since much of this prose remained in typescript until the 1970s and 1980s, few of her readers knew of its extent, even of its existence. She completed and prepared for publication thirteen full-length novels, for example, only three of which were published in her lifetime. The fiction that she called her "Dijon series" – five novellas and a sketch – was privately printed and distributed in editions of 100 by the same Dijon printer, Maurice Darantière, who produced Joyce's *Ulysses.* Of the eight memoir/journals she wrote, only one, *Tribute to Freud,* was published. *Notes on Thought and Vision,* the

first extended critical/personal essay she wrote, in 1919, remained unpublished until 1982. But she wrote several other such critical commentaries, a number of reviews, and ten essays on avant-garde cinema for
the journal *Close Up*. Some twenty-five stories remain unpublished, including a carefully put together selection she called *The Moment* and the
volume of fourteen sketches entitled *Within the Walls* written in the early
days of World War II that is currently in press.[7]

This extensive production of prose was highly unusual for a writer
who was primarily identified as a poet. Of the modernists, perhaps only
Lawrence and Stein balanced efforts in prose and poetry with as much
attention to each.[8] For H.D., this double discourse – this split between
poetry and prose and the symbiosis between them – was essential to the
formation of her modernism. As she reflected about the writing of her
verse drama, *Hippolytus Temporizes,* her poetry "was realizing a self, a
super-ego, if you will, that was an octave above my ordinary self"
represented in her prose (*Compassionate Friendship* 28). "I was working
at prose too," she continued, "there is a bridge needed, but possibly if
there had been the bridge, I would have worked at neither. *Palimpsest* is
what I am thinking of, published in 1926, in Paris. I must have been
working on the two, the poetry and the prose, at about the same time"
(28). Looking back in the memoir *Compassionate Friendship* on the decades
in which she produced prose and poetry "at about the same time," H.D.
asserted that the symbiotic separation of prose and poetry had made each
voice possible.

The formation, function, and form of difference between H.D.'s poetry and prose is the focus of Chapter 1. Suffice it to summarize here
that as she initiated the different discourses, her poetry was lyric, impersonal, and clairvoyant while her prose was narrative, personal, and
"ordinary." Of course, her novels were, like Woolf's, lyric and increasingly hermetic; her poetry, in turn, became increasingly narrative, even
personal, as *Trilogy, Helen in Egypt,* and *Hermetic Definition* demonstrate
vividly. But as *Compassionate Friendship* suggests, she needed to establish
the polarity in order to deconstruct it.

Barthes's contrast between prose and poetry in *Writing Degree Zero* is
instructive for H.D. He stressed that poetry and prose in the modern
period are "the product of a particular sensibility" and constitute "a
different language": "poetic language and prosaic language are sufficiently separate to be able to dispense with the very signs of their difference" (42–3). Poetry and prose may look more like one another in
modern literature, but they are fundamentally different discourses. Prose,
he argued, centers in a narration of the relational, the human, the ordered.
Poetry, he countered, is "inhuman," connecting the poet not to the
world, other people, or history, but to "Heaven, hell, holiness, child-

hood, madness, pure matter, etc." (50). Whereas the "Novel," like "History," relies on narration (29), "poetic speech [is] terrible and inhuman. It initiates a discourse full of gaps and full of lights, filled with absences and overnourishing signs, without foresight or stability of intentions, and thereby . . . opposed to the social function of language" (48–9). With all the "splendour and freshness of a dream language," modern poetry is a kind of "discontinuous speech," an "erect discourse . . . full of terror. . . . and a violent drive towards autonomy" (50–1).[9]

The way in which Barthes's binary does and does not apply to H.D. clarifies, on the one hand, the difference in her double discourse, and signals, on the other hand, the significance of gender for modernism. As in Barthes's formulation, prose and poetry were for her different languages emergent from different sensibilities. Poetry, at least during the 1910s and 1920s, was predominantly impersonal ("inhuman"), nonnarrative, a dream language that projected a "bridge to the sacred," as Adalaide Morris has written ("Projection" 416). Prose focused on the relational in history, the impulse in narrative to make sense of human relations in the "real" world of historical time. But Barthes's masculinization of modern poetic discourse (its erection, violence, and autonomy) does little more than articulate the phallocentric poetics within which H.D.-as-poet had to establish herself. Not "erect" or penile, her poetic discourse was nonetheless "hard," its vulnerabilities as a female voice deeply encoded beneath its crystalline surface. Like her nom de plume, H.D., gender in her early poetic discourse was suppressed – still there, but buried, screened. Her prose discourse, in contrast, as the language of history, unveiled the woman and directly narrated the story of her social relations in the world.

Precisely because H.D.'s prose discourse was relational, set in the narrative of history, it was more directly gendered than her poetic discourse. Her Penelope, it will be recalled, was weaving a *novel,* not a poem. Compared to the contained and ordered discourse of her early innovative poetry, her prose is the language of excess, of plentitude, leaking its feminine fluidity all over the surface of the text. Directly about her self as woman/poet in the world, her prose narrated the formation of a gendered subjectivity in an avant-garde language that anticipates post-structuralist experimentalism, especially as it overlaps with *écriture féminine.* Although theorists of post-structuralism often look to poetry as the privileged discourse of the avant garde, prose was for H.D. (especially in her fictions of the 1920s and 1930s) the discourse of disruption and the decentered self. Indeed, portions of Barthes's description of modern poetic discourse serve admirably for her prose: It was a form of "discontinuous speech," a "discourse full of gaps and full of lights, filled with absences and overnourishing signs, without foresight or stability of intentions," with all the "splendour and freshness of a dream language." Her prose experimentalism, written in "white ink," to echo Hélène Cixous's "The Laugh of the Medusa," in turn transformed the poetic discourse of the 1940s and 1950s into one that no longer veiled the woman.

H.D.'s prose, then, played a special and complex role in the (en)gendering of modernism. It provided the verbal space in which she could weave the voice and vision of a woman in the modern world. These experiments, in turn, fundamentally altered her poetry, which increasingly put into play the gendered subjectivity formulated in her prose. Written in the early 1950s, *Helen in Egypt,* for example, is a postmodern poem, "a discourse full of gaps and full of lights, filled with absences," a "discontinuous speech." Its postmodernist discourse was first formulated in the novels of the 1920s and 1930s and in the memoirs of the 1940s. Its implicit poetics had been verbalized in a series of little-known or unpublished prose texts written between 1913 and 1947.

II. FORMING A CRITICAL VOICE ON MODERNISM

Eliot, Pound, Woolf, Lawrence, and Stein (among others) published critical essays on literature and poetics that established them in the public eye as important articulators of modernity. In spite of H.D.'s leadership role in the imagist anthologies of 1915, 1916, and 1917 and as assistant editor of *The Egoist* in 1916–17, she appeared to be removed from theorizing about the modern and to be, instead, immersed in the production of her own version of it. This view is, however, only partially accurate. Although alienated from the theoretical posturings that produced vorticism, futurism, and such ventures as *Blast,* H.D. wrote prose during the 1910s from which the beginnings of a modernist poetic can be extracted. "The Suffragette," a narrative sketch probably written about 1913, is the first of these, and although it proposes no aesthetic, it centrally identifies feminism with the new age dawning in the prewar world. The brief narrative, which H.D. did not publish, retells the Jamesian story of American innocence coming to Europe. But instead of finding moral corruption fed by sexuality and greed, the young American girl meets a "new woman," a feminist organizer who convinces her to attend a suffragist meeting devoted to the victimization of working-class women. This organizer, a note on the manuscript says, was modeled on Dora Marsden, the British feminist and founder/editor of the journal *The Freewoman,* which became *The New Freewoman* in 1912 and then *The Egoist* in 1913. "The Suffragette" was probably written about the time *The New Freewoman* changed its name to *The Egoist,* and consequently inscribes the gender-inflected contradictions of the early Anglo-American modernist agenda. Pound had found in *The New Freewoman* a place from which to propound his theories and support avant-garde poetry. Ignoring Marsden's feminist editorials, he developed a new poetic within its pages and finally, in 1913, pushed successfully to change its name. As DuPlessis has pointed out, the name change was symptomatic of (male) modernism's resistance to the feminist project which formed a central part of its challenge to the "old" order ("Modernism").[10] Was H.D.'s socialist/feminist sketch an answer to this resistance? Did she intend to publish it in *The Egoist*? Was it rejected? Did she suppress it?

The fact that we can't answer these questions is emblematic of H.D.'s position as prose writer within modernism. She actually wrote far more prose, including critical essays, than was actually published. Was her prose censored by the men, like Pound, who nonetheless supported her poetry? Did she herself engage in self-censorship, suppressing what might not please? In assessing who should and should not be published in *The Little Review*, Pound wrote its editor, Margaret Anderson, in 1917: "H.D. is all right, but shouldn't write criticism" (*Selected Letters* 107). Pound's judgments were harsh on many, men as well as women. But did this view of modernism's tireless impresario have a chilling effect on H.D.'s criticism, particularly on her desire to define a modernist poetic in prose?

By 1917, H.D. had already published in *The Egoist*, during her stint as assistant editor, three critical reviews of modern poets: Marianne Moore, Charlotte Mew, and John Gould Fletcher. A fourth review, on W. B. Yeats's *Responsibilities*, was written, probably in 1916 or 1917, but left unpublished. The tone of these reviews – at times conversational, at times lyrical – is generous: out of step with the distant authority of Eliot or the abstract blasts of Wyndham Lewis, Filippo Marinetti, or Pound; but very much in tune with the persona that was becoming Woolf's trademark as "the common reader" in her critical essays. Praising aspects of the poetry with which she identified, H.D. defined her own aesthetic by describing the poetic of others. As Gary Burnett argued in "A Poetics out of War," these reviews establish an antimilitarist, antimechanistic poetic that opposes the celebration of violence and machines in vorticism and futurism. Poetry – represented by Moore, Mew, and Fletcher – is her avant garde against an aesthetic of militarism, patriotism, materialism, and nihilism.[11] During World War I, H.D. fought for a view of modernity based in the spirit, one that anticipated Woolf's vision in "Modern Fiction," "Mr. Bennett and Mrs. Brown," *Jacob's Room*, and *Mrs. Dalloway*. Like Woolf, she believed that the particular contradiction of modernity lay in the opposition of ephemeral moments of being and the engines of death epitomized by war. Fletcher's poetry "of suggestion" (not "of direct presentation") includes "the whirling of flowers, of boats, of the sea-water, of rain slanting and beating," but also "in grimmer moods," the "swirl of guns, cannon, terror, destruction" ("Review of

Goblins" 183–4). In the post-Romantic age of modernity, the poet is "the soul or mind or inspiration . . . knowing within itself its problems, unanswerable; its visions, cramped and stifled. . . . but flaunting in the face of its own ignorance, its own undaunted quest" (184).

The muted gender inflection of H.D.'s modernism in these reviews developed into a full-blown Eleusinian gynopoetic in *Notes on Thought and Vision,* a generic hybrid of personal meditation on creativity that she wrote in July, 1919, during a healing visit to the Scilly Isles with Bryher.[12] Motivated by what she called her "jelly-fish" and "bell-jar" experiences, H.D. wrote *Notes* to define the layers of consciousness that condition "the soul or mind or inspiration" of the poet and artist. *Notes* belongs alongside Lawrence's cultural/aesthetic treatises, hybrid essays such as *Study of Thomas Hardy* and *The Crown.* Like his, her tone is prophetic, addressing itself to the spiritually dead and embattled modern moment much in need of rebirth. Like Lawrence, she insisted that the reawakening of the spirit had to be based in the body. The intellect and the soul of the artist must, she insisted, be anchored in the material life and desire of the body. Unlike Lawrence, however, H.D. developed her model of awakening out of her postpartum experience, out of the specifically female body that gives birth.

The bell-jar experience in the Scilly Isles occurred about three months after H.D. miraculously survived the birth of her daughter Perdita while she had the war influenza. Her sensation of being suspended in a luminous globe of fluid recapitulated that birth, with herself as mother now in the position of her daughter. Having birthed a child, she herself becomes the fetus who will be born, with Bryher as mother/midwife/lover to the soul:

> We were in the little room that Bryher had taken for our study when I felt this impulse to "let go" into a sort of balloon or diving-bell, as I have explained it, that seemed to hover over me. . . . When I . . . told her [Bryher] it might be something sinister or dangerous, she said, "No, no, it is the most wonderful thing I ever heard of. Let it come." . . . There was, I explained to Bryher, a second globe or bell-jar rising as if it were from my feet. I was enclosed. I felt I was safe but seeing things as through water. I felt the double globe come and go and I could have dismissed it at once and probably would have if I had been alone. But it would not have happened, I imagine, if I had been alone. It was being with Bryher that projected the fantasy. . . . (*Advent* 130)

Notes, H.D. explained in *Advent,* is "a rough account of this singular adventure" (130), but not in any literal sense. Rather than narrating the experience (as *Advent* does), *Notes* projects the mother–daughter dyad of the bell-jar fantasy into the mysteries of Eleusis, which are held up as the model for fully integrated creativity.[13] "The new schools of destructive art theorists are on the wrong track," she wrote, with an oblique allusion to the "make it new" modernism of vorticism and futurism (24). Rejecting both the new modernism of violence and the old Judeo-Christian binaries of the body and soul, spirit and matter, she followed the path of the "Eleusinian mystic" initiated into the "mystery of Demeter, the Earth Mother" (52). In the Eleusinian mysteries, she reminded us, the initiate passed through three rooms representing the dimensions that must be experienced and integrated: the passion of the body; the detachment of the intellect; and the mystery of the spirit (29–30). Like Eleusinian mysticism, creativity of the highest order incorporates the body, the mind, and the spirit, to which she gave the name "over-mind" in the essay.

The over-mind is a state of consciousness to which she gained access through the body, specifically through the experience of pregnancy and childbirth. Defining the over-mind as a "jelly-fish consciousness" whose "feelers" reached down into the brain and the sexual/reproductive body, she described the state in terms that echo her globe experience in the Scilly Isles:

> If I could visualise or describe that over-mind in my own case, I should say this: it seems to me that a cap is over my head, a cap of consciousness over my head, my forehead, affecting a little my eyes. Sometimes when I am in that state of consciousness, things about me appear slightly blurred as if seen under water. . . .
>
> ————————
>
> That over-mind seems a cap, like water, transparent, fluid yet with definite body, contained in a definite space. It is like a closed sea-plant, jelly-fish or anemone.
> Into that over-mind, thoughts pass and are visible like fish swimming under clear water. (18–19)

The over-mind is imaged as an amniotic globe, the maternal body in which the poet is encased "like a foetus in the body" (19). The poet-as-fetus is in turn the enclosed sea in which her thoughts swim like fish. She is both contained and container, both inside and outside, child of the mother and mother to the poem, her child.[14] Recognizing that her images privilege the female procreative body, she asked: "Is it easier for a woman to attain this state of consciousness than for a man?" (20). The question remains unanswered as she noted that "For me, it was before the birth of my child that the jelly-fish consciousness seemed to come definitely into the field or realm of the intellect or brain" (20). Man's over-mind reaches down into his "love-region," she wrote, and, "My sign-posts are not yours" (24). *Notes* continues its exploration of the mysteries by examining the "love-mind" and the place of sexual ecstasy in the over-mind, open to men as well as women (22–3). But the essay's gynopoetic insistently returns with the reflection that "The majority of dream and of ordinary vision is vision of the womb. The brain and the womb are both centres of consciousness, equally important" (21).

The Eleusinian gynopoetic of *Notes* establishes a revelatory poetics akin to but different from Joycean epiphanies and Woolfian moments of being. Like both Joyce and Woolf, H.D. promoted a modernist poetic centered in heightened moments of consciousness in which the transcendent manifests in the garments of time. As in Joyce, her poetic involved the psychodynamics of desire. As in Woolf, her poetic was anchored in the maternal.[15] Written at about the same time as Woolf's essay "Modern Fiction," *Notes* advocates the kind of "spiritualism" that Woolf associated with the moderns like Joyce who had (according to Woolf) rejected the materialism of writing based in the external (*Common Reader* 153–5). "Life is not a series of gig lamps symmetrically arranged," according to Woolf, "but a luminous halo, a semi-transparent envelope surrounding us from the beginning of consciousness to the end" (*Common Reader* 154). Woolf's amniotic image for the "spirit" the moderns attempt to inscribe resonates vividly with H.D.'s gynopoetic. But, unlike Joyce and Woolf, H.D. formulated in *Notes* a revelatory poetic that directly writes the female body, female desire.

Notes on Thought and Vision not only defines a modernist gynopoetic; it also performs it. Some fifty years before Hélène Cixous and Luce Irigaray called for an *écriture féminine,* for women to *"parler femme,"* H.D. forged a prose discourse that wrote the female body and expanded the boundaries of the philosophical essay to inscribe it.[16] Highly experimental in form (much more so than Lawrence's prophetic essays), it weaves together the meditation with the essay, the parable with the prose poem, the aphorism with the prophecy, the autobiographical with the philosophical and religious. The text is a fabric of brief fragments, blocks loosely stitched by juxtaposition, interrupted by lines that join what they divide.[17] Riddled by gaps and fissures, the text riddles the reader with unanswered questions, Delphic enigmas, Taoist puzzles, Hebrew parables, Christian symbols, and precipitous leaps of fact, fantasy, and faith. Punctuated itself by the revelatory moments it defines, the text's structure is rhythmic, repetitive, multiorgasmic.

H.D. never published *Notes on Thought and Vision.* Any impact it might have had on the theorization of modernism was aborted by Havelock Ellis's negative response. As the distinguished essayist and sexologist most associated with "modern" ideas about the body in the early twentieth century, Ellis was the man to whom H.D. had turned eagerly for help during the traumatic months of her pregnancy, illness, and postpartum recovery. Much a member of her intimate circle in 1919 and 1920, Ellis accompanied H.D. and Bryher on their healing trip to Greece. But when H.D. showed him the manuscript of *Notes on Thought and*

Vision, he disapproved, much to her surprise and pain: "I thought he would be so interested. But he appeared unsympathetic. . . . It had really been a great shock to me as I had visualized Dr. Ellis, during the time of writing my *Notes on Thought and Vision,* as a saint as well as a savant" (*Advent* 130, 148). Perhaps because of his response and the authority with which she had invested him, H.D. left the manuscript unpublished and never again tried to write an essay like *Notes on Thought and Vision.*

But many of the ideas H.D. had formulated in *Notes* reappeared in different form when she became deeply involved in avant-garde cinema in the late 1920s and early 1930s.[18] The fragmentary flashes and radical juxtapositions in the visual surface of *Notes* anticipated the moving images of light – cut, edited, and joined according to the principles of montage – that fascinated her in the silent film, which she considered a major new art form and the most important innovation since the Renaissance. Quintessentially modern in its reliance on advanced technology to project flickering images of silent light, cinema was supremely able to render "psychic manifestations done with intricate but simple fade-outs or super-imposed impressions. Here the camera has it over all other mediums" ("Cinema and the Classics II" 35). Breaking down distinctions between "high" and "low" art, cinema is "a universal language, a universal art open alike to the pleb and the initiate" ("Conrad Veidt" 44). Seeing G. W. Pabst's *Joyless Street,* with Greta Garbo, was, she wrote in "Cinema and the Classics I," a revelatory experience signifying the potentiality of silent film and the essence of the modern in the postwar historical moment. Vienna, in the film, is a microcosm of postwar dispersion: "Before our eyes, the city was unfolded, like some blighted flower, like some modernized epic of Troy town is down, like some mournful and pitiful Babylon is fallen, is fallen. The true note was struck, the first postwar touch of authentic pathos" (28).

The ten review essays on cinema that she published in the journal *Close Up* between 1927 and 1929 forged the critical voice of a "common viewer" akin to Woolf's "common reader," one whose authority resided in her position as outsider. But, just as Woolf's essay persona obscured her critical expertise, so H.D.'s "common-viewer" stance screened her extensive involvement in cinema, which deeply influenced the direction and development of her gendered modernism. *Close Up,* the first theoretically sophisticated journal on film as an art, was founded, funded, and in fact (though not in name) coedited by Bryher from 1927 to 1933. Kenneth Macpherson – a talented Scotch artist, writer, and H.D.'s lover from about 1926 to 1928 – was the editor of *Close Up.* He also directed two short films featuring H.D., under the screen name Helga Doorn: *Wing Beat* (1927) and *Foothills* (1927–8), both of which have been lost. Pabst became an intimate friend, a member of H.D.'s circle, and a great supporter of Macpherson's work as a director and H.D.'s efforts as an actress. Swept up in the experience of being a (private) "star" fixed by the camera gaze of the director who was her lover, H.D. identified deeply with widely known stars of the avant-garde silver screen like Greta Garbo, Marlene Dietrich, and Elizabeth Bergner.[19] She jokingly signed some of her letters to friends during this period with a star under her name. But she also critiqued the transformation of brilliant actresses like Garbo into commodified stars ("Cinema and the Classics I"). As a "common" viewer resisting the star system and the elitism of the avant garde, H.D. wrote, "we are all 'stars'. . . . We want films of the people for the people, and this...and this...and this...BY the people" ("Russian Films" 27–8).

Engagement with a European avant garde matched an extensive, cross-Atlantic involvement in an American avant garde, specifically the art, music, writing, and politics of the Harlem Renaissance as it intersected with and influenced the white avant garde on both sides of the Atlantic. Through Macpherson and Robert Herring, another member of her intimate circle, H.D. followed with great fascination the interracial ferment centered in Harlem, Paris, and London. Herring introduced his friends to Paul and Eslanda Robeson, who became frequent guests and correspondents in the late 1920s and early 1930s. H.D. identified especially with Paul Robeson as an expatriate American who was free to practice his art only in the position of exile. The influences of the Harlem Renaissance and cinema coalesced in Macpherson's first and (as it turned out) only feature-length film, which starred both Robesons, H.D., and Bryher. *Borderline,* Paul Robeson's second experience on screen, appeared in 1930 to the acclaim of Pabst, the ambivalence of many reviewers, and the confusion of the general viewing audience. Impounded by U.S. Customs for its treatment of miscegenation, the film was not shown in the United States until 1978 (Friedberg, "Approaching *Borderline*").[20]

H.D.'s essays about cinema provided her with a screened arena in which to formulate her postwar perspective on modernism. Perhaps reflecting the impact of Ellis's stinging rejection, these essays abandon or suppress the direct and unabashed Eleusinian gynopoetic of *Notes on Thought and Vision,* based in her personal experience of body and soul, to focus on the modernist expressions of others. But they are, nonetheless, pervasively marked by the politics of gender, race, and, to a lesser extent, class. The concept of the modern that emerges from these essays focuses on the historical moment, the intersection of a modernist aesthetic with the blighted "lost generation," deeply scarred by the violence of a war in which all sides were losers. But this attention to the immediate era does not mean that she regarded the modern as an exclusively twentieth-century phenomenon. More in tune with Paul de Man's concept of "the modern" in *Blindness and Insight,* H.D. saw history as a cycle that periodically fostered the creative explosion of a "modern" sensibility, often produced by violent and anguished moments of severe cultural disruption and ferment. Thus the blight of *Joyless Street* recapitulates in historically specific terms the diaspora occurring after other falls – the destruction of Troy, of Babylon. Garbo is a modern Helen after the fall. The stark simplicity and harshness of Pabst's "true modernity" approaches the "chiselling and cutting" of "the pure classic" ("Cinema and the Classics II" 32–6).

For H.D., Carl Dreyer's silent masterpiece *The Passion and Death of a Saint* embodies this true modernity in representing another period of societal upheaval with the hard, clean lines of an absolute "simplicity." But her review demonstrates her ambivalence as a woman to the visual forms of male modernity in which the director invites the viewer to join in his gaze at female victimization. Positioned as a "common-woman" viewer both inside and outside male representations of woman, H.D. greatly admired the film, whose technique so mirrored the chiseled quality of her own imagist lyric. But she was also a "resisting" reader, deeply troubled by Dreyer's emphasis on Joan's victimization. Joan of Arc had been for H.D. a symbol of female difference and defiance associated with lesbianism in her earlier novel *Asphodel.* In seeing only her victimization, Dreyer made victims of his (female) viewers – "we are numb and beaten" ("Joan of Arc" 23). The film "bullied me as no film has yet done. I was forced to pity, pity, pity. . . . I was kicked. I was throttled. I was laid upon a torture rack. Quite solemnly I was burned at the stake" ("An Appreciation" 59). Implicitly, H.D. asked if the price of Dreyer's "incomparable" artistry is that women – as his objects or as viewers of his objects – must be bullied by modernity as Joan of Arc was bullied into submission.[21]

Twentieth-century forms of cinematic modernity meant, for H.D., coming to terms with the brilliance, passion, and politics of Russian film. Her review essay entitled "Russian Films" comments politically and radically on the current scenes of history in a way that defies the common association of her poetry with an escapist Hellenism.[22] Epical, Biblical, "Russian Film at the moment deals with hunger, with starvation, with murder, with oppression, with adultery, with incest, with infanticide, with childbirth, with the very throes of childbirth itself," she noted about films like Sergei Eisenstein's *Potemkin, Mother,* and *Ten Days That Shook the World* (18). Anticipating the fusion of the political and spiritual in contemporary black women writers like Alice Walker and Audre Lorde, she saw Russian film capturing in epic proportions the "spiritual hunger" in all people for justice and peace. She argued strongly for a revisionist history of "this so-called Great War," one that recognized the complicity of all sides. The modernity implicit in "Russian Films" is akin to the antinationalism and pacifism of Woolf's *Three Guineas*:

> We are no longer nations. We are or should be *a* nation. We all know everything about the so-called Great War, that A was base, that B was good, that C was heroic, that D lost some diplomatic papers, that E was really to blame, that it was all caused by F shooting G. We know that. We have witnessed it, died for it. Well, then let us shuffle the cards, get down and back to values. Say I *am* my brother's keeper, and if A suffers, B suffers. If C has smallpox, no doubt D will catch it and hand it on to E, and maybe F even.... For if one suffers, eventually the other must, and if one nation to-day befouls its own integrity and strikes blindly at a lesser nation, the whole world, willy (as they say) nilly must be sooner or later dragged into the fray. Men must fight, it is true just as women must have children. But don't let's fight if we must fight, blindly, let us *know* what it is all about.... One of the most distinguished women of the political non-militant suffragette period [probably Marsden] said to me (in 1914) "I have studied the problem from every angle, but I can dare not question our cause for going to war. If I questioned it for one moment, I should go mad." I did not say to her then, "well, go mad." I would now. (23–4)

H.D.'s essay on the film *Borderline*, published as an unsigned pamphlet to promote the film in 1930, represents the culmination of her cinematic essays on modernity. Its ostensible objective is to celebrate the genius of the film's director, Macpherson, and to situate him within the contemporary currents of what H.D. herself called modernism. But, like her essay on Pabst ("An Appreciation"), and later tributes to Freud in *Tribute to Freud* and Shakespeare in *By Avon River*, focus on another screens a major statement of her own views. In the guise of praising another, she formulated the vision and aesthetic of her own modernism.[23]

Borderline, both film and essay, articulates a modernism of the margins – one closer in spirit to the Society of Outsiders Woolf envisioned in *Three Guineas*, one different from the currents of Anglican Toryism in Eliot, elitism in Yeats, and fascism in Pound, Lawrence, and Wyndham Lewis. "Borderline" serves as a multifaceted metaphor for a geographical, psychological, historical, and moral state of mind H.D. associated with modernity. As Louis Martz has pointed out in his introduction to H.D.'s *Collected Poems*, the metaphor characterizes the psychological geography of H.D.'s poetry in general (*xi–xii*). But the multilayered discourse of borderlines in *Borderline* more specifically maps H.D.'s modernism as the experience of diaspora.[24] *Borderline* foregrounds race as an emblematic issue for the "lost generation" in the postwar world. As the pamphlet emphasizes, the film was a bold examination of a tabooed subject – interracial sex and violence. Two couples, one white and the other black, meet in the limbo of a Swiss village; the white man

(Thorne) makes love to the black woman (Adah), leaving the white woman (Astrid) enraged and the black man (Pete) humiliated. All four are "borderline social cases," but differently constructed by history:

> [The white lovers Thorne and Astrid] are borderline social cases, not out of life, not in life. . . . Thorne has not reached the end of his cravings, may step this side, that side of the border; Astrid, the white-cerebral is and is not outcast, is and is not a social alien, is and is not a normal human being, she is borderline. These two are specifically chosen to offset another borderline couple of more dominant integrity. These last, Pete and his sweetheart Adah, have a less intensive problem, but border; they dwell on the cosmic racial borderline. They are black people among white people.
>   . . . the everlasting black–white Problem with a capital . . . [means that] Pete and Adah must inevitably remain "borderline," whether by their own choice and psychic affiliation or through sheer crude brute causes. (29–30)

The elusive narrative of the film combines the explosive plot of a Eugene O'Neill or Faulkner text with the avant-garde formalism of German expressionism, G. W. Pabst's social realism, and Russian film. White abuse of two black human beings uncovers the disease of master–slave relations that has produced a generation of alienated, shattered, "borderline" personalities. Like the film, the essay does not shrink from the brutality of racism – indeed, H.D.'s character Astrid is the most racist; but it also emphasizes the fragile thread of connection between "borderline" blacks and whites. The director, too, as a manipulator of the "ultra-modern" cinematic techniques of superimposition, montage, and focalization, is "borderline." In his hands, film fosters identification with difference. She described how, for example, "In the little café through which Pete stalks and his mistress turns, gazing with great eyes at a vague conglomeration of whites, we have something of the nightmare that we would image [imagine?] a sensitive negro might have, on facing a room full of antagonistic presences" (45).

The essay *Borderline* uses the racial experience of marginality as a paradigm for the spiritual affliction of many postwar wanderers.[25] It formulates a modernist poetic in which race, gender, and politics thoroughly pervade the aesthetic, without reducing art to the ideologically didactic. And it prefigures H.D.'s later modernist identifications with other marginalized and persecuted groups in texts like *Tribute to Freud* and *The Gift*. "Perhaps dispersion is the key-word," she wrote about the diaspora of her companions; "We were dispersed and scattered after War I" (*H.D. by Delia Alton* 184). Working through issues of race in *Borderline* played a significant part in the development of her syncretist modernism of the margins. As an outsider herself, she identified with all the others who have been "dispersed and scattered" by the forces of history: blacks, Jews, American Indians, Moravians, homosexuals and lesbians, women, and even artists. "There is a legend," she recalled in relation to her own work, "of a Wandering Jew, of a Hidden Church, of an unrecognized Divinity or of a reviled Humanity" (*H.D. by Delia Alton* 189). These legends, not the totalizing mythos of the reactionary center, are part of what H.D. wove into the web of her modernity.

But, paradoxically, while the borderline metaphor for modernism reflects H.D.'s own gender-inflected position as an outsider, the essay does not promote the gynopoetics of *Notes on Thought and Vision*. Indeed, the extravagant celebration of Macpherson as the supreme example of "modernity," as an avatar of an earlier genius of modernity, Leonardo da Vinci, borrows masculinist and militarist discourse to highlight "the problem in every art period" to present "beauty in a form allied to its environment and its time" (35). Linguistically excluding women from the production of film, H.D. wrote: "An advanced and intellectual film-director must be mechanic, must be artist, must be man, must be warrior" (36). Watching him work with a camera was like "watching a young gunner alone with his machine gun" (34). Film is a medium dependent on the machine, which, in H.D.'s representation, takes on the qualities of "the lean skyscraper" of "ultra-modernity," of a steely phallus (37, 35). Instead of writing the female body as she did in *Notes on Thought and Vision*, H.D. appeared to promote in *Borderline* a modernity in which the phallus is the precondition and expression of creativity.

The essay *Borderline*, however, suppresses more than the gynopoetics of *Notes on Thought and Vision*; it also conceals the gender narratives woven into its very production. Thus, as a modernist poetic, it not only promotes a modernism of the margins, but it also enacts one. H.D. published the pamphlet anonymously, not to protect herself, but to push Macpherson into the limelight. Sixteen years younger than H.D., Macpherson was something of a talented drifter when H.D. met him in 1926. Catalyzed by her novel *Palimpsest,* he wrote a derivative novel about their affair (*Poolreflection*) and turned enthusiastically to film in 1927 with Bryher's gift of a camera. Both H.D. and Bryher believed in and nurtured his talent, even after he began pursuing liaisons with young black men in 1929. Supporting him emotionally and financially, they urged him to focus his talents and to pursue the film career Pabst offered. But, by 1930, Macpherson's creative drive began to dissipate, finally dissolving into neurosis by the early 1930s. As I will discuss in Chapter 4, H.D. was deeply hurt by this loss, and saddened as well by what she saw as Macpherson's abandonment of his creative daemon.

Within the context of its production, the pamphlet *Borderline* is something of a love letter to a lover already gone, one that projects the role of disciple/lover admiring the artistic genius of the director/beloved. In handing the torch of modernity to Macpherson, H.D. effaced her own role as catalyst and her achievement as the best-known and hardest-working artist in her immediate circle. This feminine narrative is symptomatically evident in her erasure of her role in producing the sophisticated montage of the film. The essay credits Macpherson entirely for the montage, with a bow to the "delicate" technical help provided by Bryher's brother. But in "Autobiographical Notes," a text probably written in 1949 to establish basic biographical "facts" for Norman Holmes Pearson, H.D. noted that, when Macpherson fell ill, she and Bryher did the entire montage for the film.[26] The film was certainly Macpherson's project, but, in loving its director, H.D. fell into the conventions of the romance plot, eager to enact the part of the hysterical woman, captured on screen by the camera gaze of the male director for whom she ostensibly served as the medium for his genius. The production of the essay *Borderline,* like its anonymous title page, enacts the marginalization that its own view of modernism theorizes.

Taking *Notes on Thought and Vision* and the *Borderline* pamphlet as exemplary signposts for H.D.'s theorizations of modernity, we are faced with the Penelopean contradictions with which this introduction began and which, in turn, H.D.'s autobiographical prose narrates. Within the framework of arachnology, H.D./Penelope in *Notes on Thought and Vision* is the weaver whose (pro)creative agency embodies a modernity to which women implicitly have privileged access. But within the framework of gynesis, H.D./Penelope in *Borderline* plays out the role of loyal wife whose artifice preserves her and ultimately provides the preconditions for male modernity. H.D.'s prose oeuvre is positioned at the borderline of these two Penelopes, two modernities. The contradictions and negotiations between them fuel the narrative line of her fictions and motivate the reflections of her personal essays, memoirs, and journals.

III. MAKING A DIFFERENCE: H.D.'S PROSE OEUVRE

In relation to H.D.'s better-known poetic oeuvre, the Penelopean web of her prose oeuvre occupies a liminal position, always already read as less significant, less visible, less perfect, less naturalizable within the conventions of male modernism. More is at stake here than aesthetic standards and value. H.D.'s prose has existed as uncertain shadow to the sculpted brilliance of her crystalline, prophetic poetry. In relation to the oeuvre of the male modernist poets with whom she had so much in common, H.D.'s poetry has been imperfectly seen, often trivialized and dismissed, especially as it became philosophically and linguistically more complex. With the advent of feminist/revisionist readings of modernism in recent years, however, this poetry has become more visible, has even been marked by the terms mainstream, major, magisterial, even though such judgments remain controversial.[27] Gender certainly marks this poetry profoundly and accounts partially for the history of its readings. But the shape of her poetic oeuvre—from innovative imagist to cosmic epic – tracks that of her male peers, especially Pound and Williams, the two Americans with whom she was intimate as a beginning writer. The developmental curve of H.D.'s poetry is naturalizable within many of the traditional categories of (male) modernism.

Not so, H.D.'s prose. In relation to her poetry and to modernism in general, H.D.'s prose is *outré*. Its shape is outside the patterns of conventional readability. Its confessional excesses stutter, start, and stop, often caught in the cycles of repetition, hesitation, and incompletion instead of the developmental pattern of conflict, resolution, and progression. "The novel" she perpetually wove, unwove, and rewove inscribes a feminine metanarrative. Its production, publication, and reception is the story of the borderlines, the threshold to what Elaine Showalter has called the "wild zone" and what Irigaray has posited as the "other" side of the mirror.[28] As H.D. wrote to H. P. Collins in a letter about her prose, "I seem a very between-worlds person" (13 May 1925). H.D.'s prose is a case history which invites transference in the scenes of writing and reading. It is also a case in point for the gendered history of modernism, for the situation of a woman who writes out of the position of the Other.

The history of the production and publication of H.D.'s prose synecdochically emblemizes the difficult position of the woman writer in relation to the male world of letters and the phallocentrism of its traditions. Whereas Penelope tropes the unending process of H.D.'s prose writing, the Pythoness of Delphi, whose cryptic utterances emerged from trance complete, is the dominant figure for the poet. Although H.D. tended to complete her poems and get them into print quite rapidly, she had considerable trouble finishing many of her prose texts, particularly her fiction, most of which she left unpublished. She once told Pearson that poems just "come" to her: "I have to let them come, as they come in they come" (24 December 1953).[29] But her prose, as she frequently reflected, took years to complete as she wrote and rewrote her autobiographical narratives. Herring reminded her at one point: "You wrote to me not very long ago, ... how awful it was to collect manuscripts and have them put by to 'revise'" (2 July 1930). The domestic metaphors for prose composition that prevade H.D.'s letters and memoirs are symptomatic, as I will discuss in Chapter 1, of how she regarded writing prose (never poetry) as a kind of household chore characterized by unending process, instead of completed product. In contrast to the poetry's authoritative and ecstatic arrival (it "comes"), her prose had to "simmer," "ferment," and "foment" over a long period of time. "Untidy" in its first appearance, rewriting was a process of "cutting," "shaping," "sorting," and "tidying-up." "Stitching," "spinning," "knitting," "embroidering" the fabric of her prose texts was a process for H.D. whose completion was endlessly deferred. As Penelopean housework, H.D.'s prose work was a kind of women's work: never done, perpetually undone and redone.[30]

The difficulty of finishing what could never be done was inseparable from the problem of publication. H.D.'s prose often existed at the border between private and public worlds. Completion meant letting go, the release of a private text to the public world that inevitably involved disclosure, more self-revelation than her impersonal poetry. This liminal space between worlds – precisely the limbo that caused Woolf so much anxiety – became filled with an ever-increasing mound of prose manuscripts that H.D. once called her "hay-stack" in a letter to Robert McAlmon (28 January 1949). Some of these manuscripts gradually worked their way first into typescript, then into publication, often to H.D.'s great relief because she felt "tangled or confused" in the web of undone work, as she explained in a letter to Robert McAlmon (24 February 1949). "I agree it blocks one not to have things published," she had written him twenty years earlier (29 January 1929). And, after temporarily blocking publication of Bid Me to Live (A Madrigal), H.D. wrote Pearson: "forgive Madrigal hysteria of my last letter. I am afraid to be unpublished, but feel the MSS are sprouting wings and want to get out" (17 September 1959).

However, H.D.'s desire to be freed of this tangle of unpublished work was often blocked by painful rejections. She wrote The Hedgehog, for example, at the request of Houghton Mifflin, who then rejected it. She tried unsuccessfully to place Pilate's Wife in the 1930s, and she was clearly disappointed when friends could not find a publisher for The Sword Went out to Sea (Synthesis of a Dream), White Rose and the Red, and The Mystery, her trilogy of the late 1940s and early 1950s. Since Oxford University Press had done such a beautiful job of setting up Trilogy during the war, H.D. was particularly disappointed when they "had practically accepted" Tribute to Freud in 1946, but then rejected it because "it was 'neither biography nor autobiography' " and "did not fit in their files" (Letter to Pearson, 25 July 1953). Unwin also rejected this tribute/memoir, but she refused to let "a second-rate publisher" have it and was content to wait until Pearson could place it with a first-class house (Letter to Pearson, 1 September 194[4 or 5]).[31] Her delight in the acceptance and appearance of her work, however, suggests that this patience was partially a screen for feelings of rejection. When her translation of Ion appeared in 1937 with the prestigious Chatto and Windus, she was delighted and quipped to Bryher that her analyst Walter Schmideberg "says a publisher is a proper 'father' for a MSS, so ION will have a legalized position" (26 February 1936). Unpublished manuscripts are illicit, in limbo, without "proper" place.

Like many modernist writers, H.D. was protected from the full blast of rejection by the complex network of friendship and patronage that made up the world of avant-garde little magazines and presses. Before the days of institutionalized literary agents, writers got other writers published, often serving informally as agents for each other. H.D. and Bryher published Moore's first collection of poems, while Moore in turn often helped place H.D.'s work in American presses.[32] Patrons like Harriet Shaw Weaver and Sylvia Beach kept writers like Joyce afloat, writer patrons like Margaret Anderson and Bryher founded magazines that promoted avant-garde writing, and Pound's tireless efforts to place work he believed had talent are an essential component of the history of modernism. However, this matrix of interdependence often carried a special resonance for women and otherwise marginalized writers. Dependency and rejection – endemic to the production and publication of literary discourse – were overdetermined for writers who existed at the periphery of literary centers of power. For women in particular, the increasing marginality of "high" culture overwhelmed by the production of mass culture intersected with the ideology of their relative insignificance as women in the world of letters.[33] To protect themselves from this double vulnerability, many women writers found alternate means of support, as Gillian Hanscombe and Virginia Symers have shown in *Writing for Their Lives: The Modernist Women, 1910–1940*. In particular, Woolf used the Hogarth Press that she and Leonard founded in 1917, which guaranteed that she would not have to suffer the agonies of suspense she had felt as she waited to hear if her half-brother Gerald Duckworth would accept *The Voyage Out* for his publishing house (Bell, II:10–11). Disgusted by the problems Stein had in finding publishers, Alice B. Toklas worked tirelessly to get her work into print, and from 1930 through 1933 ran Plain Edition, the press they founded to publish Stein (Mellow 361–73). Similarly, Bryher funded McAlmon's Contact Press, which put out *Palimpsest*, H.D.'s first extended prose fiction to be published. After Houghton Mifflin rejected *The Hedgehog*, Bryher arranged for its publication in 1936. When McAlmon refused to help H.D. get her Dijon series published in 1932, Bryher paid the Dijon printer to do private editions of these novellas. Bryher also funded two journals, *Close Up* and *Life and Letters Today*, both of which printed H.D.'s work, along with that of many of their friends.

Pearson replaced Bryher as H.D.'s main buffer and agent after World

War II.[34] His importance to her literary production – in both prose and poetry – for the last fourteen years of her life cannot be overestimated. His negotiations with publishers brought many texts into print and protected her to some extent from the hurtful rejections. Equally important, he encouraged her to prepare typescripts such as *The Gift* and *Bid Me to Live (A Madrigal)* for publication and arranged for their safekeeping at Yale.[35] By giving her a place to send her unpublished work, he released her from the sensation of paralysis so that she could go on writing. In effect, he created a category of liminal or deferred "publication" that bears some relationship to Emily Dickinson's private "publication" of her poems in letters and handmade books. As H.D. wrote to McAlmon, "I tend to re-write unless I get a thing neat and finished; that is why Pearson has been such an incentive" (24 February 1949). H.D.'s "shelf" at Yale was both public and private, and yet neither fully public nor private. Out of her hands, with an audience of one, her manuscripts existed in twilight limbo that might lead, some day, to a wider audience. "It is such a comfort that the MSS are with you," she wrote to Pearson, "but I don't worry about publication" (22 March 1951). As she explained to Viola Jordan, "I do feel very proud of it [the "shelf"], even if I am shelved, though I feel that I am being shelf-ed, a different matter" (15 March 1949). Being "shelf-ed" at Yale assured her of a material existence among other "shelf-ed" authors at the heart of cultural reproduction, a prestigious university.

This narrative of deferred publication featuring H.D.'s prose oeuvre has a subtext of suppression and self-censorship. Unlike her poetry, most of which she saw into print (or, in the 1950s, gave to Pearson for publication), H.D.'s prose was subject to erasure. Occasionally, suppression was complete. She destroyed a number of prose manuscripts, especially from the 1920s and 1930s; just how many, we will probably never know.[36] *Niké*, a prose text to which she referred in a letter to Moore in 1922 and at which she "worked feverishly" in 1924, she destroyed "some years later" because "It is discursive and plot-less" ("Autobiographical Notes" 14). To John Cournos, she wrote in 1922 about an experimental prose text whose form prefigured *Palimpsest:* "I have written two long short stories, a little in the manner (I am told) of the late Henry James. . . . Then I have another 'impressionistic' bit, not a story, not long enough for a novel. But the three would make a moderately solid prose work: 1. Floriel. 2. Behind me a Sword. 3. Beryl" (15 September 1922). Not a trace remains of this manuscript, although the name Beryl appears in *Asphodel* for the Bryher figure and the second story may well be one of H.D.'s many texts about the war.[37] In *Thorn Thicket,* she noted "a certain satisfaction in tearing up a rather salacious sketch that I did in Monte Carlo – was it about 1932? It was about a three-cornered affair, two men and myself, the woman" (38). Scattered references in her letters to other prose texts in process, especially in the 1920s and 1930s, suggest that many more manuscripts may have been destroyed.

Aesthetic considerations may certainly have played a part in these destructions – writers often toss out work they consider bad. But aesthetic judgment is seldom, if ever, uncomplicated. Performed by the writer herself, such judgments can easily screen conscious and unconscious motivations to conceal what the writing has revealed. This desire to hide is evident in the manuscripts H.D. suppressed, but did not destroy. Sometimes this suppression was temporary, the result of a sudden fear of attack or loss of privacy. After Pound wrote her a nasty letter about Freud, for example, she responded by telling Pearson that he could not publish *Tribute to Freud,* even though the book had already come out in serial form in 1945–6; she further instructed him to withdraw *The Sword Went out to Sea,* which Bryher had sent to Pantheon (Letter to Pearson, 4 June 1954). At other times, however, she completed carefully corrected typescripts, and yet made no effort (as far as we can tell) to get these prose works into print or to instruct Pearson to do so at a later date. She wrote "DESTROY" across the typescript of *Asphodel* and probably suppressed its companion volumes *Paint It To-Day* and *HER* because of their bisexual love plots and the story of illicit motherhood, as I will discuss at length in Chapter 3.[38]

The publication history of H.D.'s prose oeuvre, then, is the story of partial revelation, endless deferral, fragmentation, destruction, and suppression. The gaps are resonant with the presence/absence of women as cultural producers in the history of literary discourse. Susan Gubar has described Sappho's mutilated texts as synecdoche for the position of literary women in a phallocentric tradition ("Sapphistries"). Similarly, H.D.'s prose oeuvre as a whole occupies the place of Sappho in relation to the more complete and distinct shape of both her poetic oeuvre and male modernism in general. Reflecting its pervasively gendered slant on modernity, H.D.'s prose has been scarcely visible, scattered, and fragmented.

Moreover, this prose oeuvre enacts the kind of negotiation between speech and silence in which women writers variously engage because of the phallo(go)centrism of the social order. Freud's concept of speech and resistance in the context of the "talking cure" is instructive for reading this gender-inflected negotiation, as Chapters 3 and 5 discuss at length. The drama of analysis, Freud wrote, centers on the analysand's resistance to ending repression – the resistance, in other words, to hearing the speech of the unconscious. Repression is a potent force against direct speech because the unconscious seeks to express desires that are culturally forbidden. The ego (tied to "the reality principle") and the superego (tied to cultural norms, imprinted especially by parental figures) act together to prevent the analysand from "speaking" the forbidden desire, particularly in a comprehensible, public discourse. As the talking cure, analysis attempts to "work through" the hieroglyphic speech of the dream or the mute speech of symptom toward the direct speech of the conscious mind. The scene of analysis is consequently, in Freud's view, a site of negotiation between the need to repress and the desire to speak.[39]

Woolf's "Professions for Women" fictionalizes this psychoanalytic dynamic in relation to the woman writer. The scene of women's writing, Woolf argued, is the site of an interior civil war in which the woman must battle the image of feminine perfection internalized from patriarchal norms – the famous "Angel of the House," taken from Coventry Patmore's poem idealizing the self-less and asexual lady of the Victorian era.[40] Woolf's violent allegory for the murder of this paralyzing repressive force imagines, but cannot complete, the explosive release of forbidden speech. She said she had succeeded in killing the internalized feminine censor, but not the masculine superego. Her attempts to speak her desire, to write "the truth about the body" end in silence. The image of the writer as a young girl fishing in the streams of the unconscious (an intertextual resonance with H.D.'s *Notes on Thought and Vision*) fictionalizes the woman writer's struggle against the internalized censor-as-phallus, "something hard":

> Her imagination had rushed away. It had sought the pools, the depths, the dark places where the largest fish slumber. And then there was a smash. There was an explosion. There was foam and confusion. The imagination had dashed itself against something hard. The girl was roused from her dream. She was indeed in a state of the most acute and difficult distress. To speak without figure she had thought of something, something about the body, about the passions which it was unfitting for her as a woman to say. Men, her reason told her, would be shocked. The consciousness of what men will say of a woman who speaks the truth about her passions had roused her from her artist's state of unconsciousness. She could write no more. The trance was over. Her imagination could work no longer. (240)

Desire – forbidden desire – cannot speak itself directly, in public. The doors of repression slam shut. However, the indirection of fiction allows for some encoding of that desire, as Woolf well knew. Like a dream, fiction can disguise forbidden desire so that it can escape the censor to find some sort of screened expression in the public domain of letters. Freud's talking cure becomes a writing cure, in which the scene of writing enacts the drama between repression and expression. *Mrs. Dalloway,* for example, written during the period when Woolf was falling in love with Vita Sackville-West, presents that "pressure of rapture, which split its thin skin and gushed and poured" in Clarissa's memory of "the most exquisite moment of her whole life" – when she and Sally had kissed (47, 52). But this "moment of revelation," in which "the whole world might have turned upside down," is safely encased in a novel which shows that Clarissa's marriage to Richard is what has kept her from madness and suicide, the fate of her double, Septimus. The lesbian desire that fuels *Orlando,* Woolf's barbed gift to Sackville-West, who had by 1928 gotten involved with another woman, is both revealed and concealed in the text's satiric humor and fantastic narrative of a sex-changing hero/heroine who is predominantly heterosexual. Woolf's texts fish in the streams of female desire, but embed that desire in narratives that reaffirm its repression.

Woolf's articulation and enactment of the problems of writing female desire highlight H.D.'s different negotiation of the same issue. As DuPlessis commented about H.D.: "To speak Otherness meant a special commitment to speak of sexuality" (*Career* 39). Instead of screening that desire in public texts whose narratives undermined it, H.D. wrote about it more directly than Woolf. But then she suppressed the text. The more forbidden that desire, the more H.D. repressed the text – that is, she wrote and rewrote the story, but she had difficulty *finishing* or *publishing* what she had written, particularly those that dealt with lesbian desire. With acute suffering in fear of possible criticism, Woolf published what she wrote with relative "silence" about the body. H.D. tried to "tell the truth about the body," but she ended up repressing or suppressing much of what she had written from the public eye. For Woolf, the price of public speech was (relative) silence about the body; for H.D., the price of private speech about desire was (relative) public silence.

In their different negotiations of the desire to speak and the pressure to censor, Woolf and H.D. anticipated the psychodynamics of suppression that Cixous identified in "The Laugh of the Medusa." But H.D.'s choice of her prose rather than her poetry as the primary site of her attempt to write the desire of the Other exists in curious opposition to Cixous's poetics. Poetry, not prose, Cixous argued, will be the discourse of *écriture féminine* because novelists have been "allies of representationalism," while poets have been more centered in the unconscious, "the place where the repressed manage to survive" (250). With H.D., however, prose was the discourse in which she wrote more directly and personally about gender; therefore prose, not poetry, was where she first developed a discourse of female desire.[41]

The reception as well as the publication of H.D.'s prose oeuvre placed her fictions in the shadow of her poetry. As many have shown, readers of her poetic oeuvre frequently fetishized the perfect imagist in the position of man's Other and Muse; in no sense did readings of H.D. position her as "male" poet.[42] However, readings of her prose frequently privilege her poetry and project onto the body of her prose the ambivalence which WOMAN as mysterious Other has provoked in the *gynesis* of modernity. The narrative of the readings of H.D.'s prose constitutes what Shoshana Felman has called a "case history" of "Poe-etic Effect" (*Lacan* 28, 50–1). Literary history, she argued, has an unconscious which erupts into its critical texts, themselves the scene of resistance, repression, and transference. Using the reception of Poe's poetry as a case in point, Felman reads these readings as a case history invoked by what "seemed to be at once the most *irresistible* and the most *resisted* poetry in literary history" (50). His poetry, she concluded, "is precisely the effect of a deadly struggle between [the reader's] consciousness and unconscious; it has to do with resistance and with what can neither be resisted nor escaped. Poe is a symptom of poetry" (50–1). Similarly, H.D.'s prose corpus, occupying the position of alterity in modernity, has invited reading practices that repeat the cultural attraction for and repulsion against that ever-elusive feminine Other. Captured in the snares of Penelope's web, readers have often resisted the compelling return of that which they would escape in H.D.'s prose.

    H.D.'s first reader so ensnared was H.D. While she tended to accept her poetry as inscriptions satisfyingly complete and separate in themselves, she engaged constantly in rereading and reassessing her prose, sometimes positively, sometimes negatively. In *Advent,* for example, she contrasted her poetry and prose: "My [prose] books are not so much still-born as born from the detached intellect. . . . The poetry is another matter. Yes, the poems are satisfactory but unlike most poets of my acquaintance (and I have known many) I am no longer interested in a poem once it is written, projected, or materialized" (149).[43] Boundaries were not so clearly drawn between the writer and her prose, as if the prose texts retained their fetal bond with their (pro)creator, or as if (in Nancy Chodorow's terms) the prose text enacted the position of daughter in fluid identification with the mother from whom she could never fully separate. H.D.'s poems were individuated, separated; her prose remained bonded, bound in the threads of the Penelopean weaver.

    As reader of her prose texts, H.D. was caught up in the dynamics of ambivalence, a cycle of feelings complicated by her identification with the body of the text and inseparable from a sense of how "she" (the writer *as* the text) would be read by others. (Re)reading, in other words, often reduplicated the process of writing and repeated the narrative of the text itself. For example, a letter she wrote to Conrad Aiken after she read his novel *Great Circle* conflates the labyrinths of psyche and prose text in a defensive apologia of her self and her fictions that replicates the autobiographical narrative core of *Palimpsest*'s three stories:

I appreciated always a review you wrote of some of my prose [*Palimpsest*], such bad prose too. Yes and no. I mean it was trying to do the impossible. Which I am still trying for – but this time in a bigger way – a "Circle." I didn't want to see you some years ago, with Mr. Fletcher. I knew how bad my writing was. . . . and I had a panic. I think I know myself a little better now – there is still the panic – but like you in your "circle," I have now the clue, the Ariadne thread. I tell you again, I am very envious of the book [*Great Circle*] – but someday – I give myself five years – I will want to demonstrate my own idea – show my own Ariadne thread, and how it wove over the world and under. (6 August 1933)

Penelope weaves with Ariadne's thread. The body of the text and the mind of the writer form a single labyrinthine tapestry. Since the psyche of the writer narrates the story of life in a female body, since the body of the text is linguistic, this identification of weaver and woven anticipates Cixous's *écriture féminine*, the "sexts" of feminine difference ("Laugh of the Medusa").[44] Reading these sexts from which she was not at all separated meant being captured by their sexual and gender dynamics. As read, both the texts and their umbilically connected reader/writer took on many of the conventional attributes of the feminine – something to be loved, trivialized, despised, dismissed, feared, revered. She wrote McAlmon, for example, about *The Sword Went Out to Sea (Synthesis of a Dream)*, "I love my real this-war novel too, to distraction" (29 November 1950), and she referred to "Hesperia" as "a beautiful sequel to Secret Name" (6 November 1950). In *Compassionate Friendship*, she called *By Avon River* "a little bundle of dandelions" compared to the inspired "laurel" of books by G. Wilson Knight and E. M. Butler (62). "The early ones, *HEDYLUS* and so on taste of icycles to me now," she wrote to Pearson (22 June 1949 [?]). *Palimpsest* she called "weedy," "baffling," and she told Erich Heydt "not to read *Narthex*, as the prose was involved and repetitive" (*H.D. by Delia Alton* 218; *Compassionate Friendship* 90). Looking back on *Asphodel* and *HER*, she noted to Pearson that "the 'story' without the *daemon* makes pleasant reading, at the moment" (14 October 1959). "It is cold and misty but I am so snug and happy here," she wrote Silvia Dobson on November 21, 1948, "going over a heap of note-books I did in the 1930 period or decade rather. They are not as bad as I feared. I was terrified to touch them . . . " (H.D., "Friendship Traced" 146). About her prose of the 1920s, she reflected in *Advent*, "Perhaps the books I last wrote of were too self-centered or 'narcissistic' to satisfy my heart" (151). Rejecting the self with the fictions that inscribed the self, she concluded: "I don't think my own personal patterns of husband–friend–self or of mother–father–child and the various elongated or squat shapes of the eternal triangles was ever as important as

my mind seemed to make it or as my mind seemed to want to make it.
That is why the various stories or the novels has proved unsatisfactory,
had been a lot of useless stuff" (quoted in Guest, *Herself Defined* 169).
But, to Pearson, she wrote about her unpublished manuscripts, "I can
see, taken all in all, that there is a sequence, it is my *COMMEDIA*" (16
March 1949). From "useless stuff" to Dantesque is quite a leap.

H.D.'s self-judgments no doubt reflect the writer's critical eye on her
achievement. But the range and intensity of her feelings suggest that this
detachment at least partially screens an overdetermined identification
with and ambivalence toward writing that she perceived as "different."
Similarly, other readers of her prose have had multilayered responses,
which in part reflect aesthetic judgment, but which also fall into the
transferential pattern that Felman identified. Established first in the minds
of her readers as the poet of "perfect" lyrics, much resistance to her prose
began with its difference from her poetry. "No one really much likes
my prose," H.D. wrote to Viola Jordan about *Palimpsest;* "people don't
think [it] 'worthy' of H.D." (29 March 192[7?]). Aiken was the one
reviewer who insisted that her prose was superior to her poetry; *Palimpsest*
was more "impressive" than her coldly perfect poems because it was
more "disturbing"; its range of emotion, subtlety of nuance, and stylistic
beauty invite "comparison with the very best fiction which has been
written, in any language, in this century" (309).[45] Nonetheless, his crit-
icisms of the novel, "if novel it can be called," question the stylistic
aspects of it that most link it to modernity, particularly to those qualities
most associated in current theory with feminine writing:

> There are stylistic oddities – elisions and abruptness – which pull one
> up, and occasionally carelessnesses . . . one now and then founders a
> little in the fragmentary and chaotic and repetitive welter of the interior
> monologue. One would have preferred, in the second section, a little
> more stiffening – more of the direct narrative . . . and less of the obsessed
> round-and-round of the heroine's mind, which sometimes, in its endless
> repetitions of certain leit-motifs, goes beyond the limits of the credible,
> as also of the aesthetically endurable. . . . H.D. overdoes a little the
> interpolative method, with its interjections, qualifications, parenthetic
> questions, parenthetic reminiscences – one feels, in the midst of this
> burning subjectivism, this consuming Narcissism, that it would be a
> relief to come oftener upon a simple narrative statement or a connected
> bit of dialogue. (309)

Aiken's longing for the "stiffening" of "direct narrative" betrays the
boundaries he attempts to maintain between himself as reader and the
feminine excess of the text he nonetheless defends. McAlmon, *Palimpsest's* publisher in its 1926 Contact Edition, was similarly conflicted, both
attracted to and afraid of the engulfments of the text. He wrote a preface

for the novel that attempts to set up a buffer zone between the novel and its readers, presumably to protect H.D. from the expectations of her readers, but also to forewarn the readers against the invasions of the text. Entitled "Forewarned as regards H.D.'s Prose," it called *Palimpsest* a "tapestry hung between heaven and hell" and begged its readers to allow H.D. to go beyond her early "frozen lyrics" and to recognize that the war had changed the landscape of serious literature forever:

> Here is a generation split like the quick crack of doom by war, and she was aware that there is no leaping back across mountain crevices; and she has no crawling nature, and wanted no haven of security now that her poetry is used as a textbook in girls' colleges, and given patronizing admiration by hack reviewers in London papers. Things do go on and can be more interesting than that; and to artists literature is not a haven; it is an assertion. (241–2)[46]

McAlmon's stern warning buffering the poet's prose also revealed, perhaps in spite of itself, his own discomfort with what he was promoting. In defending its difference from her poetry, he pointed to its other difference, that is, its gendered alterity. Men, he explained, have been so destroyed by the war that it is to the women writers of modernity we must turn for creative power. Conflating her prose with its creator, he used H.D. as his prime example, but in terms that recapitulate the conventional Otherness of WOMAN: "HD's intellect is more intuitive than logical, more sensitive than practical. It mumbles in stumbling through the objective world. It is a bit wind-broken, somewhat the overstrung racehorse, ready to take fright unduly, ready to shy and bolt in a quick hysteria of panic, but once underway it takes the hurdles and is not the last to arrive at the goal-post" (243). What he perceived as the overstrung body of hysteria both attracted and repulsed him. She was the Other to which men were drawn, "with draggingly weary and despairing bodies," sunk "into despondence" and "stylistic manners" (242–3). Her "mumbles" appear as hysteria and panic on the racetrack of masculine teleology.

McAlmon's veiled discomfort with H.D.'s prose intensified by the early 1930s when she responded to his request for manuscripts for Contact Editions by sending him what she had recently written, probably her first draft of *Nights*. He refused to publish it because it upset him too much: "About the story. It rather distressed me. I spotted too much to it, and it set up a vibration whirring which had me worn nervously and crazily to a frazzle" (30 October 1932).[47] Typically, H.D. responded ambivalently and defensively to his distress. "You were so right about that series of impressions I called NIGHTS that I sent you," she wrote him (6 December 1933), and in defense of her decision to undergo analysis, she acknowledged the way in which her prose tended to capture its readers in a web of Otherness woven out of unconscious threads:

But you yourself have been pointing out – and rightly – that my writing had reached a vanishing point of sterility and finesse. Awful – I feel it when I read the stuff. All the same, though I have destroyed much – a lot – I have not been able to do away with more than one half of my last ten years output. I am sorting and arranging – don't care for the stuff – but have about four stories, all on that high-vibration-to-the-breaking-point level. As I say – I hate them. But one has to be true to one's Daemon – or what is one true to?????? And there it is – I felt the old man [Freud] does burn away like radium – that sort of crystal surface in me, anyhow. (18 August 1933)

McAlmon's response to H.D.'s prose was not unusual, either for her contemporaries or for more recent readers. Her prose fictions in particular tend to disturb, disrupt, decenter, unbalance, enchant, or irritate her readers, who often hate, love, or love–hate them. Indifference is seldom a response because, in Barthes's terms, her prose is never a "neutral" discourse of "zero degree" writing (*Writing Degree Zero*), but rather initiates a "vibration" that sets nerves "whirring," "crazily to a frazzle." Deborah Kelly Kloepfer, in discussing the effect of *Palimpsest,* has captured the range of intensities: "the movement in this section is both maddening and radiant. . . . The 'Hipparchia' section of *Palimpsest* is itself a journey into linguistic madness, both disorienting and exhilarating to read" ("Flesh Made Word" 34–5). Perdita Schaffner further articulated how the experimental stylistics of *HER* invite reader disorientation:

> Not an easy book. It shifts and jumps, and repeats itself. The voice is frequently overwrought – just like the author's in real life. Yet there is a strange hypnotic force. I'm caught up in the momentum. Then held up by jolts of recognition, clues and double clues, references and cross references – and the play on names. ("Pandora's Box" *xi*)

Whether in love, or hate, or ambivalence, readers have often expressed their responses to H.D.'s prose in terms that covertly invoke the feminine by conflating the text with the body of woman or with the Otherness of the unconscious. "Rapunzel, Rapunzel, Let Down Thy Long Hair" is the title of Babette Deutsch's review of *Palimpsest,* in which she announced that the cold poet had come out of her "alabaster tower" (2). A cluster of reactions in 1934 to the two privately printed and distributed volumes of novellas or stories (as she called them) – *Kora and Ka* (which also included *Mira-Mare*) and *The Usual Star* (which also included "Two Americans") – is exemplary. Moore, for example, greatly admired the two books. Especially moved by the concept of the ghostly Ka, she playfully rescripted Pound's famous "In the Station of the Metro" to describe the books as apparitions of petal-faces: "The apparition of these two white books so suddenly in my hands makes me very happy" (Letter to H.D., 15 October 1934).[48] Aiken also liked the group, particularly the "skillful[ly]" drawn layers of consciousness in *Kora and Ka,* but with certain reservations. "What you are doing with *form* interests me profoundly," he wrote; " – what a lot of things lie ahead in that path!" (31 October 1934). But "Two Americans" was too "autobiographic," and *The Usual Star* was "a little too upholstered, too patterned, too stiff with decoration, like a brocade," with "the rather precious preoccupations and finicking finesses" of its "languid" people (31 October 1934). The emotional nuance that distressed Aiken intrigued Herring, who wrote H.D. that reading *Kora and Ka* was like having "dreamed–lived it":

> "Kora and Ka" caught me up in its currents. I was a fish, swimming back and forth, each time in a new current. You know how the silent and swift glide of fish in a tank are like electricity in being? It was like that, (I always think that fish, with their darting pushing and inter-patterning and displacing of each other, are like one's mind)....only one wasn't looking at them, but inside with them...I have never read anything like this before. (Saturday 1934)

Moreover, the same text – as well as her prose oeuvre in general – often produced violently different responses in people, even her close friends. Pound hated *Hedylus,* but Edith Sitwell was enthralled by its "hallucinated writing": "I cannot tell you how much I have loved the beautiful Hedylus...with those rhythms like water flowing, and the blueness of the water, and the folds of the gown like water, what a lovely book it is" (Letter to H.D., n.d. [1940s?]).[49] The ghostly traces and fluidity that Sitwell, Moore, and Herring loved disconcerted more recent critics, Bernard Engel and Jeffrey Meyers, who, like Aiken in his review of *Palimpsest,* longed for conventional narrative. To Engel, "her prose works are crippled by her inability to characterize and to write narrative, resulting in a coldness without beauty. There is often, finally, concentration on a plaintive or mournful or hysterical self at the expense of the observation or experience to be presented" (515). For Meyers, "she lacks the essential quality of a novelist: the ability to create an imaginative world and bring her characters to life. Her prose is filled with self-indulgent passages" (632).[50]

The "truth" about H.D.'s prose resides not in any one of these reactions, but in the pattern of response, which reads like a case history of resistance and attraction to what has been coded as the feminine Other. Resistance to her prose often centers on what its readers experience as "H.D.'s" narcissism, hysteria, plotlessness, stylistic repetitions, and obsessive attention to nuanced layers of consciousness and dream. Fascination for her prose often revolves around these same qualities, valued positively instead of negatively, and within a post-structuralist framework renamed as aspects of *écriture féminine*: fluidity, deferral of closure, self-reflexivity, mirroring identifications, self-conscious textualization and linguistic play, dreamscapes and sex(t)ualities, broken sequences and boundaries, reconstitution of the writer/text/reader relationship as an intersubjectivity – the very qualities, we might add, that are most admired in works such as Joyce's *Finnegans Wake* and postmodernist modernity in general.[51]

Penelope's Web sets out to explore the *difference* of H.D.'s prose oeuvre: its difference from her poetry, its difference from male modernism as the Penelopean Other enacting its own agency, and the difference it makes to a literary history of modernity. The production, publication, and reception of her prose enact that difference. Its Penelopean discourses articulate a gynopoetic modernity generated at the margins that explores a woman's capture in the cultural web and affirms her agency in the (re)weaving of it. Gendered more directly than her lyric poetry, linguistically more experimental in its excesses, her prose is a difference that necessarily makes a difference in our reading practices. H.D. once wrote Bryher how much she appreciated Aiken's review of *Palimpsest,* not so much for what he argued, but for his willingness to take her seriously as a prose writer: "C. A. has always boosted my prose, one of the few people, who takes my prose AS PROSE, not as an aberration of a poet" (30 May 1933). *Penelope's Web* takes H.D.'s prose AS PROSE, a difference that makes a difference: first, as a body of experimental work that profoundly changed H.D.'s poetry to make possible the personal/ cosmic, lyric/narrative, mythic/historical long poems of the 1940s and 1950s; and second, in and of itself as a corpus that changes how we read modernism.

1

"H.D. – WHO Is She?": Discourses of Self-Creation

"All books are about oneself," my mother used to say. She was referring
to fiction. Poetry came from a different distillation.
                                                    Perdita Schaffner,
                                                    Introduction,
                                                    The Hedgehog (vii)

"Prose? No!" Richard Aldington wrote H.D. from the embattled
trenches in France: "You have so precise, so wonderful an instrument –
why abandon it to fashion another, perhaps less perfect?" (4 July 1918).
Writing prose meant defying a husband still eager to shape her career,
meant blurring the precision of her lyric instrument, meant risking the
loss of her perfect success as poet. But, predictably, H.D. was a risk
taker. It had been, after all, her rebellious desire for difference that
brought her in 1911 to London in the first place. Resistance to authority
had been essential, in fact, to her escape from the conventional life of a
professor's daughter in proper Main Line Philadelphia. Resistance became
central once again in the flight from her perfection as an imagist poet
into the indeterminate experimentalism of her prose.

The sharp sea air, brilliant sun, jagged rocks, and tidepools of Cornwall
provided H.D. with a Druidic setting far from the London scene of the
war at home in which she began "really seriously" to work "on a novel,"
as she wrote John Cournos on July 17, 1918. He was the Jewish American
imagist poet and novelist to whom she had been particularly close during
the months of Aldington's training in 1916, when her husband had an
affair with Flo Fallas. She felt certain that Cournos would approve because she saw her experimental novel as "a sort of imaginative series of
scenes" layering her life in America and England, sketches that resembled
his recreation of his Russian, American, and expatriate American experience in *The Mask* (n.d. [July 1918?]). She promised to send him "a
hunk of this opus" (17 July 1919). But, like Aldington, he must have

33

advised her to abandon the project because she wrote back defending her
prose project. Her apologia is worth quoting in full because it encapsulates the major themes of this chapter:

> You are quite right about the novel and I shall certainly chuck it. But
> I must explain to you first that the novel is not intended as a work of
> art – at least, not as it stands. It is a means to an end. I want to clear
> up an old tangle. Well, I do not put my personal self into my poems.
> But my personal self has got between me and my real self, my real
> artist personality. And in order to clear the ground, I have tried to write
> things down – in order to think straight, I have endeavoured to write
> straight.
> But I hope to come clear and then turn to my real work again.
> You must remember that writing poetry require[s] a clarity, a clair-
> voyance almost. I have been too weak to dare to be clairvoyant. I have
> tried instead to be merely sensible. I mean in the common sense of that
> word. In the long run, the clairvoyance is the only real sanity for me.
> But in the novel I am working through a wood, a tangle of bushes
> and bracken out to a clearing, where I can see clear again. (9 July [1919?])[1]

This is a strange defense – to disparage what is affirmed essential; to
connect what is separated. It perversely depends upon a binary opposition
that privileges poetry over prose, the end over the means to an end, her
"real self" over her "personal self," clairvoyance over sensibility, and
art over therapy. Writing poetry is her "real work," the extension of her
"real artist personality," while writing her novel is a devalued activity
which is nonetheless essential to the poet. Writing prose about the personal self will reconstitute the impersonal self of the clairvoyant poet,
who does not put her personal self into the poem. Echoing the cultural
division of labor into (male) production and (female) reproduction,
H.D.'s poet is the primary producer of art, while the prose writer is the
secondary reproducer of the poet, merely a means to a poetic teleology.
The novelist fills the position of wife, handmaiden and helpmeet to the
authentic artist, the poet.

No doubt H.D.'s letter to Cournos adapts a rhetoric of duplicitous
self-effacement that reflects their different positions within the gender
system. But her letter also indicates a belief in the interpenetration of
writing and identity. The writer, in H.D.'s view, not only creates the
self-in-the-text, but more fundamentally constructs the author in the
process of writing. The "authors" of her poetry and prose are different
– the one visionary, the other personal. They are personae, who originate
in and refer back to the historical writer, but are never her equivalent.
Fabricated, but not false, each "author" has her own voice and serves a
special function within the evolution of the living woman writer.

H.D.'s self-reflexive construction of these "authors" is characteristically modernist, analogous to Yeats's self-conscious theorizing about masks and to Pound's statement on poetic identity in "Vorticism": "In the 'search for oneself,'... one gropes, one finds some seeming verity. One says, 'I am' this, that, or the other, and with the words scarcely uttered one ceases to be that thing. I began this search for the real in a book called *Personae,* casting off, as it were, complete masks of the self in each poem" (85).[2] Like Yeats's masks, H.D.'s personae operate within a dualistic, ultimately dialectical schema. Like Pound's masks, H.D.'s personae emerge as the product rather than the producer of the writing.

Anticipating a post-structuralist emphasis on language, H.D. explored more intensively than Yeats or Pound the linguistic processes of masking – the way in which language mediates the relationship between the literary mask and the person behind the masks who is both their maker and their product. There is for H.D. a living writer who creates the clairvoyant poet and the personal prose writer. But also, H.D., as writer, is endlessly (re)made by what she writes. As she said in her final memoir, *Thorn Thicket,* a text in which she reflected on the palimpsest of selves she had previously written, "The story writes *me*" (42). Consistent with Julia Kristeva's concept of the subject-in-process, H.D.'s written selves both perform and thematize the post-structuralist "I" constituted in, by, and through language.[3] H.D.'s apologia to Cournos, then, suggests that the poet, prose author, and living writer exist within a symbiotic economy in which each nourishes and feeds from the others. The nature and dynamics of that system is the focus of this chapter.

I. NAMES: NOMS DE PLUME, NOMS DE GUERRE, NOMS DE PAIX

Names are in people, people are in names.

H.D., *HER* (5)

H.D.'s creation of prose and poetic personae focused on names as the medium of literary masks and masking. Identity resides *in* words, not as an entity outside language. Her poet and prose "authors," constituted in language, were separate voices whose difference required names to embody and ensure the essential distinction. Like Michel Foucault, H.D. believed that an author's name is more than a proper name. It "serves to characterize a certain mode of being of discourse," he wrote in "What Is an Author?" (147). With one early exception, H.D. never published anything under her legal names – Hilda Doolittle, Hilda Aldington.[4] Her search for the authority of authorhood involved the identification of the right names. Never a unitary gesture, this (re)naming was an endlessly repeating act that signified the self as a process (not a product) of becoming. For H.D., words, most especially names, were potent forces that not only signified, but also called into being what they named. "People, names," Hermione reflects in *Asphodel*, "Names are people and hold light and seem to gleam with light within themselves" (II 139).[5] "Spelling words," the autobiographical narrator in *The Gift* thinks, "in fact . . . was a *spell*" (10). Her father, she remembers, had found her name Hilda by running his fingers down a list in the dictionary. "Who would I have been," she wonders, if "he had put his finger on Alice?" (*Gift* 8). Alice was the name he had chosen for her half-sister who had died. Is the father's control of naming, the child wonders, a power over life and death?

Doolittle – H.D.'s patronym – seemed to predict a mock-heroic destiny. "Doolittle, it *is* rather odd," a "funny name," she wrote Eric Walter White.[6] Not only did it make people laugh, but it also carried the threat of *doing little,* a mockery of her ambitions. The narrator in her roman à clef *Paint It To-Day* explores this deflation as she recalls her debut in London's literary society in 1911:

> Myself, who was an unformed sort of nebulous personality . . . shall have no name. People called me Miss Defreddie which was surely not a name, or if it was a name it was a thing to be laughed at. If people laughed I was embarrassed and tried to laugh with them as if I had never heard just that laugh at just that particular name before. If they did not laugh, it was equally embarrassing, because one wondered if they had not heard properly, or if they were concealing the laugh and would suddenly burst forth with it like someone who has inadvertently swallowed a bit of hot potato. (460)[7]

Creating an author – a linguistically formed entity with a public presence – meant finding the right name that could materialize that author, bring her into visible existence. As DuPlessis wrote, "H.D. began her official career as a writer with a crisis of naming" (*Career* 6). Pound's creation of "H.D." in the tea room of the British Museum to launch H.D.'s poetic career has acquired the status of legend, in large part fueled by her own mythologizing of the exchange with Pound some forty-five years later in *End to Torment:*

> "But Dryad," (in the Museum tea room), "this is poetry." He slashed with a pencil. "Cut this out, shorten this line. 'Hermes of the Ways' is a good title. I'll send this to Harriet Monroe of *Poetry*. Have you a copy? Yes? Then we can send this, or I'll type it when I get back. Will this do?" and he scrawled "H.D. Imagiste" at the bottom of the page. (18)

Pearson recalled H.D. telling him the story somewhat differently, with *her* initiation of a nom de plume, the initials already on the page, and Pound's contribution centered on the word "Imagiste":

She told of how he had gone over with her the poetry of some of the
second-rate contemporaries of the 1912 period – criticising, showing
how this and that was wrong, but never asking for her own, until one
day he said "Now it's about time I saw some of your poems," and so
she brought them to a tea-room opposite the British Museum, where
they went. He took the pages, set them on the table – then with his
pencil (and she illustrated with her hands the dash of his pencil) – slash,
slash, slash."That line, you know was Ezra's. He made it; it wasn't
there as such, until he showed it to me within it." "Then he said," 'I'll
send them to Poetry'; and that's the way it was." "I said, 'I've got to
have a name' (to me: "You know, Doolittle was too comic for a name,
and I wanted to get away from it all anyhow";). I just had my initials
on the page for no reason, but he said 'H.D.'s all right,' and then added
'Imagiste' after it."[8]

H.D.'s public version in her memoir of Pound streamlines and dram-
atizes the naming, a condensation that ritualizes the act by evoking prior
male inscriptions or figurations of women: Adam, who names Eve; Zeus,
who births Athena out of his head; Pygmalion, whose desire brings to
life the statue he has made; Professor Higgins, who gave another Miss
Doolittle the power of speech in Shaw's *Pygmalion,* a play that was the
rage of London in 1912, not long after H.D. arrived on the scene, as
Robert Duncan has astutely reminded us ("H.D.'s Challenge" 23); and
Shakespeare, who, in H.D.'s own tribute to him, inscribes Claribel on
the blank page of *The Tempest,* in which she is the "invisible, voiceless"
woman who appears only in name as the bride whose marriage initiates
the king's journey:

> I only threw a shadow
> On his page,
> Yet I was his,
> He spoke my name;
>
> He hesitated,
> Raised his quill,
> Which paused,
> Waited a moment,
>
> And then fell
> Upon the unblotted line;
> I was born,
> Claribel.
>
> (*Avon* 15)

H.D.'s telling of the story suggests that Hilda Doolittle, like Claribel,
was (re)born as "H.D." through the agency of a male poet's pen. It may
also encode the kind of critique of male modernism that Elizabeth Hirsh
reads in this scene – Pound's need for the "Image" of the silent Other

to make possible his own poetics of presentation ("Imaginary Images"). As I will discuss in Chapter 3, H.D. narrated other versions of her poetic genesis, particularly in her *Kunstlerroman HER*. Nonetheless, Pound's naming of "H.D. Imagiste" remained for her a potent metonymic gesture that signified his larger role in her entrance into the public domain of letters as "the poet," specifically, of course, as the imagist poet.[9]

The H.D. *Imagiste* who appeared so mysteriously in the pages of the avant-garde little magazines of the prewar and early war years took on an existence and identity created and recreated jointly by the living writer and her readers. H.D. was widely read, reviewed, and frequently touted as "the perfect imagist," even the "most perfect" American poet.[10] In 1915, her poems were chosen over Eliot's "The Love Song of J. Alfred Prufrock" for *Poetry's* Guarantor's Prize, and in 1917, she won the Vers Libre contest sponsored by *The Little Review*. She, in turn, was deeply aware of this success and closely attuned to what her friends and reviewers thought about "H.D." Woolf, it should be remembered, characteristically suffered extreme stress in anticipation of criticism from reviewers and Bloomsbury friends as her work made its way from private to public domain. While H.D.'s response was not nearly so intense, she read her reviews carefully and repeatedly answered them in subsequent works and letters to sympathetic friends. "I can't be held up by what the critics think H.D. ought to be like," she wrote defiantly to Viola Jordan (29 March [1927?]). But, in fact, she and her critics collaborated in the construction of a rigidly, even narrowly defined "H.D." whose reputation she both enjoyed and resisted as she sought new directions for her work. "They squeal that H.D. is no longer the pure crystalline," she wrote to Bryher; "I suppose there is nothing for it but a shell of water-tight and fool proof M. Moore variety, or T. S. E. [Eliot] wobbling mass-ward . . . or else fighting it out...but how about and why and in what manner?" (13 May 1936).

The crystalline "H.D." was, above all, a literary identity, a mode of discourse tied to "the poet," especially the early imagist poet, as H.D. remained acutely aware. In the 1920s, she clearly instructed Houghton Mifflin: "My writing name is 'H.D.' Any position that I may have attained in the literary world was attained solely under the pseudonym 'H.D.' and I have resented the attack made on my anonymity" (6 February [1924?]). When she sent them the manuscript for *Hippolytus Temporizes,* she wrote: "I think you may like it as it is in what people now refer to as 'my early style.' That is it is exactly what one would expect of H.D" (25 March 1926). Bryher received similar instructions for her communications with H.D.'s publishers: "will you say for ALL anthology reference I am 'H.D.,' not Hilda D., that last is someone quite different" (27 October 1937). This identification of "H.D." as a distinctive "literary personality" and discourse continued throughout the 1940s and 1950s. In sending poems from *Trilogy* to George Plank, she felt compelled to justify why they were not "H.D.": "Please do not take them too seriously as I can re-set bits – XXIX and XXX are not 'H.D.' but they wrote themselves and I did not like to tamper with the idea" (15 June 1945). About the German translation of *By Avon River*, she wrote to Pearson: "I do hope they realize that H.D. is *H.D.*, a literary personality. I don't care what they put on jacket but do hope they realize that H.D. is to feature as the only begetter, on the title-page, as in *Avon*" (14 April 1955). To Aldington, she explained how long ago and far away "H.D." seemed from herself in the 1950s: "No, I do not feel all that young but I do think that E.[zra] and H.D. did come from a different vibration, and a vibration that did dart ahead, for all the zig-zag and the bogged-down periods" (23 February 195?).

More than a nom de plume, "H.D." was a name she performed. She inhabited it, just as it conversely lived in her as one part of a multifaceted whole. She felt both identified with "H.D." as a material signifier that gave her existence in public, and dissociated from it as an entity forever cut off from the private identity to which it did and did not refer. She regularly signed some letters to literary friends with her public name – first "H.D.," with self-conscious quotation marks, then, more simply, just H.D. Many friends, even intimate ones, addressed her as H.D. Personally designed bookplates and stationery featured "H.D." in their design. But she and her friends regularly detached "H.D." from her other selves, a dissociation alternately established by playful wit, alienation, and nostalgia. Humorous references to "H.D." as someone who did not encompass other selves are frequent in her correspondence. To Bryher, for example, she wrote one day: "I don't feel that H.D.-ish at all" (19 April 1935); and again, "I am so overwhelmed by H.D. in Jim [Whitall]'s book that I can hardly endure my present-day drab self" (28 October 1935). Alluding to H.D.'s film name, Helga Doorn, Bryher quipped "have an HD winter and a Doorn spring" (October 1929), while Robert Herring wrote "Whatever happens with Dohrn [Doorn], don't lose H.D., *please!* There are so many to whom she means so much – worthless Buddy [Herring], for instance! In this case, not 'H.D., author of – ' but H.D., whose letters have a habit of arriving at the right, because one's own worst, moments. . . . I really know what you mean about reincarnating as Dohrn, but but BUT – Don't lose 'H.D.' She wrote just like herself, in the midst of cold shoulders" (3 January 1932). The "author H.D.," Herring understood, invaded the living woman just as often as she projected herself into the public persona. " 'H.D.' may be a bore to you," Herring later wrote her about her performance in divorce court, "but she was 'H.D.' on the stand" (13 May 1938).

Sometimes a "bore," "H.D." was also intimidating, a public personality that must be demystified. In writing Bryher about taking a different nom de plume, she used "chemistry" to reduce the formidable "H.D." into the sea, mother of all life: "It is odd how the H.D. is a sort of chemical like H₂O or NACL, but as you never studied chemistry, that can't mean much, only it is water, the first and the other salt. I mean. I am seeing the H.D. as that thing [salt water], and it makes it easier to approach H.D. and also to think of forming the other pages into some tidy shape" (29 February 1936). On the other hand, "H.D.'s" powerful personality could draw her out of a too-private reclusivity. As she wrote to Plank about Pearson's impending visit, "it *should* be bliss if I don't go & crawl into my tortoise-shell & have to yank same-self into manifestation again. I think I will be all right, this time, as N. is so exquisite about H.D. & will have much literary news & gossip" (9 July 1949). She later wrote Pearson "How old and long ago does H.D. seem to me" (4 October 1951). Identifying "H.D." clearly with the past, she reported to Aldington that "Norman entered so thoroughly into the early HD legend" (27 June [1950s?]).

This dissociation from "the early H.D. legend," which she had begun to feel as it was being made, provided the immediate impetus for her desire to write prose. The poet "H.D." was too rigidly defined to encompass other aspects of the self she wanted to make manifest through linguistic self-creation. The connection between her resistance to "H.D." and her desire to write prose under a prose name is evident in a letter she wrote in 1932 to White, the composer who had set some of her poems to music:

> Is your literary agent any good? I often wish I could find a good one. I want to do prose later, under a pseudonym. People will say H.D., the poet, should let prose alone in reviews, and it's all uneven and wrong. (Of course it does not matter what reviews say, but one gets hypnotised in time, and sterilized by other people's attitude. At least there is always danger in a niche.) I have been doing sort of queer half-mad phantasies of modern people IN Greece. They are real and different but not "H.D." (White 19)

Writing prose under a new name, in other words, was one way of writing herself out of the "niche" she and the critics had built in collaboratively constructing the "early H.D. legend."[11] A new name would allow her to write differently, to form a new discourse. She instructed Richard Johns, the editor of *Pagany,* to use the name "Rhoda Peter" for her 1920 sketch entitled "Pontikonisi (Mouse Island)," which he published in 1932: "It is rather important to me that the H.D. and the Rhoda Peter are not confused as I find it increasingly difficult to remain MYSELF when writing; the two manners and personalities are quite distinct. However, as I am anxious NOT to have Rhoda Peter incriminated with H.D., will you please, if you want this PONTIKONISI (Mouse Island) keep Rhoda Peter apart from H.D." (14 March 1932, in Halpert 444).

The creation of "Rhoda Peter" reflects a deeper psychic division than H.D.'s desire to fool the reviewers might suggest, a split that takes its manifest form in the formation of opposing prose and poetic discourses. While the public name "H.D." appears on all her poetry, no corresponding single name for her prose exists. Instead, "H.D." stands as a unitary gesture on her poetry that contrasts with a fragmentary proliferation of prose pseudonyms that span her entire writing career. She did, of course, use the name "H.D." for some of her prose, whether by choice or pressure from publishers – Palimpsest and Hedylus, the "Greek" narratives of the 1920s; the reviews for Close Up, the privately circulated Dijon series, and the "children's" fable The Hedgehog in the late 1920s and 1930s; the essay/poem By Avon River in the late 1940s; and her memoirs of the 1940s and 1950s, Tribute to Freud, The Gift, End to Torment, and Bid Me to Live (A Madrigal). But her correspondence about her published prose suggests that she would have used a different name in several cases if publishers would have allowed it. Moreover, most of her unpublished and a few published short pieces bear various gendered and ungendered names that contain secret allusions to different identities. Her poetry, in other words, had one "author" – signaled by the constant and authoritative "signet" "H.D.," a "royal signature" of "sovereignty" (Tribute to Freud 66). Her prose, in contrast, had many "authors," none of which had the "royal manner" of "H.D." Read together, "H.D." and the proliferation of prose names posit the poet as a modernist subject whose fragmented selves have been pieced together into a coherent voice and the prose writer as a postmodernist subject whose selves engage in the processes of endless splitting.[12]

For H.D., these prose names acted as a "focus," calling into existence latent potentialities. Metonymns for language itself, names are like the words of Trilogy, "anagrams, cryptograms, / little boxes, conditioned / / to hatch butterflies" (Collected Poems 540). With their secret histories, names have what Michael Riffaterre called an "intertextual unconscious" accessible through decoding the wordplay that reveals and conceals buried identities. For H.D., names were texts that could be read for the selves they constructed, for the "spell" they cast in an endless process of self-conscious self-making.

A number of her earliest short stories, written before H.D. went to Europe in 1911, use the name Edith Gray, thereby giving her sister Edith, who died in infancy, a life of sorts and foreshadowing the significance of Cecil Gray, the man who fathered her own daughter in 1918.[13] "The Suffragette" bears the gender-free name J. Beran, whose possible reference has yet to be deciphered. In the 1920s, Helga Dart appears on the typescript of *Paint It To-Day* as a name that fleshes out her poetic signature, replaces Do-little with *D'art* (of art), and prefigures the goddess of "The Master," the woman in H.D.'s poem of the mid-1930s who "*is perfect,*" who "needs no man, / herself/ is the dart and pulse of the male" (*Collected Poems* 455, 456).[14] Helga Dart became the softer Helga Doorn as H.D. created a film personality for her three films. In a letter to Viola Jordan, H.D. referred to her "film personality, a thing, as you know that is separate from ones everyday self" (15 June 1930). Suggesting the significance of cinema for her narrative technique, the title page of *HER* bears the name Helga Doorn. Creating personalities for cinema may have further reinforced the text as a scene of performance, the acting out in public of a textual identity signaled by the "stage name."

In the 1930s, Rhoda Peter feminized the name of Peter Rodeck, the man H.D. met on the 1920 cruise to Greece upon which "Pontikonisi" is based.[15] John Helforth is the name she used on her novella *Nights* to signal with Dickensian appropriateness the conventionally masculine, moralistic nature of her narrator. Helforth is the reluctant, somewhat scandalized editor of the writings left by Natalia, the suicide, whose life recapitulates the patterns of H.D.'s. Referring to Ernest, the male mask Bryher used in *Manchester* to narrate her passion for Elizabeth Bergner, H.D. wrote gleefully to Bryher that she had "suddenly discouvered an 'Ernest' " of her own, one whose introduction "makes me scream with mirth... to comment morally on the lapses of the late H.D. It makes me laugh so" (16 and 17 December 1935). But she wrote more seriously about Helforth in a letter to Silvia Dobson: "I use a new name, and it seems to have come off, JOHN HELFORTH. . . . I kept saying there, 'I am John Helforth' – and all at once, it seemed I was. I was very happy at last to find a nom-de-plume, but I don't want people to know it – so will you keep it quiet. . . . I am very glad to see J. H. in print, and feel very Gemini–Aquarius, as I feel also Johanna Helforth might materialize, my twins" (27 July 1935, in H.D., "Friendship Traced" 128). In turn, John Helforth's matter-of-fact ability to cut through personal tangles reappeared as an identity that could potentially solve some of her problems. "I feel sure that J. Helforth will clear up the uc-n [unconscious] tangle of novels and so on," she wrote to Bryher (14 August 1935), and some three years later she responded to tales of Aldington's affairs with "Akk such a jungle, but I am afraid sooner or later 'John Helforth' will have to get on the job" (3 July 1938).

Rhoda and John were complemented in the 1930s by the androgynous or gender-neutral names Alex Dvorat and D. A. Hill. Alex Dvorat does not appear on any writing, but a letter to Dobson details how H.D. fabricated names: "I got the Vorat or Vorrat from a fortune-telling pack

– it means 'store' or 'treasure.' I like the sound – but didn't want to commit myself entirely to German, and the D. came to me in the car, one day. It makes really 'Alex D. V. Orat,' or 'Alex, D. V., prays,' a Greek–Latin combination. Alex meaning 'helper' in Greek, I think I told you, and old D. V. is such a friend of mine. How does it LOOK?" (22 October 193[5?], in H.D., "Friendship Traced" 125). A bisexual disguise, D. A. Hill is an anagram – "Hil-D-A" she explained to Pearson (20 April 1949) – that appeared in *Life and Letters Today* with the sketch "Ear-Ring" and a fabricated life history in the "Notes on Contributors." She liked the name Hill enough to write Bryher that "The Hedgehog... must not be printed as H.D. but D. A. Hill" (29 February 1936), a wish that was not fulfilled. But in the writing process "D. A. Hill" helped her surmount the confinement "H.D." represented. As postwar and pacifist texts, "Ear-Ring" and *The Hedgehog* share an authorial name that materialized a certain perspective on war. As H.D. wrote Bryher, "I find D. A. Hill rather 'thin,' but don't care, its a step out, and the name acts as focus for a lot of old war-stuff that I will gradually 'eliminate.' Don't TELL about HILL, it better stay like that for a time, if you don't mind" (29 May 1936).

In the 1940s and 1950s, she settled on one prose name – Delia Alton – as the author of her fiction, a total of six novels: *Majic Ring, The Sword Went out to Sea (Synthesis of a Dream), White Rose and the Red, The Mystery, Magic Mirror,* and *Bid Me to Live (A Madrigal).* Like D. A. Hill, the name Delia Alton served as a focus for her war experience and its parallels in history. But the "thin" initials D. A. are filled out in female form in Delia Alton. Alton is clearly an abbreviated form of Aldington, H.D.'s married name, and so it is no surprise that Alton's fiction deals overwhelmingly with heterosexual pairs – with the male "initiators" and "heros fatal" to whom H.D. was herself repeatedly attracted, with the patterns of what DuPlessis has termed "romantic thralldom" in the romance plot (*Writing* 66–83).

Almost an anagram for Hilda, Delia may also encode a layered identity – overtly feminine in its onomatopoeic seductions of dahlias, Delilahs; but also covertly androgynous in its austere etymological meaning, "she of Delos, i.e., Artemis." In sending various prose manuscripts to Pearson for possible publication and her shelf at Yale, H.D. repeatedly stressed that they were "by Delia Alton," her "nom de guerre," a phrase that highlights Alton's primary concern with war. A nom de guerre is usually a nom de plume for a soldier, freedom fighter, or war journalist for whom a secret identity is necessary. H.D.'s reference to Delia Alton as a nom de guerre emphasizes that there is another story of war, the war at home from a civilian perspective, specifically a woman's perspective, and, in the case of *The Sword Went Out to Sea,* a pacifist perspective.

"What I HAD to say at that point," she wrote to Aldington about *The Sword,* "was that WAR had got to stop" (6 June 194[8 or 9?]). Pearson's reference to Delia Alton as H.D.'s "nom de paix" was a playful renaming of the conventional nom de guerre.[16]

Delia Alton's defining characteristic, however, is that she was *not* "H.D." "They all pounce on 'early H.D.,'" she complained to Aldington, "but I have my own Delia Alton, three monstrous opus-es – and don't care, don't care" (18 March [194? or 195?]). "I use the name DELIA ALTON," she wrote Aldington in another letter about *The Sword.* "The point is," she explained, "the Oxford press set up three books of poems of mine during the war – a Trilogy – and they asked me for some prose. But the poetry was H.D., of course, and you will see, if you read this, that I do not want it to appear too blatantly 'historical.' . . . I do not want to submit this to Oxford, that is all. Nor do I want to enter into explanations as to WHY H.D. is not used" (1 June 19??). To Pearson, H.D. revealed that the genesis of Delia Alton went deeper than the need for disguise. Purely and simply, "H.D." could not have authored Delia Alton's novels. Her reasons resurrect the early categories of her letter to Cournos about the personal prose writer and the transcendental poet:

> I have been so very happy with this "novel" [*White Rose and the Red*]. I am writing it under a real nom de plume, I mean, one that fits me and fits the book, so it is not actually H.D. writing it. Not that it really matters. It started – the non[m] de guerre (literally), as I wrote in London, and it is too near and too intimate for H.D.; anyhow, I could not have written it as H.D. All this in time, I call the first vol. THE SWORD WENT OUT TO SEA (Synthesis of a Dream). . . . It has the old repercussion of war, war, WAR. . . . THE SWORD is too near and too intimate. (31 July 1948)

Like the "early H.D." of 1917, the "H.D." of the post–World War II world was not "intimate" enough to tell the personal story of love and war. H.D. was adamant with Pearson that *Bid Me To Live* must appear with Alton's name, but he was just as insistent that her recognized pen name be used. Their letters back and forth show the intensity of H.D.'s feelings about her names. She first raised the issue seemingly casually: "I presume the book is by *Delia Alton*. I, as H.D., could never have done it or the other later ones" (14 September 1959).[17] Pearson wrote back a tactful, but stern letter that respectfully acknowledged the importance of a fictional author for the creative process, but firmly insisted on the practicalities of publishing:

> You mention the question of the book as 'by Delia Alton.' It is quite understandably by her, as you needed, had to have, a persona in order to get the aesthetic distance in the actual writing of the manuscript. A

curious progression of personae in which H.D. is one remove from Hilda Doolittle, and Delia Alton a further remove from H.D. and Hilda Doolittle Aldington. So I shall always be grateful to Delia Alton for the gift of this and the other later books. But I had not mentioned this to Grove who of course have been thinking of it as an H.D. listing on their books. In fact one wonders whether people being what they are, and since it will be evident enough that it was written actually by you, it will not be misinterpreted as coy if it were to be published as anything but by H.D. I rather feel that Grove would have this reaction, and might indeed blame me for not telling them that it must appear otherwise than they would interpret. I repeat, I think the important thing about Delia Alton is that she enabled you to write the book, and now gives it back to H.D. (18 September 1959)

Not wanting to appear "coy," not wanting to compromise Pearson, above all wanting *Bid Me To Live* in print, H.D. succumbed to the combined pressure of Pearson and Bryher.[18] But she remained reluctant to "say *yes* to *Madrigal,* without its wind-screen or very obvious protective coloration of *D. A.*" and furiously vulnerable at Grove's proposal of a cover photo: "I feel denuded, naked, my original name, Delia Alton, gone, my title [*Madrigal*] gone. Now this [the photo] – can they leave me a shred of protection on the blurb?" (24 September 1959 and 10 December 1959).

Revealed in all her fictionality, the Delia Alton of H.D.'s letters takes on a powerful psychic reality – so real, in fact, that when she wrote an extended commentary on the development of her writing in 1949–50, she titled and later referred to the text as *H.D. by Delia Alton.* The typescript, which carries no authorial signature, bears a title in which the distinction between author and text has vanished. Each is a product of the other. Pearson was astute as well as tactful in granting H.D. the necessity of a distancing mask for writing her war novels. However, the psychodynamics of naming in H.D.'s fictional constructions of authors suggest that her personae were masks in a Yeatsian rather than a New Critical sense. The names did not so much provide "aesthetic distance" as they governed the linguistic process whereby an aspect of her identity was drawn into manifest existence. The name acted as a focus which allowed her to crystallize and project certain dimensions of the self into language. Linguistic incarnation – the word or name made flesh – meant the creation of a self, one self among many selves, or, to paraphrase the central metaphor in D. A. Hill's "Ear-Ring," one facet of a diamond made up of many facets.

As Pearson said, "H.D." preceded "Delia Alton." The seeds of the novelist lay within the identity of "H.D.," or to be more precise, in what "H.D." was not. "H.D.," particularly "the early H.D.," left gaps that Hilda Doolittle Aldington had to fill through the creation of

"H.D.'s" antithesis: "Delia Alton." The key, in other words, to the development of the prose writer lies in the identity of the early poet which was in some form inadequate as a representation of the woman behind the mask. *Who*, then, was "the early H.D.?" For, in Yeatsian fashion, the "H.D." mask served as dialectical origin for its opposite, the processus of prose personae that culminated in two decades of "Delia Alton."

II. "THE EARLY H.D.": LYRIC IMPERSONALISM

I will get a hut on an isle if there is war, and there will I sit and be a sea-gull in the best early H.D. manner.

H.D., Letter to Bryher
(15 June 1936)

As she burst on the poetic scene of early modernism, "H.D." was, above all, "the invisible poet," to borrow a phrase later associated with Eliot.[19] Eliot's "impersonal poet," first described in "Tradition and the Individual Talent" (1919) and later refined in subsequent essays, had its antecedent in H.D.'s imagist persona and poetics. Lauding efforts to "divert interest from the poet to the poetry," Eliot advocated lyric impersonalism (*Selected Prose* 44). The creative process involves, he claimed, a "transmutation" or "depersonalization" of the poet's passions, not an expression of them (40–2). While the poet's emotions constitute the poem's raw material, writing involves "a continual self-sacrifice, a continual extinction of personality" (40). "Poetry," Eliot concluded, "is not the turning loose of emotion but an escape from emotion; it is not the expression of personality, but an escape from personality. But, of course, only those who have personality and emotions know what it means to want to escape from these things" (43). Apparently sensitive to the misreadings of his "Impersonal theory of poetry" which associated him with "coldness," Eliot subsequently stressed that the poet must have personality and passion, indeed agonies, and that the poem, too, has intense, concentrated emotion.[20]

What Eliot insisted upon, however, was that the emotions of the poet and the poem were not equivalent. Mediating between the two was the linguistic process of *transmution* that distilled the historical personality of the poet into the universal impersonalism of the poem. The poet's struggle, he wrote in "Shakespeare and the Stoicism of Seneca," is "to transmute his personal and private agonies into something rich and strange, something universal and impersonal" (*Selected Essays* 17). The *objective correlative*, Eliot's term for what the imagists had more simply called "the image," was central to aesthetic transmutation.[21] It serves, as Frank Kermode wrote, as a "mask" for "the originating emotion" (17). The critic's proper task was not biographical readings of the poem, but the apprehension of the poem itself, forever cut off from its creator. As Stephen Dedalus says in Joyce's *Portrait of the Artist as a Young Man,* "The personality of the artist . . . finally refines itself out of existence, impersonalises itself, so to speak. . . . The artist, like the God of the creation, remains within or behind or beyond or above his handiwork, invisible, refined out of existence, indifferent, paring his fingernails" (215).

Eliot's impersonal theory of poetry may have been an abstraction of his struggle at the time to transmute the agonies of his personal life into the spiritual waste land of the postwar era. But his concept of impersonalism also had its roots in the poetics of imagism – particularly in the impersonal lyrics of H.D. and Pound.[22] "H.D. *Imagiste*" contemporaneous with, probably even influencing Pound and Eliot, separated the poet from the poem, stressing impersonality by refusing in her choice of signature to identify the private person behind the public persona. Emptied by identity, her initials disembodied the timeless poet from the living woman. She allowed no pictures to accompany her early work, no biographical detail. She left unanswered Amy Lowell's request for "slight biog" and "some anecdotes" for *Some Tendencies in American Literature* (1917).[23] "I have an extreme aversion to personal publicity," she told Houghton Mifflin and condemned any "attack made on my anonymity" (6 February 1924[?]). When a photo appeared in Louis Untermeyer's *American Poetry Since 1900* (1923), H.D. was outraged, according to the report of her Aunt Belle, who was visiting at Territet at the time. "It's not that picture, but any picture!" H.D. said to her mother. "The initials, 'H.D.,' had no identity attached; they could have been pure spirit. But with this I'm embodied!" (Wolle 58).[24] H.D. was still opposed to photos in the 1950s when she objected to Pearson about the projected photos for *Tribute to Freud*: "you know how I like to be 'incog'; after all, that was always *H.D. –,* wasn't it?" (15 March 1956).

Initials as a nom de plume symbolized in the name itself the anonymity and privacy of the impersonal poet. Further, initials obscured the poet's sex. Unlike the assumption of masculine authority evident in various nineteenth-century male pseudonyms adopted by women writers, the initials H.D. suggested the transcendence of gender itself, an ultimate impersonalism that creates an authorial identity beyond masculine and feminine, male and female. A photo fleshed out the genderless initials, forcibly embodying the poet in a female body and initiating conventional expectations for femininity in her readers. Without photos and biography, initials fostered the illusion that the poet-in-the-poem, constituted by language instead of mortal flesh, transcended gender, achieved, in other words, the "incandescence" Woolf associated with the writers she most celebrated as androgynous in *A Room of One's Own*: Shakespeare and Austen.[25]

Consider "Mid-day," a superb example of the crystalline imagist "perfection" for which H.D. was praised, a demonstration as well of the poem dominated by a cluster of related images, each of which is an objective correlative for a state of mind. First published in *The Egoist* on May 1, 1915, the poem predates but perfectly illustrates Eliot's theoretical definitions of impersonalism and the objective correlative as "formula" for emotion.

> The light beats upon me.
> I am startled –
> a split leaf crackles on the paved floor –
> I am anguished – defeated.
>
> A slight wind shakes the seed-pods –
> my thoughts are spent
> as the black seeds.
> My thoughts tear me,
> I dread their fever.
> I am scattered in its whirl.
> I am scattered like
> the hot shrivelled seeds.
>
> The shrivelled seeds
> are split on the path –
> the grass bends with dust,
> the grape slips
> under its crackled leaf:
> yet far beyond the spent seed-pods,
> and the blackened stalks of mint,
> the poplar is bright on the hill,
> the poplar spreads out,
> deep-rooted among trees.
>
> O poplar, you are great
> among the hill-stones,
> while I perish on the path
> among the crevices of the rocks.
> (*Collected Poems* 10)

The poem oscillates brilliantly back and forth between natural phenomena and human feeling, thereby establishing the linguistic link between object and emotion. The landscape of light, split leaf, and seed-pod is an exteriorization of the mind, accomplished by rapid superimpositions and sharp juxtapositions. The line between dashes in the first stanza – "a split leaf crackles on the paved floor" – presents an image for the emotion flatly stated in the lines that immediately precede and follow:

"I am startled" and "I am anguished – defeated." By metaphoric equation, the speaker's thoughts are the split leaf, the rattling seed-pod, the shrivelled seed whirled and scattered in the hot, mid-day wind. The verbs further conflate mental and physical agony with passivity in repeated images of being beaten, broken, torn, split, shrivelled, scattered, and bent. The funereal rhythm of spondees – "A slight wind shakes the seed-pods," for example – intensifies these images of defeat.

The poem's emotion is anguish, the sensation of defeat. Intense, concentrated, and passionate, the poem is nonetheless completely impersonal in Eliot's sense of the term. The anguish belongs to the poem, to the poet constituted as "I" in the poem; it is disembodied emotion distilled of any reference to the living writer. To emphasize these images as masks that transmute the originating emotion of the poem, H.D. provided not a single clue about the cause of anguish or defeat – neither in her own life, nor in the world of the poem. The sudden introduction of the poplar after the pivotal colon intensifies the mystery of origins. The speaker addresses the poplar as a binary opposite – bright, not black; deep-rooted, not scattered; on the hill, not in the crevice; victorious, not defeated. But why, we are not told. We don't even know the sex of the speaker. The hint of womb-like seed-pods and phallic poplar offer only the barest evocation of masculine and feminine.

"Mid-day" refuses an autobiographical reading. We can speculate about the emotions that provoked the poem. The image of a triumphant poplar which contrasts with the speaker may answer Aldington's poem "The Poplar," published in his first volume, *Images,* in 1915. Like a number of his imagist poems, "The Poplar" may screen a description of his wife, whom Pound called "Dryad." "Why do you always stand there shivering / Between the white stream and the road?" the poet asks, as he repeatedly tries to convince the poplar that she is loved, adored, and caressed (*Complete Poems* 43). If "Mid-day" was written after Aldington's poem, it may reverse his poem by insisting that she feels like a shrivelled seed, not a poplar, no matter how she is adored.

Probing more deeply, we might speculate that the poem's anguish originated in H.D.'s interlocking feelings about war and pregnancy. "Mid-day" was published just three weeks before her first child was stillborn, a death she linked with the war. "Khaki killed it," she wrote bluntly about the baby in *Asphodel* (II 3). Hermione, H.D.'s persona in *Asphodel,* is very distressed by the war, by propagandistic appeals for patriotic volunteers, by accusations of cowardice against those not in khaki, by the possibility of her husband's enlistment or conscription into a war he did not support. Echoing imagery from "Mid-day," Hermione in *Asphodel* thinks, "I feel Europe is splitting like that pomegranate. . . . The guns went on, went on, went on . . . guns dropped sound like lead-

hail. . . . an enormous shattering, breaking and tearing...guns over-head
were better though they dropped lead hail that beat and seared her brain,
brought pain back to her consciousness" (II 5, 10). For Hermione in
Asphodel, as most likely for H.D., these guns were inseparable from her
pregnancy. "Men and guns, women and babies," Hermione thinks. In
childbirth, women go "over the top" (II 16). As a threat not only to her
life, but also to her art, the pregnancy itself caused anguish: "almost a
year and her mind glued down, broken, and held back like a wild bird
caught in bird-lime. The state she had been in was a deadly crucifixion.
Not one torture . . . but months and months when her flaming mind beat
up and she found she was caught, her mind not taking her as usual like
a wild bird but her mind-wings beating, beating and her feet caught, her
feet caught, glued like a wild bird in bird-lime" (II 12).

There are, in other words, many sources that suggest biographical
referents for the anguish in "Mid-day." However, the whole point of
H.D.'s impersonal technique in "Mid-day" is to block such connections.
The text denies a context. The emotion is depersonalized and univer-
salized so that we can never locate with any certainty its concrete origins.
To read the poem biographically as a representation of Hilda Aldington's
tortured thoughts during a pregnancy in wartime defies the transmutation
of the emotions of the living woman into the anguish of a "universal,"
disembodied, genderless H.D. – "the early H.D." – constituted "incog[nito]" in the poem. We may (or may not) be "right" in guessing
the "originating emotion" for "Mid-day." But in piercing the textual
screen for its origin, we are missing a key element of "the early H.D."
– the poet's deliberate impersonalism. As H.D. wrote to Cournos, "I
do not put my personal self into my poems." The distinction H.D. made
between "my personal self" and "my real artistic self" anticipates the
distinction Eliot made between the "personality of the poet" and the
impersonalism of the poet the reader meets in the poem.

More than Eliot, however, H.D.'s artistic self, the depersonalized self
projected into and by the poem, was removed from not only her personal
history, but also the history of her times. Eliot anchored his personae in
concrete space and moved them through linear time: the streets, drawing
rooms, offices, and cafés of a modern city in "Prufrock" and the postwar
metropolis of *The Waste Land.* In contrast, the transcendental clairvoyance of "the early H.D." transported her into another realm, one further
removed from recognizable contexts. Her lyrics seemingly take place
outside the social order, in another dimension of space and time that she
later came to call "the fourth dimension," as I will discuss in Chapter 4.
As F. S. Flint wrote about "Hermes of the Ways" in "The Poetry of
H.D.," "the sea that breaks over it surges in some far country of her

imagination; and the wind rushes upon her from the four caves that are in no charted range of mountains" (72–3).

Theocritus, the Hellenist poet and father of the pastoral, was, significantly, one of H.D.'s earliest models. As a genre, the pastoral suggests a binary opposition between nature and culture in which the poet is located in an imaginary realm temporarily removed from the confinements of the social order. *Sea Garden* is a sequence of modern pastorals set in a symbolic green world removed from conventional space and time. In contrast to the harmonious, domesticated nature of traditional pastorals, *Sea Garden's* landscape is wild and dissonant. But it nonetheless gains its revisionist impact by its invocation of a pastoral world of nature.[26] A stone, a pool, a cliff, a shore, a flower designate space. It is a landscape of the imagination in which nature is an exteriorization of the poet's consciousness. The occasional things made by human hand – the shrine in "The Shrine," the temple in "The Cliff Temple," the "rough-hewn god" of "Orchard," the boat in "The Helmsman" – are points that mediate between nature and culture, things that transport the poet into the realm of the sacred. Time exists in this realm – but not historical time. Rather, the elemental cycles of night and day or seasons of the year rhythmically punctuate the volume in poems like "Mid-day," "Evening," "Garden," "Orchard," "Night," and "Hermes of the Ways." Without clocks and calendars, the poet experiences time through light and dark, through the ripeness of the fruit and the heat of the sun. As the final poem in the volume, "Cities" is the exception that proves the rule. It moves the unwilling poet from the natural order back into the social order, symbolized by its construction of crowded cities where the poet can "find no honey of flowers in this waste" (*Collected Poems* 41).

While Theocritus and the Greek lyric poets whom she was translating in the British Museum with Aldington were a profound influence, the poems of *Sea Garden* are, significantly, not set in Greece. Sappho, as Eileen Gregory argued, is a liminal presence throughout *Sea Garden* ("Rose Cut in Rock"), but the poems have no human geography. Temples and shrines, dryads and daemons, gods and goddesses evoke a pre-Christian era, which in turn suggests a Mediterranean landscape. But deities are not named; places are not specified. H.D. even changed the title of "Priapus," one of the three poems Pound sent to *Poetry* in 1912, to the more generalized "Orchard." "Huntress" only alludes to Artemis, goddess of the chase, while the shrine of " 'She who watches over the sea' " merely hints of a goddess who might be Artemis of Tauris or Aphrodite Pelagia.[27] The only poems in *Sea Garden* that specify locations or name deities are "Hermes of the Ways" and "Acon," but both are loose translations and expansions of preexisting poems. Just as the personal self has been distilled into the disembodied poet, so the geography of *Sea Garden* has been deliberately removed from human history.

The predominant tense of *Sea Garden* is the present, what George Wright has called "the lyric tense," a poetic form that dislocates ordinary space and time and asserts the "presence" of past and future in the lyric moment (563–79). "A split leaf crackles on the paved floor," "a slight wind shakes the seed-pods" in the present moment of "Mid-day" – which is forever. Like the moment frozen into timelessness on the Greek vase painting in Keats's "Ode on a Grecian Urn," like "the still point of the turning world" where "the dance is" in Eliot's *Four Quartets* (*Complete Poems* 119), the moment in H.D.'s classic lyric encapsulates past, present, and future.

Like Emily Dickinson, with whom she felt a strong affinity, H.D. pushed the lyric to the borders of generic expectations. What happens in a lyric, as Sharon Cameron wrote in *Lyric Time: Dickinson and the Limits of Genre*, "is arrested, framed, and taken out of the flux of history. ... in lyric poems history gets sacrificed to presence" (70). The lyric attempts a "banishing of the social world" as it "retreats from the telling of stories" (119, 57). Like many other theorists, Cameron described lyric and narrative as opposing discourses.[28] Narratives "are time-and-space-bound," she wrote. They connect "isolated moments of time to create a story multiply peopled and framed by a social context" (56, 22–3). Narrative may be implicit in the lyric moment, but its plot must be reconstructed by the reader (70). For the lyric "resists" narrative by focusing on insight, not action. It interiorizes the conflicts that other genres exteriorize in narratives of the self in relationship to the social world. Not expansive and digressive like the novel, "the lyric is a still life" (241). It features a "solitary self" and celebrates the authority of "the revelatory moment" (22, 71).

Cameron's delineation of lyric discourse conflates exaggerations of the genre with definitions of it, a slippage that ignores theoretically and empirically the existence of lyrics that explore the self-in-history (Yeats's "Easter Morning 1916," Plath's "Daddy," or Rich's *Twenty-One Love Poems,* for example). Nonetheless, her view of the lyric in general captures essential features of "the early H.D." in particular. Like Dickinson, H.D. intensified the tendencies in the lyric for a discourse that privileges vision over action in a landscape of the imagination seemingly constituted outside the social order. H.D.'s later reflections back on her earlier poetic persona identify the poet of *Sea Garden* with the lyric as Cameron has defined it. In *H.D. by Delia Alton,* for example, she commented that some of her World War II poems "differ entirely from the recognized H.D. of the 'early poems.'. . . these are not fundamentally 'H.D. poems' " because they are "narrative" (38–9). The early poems do have progressions, structural movement through states of mind. But they are not "narrative" in H.D.'s view because they do not tell a story within the coordinates of historical space and time. The nonnarrative, dislocated space and time of her *Sea Garden* poems became the butt of ironic humor in her correspondence with Bryher – as the epigraph to this section indicates. In another letter to Bryher, she wrote: "My idea of Paris is a sort of holy, holy pilgrimage to the Louvre to see the lights and shadows on the marbles and wings of marble. All very early H.D." (5 April 1936). Like Yeats's poet sailing for Byzantium, "the early H.D. manner" transported her to a marbled realm frozen forever in the lyric moment.

The association of "the early H.D." and the marble of the Louvre is not a casual comparison. H.D. regarded her early work as sculpted and visual, as well as nonnarrative. She refused to record her early poems, writing to Pearson that "I feel that the early poems were written to be seen, painted or chizzled, rather than to be dramatized" (25 February 1955). This view echoes the discourse of "the early H.D.," as it was collaboratively constructed by the poet and her critics. As Louis Untermeyer wrote, "More than any of the Imagists, H.D. has the sculptor's power of transfixing a gesture and yet not making it static; she can capture a movement without seeming to arrest it" ("Fire and Ice" 134). Her early lyrics were, in short, carved (e)motion, a seeming contradiction that partially accounts for the extraordinary tension in her concentrated verse. Untermeyer called this quality "fire and ice," asserting that in her best poetry "H.D. accomplishes the miracle of fusing warm blood and chill stone. Her marble palpitates" (134). Perhaps in answer to Untermeyer, the poem "Gift," written later but in "the early H.D. manner," presents a poet who imagines herself as a sculptor, "Ardent / yet chill and formal" who will chisel flowers "bled in some ice of fire, / or fire of snow" (*Collected Poems* 338–9).[29]

Both "Gift" and Untermeyer's "Fire and Ice" contributed to a debate about lyric impersonalism running through the reviews of "the early H.D." Like Eliot, H.D. was often charged with "coldness." Indeed, Untermeyer's defense of *Hymen*'s "fire and ice" critiques the "coldness" of *Sea Garden*, which, he reminded readers, had led some to say that it had been written by "a frozen Lesbian" (*American Poetry* 309). While Untermeyer and others like Marianne Moore, Bryher, and May Sinclair defended the vibrancy of the poems, some critics found the chiseled perfection of her imagist lyrics "inhuman," "cold," "passionless," "remote," like a statue that refuses to come to life, like a Galataea who will not reward Pygmalion's desire. Eliot's impersonalism was of course ultimately accepted as quintessentially modernist. But many of H.D.'s readers identified the living writer with the poem-as-statue and fetishized her sculpted perfection as something to both adore and reject, as if it were impossible to grant her the distilled identity of Eliot's Tiresian mask. Marcia Nardi, for example, wrote in praise and condemnation: "Poetry becomes a wall shutting one away from life instead of a gate leading into it. . . . As a chiseled sea-shell, or one upon a canvas, H.D.'s poetry is perfect, but as such, it also lacks those echoes of the heart's depths or the mind's that we always listen for in literature of any kind." "The early H.D.," in the eyes of many readers, *was* the imagist lyric, rather than its Pygmalion. "H.D." was a still life, an "exquisite cameo," perfect in her frozen limitation.[30]

H.D.'s sense of entrapment in the words of her reviewers centered on a word many used about her early imagist lyrics: *crystalline,* which reflects the sculpted quality of "the early H.D." and suggests poems carved in rock. She, like her poems, was imaged as immutable, timeless, impersonal, universal. But in attempting to write herself out of the word that immobilized her, H.D. redefined the word crystalline to mean "of crystal," a mineral that she called a matrix of concentrated energy: "For what is crystal or any gem but the concentrated essence of the rough matrix, of the energy, either of over-intense heat or over-intense cold that projects it? The [early] poems as a whole . . . contain that essence or that symbol, symbol of concentration and of stubborn energy. The energy itself and the matrix itself have not yet been assessed. It is difficult for a critic to do this, it is difficult for me to do this" (*H.D. by Delia Alton* 184).

This crystalline matrix suggests a poetics of psychic intensity. The poem – with its imagist condensation and visual presentation – is a "still point" of fire and ice, of concentrated energy that projects the mind into a transcendental realm, a fourth dimension outside ordinary space and time. As a descendant of the Emersonian transcendentalist whose communion with nature transports the poet to "the over-soul," the poet is "a clairvoyant" – to echo H.D.'s letter to Cournos – that is, a medium whose mind functions as a matrix jewel mediating between the transcendental and the linguistic.[31] As "crystalline," the poem incarnates the transcendental for which the clairvoyant poet serves as medium. The objective correlatives of these early poems pulsate with animistic presences. Ultimately not distinct as tenor and vehicle, the images of "the early H.D." break down the boundaries between mind and matter. This transcendental, even hieratic quality of "the early H.D." has led Robert Duncan to describe even her earliest work as poetry which animistically *presents* (not represents) "the sacred" ("H.D.'s Challenge" 27–8). "The poems of *Sea Garden,*" Adalaide Morris has also written, "are thrown out as bridges to the sacred" ("Projection" 416). Her technique, Morris concluded, broadened Pound's concept of *phanopoeia* "into a technique of meditation or prayer: an imaging used to summon a being from another world" (416).[32]

"The early H.D.," then, was hieratic, not personal; transcendental, not intimate; out-of-time, not in-time; and lyric, not narrative. It is important, however, to recognize that these qualities are part of a *discourse* constructed through the interplay of the historical moment and the conventions of the lyric. Rather than reading H.D.'s lyric as a "cri de coeur," as C. Day Lewis's definition of the genre would suggest (*Lyric Impulse* 4), we do better to remember what W. R. Johnson has argued in *The Idea of Lyric*. The lyric, he maintained, transmutes the personal into the impersonal by submitting feeling to "the needs of discourse" through the mediation of the rhetorical (31–3). Moreover, as Margaret Homans pointed out in adapting Theodor Adorno's discussion of the lyric, the "lyric's insistence on its ahistoricity indicates the nature of its participation in history" ("'Syllables'" 570). The seemingly timeless discourse of the lyric is based, Adorno argued, on the concept of individualism that is itself a product of the history it represses. In the early modernist period, lyric impersonalism involved the repression of history as a factor in the poem's production. The lyric discourse of "the early H.D." transmuted the personal, intimate feeling of the living woman into the "universal," timeless, hieratic language of the disembodied "poet."

Read historically, the repression of history in H.D.'s lyric impersonalism signals her attempt to escape the confinements of history specific to women. Overtly, "H.D." was genderless, beyond the categories of male and female. The impersonal discourse that constructed this persona represented H.D.'s first solution to the problem of gender posed by the post-Victorian male world of letters. As Cassandra Laity suggested, modernist impersonalism was at least partially a masculinist response to the nineteenth-century feminization of the (male) poet which culminated in the personal effusions of Aestheticism and Decadence ("H.D. and Aestheticism"). But, for H.D. (perhaps also for Marianne Moore), impersonalism allowed an escape from femininity – not only from the feminine destiny of hearth and home, but also from the feminine discourse of the Decadents and the Victorian "poetesses" from whom the male modernists were insistently separating themselves. H.D.'s "hard," "clean," "crystalline" lyric discourse cut her off from the dreaded "excesses" of the feminine. The disembodied "H.D." created in *Sea Garden* consequently mirrored her expatriation, her flight from her father's house. Flight is a double word, like exile. It suggests both fleeing from oppression and flying in freedom. The modern pastorals of *Sea Garden* are poems of flight. They represent her exile from the web of social obligation embedded in conventional feminine norms; from the fatherland and motherland of the social order; and from the traditional division of labor that her parents represented – her father, the austere professor and astronomer; her mother, artistically gifted, but "morbidly self-effacing" and dedicated to the career of

her brilliant husband (*Advent* 164). They celebrate as well her flight into
the relative freedom of a landscape of the imagination seemingly removed
from the social order in which women are daughters, wives, mothers,
muses – and "poetesses," if they write verse.[33]

Overtly genderless, this landscape is thus covertly gendered. The seeming absence of gender in *Sea Garden* is in fact its most prominent trace.
The volume's pastoral realm provides an arena for the poet to explore
the gendered questions of identity and desire in highly coded forms.
Freud's concept of the *dream-work* is useful in illuminating the kind of
gendered encoding that *Sea Garden* represents. The dream-work, he argued, negotiates between the dreamer's conflicting needs to reveal and
conceal forbidden desire by "translating" latent thoughts into manifest
content. This disguise both serves and defeats the ego's need for cen-
sorship – serving, by obscuring meaning; defeating, by expressing desire
through indirection. The dream is an expression in code. The grammar
of the dream-work Freud identified – displacement, condensation, visual
(and other nondiscursive) modes of representation, and secondary re-
vision – invite comparison with literary production, particularly with
the poetics of imagism.[34] *Sea Garden* is just such an encoded text, in
which the techniques of the impersonal imagist both reveal and conceal
a forbidden gendered rebellion and eroticism.

Take, for example, the poem "Sheltered Garden," in which H.D.'s
indirect language of flowers serves as a key to unlock the flower codes
throughout the volume, particularly the five sea garden poems scattered
strategically to give the book coherence: "Sea Rose," "Sea Lily," "Sea
Poppies," "Sea Violet," and "Sea Iris." "Sheltered Garden" encodes a
lyric flight from the suffocations of conventional femininity. To quote
in part:

> I have had enough.
> I gasp for breath.
> ....
> I have had enough—
> border-pinks, clove-pinks, wax-lilies,
> herbs, sweet-cress.
>
> O for some sharp swish of a branch—
> there is no scent of resin
> in this place,
> no taste of bark, of coarse weeds,
> aromatic, astringent –
> only border on border of scented pinks.
> ....
> O to blot out this garden
> to forget, to find a new beauty

in some terrible
wind-tortured place.
                    (*Collected Poems* 19–21)

"Sheltered Garden" presents a microcosmic version of the polarities
permeating the volume, including the binary opposition between nature
and culture. The poet's flight from the sheltered garden and longing for
"some terrible / wind-tortured place" enacts on a small scale the movement of the volume as a whole. The celebration of the sharp and coarse,
the hard and harsh, the unripe and unlovely throughout the book encodes
H.D.'s desire to escape from the sweetness and softness, the delicacy and
lushness associated with the "pinks" of conventional femininity. "Sea
Rose," the volume's opening poem and the first of the five sea garden
poems, encodes this gendered rebellion. Overtly, the poem is about a
sea rose, to which the poet speaks, contrasting it with the domestic "wet
rose / single on a stem." Covertly, however, the poem encodes a contrast
between two kinds of womanhood. The traditional association of the
rose with feminine beauty, eroticism, and even female genitalia helps to
evoke this human reference which nonetheless does not appear in the
literal surface of the poem.

> Rose, harsh rose,
> marred and with stint of petals,
> meagre flower, thin,
> sparse of leaf,
>
> more precious
> than a wet rose,
> single on a stem —
> you are caught in the drift.
>
> Stunted, with small leaf,
> you are flung on the sand,
> you are lifted
> in the crisp sand
> that drives in the wind.
>
> Can the spice-rose
> drip such acrid fragrance
> hardened in a leaf?
>   (*Collected Poems* 5)

The meagre sea rose, wild and wind-blown in the sand, is an objective
correlative for the poet's own difference, her flight from Victorian femininity. Viewed from a conventional perspective, the sea rose is "harsh"
and "sparse," "marred" and "meagre," "stint[ed]," "thin" and "stunted"
– H.D.'s randomly scattered, internal off-rhymes intensify the sea rose's

status as outcast. The syntactic repetition of passive verbs whose actors
are absent – "you are caught," "you are flung," "you are lifted" – suggests
the vulnerability of the sea rose. Nonetheless, the poet praises what is
despised and rejects what is typically valued – "you are more precious";
its "acrid fragrance" is superior to the soft rose of the sheltered garden.

While the poet's preference for the wild rose represents H.D.'s alienation from conventional femininity, it does not mean a flight from eroticism. Permeating the "wind-tortured" realm of *Sea Garden* is an austere
sensuality, an erotic dimension of repressed yet explosive sexuality that
is nonreferential in nature. Related to her animistic sense of the sacred,
H.D.'s flowers often radiate erotic energy and rhythm. They are the
crystalline matrix of "over-intense heat" and "over-intense cold," like
the sea violet, white on the sand-hill that catches the light: "frost, a star
edges with its fire" (*Collected Poems* 26). Like the potent flowers in Lawrence's early novels and in Georgia O'Keeffe's flower paintings of the
1920s, the flowers in *Sea Garden* pulsate with an ecstatic eroticism whose
power comes precisely from its elusive, impersonal expression.

Harriet Monroe wrote astutely about these encoded dimensions of
H.D.'s early poetry, which she called "mystic" and "super-sensuous":
the "flowers and trees she writes about . . . are symbols of the soul's
adventures, of a soul which discards and transcends and sublimates the
daily events and emotions of ordinary life" (*Poets* 96). Like May Sinclair
and Bryher, Monroe loved the wildness of H.D.'s lyric gardens. Like
Bryher, she considered this quality distinctly American, attuned particularly to the pioneers and Indians who took "civilized" Europeans "out
of doors":

> The astonishing thing about H.D.'s poetry is the wildness of it. . . . She
> is as wild as deer on the mountain, as hepaticas under the wet mulsh
> of spring, as a dryad racing nude through the wood. She is never
> indoors, never even in a tent. Her feet know the harsh rocks, but never
> the ordered hardness of pavements. Her breath is drawn from bright
> breezes and bold winds, but never from the walled-in atmosphere of
> rooms. . . . never was a poet more unaware of civilization, more inde-
> pendent of its thralls. (*Poets* 92)

This lyric wilderness externalizes H.D.'s alienation from conventional
femininity. It parallels the "murder" of the internalized phantom of the
selfless and pure angel in the house Woolf described in "Professions for
Women" as the precondition of women's creativity. It also represents
H.D.'s flight from the stereotype of the poetess, the sentimental versifier
of soft love and sweet sighs from whom women poets often felt they
had to separate in order to establish their own poetic authority in the
male-dominated world of letters. Untermeyer reinforced this need for
separation in his review of three women poets, one of them H.D. They

"are not," he wrote approvingly, "the manufacturers of traditional, po-
litely feminine verse; they care about many things too much to write,
as so many of their sisters have been doing, the sort of nature-poem that
seems designed for a wall calendar or the type of love-lyric that appears
to have been concocted in a candy-factory" ("Fire and Ice" 133). The
serious woman artist, he seemed to say, must disparage her "sisters,"
must signal her difference from other women.[35]

Such stereotypic poetesses posed a threat to the young Hilda Doolittle,
who needed the approval of the male masters to establish her authority
as a poet. H.D.'s harsh flowers reflect a repudiation of the sentimental
language of flowers popularized by the Victorians, especially the widely
known poet and illustrator Kate Greenaway, whose books *Under the
Window, Language of Flowers,* and *Marigold Garden* were best-sellers. The
first poem H.D. ever learned, as she recalled in *The Gift* (73), was a
Greenaway poem she had to recite in a school play:

> Under the window is my garden,
>> Where sweet, sweet flowers grow;
> And in the pear-tree dwells a robin.
>> The dearest bird I know.
>> (Greenaway 35)

Greenaway's garden is a sheltered one; her pear tree has none of the
"great mass" or "staunch" height of H.D.'s in "Pear Tree" (*Collected
Poems* 39). *Language of Flowers* establishes a code whereby messages could
be secretly transmitted in a gift of flowers or a flower poem. A rose, for
example, meant "love," a violet meant "modesty," a lily meant "purity,"
an anemone meant "forsaken," and rhododendron meant "danger"
(Greenaway 77–80). In *Marigold Garden,* "love" and "purity" dance "under Rose Arches to Rose Town" as the poet sings: "Twist and twine
Roses and Lilies / And little leaves green, / Fit for a queen" (Greenaway 85).

By the time H.D. wrote *The Gift,* she linked the origins of her creativity with such marginalized art as Greenaway's enchanting verse and
illustrations, Harriet Beecher Stowe's popular fiction, and the domestic
art of the folk tradition (see Chapters 2 and 5). But as an emerging poet
in prewar London, H.D. had to exorcise the poetess to become the poet.
As she wrote in her autobiographical sketch "Pontikonisi (Mouse Island)"
about "the early H.D.," "she offered cast-iron exterior to cover, if possible, the suppressed Victorian sentiment" (2). And Alfred Kreymborg
wrote about her early poetry: "Never the soft, the effeminate, is allowed
to intrude, not even among the flowers" (350). "The early H.D." was
akin to Woolf's fictionalized modern woman writer, Mary Carmichael,
whose prose sentence sounds much like H.D.'s crisp lyric line: "This
terseness, this short-windedness, might mean that she was afraid of some-

thing; afraid of being called 'sentimental' perhaps; or she remembered
that women's writing has been called flowery and so provides a super-
fluity of thorns" (*Room* 85). *Sea Garden* is a garden of thorns whose
radiant flowers sting with the brine of salt air.

This "wind-tortured" garden represented H.D.'s first solution to the
problem not only of femininity, but also of masculinity – specifically,
the war, as a reflection of patriarchal patriotism run riot. Most of the
poems of *Sea Garden* were written after war was declared in August,
1914. Like Dickinson, whose powerful lyrics of the early 1860s did not
mention the Civil War, H.D.'s first volume seems to avoid entirely the
cataclysmic Great War which was tearing apart the fabric of her artistic
community and destroying once and for all the grand illusions of Western
civilization. Related to the debates about "coldness" and "passion" in
the reviews of her work, critical views of H.D. in the 1910s and 1920s
circled around her "exquisite" otherworldliness and "true" Greekness.
Some, like Sinclair, defended it; others, like Harold Monro, attacked it
as escapist. Many were ambivalent, as they criticized precisely what so
attracted them. Lowell, for example, celebrated H.D.'s perfection, but
ultimately trivialized it by complaining of her "narrowness": "She seems
quite unaffected by the world about her. . . . The everyday world startles
her as though she really were the dryad," "just startled from a brake of
fern" (*Tendencies* 275, 251). Untermeyer's praise of *Hymen* was qualified
by his distaste for *Sea Garden,* which featured, he wrote, a "wood-nymph
lost in modernity, a Greek marble faintly flushed with life, a delightful
but detached anachronism" ("Perfect Imagist" 260). In 1937, Douglas
Bush canonized the criticism of H.D. as escapist, capping his dismissal
with a judgment that she wasn't even authentically "Greek" (497, 506).[36]

Acutely aware of the critical debate about her timeless landscape, H.D.
defiantly accepted, by redefining, the term "escapism" for her early
poems in a letter to Pearson, which she allowed him to print in his 1938
Oxford Anthology of American Literature: "They are, I suppose, an inner
region of defence, escape; these are the poems of escapism" ("Note"
73).[37] But she and her critics meant something quite different by "escape":
not retreat, but rather "an inner region of defence" against the horror
of the war. Poetry, she believed, offered a means to keep alive the best
in human nature and civilization, to counter the forces of destruction
and death. Where the war bred nihilism, poetry fostered faith. To explain
the "aims" of her early poetry to Pearson, she told him a story about
receiving a letter from Harriet Monroe urging her to give up her "ivory
tower," to "get into 'life,' into the rhythm of our time, in touch with
events, and so on and so on and so on" (72). The irony of this letter from an American living far from the bombs is that H.D. read it
just having come home after a bombing raid, "exhausted and half-

asphixiated." A house next door, she continued, had been struck one night and her flat was filled with shattered glass.

> What does that sort of shock do to the mind, the imagination – not solely of myself, but of an epoch? One of the group [Aldington] found some pleasure in the sight of the tilted shelves and the books tumbled on the floor. He gave a decisive foot-ball kick with his army boot to the fattest volume. It happened to be Browning. He demanded dramatically, "what is the use of all this – now?" To me, *Fortu* and the *yellow-melon flower* answered by existing. They were in another space, another dimension, never so clear as at that very moment. The *unexpected isle in the fair seas* remained. Remains. (72)

Sea Garden remains – a linguistic hold on beauty, music, and desire "in another space, another dimension." As an alternate and higher reality of the imagination, poetry was the basis, H.D. believed, for the regeneration of civilization after the war. The poet's task in wartime was to keep the flame alive, to witness and record the existence of "another dimension" of reality, to answer with faith the nihilism of kicking books and asking "what is the use of all this – now?" Martz has recognized this aspect of H.D.'s early poetry, which he situated within the tradition of the Biblical prophets, who exhort a wayward generation to return to God ("Voices"). Always deeply aware of the historical moment, the prophet's task is to remind those immersed in-time of the out-of-time, the eternal realities of the spirit. What is implicit in *Sea Garden* was to become explicit in *The Walls Do Not Fall,* her next wartime volume of poetry. "The new heresy" the poet attacks in the 1940s is reminiscent of Monroe's charge of escapism. "Poets are useless," " 'nonutilitarian,' " " 'pathetic,' " "they say"; "So what good are your scribblings?" (*Trilogy* 516, 518). "This –" the poet responds, "we take them with us / beyond death / . . . / remember, O Sword, / you are the younger brother, the latter-born, / . . . / *in the beginning/ was the Word*" (*Trilogy* 518–19).

The poet/prophet's call to renew "spiritual realism" in *Trilogy* is direct, indeed exhortatory. But the related prophetic function of *Sea Garden* is submerged. Once again, the concept of literary encoding is useful for decoding the hidden historical reference in the seemingly timeless surface of *Sea Garden*. As the opening poem "Sea Rose" indicates, the pastorals of the volume are hardly suggestive of an idyllic Golden Age. Not harmony, but conflict, both inner and outer, pervades the volume, whose overall tone suggests a siege against unnamed and overwhelming forces. Verbs and sparse adjectives continually evoke violence, not peace – even in the pastoral gardens of the five flower poems. The sea rose and the sea poppies, for example, are "caught" and "flung"; the sea lily is "slashed and torn"; the "fragile" sea violet "clings" to the sand; the "brittle" sea iris is "tangled." A fierce "wind-blast" circulates throughout the volume, introduced first in the driving wind of "Sea Rose" and increased in intensity in poems like "The Shrine," "The Wind Sleepers, "The Cliff Temple," and "Storm." The landscape of the poems is "charged" with "sacred energy," as Morris argued ("Projection"). But the "spiritual force" to which the poems would recall us, is "vanished or vanishing," a presence the poet must pursue, "compelling" it "from immanence to manifestation" ("Projection" 416–17). The cause of the poet's urgency to "track" the signs of the sacred is itself absent in the volume. But the final poem, "Cities," which ushers the reader back into the social order of civilization, reverberates back to the volume's other poems about unspecified conflict: "The Shrine," "Pursuit," "The Contest," "Loss," "Prisoners." These six long poems, comprising over a third of the book, punctuate the volume just as the sea flower poems do. The setting is mythic, the full narrative of violence is veiled, but the omnipresence of struggle is fundamental. Never directly *about* it, Sea Garden is nonetheless *of* the Great War.

However, decoding historical and gender contexts inscribed in the texts of *Sea Garden* runs the risk of obscuring the nature of the *discourse* H.D. devised early in her career – as if we were to analyze only the latent content of the dream, not its manifest surface as well. Like the search for a biographical origin in a poem like "Mid-day," such decoding threatens to ignore the impersonal poetics of "the early H.D.," for whom the historical was transmuted into the mythic, the gender-bound into the gender-free. Johnson's concept of the lyric as a "discourse" in which feeling is mediated by rhetoric is a useful reminder (*Idea of Lyric* 31, 33). We ignore the rhetoric of the disembodied "H.D." if we read only the embattled and battling feeling of the woman/poet in *Sea Garden*. The discourse of "the early H.D." repressed and encoded the gendered shapes of history – both feminine and masculine – so as to defend herself against their constraints and violence.

As initial solution to the problems of gender and war, however, the transcendental discourse of "the early H.D." became its own problem. It left her no discourse in which to tell her *personal* story, the embodied narrative of a woman whose life was being shattered by the intersecting public and private catastrophes caused by the Great War. A reconstructed outline of these events which took place when H.D. was in her late twenties and early thirties is worth reviewing.[38] Shortly after the Germans sank the *Lusitania*, H.D.'s first child was born dead in May of 1915, "from shock and repercussions of war news broken to me in a rather brutal fashion" (*Tribute to Freud* 40; *Magic Mirror* 7–8). Critical of Aldington's civilian status, the matron at the nursing home probably told H.D. to avoid another pregnancy until after the war to save the doctors for the wounded soldiers. Aldington's affairs with other women started as early as the spring of 1916. Although he opposed the war bitterly, Aldington enlisted in the summer of 1916, had a passionate affair with Flo Fallas, the wife of his close friend in training camp, and left for the front in 1917. Enlisting the support of John Cournos, H.D. was determined to keep Aldington's spirit alive, even if it meant sacrificing the man she loved "with a searing, burning intensity" to another woman (Letter to Cournos, 5 September 1916). But as Aldington donned his Tommie uniform in spirit as well as flesh, his leaves became increasingly disastrous. Disillusioned and despairing, he mocked poetry and sought passion in the arms of Dorothy Yorke, the woman H.D. was protecting for Cournos at 44 Mecklenburgh Square. In the fall of 1917, H.D. was also sheltering Frieda and D. H. Lawrence, expelled from Cornwall for suspected spying. But her vitally important friendship with Lawrence fell apart as the affair between them that Frieda apparently fostered never materialized and as H.D.'s relationship with Cecil Gray began in early 1918. Her escape from London's bombs to Gray's house in Cornwall in March of 1918 was healing, but left her unexpectedly pregnant in July of 1918, at about the same time Bryher first came to visit. Aldington approved of the affair with Gray and hoped for the restoration of their marriage after the war. But he was very upset by her consequent pregnancy, saddened by the memory of their own lost daughter, and hopeful (at least temporarily) that she would abort the child in August of 1918. His letters alternately expressed anger and promised support, with the constant threat of his passion for Yorke in the wings. Compounding this ambivalence was his continued enthusiasm for her talent, his adoration of her "spirit," and his passion for the "body" of Yorke.

The war continued to intensify H.D.'s personal suffering. Her brother Gilbert died in France in September of 1918; her father's subsequent stroke led to his death just weeks before the baby was due. Gradually, a certain intimacy developed between the thirty-one-year-old woman and the troubled, twenty-five-year-old Bryher, who was adoring, but suicidally in need of support. Pound, whom H.D. had barely seen in years, appeared at the nursing home to tell her that the baby should have been his. Contraction of the deadly epidemic flu in the final period of pregnancy spelled death, but mother and babe miraculously survived the birth on March 31st, due in part to Bryher's devotion and promise of a trip to Greece. A shell-shocked Aldington appeared with daffodils and a plea for reunion. But when she arrived at his hotel in April, he brutally rejected her and threatened prison if she dared to register the child with his name. Emotional breakdown followed. Recovery came with Bryher on an idyllic trip to the Scilly Isles in July of 1919, where H.D. had the first of several visionary experiences she experienced in her travels with

Bryher, culminating in the "writing on the wall" in Corfu in the spring
of 1920. Cut off completely from the community of artists with whom
she had forged her early success, H.D. lived out the first year of the new
decade with Bryher and her fatherless child. "If I had been a little mal-
adjusted or even mildly deranged," she later quipped, "it would have
been no small wonder" (*Tribute to Freud* 41). Love and war, birth and
death, betrayal and loss were inseparably woven together into her psyche.

Writing about these events was essential to recovery from them. But
the impersonal discourse of H.D. *Imagiste* was not suited to that need.
To work through these events, she needed a personal, narrative, directly
gendered and historical discourse. Woolf, in an essay called "The Narrow
Bridge of Art," suggested that the lyric was entirely unsuited to the
pressing needs of the age: "it is in this atmosphere of doubt and conflict
that writers have now to create, and the fine fabric of a lyric is no more
fitted to contain this point of view than a rose leaf to envelop the rugged
immensity of a rock" (*Granite* 12). The "emotions" of the "modern
mind," she concluded, "submit more readily to prose than to poetry"
(18). In concert with Woolf's view, prose did become the discourse that
freed H.D. to narrate her experience of modernity. But she first tried to
meet the pressure of events by changing her poetry. After the publication
of *Sea Garden,* she began altering the absolute impersonalism of "the
early H.D." in two distinct ways. First, she wrote a few intensely confessional poems that she suppressed; second, she began writing and publishing more explicitly gendered poems anchored specifically in classical
space and mythic time. These poems, which are not "imagist" in the
narrow sense of the term, charted important pathways away from "the
early H.D." for her poetic development, but could not fully suffice as a
personal discourse.

As Martz has pointed out, she "was beginning [in 1916] to create a
strongly personal voice, breaking out of the Imagist confines" (Introduction *xviii–xix*). Her exchange of manuscripts with Lawrence in 1916
and 1917, Martz argued, was an important influence. The events of her
own life and times, I would add, compelled her to seek a more intimate
and narrative discourse. While Aldington began his training near Corfe
Castle in the summer of 1916, she wrote three personal poems that Martz
rightly identified as a major shift in her poetry. As autobiographical and
intimate as Lawrence's own *Look! We Have Come Through!,* "Amaranth,"
"Eros," and "Envy" explore her anguish over Aldington's affair with
Fallas after the stillbirth of their child (*Collected Poems* 310–21). So personal were the poems, in fact, that she did not publish them until 1924.
Even then, she used a lesbian screen to hide the heterosexual base, as
Martz noted. Deleting sections, altering pronouns, separating the poems,
and changing the order, H.D. published them as expansions of Sappho

fragments to disguise the biographical reference (*Collected Poems* 173–5, 181–4, 187–9). Instead of transmuting the personal into the impersonal, H.D. had written a sequence of lyric confessions. According to her own account in *Bid Me to Live (A Madrigal)*, she was following Lawrence's advice. Rico, the novel's Lawrence figure, "jeered" at Julia, the H.D. figure, by calling her a "frozen lily of virtue" at "frozen altars," who wrote about people as if they were deities instead of human beings (51, 138–9, 159, 164). "Amaranth," "Eros," and "Envy" are intimate, not hieratic, poems that attempt to work through the personal tangle into a clearing. Perhaps because their intensely confessional tone was inconsistent with her notion of the poet-as-clairvoyant, or possibly because these poems were too painfully private for her to publish, H.D. did not continue to develop this personal lyric discourse.[39]

The publication of "Eurydice" in 1917 represented the second major shift away from the lyric impersonalism of *Sea Garden*. Written during the same period as her three confessional poems, "Eurydice" established the kind of myth poems H.D. was to write for the next twenty-five years. Like most of the poems in *Hymen* and *Heliodora,* "Eurydice" is specifically Greek, anchored in the space and time of classical myth. Its speaker is overtly and defiantly female. While the focus is still on feeling, the poem has a strong narrative drive: the transformation of Eurydice's despairing anger at Orpheus's backward look into her rebellious affirmation of her own power. The spare line and sharp image of her imagist craft now serves a larger story – Eurydice's release from the gaze of the archetypal male poet whose love confines her to the mute underworld of silence. Superimposed on imagist "presentation" is a revisionist examination of cultural "representation," particularly male representations of WOMAN embedded in mythic texts. As DuPlessis has argued, "Eurydice" is a poem that dismantles the "romantic thralldom" of the cultural love plot and authorizes the autonomous voice of the woman poet (*Writing* 70–1, 109–10). "Eurydice" is the first of many poems in which H.D. deconstructed a masculinist cultural text and reconstructed a female text by making the woman speak. Poems like "Leda," "Cassandra," "Demeter," "Helen," "At Ithaca" and "Calypso Speaks" all rely on the imagist discourse developed by "the early H.D." But their directly gendered re-presentations of dominant mythic discourse mark a substantial departure from the timeless, disembodied presentations of *Sea Garden*.

The assumption of a Greek mask in "Eurydice" also represents a shift away from transmutation toward disguise, a different kind of encoding of the personal than the type represented in poems like "Sea Rose." Unlike "Mid-day," whose anguish has no story, "Eurydice" suggests an analogue between mythic time and ordinary time. Eurydice masks the modern woman whose husband has betrayed their love and left her to the underworld of despair. She also disguises the woman poet who, we learn from *Bid Me to Live*, had the audacity to try to speak for Orpheus as well. Rico wrote to Julia about the manuscript of her Orpheus and Eurydice sequence, "Stick to the woman speaking. How can you know what Orpheus feels? It's your part to be woman, the woman vibration. Eurydice should be enough" (51). Read in the context of the novel about the poem's creation, "Eurydice" becomes in part a kind of mythic autobiography. Orpheus, who conflates and masks the different betrayals of Aldington and Lawrence, consigns Eurydice to the emotional hell of the rejected, chastised, and silenced woman. She in turn, like H.D. herself, refuses to accept this fate and transforms her living death into the basis of rebirth: "At least I have the flowers of myself, / and my thoughts, no god / can take that" (*Collected Poems* 55).

In many of H.D.'s subsequent poems, Greek times, places, and names serve as palimpsestic analogues to the modern world and the people in her circle. The poems can and should, of course, be read without reference to their analogues, just as the more impersonal poems of *Sea Garden* should be read. But as Bryher wrote in her review of *Hymen*, "Thetis, proud, beautiful and alone; Simaetha, wrecked by war; Phaedra, smashed by alien forces – it is only their names (perhaps their personal beauty) that differentiate them from the individuals who struggle and suffer in this present world" ("Spear-shaft" 336). H.D. herself wrote to Pearson that things Greek functioned as "symbols," by which she meant an evocative and talismanic disguise for the personal:

> "Leda" was done at the same time as "Lethe." Lotus-land, all this. It is nostalgia for a lost land. I call it Hellas. I might, psychologically just as well, have listed the Casco Bay islands off the coast of Maine, but I called my islands Rhodes, Samos and Cos. They are symbols. And symbolically, the first island of memory was dredged away or lost, like a miniature Atlantis. It was a thickly wooded island in the Lehigh river and, believe it or not, was actually named Calypso's island. . . . The "lost" world of the classics and the neo-classics is the world of childhood. "What are the islands to me?" . . . [They are poems] of memory – suppressed memory, maybe. (And what about the mother of the Muses? Mnemosene, if I remember?) ("Note" 72–4)

As different as they were from the poems of *Sea Garden*, however, these Greek poems were also "an inner region of defence, escape; these are the poems of escapism," as H.D. wrote to Pearson ("Note" 73). H.D. *Imagiste* had changed in *Hymen* and *Heliodora*, becoming more narrative, more secretly personal, more centered in culture, more directly female. But her critics scarcely noticed the change as they continued to encase her in the perfection of her impersonal lyric discourse. More fundamentally, however, the mythic masks of *Hymen* and *Heliodora* still removed her from direct engagement in the modern world, from the tangled story she felt compelled to tell about her self – the story of a woman, a wife, a mother, a daughter, a sister, a lover caught in the interwoven webs of love and war. She required an intimate, narrative discourse to tell her story, to examine the self-in-the-world that has traditionally been central to the novel. As a method of disguise, the encoding that had worked for "the early H.D." was too indirect. Rather than transmute the personal into the impersonal, she wanted to know the personal in all its particularity. She regarded her own life as a text to be read and to be reread in a subsequent text characterized by its reflexivity. To restore the sight of the shattered clairvoyant poet, H.D. moved toward autobiographical prose, the story of "my personal self." As she wrote Pearson many years later, "For me, it was so important, my own LEGEND. Yes, my own LEGEND. Then, to get well and re-create it" (17 June 1951).

H.D.'s fashioning of a narrative author during World War I represented a flight from the lyric poet, an escape that recapitulated the origins of the English and American novel, in whose development women played such an important role as writers and readers. As many have argued, the novel in the West developed out of a rising middle class wanting a narrative discourse of the here and now, of the self in the social order, of the self in relationship to others.[40] The rapid expansion of middle-class women as a newly literate and partially leisured readership encouraged the development of narrative conventions centered on issues of great concern to women, especially the plots of seduction, courtship, and marriage. As stepchild to genres higher on the literary hierarchy, the novel did not initially have the prestige of the epic, drama, or lyric. Consequently, women writers, whose numbers were greatly on the rise in the eighteenth century, felt freer to make their foray into the male domain of public letters in the novel.[41]

As a genre centered on the story of the self in the world, "The novel," wrote Jonathan Culler, "is conventionally tied to the world in a way that poetry is not" because "the novel serves as the model by which society conceives of itself, the discourse in and through which it articulates the world" (Structuralist Poetics 189–90). The conventions of the novel have created in its readers an expectation of mimesis, that the world of the novel is a representation of a recognizable historical reality (193). Moreover, the rise of the historical novel in the nineteenth century contributed to this association of the novel with a consciousness of history. As Georg Lukacs argued in The Historical Novel, the post-Enlightenment "awakening" of a "conscious historicism" that was the product of the changing nature of war in a post-Napoleonic world fed the development of a narrative genre centered on charting "the historical character" of individual experience and the "mass experience of history" (23–5). In formulating a personal discourse that could narrate her experience as a woman caught in the scripts of love during the war, H.D. repeated in microcosm the developmental patterns of the discourse in which she fashioned her legend. The disembodied lyric flight of the poet was historicized into the directly gendered articulations of the prose writer.

III. SELF-FASHIONING: NARRATIVE PERSONALISM

> It is a very long story or it is a very short story, depending on how you look at it. I could more or less tell it in a paragraph. I could spend my life on ten long volumes and just begin to get the skeleton frame-work of it.
>
> H.D., *Paint It*
> *To-Day* (461)

In the context of war and the postwar world, lyric impersonalism created in H.D. the need for its opposite, narrative personalism. But what began as a therapeutic discourse, a "means to an end," became an unending process, an open-ended end in itself. Writing prose *about* "my personal self" led to a lifelong autobiographical project that fashioned and refashioned the self in the writings of it. "The writing itself . . . constitute[s] the creation," as Patricia Meyer Spacks wrote about autobiography in general (*Imagining a Self* 16). Not a preexisting entity to be authentically (or inauthentically) expressed, the personal self of H.D.'s prose oeuvre was a fiction self-consciously created and re-created in the reflexive acts of writing about it. Like the depersonalized persona of "the early H.D.," the selves constituted in her autobiographical prose are the product of a distinctive discourse, one that anticipated post-structuralist debates about the status of the "author," the issue of referentiality, and the position of women in language.[42] This section will examine the genres of H.D.'s life-writing and demonstrate how her self-fashioning negotiates between fictionality and historicity. The two subsequent sections will further define H.D.'s narrative personalism by identifying its textually, psychologically, and historically determined split female subject and by exploring the stylistics in and through which she (re)fashioned the self.

While the project of H.D.'s prose was autobiographical, its form was never autobiography in the narrow sense of the term. Unlike such (male) classics of the genre as *The Confessions* of St. Augustine and Rousseau, H.D.'s life-writing was not a "confession" cum apologia, not a developmental reconstruction of her life in its totality, not a summary interpretation imposing coherence in its creation of order and meaning. Such

teleological projects are fundamentally at odds with historical constructions of femininity and modernist perspectives on the self.[43] Like Woolf
(and many other modernist writers), H.D. never wrote a single sum-
mation of her life. When Viking Press asked her to write an " 'honest'
autobiography," she adamantly refused.[44] Although she did not explain
her refusal, she wrote elsewhere about the artistic freedom she required
to write about the personal self. About *The Gift,* for example, she reflected, "[it] is autobiographical, 'almost.' The author has the privilege
of trimming or paring, of concentrating or expanding where it will best
suit his purpose or where his purpose will suit him" (*H.D. by Delia Alton*
17). In *Compassionate Friendship,* she noted how she had changed some
dates in *Bid Me to Live* to highlight the significance of her meeting
Lawrence on the eve of war (53, 57). In *HER,* selection and alteration
of chronology are radical. The events of the novel, which take place in
a gestational nine-month period, correspond to a four- or five-year period
in her life. H.D.'s successes at night school at the University of Pennsylvania are missing from the novel, which emphasizes Hermione's academic failure. H.D. wanted the freedom to tell the "truth" by
fictionalizing, the same liberty Woolf took in *A Room of One's Own* when
she said "Lies will flow from my lips, but there may be some truth mixed
up with them" (4).

Privacy as well as aesthetic license was also at issue. The personalism
of H.D.'s prose discourse did not eliminate her desire for screens, especially in texts written for immediate publication. "Selves in Hiding"
– Spacks's descripter for women's characteristically disguised self-
revelations – is an apt phrase for H.D.'s prose personae. As Spacks noted,
the genre of autobiography "implies self-assertion and self-display," a
confident exposure at odds with cultural prescriptions for femininity
("Selves" 114). Fictionalizing conventions served for H.D. as "protective
colouration" in autobiographical self-fashioning. *Tribute to Freud,* for
example, is a cautious text whose personal revelations discreetly screen
her frank exploration of eroticism and gender in the analytic situation,
a part of which she confided to Bryher in her daily letters from Vienna.
As she later reflected about her tribute, "In a very superficial account
that I give of some of our sessions at *Bergasse,* in Vienna, I touch on the
family-scene, as presented in *The Gift*" (*H.D. by Delia Alton* 22). In a
similar vein, she wrote to Aldington, "I have been going over about 20
old note-books, or slopped-down impressions, Vienna, London, Paris,
New York, and combing out all sorry, unpleasant, unhappy references
to anybody, more or less. I get in a few digs at the elite and the high-
brow but personal revelations, I really do bar. This sounds as if my 'For
Remembrance' may read pretty insipid" (28 November 195[?]). In part,

H.D. was eager to reassure Aldington, who might well have been concerned about her disclosure of his personal life. But disguise remained important for H.D., even as she created a personal discourse more intimate than the distilled lyric impersonalism of her imagist and mythic poetry in the 1910s and 1920s.

H.D.'s multivolume remembrances of things past are no more "insipid" than they are "superficial." Rather, their discourse is characteristically modernist in its reflexivity, formal experimentation, and preoccupation with the fragmentary, discontinuous, and decentered nature of the self in the modern world.[45] A narrow definition of autobiography is particularly unsuited to modernism in general and to H.D.'s prose in specific. William Spengemann has characterized modernism as a movement whose epistemology fostered autobiograph_y in the broadest sense of the term. Modernism brought about a move "away from representational discourse toward self-enacting, self-reflexive verbal structures" in which the self is pervasively present – so much so that "the very idea of literary modernism seem[s] synonymous with that of autobiography" (*xiii*). Like many other recent critics, Spengemann has urged a much broader understanding of autobiography, one that recognizes the varied genres in which the autobiographical impulse has found expression. Generic forms of self-presentation, according to Spengemann, have varied – the novel, the poem, the play, the essay, the diary are equally available for life-writing. Poetic and fictive genres have been especially common in the modernist period (*xiii*). What autobiographical writings share is that "the writer's self is either the primary subject or the principal object of the verbal action" (*xvi*). For James Olney, the definitional core resides in the root meanings of the word: *autos* (self), *bios* (life), and *graphe* (writing). Whatever the genre, autobiography is a text that inscribes the life of the self (*Autobiography* 3–6).[46]

The protean forms of H.D.'s autobiographical self-creations in prose inscribe not only her "personal" story, but also her sense of marginality as a woman writer. The genres she chose – roman à clef, historical novel, children's novel, novella, sketch, memoir, journal, and personal essay – are themselves marginal to more prestigious literary forms. The novel's importance as a genre authorizing women writers and readers may have attracted H.D. in her initial escape from "the early H.D.," for her first attempts to write about her personal tangles were novels. But even her novels stand outside the tradition's mainstream. By the beginning of the twentieth century, the newest genus of literary species had established its own "great tradition," but instead of situating her prose at the center of that tradition, H.D. grafted the principles of modernist epistemology and style to the less prestigious subgenres of the novel – the roman à clef and the historical novel. The roman à clef flourished as a literary and sexual scandal sheet in the satiric war of words common in the eighteenth century, not a promising resonance for a high modernist novel. The roman à clef also fosters a mimetic, even allegorical reading that is at odds with most modernist fiction. The "key," known to initiates, invites the reader to make one-to-one equivalences between fictional and real people and events. Similarly, the historical novel developed in the eighteenth century as an arena for nostalgic pageantry. "History," according to Lukacs, was "treated as mere costumery: it is only the curiosities and oddities of the *milieu* that matter" (19). Its rise during the nineteenth century as a probing exploration of the interaction between individual and history was followed in the early twentieth century by the rise of the form as popular fiction replete with costumery, exoticism, and settings far removed from the present.[47] Like the roman à clef, the historical novel hardly appears to be an encouraging mode for a discourse about the personal self in the modern world at war. Nonetheless, to construct the legend of the poet, H.D. transplanted the narrative conventions of the *Bildungsroman* and *Kunstlerroman* into the unlikely framework of the roman à clef and the historical novel.

Her first and last novels were romans à clef: *Paint It To-Day,* completed in 1921, but possibly a version of the novel about which she wrote Cournos in 1919; and *Magic Mirror,* written in 1955 about life at Küsnacht Klinique in Switzerland. Six additional novels, only two of which she published, are romans à clef: *Asphodel, Palimpsest,* and *HER* from the 1920s; *Majic Ring, The Sword Went Out to Sea (Synthesis of a Dream),* and *Bid Me to Live (A Madrigal)* from the late 1930s and 1940s. She also used this form for her Dijon novellas (*Narthex, The Usual Star, Kora and Ka, Mira-Mare,* and *Nights*) of the late 1920s and early 1930s; an unpublished collection of World War II sketches (*Within the Walls*); a 1930 sketch about Paul Robeson ("Two Americans"); and her pacifist children's book, *The Hedgehog,* published in 1936. When *Bid Me to Live* finally came out in 1960, the reviewer from *Newsweek* wrote "H.D. had no hesitation in admitting that the book she had written was completely autobiographical. 'It's just that, word for word,' she said. 'It is a roman à clef, and the keys are easy enough to find. I even thought there might be some libelous material in it, but some lawyers said no. I am Julia. And all the others are real people" (2 May 1960). She provided the "keys" to Pearson for the novel, just as she did for *The Sword Went out to Sea.* As if they were the credits for a play or film, she called these keys a "dramatis personae." The typescript of *HER* contains a handwritten dramatis personae equating fictional and actual names on the title page, a list that can be made with relative ease for all her romans à clef.

The historical novels contain no such keys, in part because the characters seldom have a one-to-one correspondence to the people in H.D.'s life. The autobiographical core of the history novels is more coded, partial, and displaced than it is in the romans à clef, but it is still recognizably present, particularly for the central female character. Published in 1926 and 1928, *Palimpsest* and *Hedylus* feature Greek heroines in the ancient world. Three subsequent historical novels were rejected by publishers: *Pilate's Wife* (1924, 1929, 1934), set in the time of Jesus; *White Rose and the Red* (1948), about Elizabeth Siddal and the Pre-Raphaelites; and *The Mystery* (1949, 1951), about eighteenth-century Moravians. An avid reader of popular historical fiction, H.D. found the form useful for hiding an autobiographical impulse in the settings of another era. During the final stressful days of her divorce proceedings, for example, she wrote Bryher that she was enjoying going over "some of my old historical novels at Harrods," including "a popular vol." on Henry VIII that "also helps and links straight on to Bluebeard and evidently in UNK [unconscious], I was Catherine of Aragon – all very odd, and such a relief to have escaped from R. A[ldington]" (7 and 11 July 1938).

H.D. regularly bridged the gap between the roman à clef and the historical novel by creating generic hybrids. *Palimpsest* is ostensibly a collection of three unrelated short stories, but the text is an interlocking triptych, one story of which is set in classical Rome, while the other two stories are set in the 1920s. All three stories are like roman à clef in that the characters clearly correspond to each other and to the people in H.D.'s life "story." *The Hedgehog* combines the autobiographical correspondences characterizing H.D.'s romans à clef with the displacements common in her historical novels. The central figure in *The Hedgehog* is the child Madge, modeled on and created for Perdita. She is the child of Bett, a mother figure who combines aspects of both H.D. and Bryher, Perdita's two mothers. In the course of the story, Madge's mountain climb takes on the qualities of transcendental quest that H.D. particularly associated with her stays at Kenwin in the Swiss Alps.[48] Like *White Rose and the Red* and *The Mystery*, *The Hedgehog* presents a psychological autobiography in the form of a story about another.

While H.D.'s autobiographical writings began with forms of prose fiction, she also explored several related forms of the personal essay, each one of which enacted a marginality to more established genres. *Notes on Thought and Vision* was the first of these, completed while she was in the middle of writing *Notes on Euripides, Pausanius, and Greek Lyric Poets*. Her *Close Up* reviews and the *Borderline* pamphlet strongly personalized the critical essay. Then, after her experience with psychoanalysis in the 1930s, she adapted the conventions of the memoir and journal – stepchildren to autobiography proper – to write eight more such texts: *The Gift, Tribute to Freud, Advent,* "The Guest" in *By Avon River,* and *H.D. by Delia Alton* in the 1940s; *Compassionate Friendship, End to Torment,* and

Thorn Thicket in the 1950s and 1960s.[49] With their free-associational structures, these personal essays resemble both the psychoanalytic process H.D. learned from Freud and the interior monologues of the modernist novel.

The memoir, Roy Pascal wrote, differs from "autobiography proper" in its focus on others instead of the self (5–6). *The Gift,* written from 1941–3, is the first of three tribute/memoirs. It is a gift to her mother and the Moravian heritage which was her mother's gift to her daughter. *Tribute to Freud* (first published in serial form in 1945 and 1946) and *End to Torment* (written in 1958) are tributes that both praise and resist a famous man, thereby invoking the double meaning of the word "tribute," as Adalaide Morris has argued ("Relay of Power"). As Mary Mason hypothesized about women's autobiographies in general, H.D.'s tribute/memoirs have a "double focus" – they engage in self-creation through a focus on an Other. "The discovery of women's identity [in their autobiographies]," Mason argued, "seems to acknowledge the real presence and recognition of another consciousness, and the disclosure of female self is linked to the identification of some 'other.' This recognition of another consciousness . . . this grounding of identity through relation to the chosen other, seems . . . to enable women to write openly about themselves" ("Other Voice" 210).[50] The historically determined construction of feminine identity, Nancy Chodorow argued, fosters a relational identity for women, a self whose "permeable ego boundaries" suggest a network of relations rather than an isolate unit of being (*Reproduction* 169). Like Gertrude Stein's *The Autobiography of Alice B. Toklas* and Maxine Hong Kingston's *The Woman Warrior: Memoirs of a Childhood among Ghosts,* H.D.'s tributes to others allowed for an indirect exploration of her self in a text whose form inscribes what Chodorow calls the "complex relational constellation" of the female psyche.[51]

As a tribute in journal form, *End to Torment* forms a generic bridge to H.D.'s other personal essays, those written in the form of the diary. With their carefully dated entries, these texts appear to have the immediacy and open-endedness of a journal, qualities at odds with the ordering principle of "autobiography proper," according to Pascal (5).[52] These journals, however, are unlike daily diaries that reflect on the events of the day, even diaries as carefully composed as the multivolumed *Diary of Anais Nin.* Instead, they are carefully directed reflections on specific topics related to her own unfolding artistic development. *Advent,* which purports to be the daily entries she wrote about Freud during March of 1933, is actually a text based on her Vienna notebooks, but composed in 1948 in the form of a journal, which gave her the license to be less censored about her analysis than the more formal *Tribute to Freud. H.D. by Delia Alton* (1949–50), *Compassionate Friendship* (1955), and *Thorn*

Thicket (1960) are all centered on her own oeuvre, both poetry and prose. Like the prose insets in *Helen in Egypt,* written after the lyric sequences of the epic, these "journals" reflect upon the texts she has written – their meanings, their intertextual resonances, their relationship to her life, their significance for the future. Written during periods when she was re-reading her published and unpublished work, her self as *text* is the subject of these "journals." Like Helen, "she herself is the writing" which she must (re)read in an endless process of deciphering (*Helen in Egypt* 91). Borrowing from the journal's characteristic, unabashed narcissism, H.D.'s "journals" perform the task of the critic. They are a self-assessment that fortified her for future creative work.

The protean generic shapes of H.D.'s autobiographical prose tend to obscure the complex negotiation between fictionality and referentiality that characterizes her personal discourse. As a genre, the novel is a fictional form that makes no claim to historical or biographical fact, whether or not the text is understood to be mimetic, an accurate representation of reality. It tells "the truth" by lying, by fictionalizing; its perceived authenticity resides in the writer's imaginative powers. The memoir or journal, on the other hand, does claim historicity. These genres, like the "autobiography proper," foster the reader's expectation that the narrative records things that really happened; that the people named really exist; that the writer, the speaking subject, and the person in the text are one and the same, however much he or she might have changed over time. A reader might understandably feel betrayed to discover that the author "made up" things that were presented as "facts." Given these differences, it seems confusing to place H.D.'s novels and memoirs in the same category of discourse – as mystifying as the title page of Charlotte Brontë's first-person novel, "*Jane Eyre, An Autobiography,* by Currer Bell."

However, this polarity of generic expectations between the fictionality of the novel and the referentiality of autobiography obscures the degree to which each regularly partakes of the other. The novel can and does exhibit referentiality – no matter how displaced or encoded. Its text gestures to a context beyond itself and its literary intertexts; it contains a reference back to the life of its author and more broadly to the historical world from which it emerges. As a verbal act, autobiography inevitably shares with fiction linguistic strategies for telling stories. No matter how "factual," its text borrows its shape from literary conventions and its discourse from fictional representations.[53]

This interpenetration of referentiality and fictionality that I claim for H.D.'s life-writing appears at odds with my Foucaultian assertion that "the early H.D." and the "H.D." of her prose oeuvre represent constructed "discourses." But in fact, H.D.'s life-writing anticipated structuralist and post-structuralist views of the "author" and "the subject." Because H.D. self-consciously disrupted so many of the conventions that later theorists unraveled, it is especially useful to read her texts within the grid of recent critical theory. Influencing many theorists of auto-biography, structuralism has challenged the referentiality of texts on the grounds of the nonreferentiality of language itself. Words are part of an endless chain of signifiers that refer only to other signifiers within the semiotic system. As empty signs, words are an absence that cannot contain the presence of the signified. The "reality effect" in the novel or autobiography is merely a "referential illusion" based on convention, according to Barthes in "The Reality Effect" (*Rustle* 148). Writing is not "expression," which presumes the preexistence of an author, but rather a "pure gesture of inscription." The writer is an "agent... not interior but *anterior* to the process of writing," Barthes insisted in "To Write: An Intransitive Verb?" (*Rustle* 19). "To write" is "intransitive," an act that does not *express* the author, but rather *constitutes* the subject "as immediately contemporary with the writing" (*Rustle* 19). In "The Death of the Author," Barthes described writing as "the destruction of every voice.... where our subject slips away, the negative where all identity is lost, starting with the very identity of the body writing" (*Image* 142). The impersonalism of the poet in Eliot's theory is expanded in Barthes into the "requisite" of writing itself: "voice loses its origin, the author enters into his own death" (*Image* 143, 142). Given impetus by the rise of individualism as ideology in the nineteenth century, the "author" is a construct, a convention of literary discourse.

From the structuralist perspective, the "death of the author" marks the "I" (particularly the autobiographical first person) as a "poseur," and "writing" as a "species of imposture," an " 'artifice' of sincerity" (Kennedy 385).[54] As Sidone Smith summarized the structuralist and post-structuralist "challenge" to "confidence in the referentiality of language" and "comfortable assumptions about an informing 'I' ": "The *autos,* shattered by the influence of the unconscious and structured by linguistic configurations beyond any single mind, may be nothing more, and certainly nothing less, than a convention of time and space.... The auto-biographical text becomes a narrative artifice, privileging a presence, or identity, that does not exist outside language" (5–6). The title of Barthes's own autobiography, *Roland Barthes by Roland Barthes,* highlights this artifice. "Barthes" appears in the text variously as "I," "you," "he," or simply "R. B." In one fragment titled *"Le livre du Moi – / the book of the Self,"* these alternating pronouns emphasize the fictive nature of the autobiographical self, which exists only in the empty signs on the page: "Though consisting apparently of a series of 'ideas,' this book is not the book of his ideas; it is the book of the Self, the book of my resistances to my own ideas. . . . All this must be considered as if spoken by a character in a novel – or rather by several characters. . . . The substance of this book, ultimately, is therefore totally fictive" (119–20). Barthes's view in this book, if we can even presume a "Barthes" who has a view, comes close to asserting that there is nothing but representation, which refers to nothing but other representations. *Roland Barthes by Roland Barthes* has "expelled" the signified from the signifier, the life from the sign (*Rustle* 147).

The "death of the author" replicates the broader "death" or decentering of the unitary subject (or self) in structuralist and especially post-structuralist theory. Like the author, the subject is a construct of language, not an essence that lies outside language. As David Carroll wrote in *The Subject in Question,* the impact of structuralism has been that "the subject finds itself now within, not at the source of, language, a function determined by language and not an origin 'outside' the textual–linguistic systems surrounding it" (14–15). For Lacanians, this fictive constitution of the subject goes back to the beginnings of "identity" in "the mirror stage," when the child first knows itself by seeing an empty image in the mirror. "The subject," Lacan wrote, "originally identifies himself with the visual *Gestalt* of his own body," which represents "an ideal unity, a salutary *imago*" (*Ecrits* 18–19). This experience points the formation of the ego in an "alienating" and "fictional direction" from which it never departs as the subject moves from the Imaginary stage into the Symbolic. As the Oedipus complex ushers the child into the realm of the Symbolic, the empty image in the mirror is replaced by empty words in a semiotic system that constitutes the subject. Identity remains a false construct, a rigid imago, an Other whose unity and coherence represent an alienation from its fragmentary, discontinuous origin (*Ecrits* 2, 19–26). For autobiographical texts, let alone fictional ones, this dismantling of the unitary subject denies the referentiality which generic conventions foster. As Willis Buck argued in his Lacanian study of autobiography, "Identity is thus constituted in the image of an image, and marks the individual's alienation from his own reality" (481). An autobiography simply extends into a public text the fictionalizing or – what Buck termed "autobiographizing" – that characterizes the private formation of identity (482). Like the analyst who seeks the fragmentary entity in the mute speech of the unconscious, the reader of an autobiography looks past the constructed imago ultimately to the "unconscious of the text" (482).

The discourse of H.D.'s prose oeuvre insists on a both/and rather than an either/or approach to the debate about the referentiality and fictionality of the author, subject, and text. In doing so, it demonstrates how her work anticipated structuralist and post-structuralist critical theory. It further points beyond post-structuralism toward a dynamic interplay of linguistic and materialist perspectives on language and reality.[55] Mediating in this dialectic is her gender – the gendered dimension of her discourse – that, on the one hand, recognizes the (female) self as a cultural construct rather than an essence and, on the other hand, insists on her (female) "presence" rather than "absence" in her self-begetting texts. In her reflexive works, language is both empty and full, nonreferential and referential; it gestures to other texts and to the world that produced them. The self is both a linguistic entity and a speaking, writing subject – not "killed" in the process of entering language, but reborn. In the words of Ntozake Shange, language is "a tool for exploring space" – a potency, not a lack, that makes its mark on history (*Nappy Edges* 17). "Words were her plague and words were her redemption," H.D. wrote in *HER* (67).

The terms *representational, referential,* and *mimetic* – all associated with the concept of literary discourse as a transparent medium for "expressing" the "real" world – actually suggest this both/and dialectic of fictionality and referentiality. The *representation* of self in an autobiography is a *representation*, not the thing itself. Textual *reference* to an external context *refers* one thing to another; it doesn't conflate them. Mimesis means imitation, a *mimicking* of reality rather than a (re)incarnation of it. Referential, representational, mimetic are all terms that suggest correspondence between the signifier and the signified, not an equivalence. Although it can and has been read in a number of ways, Barthes's puzzling final book, *Camera Lucida,* can be seen as an argument for this dialectical view of literary representation. Apparently, his mother's death, which disturbed Barthes profoundly, led him to rethink his earlier position on language in which everything (even "fact") ultimately becomes a form of textuality, thereby empty of reality. His mother's death was "real"; its consequence was "real." *Camera Lucida* records Barthes's movement away from linguistic solipsism into an exploration of the representation of the "real," as Gerald Kennedy has pointed out. A photographic image – a picture of himself as a young boy in his mother's lap – becomes emblematic of such representation. This image is both empty and full. As an image, it is not himself and his mother – he in fact playfully labels it "the mirror stage" to highlight its fictionality. The photo's replication of the madonna-and-child archetype further stresses its existence as cultural text. But as an image, its existence refers back to a real point of origin. He is both absent and present in the image – the image is an empty sign whose existence testifies to a real fact: He did sit on his mother's lap.

Camera Lucida may represent Barthes's move from the Symbolic realm of words back to the Imaginary realm of images; or it may reflect a retraction of his earlier work on the illusion of referentiality.[56] But it is useful to see this image of a young Barthes on his mother's lap as an emblem of verbal as well as visual representation, one that shows signifier mothered by signified, one that captures the complexities of interlocking autobiographical and fictional discourses, one that thereby illuminates H.D.'s discourse of self-creation. Like the photo, the literary text, especially the autobiographical one, originates in and refers back to the real, but is never its equivalent. The autobiographical self is created within the text, but such construction does not mean that the self has no reference to the world beyond the text. Rather, it is *both* created in language *and* tied umbilically to its origins in experience; it is composed of and by words, but is not merely empty characters on a page, a "poseur" without historical mediation. Further, as a linguistic act, the text is *of* the world, not autonomous from it. As Linda Hutcheon argued in *Narcissistic Narrative* about self-reflexive texts, "the Romantic 'author,' as originating and original source of meaning may well be dead," but fiction "is always mediated by contextual forces, including its historical, social, and ideological determination" (*xv*). A self-referring text, what Hutcheon called a "metafiction," "provides within itself, a commentary on its own status as fiction and as language, and also on its own processes of production and reception" (*xii*). It "works to situate itself in history and in discourse, as well as to insist on its autonomous fictional and linguistic nature" (*xiv*).

Anticipating the issues Barthes explored in *Camera Lucida*, H.D.'s *H.D. by Delia Alton* repeatedly demonstrates an awareness of the fictionality and referentiality of her prose works. Even more radically than *Roland Barthes by Roland Barthes*, *H.D. by Delia Alton* suggests in its processus of pseudonyms the linguistic construction of identity – the self as the product of naming. As she wanders through the labyrinth of her writings, rereading and reconstituting them, the autobiographical selves she finds are fictive loops that originate in and refer back to a living woman whose identity is inseparable from its many inscriptions. Self and text, language and reality are entangled: "she herself is the writing" that she herself has written. As she reflected on her purpose in *H.D. by Delia Alton*, "I am trying to pin down my map, to plot the course of my journey, to circumscribe my own world or simply to put a frame around my clockface. I repeat these dates, these names and titles for they are important to me, in this PLOT" (220). On the one hand, she recognized that each persona in this "plot" is a fiction "dressed up" in linguistic costume. Alluding to the various personae that "ghosted" for her own experience, she noted that her books seem

> "dressed up." But why not dress up? We are not Margaret [Fairwood of *Palimpsest*], we are not Julia Ashton of the War I *Madrigal*. We are not one or any of these whose lovely names startle and enchant me, as

I read them now as if for the first time. . . . We are not Hedyle, . . . nor the exquisite child of Hedyle, Hedylus who gives his name to that book. . . . We are not Raymonde of the first "contemporary" *Murex* [in *Palimpsest*] nor yet the later Raymonde of *Narthex*. (220)

On the other hand, H.D. regarded these dressed up personae as projections of some "real" aspect of her self, some matrix of experience that "comes true" as she writes about it.[57] They "overlap, or the names change though the 'characters' are the same" (219). As her persona Erica in *Magic Mirror* reflects, "I am Julia of that period, of that story, she thought. I am various other people, Stella in particular, of the second war series (*Sword, Rose*). O – so many" (8–9). These personae are superimpositions for fictional others, but also for herself as living woman who (re)creates herself in the writing.

Like the names she chose for her noms de plume, the names of her personae exemplify H.D.'s double discourse, one that gestures simultaneously at fictionality and referentiality. The name Erica in *Magic Mirror* points to both texts and contexts. Rica, Erica's nickname in the novel, echoes Rico, the name Lawrence used in *St. Mawr* for an impotent dullard. It also reproduces the Lawrence figure named Rico in *Bid Me to Live,* in which H.D. appears as Julia, the same name Lawrence used for her in his vicious portrait in *Aaron's Rod,* as Martz has pointed out ("Voices"). With its multiple codes, the name Erica in *Magic Mirror* is well worthy of an eighteenth-century scandal sheet, but it is also more than an intertextual joke. Erica refers to the real relationship between H.D. and Lawrence, which she saw superimposed on her relationships with her favorite brother Eric and her analyst Erich Heydt, for whom her novel is a kind of "tribute." She experienced all three men as her doubles, as twin souls with whom she had a cerebrally intense, erotically sublimated relationship that fueled her creativity. Further, the name Erica evokes H.D.'s American origin. Erica sees her name as an anagram for her American identity – "Am-Erica" is "America," she thinks (24). "Erica" both is and is not "H.D."

This complex interplay between intertextual and biographical reference in H.D.'s choice of names is a consistent feature of her prose and anticipates current debates in feminist literary theory about the significance of "signature" and the status of the gendered subject. H.D.'s elaborate play with textual naming simultaneously asserts the fictional and historical constructions of female identity and it consequently requires Nancy K. Miller's arachnological method of *overreading*. "When we tear the web of women's texts," Miller wrote, "we discover in the representations of writing itself the marks of the grossly material, the sometimes brutal traces of the culture of gender; the inscriptions of its political structures" (*Subject* 84). The historical remains in the textual. This double

trace of the linguistic and the historical requires "reading for the signature
. . . to put one's finger – figuratively – on the place of production that
marks the spinner's attachment to her web" (96–7). It is Miller's "con-
viction" that "it matters who writes and *signs* woman" and that "by
glossing 'woman' as an archaic signifier, it ['the metalogically "correct"
position'] glosses over the *referential* suffering of women" (69, 71). Although she adapted Barthes's concept of the text as textile, a weaving
of textual practices, Miller argued that

> the postmodern decision that the Author is dead and the subject along
> with him does not . . . necessarily hold for women, and prematurely
> forecloses the question of agency for them. Because women have not
> had the same historical relation of identity to origin, institution, pro-
> duction, that men have had, they have not, I think, (collectively) felt
> burdened by *too much* Self, Ego, Cogito, etc. (106)

Consequently, Miller concluded, we need to develop reading strategies
that examine the contradictions between textual and historical constructions of female identity (103). Arachnology involves "a critical positioning" that allows us "to recover within representation the emblems of
its construction" (80). H.D.'s self-reflexive play with naming and self-
fashioning both enacts and is illuminated by the "critical positioning"
Miller proposed.

IV. SPLITTING THE SUBJECT: MODERNISM, GENDER, AND AUTOBIOGRAPHY

I am Her, Her, Her.

H.D., *HER* (3)

Psychological, textual, linguistic, and material conditions shaped
the self H.D. fashioned in her prose into a multiply split, gendered subject
characteristic of both modernism and an oppositional discourse that positions woman within, yet against, patriarchal representations of female
identity. One could certainly argue that these same splits are encoded in
the lyric impersonalism of "the early H.D.," in spite of H.D.'s insistence
to Cournos that in her poetry, she was her "real self," a "clairvoyant,"
disembodied presence. But *Sea Garden*'s covert splits between the conscious and unconscious, between her status as object and her desired
agency as subject, overtly structure the reflexive play and narrative movement in her autobiographical prose.[58] These splits are themselves the
central focus of the narratives produced by fully fleshed-out writers like
Helga Dart, Helga Doorn, Rhoda Peter, and Delia Alton and specifically
female subjects like Midget, Madelon, Hermione, Julia, and Erica. As
H.D. wrote to Cournos, in the prose she was "working through a wood,

a tangle of bushes and bracken." Her autobiographical project was therapeutic, a writing cure based increasingly on the patterns of the psychoanalytic talking cure. Its textualizations achieved no permanent cure, no reunification of split selves, but rather the endless process of "working through" the tangled forest of female subjectivity within a culture and language that perpetually positioned her as an object.

The split subject in H.D.'s prose articulates what Jardine has called "the demise of the Cartesian subject," the overthrow of the "imperial speaking subject" (112, 118) and the deconstruction of what Domna Stanton has described as "a notion essential to the phallogocentric order: the totalized self-contained subject present-to-itself" (16). As a vanguard of modernity, psychoanalysis theorized this demise by positing the existence of the unconscious to which we have access only through its disguised, distorted, displaced speech. From writers like Stein to analysts like Lacan, the very concept of identity has undergone radical disruption in both modernist and postmodernist thought. Discontinuity, fragmentation, alienation, enigma, gaps, and traces predominate in the post-Romantic concepts of the subject caught in the psychodynamics of desire and necessity. While Freud himself continually voiced faith in the capacity of psychoanalysis to become a *science* of the unconscious, his impact on twentieth-century thought, particularly on Lacanian post-structuralism, centers on his admissions of the ultimate unknowability of the unconscious and his analysis of the role of the unconscious in the production of the ego.[59] The split he posited between the conscious and the unconscious led to the decentering of the unitary subject, to the fragmentation of the self, which could no longer be equated with the conscious mind or the ego. Consciousness itself he redefined in *Beyond the Pleasure Principle* as "the borderline between outside and inside; it must be turned towards the external world and must envelop the other psychical systems" (18). Caught between the vast continents of the interior and exterior worlds, consciousness came to be viewed as a threshold, a point of mediation in the civil war between the demands of the material world and the drives of the unconscious.

It is on this borderline between the known and the indeterminate that H.D.'s prose is positioned. Many critics have demonstrated the importance of borderlines in H.D.'s imagist lyric.[60] But, in the poems, the clairvoyant poet stands either on the threshold of the sacred, as a medium of Presence, as Duncan and Morris argued, or on the borderline between oppositions that are not *explicitly* gendered, but rather exist as a universal, untranslatable polarity like the land and sea in "Hermes of the Way." In H.D.'s prose, on the other hand, the threshold represents the border between necessity (the external realm of history) and desire. Her experimentalist texts explicitly follow the gendered train of associations in a stream of consciousness that perpetually engages with both the modern world and with the unconscious. Representing the gendered self-in-the-world, the unconscious surface of the text exhibits competing desires to forget and remember constantly ruptured by traces of a textual unconscious.

Raymonde Ransome in "Murex," the second story of the triptych of *Palimpsest,* enacts this split consciousness, caught on the threshold between awareness and amnesia. Her repetitive stream of consciousness resists knowing what the text insistently reveals: the break-up of her marriage during the war. As she gradually is forced to remember the wartime pain she had repressed, she occupies the shifting borders between the conscious and unconscious:

> Layer and layer of pain, of odd obliteration had forbidden Raymonde Ransome to see into the past that was to her further than an Egyptian's coffin. The past is somewhere about 1917.... London was a foggy Limbo and one's only hope was to be drowned out in it. One's only hope was drift and obliteration. Feet, feet, feet, feet, feet.... By facing that straight, a whole area of Raymonde's subconsciousness was shifted, was opened up as if a layer of hardened, protective sand and lava had been shifted. (109, 121, 143)

"Modernity," Raymonde reflects, "was the unfamiliar, always baffling substance": "all of modernity (as she viewed it) was the jellified and sickly substance of a collection of old colourless photographic negatives through which gleamed the reality, the truth of the blue temples of Thebes, of the white colonnades of Samos" (158). The "early H.D." articulated "the truth of the blue temples," but the prose writer was enmeshed in the sticky substance of modernity.

The narratological structure of autobiography itself intensified modernity's destruction of the unitary self. Autobiography splits the self telling and the self told – what Woolf called in "A Sketch of the Past" the "two people" of "life-writing": the "I now" who writes and the "I then" whose story is told (*Moments of Being* 75, 80). Moreover, Sidone Smith argued that this splitting results in a textual "doubling of the 'self' into a narrating 'I' and a narrated 'I' and further, the fracturing of the narrated 'I' into multiple speaking postures mark the autobiographical process as rhetorical artifact and the authorial signature as mythology" (47). For Louis Renza, this "divorce between the writing subject and his textual rendition" entails a "split intentionality" in which the text presents the writer "with an empty or discursive 'self,' an 'I' never his own" (278–9). This inevitable split renders autobiography, in Renza's post-Lacanian view, a fundamentally "alienated" and "entropic... enterprise" (273). Given the thoroughly rhetorical nature of the "autobiographical contract," Smith further argued, the autobiographical self is also split as a writer and reader. The "I" is a reader, an interpreter whose writing is shaped by the already written (48). Adapting Elizabeth Bruss's move from the verbal "I" to the filmic "Eye," we might also say that the "I now" is an "Eye" that reads not only the ideological conventions of the self, but also the "text" of the "I then." In its appeal to its own historicity, autobiography heightens its fictionality, its origin in a splitting that multiplies the self. Modernist autobiographical writings in particular tend to foreground this split as they self-consciously call attention to the text and its process of construction. Experimentalism further highlights the gap between the self-as-narrator and the self-as-object of narration. H.D.'s split autobiographical "I" is no exception to this post-Romantic separation of narrating and narrated selves.

The initial therapeutic impetus behind H.D.'s prose gave this split subject a psychoanalytic cast even before she entered analysis with Mary Chadwick in 1931 and then with Freud in 1933 and 1934. The scene of autobiographical writing can correspond to the scene of analysis. As analyst, the "I now" who narrates eyes the "I then." As analysand, the narrated self is positioned in the part of the resisting analysand whose unfolding story works through the tangle of repression into the clearing of recovered memories. Freud's preface to the second edition of *The Interpretation of Dreams* claims just such a bold comparison between therapy and autobiography. The book, which proposes his general theory of dreams and their interpretation, is a record of his self-analysis, undertaken to work through his feelings about his father's death.[61] Freud's self-analysis broke the "rules" for analysis he later formulated in his papers on technique in the 1910s. Training analyses were established to circumvent the impossibility of a person working through his or her own resistance and transference. But H.D. claimed the privilege of the progenitor of psychoanalysis. Like Freud, H.D.'s self-analysis in the scene of writing boldly asserts that she can split the subject so as to reconstitute it – not as a unitary subject, but as a self with unconscious as well as conscious manifestations.

HER, written in 1926–7 after H.D. had read a good deal of psychoanalysis, demonstrates a self-conscious play with splitting, then doubling, the self into analyst and analysand. It opens with Hermione's mad circling in the woods near her home, a symptomatic acting out of interior circles. It moves into the reflective commentary of the more knowledgeable narrator, and continues to oscillate back and forth between the reflections of the "I now" and the interior thoughts of the "I then." Invoking psychoanalysis, the narrator is analyst to her own troubled younger self whose fragmented story is recovered in the free-associational text. H.D.'s linguistic play with object pronouns in the subject position – based on Hermione's nickname Her – intensifies the split between the narrating "I" and its object, the narrated "Her":

> Her Gart went round in circles. "I am Her," she said to herself; she repeated, "Her, Her, Her." Her Gart tried to hold on to something; drowning she grasped, she caught at a smooth surface, her fingers slipped, she cried in her dementia, "I am Her, Her, Her." Her Gart had no word for her dementia, it was predictable by star, by star-sign, by year.
>
> But Her Gart was then no prophet. She could not predict later common usage of uncommon syllogisms; "failure complex," "compensation reflex," and that conniving phrase "arrested development" had opened no door to her. . . . She could not see the way out of march and bog. She said, "I am Hermione Gart precisely."
>
> She could not know that the reason for failure of a somewhat exaggeratedly-planned "education," was possibly due to subterranean causes. She had not then dipped dust-draggled, intellectual plumes into the more modern science that posts signs over emotional bog and intellectual lagoon ("failure complex," "compensation reflex") to show us where we may or where we may not stand. . . .
>
> It was summer. She wasn't now any good for anything. Her Gart looked up into liriodendron branches and flat tree leaf became, to her, lily pad on green pool. She was drowned now. (3–4)

"Her" is not only the narrated "I" of an autobiographical text, the analysand in the scene of a writing cure, but also the "her" objectified in the male texts of masculine desire. The split subject of all autobiography takes on a special cast in women's life-writing. Positioned between patriarchal definitions of WOMAN and the historical experiences of women, the female subject in women's autobiographical writing often negotiates a difficult split between recognition of the self as signifier in the male texts of culture and desire for the self as subject in and of a female textual practice.[62] As Stanton argued about women's autobiography: "Woman's different status in the symbolic order . . . involved a different plotting and configuration of the split subject. . . . In a phallocentric system, which defines her as the object, the inessential other to the male subject . . . the *graphing* of the *auto* was an act of self-assertion that denied and reversed women's status" ("Autogynography" 15, 16). Encoded in H.D.'s early poetry, this position is more directly inscribed throughout her prose, more frankly the subject of her personal discourse. The "legend" she felt compelled to define in prose centered on the gendered problematics of authority – her erotic and aesthetic authority to fuse the woman and the writer in a world that steadfastly separated creation and procreation, in a world where the dominating economy of male desire would fix her in the position of man's muse, the object rather than the subject of discourse. Whatever its form, H.D.'s prose is overwhelmingly centered on the legend of the woman writer for whom the erotic and the linguistic are inseparable.

This gendered dimension of the split subject inflects the intertextuality of writing itself. The "I" that writes is first an "Eye" that reads. In Kristeva's words: "the one who writes is the same as the one who reads" (*Desire* 86–7).[63] Or, as Carolyn Heilbrun pointed out in *Writing a Woman's Life*, "we live our lives through texts. . . . Whatever their form or medium, these stories have formed us all; they are what we must use to make new fictions, new narratives" (37). The presence of prior reading in women's life-writing includes an interrogation of what men have written about women.

Like Woolf in *A Room of One's Own,* whose search for women writers begins in the British Museum, like Christine de Pisan, whose vision in *The Book of the City of Ladies* begins in the library of men, H.D. confronted male representations of women as a necessary part of telling her personal story. Reading what men have written of women informs H.D.'s narrative reading of her past self – most especially the writings of men like Pound, Williams, Lawrence, and Aldington, who fixed her into their texts as the object of their authoritative, often desirous gaze. Susan Howe's description of Emily Dickinson's intertextual engagements accurately captures the reading that informs H.D.'s life-writing: "Forcing, abbreviating, pushing, padding, subtracting, riddling, interrogating, re-writing, she pulled text from text" (29). Tugging at male texts, H.D. riddled, interrogated, and rewrote their scripts – split between her sense of how she had been defined and how she would define herself.

This split gives to her prose texts the "double consciousness" Sheila Rowbotham identified as characteristic of women's consciousness:

> But always we were split in two, straddling silence, not sure where we would begin to find ourselves or one another. From this division, our material dislocation, came the experience of one part of ourselves as strange, foreign and cut off from the other which we encountered as tongue-tied paralysis about our own identity. . . . The manner in which we knew ourselves was at variance with ourselves as an historical being–woman. (31)

Alienation, central to Lacan's concept of identity, is historically rather than psychosexually determined for Rowbotham; alienated from WOMAN as cultural representation, women have appropriated language – phallocentric as it is – to break through culturally imposed "silences" and "invisibility" to bring themselves as speaking subjects into history. As for Lacan, mirrors are a central image for Rowbotham, but, once again, the mirrors are historically constructed: "The prevailing social order stands as a great and resplendent hall of mirrors," a "self-reflecting world which encircles" women, mirrors that women must "shatter" to "project [their] own image onto history" (27). H.D.'s prose texts both engage with and shatter male representations of women's nature – sometimes literally reinscribing the words men wrote about her into a gynocentric context; sometimes more generally re-visioning male myths and texts from a female point of view.

H.D.'s dialectical engagement with male texts places her work within the larger tradition of autobiographies by marginalized groups whose race, religion, class, gender, or sexuality are different from those in the cultural mainstream. Rowbotham's metaphors for women's consciousness came from W. E. B. DuBois's *The Souls of Black Folks,* which early in the century defined the invisibility and double consciousness of blacks in a white world. Minorities, as well as women, have created an autobiographical discourse in which the split subject moves from the story of alienation to an enactment of self-creation through the agency of the word. As Albert Stone wrote about autobiography, "social selves, especially for women and blacks, are partly masks or imposed identities." Consequently, "to stress the self as the creator of history – even, at times, as the fabricator of fantasies – maximizes one's freedom from circumstances and social stereotypes" (13). These autobiographies establish a discourse of the Other in which the narrator creates a self through a dialectical negation of the dominant discourses of the social order. This self, made in the act of writing about it, not only records the role of history in its formation, but also counters the dominant ethos by posing an alternative identity from the one imposed by history. Like H.D.'s dual discourse, the discourse of the Other in autobiography is both fictional and referential. On the one hand, the autobiographical self is created by a process of inscription, not expression; but on the other hand it is not a Barthesian poseur, empty of reference. The narrative originates in and refers back to a living person; but it is precisely the fictive nature of the autobiographical I that allows it to move through a culturally imposed alienation to a linguistically accomplished self-creation. Gordon Taylor's description of the task of black autobiography applies as well to H.D.'s autobiographical prose: "the act of writing is the way to become oneself," "to speak oneself into being, to enter through words the world from which one feels an exile" (342). "The story writes me," H.D. reflected in *Thorn Thicket* upon rereading *Bid Me to Live.*[64]

V. PENELOPEAN TEXT(ILE)S: REPETITION, REMEMBERING, AND THE WRITING CURE

At least, I could record the details of my experience, could note them down, could weave and re-weave the threads, the tapestry on this frame.

H.D., *Advent* (163)

The self perpetually split and doubled in a process of becoming in H.D.'s life-writing led to a Penelopean discourse in which writing became an endless form of weaving, in which one work rewove another, in which repetition shaped the narrative and lyric poetics of each text.[65] Driven "to begin again and again a fresh outline of the 'novel,' " H.D. was continually weaving, unweaving, and reweaving text (ile)s that went over and over the defining events in her life (*Advent* 153). Like Penelope's unfinished tapestry, woven and unwoven as a defense against the pressing plague of suitors, H.D.'s textual weavings were a ruse, an artifice whose undoing and redoing therapeutically ensured her survival. Each text, focusing directly or indirectly on her self as poet, unwove and rewove the one that preceded it so that, taken together, her autobiographical writings are a composite tapestry of intertextual threads. Moreover, the linguistic weave of each text established repetition as the defining principle of its stylistics. Karen Lawrence's reading of Penelope articulates her significance for H.D.'s autobiographical discourse: "As weaver and unweaver, she is the spirit of narrative repetition, defending against the premature closure of the story" (*Penelope Voyages* 11).

H.D.'s invocation of Penelope in *Advent* (quoted in full as the Epigraph for this book) to describe her novel writing looks back to her poem "At Ithaca," first published in 1923, and looks forward to the structuralist and post-structuralist tropes for writing as weaving, text as textile, and verbal surface as texture. In the poem, Penelope's "weary thoughts" move "over and back," like the waves that "track the sand with foam," like "tangled thread" in her loom, like the pattern that must be torn only to be made again (*Collected Poems* 163). As a re-vision of the archetypical, faithful wife, however, H.D.'s Penelope is weary with the task of virtue because her ruse requires her to destroy "that web of pictures," what she has so "deftly wrought." The demands of love and the enchantments of art are at odds in the poem, the very conflict that is so often narrated in the prose webs that H.D. repeatedly wove and rewove. Her re-visionist Penelope wrote to protect the poet as speaking subject, rather than to preserve her self as property of her husband and sign of his honor.

"At Ithaca" prefigures Barthes's trope of the text-as-textile and the debate about the place of the weaver/author in its making. As Nancy K. Miller has pointed out, Barthes imaged writing as secretion. The making of a text involves the unmaking of its author who must disappear in its construction, "like a spider," he wrote, "dissolving in the constructive secretions of [her] web" (*Pleasure* 64; *Subject* 79). Barthes's reading of his own trope reinforces his view of the death of the author and the concomitant rise of the text and its reader. But spiders do not, of course, dissolve as they spin. Their labor makes a home that they occupy and endlessly repair. Miller noted that Barthes's "hyphology" "chooses the spider's *web* over the spider," a method in which "the subject is self-consciously erased by a model of text production which acts to foreclose the question of agency itself" (*Subject* 80). Miller's insistence on restoring the spider as central agent in and for the web extends her earlier argument that "the signature matters." The gender of the writer is marked in the web she weaves as a sign of her agency, even as that web patterns the significance of her status as object in the dominant discourses of culture.

Similarly, H.D.'s Penelopean textiles, as representations of the tangled web of female existence in modernity, insist upon the significance of the signature and the conditions of textual production. Penelope in "At Ithaca" does not secrete herself out of existence, but remains the central defining consciousness weaving the stories of her marriage and Odysseus's exploits. In *Advent*, H.D.'s identification with Penelope similarly emphasizes the connection between "the novel" she weaves and the highly gendered experiences which initiate the process of their representation. "Penelope's web" signifies her effort to hold onto the "experiences" and "fantasies" that are "residue of the war, confinement and the epidemic" (153).

In developing the tropes of text-as-textile, author-as-weaver, neither Barthes nor Miller distinguish poetry from prose; both discourses are textual webs. But, for H.D., these Penelopean tropes are specifically associated with her life-writing in prose, not her poetry. The "Penelope's web I am weaving" is not a poem, but a "novel," or to be more precise, "the novel," which is the term, in quotes, that H.D. often used to describe whatever prose fiction she was engaged in writing. Penelope represents the discourse of narrative personalism, not of lyric impersonalism, the discourse of what is forever undone and redone. Writing poetry, in contrast, evoked tropes of sculpting, particularly for "the early H.D." and even the poet of the 1920s and 1930s. The poet-as-sculptor of words carved "crystalline" poems. As H.D. explained to Pearson, she liked to "let my pencil run riot" with "automatic or pseudo-automatic writing" and then "shape" or cut them back ("Note" 73). Revision involved chiseling away the excess. To Bryher, she described the process of producing the "seven chiseled, polished gems I so laboriously wrought" as a birthday gift: "You might think they cost me no sweating so perfect is the slight crystalline finish" (2 September 1924). In contrast, tropes for her prose fiction revolve around fabrics, soft materials that are the product of excess, of repetitive movement. As she wrote to Pearson about *The Sword Went Out to Sea*, "I just wanted them ["Freud and others"] like that in the texture of the cloth or the weave or the 'broidery" (14 August 1948). About the pile of typescripts of her unpublished prose that she sent to Pearson, she told him: "I am so relieved to think of all that rag-bag of old MSS being with you. It [is] heavenly of you to harbor old grandma's horse-hair trunk, as it were" (27 December 1950).

The text-as-textile trope for H.D.'s prose fiction is complemented by a constellation of related images for writing fiction that are based in repetitive domestic tasks, in the routine work that women have always done and redone daily. Not only weaving, but also spinning, sewing, cooking, gardening, and "tidying up" recur constantly in her journals and letters as metaphors for her prose life-writing. To George Plank, for example, she wrote in response to his praise for *Kora and Ka,* "I had three letters, yours, one of them, that made me feel it entirely worth while to go on and on spinning, as I do. The spinning is a sort of necessity, to me, or a dope, if you will – sometimes, it has seemed, I ought to try to do without it" (16 October 1934). Perdita Schaffner recalled that her mother once explained why she had to write every day by saying that writing was "like working on a sampler": "So many stitches and just so many rows, day after day. If I miss even one day, I drop a stitch and lose the pattern and I feel I'm never going to find it again" ("Egyptian Cat" 145). Trying to write during a period of frequent writing blocks in the 1930s, she wrote to Bryher, "Its only to keep little stitches in the tapestry, so easy to let things go. . . . I am writing again, and try not quite to lose touch" (12 July 1936).[66] About *The Gift* as autobiography, she compared the process of selection to the cutting that accompanies sewing: "The author has the privilege of trimming or paring" (*H.D. by Delia Alton* 188). Images of fermenting and cooking occur to emphasize the process of writing. To Bryher, she wrote "I did not want to begin pages again with the wrong vibration or the wrong pattern, so have let them go on fermenting in my file. There must be a fine foment by now. . . . I am sure everything is boiling and simmering in the UNK [unconscious] like mad" (30 August 1936). Comparing herself to Marie Curie, the woman Professor Doolittle had held up for her as a model, H.D. described Curie's science and her own writing as exhausting kitchen work, a kind of domestic creativity:

> I think in a way, the old MSS in the end, becomes a comfort to one; I did so hate the idea of going over my hay-stack, but now after destroying rought [sic] pencil note-books by the dozen, I seem to have got out the core of the thing; I remind myself of that scene in the Curé [sic] film (a good film, that) where she boiled and boiled cauldrons of whatever-it-was and distilled thousand[s] of saucers – and finally there was 'only a stain in the bowl.' You saw the film? Rushing back at night, she sees the 'stain' glowing....RADIUM. This is rather cheeky, comparing my stuff to Curé, but there it is....(Letter to McAlmon, 28 January 1949)

Dealing with the ever-increasing pile of unfinished, unpublished prose manuscripts led H.D. into frequent comparisons of revision with repetitive housework and gardening. "I suppose if I am ever to get on with my life," she wrote Bryher, a passionate gardener, "I must weed out MSS, and it is slow work, like an over-grown garden – and it takes time and patience" (n.d.). As if rewriting were picking up the mess of daily life, the phrases "tidying up" and "shaping up" appear almost formulaically in her letters.[67] "I myself," she wrote Bryher, "at present am calm here, working out these notes, daily. That helps much, it is a sort of tidy-up" (19 March 1938). Self-conscious about the term tidy-up for revision, she told McAlmon that the expression came from Mary Butts (18 August 1933), and, during a period of extensive rewriting in the summer of 1936, she wrote Bryher that she was weary of the word tidy (12 July 1936). Like a messy house that disturbs the routine of daily life until it is straightened up, H.D. felt trapped by the "old un-tidy MSS" (Letter to Bryher, 9 July 1936). As discussed in the Introduction, Pearson proved to be an enormous incentive to H.D. in tidying up her piles of manuscripts because the shelf he established for her at Yale encouraged her to prepare typescripts for future publication and thus achieve a closure of sorts on individual texts. "I tend to rewrite unless I get a thing neat and finished," she told McAlmon (24 February 1949).

The Penelopean repetition that pervades H.D.'s domestic tropes for the process of writing also governs the succession of prose texts and the poetics of the prose itself. Breaking the rigidity of textual autonomy, H.D.'s prose fictions are protean versions of each other as well as distinct texts. Not progressively linear in relation to each other, one text repeats another in a seemingly endless and circular succession. Like a cubist painting, H.D.'s fiction examines again and again the same kind of events and people, each from a different angle of vision. *Paint It To-Day, Asphodel,* and *Bid Me to Live,* for example, all tell the same story of a woman poet and her lovers set in London about the time of the war. "Hipparchia" and "Murex," the first two sections of *Palimpsest,* not only repeat each other as a palimpsest whose layers are different archeological strata, but also retell the story of *Paint It To-Day, Asphodel,* and *Bid Me to Live.*

Less directly autobiographical than the romans à clef, the history novels nonetheless continue the pattern of repetition. *Hedylus,* set in Greece, and *Pilate's Wife,* set in Palestine, have different plots that nonetheless recapitulate the events and characters of the other novels. *White Rose and the Red,* about the Pre-Raphaelite circle in nineteenth-century England, is more distantly related, but is nonetheless a transposition of H.D.'s situation in her imagist circle of the war years. As she explained in *H.D. by Delia Alton,*

> I do not actually mean that I and my group of *Madrigal* were living in
> the days of our grandfathers, that is in the mid-years of the last century.
> But something of my early search, my first expression or urge toward
> expression in art, finds a parallel in the life of Rossetti and Elizabeth
> Siddall. So, as a very subtle emotional exercise, I go over and over the
> ground, find relationships or parallels between my own emotional star-
> vation and hers, between a swift flowering soon to be cut down, in her
> case, by death, in mine, by a complete break after War I, with the group
> of artists described in *Madrigal*. (194)

Superimposed on these fictions, H.D.'s personal essays unveil the cast
of characters in the novels as versions of the same people she explored
in her memoirs.

   To develop H.D.'s own scribal trope, her prose oeuvre is a palimpsest,
"a parchment from which one writing has been erased to make room
for another," with, as Deborah Kelly Kloepfer has shown, one text
bleeding into another.[68] A palimpsest, for H.D., is a repetition, not a
progression, of layers, "different yet the same as before." "Faces," Raymonde thinks in *Palimpsest,* "overlaid now one another like old photographic negatives and faces whirled on and on and on, like petals down,
down, down as if all those overlaid photographic negatives had been
pasted together and rolled off swifter, swifter, swifter from some well
controlled cinematograph" (157). The people in one text who repeat the
people in another are a "superimposition or *montage,*" H.D. wrote Bryher
(25 March 1955). The "superimposition" of text-on-text in the moving
pictures of H.D.'s prose oeuvre suggests the overlaying of a perpetually
unfinished and open-ended process.

   Repetition in the form of stylistic and structural "returnings, knottings,
recrossings, crinklings to and fro, suspensions, interruptions" – to quote
J. Hillis Miller on narrative in general – also characterizes the discourse
of each prose text. In "Ariadne's Thread," Miller justified his project of
deconstruction by arguing that *repetition,* not *linearity,* is the principle of
narrative (68– 9, 70). His adaptation of the text-as-textile trope is useful
for unraveling the Penelopean discourse of H.D.'s prose, although he
warned readers that the textual web is a verbal labyrinth that traps those
who strive to find some Ariadne's thread in the text's repetitions.[69] The
experimentalism of H.D.'s texts – so much more strongly marked in her
novels than in her poetry of the period – takes the form of hypnotic
repetition, a latticework of interlocking motifs, extended passages of
staccato interior monologue, unstable narrative points of view, and oscillating pronouns. Less repetitive on the textual surface, the memoirs
nonetheless break up the linear sequence of conventional chronology by
following the associational movement of memory. "The years went
forward, then backward," H.D. wrote in *Tribute to Freud.* "The shuttle

of the years ran a thread that wove my pattern into the Professor's" to
make "a present that was in the past or a past that was in the future"
(9). H.D.'s Penelopean discourse shares the broken sentences and sequences of Woolf's fictionalized modern writer, Mary Carmichael, in
Life's Adventure (A Room 84–5). But, even more than Woolf's experimentalism, H.D.'s ruptured sentences depend on repetitive excess, on
verbal vertigo.

H.D.'s assessment of her style in *Palimpsest* exaggerates and consequently highlights qualities present to some extent in all her prose, especially her fiction of the 1920s and early 1930s: "The writing is weedy
and involved, with many baffling parentheses. It is sometimes difficult
to disentangle the central theme from the turnings and involutions. . . .
But we are, as I have said, in the labyrinth and no formalized (however
intricate) static labyrinth. It does not stay, with all its meanderings, on
one plane and time goes slowly, goes swiftly; our dream-time is relative
but we have yet no formula for this relativity" (*H.D. by Delia Alton* 218,
220). The opening of "Murex," the second story of *Palimpsest,* fits her
description and gives some sense of the repetitions that accumulate in
this "weedy" text, so unlike the spare lines of "early H.D." in its excess
of words:

> Raymonde didn't know what to think. But why think? London did
> this to her, blurred her acute perceptions so that inevitably at the end
> of her half-year visit (she always seemed to be in a state of expectation,
> of laisser-aller in London that made her feel, for all her definite little
> address, that she was a bird of passage) she would let go perception,
> let go arrow-vibrant thought. London did this to her. It blurred over
> too alert perception, it, so to speak, snuffed out vibration of too keen
> thinking. In London her fatalistic Eastern attitude was apt to become
> an obsession. Things were so and so. In London (from the first she had
> been forced to this) people did so and so, as inevitably as sun-rise and
> sun-set which here too, in London, had an ineffable quality of merging
> so that one never knew the barrier of day and night, one never outlined
> accurately the barrier of summer, spring, and autumn. London had one
> season. Spring, winter, summer, they were all blurred in an ineffable
> half-light. Raymonde found here that corresponding twilight of the
> spirit. (95)

The narrator – or Raymonde, we can't tell who – interrupts herself
three times, twice with parentheses and once with a question that undermines her authority to ask anything – "Why think?" "London" is
repeated seven times in a passage that stammers its way through correspondences between interior and exterior worlds – with consciousness,
as Freud said, a tenuous threshold between the two. "Things were so
and so" is a definitive statement of indeterminacy, intensified by its

repetition in "people did so and so." "Blurred," repeated three times, succeeds in snuffing out the reader's as well as Raymonde's "too alert perception," "too keen thinking," to such an extent that the reader feels trapped in a textual obsession for which there are no clear boundaries, barriers, or markers of space and time. What London does to Raymonde, the text does to the reader.

As these repetitive motifs accelerate hypnotically in the unfolding text the passage introduces, the reader is increasingly drawn into the vortex of Raymonde's thought. Raymonde, having repressed the story of her husband's betrayal during the war, is forced to remember by a woman who comes to tell her of a similar loss. She is compelled to emerge from "this last cocoon-blur of not-thinking that was her fixed and static formula for London," to follow "a thread that ran on and on and through and through" the labyrinth of forgotten memories (96, 101). Oscillating between the drive to repress and the drive to know, Raymonde – and the text – is caught in repetitions. "O, do keep quiet," she thinks at one point. "Let it alone. Feet, feet, feet, feet, feet. London had forgotten. Raymonde wanted to shout at Ermy, 'play the game. Shut up. Don't you see I am, everyone is always fighting, always fighting to – forget? Like London – to forget – feet – feet – feet – feet – feet?' " (100). The feet are the marching feet of the men in khaki, a kind of metrical rigidity that had killed poetry. Raymonde thinks:

> Art was magic – but it had lost – had lost – its savour. Joyce was right. It had lost. Art was magic but it had lost. Must get back into art the magic it had had in Egypt, Greece even.... Faces, people, London. People, faces, Greece. Greece, people, faces. Egypt. James Joyce was right. On, on, on, on, and out of it like some deep-sea-jewel pulled up in a new squirming with an enormous catch of variegated squirming tentacled and tendrilled memories, just this, this – *who fished the murex up?* (155–7).

Running "on, on, on, on," Raymonde's thoughts transform the marching feet into the musical rhythms of a reawakened poet whose "fishing" in the unconscious "brings up" the writing of the poem whose gradual emergence forms the final pages of the story. In the excess of the text, waves of repetitions overflow and overwhelm the page. Not only Joyce, but Stein "was right" in *Palimpsest*. Images float without predicates. Staccato stutters jerk syntax. Presence, then absence of punctuation accelerates the mind's flow. Pound had defined modernist prose through the exemplum of Joyce's *Portrait of the Artist as a Young Man* in the same terms as modernist poetry: "hard, clear-cut, with no waste of words, no bundling up of useless phrases, no filling in with pages of slosh" (22).[70] But, for H.D., modernist prose meant abandoning the condensed discourse of the poet to spill out pages and pages of slosh –

a plenitude from the unconscious sea so contained in the crystalline carvings of "the early H.D."

Joyce, Stein, Woolf, and H.D. – all experimented with stylistic repetitions linked with modernist forms of linguistic play and psychological realism.[71] H.D.'s repetitions are less abstract and philosophically based than Stein's in *The Making of Americans,* which McAlmon published the year before he brought out *Palimpsest.* They are far more irritating and less "beautiful" than those of Woolf in *The Waves.* Less a representation of subjectivity than a performance of it, H.D.'s repetitions emerge out of the borderline between the unconscious and the conscious, more like the Joyce of *Finnegans Wake* than the Joyce of *Ulysses.* What distinguishes H.D.'s linguistic stammers and repetitions (particularly in her prose of the 1920s and 1930s) is her emphasis on the psychodynamics of language and the linguistic principles of psychic structures.

Consequently, H.D.'s Penelopean repetitions particularly anticipate and are illuminated by Kristeva's work, as DuPlessis has argued in another context.[72] In reading the text-as-psyche and the psyche-as-text, Kristeva theorized that texts are a dynamic site of dialectical interplay between what she called the *Semiotic* and the *Symbolic* modalities of language. Following Lacan, she identified the Symbolic with the Oedipal stage which ushers the child into the realm of signification, governed by the "Law of the Father" in the social order. Texts that foreground the Symbolic emphasize signification, linearity, and causality. The Semiotic register of language represents the "trace" of the pre-Oedipal stage, which resides within a text just as it remains largely unconscious in the layers of the adult psyche. She characterized the Semiotic modality of a text as a kind of "rhythmic space" that recalls the preverbal stage of the pre-Oedipal period centered in the child's desire for the mother. Semiotic discourse recapitulates the *"chora,"* the "maternal matrix" of desire in which the child is enveloped before the acquisition of symbolic language. The Semiotic lacks boundaries, temporality, spatiality, and causality. Instead, it highlights sound, rhythm, repetition, movement, color, and waves of desire in a babble that is anterior to signification (*Revolution* 25–9).[73] No text, she insisted, could be " 'exclusively' Semiotic" or " 'exclusively' Symbolic," but the specific dialectic between modalities in any given text "determines the type of discourse (narrative, metalanguage, theory, poetry, etc.)" (*Revolution* 24). Poetry, as the more lyric and less narrative discourse, is more likely to foreground the Semiotic, while fiction emphasizes the Symbolic.

Modernity, Kristeva argued, highlights the Semiotic register of language; consequently, poetic discourse is for her the avant garde of the avant garde. But in H.D.'s oeuvre, the Semiotic register is intensified in the prose, not the poetry. Kristeva's description of the Semiotic in Mallarmé is more suited to *Palimpsest* than to H.D.'s poems of the period: "Indifferent to language, enigmatic and feminine, this space underlying the written is rhythmic, unfettered, irreducible to its intelligible verbal translation; it is musical, anterior to judgment, but restrained by a single guarantee: syntax" (*Revolution* 29). As the more directly gendered discourse devised to examine the "personal" tangle of the woman/poet, H.D.'s prose heightens the Semiotic register in an excess of rhythmic repetitions just barely fettered by a fractured syntax. Like Woolf in *A Room of One's Own*, H.D. conflated modernity and womanhood in the experimental discourse of her autobiographical writings, one that anticipates the current debates about *écriture féminine*, but one that locates this speech of Otherness in the agency of the woman writer.[74]

As Kloepfer argued, the Semiotic in H.D.'s prose inscribes the dialectic of maternal loss by "invoking a universal and archaic mother who will manifest herself not only within an arcanum but within *language:* a maternal voice and rhythm, a mutter-ing, a grotto in language which is the mother's space" ("Flesh Made Word" 27). Textual repetitions can be read as psychosexual residue, as inscriptions of psychic drives, specifically the repressed desire for the mother. J. Hillis Miller associated repetition with the compulsion to repeat ("Ariadne's Thread" 62). In *Beyond the Pleasure Principle,* it will be recalled, Freud theorized that the compulsion to repeat in both children and adults replicated an early stage of development when the child is willing to risk pain for the pleasure it will bring, as in the "*fort-da*" game in which a child he observed threw down an object so that he could enjoy its return. This repetitive game, Freud believed, enacts the child's fear of its mother's absence and pleasure at her return; at the same time, it reproduces the loss and recovery of the mother as if the child controlled the process. Adapting Freud, Miller viewed the text as the scene of the repetition compulsion, a linguistic site for playing a "*fort-da*" game of pain and pleasure. Relating Miller's idea to Kristeva's concept of the *chora,* we can connect the "compulsion" of textual repetition evident in much modernist writing, including H.D.'s, to a maternal matrix, a linguistic return to desire for the mother and resistance to the Oedipal patterns of the social order. As Kloepfer noted, "in H.D. maternal form and language are intricately related" (28). The repetitions of H.D.'s (re)woven "novel" reenact and substitute for the "*fort-da*" game of maternal loss and return.

The psychodynamic element of these repetitions return us to the therapeutic dimension of H.D.'s life-writing, which is greatly illuminated by Freud's suggestive theories of transference.[75] Within the context of analysis, Freud linked repetition to transference and resistance and argued that analysis should ideally free the analysand from repeating by helping him or her to remember. In "Further Recommendations: Recollection,

Repetition and Working Through" (1914), Freud argued that the aim of all analysis was "descriptively, to recover the lost memories; dynamically, to conquer the resistances caused by repression" (158). Forgetting, which often consists of losing the links between fragments of memory, is the result of repression, he argued. Through the encouragement of free association, the analyst engages in a war against repression to restore what has been forgotten to consciousness. This process is not a linear or rational one, however. Instead, it is a dynamic and conflictual drama dominated by transference and resistance. The analysand, resisting the recovery of memories containing forbidden desires, transfers to the analyst the feelings he or she had in childhood toward various family members, especially the mother and father. By reenacting childhood patterns through the transference in the analytic situation, both analyst and analysand succeed in recovering what has been repressed. Transference, according to Freud, was essential to the success of analysis. But it was also a form of repetition, an acting out of the "compulsion to repeat": "the transference is itself only a bit of repetition, and . . . [it is] the transference of the forgotten past not only on to the physician, but also on to all the other aspects of the current situation" (161). Repeating, he concluded, is resistance to remembering: "the greater the resistance the more extensively will expressing in action (repetition) be substituted for recollecting. . . . From then onward the resistances determine the succession of the various repetitions. . . . The patient reproduces instead of remembering, and he reproduces according to the conditions of the resistance" (161). Analysis, he believed, was a working through in which the analysand moved from repeating into recollecting. "The main instrument," he advised, "for curbing the patient's compulsion to repeat and for turning it into a motive for remembering consists in the handling of the transference. We render it harmless, and even make use of it. . . . The transference thus forms a kind of intermediary realm between illness and real life, through which the journey from the one to the other must be made" (165).

Among the many reasons (or versions) H.D. gave for going to Freud in *Tribute to Freud,* she wrote: "I wanted to free myself of repetitive thoughts and experiences – my own and those of many of my contemporaries" (13). For a decade, she had been trying to do just that in her writing – to free herself of repetition by remembering through her writing. Her Penelope, it should be recalled, wove and rewove her web so as not to forget what she could only incompletely remember. Analysis with Freud took the place of writing. During her relatively brief, but intense spurts of analysis during the 1930s, her writing slowed to a trickle, in part because writing autobiographical prose and undergoing analysis for H.D. were two ways of addressing the same problem – her sense of entrapment in a cycle of repetition. Before and after her analysis with Freud, the prose text reproduced the scene of analysis for H.D. As analogue to the analytic situation, the text is thus the site of transference and resistance, of the conflict between repeating and remembering. Repetition is not only the text's "illness," but also its necessary reenactment of transference in the effort of working through to remember.

This dynamic struggle between repeating and remembering, evident in H.D.'s prose oeuvre, is paradigmatically clear in *Palimpsest,* one of the most repetitive ("weedy") of her texts and the novel that Freud read before her analysis (*Tribute* 190). The palimpsestic structure is itself a repetition, with each of the seemingly unrelated stories in the triptych presenting versions of each other set in different time periods, with different characters. "Murex," the central panel of the triptych or middle layer of the palimpsest, is stylistically the most repetitive. Its plot moves forward as the literal battle between Raymonde's desire to forget and her need to remember. Her endlessly repeated resistance to memory gradually yields to the force of the young woman, her double, who insists that she recall the story. Her success in remembering the pain of the war years breaks the cycle of repetition and makes possible the writing of her poem. However, stylistic repetitions are as pervasive at the end as at the beginning, which perhaps helps to account for a certain tentativeness in an end that invites, but does not fulfill, a sense of authority. Yes, we feel, Raymonde has written her poem, but somehow, as readers, the weight of the web is still upon us. Sure enough, this is not the end. The story starts all over again as "Secret Name," the last section of the novel, begins.

As a scene of transference, writing for H.D. negotiated between the resistance against and the drive to work through her personal tangles into the clearing of memory. This accounts for the omnipresence of stylistic repetition in her prose, as well as the repetition of story and characters from text to text. It also accounts for the centrality of associative memory as the structuring principle of narrative in so many of her prose works. The "plot" in many of her texts, particularly the memoirs, is not made up of actions, but rather reflections on actions.

Writing as a transferential scene also invites transference in the scene of *reading.* Felman and Culler have theorized that the text engenders the *reader's* transference, so that the reader, drawn into the vortex of the text, either reenacts his or her own unconscious drives in reading or repeats the unresolved conflicts of the text itself.[76] Readers of H.D.'s prose, particularly her fiction, are perhaps so often disturbed by it because it heightens the reader's transference. Caught as her texts are in repetition – both structural and linguistic – the reader is ensnared in a verbal maze. The hypnotic effect of Raymonde's stream of consciousness induces ver-

tigo, severe enough at times to lead the reader to slam the book shut as
the ultimate defense against the textual maw. As J. Hillis Miller argued
in general about reading, our search for "the command center" of the
textual labyrinth is doomed because "the Minotaur . . . is a spider, Arachne – arachnid who devours her mate, weaver of a web which is herself,
and which both hides and reveals an absence, the abyss. Her text is a
mise en abyme" (72–3). Understood as the idea of endless repetition,
internal and reflexive mirrorings without origin and end, the text as *mise
en abyme* suggests both writer and reader caught in a chain of devouring
repetitions. The repetitions in at least some of H.D.'s prose are not an
idealized reunion with the maternal body. They can be frightening, particularly when the "I then" swallows the "I now."

However, the dialectic between repetition and remembering, between
the Semiotic and the Symbolic, gradually shifted in H.D.'s prose over
time. Her brief, but intense analysis with Freud in 1933 and 1934 contributed greatly to this shift, perhaps by strengthening the control of the
"I now" over the "I then," perhaps by providing her with a more sys-
tematic model of self-analysis.[77] After her analysis with Freud, she began
to develop the personal essay/memoir, a genre that she first attempted
with *The Gift* in 1941–3 and followed up with *Writing on the Wall* in 1944
(the text that became *Tribute to Freud* in 1956). *The Gift*, as we shall see
in Chapter 5, explores the repetitive pattern of violence and terror imprinted in H.D.'s psyche and on human history when she, only ten at
the time, found her father covered with blood standing in a daze at the
front door. Linking the recovery of personal memory with the restoration
of cultural memory breaks the cycle of repetition in *The Gift*.

H.D.'s memoirs extend the analytic practice she learned from Freud
into her writing. Whereas her autobiographical prose was, right from
the beginning, a kind of textual self-analysis, the narrating I/Eye in all
her memoirs is a much stronger "analyst" than it is in the fiction of the
1920s and 1930s, when the "analysand" often overwhelms the "analyst"
in the wave and weave of linguistic excess. The style in the memoirs is
not only less "weedy," but the associative play of memory is far less
repetitive and more reconstructive. Further, instead of playing and re-
playing the story of the war years, the memoirs focus more specifically
on working through a particular aspect of the self – her family in *The
Gift;* Freud in *Tribute to Freud;* her oeuvre in *H.D. by Delia Alton;* Pound
in *End to Torment,* as so on. Even the fiction she wrote after analysis is
less stylistically repetitive and more varied in overt subject matter than
the fiction she wrote before she went to Vienna. Repetition does not by
any means disappear, but the interplay between remembering and repeating is often different. Perhaps the predominance of recollecting in
this later prose accounts for its less linguistically experimental nature.

The Kristevan Semiotic is more muted in these later prose texts than it was in earlier novels like *Palimpsest* and *HER*, in which the verbal textures resonate strongly with the most experimental writing of Joyce, Woolf, and Stein.

This linear drift in H.D.'s prose discourse – from repetition to re-membering – does not, however, signify teleological development. Like Freud's concept of the talking cure, the writing cure seems to imply an endpoint to analysis, consequently, a linear movement from the "illness" of repetition to the "cure" of remembering. But this binary of illness and cure is one that both Freud and H.D. deconstructed, to propose in its place a narrative of endless, multifaceted search. Freud's early papers on technique suggested an optimism about cures, but his experience in clinical settings and his observations of the violent repetitions of history led him to be much more pessimistic. One of his final essays, "Analysis Terminable and Interminable" (1938), suggests that an analysis can never be finished, that what psychoanalysis offers is the process, not the prod-uct, of interpretation. This conclusion highlights the indeterminacy that had been present right from the beginning, even in the inauguration of his hermeneutic. In *The Interpretation of Dreams,* he noted that the meaning of a dream cannot be finally determined: "There is at least one spot in every dream at which it is unplumbable – a navel, as it were, that is its point of contact with the unknown" (*Interpretation* 143).

Like the talking cure, the writing cure proposes a process, not an end-point. There was no end to the weaving, unweaving, and reweaving of Penelope's web for H.D. In the midst of war and the dissolution of her marriage, she began writing fiction as a means to an end: to save the impersonal, clairvoyant poet by writing the personal, tangled fictions of the woman. Originally handmaiden to the poet, the prose author de-veloped her own gender-inflected authority and agency. Anticipating *écriture féminine,* H.D.'s Penelopean discourse abandons the phallogocen-tric authority of the masculine position to inscribe the marginal position of a woman who must endlessly reweave her exploits as the ruse that makes possible her survival. Rather than saving the poet, the prose writer continually reconstituted her and in the process changed her profoundly. The signature of the poet of *Trilogy, Helen in Egypt,* and *Hermetic Defi-nition* is still "H.D.," but the poet's voice is fully fleshed out as the speech of a woman, the woman made and remade in Penelope's web.

2

Origins: Rescriptions of Desire in *HER*

Women, who for centuries had been the *objects* of male theorizing, male desires, male fears and male representations, had to discover and re-appropriate themselves as *subjects:* the obvious place to begin was the silent place to which they had been assigned again and again, that dark continent which had ever provoked assault and puzzlement.

> Susan Rubin Suleiman,
> "(Re)writing the
> Body" (7)

What does it mean to claim Otherness? In H.D.'s terms, it is to claim 'Her' . . . the subject claims its dominated, object case for scrutiny.

> Rachel Blau DuPlessis,
> *H.D.: The Career of*
> *That Struggle* (34)

They themselves will have no Shes, unless some Her puts them forth!

> Djuna Barnes,
> *Ladies Almanack* (13)

The movement from *object* to *subject* status in literary discourse – from *Her* to *She* – pervades the question of origin for women writers. How does a woman writer come to be, come into being, when the very thrust of culture has been to deny her access to the authority and process of naming? When the very presence of woman as object in male texts is the sign of her absence as subject? When the very motive for representation has so often been man's desire to fix woman in the stasis of his own word? When, in the words of Teresa de Lauretis, woman has been "the very ground of representation, both object and support of a desire which, intimately bound up with power and creativity, is the moving force of culture and history" (13)? How, in other words, have actual women created themselves as subjects, as producers and reproducers of texts, when the dominant discourses in which they are inescapably immersed repress such self-creation? In the contemporary rush to "problematize" the question of origin, to deconstruct the Romantic concept of the poet as Creator, and to discard the notion of "author" as point of origin, the compelling need of women writers to confront the issue of their own origins gets lost. The historical conditions inhibiting women's creativity – ideological and material – have led many women to explore the origins of their rebellion, to examine the narrative of their birth as subjects into the public domain of letters, into author-ity. This historically determined imperative to identify and justify the origin of their resistance to cultural norms often has a double reference in women's writing – on the one hand, to their personal histories; on the other hand, to their literary precursors. Both biographical and intertextual resonances pervade the apologia of women writers.

H.D. was fascinated with the question of origins – she returned to it again and again in her writings, in most of her prose and in much of her later poetry. Anticipating post-structuralist critiques of origin, however, she never presented the making of "H.D." as a single point of origin or a completed act of creation. Rather, in each work and in the palimpsest of her oeuvre, H.D. reexamined the origins of the self anew and newly through the agency of the potent word: She was "Psyche, the butterfly, / out of the cocoon" each time a new text emerged in a lifelong and unending process (*Trilogy* 570). Each text repeats the narrative of beginnings. Each explores in its own dazzling specificity the question of origin – perhaps most dramatically in her final poem, *Hermetic Definition*, written on the threshold of her death in 1961, but structured as a pregnancy resulting in the multiple births of a fecund desire. The poem ends with the poet reborn in the process of birthing the poem, but for what future, as she draws her "nun-grey" about her, neither she nor we really know. Like *Hermetic Definition*, no one text completes the process of becoming. To "beget, self-out-of-self," to echo *Trilogy* (514), is a *mise en abyme* of endlessly repeated, indeterminate acts for which the constant is the question of origins itself – the need for a narrative of awakening, transformation, birth.

HER is a gestational narrative of artistic awakenings that serves vividly as a microcosm of this larger pattern in her work.[1] The story is really two stories, a birth and a rebirth, in which the second undoes the first to suggest the endlessness of the process of becoming. The first story takes place over a nine-month period, from early summer to late winter, in the life of Hermione Gart whose emergence as a writer depends upon intersecting plots of heterosexual and lesbian desire. It is a fictional reconstruction of a five-year period in H.D.'s life from about 1906 to 1911, during which she withdrew from Bryn Mawr College, wrote her first published work, became engaged to and disengaged from Ezra Pound, and fell in love with Frances Gregg, with whom she went to Europe in the summer of 1911. The autobiographical reference of this story is the making of H.D. *Imagiste* in Pennsylvania through her love for Pound and Gregg in the years before she went to London. The second story of origins is about the unmaking of H.D. *Imagiste*. Not itself told as a direct narrative, this "story" is embedded in the way the autobiographical narrator tells the story of Hermione, her younger self. It refers obliquely to the "H.D." who was writing the novel in the mid-1920s, that is, to the writer who felt confined by the persona of "the early H.D.," whose making is the dominant story of the book.

I. THE MAKING OF H.D. IMAGISTE

Writing. Love is writing

H.D., *HER* (149)

As a roman à clef about well-known literary people, *HER* is a scandalous story of forbidden desires. As a *Kunstlerroman,* it invokes the patterns of the genre to examine the interpenetration of sexuality and textuality in a narrative of development – "Writing. Love is writing." Unpublished until 1981, *HER* is a literally suppressed, figuratively re-pressed story of origins whose private telling was essential to subsequent public retellings of how Hilda Doolittle became "H.D." The typescript for *HER,* dated "about 1927," contains H.D.'s penciled corrections, as well as her key for the "real" identity of the characters. The name Helga Doorn appears as author on the title page, but with a gesture that inscribes a palimpsestic identity, H.D. penciled out this pen name at some later date. "Autobiographical Notes" includes *Asphodel* and *HER* in its list of "unpublished" work for 1926 (16), and a letter to Bryher in 1930 mentions that she was working on the typescript of *HER.* In 1959, she was rereading both *HER* and *Asphodel* when she wrote Pearson to destroy any carbons he might have because she felt they lacked the "daemonic drive" of *Madrigal,* but she confessed that they made "pleasant reading" and that she enjoyed following how they were "put together" (14 October 1959). Her carefully corrected typescript remained on her shelf at Yale for safekeeping. H.D. appears to have made none of the efforts that she made for some of her other unpublished novels to find a publisher for *HER.*

This probable suppression of *HER* embodies the contradictory choice between silence and public speech that characterizes H.D.'s prose oeuvre in general and the more specific dilemma of the novelist of lesbian desire in particular. "Being quiet," Catharine Stimpson wrote about the lesbian writer in the early twentieth century, "would enable her to 'pass.' Silence could be a passport into the territory of the dominant world. . . . Silence is also a shrewd refusal to provoke punitive powers – be they of the family, workplace, law, or church. Obviously this survival tactic makes literature impossible" ("Zero Degree" 366). DuPlessis and I have speculated that *HER*'s undisguised and quite positive exploration of lesbian desire as an alternative to a suffocating heterosexual engagement may have led H.D. to leave the novel in the silent speech of an unpublished manuscript.[2] The suppression of *The Rainbow,* ostensibly because of its explicit chapter on Ursula's lesbian affair, no doubt made a great impression on H.D., who must have noticed the treatment Lawrence received even though his portrait of the affair was very negative. The 1920s, which Elaine Marks has called "the *anni mirabiles*" of women's novels depicting lesbian characters, culminated in a storm of abuse against Radclyffe Hall and the notorious obscenity trial for *The Well of Loneliness* in 1928, about which H.D. and Bryher were deeply concerned.[3] Barnes's *Ladies Almanack,* Woolf's *Orlando,* and Stein's *Tender Buttons* were far more safely disguised than *HER* in their celebrations of lesbian eroticism. Not concealed by such extremes of fantasy and obscurity, *HER* presents a code that is relatively easy to break. Once the biographical key for the roman à clef is discovered, the novel's disguises dissolve. As a person for whom privacy was essential, H.D. wrote the personal story of her love for Frances Gregg but chose not to risk provoking punitive authorities by publishing the novel.

As a repressed narrative of origins, *HER* examines what is invisibly present in the public story of Pound's creation of H.D. *Imagiste,* the story that she and her friends all knew, the story that she herself gave the status of legend in the much later *End to Torment.* In this later version, as I have discussed in Chapter 1, H.D. made Pound into Adam, herself into Eve. As his pen slashes and shapes the lines of her poems in the tea shop near the British Museum in September of 1912, his power to name her resonates with the religious authority of God, the linguistic authority of the (male) poet, and the sexual authority of the (male) lover. With the signature H.D. *Imagiste,* he named her a serious poet with an exalted poetics. By serving as her conduit to the world of publishing, Pound gave her a public identity, for which she was always grateful, as she wrote in *End to Torment*: "The strange thing is that Ezra was so inexpressibly kind to anyone who he felt had the faintest spark of submerged talent" (10). DuPlessis has explored how a subtext of ambivalence toward Pound pervades this story of her beginnings, this tribute to Pound's significance, that also explains why "Ezra would have destroyed me and the center they call 'Air and Crystal' of my poetry" if they had married (*End* 35).[4]

However, even this account of the famous scene in the British Museum paradoxically gestures toward a hidden origin prior to itself. "But Dryad, this *is* poetry," Pound apparently pronounced, *before* his slashing pen began to do what it was to do for another poet whose talent Pound admired – T. S. Eliot, whose draft of *The Waste Land* underwent probably more changes under Pound's pen than H.D.'s three poems. The *making* of "H.D." precedes the *naming* of "H.D.," even in her public tribute to the impresario of modernist poetry. In relationship to *End to Torment*, which H.D. tried to publish, the suppressed *HER* contains the repressed narrative of prior beginnings. Beneath the erotic dyad in *End to Torment* – Pound and H.D. – is the erotic triad in *HER* – H.D., Gregg, and Pound. The origin of H.D. *Imagiste, HER* heretically suggests, lay not in the heady, intellectual crosscurrents of Pound's London, but in the erotic triangle of three poet/lovers meeting in the fields, forests, and drawing rooms of Pennsylvania.

Sources outside the novel tend to reinforce the complex triangle portrayed within it, suggesting an important biographical reference. As Barbara Guest has discovered, Gregg recorded in her diary: "Two girls in love with each other, and each in love with the same man. Hilda, Ezra, Frances" (*Herself Defined* 26). In an unpublished memoir written in the 1930s, Gregg recalled "That kiss of Ezra's stirred me to the unsounded depths of my undiscovered womanhood... Nothing has ever happened that has bourne any relation to that first kiss" (quoted in Hanscombe and Smyers 20). Although H.D. and Pound were the "official" couple, engaged at least for a time, H.D. was devastated by Pound's liaison with Gregg and at the same time increasingly committed to Gregg, especially in 1910, the year she called "the Frances Gregg period" in "Autobiographical Notes" (1). Pound was apparently jealous, telling them that they would have been burned as witches in the Middle Ages, an accusation that the Pound figure makes in both *Paint It To-Day* and *Asphodel*.

Inseparable from the erotic triangle was the poetic one. Pound was the "official" poet of the group, with several books already published and a literary reputation in London. But both women were writing as well, each competing to some extent for Pound's approval by the time they arrived in London. In "Autobiographical Notes," H.D. noted that in 1910, "I write my first poems to Frances, modelled on Theocritus trans. that E[zra] brought me; I am satisfied with these few poems" (1). Her first of two accounts of the British Museum scene in "Autobiographical Notes" indicates further how poetic jealousies were entangled with erotic ones: "Autumn in London, at Museum Tea Room, Ezra picks out certain poems to be sent to Poetry, Chicago. E had hurt me, the previous autumn [1911], by picking out some rather Celtic conventional poems of F[rances] and ignoring mine. *Hermes* and *Orchard* are cut and line form changed, E signs them H.D. *Imagist*" (2).[5] Further, in stating that Pound chose Gregg's "conventional" poems over her own, she confirmed that she had shown Pound poems long before September of 1912, and she strongly implied that these poems were highly innovative, perhaps precursors to those of the startlingly original H.D. *Imagiste*. Pound, it seems, attempted to launch Gregg before H.D., thereby annointing the poems of one lover before the other. Perhaps it was with his help that Gregg's "La Mendiante," a sequence of four longingly wistful love poems, was published in the December 1911 issue of *Forum*.[6] In London, H.D. reported in a letter to Pound's mother, Pound introduced Gregg to his literary friends "as the rising American poetess, and I as – well, just a friend of great people" (quoted in Pound and Spoo 86). Completing the weaving together of the poetic and erotic strands of the triad, H.D. gave the handwritten, hand-bound, untitled "volume" of poems Pound had written for and about her to Gregg, who wrote on the front page, "Hilda's Book," the title under which the poems have since been published as a coda to *End to Torment*. *Hilda's Book* was found in what remained of Gregg's bombed apartment, where she and her daughter died after a Nazi raid in 1941.

HER fills the gap in *End to Torment* and expands on the cryptic triangles alluded to in "Autobiographical Notes." As a narrative of origins, it suggests that the making of a modernist poet lay not in the metropolises of Europe, where critics like Hugh Kenner tend to locate the origins of modernism, but in the psychodynamics of desire, in the superposition of erotics and poetics evident in the novel's fundamental, impossible equation – "Love is writing." Yoking two abstract and grammatically unbalanced nouns, the formula's linking verb "is" oscillates between the metaphoric and the literal. Since "love" is not literally "writing," the "is" suggests metaphoric comparison. But when the metaphoric structure produces no meaningful analogy, the "is" ultimately reasserts, without clarification, its literal meaning – Love *is* writing. The novel explores the conflicts embedded in this difficult formula for living and creating as a woman, conflicts that contain a double reference to H.D.'s own life and to literary representations of WOMAN.

H.D.'s equation of erotics and poetics is a radical renunciation of the culturally imposed choice many women artists felt compelled to make, a choice that often fuels narrative movement in women's *Kunstlerromane* – the choice to be an artist or a woman, categories culturally constituted as mutually exclusive.[7] H.D.'s negation of that binary opposition stands significantly at odds with Woolf's autobiographical *Kunstlerroman* published in the same year H.D. completed her own – that is, of course, *To the Lighthouse,* in which Lily Briscoe confronts the specter of Victorian femininity, redefines it as a source of maternal empowerment for the daughter artist who nonetheless must repudiate it as a model, and ultimately pours her erotic fountain of energy solely into her creativity.[8] Lily resolves the double bind of the woman artist by channeling eros into art, by ecstatically painting her vision of the relation between masses, by renouncing the exploration of erotic relation in the realm beyond the boundaries of the canvas.

While Woolf's *Kunstlerroman* focuses on the threat and potential empowerment the procreative mother poses for the woman artist, H.D.'s novel emphasizes the story of the lover, of the woman artist who would renounce neither writing nor adult sexuality. *HER*'s narrative invokes in order to revoke the male economy of desire, specifically the muse tradition in which the male artist's desire for woman is inscribed in a text that becomes the sign, symptom, and scene of his possession. Possessed by desire, the male artist comes to possess the object of his desire through the act of representation, especially in the love lyric. This loop of desire circulating through the male subject and text presumes a silent muse, a woman who inspires, but does not speak, who is called into being by his act of naming, never by her own. "The traditional muse," wrote DuPlessis in "Family, Sexes, Psyche," "is a contact with a pure force, yet, at the same time, is a voiceless, wordless figure who needs you (a male poet) to interpret and articulate what it is she represents" (74). The "romantic lyric," wrote Margaret Homans in " 'Syllables of Velvet,' " depends on an "implicit plot" of "masculine heterosexual desire" in which the male poet gazes on "the silent object of desire" whose very absence ensures the production of the poem (570, 573). The muse tradition is a particularly acute example of the larger problem of representation. As Gilbert and Gubar have punned, women have been "penned in" by men's "sentence" (*Madwoman* 13). Women are both "absent" and "captive" in the representations of which they are "both telos and origin," de Lauretis wrote (13–14). Within this closed system of male desire, "love *is* writing." But neither the love nor the writing belongs to women.

H.D.'s project in *HER* is to maintain the equation of love and writing by redefining its terms and consequences for the woman writer. Claiming subject status for the muse, H.D. reconstituted woman as desirous, not simply the object of desire; as namer, not the thing named. To accomplish this re-vision, H.D. engaged in a self-reflexive, combative intertexuality. *HER* resonates with a number of specific formulations that epitomize the muse tradition – from the mythic figures of Pygmalion and Galataea, Orpheus and Eurydice, and the mermaid Undine; down through the lyric conventions established by the troubadours, Petrarch, Dante, and

Shakespeare; into the contemporary period in which Joyce's *Portrait of the Artist as a Young Man* and Lawrence's *Sons and Lovers* stand as literary beacons; and finally, into *Hilda's Book*, Pound's early private love poems for her. However, H.D. activates these vibrations of male convention only to transform this initial resonance into dissonance. Present in the textual grid of *HER*, they are ultimately rescripted into a gynocentric version of the equation, "love is writing." A gynopoetic, a lesbian erotic, displaces the male loop of textual desire.

The avant-garde self-reflexivity of *HER*, a major mark of its modernism, is also the key to its type of self-conscious intertextuality. Operating more like a camera than a Jamesian center of consciousness, the narrative point of view is highly unstable, as it zooms from its position of distance and knowledge into the interior of Hermione's consciousness, often rendered in sequences of images, like the expressionist/impressionist silent films in which H.D. acted for Macpherson about the time she was writing the novel. At times, the narrator collapses the distinction between the split subjects of autobiography – between the "I" (eye) who wisely regards the past self and the "I" who enacts the present story being regarded. The reader, like the narrator, becomes immersed in the repetitive discourse of Hermione's troubled consciousness. But, at other times, the narrator invites the reader to identify with her position of distance and authority as she inserts authoritative commentary into her narrative, as I have discussed in Chapter 1. One source and sign of the narrator's privileged knowledge is her transposition of male texts into a female (con)text. The narrator is present in the text as the *reader* who "eyes" male texts that she deconstructs and reconstructs in the act of telling her story. This reading is not the creative "mis-reading" Harold Bloom identified as essential for the writer who must displace his literary fathers. Rather, it is a deadly accurate deconstruction, a re-reading of convention from a feminist slant, analogous perhaps to the Hegelian slave whose survival depends on "reading" the master more accurately than the master "reads" himself. In the case of *HER*, the texts of Pound, Joyce, and Lawrence reappear as rescriptions of desire accomplished by an authoritative narrator who "knows" what Hermione "could not know," what Hermione painfully learns in the course of the story the narrator teleologically unfolds – that Hermione's "failure to conform to expectations was perhaps some subtle form of courage" (4).

Because H.D. was herself the object of *Hilda's Book*, and because she so admired *Sons and Lovers* and *Portrait of the Artist as a Young Man*, it is worth articulating the patterns of the muse tradition they embody, structures and rhetoric to which *HER* is a response.[9] In *Hilda's Book*, the poet invokes the tall, beautiful Hilda as his lady love and muse. Adapting the pastoral idylls of Theocritus, troubadour lyrics, and Swinburne's *Poem and Ballads,* Pound self-consciously explored the connections between making poetry about and making love to a woman brought to full being by his words. The setting is the woodlands, meadows, and streams of the pastoral, the world of "nature" imaginatively reconstituted as temporarily outside culture. Reproducing the muse tradition of the romantic lyric, Pound's Lady says not a word, but rather stands impassive and elusive as the gentle winds of poetic imagination circulate about her and through the poems. The scene of desire is the male poet's text; his gaze and speech repeatedly fix her as his creation – like Pygmalion and his statue Galataea; like Petrarch and his Laura; like Dante and his Beatrice.

The dominant metaphor of *Hilda's Book* epitomizes the silent presence of the Lady – she is repeatedly imaged as a tree, an image that invokes Pound's nickname for H.D., Dryad. Their trysts in the fruit trees of her yard, their walks in the nearby forests, her animistic identification with the natural world, and her unusual height – nearly six feet – probably all contributed to his choice of a name. Dryad – partly mystic, partly mock heroic – is also a name that suggests the Greek and Druidic resonances of the poetry the young Pound was reading and writing in the years that led to *A Lume Spento, Lustra,* and *The Spirit of Romance.* Swinburne's "Aholibah" might have been one of the poems he read to Hilda; Pound appears to have recreated it in *Hilda's Book.* "Aholibah" opens with the image of the Lady as a tree:

> In the beginning God made thee
> A woman well to look upon,
> Thy tender body as a tree
> Wherein cool wind hath always blown
> Till the clean branches be well grown.
> *(Poems and Ballads: First Series* 266)[10]

While Pound's "Domina" introduces the mock heroic, the specular metaphor of the poem still centers on the gaze of the poet, whose desire is like the wind that caresses the textual body:

> My Lady is tall and fair to see
> She swayeth as a poplar tree
>   When the wind bloweth merrily
> Her eyes are grey as the grey of the sea
> Not clouded much to trouble me
>   When the wind bloweth merrily
> . . . .
> Her lips part, tho no words come
>   When the wind bloweth merrily
>   *(Hilda's Book* 73–4)[11]

In "Rendez-vous," the Dryad's dreams inspire the songs of the poet, while she herself still maintains the "dumb semblance" of a tree:

> She hath some tree-born spirit of the wood
> About her, and the wind is in her hair
> ....
> The moss-grown kindly trees, meseems, she could
> As kindred claim, for tho to some they wear
> A harsh dumb semblance, unto us that care
> They guard a marvelous sweet brotherhood...
>
> (*Hilda's Book* 84)

Like trees and muses, the Lady inspires the poet by being a mute spectacle, inviting what Homans has called the "story of looking" implicit in the conventions of the romantic lyric (" 'Syllables' " 572). Homans further described the specular metaphor as "a hierarchy that permits one term – whether the romantic (male) subject or one term of a metaphor – to claim the authority to define the other – whether the feminine object of romantic desire or the second term of a metaphor" (573). There is only one poem in *Hilda's Book* in which the Lady herself speaks. But what she says reaffirms the rhetorical and cultural hierarchy implicit in the muse tradition. She speaks with the mute voice of a tree, like Daphne, who became a tree to escape the poet Apollo's assault:

> I stood still and was a tree amid the wood
> Knowing the truth of things unseen before
> Of Daphne and the laurel bow
>
> (*Hilda's Book* 81)

Pound developed the satiric undercurrent in his metaphor of the tree-lady in a slightly later poem that directly alludes to his role in getting H.D.'s poetry published, as Guest has suggested (*Herself Defined* 36). "Tempora" presents Dryad as a speaker, a poet with a voice, but a voice to be mocked by the male poet, who compares it to the frenzied cries of the maenads. In the sexual economy of his own poems, his yearning for the silent Dryad led to his poem, but in "Tempora," the Dryad's cries are the butt of his humor:

> Io! Io! Tammuz:
> the Dryad stands in my court-yard
> With plaintive, querulous crying.
> (Tammuz. Io! Tammuz!)
> Oh, no, she is not crying: "Tammuz."
> She says, "May my poems be printed this week?"
> The god Pan is afraid to ask you,
> May my poems be printed this week?"
>
> (*Lustra* 110)

For the early Pound, then, the Lady who speaks does so out of a position of silence – either as an avatar of the victimized Daphne or as the plaintive woman who must depend upon the male poet to make her speech public. The Lady the poet loves is silent, caressed by his eyes and words. As an image of his desire, she is untouched and untouchable, a perpetual lure whose eroticism is displaced onto the poet's page.[12]

The "story of looking," as the hierarchical plot of male desire implicit in the romantic lyric, is explicitly narrated in *Portrait of the Artist as a Young Man*. Oscillating between the heroic and the ironic, *Portrait* brings the Romantic image of the artist into the twentieth century, as Pound was just beginning to do in his post-Swinburnian poems. Even more than Pound, Joyce was particularly interested in exploring the connection between erotic and aesthetic desire. Sexuality is central to Stephen's *Bildung* as an artist in the making (on the make) – from the infant sexuality of the novel's opening page to the early morning production of his villanelle in a scene whose aesthetic reveries emerge out of erotic ones – the poem as wet dream. From mother to imagined lover, from virgin to whore, from Mary to the bird-girl, woman serves as the elusive matrix of body and soul, the longing for which leads Stephen into the theory and practice of representation. Reflecting its Jesuit context, Stephen's muse is split into spirit and flesh, purity and sexuality, grace and guilt. The Virgin Mary, Mercedes, and E. C. form one untouchable pole, while the prostitute represents the other. Swerving from one to the other, Stephen seeks to reunite the two, to recover the prelapsarian bliss evoked on the novel's first page, when his mother's smell and music merged with the smells of his own body, when his mother's flesh had not yet become taboo.[13]

The bird-girl, the novel's major muse who initiates Stephen's vocation into the secular religion of art, unites the sexual and the spiritual. As Stephen gazes at the silent girl standing in the water, strands of the novel's virginal and erotic imagery weave together (171). Called to his destiny as Daedalus by his desire for the image of woman who possesses him, Stephen becomes the artist in Chapter 5 who discourses on a theory of aesthetics and produces a love poem for E. C. that gives him linguistic possession of the image he desires. While the novel's pervasive irony suggests that Stephen may be Icarus rather than Daedalus, the muse figure of *Portrait* remains a figment of Stephen's desire, the silent object of his longing, a presence without autonomous voice, a creature fixed in his gaze and by his pen. For Stephen, love is writing.[14]

Like *Portrait*, *Sons and Lovers* locates the making of the artist in the matrix of desire, where the image of woman serves as catalyst for and consequence of the act of representation. Even more than Joyce, however, Lawrence regarded the psychosexual dynamics of the family as central to the artist's *Bildung*. The Oedipal narrative suggested in Stephen's attraction to and repulsion from religion and state is more directly examined as a family plot in *Sons and Lovers*.[15] Paul

Morel's youthful loves for Miriam and Clara reenact in split form his forbidden desire for his mother and his deeply repressed desire for his father. But like *Portrait*, *Sons and Lovers* explores the young artist's conflicted sexuality in terms of binary opposition: spirit and flesh, body and soul. The dissolution of the Morel marriage leads the young Paul to see his parents in dualistic terms – his middle-class mother representing the spirit and the mind while his working-class father represents the mute body.

In his struggle to pass into sexual and vocational adulthood, Paul replicates that dualism in the two women he loves – Miriam representing purity, whose eroticism is displaced into a passion for flowers, just like his mother; and Clara representing passion and consummated sexuality, allied therefore with his father, but also with the maternal body.[16] With delicate irony, Lawrence shows Paul repudiate Miriam's sexual advances in his insistence that she fulfill his need for her as an asexual, purely spiritual image of woman. To touch Miriam is to touch his mother, what he both fears and desires. With her open sexuality, Clara seems to free Paul from his mother, but he is unable to establish a full relationship with her because he is compelled to see her only in terms of sexual desire and satiation, compelled as well to return wordlessly to her breast like a child to his mother. Paul has split the mother/muse he desires into two muses, both of whom are essential to his art. With Miriam, he discusses his work, listening to her criticism, desiring her praise, drawing vitality from her spiritual apprehension of his art. With Clara, he never talks about his work. Instead, Clara is the image he draws and redraws, the sight that leads him into the act of representation. With his two muses, Paul enacts the two sides of his desire for his mother. For Paul, love is painting.

In *HER*, the muse speaks. She refuses to be the object of the male gaze, refuses to be caught in the male loop of desire, refuses to be split into body or soul, refuses to choose between love and writing.[17] The birth of the woman as subject begins in refusal, a deconstructive stance toward her self and culture, a negation that is fertile ground for new beginnings. In *HER* these creative negations take both narrative and lyric forms. First, the novel's narrative invokes in order to revoke the implicit narrative of *Hilda's Book* and the explicit narratives of *Sons and Lovers* and *Portrait of the Artist as a Young Man*. Second, the lyric elements of this imagist novel literally replace Pound's images for her in *Hilda's Book* by re-placing them into the story of Her.

To begin with H.D.'s narrative rescriptions of Joyce and Lawrence, we notice immediately that where the male texts begin in a harmony that is lost as an Oedipal plot unfolds, *HER* begins with failure and absence. The novel opens with Hermione in a state of acute distress.

Having flunked out of college and still unmarried, she feels "she was good for nothing. . . . She did not know what it was she wanted" (6–7). In this state of paralysis, Hermione has no muse to propel her forward into the linear plot of development. Instead, she walks in circles in the woods near her home:

> Her Gart stood. Her mind still trod its round. I am Her Gart, my name is Her Gart. I am Hermione Gart. I am going round and round in circles. Her Gart went on. Her feet went on. Her feet had automatically started, so automatically she continued, then stumbled as a bird whirring its bird oblivion into heavy trees above her. Her Gart. I am Her Gart. Nothing held her, she was nothing holding to this thing: I am Hermione Gart, a failure. (4)

Hermione's feet are a mute form of speech as they act out the repetitive, rhythmic, visual discourse of her consciousness, in which, to use Kristeva's terminology, the Semiotic register overwhelms the Symbolic modality of language. Caught in "a patchwork of indefinable association" and visual image, Hermione is without meaningful language or "formula" for living (24). "Words beat and formed unformulated syllables" for her instead of falling into the ordered patterns of the Symbolic (13). In this state of negation "she could put no name to the things she apprehended. . . . It had not occurred to Her to try and put the thing in writing" (25).

Like Stephen and Paul, Hermione sees her parents as symbolic opposites, incarnations of masculine and feminine. But like Woolf in *To the Lighthouse,* H.D. revised the nature and significance of the binary system for the artist who is a daughter. Hermione's father and mother do not embody a patriarchal split between body and soul; rather they represent the culturally constructed structures of power and powerlessness. Her father, Carl Gart, is a famous scientist who peers through the microscope to make the invisible visible; her mother, Eugenia Gart, is a devoted housewife who graces the home with her domestic artistry. "Eugenia is Eleusinian," Hermione thinks at one point; "My father is Athenian" (31). One is the mind, the other is the mysteries. Her father is "the stark glare of inimical Atlantic tumblers," the freedom of the sea; her mother is "the fibres . . . rooted and mossed over and not to be disrupted," the confinement of the "cumbrous . . . subsoil" (9). The Oedipal plot that turns the son into the artist in *Sons and Lovers* and *Portrait* cannot serve for the daughter who would be a poet. To take the place of the father, as Stephen and Paul do, would cost Hermione her womanhood. To take the place of her mother would cost Hermione her potency. Eugenia is like Demeter who is looking for her lost daughter as she moves through the world of her husband's laboratories, "moving through it powerless, all-powerful...one should sing hymns of worship to her, powerful, powerless, all-powerful" (81). Unable to identify with either parent, she is also unable to unite the two: "In Hermione Gart, the two never fused and blended, she was both moss-grown, imbedded and at the same time staring with her inner vision on forever-tumbled breakers. If she went away, her spirit would break; if she stayed, she would be suffocated" (9).

Like *Sons and Lovers* and *Portrait,* initiation into adult sexuality in *HER* signifies a break from, even as it replicates, the erotic triad of mother–father–child. This break, essential to the *Kunstler* plot in all three novels, substitutes a new triangle for the old one. But where Lawrence and Joyce feature a youth oscillating between desire for woman-as-soul and desire for woman-as-body, H.D. reveals a woman moving from heterosexual to lesbian desire. The triangulation of desire in *Sons and Lovers* and *Portrait* inscribes patriarchy, while *HER*'s reformulation of that triangle critiques it. Evoking the interpenetration of erotic and linguistic initiations, the arrival of two letters in the first chapter sets the narrative of *HER* in motion by propelling Hermione out of the stasis of psychic paralysis into the kinesis of love, first for the disreputable poet George (the Pound figure), who dominates Part 1 of the novel, and then for the visionary Fayne (the Gregg figure), who dominates Part 2.

The first letter announces George's return from Europe and leads to Hermione's engagement to a poet she hopes will free her from the conventionality of her family and initiate her into his bohemian world of art. But as the relationship unfolds, she gradually realizes that his kisses "suffocate" her, that his "sea-green eyes that became sea-grey" as they lie on the forest floor press her into the moss beneath her body: "Kisses forced her into soft moss. Her head lay marble weight in cushion of forest moss. . . . Smudged out. I am smudged out" (65, 73). In the romance plot of heterosexual love, George becomes her father and she becomes her mother – a superposition revealed through the parental imagery of seawater and moss. After their engagement is official, the suffocation of his kisses in what was "almost the forest of Arden" in Part 1 becomes in Part 2 downright assault in the drawing room of what seemed like "some bad novel": "Sound of chiffon ripping and the twist and turn of Hermione under the stalwart thin young torso of George Lowndes" (65, 173).

In contrast to *Sons and Lovers* and *Portrait,* the heterosexual love plot ultimately inhibits the development of the *Kunstler* plot instead of moving it forward. George initially draws her out of psychic paralysis, with the result that Hermione begins to write, moves out of the undifferentiated syllables in which she had been caught, tries "to put the thing in writing." But George is upset and ambivalent about the poems she tentatively shows him: "Pages fluttered in the hands of George Lowndes. His hands

fluttered white pages. What George holds in his hands is my life's beginning" (148). On the one hand, he doubts that she did them herself,
the classic charge that women artists have faced: " 'Who helped you do
this thing, Hermione?... Well I'm ballyho damned if I'm going to help
you with your bally writing' " (147). But, on the other hand, he says,
" 'I tell you *this is writing,*' " a statement that prefigures H.D.'s account
of Pound's words in the British Museum, "But, Dryad, this is poetry."
In explaining his praise, he says her writing is like Theocritus, "like the
choriambics of a forgotten Melic" (149).[18] As their engagement pro-
gresses however, he becomes less sympathetic. "Your melic choruses
aren't half so bad as simply rather rotten," he says (167), and finally,
"You are a poem, though your poem's nought" (212).[19] She concludes
that George "wanted Her, but he wanted a her that he called decorative.
George wanted a Her out of the volumes on the floor.... He wanted
Her from... the Great Painters (that came under Florence) section....
George saying 'Choriambics of a forgotten Melic' was flattering her,
tribute such as some courtier might pay to a queen who played at clas-
sicism; he did not proffer her the bare branch that was the strip of wild
naked olive or the tenuous oleander" (172).

As muse for his poems, she cannot also be the poet. This is the significance for Hermione of the story of Undine, to which she returns
repeatedly after her sessions with George. Undine is connected to the
Little Mermaid from Anderson's fairy tale, the creature whose fate embodies the price love exacts for women in the male economy of desire.
To win the love of the prince, the Little Mermaid has to get the feet of
a mortal woman. To get the feet, she has to give up her voice. When
George's mother calls her Undine, Hermione suddenly realizes that she
can never marry George: "Undine was not her name, would never be
her name.... 'I am not Undine,' she said, 'for Undine or the Little
Mermaid sold her glory for feet. Undine (or the Little Mermaid) couldn't
speak after she sold her glory. I will not sell my glory' " (120). For
Undine, love was *not* writing. The loss of her voice, of her status as
subject, is the price of love.

The second letter brings an invitation to a party where Hermione meets
Fayne, with whom she falls in love, thereby breaking the heterosexual
romance plot of *Sons and Lovers* and *Portrait of the Artist*. Disengaging
from George, Hermione finds in Fayne the "sister" who can offer her
the bare branch of wild olive, the one who sees her "stripped of decoration," as Artemis rather than a Florentine Diana encased in a book
(172–3). George brings out her conventional feminine side – "She wanted
George as a little girl wants to put her hair up or to wear long skirts"
(63). But Fayne draws out her unconventional, visionary, and creative
potential, that secret self that had always yearned for "a sister [who] was

a creature of ebony strung with wild poppies..., [who] would run, would leap, would be concealed under the autumn sumac or lie shaken with hail and wind, lost on some Lacedaemonian foothill" (10). *Sight* and *seeing* are central to their love, as it is for Paul and Stephen. But in *HER,* the gaze is mutual, not hierarchical.[20] "Prophetess to prophetess on some Delphic headland," they sit gazing into each other's eyes until, one afternoon, "Eyes met eyes and the storm held, storm of ice, some storm in an ice crater" (180, 161). Syntax dissolves linearity into circularity and differentiation into sameness, thereby fusing the two women "into a concentric intimacy" at the moment they kiss: "Her face bent forward, face bent toward Her" (163). This touch that erases the difference between the women contrasts greatly with the distance between the male artist and his muse figure not only in Joyce and Lawrence, but also in the romance tradition of the lyric described by Homans, for which the maintenance of distance and specularity is essential to the production of the poem.

HER's transposition of the erotic from heterosexual passion to lesbian love is connected with Hermione's development as an artist. Hermione shows her poems to Fayne, as she did to George. Instead of his scorn, based partially in jealousy, Fayne tells Her that she is not threatened by her writing: "Your writing is the thin flute holding you to eternity. Take away your flute and you remain, lost in a world of unreality" (162). Fayne's betrayal of this love in her secret affair with George leads Hermione into the underworld of madness, which recapitulates and intensifies the anguish at the beginning of the novel. But this psychic death becomes the chrysalis of rebirth, the emergence of a healed Hermione. Nine months after she received the letters, her body itself has become the artist's pen. Once again she walks through the woods near her home, but this time, her body writes across the virginal text of fresh snow: "Her feet were pencils tracing a path.... Now the creator was Her's feet, narrow black crayon across the winter whiteness" (223). A matrix of desire, Fayne's image accompanies her as she pencils her path into the future: "When she said Fayne a white hand took her.... Her saw Her as a star shining white against winter daylight" (225). Fayne, the woman who betrayed their love, has become the ideal image of Fayne, the muse who takes the fledgling poet by the hand and makes her a "star."

Like Paul and Stephen, Hermione discovers that love is both essential and nonmaterial to the birth of the artist. All three novels conclude with their central figures alone, empowered by love relationships that they leave behind as they initiate a flight from home. Hermione's determination on the final page of the novel to use her trousseau money for travel to Europe evokes both Paul's decision to go to London and Stephen's exile in Paris in the final pages of the other novels. But the very strength of the textual echo intensifies H.D.'s radical departure. The last line of *HER* breaks across that resonance by suddenly, unexpectedly, and without explanation reintroducing the "real" Fayne. "Oh, Miss," says Mandy. "I thought you was back long since. I done left Miss Fayne all alone upstairs in your little workroom" (234). Fayne, we learn, is waiting for Hermione in her room, an open ending that may mean everything, or nothing – we never learn. But it suggests the reconstitution of the lesbian lovers, a reaffirmation that "Love is writing" realized not only in the psychodynamics of muse and writer, but also in the "real" realm of lovers.

H.D.'s intertextual transposition of *Sons and Lovers* and *Portrait of the Artist* forms a kind of metanarrative in *HER,* a "story" of intertextual action (or textual interaction) that sits on top of (or underneath) the story of Hermione. This commentary on Lawrence's and Joyce's texts is generally evident in the way *HER* both echoes and alters the complex triangulations of desire in the earlier novels. The *Kunstler* narratives of both *Portrait* and *Sons and Lovers* are fundamentally Oedipal. The son, desiring the forbidden mother, displaces onto the women he loves his feelings for his mother. Mothered by these muses, the youth passes into adulthood, erotically charged and alone, ready to spill his seed onto the blank page and canvas of his art. The *Kunstler* narrative of *HER,* on the other hand, is fundamentally pre-Oedipal. The daughter, rejecting Oedipal love, returns to the fusion of the pre-Oedipal in her love for Fayne, to the merged identities of two women evident in the formula "She is Her. I am Her. Her is Fayne. Fayne is Her" (181–2).

H.D.'s narrative rescription of *Sons and Lovers* and *Portrait* also critiques the romance plot implicit in the lyrics of Pound's *Hilda's Book.* But H.D.'s intertextual combat with Pound's poems takes place on the lyric as well as the narrative level. In this imagist novel, the authoritative narrator literally appropriates lines and images from *Hilda's Book,* deconstructs these *words* as textual sources of her own objectification, and finally reconstitutes them as lyric expressions of a forbidden female identity as speaking subject – not the object of desire, but desirous; not a cultural product in man's text, but a cultural producer through the agency of the poetic word. In short, Pound's love poems for H.D. are transposed into lyric celebrations of Her's love for Fayne. In their new context, the images do not reproduce the male economy of desire, but rather create a scene in which the two women are mutually desirous and creative, neither fixed in the text of the other. For H.D., as for Her, "Words were her plague and words were her redemption" (*HER* 67).

The dominant metaphor of *Hilda's Book* – H.D. as Dryad, the tree spirit – is also the pervasive motif of *HER.* "I am TREE," Hermione repeatedly thinks, a refrain that places Pound's metaphor into the sequence of Her's consciousness. The (r)evolution of the tree metaphor in the novel contributes lyrically to the narrative of how the mute muse of Pound's volume comes to speak in her own book. The novel opens, it will be recalled, with Her stumbling into oblivion underneath the trees. "Trees were suffocation" that "walled one in," Hermione thinks (8). Peering up into the branches, she thinks: "Pennsylvania. Names are in people, people are in names. Sylvania. I was born here. . . . I am part of Sylvania. Trees. Trees. Trees. . . . Trees are in people. People are in trees" (5). Even the shape of the trees entrap – they are the "conic sections," the "concentric" cones of the math test she failed (5).

When Hermione first reaches out to George as a possible solution to her sense of failure, the tree motif develops into direct echoes of poems like "Domina" and "Rendez-vous." Hermione thinks of herself as a tree called into being by George: "She wanted George to define and to make definable a mirage, a reflection of some lost incarnation, a wood maniac, a tree demon, a neuropathic dendrophil" (63). But as she discovers that George's desire is a trap, the trees become a kind of prison: "Trees swung and fell and rose. Trees barricaded her into herself, Her into Her. . . . Her was received into trees that swung and billowed and swung" (64). On one level, the trees are the woods in which they walk; but on the metalevel, the trees are the imprisoning words of Pound's poems in which he has worshipfully named her "Tree" or "Dryad," his silent muse.

When George's approach becomes openly sexual, Pound's poem "Tree," with its evocation of Apollo's assault on a silent Daphne, is recast into H.D.'s narrative: "George turned facing Her, rubbed cheek against a tree trunk. 'Don't talk,' he now said, 'don't talk.' . . . She now braced herself decisively against her own tree. She rubbed her shoulder blades against that small tree. Small hard tree trunk . . . swayed a little, upright swaying little tree swayed. She was stronger than the upright little tree" (68). The ominous swaying in H.D.'s text echoes the refrain in Pound's "Domina:" "She swayeth as a poplar tree." The "dumb semblance" of Pound's Lady, whose "lips part, tho no words come" in "Domina" is transposed into George's command in *HER:* "Don't talk." Similarly, the "moss-grown kindly trees" of his poem "Rendez-vous" become in H.D.'s text "the soft moss" into which his kisses force her, thereby invoking her mother's powerlessness (73). The imagery of Pound's lyric eroticism is repeatedly transformed in H.D.'s narrative into a plot against Her's autonomy, an assault on her self as a speaking subject of her own desire.

Pound's words in *Hilda's Book* are literally – literarily – H.D.'s "plague." Her own words, rescripting his text, are her "redemption." Trapped as a "tree" in Pound's text, H.D. freed herself by reclaiming "treeness" for Hermione in her own text. Gradually, trees become the motif of Hermione's autonomous inner self. This transformation from the word as trap to the word as creative force is evident in the repetitive circlings of Hermione's thought: "Tree on tree on tree. TREE. I am the Tree of Life. Tree. I am a tree planted by the river of water. I am...I am...HER exactly....I am in the word TREE, I am TREE" (70, 73). By the end of the novel, Hermione thinks: "I am Tree exactly. George never would love a tree, she had known from the beginning. . . . I knew George could never love a tree properly" (197). The parodic effect of this culminating accusation anticipates the "playful repetition" that Irigaray associated with feminine mimicry. "To play with mimesis," she wrote in "The Power of Discourse," "is thus, for a woman, to try to recover the place of her exploitation by discourse, without allowing herself to be simply reduced to it" (*This Sex* 76). H.D.'s repetitions of "Tree on tree on tree" mimic Pound's poems so "as to make 'visible,' by an effect of playful repetition, what was supposed to remain invisible" (76).[21]

H.D.'s playful transformation of Pound's words records not only Hermione's disengagement from George, but also her engagement with Fayne. The complicated wordplay and syntactic disruptions surrounding Hermione's nickname "Her" are key to these lyric intertexts. Many critics have noted how the disturbing impact of the object case "Her" in the syntactic position of the subject inscribes the objectification of woman within the phallo(go)centric systems of desire and language.[22] But the awkward "Her" is also an intertextual play on Pound's poem "Shadow." In this poem, the poet flirts with deserting his Lady for the attractions of a golden-haired woman, but each time his thoughts wander, he is recalled to his true love by the recollection of *seeing* "HER." Without "HER," he is in darkness, stifled:

> Darkness hath descended upon the earth
> And there are no stars
> The sun from zenith to nadir is fallen
> And the thick air stifleth me.
>> (*Hilda's Book* 75)

But recalling his vision of "HER," whom he saw just yesterday, restores the light and air. Four times he recalls his gaze, in a refrain that structures the poem:

> I saw her yesterday.
> And lo, there is no time
> Each second being eternity.
> ....
> I saw HER yesterday.
> ....
> I saw her yester e'en.
> ....

I saw her yesterday
Since when there is no sun
(*Hilda's Book* 76).[23]

In *HER,* H.D. picked up on Pound's repetition and capitalization of "HER" to establish the same pattern of textual entrapment and liberation evident in the evolution of the tree motif. In the novel, Hermione is literally the "HER" of Pound's text. The opening lines of the novel suggest this intertextual reference and her related distress: "Her Gart went round in circles. 'I am Her,' she said to herself; she repeated, 'Her, Her, Her' " (3). Hermione is the "HER" of Pound's poem, an object in his text and of his gaze. The disturbing disruption of grammar ostensibly justified by Hermione's nickname points to her object status. "I am Her" is correct from the standpoint of naming, but incorrect in relationship to pronouns. This ambiguity emphasizes that linguistic objectification embodies a corresponding cultural objectification of which Hermione gradually becomes aware: "There was that about George, he wanted to incarnate Her, knew enough to know that this was not Her. There was just a chance that George might manage to draw her out half-drowned, a coal scuttle, or push HER back, drowned, a goddess" (64). As George's Lady, she is his text. HER *is* text, that is, a word without its own voice, the object of its male speaker.

Having deconstructed Pound's "I saw HER," H.D. reconstructed Hermione's identity through a forbidden love of doubled "Hers," which changes the scene of desire from heterosexual to lesbian. When Hermione tells George that she can never marry him, she says: "Anyhow I love – I love Her, only Her, Her, Her" (170). "Her" is simultaneously Hermione and Fayne – loving Fayne teaches Hermione how to love herself. George taunts Hermione with the name "Narcissa," evoking not only the myth of Narcissus, whose self-love led to his death, but also Freud's theory of narcissism, which regards homosexual love as a return to an infantile stage of object choice. But Hermione's narcissistic love is creative, not regressive. It accomplishes the birth of the subject "She" and "I" out of the object status of "Her" with which the novel opened. Her thinks: "I know her, I know her. Her. I am Her. She is Her. Knowing her, I know Her. She is some amplification of myself like amoeba giving birth, by breaking off, to amoeba" (158).[24]

The novel records this birth of twin selves in a series of ecstatic lyric moments in which ordinary space and time vanish, in which the repetitive rhythms of ungrammatical and circular sentences interrupt the sequence of both language and narrative. It is the voice of the Kristevan Semiotic disrupting the linearity of the Symbolic when Her thinks, for example: "Fayne being me, I was her. Fayne being Her I was Fayne. Fayne being Her was HER so that Her saw Fayne" (210). Yet these moments of repetitive eruption and syntactic breakdown also have an intertextual dimension as deliberate rescriptions of prior male texts by the narrator. At another point, for example, Her lays her cool white hands on Fayne's eyelids. "Your hands are healing," Fayne tells her. "They have dynamic white power. . . . Your hands are white stars. Your hands are snowdrops" (180). Ignoring the voices calling her from downstairs, Her locks the door and watches the sleeping Fayne: "I will not have her hurt. I will not have Her hurt. She is Her. I am Her. Her is Fayne. Fayne is Her. I will not let them hurt HER" (181). This passage transposes Pound's poem "Sancta Patrona Domina Caelae":

> Out of thy purity
> Saint Hilda pray for me.
> Lay on my forehead
> The hands of thy blessing.
> Saint Hilda pray for me
> Lay on my forehead
> Cool hands of thy blessing
> Out of thy purity
> Lay on my forehead
> White hands of thy blessing.
> *Virgo caelicola*
> *Ora pro nobis.*
> (Hilda's Book 83–4)

In the novel, Hermione lays cool white hands not on George's forehead, but on Fayne's. Saint Hilda's virginal innocence in Pound's poem becomes the "indecent" innocence of lesbian love in *HER*.[25] The Swinburne poems that Pound brought to H.D. in their courtship become in the novel the code for the lesbian love through which Hermione creates both her self and her sense of artistic vocation. Fayne asks, " 'Isn't Swinburne decadent?' " " 'In what sense exactly decadent, Fayne?' " Hermione responds. " 'Oh innocence like thine is totally indecent,' " Fayne replies (164). Swinburne's coded lesbian poems "Itylus" and "Faustine" provide refrains for their love – " *O sister my sister Oh fleet sweet swallow*" from "Itylus" and "Curled lips, long since half kissed away" from "Faustine" (158, 163–4). The erotic decadence of Swinburne's sapphics, however, appear transformed in *HER,* as Cassandra Laity has shown. The Circe-like Faustine and the lesbian "sisters" Philomel and Procne of Swinburne's poems both attract and disgust a voyeuristic poet, who ultimately associates their love with Procne's murder of her son Itylus and Faust's pact with the devil.[26] But in *HER,* Hermione quotes Swinburne's lines about Itylus to vow that she will never forget Fayne – "*Thou has forgotten O summer swallow but the world will end when I forget*" (160). She quotes lines from "Faustine," not to condemn, but to celebrate their kiss: "Lips long since half kissed away. Curled lips long since half kissed away. In Roman gold. Long ere they coined in Roman gold your face – your face – your face – your face – your face – Faustine" (163–4). In the reversals that characterize the novel, what is conventionally moral – such as a proper engagement to George – becomes immoral. What is conventionally indecent – such as lesbian love – becomes the sacred center of innocence.

HER's combative intertextual rescriptions and transpositions of Pound, Joyce, Lawrence, and Swinburne are complemented by the novel's intricate restaging of Shakespeare's *The Winter's Tale,* which in its own revisionist telling of the Demeter–Koré myth acts as midwife to the story of birth in *HER*.[27] As a romance, *The Winter's Tale* presents a conventional narrative and an unconventional subtext of mother–daughter love submerged within the dominant plot. In a blind fit of jealousy, Leontes, a Sicilian king, condemns his wife Hermione to death and orders that her infant daughter be exposed in the wilderness as a bastard. Under the guidance of Paulina, a sculptor stealthily makes a statue of the dead queen while Paulina's husband secrets the baby to safety in Bohemia. Deeply remorseful for his crimes, Leontes is rewarded for his penitence sixteen years later. The lost child, named Perdita by the ghost of her mother, is found as a beautiful shepherd girl by Prince Florizel. When Perdita returns to Sicilia, Paulina reveals the statue of Hermione to Leontes, who watches in amazement as it comes to life. The marriage of king and queen is reestablished just as the union of Perdita and Florizel is celebrated.

However, the double marriage plot only seems to dominate. The play's conclusion depends entirely on a subtext of maternal desire, in which mother and daughter double for each other as Demeter and Koré. In the myth, the daughter dies, raped into the underworld by the unjust might of Hades. In the play, the mother dies, forced into death by the unjust power of the king. In the myth, the mother seeks for her daughter, whom she brings to life for half of each year. In the play, the daughter, who survives her initial exposure like Oedipus, travels to Sicilia and requests to see the statue of her mother kept in the chapel. The statue is not brought to life by the gaze of Leontes, who is indeed spellbound by the sight. Instead, Paulina is the *sage femme* who assists at the "birth" of the statue, which comes to life because Hermione desires her daughter. It is not love from or for Leontes that makes the miracle happen, as we learn when Hermione finally speaks in the final moments of the play. Ignoring her gazing husband, she says to Perdita: "Tell me, my own, / Where has thou been preserved? Where lived? How found / Thy father's court? For thou shalt hear that I, / knowing by Paulina that the oracle / Gave hope thou wast in being, have preserved / Myself to see the issue"

(V, *iii*, 125–8). The mother saved herself in order to be saved in turn by
her daughter. The play reunites mother and daughter, Demeter and Koré,
whose love for each other signals the return of spring in "a winter's
tale."

The birth of Her similarly depends on an Eleusinian subtext that resides
in lost and muted form within the dominant family romance of the
traditional Victorian family. In the novel, Her plays the role of both
mother and daughter: She is the frozen statue and the lost child. As
Hermione, Her feels like heavy marble under the ardent body of George
(73–5). She is only "Hermione from the *Winter's Tale* (who later froze
into a statue)," not "Rosalind with sleek, deer-limbs and a green forester's
cap with one upright darting hawk quill" from *As You Like It* (66). Statue
imagery pervades the heterosexual love plot to signal Hermione's frozen
existence as the object of George's desire. But as Perdita, Her suffers a
kind of exposure, a near-death imaged by the mad circling of her mind
and body at the beginning of the novel. Just as Shakespeare reversed the
myth to have the daughter seek her mother, Her keeps looking for the
spirit of Demeter that lives inside Eugenia Gart.

On the surface, Eugenia epitomizes the selflessness of a Victorian "angel in the house." Like Hermione in the play, she is "frozen" into a
statue; like Perdita in the play, she is "lost" in the world of men. She
has given up sewing in the evening, she explains to her daughter, because
"Your father likes the light concentrated in a corner. He can work better
if I'm sitting in the dark" (79). As arbiter of convention, Eugenia responds
to Hermione's romance with the disreputable George by wondering what
the "university ladies" would think, by further asking Hermione about
money and status. Eugenia becomes reconciled to Her's engagement only
when she learns that George's family has a villa in the south of France
and when the presence of Fayne threatens an unspeakable violation of
respectability. To Her, Eugenia appears to represent everything from
which she must escape. Their exchanges in the novel represent an absence, the separation of Demeter and Koré, of Hermione and Perdita.
Her thinks but cannot say at one point: " 'You never listen to what I
say mama. Your throat looks so pretty coming out of that ruffle...like
a moonflower.... You have no midwife power, you can't lift me out
of this thing' " (80).

Yearning for her mother's presence – the maternal body, in Kristeva's
terms – Her attempts to see beneath the frozen surface of her mother to
Demeter, to the powerful mother who can nourish her lost daughter.
But Eugenia, she realizes, is also caught in the world of the fathers,
"moving through it powerless, all-powerful...one should sing hymns of
worship to her, powerful, powerless, all-powerful" (81). Her can come
into touch with Eugenia's hidden power only by thinking of her in

childbirth.[28] During the brutal thunderstorm that breaks the summer heat, mother and daughter break through their conventional discourse into a moment of nourishing communion, "all their past million-of-years-ago quarrel forgotten in the firelight" (89). In something of a trance, Eugenia recounts how she gave birth to Her in the middle of a terrible storm, all alone, before the arrival of doctor and midwife. For a moment, the daughter is empowered by this scene of maternal power: "*The morning stars sang together.* Words of Eugenia had more power than textbooks, than geometry, than all of Carl Gart.... Carl Gart wasn't brilliant like Eugenia" (89).

   HER's Eleusinian narrative of maternal desire has its own subtext of homoerotic love signaled by the novel's double inversion of the Pygmalion myth, itself transformed in *The Winter's Tale*. Hermione is frozen into a statue, instead of brought to life, by George's passion. Moreover, as the frozen statue, she wakens and is awakened by not only Eugenia, but also Fayne. Hermione begins to escape George's ardent "almost Arden" when she sees the statue of an ecstatic boy praying on top of the piano at George's house. A prophetic Helios figure, the statue makes her see that she cannot become Mrs. George Lowndes (106–12). Fayne brings the boy statue to life by playing the role of Pygmalion dressed as a boy in a Greek tunic (162). This conflation of statue and sculptor rescripts the traditional myth in which the desire of Pygmalion, the male artist, brings to life Galataea, the object of his gaze. Like Fayne, Her is both artist and statue. When the two women kiss, one says to the other, "I'll make you breathe, my breathless statue" (162). Significantly, the speaker here is ambiguous. In the mutuality that characterizes their ideal moments, both women are statues that come to life; both women are subjects in the story of desire. Like her Shakespearean namesake, the frozen Hermione has stepped off the pedestal where George's love had placed her. Fayne's confession on the phone that she has been with George refreezes Her into white marble (186). Her emergence out of madness is the breaking of "frozen surfaces" (215). As she walks in the wintery woods at the end, she stamps her feet into the ice until it cracks. For a moment, "her feet were held, frozen to the cracked ice surface. Her heart was frozen" (226). But she suddenly breaks free and runs to the Farrands' where she accepts their offer to accompany them to Europe. "Feet pulsed forward," now unfrozen, as she rushes to her room in the last lines of the novel (234). Like Shakespeare's play, the "winter's tale" in *HER* ends with the resurrection of Hermione.

   H.D.'s rescriptions of *The Winter's Tale* and the myths of Pygmalion and Demeter/Koré consequently weave together two strands of desire, the maternal matrix of a revisionary mother–daughter bond and the sister nexus of a lesbian love. These narratives appear to be at odds with each other and in fact coexist in a certain tension that covertly points to the state of mind of the psychoanalytically knowledgeable narrator, the "I now" of 1926–7. The mother and sister narratives of desire connect to different phases of Freud's evolving theory of homosexuality. As early as *Three Contributions to the Theory of Sex*, Freud had attacked the concept of inborn homosexuality promoted by sexologists like Havelock Ellis to argue that most homosexual "object choice" was acquired. Normal passage through the Oedipus complex, he thought, led heterosexual adults to repress homosexual desire. Homosexuals, in turn, regressed to a pre-Oedipal stage of desire. In "On Narcissism" (1914), he suggested that (male) homosexual love represents a regression to primary narcissism: "in the choice of their love-object they have taken as their model not the mother but their own selves. They are plainly seeking themselves as a love object and their type of object-choice may be termed narcissistic" (69). By the 1920s, when Freud began to address women's different passage through the psychosexual stages, he explained lesbian desire not in terms of narcissism, but as the daughter's pre-Oedipal desire for fusion with the "phallic" mother, that is, with the potent mother she loved before she learned of her mother's "castration" ("Psychogenesis of a Case of Homosexuality in a Woman").

Ignoring Freud's normative bias, H.D. embedded both theories of same-sex desire in *HER*, signaled by the narrator's references to what she knows that Her does not: concepts like "arrested development" and "mother fixation." The lyric and linguistic fusions of Her and Fayne celebrate sister-love as the narcissistic passion of twin souls for themselves in each other – as in "I love Her, only Her, Her, Her" (170). George's taunt – "Narcissus in the reeds. Narcissa" – evokes Freud's earlier theory. But, instead of spelling sterility and death, sister-love as self-love leads to Her's birth as butterfly, as psyche, by the end of the novel.[29] Her's search for the Eleusinian Demeter represents Freud's later theory of lesbianism as pre-Oedipal desire. She connects with the lost mother, the powerful mother layered beneath the powerless mother, when the furious storm leads the mother to re-create the scene of the daughter's birth. Longing for the all-encompassing maternal body is displaced, according to Freud's later theory of "mother fixation," onto other women, especially Fayne, but also onto a series of marginalized women in the novel, each of whom nurtures Her in a way that the more conventional and privileged Eugenia is not able to do. First, there is the family's black cook Mandy, with whom Her pits the cherries, merging "white hand" and "black arm" in a pre-Oedipal fusion of selves[30]; then, Lillian, George's iconoclastic mother, who gives Her the statue of the praying boy, a "phallic" gift that leads Her to reject her son and embrace Fayne;

and finally, Amy, the working-class nurse whose matter-of-fact care loosens Her's tongue so that she is able to articulate all the things she has thought, but never said, especially to her mother. Each woman has a certain kind of power that Her desires: "Mandy had her formula" and the power of speech (27); Lillian is associated with the power of music and ecstatic prophecy; and Amy represents the power of healing. Figures of displaced maternal desire, these women function as surrogate mothers who "lift up" the lost daughter from the underworld into the light of clear thought. They are precursors to the goddesses in H.D.'s later poetry who heal the daughter–poet and inspire her visionary poetry.[31]

Re/membering Eugenia as Demeter helps usher Her into a symbolic world of language essential to her development as a poet in the course of the novel. The recovered birth scene, it will be recalled, led Her to perceive her mother's "brilliant" words as more powerful than the "text-book," "geometry" words of her father (89). Not the prestigious language of Western male discourses, this maternal language is a precursor of the discourse of H.D. *Imagiste*. Highly visual, it is clustered in the novel with flowers and fruit, women's domestic art, and Japanese painting and poetry. Peony petals, cherries, cherry blossoms, moonflowers, snowflakes, and cranes reappear as a lyric subtext in the novel that links the fragmentary perceptions of Her's "octopus" mind with her maternal desire. At first, George's discourse fully represents "writing" to Her: "Writing had somehow got connected up with George Lowndes who even in his advanced progress could make no dynamic statement that would assure her mind that writing had to do with the underside of a peony petal that covered the whole of a house" (71). But after the storm, when Eugenia tells her " 'My darling child. You're far too Fujiyama. . . . too those sketches, you know Hokusai, whatever his name is, Japanese snowflakes, cherry trees, obvious cherry tree snowflakes on water,' " Her thinks: "My mother is a poet. Cherry flakes on water" (126). Her's metonymic condensation of her mother's visual image anticipates the lyric discourse of H.D. *Imagiste*, the visual discourse of *Sea Garden*, as L. S. Dembo has pointed out ("H.D. *Imagiste*").

In the *Kunstler* narrative of *HER*, Her distances herself from George's influence by drawing closer to Eugenia as the prototypical figure of the artist. The scene in which Her first shows her poems to George is pivotal. The "white pages" – "my life's beginnings" – that "fluttered" in his hands reproduce the "peony petals" and "cherry flakes" associated with her mother (148). Her fear at his response is interwoven with thoughts about a watercolor her mother painted as a young woman (147–9). She recalls telling Fayne and George that this painting always made her want to paint like her mother (147–8). Fayne, she remembers, had admired the painting, but George snorts "Painted? You call that painted?" (148–9). Her's key revelation in the novel – "Writing. Love is writing" – significantly comes in defense of her mother's painting:

> "You must see how she loved it." "Love doesn't make good art, Hermione." George Lowndes bounced forward like someone who has had a tooth out. "I tell you *this* *is* *writing*."
> Hermione faced George Lowndes across a forest jungle. Writing. Love is writing. (149)

George's praise attempts to separate Her from Eugenia and the domestic creativity she represents. Her does not voice open resistance to George, but she silently identifies with her mother's art, based as it is in desire. As wife, Eugenia is the powerless Demeter unable to end her daughter's winter death. But, as artist, Eugenia is the powerful Demeter who helps to "lift" her daughter out of the underworld of spiritual paralysis to a springtime of peony petals and cherry flakes, to a language of flowers.

As H.D. re-created the origins of H.D. *Imagiste* in *HER*, the poet was "born," not in the tea shop of the British Museum under the maestro's pen, not in the powerful urban centers of international modernism, but rather in and through the "words" and domestic creativity that the daughter learned from her mother. *HER* narrates how the young woman slipped the noose of the male words that were her "plague" and formulated her own agency with words in the matrix of maternal and lesbian desire. This story of origins rewrites the narrative of creation in Pound's poem "Ortus," which is often read as a general poem about creativity, but which may also be, as Cyrena Pondrom suggested, a specific poem about the origins of H.D. *Imagiste*. Pound originally published "Ortus" in April of 1913, in the same issue of *Poetry* in which he and Flint laid out imagist doctrine for the first time and just one issue after H.D.'s first three imagist poems had appeared. Whether or not the poem alludes to H.D., the creator in the poem is male and the text is female. The poet's labor reproduces the creation of the universe by the potent Word. "In the beginning was the Word, and the Word was with God, and the Word was God," the Gospel of John reads. The linguistic authority of the poet to name a thing into existence resonates with a corresponding religious and sexual authority as well:

> How have I laboured?
> How have I not laboured
> To bring her soul to birth,
> To give these elements a name and a centre!
> She is beautiful as the sunlight, and as fluid.
> She has no name, and no place.

How have I laboured to bring her soul into separation;
To give her a name and her being!

Surely you are bound and entwined,
You are mingled with the elements unborn;
I have loved a stream and a shadow.

I beseech you enter your life.
I beseech you learn to say "I,"
When I question you;
For you are no part, but a whole,
No portion, but a being.

(*Lustra* 84)

For H.D., the poem may have represented the problematic nature of the artistic, sexual, and religious authority Pound and later men repeatedly assumed in relationship to her. The significance of words and naming in *HER* can be read as H.D.'s rewrite of Pound's poem celebrating his role in the creation of H.D. *Imagiste*. The butterfly and birth imagery pervasive throughout *HER* may well be an intertextual echo of the birth imagery of "Ortus." Just as likely, the refrains in the novel about identity – names, places, and things – may answer Pound's lament: "She has no name, and no place." Hermione variously thinks: "Names are in people, people are in names" (5); "she could put no name to the things she apprehended" (13); "Things make people, people make things" (25); "People were in things, things were in people. Names were in things, things were in names" (74); "I don't know what her name is. . . . She was nameless" (81); "People are in names, names are in people" (131); "Things are in people, people are in things" (134); "People are in things. Things are in people and people should think before they call a place Sylvania" (198). Her's resistance to marriage centers synecdochically on her name: "I am Hermione Gart and will be Hermione Lowndes...it wasn't right. People are in things, things are in people. I can't be called Lowndes" (112). Within this context, the slip in the manuscript of *HER* takes on added significance. George's name is alternately spelled as "Lowndes," as it is printed, and "Lowdnes," perhaps an unconscious gesture at Pound's "loudness" that would mute the voice of his muse.

HER narrates how Hermione finds her own "center," "place," and "name" within and through language. But the agent of creation is not the potent male poet who brings her into existence. Instead, her self-creation emerges out of her disengagement from George, engagement with Fayne, and re/membering of the mother–daughter bond. This re-definition of the role of desire in the making of identity coexists with Hermione's reclamation of the word, the power to name, which she appropriates in acts of self-conscious blasphemy: "God is in a word. God

is in a word. God is in HER. She said, 'HER, HER, HER. I am Her.'
. . . I am the word...the word was with God...I am the word...HER"
(32). Through opposition to George rather than obedience to his command, Hermione transforms her very body into the poet's pen; she writes
herself into the role of Creator as she walks across the virginal text of
snow at the end of the novel. This phallic shape occupying John's position, however, does not simply reproduce the narrative of masculine
parthenogenesis. Like "Ortus" itself, *HER* contains a more subversive
story of birth based on the procreative metaphor for artistic production.
This metaphor feminizes the poet, who is mother to herself, producing
her word out of the labor of her body. Completed in the year of Helen
Doolittle's death, *HER* returns to the gynopoetics of *Notes on Thought
and Vision,* written in the year of Perdita's birth.

II. THE UNMAKING OF H.D. IMAGISTE

O to go down as one who remained true to the Imagists. I could
turn them out by the barrel.

H.D., Interview
with Pearson[32]

The split subject of H.D.'s therapeutic narrative points to another
birth, another mother–daughter connection between the "I now," who
writes in a postwar, psychoanalytically informed moment, and the "I
then," the young woman brought to life (again) by the older woman's
act of writing. The narrator is a representation of H.D. in 1926–27, who
is, like Hermione in Greek myth, the daughter of Helen and like Hermione in Shakespeare, the mother of Perdita. Also like Shakespeare's
Hermione, she is frozen, waiting to be reawakened by the return of her
"daughter" who comes back in the form of the story about her younger
self that she tells. Her fixed identity as H.D. *Imagiste* has stiffened her
into a marble statue, an icon for worship or hate, rather than a living,
breathing, aging, and changing writer. Narrating the making of H.D.
Imagiste unmakes "H.D.," brings the frozen statue back to life. It writes
H.D. out of the imagist cage to which she had been confined by the very
successes of the poet whose birth is told in the novel. This *mise en abyme*
sets up a second story that deconstructs the first.

The second story is a metanarrative, embedded in the way the narrator
tells the first story. The natural landscape of H.D.'s early poems, with
its characteristic polarities, forms the backdrop for Hermione's *Bildung.*
Oppositions of land and sea, fire and ice, hard and soft, domestic and
wild structure the novel's imagery just as much as they do poems like
"Hermes of the Ways," "Sea Rose," "Sheltered Garden," and "Or-

chard." Additionally, H.D. wove a number of her early imagist poems
into the narrative discourse of the novel. Just as she rescripted the narrative implicit in specific poems from *Hilda's Book,* so she recast some
of her own best-known poems into Hermione's imagistically rendered
stream of consciousness – particularly poems such as "Oread," "Garden," "The Pool," "Storm," "Sheltered Garden," and "Huntress." In
effect, providing a narrative context for these early lyrics embodies the
disembodied H.D. *Imagiste,* repersonalizes the carefully depersonalized
discourse of the imagist poet, unveils the early poet's androgynous persona as a woman. *HER* is the kind of personal, intimate *story* of desire
that was removed from the lyrics of "the early H.D." Giving the images
of her lyric poems a narrative context breaks their hold over H.D. Caught
like a butterfly in the web of her own brilliant lyrics, H.D. frees herself
by setting the poems in prose, in a fiction that tells the story of the female
self-in-the-world. She resorted to narrative to write herself out of a
particular lyric discourse in which she felt trapped. Consequently, the
interplay of lyric and narrative discourses in *HER* encapsulates the more
general conflict H.D. had felt for some ten years between impersonal
poetry and personal prose.

Consider, for example, "Oread," first published in 1914 as "Pines,"
and then widely quoted, discussed, and anthologized during the 1910s
and 1920s.

> Whirl up, sea –
> whirl your pointed pines,
> splash your great pines
> on our rocks,
> hurl your green over us,
> cover us with your pools of fir.
> (*Collected Poems* 55)

The image of tree-waves that dominates the poem signals the Oread's
ecstatic embrace of her opposite. While the progression of verbs evokes
without specifying an orgasmic rise, climax, and fall, the poem does not
exhibit the kind of social narrative characteristic of a novel. In *HER,* the
poem's central image and opposition reappears in the consciousness of
another tree spirit, the "Dryad" Hermione. In the novel, however, the
basic image of tree-water undergoes an evolution tied to the unfolding
narrative of Her's development. At first, the trees are pools in which
Her drowns: "Her Gart looked up into liriodendron branches and flat
tree leaf became, to her, lily pad on green pool. She was drowned now"
(4). Echoing "The Pool" as well as "Oread," the pools of trees become
mirrors – not alive, as they are in the early poem, but blank, a Lacanian
mirror stage that produces only absence: "Her eyes peered up into the
branches. . . . She tried to concentrate on one frayed disc of green, pool

or mirror that would refract image. She was nothing" (4–5).[33] Under the pine trees, whose conic shape recalls the class in conic sections she has just failed, she thinks: "Another country called her, the only thing that would heal, that would blot out this concentric gelatinous substance that was her perception of trees grown closer, grown near and near, grown translucent like celluloid. The circles of the trees were tree-green; she wanted the inner lining of an Atlantic breaker" (6–7).

At first, seeing the sea breakers in George's gray eyes, Her thinks that these "pools" will reflect back an identity for her. As she tests out their relationship, land and sea, pines and pools begin to fuse, as they earlier did in "Oread." Walking in the forest with him, she "sees" his hair as watery leaves, much like the Oread had seen pine-tree waves: " 'It's under water' she wanted to say; 'It's under deep-sea water,' she didn't say. Her eyes half-closing saw George gone tawny, leaf-colour, his hair is the colour of leaves drifting down, he had drifted down from trees" (65). However, as the erotic narrative of the poem's images unfolds, the union of land and sea shades into images of stagnation: "Heat seeped up, swept down, swirled about them, with the green of branches that was torrid tropic water. Green torrid tropic water where no snow fell, where no hint of cold running streams from high mountains swept down, was swept into and under branches that made curious circle and half circle and whole circle...concentric circle of trees above her head" (70).

The "heat" that swirls around the lovers like torrid water is one of the many echoes of H.D.'s poem "Garden," Section 2 of which was frequently anthologized as the poem "Heat" (*Collected Poems* 24–5). In the early poem, Section 2 begins: "O wind, rend open the heat, / cut apart the heat, / . . . / Fruit cannot drop / through this thick air –" (25). Like "Oread," "Garden" suggests without direct reference a covert eroticism. The heat thickens the fruit, rounds the grape – encoded allusions to ripening sexuality that lead to the poem's concluding evocation of sexual intercourse as man ploughing the earth: "Cut the heat – / plough through it, / turning it on either side / of your path." Set in the context of the novel's narrative, the imagery of "Garden" becomes overtly sexual. The oppressively hot summer weather becomes an objective correlative for the heterosexual passion that stifles and suffocates. "He wanted trees, because it was hot, he wanted her because it was hot. It was hot," Hermione thinks (43). As George chases her through the woods, she focuses on "his odd tawny hair gone (in small rings) hot on his damp forehead" (65). Later, she recalls him "finding her flung down under the seven larches, the seven small larches making a circle where moss spread in a circle for Hermione to lie on. Hermione tried to visualize moss under her hot flanks. It was too hot" (85).[34] In the novel, then, the image of oppressive heat takes on a narrative function that it did not overtly have in the poem: the critique of oppressive heterosexuality.

Curiously, this narrativization of "Garden" in *HER* helps us from the perspective of hindsight to decode the deeply encoded dimension of the earlier poem. Section 1 of "Garden," often not printed with Section 2, appears totally unrelated. It opens with the poet addressing a rose whose harshness evokes "Sea Rose" and the "wind-tortured" landscape of "Sheltered Garden": "You are clear / O rose, cut in rock, / hard as the descent of hail" (24). To define just how hard this rose is, the poet fantasizes violence: "I could break you / I could break a tree." Sections 1 and 2 of "Garden" superimpose opposites, the hard rose and the oppressive heat, in a way that prefigures montage. The poet seems to valorize the strong rose over the ripening fruit, but we can't be sure and we don't know why. The poem's lyric juxtaposition remains largely nonreferential. The poem does not invite a metaphoric reading, nor any attempt to translate the lyric into a discursive statement about sexuality. The reappearance of the images in *HER*'s narrative context, however, does invite such a reading. The images of tree and rose in Section 1 are recast as motifs for Her's inner self, which is not broken by the "heat" of heterosexuality. She is not only a "tree" that resists George's heated passion, but also a rose, particularly the "black rose" associated with her dead grandmother (41). Long ago, her grandmother had planted a strange rose bush in the corner of the garden, near which she had died. The scraggly bush became "a sort of sacrament" that no one touched until Her's conventional sister-in-law Minnie cuts it down to tidy up the garden (20–1). Her carries on the tradition of that "riotous" rose bush by remembering her grandmother's mysterious proverb: "there's a black rose growing in your garden." The narrative context of the images in *HER* suggest a new reading of the earlier lyric, one that opposes a maternal matrix to heterosexual passion.

The soft heat of heterosexual passion contrasts not only with the strange, harsh rose of difference, but also with the hard ice and white snow of the world in which Her's body inscribes her desire on the blank page of the earth. The poem "Huntress" is recast in the novel as a central sign and symptom of that transformation. "Huntress" is one of the few poems in *Sea Garden* that strongly suggests a gendered narrative. The speaker is a "huntress," perhaps Artemis herself, who invites the poem's "you" to join the collective "we" in the revel of the hunt. The passion of the hunt in which the women's running feet "spear" the earth's crust suggests by double entendre an erotic passion: "*Can you come, / can you come, / can you follow the hound trail / can you trample the hot froth?*" (*Collected Poems* 24). This evocation of lesbian desire in the poem is fully explicit in *HER*. Her yearns for the "great hound" of Artemis and a mountain "sister" who "would run, would leap" in the "Lacedaemonian foothill" that echoes the mountain chase of "Huntress." She finds this Spartan sister in Fayne. "You might have been a huntress," Hermione tells Fayne just before they kiss (163). The images of circles, pine trees, and water negatively connected to her relationship with George reappear with Fayne in a fully positive context: "Her Gart saw rings and circles, the rings and circles that were the eyes of Fayne Rabb. Rings and circles made concentric curve toward a ceiling that was, as it were, the bottom of a deep pool. Her and Fayne Rabb were flung into a concentric intimacy, rings on rings that made a geometric circle toward a ceiling, that curved over them like ripples on a pond surface" (164). Like the pools of fir in "Oread," the pools gently cover the women in *HER* after the passion of their kiss.

Spinning out the narratives covertly present in the overtly impersonal lyrics of "the early H.D." frees the frozen writer so that she may write anew. Narrative personalism unmakes the "H.D." still caught, in 1926–7, in the thrall of her own reputation as the impersonal H.D. *Imagiste*.

III. WHO IS "HELGA DOORN"?

I will be Beatrice to no Dante.

Kenneth Macpherson,
Poolreflection (77)

Helga Doorn, who appears as the author on the typescript of *HER*, is the name that crystallizes the identity constructed by the interlocking stories of the making and unmaking of H.D. *Imagiste*. But who is she? Her existence – partially erased by H.D.'s later editorial pencil – on the title page reminds us that for H.D. the question of origins had to be re-posed and re-solved endlessly. Tripling the layers of *mise en abyme*, the novel encodes another dimension of biographical and intertextual reference for which the name Helga Doorn is the key – namely, that of H.D.'s love affair with Macpherson and of his novel *Poolreflection*.

"Helga Doorn" fleshes out the disembodied "H.D." into an "author" who is a woman. Moreover, as the cinematic name H.D. took for the three films in which she appeared from 1927 to 1930, Helga Doorn is also a projection of the woman in love with Macpherson, the actress fixed by the cinematic gaze of her lover and director.[35] But hidden within this conventional plot is the unconventional narrative of bisexuality and homoeroticism. Like the dyad of Pound and H.D. in Upper Darby, H.D.'s relationship with Macpherson was initially triangulated by the role Gregg played in the formation of the affair. The novel written by

Helga Doorn is dedicated to "F......." The spell of H.D.'s relationship with Gregg had been broken in 1912, when Gregg refused to stay in London, returned to the United States, and then suddenly married Louis Wilkinson. Gregg showed up in London with her new husband and convinced H.D. to join them for a Continental honeymoon, but, as H.D. recalled in *End to Torment,* Pound forbade the trip (8–9). Gregg helped Wilkinson write *The Buffoon* (1916), which contains a vicious portrait of H.D.; but in 1919, Perdita, whose first name is Frances, was named after Gregg. Divorced in 1919, Gregg lived mainly in England during the 1920s, struggling to support her two children through her writing. By the mid-1920s, H.D. had renewed her friendship with Gregg, who still magnetized her with her intensity, as the portrait of Katharine in *The Usual Star* attests. Macpherson, twenty-two years old, entered the story in 1924, probably as Gregg's lover (Guest, *Herself Defined* 179). Repeating and inverting the triangle of 1910, Gregg sent Macpherson to H.D. in 1926, which resulted in his affair with H.D. It was Gregg's turn to feel hurt, but her presence was very much evident in the attraction of H.D. and Macpherson. "K and I talk much of Frances," H.D. remembered in "Autobiographical Notes" (16). In part, the charismatic, gifted, boyish, and bisexual Macpherson had taken Gregg's place.[36]

Probably written in the first year of their affair, *HER* and *Poolreflection* attest to the erotic and creative symbiosis of the relationship. It is impossible to tell whether one novel preceded the other or whether they were written together, but it is self-evidently true that each reflects the other.[37] Paradoxically, both are bisexual, ultimately homoerotic novels of development whose style and narrative structures are mirror images of each other. *HER* is a "poolreflection" about Narcissa, who is, on one level, the young woman in love with Fayne and, on another, the middle-aged woman who must "beget self-out-of-self" by staring at her own reflection, the image of her early images. *Poolreflection* is about Narcissus, who is both the young man Lex and the middle-aged Peter whose incestuous love climaxes the novel. Narcissistic love in both novels is self-love and homoerotic love, the precondition for (re)birth. *Poolreflection* is not a *Kunstlerroman* like *HER,* but its plot of erotic awakenings, like its imagistic style, is strikingly parallel. *Poolreflection* is also more fictionalized than *HER.* But its main dramatis personae are portraits of real people: Moreen is a thinly disguised version of H.D.; Peter and Lex represent two aspects of Macpherson himself.[38] Macpherson does not, of course, make a fictionalized appearance in *HER,* but Helga Doorn's novel exists in intertextual dialogue with the novel of "her" lover.

Like *HER, Poolreflection* triangulates the story of desire by invoking, then revoking, the Oedipal family romance in favor of a narcissistic love. Peter, a free-spirited wanderer and sometime lover of Moreen, returns to London to make contact with his seventeen-year-old son, whom he abandoned years before to the care of his respectable aunts. In a scene that mirrors the imagery of H.D.'s forest scenes in *HER*, Peter signals Moreen to initiate Lex into an authentic eroticism so that he can evade the clutches of the "naiads," conventional women who will "drown" him in respectability. As Lex bathes nude in a forest pool, Moreen thinks he's drowning and rushes in to pull him out of the water, an act that leads to their passionate affair and Lex's erotic awakening – an overtly Oedipal plot up to this point, including the father's unanticipated jealousy. However, the Oedipal plot dissolves when we gradually realize that Peter is jealous on account of Lex, not Moreen. It is his own son he desires, his own poolreflection, that is, a beloved of the same sex who is an image of his own younger self. Moreen fights Peter bitterly for the love of the younger man. Imaged in terms of trees, dryads, and hamadryads, Moreen has been reawakened from a period of sexual sleep by the affair with the boy.[39] Even though she resists Lex's idealization of her and refuses the role of Beatrice, she will not give him up. Accusing Peter of sodomy, she appears to win, but father ultimately defeats mother in the contest for the love of his son. The novel ends ambiguously with Lex's apologetic appeal to his father and Peter's erotic fantasies for his son, which lead him to kiss the earth and invite Lex to his secret hideaway in the mountains.

The father–son motif screens its homoerotic conclusion, its celebration of narcissistic love. The end fulfills the prophecy of the beginning when Peter looks at Lex: "Peter looked upon Lex and loved Peter, a mirrored sublimation of himself. Peter looked (Narcissus) into a pool and loved his watery image. Narcissus was the symbol of all human love, all human love was Narcissus struggling after the evasive beauty of pool reflection. All love was a figment, a stimulus of apprehension, a new angle, a new possibility of self, a new gesture, a new pathway to self. . . . There was no golden faun of Atticus, only pool reflection spiked with tangible rushes, cold water stems" (24). Like *HER*, *Poolreflection* suggests that the "pathway to self" is self-love discovered in the love of the other who physically and spiritually mirrors the self.

HER and *Poolreflection* mirror each other, not as exact replications, but as opposite images of the same thing – where the female lens reverses the male image and vice versa. Like Lex, Her is drowning in pools of water as the novel opens, clutched at and negated by the demands of conventionality. Just as Lex reaches for Moreen, Her's "two hands reached toward George like the hands of a drowned girl" (*HER* 63). The Oedipal pair of surrogate mother and son in *Poolreflection* mirrors the Oedipal pair of surrogate father and daughter in *HER*. Images of maternal nurturance and violent rape characterize the Moreen–Lex dyad, while images of paternal rescue and suffocation portray the George–Her dyad. Reflecting differently gendered origins, the negative images for both pairs prefigure the return to a homoerotic fusion with a figure who stands in for the parent of the same sex. The narrative movement of both novels breaks the conventions of the romance plot by replacing the heterosexual with the homosexual couple as the scene of desire. Images of heat and cold in both novels signify the passion of awakening, a birth signaled by the self as butterfly emerging from the chrysalis of erotic experience.

In the myth of Narcissus, the nymph Echo is doomed to the status of verbal reflection because of the youth's self-love. Unable to initiate her own speech, she can only repeat what her beloved says.[40] In the pool reflections of *HER* and *Poolreflection,* does one fill the role of Narcissus, the other of Echo? Did H.D. and Macpherson write the novels together, for each other? Or did one come first, with the other as answer? It is impossible to tell at this point from the scanty biographical record. But, as mirror reflections of each other written in the flush of their authors' affair, both novels deconstruct the patriarchal heterosexism of the traditional myth in their privileging of same-sex love, in their affirmation of narcissistic awakening. In the process, these homoerotic novels prefigure the end of the heterosexual affair of Macpherson and Helga Doorn, the love that led to the creation of the novels in the first place.

HER is a multilayered novel about the origins of the artist in desire, the emergence of "Her" in the subject position through an examination of her objectification. Like *Portrait of the Artist* and *Sons and Lovers, HER* places the nascent and nubile female subject within an Oedipal configuration; but like *To the Lighthouse,* it also reconfigures the gestational story of emergence. The pre-Oedipal narrative supplants the Oedipal plot as *HER* narrates the daughter's recovery of the mother's power and discovery of the self in the same. The infolding plots of maternal and narcissistic desire re-place the heterosexual narrative of the conventional story of the artist's origin. The dyad of male subject and female object exists in the novel in the figures of George and Her, but not as closure; rather as the beginning of a story that must be undone. To echo DuPlessis's resonant phrase, *HER* writes "beyond the ending" of the conventional *Kunstler* plot by reconstituting the dyad implicit in Hermione's oddly phrased formula for the artist. "Love is writing" in *HER* is the multilayered matrix of maternal and homoerotic desire.

3

Madrigals: Love, War, and the Return of the Repressed

Oh, the times, oh the customs! Oh, indeed, the times! The customs! Their own, specifically, but part and parcel of the cosmic, comic, crucifying times of history.

H.D., *Bid Me to Live*
(A Madrigal) (7)

All night I waked forlorn,
I waked forlorn,
Harkening the lamentation of the rain,
But daylight brought no slumber to my pain
no slumber to my pain.

Richard Aldington,
"Madrigal" (*Poetry* 1923)

I love Richard with a searing, burning intensity. I love him and I have come to this torture of my free will. I could have forgotten my pride broken and my beauty as it were, unappreciated.... Of my will, I have come to this Hell... I believe this flame is my very Daemon driving me to write. I want to write.

H.D., Letter to John
Cournos, 5 September
1916

"Things now are like Gibbon," Hermione thinks in *Asphodel* during the Great War; "The decline and Fall. This is history, I suppose" (II 6). Paradoxically applied to the here and now, the phrase "this is history" suggests the past-in-the-present and the future-about-to-become-the-past, an awareness, in other words, of the chronological passage of time and the compulsion of "history" to repeat itself. "History" forces a Fall into time, into the "real" events of time and the larger patterns of time that shape the lives of individuals powerless to halt its march – like the

136

decline and fall of the Roman Empire, like the decline and fall of European civilization in the modern world. Like so many of her generation, the great events of the modern world wrenched H.D. out of the relatively private realm of the imagination and into the public realm of "history," into the development of an historical consciousness in a post-lapsarian world. Trying to "make it new," as Pound proclaimed, many of the modernists nonetheless became obsessed with "history," with their failure to awaken from the "nightmare" of "history," and with their search to discover or create some pattern of continuity and meaning in the processes of time.[1]

H.D., forced by "history" to fall from lyric into narrative, made the self-in-history the centerpiece of much of her prose. Perhaps echoing Aldington's poem "Madrigal" (quoted above), she called her major novel about the "cosmic, comic, crucifying times of history" *Madrigal* [a title she later reluctantly changed to *Bid Me to Live (A Madrigal)*]. Later, in *Thorn Thicket,* she referred to the events in her life during World War I and her fiction about this period as "the Madrigal cycle" (28).[2] The term "madrigal" is ironic, evoking, in the midst of war, the image of a lyric form associated with Elizabethan love songs in timeless pastoral settings. Modernity superimposes the form and spirit of Afro-American blues onto the madrigal's traditional echo device in its final couplets. *Madrigal* is a novel about love – heterosexual love – caught in the monstrous cataclysm of history, what began as an out-of-time pastoral trapped in the reality of the in-time.

The Great War, ultimately, war itself, both epitomizes "history" and signifies its extremis – "this is history." "Time," in *Madrigal,* is metonymically a soldier's wristwatch, ticking away "inside its steel cage" (19). The spirit of the age, of the modern world, centers on a civilization caught in the war machine of death. It is concretely the guns and bombs of war that create and represent H.D.'s twentieth-century wasteland, her blues-scape of a "city of dreadful night, city of dreadful night" (109). The devouring labyrinth is not a web of words, but "the crucifying times of history" that reduced civilization to "Ashes and death; it was the city of dreadful night, it was a dead city" (109). "The war will be over," everyone said; "the war would sometime be over." But *Madrigal*'s repeated refrain was "(The war will never be over.)" (12, 63, 91).

For T. S. Eliot in *The Waste Land,* the war is unnamed; it is the gap in the text whose absence signifies the extremity of its horror – we witness it only by regarding its devastating personal and cultural effects. The exhilaration of early modernism celebrating its break from the absolutism of the Victorian age gave way to despair, even lamentation for what had been lost. Unlike Eliot, Pound in "Hugh Selwyn Mauberly" (1918) and Aldington in volumes such as *Reverie: A Little Book of Poems for H.D.*

(1917), *War and Love* (1919), and *Images of War* (1919) wrote directly about the shattering impact of the war. Like Pound and Aldington, H.D. felt compelled to stare her wartime experience in the face, even if she risked being turned to stone by its gaze. Like Woolf in *Jacob's Room* and *Mrs. Dalloway,* H.D. used experimental narrative, not poetry, as the medium in which she could reconstruct what had happened to "the early H.D.," the poet who had married another poet about ten months before the outbreak of war, who had watched that marriage disintegrate as a result of war.

H.D.'s prose about the war mirrored Aldington's *Reverie,* much as *HER* mirrored *Hilda's Book* and *Poolreflection.* Aldington scribbled the nine poems of *Reverie,* as well as many of those in *War and Love, Images of War,* and *Images of Desire,* in little notebooks in the trenches. The underlying battle of these poems is between the war's attempt to destroy the soul and the poet's desire to remain spiritually alive. Love – the memory of love, the desire for love, the passion of love – is the poet's ally, the only avenue of possible escape from the spiritual death that stalks the trenches and cities of Europe. Particularly in *Reverie,* poems addressed to H.D., the poet alternates between images of anguish and images of a redemptive desire. He is the "faun captive," dreaming that afar off he can see "Bent poppies and the deathless asphodel" (*Complete Poems* 68–9). The poems are "madrigals," modernist style, their pastoral passions mediated by the historical realities of war.

In this landscape, ironically titled "trench idyll" in one poem, the individual is history's victim. The poet laments the power of history, embodied in the war, to engulf the individual, whose dike against the flood of circumstance is love. For the "egoists" of prewar London, this power caused particular bitterness. Their emergence from Victorian obligation into modern egoism celebrated the freedom of the creative individual to break the chains of history, as the defiant subtitle of *The Egoist: An Individualist Review* and the individualist/feminist editorials of Dora Marsden demonstrate. The lesson of the war for Aldington was that such individualism is impossible. Particularly at times of crisis, history penetrates the individual psyche – the barriers between public and private spheres break down. Love remained for Aldington the individual's last line of defense against the tyranny of history – love, and the poetry it inspires.

Like Aldington, H.D. believed that the power of history embodied in the war held love, poetry, and beauty in its death grip. Poems such as "Cities" and "Prisoners" in *Sea Garden* mirrored Aldington's "In the Tube" and "London" in *Images* in their struggle to resist the death spiral of modern history with a vision of beauty and love. Her letters to Cournos from Corfe Castle in the summer and fall of 1916 show her intense efforts to "save" Aldington, who was in a nearby training camp. "I seem to watch this beautiful spirit suffering – and I am helpless," she despaired in one letter (July 1916). In another, she wrote: "He is like a wounded animal! – He is like some great, beautiful clean, sensual beast, captured, galled with chains" (9 August 1916). On October 16th, she wrote more hopefully, "I think of the crowd – our little spiritual army – stirring against such odds but sure to win" (1916). H.D.'s later Madrigal prose charts the chaining of Aldington's spirit, the transformation of the sensitive poet/lover into the brutal Tommie soldier.

However, H.D.'s Madrigal prose probes even more deeply and radically into the meaning of history. For women, the private sphere has never been a "haven in a heartless world," a respite from the great march of events in the public sphere. Rather, "home" is a point of instability, a place that oscillates between women's potential legitimation and victimization within the social order. Like Woolf's *Mrs. Dalloway* and *Three Guineas*, H.D.'s texts show war to be a monstrous extension of the structural violence of society that governs both the public and private spheres in times of peace and war. In contrast to Aldington's *Reverie*, H.D.'s madrigals portray romantic love as a product of history, not a force outside it; as a primal enactment of war, not a flight from it. From her perspective, one that explores women as both objects of and subjects in history, the war at home is also a war in the home. In addition to being a civilian's view of the war, H.D.'s madrigals examine the war at the front as it both creates and reflects the patterns of the battle on the home front. The marriage-bed, Julia discovers in *Madrigal,* is also a death-bed. "The war was my husband," H.D. reflected about her Julia-self in *Thorn Thicket* (13). Childbirth is "going over the top," Hermione thinks in *Asphodel*. As nightmare (to echo Joyce again), history enacts the dream-world of interlocking desire and death.

H.D.'s novels about the war deconstruct the prevailing binary oppositions between private and public, personal and political, individual and societal to suggest that no place is immune from history because the structures of the social order and of desire correspond to and replicate each other. Superimposed and interpenetrating, each is an extension of the other. This view, which anticipates contemporary feminist formulations of the personal as political, parallels Woolf's contemporaneous critique of the patriarchal family as the structural basis of oppression and war.[3] H.D.'s perspective also resonates with Freud's speculative hypothesis of the dual instincts – eros and the death drive – presented mainly in *Beyond the Pleasure Principle* (1920) and *Civilization and Its Discontents* (1930).

Beyond the Pleasure Principle was Freud's answer to the challenge of the Great War. The sight of the most "advanced" civilizations engaged in a suicidal war for which there could be no real victors led him to revise his view that the drive for pleasure – the pleasure principle – was the only instinct in the unconscious. To the dismay of many of his disciples, he posited the existence of an opposite drive, the death wish "to return to the inanimate state," to which he linked both individual and societal aggression (32).[4] *Civilization and Its Discontents* further links the psychic processes of the individual with the psychosexual dynamics of civilization. Recapitulating the history of the individual, the "evolution of civilization," Freud wrote, "present[s] the struggle between Eros and Death, between the instinct of life and the instinct of destruction, as it works itself out in the human species" (*Civilization* 69). More radically, however, he wanted to theorize not only the alternation between eros and death in human history, but also their interrelationship. "If only we could succeed," Freud wrote, "in relating these two polarities to each other and in deriving one from the other!" (*Beyond the Pleasure Principle* 47). The link, he argued, is in the dynamics of sadomasochism, in the displacement of the death drive into the erotic (*Beyond* 48). The death instinct is hard to "grasp" directly: "we can only suspect it, as it were, as something in the background behind Eros, and it escapes detection unless its presence is betrayed by its being alloyed with Eros. It is in sadism, where the death instinct twists the erotic aim in its own sense and yet at the same time fully satisfies the erotic urge, that we succeed in obtaining the clearest insight into its nature and its relation to Eros" (*Civilization* 68).

To locate that "something in the background behind Eros" is a central task in H.D.'s modernist Madrigals. Conversely, she sought the eros that lay buried in the background of the human history of violence. Within the context of Fredric Jameson's concept of the "political unconscious," H.D.'s narratives demonstrate "the return of the repressed," the playing out of the suppressed story of eros and death in which gender, not class, is foregrounded. For Jameson, "history" itself is "a single vast unfinished plot" of "class struggle" in which "oppressor and oppressed – stood in constant opposition to one another, carried on an uninterrupted, now hidden, now open fight" (*Political Unconscious* 20). The latent content of the manifest tradition of the novel, for example, is the "repressed and buried" narrative of revolt that the critic, in the position of the analyst, decodes (20). In highlighting gender, H.D. did not claim the supremacy of one story over another, as Jameson did in reflecting the theoretical imperialism to which Marxism has often been prone. But in her autobiographical stance, she, like Jameson, played the hermeneutic role of analyst to recover the political unconscious of history – the suppressed and repressed history of sexual politics that flared up with particular clarity during the Great War.

The novels that make up the Madrigal cycle repeat each other, com-

pelled by the "crucifying times of history" to go over and over the story.
Like "the compulsion to repeat," this repetition reenacts the mixture of
pleasure and pain, of eros and death, that each story narrates. And as I
discussed in Chapter 1, H.D.'s return to her personal story of the war
also represented her attempt to move from *repeating* that story to *remembering* it – that is, to work through her transference in and resistance to
the story into the analytic clearing of understanding and control. *Paint
It To-Day, Asphodel,* and *Madrigal* contain overlapping time frames and
dramatis personae, whose names are different, but whose biographical
referents are predominantly the same. Each novel records the rise and
fall of a marriage as it reflects the rise and fall of history. Each text flowed
into the other, becoming what she frequently called simply "the novel"
("Autobiographical Notes" 11; *Advent* 153).

In reflecting on the endless rewriting that led to the completion of
Madrigal, H.D. described the earlier novels, particularly *Asphodel,* as mere
drafts that "came true" in *Madrigal:*

> *Madrigal,* left simmering or fermenting, is run through a vintner's sieve,
> the dregs are thrown out. Really, this is not bad. We began on that
> vineyard in 1921. It was stony. We grubbed up dead roots, trimmed
> and pruned. But the grapes were sour. We went on. It was a pity to
> let that field (1914–1918) lie utterly fallow. We returned to it, from time
> to time. At last, winter 1949, we taste the 1939 gathering. Impossible
> but true. The War I novel has been fermenting away during War II.
> This is intoxicating, the red grapes of –
> >   War?   Love?
>
> > (*H.D. by Delia Alton* 212)

The 1921 "vintage" could refer to either one or both of *Paint It To-Day*
(written in 1921) or *Asphodel* (written in 1921–2). The unsigned title page
of the *Asphodel* typescript shows H.D.'s penciled comment "Early edition
of MADRIGAL" and bold demand "DESTROY."[5] A letter to Pearson
in 1959 makes the same point: *Asphodel* is the

> old *Madrigal* . . . material without the daemonic drive or the *daemon* that
> (or who) was released by ps-a [psychoanalysis], I suppose, & the second
> war. . . . Strange, that *Madrigal* only "came true" on the verge of War
> II, though no doubt, it Phoenix-ed out of *Asphodel* that was put far
> away & deliberately "forgotten." The *Asphodel* "nest" should, in the
> traditional manner, be burnt. Untraditionally, I am picking it apart to
> see how it was written. (19 October 1959)

Madrigal was begun significantly, in 1939, some eight months after her
divorce from Aldington and just weeks before Hitler invaded Poland on
September 1, 1939. Completing the novel during the eerie months of
the "phony war," H.D. locked up the manuscript at Kenwin when she
left for London in the fall of 1939. She returned to the manuscript in the

late 1940s, deciding to rewrite the last section of the novel in 1948 and completing her corrections of the typescript in 1950.[6] As she reread *Madrigal*, she concluded in *H.D. by Delia Alton* that "at last, the War I story had 'written itself' " (180).

From H.D.'s perspective in the late 1940s, the earlier novels appeared as "dregs" to the intoxicating "wine" of *Madrigal*, which she believed had "an unexpected force and energy" lacking in the earlier works (*H.D. by Delia Alton* 180). Whatever the merits of her aesthetic judgment, *Asphodel* and *Paint It To-Day* are no mere drafts, but rather works in their own right. Each is an autobiographical self-creation in which the "analyst" (narrator), the "analysand" (protagonist), and the "analysis" (text) have a unique shape even though they draw on the same personal history. Reflecting the concerns of the author/analyst who was writing at a given point in time, each text presents a certain slant on the past. Taken together, the novels form a palimpsest in which intertextual resonances and dissonances attest to their distinct, yet separate existence. This composite "text" in turn constitutes a multiply split self whose textualizations correspond to the overwritten layers of the palimpsest. "What else than a natural and mighty palimpsest is the human brain?" Thomas De Quincey wrote in *Suspira de Profundus* (*Collected Writings* 346).[7] Kristeva's intertextual reading of the text-as-psyche can be inverted in H.D.'s palimpsestic "text" to become, additionally, the psyche-as-text. Governing the relationship between textual–psychic layers are the psychodynamics of memory, the struggle between repression and expression.

The dissonances among the three texts highlight this dynamic. As Barbara Johnson argued in reference to Derrida and Lacan reading Poe, how the question is *framed* – in both senses of the word – is instructive ("Frame of Reference"). The different time frames of the Madrigal texts establish the boundaries of the narrative. Selectively covering the years in H.D.'s life from the early 1890s through 1919, *Paint It To-Day* begins with the narrator "painting a portrait" of a small child clawing its way through brambles, and it ends with a reference to a mysterious Brindel and a hint of a baby, just come or about to come, whose lyric rendering recapitulates the opening images of the novel. *Asphodel*, on the other hand, opens with Hermione Gart and Fayne Rabb arriving in France in the summer of 1911 and closes in 1919 with Hermione and Beryl de Rothfelt discussing Hermione's new baby. Further condensing the time frame, *Madrigal* begins in 1917, during one of Rafe Ashton's leaves, and ends in Cornwall with Julia Ashton writing a letter to Rico during the summer of 1918.[8]

These time frames point to the differing narrative emphasis in the three texts. As representations of H.D.'s relationship with Gregg in 1910–12

and with Bryher in 1918–19, the first and last chapters of *Paint It To-
Day* focus on a lesbian love: first, that of Hermione (nicknamed Midget)
DeFreddie and Josepha before the war; then, Midget and "the friend"
Althea after the war. Pound appears elusively and namelessly in the novel
as "the erstwhile fiancé," reduced hilariously to "the erstwhile." Aldington is at first "the youth," then Basil, the man whom Midget marries
after idyllic travels in Italy. With a far more complex cast of characters,
Asphodel has two parts of equal length. Covering 1911–12, Part 1 begins
with an appeal to an ideal lesbian sisterhood and ends with Hermione's
fear of remaining single. Part 2 skips to 1915, just after the traumatic
stillbirth of Hermione's child; explores the dissolution of her marriage
and the unfolding of her affair with Cyril Vane; charts her pregnancy;
and ends with the birth of her child and her new relationship with Beryl.

Madrigal, in contrast, erases the lesbian frames of the earlier novels to
focus on the story of heterosexual love – the vanishing love of Rafe and
Julia, the cerebral love of Julia and Rico, the surrogate love of Julia and
Cyril Vane. Rico, the Lawrence figure, is central to the *Kunstler* narrative
of *Madrigal,* whereas he does not exist in *Paint It To-Day* and *Asphodel.*
Not only is lesbian love dropped, but the story of birth that appears at
the end of *Paint It To-Day* and throughout Part 2 of *Asphodel* is missing
in *Madrigal.* Although the stillbirth is a crucial memory for Julia, *Madrigal*
cuts H.D.'s life story off well before the birth of Perdita on March 31,
1919, and does not even suggest the pregnancy, let alone the visionary
experience that leads Hermione to save it in *Asphodel.*

These erasures suggest the conflict between speech and silence that
pervades women's writing in general and the publication history of
H.D.'s prose in particular, as I have discussed in the Introduction. *Madrigal* is a powerful novel of "Love?   War?" – highly charged in its
condensed, often cryptic construction of H.D.'s life during the war. But
it is also full of gaps and silences – gaps for which *Paint It To-Day* and
Asphodel serve as speech. What is absent in *Madrigal* is present in the
earlier novels, most especially the stories of procreation and lesbian desire.
"The *Asphodel,*" H.D. reflected, "shows up facets of the early 'story' or
gaps rather, in consciousness" (Letter to Pearson, 19 October 1959).
While Rafe makes love to her in *Madrigal,* Julia thinks: "Corfe Castle
was after the child and they were just where they had been except for a
gap in her consciousness, a sort of black hollow, a cave, a pit of blackness;
black nebula was not yet concentrated out into clear thought" (13). Her
memory of the stillbirth is *Madrigal's* black hole, an invisible source of
immense power into which the stories of *Paint It To-Day* and *Asphodel*
have disappeared.

As a novel that brings to consciousness the political unconscious of
wartime sexual politics, *Madrigal* is also the scene of repression and re-

sistance. The missing stories of the lesbian lover and the poet mother are the political unconscious of *Madrigal,* the textual unconscious which we as hermeneutic critics can reconstruct with the help of *Paint It To-Day* and *Asphodel.*[9] Taken separately and together, the composite and distinct self-portraits in these three novels (en)gender the historical consciousness of modernism. "This is history": the stories of love and war, creation and procreation, public and private – woven of distinct, but inseparable strands into a tapestry of time.

I. MADRIGAL: *SEXUAL POLITICS AND THE CRITIQUE OF HISTORY*

The war was my husband.

H.D., *Thorn Thicket* (13)

Julia Ashton, the poet, is married to death. She is Mrs. Ash-ton in a "city of ashes." The story of *Madrigal* is her discovery of this marriage and her rebirth through art. A Lawrentian phoenix at the end of the novel, she rises out of the ashes of history into the power of *"the gloire."* Like *HER,* the novel is centrally focused on the interplay between poetics and erotics. Like *HER,* it refuses to accept the culturally mandated separation between womanhood and authorship. Julia would be both – lover and poet; and, more radically, she would insist that eroticism fueled her art. Like *HER,* this *Kunstlerroman* rescripts a series of contemporary male texts, some of which were written for or about her – namely, poems and novels by Aldington and Lawrence. But, unlike *HER, Madrigal* explores these questions solely within a heterosexual context. Lesbian desire does not exist as an alternative. Supplanting Helga Dart and Helga Doorn, Delia Alton is the author of *Madrigal.* She is not only intimate and personal, but also married, bearing a shortened form of H.D.'s married name, Aldington. Delia Alton's *Madrigal* is a story of marriage in wartime, as H.D.'s wordplay in *Thorn Thicket* demonstrates: "*Madrigal* tells the story. We repeat *Madrigal* or *Marriage* 20 years later with another war!" (17).

Like *Ulysses, Madrigal* uses mythic analogue to develop historical consciousness. Isis, not the Koré of *HER,* is the archetypal figure whose story Julia lives out. First Rafe and then Rico – the Aldington and Lawrence figures – take on the part of Osiris in the city of the dead. As H.D. reflected in *H.D. by Delia Alton:* "*Madrigal* is a story, a novel in historical time. It is the eternal story of the search. . . . 'women are individually seeking, as one woman, fragments of the eternal Lover.' As the Eternal Lover has been scattered or dissociated, so she, in her search for him. In *Madrigal,* she seeks for him in contemporary time" (2, 4). In Egyptian religion, the desert whirlwind Typhon/Set kills his brother Osiris and scatters his body all over the world. The goddess Isis, sister and wife of Osiris, gathers his parts, restores his phallus to potency, impregnates herself, gives birth to her avenging son Horus, and finally rules with Osiris in the kingdom of the dead. Revising the myth in *Madrigal*, H.D. showed Julia as Isis seeking not only the dismembered parts of the Lover, but also the fragments of herself. She does not succeed in revivifying Osiris – neither Rafe, nor Rico – but she does re-member her dismembered self, a rebirth signified by the defiant letter to Rico with which the novel closes.

To be reborn, Julia must figuratively die in the wasteland of modern history, must in the classical sense journey to the underworld for its secrets. This narrative of spiritual suffering and death unveils the configurations of desire and their relationship to the war. Love, Julia learns, is not an escape from, but a resituation of war into the private sphere. "The pleasure principle seems actually to serve the death instincts," as Freud wrote in *Beyond the Pleasure Principle* (57). Julia's lesson on *Eros* and *Thanatos* takes place within a series of interlocking triangulated relationships through which she passes in a linear progression: first Julia–Rafe–Morgan; then Julia–Rafe–Bella; next Julia–Rafe–Rico; then Julia–Rico–Elsa; then Julia–Rafe–Vane; and finally Julia–Rico–Vane. A sexual politics that fragments the body and soul of women and men constitutes the deep structure of these relationships. Julia's spiritual triumph at the end of this passage represents her affirmative stance against this dehumanizing social construction of desire and destruction. Poetry, prefigured in her letter to Rico, is her "loophole" through the trap of history.

Julia's lesson begins in medias res, during the final moments of a leave from the front, of a leave taking in a Bloomsbury flat early one Sunday morning in 1917. *Madrigal* echoes *Ulysses* – like Bloom, Rafe leaves his wife in the warm bed and gets up to make breakfast before he leaves; like Joyce, H.D. suggested that what is wrong in the marriage bed permeates what is wrong in the "outside" world to which the husband must return. But, reversing Bloom (and, by extension, Joyce's critique of culture), Rafe is anything but impotent. Facing once again death at the front, he seeks the comfort of love at home in the oblivion of sex. For Julia, sex is death centered, not life centered. Sex means pregnancy to Julia, means therefore the annihilating "wound" of the stillbirth "that gaped at her," the "gap in consciousness," the "black-hole-of-Calcutta" (13). Mother and child, not fully separated at a moment of birth, partook of each other in death. Julia remembers "1915 and her death, or rather the death of her child . . . and then coming back to the same Rafe. Herself different. How could she blithely face what he called love, with that prospect looming ahead and the matron, in her harsh voice, laying a curse of whatever might then have been, 'You know you must not have another baby until after the war is over.' " (24). Not recognizing that childbirth is women's battlefield, the matron of the nursing home wanted to save the doctors for the wounded men. As a scene in which *Eros* could become *Thanatos,* childbirth was for Julia a liminal moment between the two.

As the precondition of childbirth, sex becomes the field on which Julia must battle off her husband: The "wound" of birth is inseparable from the "wound" of intercourse. " 'I'm sorry,' Rafe says after sex, 'did I hurt you?' " (13). She must of course deny it, but she thinks "that was marriage-bed, that was death-bed, that was resurrection" (17). She wonders as he approaches her an hour later, "Surely they were too tired, surely they were worn out, surely it was impossible for him to cover her mouth with kisses" (21). Like Hermione in *HER,* Julia feels smothered by Rafe's passion.

In *Madrigal,* however, it is Rafe's participation in the war that makes his kisses repugnant. In donning the uniform of a British officer, he has unwittingly put on a militarist mind-set. The transformation seems to repeat itself before Julia's eyes as he takes off the camel's hair dressing coat and puts on his khaki: "He was strapping on his Sam Browne. He stepped to the knapsack, drew it toward him, then dragged it to the bed. He sat clothed now, a British officer on leave, on the edge of the bed. . . . His shoulders were British officer, out of a tailor's window" (28).[10] Like an Ovidian character, Rafe struggles against the metamorphosis, but is powerless before the violence of the process. He becomes "not-Rafe, . . . a stranger standing over by the book-shelf" who "is actually enjoying it [the war]," a "hearty over-sexed ('we have them on the run') young officer on leave" (45–6). Kisses which are a lifeline to him are filled with the war's poison for Julia: "He had breathed a taint of poison-gas in her lungs, the first time he kissed her" (39). *Eros* cannot provide escape from *Thanatos.* They are all "victims, victimised, victimizing" (7).

What the erotic cannot do, simple intimacy can – initiate a momentary access to "Bliss," H.D.'s version of a Woolfian moment or a Joycean epiphany (18). Watching Rafe repeat the familiar, nurturant task of preparing tea reminds Julia of their prelapsarian love, their idyll before the fall into history, before the war. "It was like that, in these moments," Julia thinks. "She touched paradise" (19). Looking at Rafe's watch in its "steel cage," the "voice of time on a table," she wonders if it might have "stopped at tea-time," at the moment of "Bliss." Julia likens the chronological march of time to a necklace in which lyric moments are shimmering beads, each one of which suspends time for the moment. "The past had been blasted to hell" by 1917, but Julia has access to the past through memory of these moments: "Words that she did not speak held old cities together; on this fine strand, this silver-cord, Venice was a bright glass-bead, certainly a translucent emerald-green, a thing in itself worth all the misery of the past two years" (24). Like Woolfian moments, this "cord" strung with memories is "frail," a "spider-web of a silver-cord that might so soon be broken" (24). Umbilical to an ideal past, the cord of memory keeps Julia alive. It reminds her of the reality of a once-upon-a-time when she and Rafe were poets and lovers, when *Eros* was not *Thanatos*. Then they were a modern version of Elizabeth Barrett and Robert Browning – equally lovers and poets; now they are like Punch and Judy, engaged in the constant warfare of sexual politics (11, 7).

Rafe's leaves from the front punctuate the novel, charting his meta-morphosis and the dissolution of the marriage. As he becomes increasingly the Tommie, his enactment of conventional sexual politics intensifies. Falling in love, first with Morgan (the Brigit Patmore figure) and then Bella (the Dorothy Yorke figure), Rafe justifies himself by resorting to the ideological split in cultural representations of woman. Bella satisfies his body, Julia his soul. "The situation," he told Julia, "was impossible. I love you, I desire *l'autre,* was impossible. . . . I'll go mad, I am torn to pieces, I love you" (70)." This split between love and desire, between the beloved as sacred and the beloved as profane, replicates the splits Stephen made in *Portrait* between the virgin and the whore, that Paul made in *Sons and Lovers* between Miriam and Clara. One woman is for inspiration, the other for sex. "Bella makes me forget," he tells Julia; "You make me remember" (71). Such a split denies the body to Julia and the mind to Bella. When Bella comes to accuse her of "tyrannizing his soul," Julia suddenly realizes her common bond with Bella as a woman caught in a patriarchal system of representation:

> The funny thing was that facing Bella, Julia felt that she was looking at herself in a mirror, another self, another dimension but nevertheless herself. Rafe had brought them together; really they had nothing in common. They had everything in common. . . . She and Bella were simply abstractions, were women of the period, were WOMAN of the period, the same one. (103)

This moment of sisterhood between the two bitter rivals reconstructs the conventional triangulation of desire in the novel. Rafe, who has the power to choose, is momentarily rendered impotent as Julia is empowered by her realization that both women are victimized by his "abstractions." This moment also deconstructs the very image of love that Julia – and the novel – has clung to as an ideal, an idyll outside time. An intertextual resonance subtly makes the point. The novel opens with a love poem by Robert Herrick called "To Anthea." It comes from Herrick's major work, the *Hesperides,* a title that invokes a pastoral paradise of love. Uttering the steadfastness and obedience of the conventional Petrarchan lover, the poet promises Anthea that he will do anything she commands: "Bid me to live, and I will live / . . . / Thou art my life, my love, my heart / The very eyes of me: / And hast command of every part, / To live and die for thee." Rafe calls Julia his Anthea and asks for Herrick's *Hesperides* and for *Madrigals,* a book of Elizabethan songs that includes Herrick's poem "To Anthea" (21, 36, 48, 129). The poem, associated with the "old" Rafe, functions first as an ideal, but then as an ironic statement in the novel. In the "real" world, in history, poets like Rafe betray their romantic oaths. "To Anthea" is an ironic comment on the love story in the novel itself. As a deflation of the poet/lover in "To Anthea," Rafe represents the imperfection of love played out in time, specifically in the historical moment of the Great War.

However, Julia's moment of communion with Bella also signifies an even more radical critique of the ideal that "To Anthea" represents. Rafe's "abstractions" recapitulate the economy of desire that structures the paradise of Herrick's Hesperides – the ideal and the real, the out-of-time and the in-time, the mythic and the historical are revealed as versions of each other. Although Herrick addressed his love lyrics to a number of beloveds, two women are the most frequent objects of his desirous speech in *Hesperides:* Anthea and Julia. These poems replicate the split in patriarchal representations of woman. The poems to Anthea portray her as the pure, sacred, and even sickly beloved. The poems to Julia stress her sensuality. The names Julia and Anthea in *Madrigal* invoke this split between woman as body and woman as soul, reflected in Herrick's lyrics.[12] Like Herrick's, Rafe's abstractions trap Julia and Bella in a semiotic system in which one functions as a spiritual muse, the other as a sensual muse. These abstractions in turn mirror and critique the parallel divisions that pervade Aldington's own autobiographical writings.

In claiming Julia as his spiritual muse, however, Rafe has commanded her speech, not her silence – unlike the poet of *Hilda's Book.* Rafe – and her love for Rafe – is inseparable from Julia's emergence as a poet. Like *HER,* the love plot and the *Kunstler* plot are interwoven in *Madrigal.* But, unlike *HER,* heterosexual erotics initially sustained poetics for both wife and husband. Their importance to each other as nascent poets is suggested through brief flashbacks in *Madrigal* (and more extensive ones in *Asphodel*). The idyll of their prewar Paris and Italy includes an emblematic scene, one of Julia's "beads" of memory. The two lovers had wandered into the cool recesses of the Cluny Museum where they sat sketching – his drawings "niggling and tight, hers better conceived but vague in outline" (33). Julia remembers how they "completed each other, even in their crude sketches; 'Between us we might make an artist,' he said" (33–4). As artists, each was necessary to the other. Incomplete

apart, together they made an androgynous unit in Paris, the city of love.
Their marriage was "different," an "experiment" that was a suitably
modern version of the poet–lover relationship of Robert Browning and
Elizabeth Barrett. (11).

Like their love, their poet/companionship is eventually split open by
the war. At first, the war intensifies Rafe's need for Julia's speech. At
the end of his first leave, he deposits her "precious" letters on the bed –
he might die, but her letters must survive. With his watch imprisoning
her wrist, she promises to write more. Letters versus time, love versus
death – the opposition is clearly delineated. Letters are the sign of love
that keeps Rafe alive, the symptom that keeps Julia alive.[13] Chapter 3
culminates in Julia's composition of a letter to Rafe, which in turn sets
in motion the beginnings of a poem – an unshaped, prose poem that
itself replicates the opposition of poetry and war with the familiar internal
rhymes, syntactic repetition, and harsh landscape of "the early H.D.":
"sing frost sing indefinite cold sweet stinging grain of white hail and
sing all formed and formative deep-sown earth-grains each separate sing
for the new-time come and out of the old war-wreck . . . " (43). Foreshadowing the failure of their experiment, Julia rips up the poem before
it is finished.

The sexual politics that destroys their love also dissolves their interdependent union as artists. Writing for Rafe's survival on the front not
only stimulates, but also narrowly channels Julia's voice. To escape, she
writes poems that she does not rip up, does not send to France. They
go instead to Rico, the poet who increasingly fills the gap between the
"Love?   War?" of her madrigals with Rafe. Having already initiated
his affairs with Morgan and Bella, Rafe is nonetheless jealous to discover
that Julia has been sending poems to Rico. This possessive jealousy is
displaced into the authority he asserts as critic of her work. Abandoning
their prewar artistic symbiosis, Rafe assumes the position of superiority
and sharply criticizes what she has written: " 'A bit dramatic, I don't
like your *look not back*. It's Victorian. . . . There aren't eight furies and
why unglorified furies? . . . You might boil this one down,' he said,
'about quarter the length and cut out the *clichés*' " (55–6). Julia is reduced
to defensive self-deprecation and silence by his criticism: "She didn't say
anything. It didn't really matter. 'It doesn't really matter. . . . I told you
it was only preliminary scribbling. . . . Give it to me' " (54–5). Having
fixed Julia in the position of the cerebral poet, Rafe compounds his
betrayal of their experiment by criticizing the writing to which he has
confined her.

As with the allusions to Herrick's *Hesperides,* an intertextual play with
Keats's "To Autumn" suggests a more radical critique of the prewar
ideal from which Rafe falls. Julia's memory of their Cluny sketches led

to a recollection that seemed to be part of the idyll, but in reality fore-shadowed their later problems. Later that afternoon, they had been sitting on a Parisian bridge. While he scribbled poetry on an envelope, she blocked a faun's head, placing herself "in the centre of a circle, which she measured, mock-professionally, with a pencil held before her" (34). "The faun," it should be recalled, was the Aldingtons' pet name for Richard. While her sketch "centers" her, makes a stable "circle, with a compass, for herself to stay in," Rafe's writing leaves him at the periphery. He is not composing, but instead merely copying another poet's words: Keats's *"Season of mists and mellow fruitfulness,"* the first line of "To Autumn" (*Selected Poems* 35). "Why can't you write your own poetry?" Julia had asked him. To give him the pleasure of correcting her, she identified the lines as Shelley, full knowing they were Keats, thereby pretending an appropriately feminine ignorance. His silence makes her suspicious – whose name was on that envelope to make him think of Keats? These undertones of inequality and possible liaison in the seemingly androgynous union of prewar poet/lovers are fore-grounded by Julia's repeated return to the poem during the war.

   The Keats poem is not an arbitrary choice. First, it echoes the importance of Keats in Aldington's war novel, *The Death of a Hero,* in which the young soldier, modeled in part on Aldington himself, went to war clutching his volume of Keats as his last hold on civilization. Second, "To Autumn" introduces an ironic commentary on the post-Romantic narrative in which it finds itself. Keats's ode, it will be remembered, is an ambiguous paean of praise to the personified spirit of autumn, whose ripe harvest connotes the sensual fullness of fruit just moments before it begins to rot. Like a seventeenth-century still life, the sensual beauty of autumn signifies the coming of death in winter. Eros and death are entangled in Keats's image of autumn, "Drows'd with the fume of poppies" (247). Against just such a Priapus, "the early H.D." had cried in "Orchard": "spare us from loveliness / . . . / spare us the beauty / of fruit trees" (*Collected Poems* 28). Foreshadowed by their presence in the seeming idyll of prewar Paris, Keats's lines return to Julia in the midst of war to signal the entanglement of *Eros* and *Thanatos.* During Rafe's leave in the autumn of 1917, she thinks, "This was the season – of – of mellow fruitfulness. A great, over-sexed officer on leave, who had thrown off his tunic, is mellow fruitfulness" (47). The "mellow fruitfulness" of Rafe's desire signifies his betrayal of their marriage with first Morgan, then Bella. Rather than a sign of life, Rafe's Keats is a harbinger of death to Julia.

   Much as Fayne replaced George in the unfolding triangulation of desire in *HER,* Rico displaces Rafe in *Madrigal.* With his refusal to participate in the war frenzy and his cerebral intensity as a poet, Rico fills the heterosexual vacuum left by Rafe's metamorphosis. Rafe's jealousy has good cause, as Julia's silent thoughts reveal to the reader. "What's this Orpheus that you've been writing for old Rico," Rafe had asked during his second leave, when Rico was still in Cornwall with his wife Elsa (51). Julia answers falsely, "I wasn't exactly writing it for Rico" and thinks, "But she had, she was; it was Rico's pale face and the archaic Greek beard and the fire-blue eyes in the burnt-out face that she had seen, an Orpheus head, severed from its body" (51). To Julia, Rico becomes the archetypal poet figure, the Orpheus whose head is split from his body by the agonies of the modern world. Unlike the "bronze," "Roman" soldier Rafe, Rico holds true to poetry, sings his prophetic song in spite of the war. Adapting Lawrence's own prose technique of clustering colors and images to characterize figures, H.D. associated Rico with "words that flamed alive, blue serpents on the page that Rico wrote her . . . that yet held the flame and the fire, the burning, the believing" (52). For sheer cerebral intensity, the communion between Julia and Rico surpasses her marriage: "she knew that the flame and the brand of this gift that Rafe and Julia had had between them was a secondary refracted light, . . . not the blaze and the blue-flame of the sun-shelf. Rico" (52).

Rico's cerebral flame ignites her own. The poem she sent to him is "Sheet lightning. Blue lightning" (55). His letters from Cornwall "empowered her, so that in the middle of the night she could strike a match, and crouched over her bed-clothes, run her pencil down a page, or rather let it run for her. She had sent copies of the poems to Rico, she had not to Rafe" (59). Echoing Lawrence's invitation to H.D. (not Aldington) to join his planned Utopian community of Rananim, Rico writes Julia: "We will go away together where the angels come down to earth" (57).[14] This line reinscribes Birkin's invitation to Ursula in *Women in Love* and thereby draws Julia into the Lawrentian circle. Rico, not Rafe, is her bridge to the sacred domain of poetry.

This communion established by letter (by *the* letter, the word) first appears in the novel as an ideal powerful enough to counter the realities of history, of war and Julia's failing marriage. But H.D. subjected the unfolding relationship to a deconstructive process that parallels her examination of the seemingly androgynous love of Julia and Rafe. The sexual politics that destroyed Julia's marriage also distorts the initially promising relationship with Rico. Even Rico, the great enemy of the war, acts out the patterns of history, of *Eros* and *Thanatos,* in his relations with women. Like H.D.'s rescriptions of Pound in *HER* and of Herrick and Keats in *Madrigal,* a metafiction of intertextual play serves as ironic commentary on the narrative, ultimately leading Julia out of Rico's circle back to a reestablishment of her own. H.D. embedded in *Madrigal* Lawrence's fiction (particularly *Women in Love, Aaron's Rod, Kangaroo,* and

St. Mawr) and poetry (especially "Gloire de Dijon," "Touch," and "Noli Me Tangere"). Recontextualized in H.D.'s roman à clef, Lawrence's texts serve two functions: first, they uncover the sexual politics that underlie the communion of Rico and Julia; second, they boomerang back to their original sources as a critique of the sexual politics pervading Lawrence's work.

The intertextual irony begins with the names Rico, Julia, and Cyril. As Martz pointed out in "Voices of the Prophet," H.D.'s choice of the name Rico for Lawrence enacts a revenge for his vicious caricature of her as Julia in *Aaron's Rod*. Begun at the end of the war, *Aaron's Rod* is a *Kunstlerroman* that explores a homoerotic poetic and politics in which the male artist defeats the female "will to power" and is empowered by his worship of a charismatic male leader who leaves him "free" in his "singleness." H.D.'s Bloomsbury appears briefly, but instantaneously recognizable, in the novel, only to be condemned as spiritually and sexually dead. Julia Cunningham, wife of Robert, epitomizes the corruption of Bohemia. "A tall, stag of a thing," she looks "hunched like a witch" (23). Echoing Lawrence's brutal portrait of Lady Ottoline Morrell as Hermione in *Women in Love*, Julia is repeatedly said to "sing" her high-pitched jibes. Manipulative and "catty," Julia is the kind of Lawrentian woman he most despised: the powerful, "mental" woman who gets erotically aroused by humiliating men. Not an artist herself, Julia is a parasite on artists, one of whom is Josephine Ford (the Dorothy Yorke figure), who is sympathetically portrayed in the novel. The scenes with Julia and her crowd center on her public display of indecision – should she go down to the country to be with Cyril Scott (the Cecil Gray figure) or should she stay with her husband Robert (the Aldington figure)? Publicly reviewing the pros and cons, she says that Cyril is "the real artist," unlike "*Rob*-ert – Robert is a dilettante, don't you think – he's dilettante" (47). She urges the reluctant Josephine to have an affair with Robert so that she can be free for Cyril: " 'And wouldn't Robert be an *awfully* nice lover for Josephine! O, wouldn't that be splendid!' she cried, with her high laugh" (47). Julia's "ritual" dance in front of the lighted Christmas tree not only symbolizes the debasement of the sacred in Bohemia, but also particularly singles out H.D. for satire, playing as it does on Pound's well-known name for her, Dryad, and on the role of Tree that H.D. played in the charade at Mecklenburgh Square. Julia cuts a ridiculous figure as she "dropped the cloak in which she was huddled, and with arms slung asunder was sliding, crouching in a *pas seul* before the tree, looking like an animated bough herself" (28).

Lawrence was notorious for satirizing the very friends to whom he was especially indebted in his fictional adaptations of his own experience. In October of 1917, H.D. had sheltered the penniless Lawrence and Frieda in her Mecklenburgh Square flat after they were evicted from Cornwall as German spies. Lawrence's highly autobiographical account in *Kangaroo* of his medical examinations by the draft board, the Lawrences' expulsion from Cornwall as possible spies, and their flight to London pays homage to H.D.'s courage and kindness. Everyone else was afraid to take them in, but the "American wife of an English friend, a poet serving in the army . . . tossed the rooms to them, and food and fuel, with a wild free hand. She was beautiful, reckless, one of the poetesses whose poetry Richard [the Lawrence figure] feared and wondered over" (275). But, in *Aaron's Rod,* Julia is a symbol of decadence. She, not her husband, first betrays the marriage; she, not her husband, manipulates the affair between Robert and Josephine.

Aaron's Rod is a novel, with no pretense of being an autobiography, or even à roman clef. But the nature of Lawrence's alteration of actual events must have hurt H.D. deeply, particularly in the context of the break in their friendship after the war. Reading Harry T. Moore's biography of Lawrence in 1954 led her to write about *Aaron's Rod* that the characters "were unrecognisable, as the characters of that war-time charade; least of all did I know myself, Julia. . . . No doubt, I did not want to recognize her. It is odd that in *Madrigal,* I called myself Julia, as he called me in the *Rod.* Could I possibly have recalled sub-consciously, 'a tall stag of a thing' who 'sat hunched up like a witch?' "¹⁵ Her response is reminiscent of Lawrence's more playful poem "I Am in a Novel," in which he said: "I read a novel by a friend of mine / in which one of the characters was me, / . . . / or what was supposed for me, / for I had to recognise / a few of the touches . . . / but the rest was a real surprise" (*Collected Poems* 489).

Madrigal's Julia Ashton is an answer to Lawrence's Julia Cunningham, a self-portrait that is closer to the biographical record and that implicitly critiques Lawrence. As the wife who has tried, but failed, to recall her husband to his prewar identity as poet, Julia Ashton leaves London for Cyril Vane's Cornwall as a response to, not the cause of, Rafe's affair with Bella. Rico begs Julia to live in his nearby Cornwall cottage where Vane could visit her: "It would make a difference" (137). Julia is in turn shocked by the hypocrisy of Rico's discomfort: "It was Rico who had stamped about, uttered his shrill peacock-cry, his death-cry, his man-is-man, his woman-is-woman. Didn't he mean any of it?" (137). In the novel, Rico's sexual double standard, so at odds with his own life and novels, effectively ends his special relationship with Julia. She refuses to write a letter to him as Cyril requests and substitutes a "letter" she will never send, a journal to Rico which begins, "I will never see you again, Rico" (171).

More autobiographical than Lawrence's account, this version nonetheless softens the harsher view of Aldington and Lawrence implicit in the events as they can be reconstructed from other sources. In *Madrigal,* H.D. reduced the time frame and number of Aldington's affairs considerably. Her letters to Cournos in July and August of 1916 indicate that Aldington's affairs began at least as early as the spring of 1916; while in training, he was having an affair with Flo Fallas, the wife of his close friend and partner in training, Carl Fallas. This affair may have been followed by a liaison with Brigit Patmore in 1917, just before he fell in love with Yorke. In *Madrigal,* H.D. erased the earlier episodes and only hinted at an affair with Patmore (65–7), who appears in the novel as Morgan.[16] Nor does the novel incorporate Aldington's enthusiasm for her move to Cornwall, including its sexual dimension, in his letters from France. H.D.'s affair with Gray may have simply made Aldington feel less guilty, but he also expressed the belief that Cornwall would be healing, would increase the likelihood that they could put their marriage back together again after the war. It was her pregnancy, not the affair, that disturbed him.[17]

As for Lawrence, he was indeed shocked by H.D.'s relationship with his friend Gray, according to Harry T. Moore, who stressed Lawrence's "ferocious sense of puritanism" (459, 482). Like Aldington, he may have been even more disturbed by her pregnancy. She told him about the child when he visited her in London in November of 1918, according to his December letter to Amy Lowell. He found her "not so very well. She is going to have another child, it appears. I hope she will be all right. Perhaps she can get more settled, for her nerves are very shaken: and perhaps the child will soothe her and steady her. I hope it will" (Moore 297). To Lowell, Lawrence expressed great sympathy for H.D.[18] But to H.D. he was silent, at a time when she most needed his friendship. She wrote in *Compassionate Friendship,* "He never wrote me after I told him that I was expecting this child" (52).

If the name Julia consciously or "subconsciously" criticizes Lawrence, the name Rico does so even more satirically. For those who know Lawrence's life story and oeuvre, *Madrigal* offers a hilarious and devastating portrait executed with a wit every bit as biting as Woolf's. Rico is the name of the weak husband in his novella *St. Mawr* (1925). An aspiring artist who ends up doing portraits of rich clients, Rico is an impotent dandy who is defeated by his wife and mother-in-law. Wandering expatriates, these American women are typical of Lawrentian heroines who are spiritually and sexually unawakened. Like the heroines in *The Virgin and the Gypsy, The Plumed Serpent,* and "The Woman Who Rode Away," Lou is a Lawrentian "princess" who searches among the "tame dogs" of European men for a "real man." She finds her "dark god" – this spirit of animal man, an intuitive, sexual, mystical being – in St. Mawr, the stallion whose fiery eyes pierce the patina of civilization, whose arching, blood-filled neck is the erection her husband cannot have: "she stroked his shoulder, and then the hard, tense arch of his neck. And she was startled to feel the vivid heat of his life come through to her, through the lacquer of red-gold gloss. So slippery with vivid, hot life!" (13). Rico is terrified of St. Mawr, and, after losing a battle of wills to the horse, he sells him to a woman who plans to tame his spirit by castrating him. Worshiping the vitality of the horse, Lou and her mother conspire to save St. Mawr by spiriting him away to the American West. The novella's themes are typical for the Lawrence of the mid-to-late 1920s. Out of the "leadership," homoerotic phase of *Aaron's Rod*, he had returned to het-erosexual awakenings in works like *St. Mawr* and *The Virgin and the Gypsy*, both of which anticipate *Lady Chatterley's Lover*. But unlike *The Rainbow* and even *Women in Love*, which promote individual androgyny or "star equilibrium" for men and women in love, *St. Mawr* advocates strong women worshipping the even stronger phallus, the "dark god" to which civilization must return to be reborn.

The name Rico in *Madrigal* satirically links Lawrence to the very qual-ities he condemned in *St. Mawr*. In his letters and their early meeting, H.D.'s Rico has some of the same qualities of Lawrence's St. Mawr – a searing vitality imaged in both texts in terms of fire, blazing eyes, light-ning, snakes, and a Greek spirit. But after H.D.'s Rico and his wife Elsa come to live with Julia, he is unmasked as entirely "cerebral," as the "mind" without body condemned in *St. Mawr*. The incident that signals Rico's bodilessness opens with Rico's pronouncement to Julia one eve-ning: " 'Elsa is there,' said Rico, 'you are here. . . . You are there for all eternity, our love is written in blood,' he said, 'for all eternity' " (77–8). Julia wonders "whose love" and concludes that "it was to be a perfect triangle" (78). "Elsa acquiesced," for she "muttered, . . . 'This will leave me free . . . for Vanio' " (78). Already rejected by Rafe, Julia is ready to consummate in the flesh what she already has in words with Rico. Like Miriam in *Sons and Lovers*, like Ursula in *The Rainbow*, Julia initiates the erotic by reaching out to touch Rico the next day, when she suddenly becomes aware that Rico has stopped writing to watch her:

> Now was the moment to answer his amazing proposal of last night, his "for all eternity." She put out her hand. Her hand touched his sleeve. He shivered, he seemed to move back, move away, like a hurt animal. . . . Yet, last night, sitting there, with Elsa sitting opposite, he had blazed at her; those words had cut blood and lava-trail on this air. . . . Yet only a touch on his arm made him shiver away, hurt, like a hurt jaguar.
>
> He was leopard, jaguar. It was not she who had started out to lure him. It was himself with his letters, and last night his open request for this relationship. Yet even this touch (though not heavy on his sleeve)

seemed to send some sort of repulsion through him. She drew back her hand. (81–2)

Rico's repulsion at her *touch* takes on tremendous irony in the context of Lawrence's words about touch in *St. Mawr* and the poems "Touch Comes," and "Noli Me Tangere." In *St. Mawr*, Rico's delight in looking at women, pleasure in being looked at himself, but fear of all touching is a sign of his sexual deadness – a distinction between *sight* and *touch* that anticipates the work of Irigaray. As a sign of her awakening, Lou moves from the specular pleasure of looking at St. Mawr to the sensual pleasure of touch. This opposition between *sight* and *touch*, between *words* and *deed*, *mind* and *body* is even more directly constituted in the poems "Touch" and "Noli Me Tangere," published in *Pansies* (1929). "Touch" utilizes dramatic irony, whereby Lawrence condemned the speaker of the poem who exhibits a fear of touching:

> Since we have become so cerebral
> we can't bear to touch or be touched.
>
> Since we are so cerebral
> we are humanly out of touch.
>
> And so we must remain.
> For if, cerebrally, we force ourselves into touch,
>   into contact
> physical and fleshly,
> we violate ourselves,
> we become vicious.
>
> *(Collected Poems 468)*

Like many of the poems in *Pansies*, "Touch" condemns the cerebral and privileges the touch of flesh uncontaminated by the mind. Desire that begins in the mind makes us vicious, self-rapists. "Noli Me Tangere" expands on this pronouncement by playing off Jesus' warning – "Don't touch me" – to Mary Magdalene, who is the first to see him after his resurrection. As spirit in the image of flesh, Christ is taboo, untouchable. In the poem, Lawrence uses Jesus as his persona to condemn "this cerebral age" dominated by "you with mental fingers," "mental bodies": "Noli me tangere, touch me not! / O you creatures of the mind, don't touch me" (*Collected Poems* 468–9). In such a cerebral world, it is better to remain "chaste," "untouched"; for contact with "mental bodies" is worse than no touch at all. The poem "Touch Comes" celebrates the redemptive touch that "comes when the white mind sleeps / and only then" (*Collected Poems* 470).

Madrigal offers a satiric gloss on these poems, an intertextual resonance that changes how we read them. Like the Rico of *St. Mawr*, H.D.'s Rico is akin to the cerebral lover condemned in the poems. It is Rico's *letters*

– a mental "touch" – that initiate their relationship. Like the Rico of *St. Mawr, Madrigal's* Rico draws back from the flesh. Julia uses the rather uncommon term "cerebral" some seven times to describe her relationship with Rico, a repetition that covertly gestures at "Touch," which also makes its point by the repetition of cerebral. More overtly, Julia directs us to Lawrence's "Noli Me Tangere" in wondering if his withdrawal were "some sort of *noli me tangere* (his own expression)" (82). Her comparison of Rico to Orpheus gives his *noli me tangere* a macabre, literal dimension: Rico *is* the head of Orpheus – a singing head without a body: "He's cerebral, he had to write to someone" (55).[19]

However, *Madrigal's* critique of Lawrence probes more deeply than this satiric inversion of his personae. To say simply that Lawrence was incapable of the touch he celebrated would still leave his economy of desire, with its worship of the phallus, unchallenged. *Madrigal* goes further by showing that for all Lawrence's differences from Aldington, his behavior enacted a similar sexual politics, one that brings history, with its interplay of *Eros* and *Thanatos,* into the private sphere just as surely – though somewhat differently – as her soldier/husband. What Julia discovers is that Rico, like Rafe, cannot resist seeing her within a system of "abstraction," that is, within an ideological semiotics of representation that divides WOMAN into the binary of body and soul. Like Rafe, like Paul in *Sons and Lovers,* like Stephen in *Portrait of the Artist,* Rico bifurcates his desire into a longing for the body of one woman and the soul of the other. One woman is for sex, for physical touch; the other is for art, for verbal communion. Like Rafe, Rico denies the body to Julia and the mind to Elsa while claiming both body and soul for himself. As a variation on Rafe, however, his yearning for Elsa is portrayed as a desire for the maternal body, for the "great goddess-mother idea" of Elsa, who "fed Rico on her 'power,'" it was through her, in her, and around her that he had done his writing" (79). More wittily, she sees Elsa as a "barnyard hen who has hatched a Phoenix" (83). Essential to his writing, Elsa nonetheless cannot engage with it, as Julia can.

At first, Julia does not understand how destructive Rico's division of women is to her own identity as woman/poet. She believes that Bella's "physicality" and Rico's "cerebralism" might in fact save her marriage by draining the excess mind and body of husband and wife:

> There was a shape to their marriage, broken now, shattered actually, yet there was a shape to it. It was Frederick who had taken her away (cerebrally), it was Bella who had broken across (physically), but all the same, there it was, the union. . . .
>
> Wife, husband. Elsa and Rico were very near, she and Rico would burn away, cerebralistically, they would burn out together.
>
> Julia existed, parasitically on Rafe, and Rico lived on Elsa.

> But once alive, fed as it were from these firm-fleshed bodies, they
> were both free, equal too, in intensity, matched, mated. (57–9)

Julia feels "mated" to both Rico and Rafe in this matrix of divisions
and desires. Inside the "stranger" Rafe, there is still "a young poet [who]
had been her lover" with whom she can still connect: "Rafe Ashton is
my husband" (134). Yet "truly, yes," she thinks about Rico, "she loved
him but loved him in another dimension, out of the body, wandering
in thought, in dream" (69). But when Rico appears to invite a sexual
relationship and then repudiate it, Julia's public humiliation leads her to
reassess this double "marriage" as a form of male egotism in which
women must serve male genius. Clearly forced back into the abstraction
of the untouchable woman, she feels used: "Julia had the sense to realise
(her own New England pragmatism) that she was to be used, a little
heap of fire-wood, brush-wood, to feed the flame of Rico" (88). Rico's
egocentrism is unveiled as androcentrism – a cerebral version of Rafe's
sexual womanizing. The "Great Goat Pan" resurrected in *St. Mawr* is
comically transformed into a red-bearded "Satyr," a goatman who cerebrally eats women to feed his genius, in *Madrigal:* "He cropped round
and round, eating up field-flowers, grass; goat-like, his teeth made fur-
rows in symbolic olive trees. When he had got his full, his genius would
demand fresh fields and up would pull the totem-pole, Germania [Elsa],
obligingly plant itself in another meadow" (89).[20]

Julia's disillusionment with Rico's cerebralism is matched by her growing recognition that he assumes a position of privileged, masculine authority in relationship to her poetry. Like Rafe, Rico consigns her to the
realm of bodiless "pure being," only to offer devastating criticism of her
work. But where Rafe's negative comments are largely technical, Rico's
words attempt to confine her discourse to what he considers appropriate
for a woman. Like Rafe, Rico believed in her poetry, validating her
efforts with strong praise. Anticipating the very phrase H.D. later used
in connection with Pound in *End to Torment* ("Dryad, this *is* poetry"),
Rico had told Julia at their first meeting in August of 1914, "Don't you
know, don't you realise that this is *poetry?*" (140). He wrote "that there
was a bite and sting in my writing" (66). He "liked her flower poems.
He had particularly liked the blue-iris" poem, which may well be an
allusion to "Sea Iris," one of the five sea-flower poems in *Sea Garden.*
He paid her the supreme compliment of sending her his work in manuscript. Julia recalls especially "the bulky manuscript" he sent her in
London, an allusion to the manuscript of *Women in Love* that Lawrence
did send H.D. in 1916 (179).

There was a price to be paid, however, for Rico's approval. Feeling
"revulsion" for his novel, Julia never told him what she thought, but
she sent him poems, particularly the "Orpheus–Eurydice sequence,"

with the "Orpheus sequence" written specifically for him (62, 173). Rico's response was a blunt command that asserted a gender-inflected, aesthetic double standard – his freedom as a male writer and her confinement as a female poet:

> I don't like the second half of the Orpheus sequence as well as the first. Stick to the woman speaking. How can you know what Orpheus feels? It's your part to be woman, the woman vibration, Eurydice should be enough. You can't deal with both. (51)

Julia knows, however, that "his novels, those heady sex-expositions that nobody would publish, after his last novel had been suppressed," demonstrate his attempt to "deal with both" (76). As androgynous artist, he allows himself to enter both the man and woman "vibration." But he would restrict her to feminine subjectivity. Julia's response is angry defiance, claiming a Tiresian androgyny for herself:

> What did Rico matter with his blood-stream, his sex-fixations, his man-is-man, woman-is-woman? That was not true. This mood, this realm of consciousness was sexless, or all sex, it was child-consciousness, it was heaven. In heaven, there is neither marriage nor giving in marriage. . . . This man-, this woman-theory of Rico's was false, it creaked in the joints. Rico could write elaborately on the woman mood, describe women to their marrow in his writing; but if she turned round, wrote the Orpheus part of her Orpheus–Eurydice sequence, he snapped back, 'Stick to the woman-consciousness, it is the intuitive woman-mood that matters.' He was right about that, of course. But if he could enter, so diabolically, into the feelings of women, why should not she enter into the feelings of men? (62)

Julia's feminist dismissal of Rico's "man-is-man, woman-is-woman" is a revisionist, intertextual play on *Women in Love,* whose very title asserts Lawrence's appropriation of female subjectivity. The novel that repelled Julia is carefully woven into *Madrigal,* changed dramatically by its new place within H.D.'s narrative. H.D. superimposed the opening scene of *Women in Love* (where Ursula and Gudrun, "sisters of Artemis," discuss sex, men, and marriage) onto the scene in which Julia and Elsa sit on the left and right sides of Rico. *Women in Love*'s opening serves as metonym for the novel's central questions about "women in love." Birkin, the Lawrentian priest and persona, is not yet present, but he will soon be there to test which woman has the capacity to be "awakened" from her sterile, Artemisian sleep. The astute reader can guess from the novel's second sentence: "Ursula was stitching a piece of brightly-coloured embroidery, and Gudrun was drawing upon a board which she held on her knee" (1). Ursula, the woman engaged in stereotypically feminine activity, is the sleeping beauty who will be awakened by the modern prince, Birkin; and though she is by no means passive, she is

womanly and maternal in a way that her more superficially stylish sister
is not. For all her beauty, Gudrun is the unconventional one – the loner,
the wanderer, the artist of uncanny power and cleverness. But, for Lawrence, her identity as artist is inseparable from her desire for power. Like
her lover Gerald, Gudrun is caught in a sadomasochistic cycle of eroticism, the kind of love that the narrative overtly condemns and covertly
finds arousing. Like *Madrigal, Women in Love* charts the course of two
"experiments" – one, the privileged relationship Ursula and Birkin develop; the other, the murderous affair that Gudrun and Gerald act out.
The woman who feeds the genius of her husband succeeds, while the
woman who is the artist does not. At the end of the novel, Gudrun has
reentered the morally corrupt world of Bohemian artists by running
away with the Jewish artist Loerke, who represents in the novel the
spiritual and sexual sterility of European culture.

   Madrigal invokes the binary representation of WOMAN in *Women in Love*
in order to reappropriate the female subjectivity Lawrence assumed. Like
Ursula, a character based on Frieda, Elsa sits sewing in the scene that
reinscribes the opening of *Women in Love:* "Elsa went on placidly hem-
ming the torn edge of an old jumper. Her work-bag spilled homely
contents on the floor" (77–8).[21] Later repetition of the "work-bag spilt"
(168) underscores its uterine symbolism – Elsa, the mother goddess,
"hatched the Phoenix" (89), the reborn bird with which Lawrence particularly identified. Like Gudrun, the character based on Katharine Mansfield, Julia represents the woman artist. She is not literally sketching,
like Gudrun at the beginning of *Women in Love* (although sketching
appears earlier in *Madrigal* to signify Julia's status as artist); but her position on Rico's *left* side signifies her status as the different woman, the
poet, in contrast to the maternal wife. In the course of the narrative,
Julia "hatches" not a man, but the word: "She brooded over each word
as if to hatch it" (163).

   In *Madrigal,* Julia echoes Gudrun in order to refuse living out her story
as told by Lawrence, thereby implicitly challenging Lawrence's belief
that he could tell the story of the woman artist from a woman's point
of view. As if H.D. were extracting the Gudrun silenced by Lawrence's
androcentric creation of her, Julia speaks what Rico would have her not
say. H.D.'s embedding of Rico's letter within Julia's narrative inverts
Lawrence's own practice of embedding the speech of women with whom
he was intimate in his own texts. Recontextualizing Rico's discourse into
the female discourse of *Madrigal* deauthorizes, even silences him. Julia's
resistance to Rico enacts H.D.'s rebellion against Lawrence.

   In speaking for Gudrun, Julia gradually develops her own "theory"
of erotics and poetics, a pathway that defies Rico's formulations. Her
reference to Rico's "man-is-man, woman-is-woman" clearly evokes Bir-

kin's theorizing about love. Subject himself to Lawrence's irony, Birkin is nonetheless the novel's prophet of a modern love based on "star equilibrium." Dismissing Ursula's desire for "intimacy" and "fusion," he "wanted a further conjunction, where man had being and woman had being, two pure beings, each constituting the freedom of the other, balancing each other like two poles of one force" (191). In contrast to the "see-saw" of sadomasochistic eroticism, in which love is death, Birkin promotes a "marriage into a third heaven. . . . into Paradise" (282–3). Repudiating his advocacy of androgyny for the *individual* in *The Rainbow*, Lawrence in *Women in Love* celebrates the *couple* as androgynous unit:

> In the old age, before sex was, we were mixed, each one a mixture. The process of singling into individuality resulted into the great polarisation of sex. The womanly drew to one side, the manly to the other. . . . There is now to come a new day, when we are beings each of us, fulfilled in difference. The man is pure man, the woman pure woman, they are perfectly polarised. But there is no longer any of the horrible merging, mingling self-abnegation of love. (193)

Ursula battles fiercely with Birkin out of an awareness that his separate-but-equal philosophy falls quickly into a separate-but-unequal reality. Lawrence qualified his own character/mouthpiece (as he so often did) by supporting Ursula's charge that the "pure man" in Birkin's system has more power than the "pure woman" – an androcentrism that includes his right to vocation and a homoerotic blood brothership with a man and that prescribes a woman's total devotion to her husband. In *Madrigal*, Julia takes Ursula's part, as well as Gudrun's, in her resistance to Rico's "sex-theories." Having learned that the androgynous *couple* is a flawed model of love from her experience with Rafe, Julia says Rico thinks only of "the man-artist," not the woman artist: "He was willing to die for what he believed, would die probably. But that was his problem. It was a man's problem, the man-artist. There was also the woman, not only the great mother-goddess that he worshipped, but the woman gifted as the man, with the same, with other problems" (136). "I could not be your mother," she writes to Rico in her journal/letter; "Anyhow, I need a great-mother as much as you do" (182).

Echoing Woolf's *A Room of One's Own*, H.D. chastised Lawrence for ignoring the question of "the woman gifted as the man," of "Shakespeare's sister" whose genius was thwarted by the material conditions of history.[22] Judith, it should be remembered of Woolf's fictionalization, died a suicide, alone and pregnant. H.D. also returns to the issue of pregnancy, so crucial to Julia's relationship with Rafe. Biology is the "catch," Julia thinks, that prevents women from having the same freedom as men: "Why this vaunted business of experience, of sex-emotion

... ? It might be all right for men, but for women, any woman, there was a biological catch and taken at any angle, danger. You dried up and were an old maid, danger. You drifted into the affable *hausfrau*, danger. You let her rip and had operations [abortions] in Paris (poor Bella), danger" (135–6). The catch that prevents star equilibrium is the cultural construction of femininity, the meaning history gives to sexuality and reproduction – specifically, the division of women into asexual "old maids," maternal housewives, and childless mistresses who need abortions. Each destiny means "danger" because each denies the sexual, reproductive, and mental wholeness allowed for men. Whereas men's danger is war in the trenches, women's danger originates in the family, in the cultural organization of sexual difference.

Adapting Woolf's concept of androgynous genius in *A Room of One's Own*, H.D. identified the loophole through the minefields of femininity: "There was one loophole, one might be an artist. Then the danger met the danger, the woman was man–woman, the man was woman–man" (136). "The great mind is androgynous," Woolf wrote – "It is fatal to be a man or woman pure and simple"; "one must be woman–manly or man–womanly" (*Room* 102, 108). H.D. glossed Woolf by having Julia think: "Frederico, for all his acceptance of her verses, had shouted his man-is-man, his woman-is-woman at her; his shrill peacock-cry sounded a love-cry, a death-cry for their generation" (136). The spiritual/sexual death of the age that Lawrence decried is inherent, H.D. said, in his abandonment of the androgynous vision for women evident in *The Rainbow*, the one novel of his she found "magnificent." The sadomasochistic alternation of *Eros* and *Thanatos* is built into his theory of sexual difference. Lawrence, a strutting "peacock" in *Women in Love*, sounds not salvation, but the "love-cry, death-cry" of the age.

Unlike Woolf, however, H.D. did not suggest that "it is fatal to lay the least stress on any grievance; to plead even with justice any cause; in any way to speak consciously as a woman" (*Room* 108). The final third of *Madrigal* represents Julia's attempt to articulate and enact an androgynous loophole, anchored in, not transcendent of, her womanhood. This begins in her affair with Vane, whom she does not "love," but with whom she feels healed. More than the man he is, it is the landscape to which he brings her, the room he gives her, and the name he calls her that signals the nature of his influence. Rosigran, his house near St. Ives (based on Cecil Gray's Bosigran), offers a temporary respite from the war: It is the pastoral setting of "the early H.D.," with its timeless rock and sand and sea. Syntax and diction take on the sparse discourse of H.D.'s imagism: "The wind was cold. Salt tasted. She tasted salt. Her lungs drank in mist and salt-mist. Under her feet was a new fragrance. ... Cliff rose defined against this mist. She was glad of the mist. It drew curtain over the startling expanse of sea-line that had stunned her into sudden reality" (143, 145). "Enclosed in crystal," situated in "some old Druid oak-circle," she is "butterfly in cocoon," "rejoicing" in her coming (re)birth (145, 154, 151). Vane calls her "Person" and offers her a room of her own for work: " 'you can choose whatever room you want to work in.' It had been implicit from the start. She was to have a room to work in" (161). She chooses a tiny "attic" room, like Clarissa's attic room in *Mrs. Dalloway*: "it was her own, empty" (165).[23] Here, she begins to write again; here, she can say to Rico, "your puppets do not always dance to your pipe. Why? Because there is another show" (164).

It is from this room, symbolically associated through Woolf with women's freedom of mind and body, that Julia launches her most extended challenge to Rico – the interior speech and journal/letter that displace his discourse and influence. Vane asks her to write a friendly note to Rico, but she refuses and instead begins a monologue that opens with "I will never see you again, Rico" (171), a statement that inverts what Lawrence in effect wrote to H.D. in his last letter: " 'I hope never to see you again,' he wrote in that last letter" (*Advent* 134). Julia's stream of consciousness merges seamlessly into "scribbling," an entrance into discourse that emphasizes Julia's replacement of Rico's "scribbling" for which she had served as the muse in Chapter 6: "I will never see you again. I will go on scribbling. This very notebook is from the Zennor post-office–stationery–cum–what-not corner shop. You know it. This notebook is a replica of the one you were writing in that day" (172).

As a labyrinthine *mise en abyme*, Julia's "letter" to Rico (re)enacts the self-analytic working through from repetition to remembering of the novel itself. "I will write these notes," Julia scribbles, "and re-write them till they come true" (176). Returning again and again in a staccato discourse to the leitmotifs of her exchanges with Rico, Julia works through the compulsion to repeat into a form of remembering that authorizes and empowers her own rebirth. Repetition of Rico's *"gloire"* becomes transformation of it as she circles round and round its meaning in his texts and her appropriation of it for her own. As Julia herself indicates, Rico's *gloire* is an allusion to Lawrence's poem *"Gloire de Dijon"* which appeared in his celebratory volume about his relationship with Frieda, *Look! We Have Come Through!* (1917)

> I remember somewhere (in Austria, I think) your writing of a terrace or a summer-garden by, overhanging, or overlooking a river ["On the Balcony"]. I don't remember anything about it but the *gloire-de-Dijon* roses. . . . this is not a red rose nor a white one, it is *gloire*, a pale gold. Not gold exactly, maize colour, pale corn-colour. . . . It's Elsa's work-bag split on the floor. (168)

In Lawrence's poem, the poet watches his beloved bathing in the sun-
beams near the window in Icking. In the pleasure of his masculine gaze,
she becomes a golden Dijon rose while the glistening petals become the
"mellow" flesh he desires;

> I linger to watch her;
> ....
> And the sunbeams catch her
> Glistening white on the shoulders,
> While down her sides the mellow
> Golden shadow glows as
> She stoops to the sponge, and the swung breasts
> Sway like full-blown yellow
> Gloire de Dijon roses.
>
> (*Collected Poems* 217)

In this classic masculine lyric, the woman is a lush Renoir nude in
words, a corn goddess whom Adonis adores, the sight (cite) that is the
scene of writing. Lawrence's *gloire* is, in short, a visualization of WOMAN
as the maternal body to which man returns in fantasy for the titillation
of his desire, for the nourishment of his genius. As a poem that forcefully
represents WOMAN as Other in the discourse of male subjectivity, *"Gloire
de Dijon"* contributes to the cultural silencing of "the woman gifted as
the man." This implicit connection between the *gloire* and (male) power
is explicitly articulated in a climatic moment of *Kangaroo*. Devastated by
the war, Richard Sommers abandons his belief in "aloneness" for the
"ritual" of "communion," the "the communion" of "blood sacrifice":
"Sacrifice to the dark God, and to the men in whom the dark God is
manifest. Sacrifice to the strong, not to the weak. In awe, not in dribbling
love. The communion in power, the assumption into glory. *La gloire*"
(312). In Lawrence's "leadership" phase (early postwar period), *la gloire*
signifies the phallic power of men.

Madrigal usurps *la gloire* of both Lawrence's love lyric and death sacrifice, the *Eros* and *Thanatos* of his poetic. In the hands of the "woman
gifted as the man," *la gloire* becomes the basis for an androgynous,
procreative, and erotic poetic, one in which the *gloire* itself has fluid and
suggestive meanings instead of a single, definitive signification.[24] But
before she can transform the *gloire,* she must confront its power in Rico's
text. Emanating from him, the *gloire* threatens to overpower rather than
empower her. His *gloire* signifies the threat of a hegemonic masculine
discourse, potentially "catching" for the woman writer. The staccato
rhythm, disconnected sentences, and abrupt paragraphs highlight her
gendered "anxiety of influence," to borrow Bloom's term:

> I am nobody when it comes to writing novels. But I will find a new
> name. I will be someone. I will write these notes and re-write them till
> they come true. Maybe you haven't tuberculosis.

I don't mean the T.B. would make any difference to me. Only, I am susceptible, would catch something. I would catch your mannerisms, your style of writing, your style of thinking, even.

But that *gloire*. I must find words to tell you.

Perhaps I caught the *gloire* from you. Was it your way of thinking? (176)

Julia's re-vision of the *gloire* supplants "your way of thinking" with her own. She sees the *gloire* as a dynamic sequence of evolving meanings, each one of which alludes to a major element in her story with the result that the *gloire* in toto recapitulates the novel. First, Julia invites Rico to understand, "The *gloire* is both," by which she means it is man/woman and woman/man: "Perhaps you would say I was trespassing, couldn't see both sides, as you said of my Orpheus. I could be Eurydice in character, you said, but woman-is-woman and I couldn't be both. The *gloire* is both" (176). The *gloire* is, in other words, the Tiresian androgyny she has claimed as woman writer against Rico's demand of her confinement to femininity. But, once asserted, this meaning of the *gloire* becomes inadequate: "No, that spoils it; it is both and neither. It is simply myself sitting here, this time propped up in bed, scribbling in a notebook, with a candle at my elbow" (177).

This tableau of the *gloire* is specifically gendered, a *gloire* in a female body. As she decodes this image of her self in bed writing, she first connects the *gloire* with an unborn child who is the unborn story. This time the abrupt style suggests a cryptic oracle, a Druidic riddle that resists translation:

The child is the *gloire* before it is born. The circle of the candle on my notebook is the *gloire,* the story isn't born yet.

While I live in the unborn story, I am in the *gloire.*

I must keep it alive, myself living with it.

It is hard not to be able to tell you of this. I want to share this with you. You will think I could not face my ordeal, when you hear I have gone back. (177)

This passage is the only one in *Madrigal* that can be read as an allusion to H.D.'s actual pregnancy, near miscarriage, and decision not to abort – all subjects that are fully explored in *Asphodel*. But, without the prior "draft," the condensed formulas in the passage unravel to define the *gloire* as a procreative poetic reminiscent of *Notes on Thought and Vision*. First, the fetus is the *gloire*. Then, the circle of light on the notebook becomes the *gloire* – that is, the pregnant page is "mother," a uterine globe of light. Next, "the story" that "isn't born yet" is the "child," the fetus in the blank page of the notebook and therefore also the *gloire*. Finally, the "I" who lives "in the unborn story" is the fetus of the *gloire*: The container (mother/writer) has become the contained (the story). Inside the uterine *gloire,* the "I" will come to term. As Julia writes a bit later, "The story must write *me,* the story must create *me"* (181). The writer is not God the Creator, projecting his vision into and by the Word; instead she is the fetus nourished in the womb of her own words. She is mother to her self; she is babe to the mother tongue. To survive, she "must keep it alive" – "it" is simultaneously the fetus, the story, and the womb. The child Julia lost with Rafe has become in her revisionary poetic the story-as-child recreated in "the ordeal" she is recording.

The *gloire* as mother, however, is succeeded by the *gloire* as lover. "The *gloire* is the candle at my elbow," as Julia goes on to think while she "scribbles," "propped up in bed." (177). We are back to "the bed" where the novel began, the "not always such a happy [marriage] bed" (36). The meaning of Julia's self-image continues to shift, resisting the assignment of static signification and suggesting the endlessly dynamic process of signification. Not only the womblike circle of light, the *gloire* is the phallic candle itself. This image of the candle as *father* of the child loops back to the dominant images positively associated with Rafe in Chapters 4 and 5. Rafe has begun his liaison with Bella at this point, the autumn of 1917. But, in spite of his distance from Julia, they continue to share brief moments of communion that bring the out-of-time, however flawed, back in time. The symbol of these moments is the bunch of chrysanthemums Rafe brings Julia after leaving Bella and sets down on the table next to a burning candle (61). It is a conventional gift, a conventional plea by a man who has "cheated on his wife." But, aware of this irony, Julia nonetheless sees the flowers as "the last link with him" as they "blossomed mysteriously," in the middle of night when she can't sleep, giving off a "heady scent of woods and wild spaces": "Now it seemed like Christmas, the bunch of chrysanthemums was like a little tree. The candle threw its circle of halo-light" (64, 61). Rico had told her to "Kick over your tiresome house of life," but the flowers and candle constitute for Julia her " 'house of life' that Rico didn't really guess at" (61). They allow her to reclaim Rafe from Bella and revise the Keatsian "season of mists and mellow fruitfulness" to make it signify the richness of their bond: "Season of mists – certainly – and mellow fruitfulness. She saw that the great yellow globe that caught the candle-flame was perfectly round as her eyes misted. . . . Something was born between them, between Rafe and herself, the Christ-child of their battered integrity, of something they had" (61–2).

The phallic candle and womblike globes of light and flowers make an archetypically heterosexual erotic and procreative unit, a *gloire* that critiques the pure cerebralism of Rico's relationship with Julia and, by extension, a poetry based on sheer "abstractions" (61). Now alone in bed, Julia has lost the actual Rafe. But as she claims the *gloire* in her attic room in Cornwall, she is neither the "frozen lily" Rico has accused her of being, nor the nunlike, celibate Clarissa in *Mrs. Dalloway.* In memory,

Julia resurrects those ephemeral moments of "bliss" and makes them the basis of her poetic. The "Christ-child" is not only their "battered integrity," but also the child-as-story, the word that emerges from the womb of history. The images of candle and red-yellow chrysanthemums that signify her "house of life" gain further intensity when read in the context of two poems Aldington wrote during the war, "Epilogue" and "Compensation." In "Epilogue," probably written in 1917–18, the light of a burning candle is the image for love, the only "Warmth and beauty of this life / Before the blankness of the unending gloom": "And in this little glow of mortal life – / Faint as one candle in a large cold room – / We know the clearest light is shed by love" (*Complete Poems* 148). "Compensation" centers on a dream the poet has while dozing "in a chilly dug-out" of "Li Taï-Pé, the sage / And Sappho, the divine Lesbian," who say to him:

> "There is no death of beauty;
> Endure – we also suffered."
> And for a token of their love they gave me
> A gold chrysanthemum, a fiery rose
> And a cleft-open, dew-wet nectarine.
>
> (Gates 267)

Julia's re-vision of Rico's *gloire* does not end, however, with her reconstitution of her broken marriage on the scribbled page. Having reclaimed Rafe, she turns back to Rico. In the final section of the novel, Julia redefines the *gloire* yet again, this time to re-create Rico so that his power empowers, rather than silences her. The room in which she sits scribbling in the candlelight is the associative key. It is not only *her* room, but also a series of rooms that bring Rico back. Above all it becomes the empty room full of the artist's presence in Van Gogh's painting, "Vincent's Room" (178ff). Rico, Julia discovers, is like Van Gogh, who "is in the *gloire*" (183). In making the connection, Julia re-creates Rico in Van Gogh's image, a figure whose *gloire* has nothing to do with the "shrill peacock-cry" of Rico's "sex-theories," "dark gods," and "bulky" novels. Van Gogh's *gloire* is his daemon, his creative drive which is inseparable from his madness, even his suicide. Not "nature-worship," but a Druidic mysticism characterizes this daemon that draws Van Gogh with the force of a vortex into what he paints: "He would get into the cypress tree, through his genius, through his daemon. Because of him alive in the cypress tree, alive in his mother, the cypress would be deified. . . . It is worship, such as the Druids felt here with their sun-circle of stones. . . . Vincent is in the cypress, he is in the blossoming fruit-tree, he is in the *gloire*" (183). Rico, Julia asserts, has this same power: "It is in everything you write; even if I don't agree with you or don't like what you're saying. I know that the genius is there" (183). Reversing Rico's authoritative advice giving earlier in the novel, Julia instructs Rico (in the privacy of her journal) by telling him to remain true to his daemon: "I could only qualify . . . by saying you should write as Vincent Van Gogh painted" (183). This Druidic genius does not threaten Julia as Rico's sex theories do. Instead, it enlivens what she now agrees is too static and one dimensional in her volume of poems, *Coronal*, that Rico characterized as the "flowers of. . . Persephone" – an allusion to *Sea Garden* (178–9). Rico's genius has helped her enter a "Druidic circle," where paths "make a pattern, letters, a sort of hieroglyph or picture-writing," not "on one plane or parallel," but "dynamically exploding inside, like Van Gogh pictures" (178–9). This *gloire*, this genius, Julia can serve, without any loss of herself, without "catching" Rico's style: "I realise this genius in this place. I would like to serve your genius, not because it is personally, your genius, but because it is part of this place" (183). Lest we think that Julia has become one of Rico's "maenads," worshiping at his feet, the novel concludes with Julia recalling Rico's ultimate affirmation of her own genius: "I can remember how you said to me, 'You were singing in a dream. I woke and found my face wet with tears' " (184).

Madrigal's conclusion exhibits a pattern that characterizes H.D.'s later textual re-visionings of authoritative men whom she revered, even loved, but whom she had to remake in her own image so that their power intensified instead of overwhelming her own – Freud in *Tribute to Freud*, Shakespeare in *By Avon River*, Pound in *End to Torment*, St.-John Perse in *Hermetic Definition*. Her resolution of the anxiety of influence avoids the patricide in Bloom's poet sons and the victimization of the daughters in some Lacanian–feminist models. Instead, H.D. marks out a dialectical interaction, one that stresses the active power of the creative woman to reinterpret, reclaim, and reconstitute these men whom she loved into a source of her own validation.

In a letter to Aldington, H.D. described the resolution of narrative conflict in *Madrigal* as "a 'happy ending,' if it could be called that" because "somehow" Julia "knows that she will live in the *gloire*, as she calls it, will, will, will sometime write, as she wants to write, not just slim volumes of Greek chorus quality, but something else" (27 December 195[?]). But this " 'happy ending,' if it could be called that" provides no final closure; rather, it concludes by reopening the questions that fueled the narrative to begin with. Julia's appropriation and re-vision of Rico's *gloire* presents itself as a "happy" victory, just as the novel itself, with its full portraits of Rico and Rafe, successfully defies the advice Rico gave to Julia to "stick to the woman." But the authority that Julia, and the novel, still give in the novel's final moment to the male poet to validate the female poet calls into question the extent of that "happy ending." Rico's dream – the power of her song making him weep –

paradoxically places him in the traditional role of a woman, but covertly reasserts his authority as a man to admit her to the company of "real poets." The dream reminds us that he had earlier proclaimed: "Don't you know, don't you realise that this is *poetry?*" (140). Male praise has its cost: the covert reaffirmation of man's position as arbiter of judgment and genius. Julia's recollection of Rico's dream at the conclusion of the novel unravels her appropriation of his *gloire.*

Rico's dream may be H.D.'s transposition of her own dream of Lawrence that she later recalled in *Compassionate Friendship:* "Lawrence did not come into War II. I hardly thought of him, though once in a dark, bomb-shattered night, I had a dream of him. It was a fiery golden Lawrence, it was nothing but a fleeting presence and the words, 'Hilda, you are the only one of the whole crowd, who can really *write*' " (54). The man who still had that kind of power in her psyche in the 1940s had in fact imposed his judgment on her in 1916. The poem "Eurydice," written in 1916 and alluded to as the "Orpheus–Eurydice" poem in *Madrigal,* has no "Orpheus sequence." Only Eurydice speaks – it is a poem passionately defying the masculine authority of Orpheus, the archetypal poet whose gaze sent her shade back to the Underworld. But, as Lawrence apparently demanded, H.D. made no attempt to speak for Orpheus in the final version of the poem.[25] *Madrigal,* completed over thirty years later, returns again to the problem that had plagued her in 1916. Unlike the poem, the novel has "an Orpheus sequence": Rico, as an in-time manifestation of the out-of-time Orpheus, is a fully drawn character, as is Rafe, the other poet figure. The novel therefore completes the defiance begun in "Eurydice" and partially withdrawn at Lawrence's insistence. But, although the novel extends the challenge of "Eurydice," its final lines return to the problem that surfaced in the revisions of the poem: Rico, however redefined through the transformation of his *gloire,* retains the authority to validate Julia's voice. *Madrigal* ends by "beginning again," by restating the questions that were fundamental to its origin as a *Kunstlerroman.*

Julia's imaginative reclamations of Rafe and Rico at the end of the novel also remind us of the semiotics of gender that initiated the triangulations of desire in wartime. Julia's pages challenge Rico and recall the chrysanthemum glow of her blissful moments with Rafe. But she is still alone in an "empty" room in which she is "Person, *Personne,* Nobody" (172, 176). Vane is only a surrogate lover, while Rafe is with Bella and Rico is with Elsa. Art has been indeed the only loophole through the danger for Julia – Rafe and Rico live with her only in the words she scribbles in her notebook. Although Julia changes her vision of Rafe and Rico, neither of the men *in fact* change with her. The "real" men are gone, and she is alone in an empty room, denied the companionship of heterosexual love. Her "madrigals" are songs in which she sings all the parts, solos rather than multivoiced lyrics. Even the parallel to Van Gogh is terrifying because the price of genius is his madness and suicide. In a "room of her own," Julia is not only Mary Carmichael, but also potentially Judith, Shakespeare's finally abandoned and crazed "sister," the "woman gifted as the man." In short, Julia's imaginative restoration of her love for Rafe and Rico does not change the fact that in "history," she occupies the position of WOMAN, specifically the place of the woman poet caught in a binary system of representation in which women are body or soul, virgins or whores, mothers or muses. History, with its intersections of *Eros* and *Thanatos* in the public and private spheres, still conditions Julia's life. The novel's refrain – "the war will soon be over. The war will never be over" – still resonates as the structuring principle throughout Julia's song. As Isis, Julia is still seeking the fragments of Osiris, the fragments of herself, shattered in the underworld of the modern world.

> *II.* ASPHODEL: *PLOTTING COURTSHIP AND*
> *SPEAKING MATERNITY*
>
> Khaki killed it.
>
> H.D., *Asphodel* (II 3)

Read in the context of *Madrigal*'s unanswered and restated questions, *Asphodel* is more than an early draft, more than an autobiographical fiction based on a larger chronological time frame. It is a different formulation of the issues, one that implicitly critiques the heterosexual boundaries for love established in *Madrigal*. *Asphodel* is the repressed story of the woman as poet–lover–mother, the political and textual unconscious of both the novel for which it became a "draft" and of the historical moment that it inscribes. I want to explore how the unpublished *Asphodel* tells a story that the more public *Madrigal* cannot tell, how *Asphodel* fills the "gap" in consciousness to which Julia alludes in *Madrigal,* and how the interplay of *Eros* and *Thanatos* in *Asphodel* expands the critique of history articulated in *Madrigal.*

Madrigal's condensed and selective plot covers about a nine-month time span from early autumn to summer, a gestational chronology that evokes the mythos of the mystery religions that underlie its narrative of the in-time. With its more expansive, nine-year chronology, *Asphodel* is more nearly akin to the multivolume and serial structure of many nineteenth-century novels with their large casts of characters – especially Henry Jame's *Portrait of a Lady,* "a novel in two volumes" whose narrative patterns H.D. evoked and revoked. Like the first volume of James's

Portrait, Asphodel's Part 1 is basically a courtship narrative that begins with an innocent American girl's journey to Europe and ends with her marriage to a foreigner. Again like James, Part 2 is the story of a marriage – its disintegration in the midst of European dissolution (the war) and its heroine's final reconciliation to her destiny.[26] *Asphodel*, however, invokes the narrative conventions James represents in order to break them. The courtship plot in Part 1 is repeatedly undermined by the story of female friendship and love. The resolution of the plot in Part 2 does not center on the American wife's return to the European husband who betrayed her faith, but rather shows her discovery of her freedom in abandonment – a liberation enacted in her decision to have an "illegitimate" child, in the return of her creative inspiration, and in the reconstitution of her family as two women and a child. Anticipating Woolf's prediction in *A Room of One's Own* that women's writing would "break the accepted sequence," *Asphodel* disrupts James's story. In so doing, H.D. continued the life story she later cut off in *Madrigal*. By representing Perdita's birth, H.D.'s relationship with Bryher, and the replacement of a heterosexual family by a lesbian one, *Asphodel* literally and figuratively "writes beyond the ending" of *Madrigal*.

Asphodel's break with the expected sequence of the nineteenth-century marriage plot rests upon its disruption of conventional narrative point of view. In contrast to *Madrigal,* the stream of consciousness in *Asphodel* runs riot in an excess of words seemingly unmediated by an authoritative narrator. *Asphodel* exaggerates the disappearance of the narrator that James's late work embodies. To represent subjectivity in novels of both first- and third-person narration, James located an invisible narrator within the various characters who served as a center of consciousness. Intensifying this technique, *Asphodel* has only one center of consciousness – Hermione Gart – and no distinctive narrative voice. The title page of the manuscript is one of the very few of H.D.'s works to bear no authorial name at all. Collapsing the distance between narrator and narrated, the text oscillates between first- and third-person narration without textual markers (such as italics, punctuation, or paragraphing). Disturbingly, even the third-person narration gives us no sensation of being "outside" of or detached from the textual vortex of Hermione's thoughts. The authoritative narrator of *Madrigal* who pronounces on the "crucifying times of history" by invoking both Cicero and Dickens in the opening line is entirely missing from *Asphodel*. Perhaps influenced by cinematic technique, *Madrigal*'s narrator zooms from the external position of a prophet of "the times" into the interior world of Julia's consciousness, only to retreat back into the position of authority. By slipping from thought into writing in her journal, Julia usurps the narrator's position in the final chapter of the novel, much as Stephen does in *Portrait of the*

Artist. But, taken as a whole, *Madrigal* projects an authoritative subject located somewhere, some time in the future tense of the novel. *Asphodel,* on the other hand, immerses the reader in its own present tense. As a profoundly nonteleological text, it weaves partial scraps of dialogue with fragments of interior monologue in a baffling way that keeps the reader grasping for the simple externalities of the plot that continue to unfold serially as if the text were a diary. The narrator does not seem to know the sequence of events she is telling until they are told. Hermione's thoughts as she stands before the statue of Joan of Arc can serve as a representative sample:

> One came to France to see something – but why this? Why had she come to France? It was only a story. . . . O God don't you see, it was something real that happened. It was written on the pavement with the date, a circle and the French words. One dared not read them. Not even herself *there*. She had gone away into the air and she was a Spirit and she was France. O book you are worse than Saint John. I could never read those terrible words and here it is written, all written on the pavement and it happened like the Crucifixion. . . . And they had caught her. Caught her. Trapped her with her armour and her panache and her glory and her pride. They had trapped her, a girl who was a boy and they would always do that. They would always trap them, bash their heads like broken flowers from their stalks, break them for seeing things, having "visions" seeing things like she did and like Fayne Rabb. This was the warning. Joan of Arc. O stop them. Stop them. . . . Streets and the heat coming back and the reality and Clara reading, "visitors would do well to profit by the neighborhood – br – br – br –" Hermione could not hear her. Clara was reading out of another book, the wrong sort of book. O France, France, terrible book. Like the revelations. . . . O moth with blue wings. They have caught you moth, moth with blue wings. The black smoke shrivels your blue wings. People are shouting, blasphemy. They curse the witch of Orleans. . . . I don't want to be burnt, to be crucified just because I "see" things sometimes. O Jeanne you shouldn't ever, ever have told them that you saw things. . . . "Yes, Mrs. Rabb. . . . Let's get out of this heat anyway."
>
> Heat roasting from the pavement. Heat with black devil wings to catch her. (I 10–13)

This nonauthoritative narrator immersed in the present contributes to the production of a narrative that appears to interrupt its own patterns as soon as they are initiated. With its mythic analogues, *Madrigal* exhibits a classical structure based on a descent to the Underworld and the rebirth of its wiser hero(ine). *Asphodel,* on the other hand, presents repeated clashes between conventional and unconventional narrative structures in which the forbidden story of the woman writer keeps reasserting itself against the formulaic plots of the nineteenth-century novel. This conflict deeply implicates the reader in the production of the narrative. We are constantly having our expectations of a familiar plot aroused, only to have them dashed and contradicted by what actually happens. In Part 1, for example, the journey of two young women to Europe invokes the conventions of feminine initiation. The novel's opening – with its focus on the two seasick women squabbling in their cabin and then later as they sightsee – suggests the novel of feminine awakening in which the innocent heroines will be inducted into the adult world of sexuality and marriage through the agency of men – when, how, and who are the questions that provide the momentum for courtship novels. The sensation of satisfaction comes at the end, when closure is achieved in the tying of loose ends into the marriage knot.[27]

Part 1 of *Asphodel* has just such an overall narrative shape. Fayne marries first, and we are left in the final chapter with the certainty of Hermione's impending marriage to Jerrold Darrington. However, narrative movement within this overall pattern is based on jarring disruptions that call into question the very expectations that are ultimately fulfilled. Hermione's entrance into France, for example, centers not on a male initiator, but on Joan of Arc, whose statue at Rouen suggests the spirit of female rebellion and the martyrdom of female difference. Hermione's meeting with the famous pianist Walter Dowel shortly thereafter appears to erase the dire warning of Saint Joan. Walter (the Walter Rummel figure) brings Hermione back to the familiar courtship plot by making her his muse. Just as we begin to expect a blossoming affair, an erotically charged scene between Hermione and Verené breaks across this plot. Verené, who loves Dowel, comes to plead her case with Hermione, but "an entente all at once flaming up between" supplants the conventional plot of female rivalry. "Don't let's talk about *him,*" the two women agree (I 58).

This exchange foreshadows a more substantial reversal in London. George Lowdnes (sometimes Lowndes), once Hermione's fiancé, greets her with enough ambiguity to suggest that they are perhaps still engaged. "Should she. Shouldn't she," Hermione wonders about accepting George's invitation to tea. "One I love, two I love" (I 73). Fayne challenges Hermione: "Well are or are you not engaged to George Lowdnes?" Hermione's answer is babble: "I mean, we did [break it off]. I mean he did. Then he came back and we got engaged again. . . . I mean we got engaged then we – I mean he – no it was I this time – I mean *I* broke – it – off – I mean it was broken off. . . . I don't know, Josepha. I had better ask him" (I 74). Hermione's uncertainty and Fayne's fear are signals to the reader to expect the resumption of the courtship plot. Even George's denial – "Gawd forbid" – does not allay Hermione's (nor the reader's) suspicion that the on-again, off-again engagement might not flicker on again – especially in light of George's deliberate orchestration of Hermione's debut into his London circle of artists and writers. Criticizing her dress, her speech, her manner, her address, George attempts to shape Hermione into the image of his desire, the "odd, exotic" American "pet" to be fêted by his sophisticated European friends.

The possible resumption of her engagement to George is radically disrupted by the narrative revelation of Hermione's love for Fayne. The muted lesbian plot, previously closeted, interrupts the dominant heterosexual plot. George's final criticism of Hermione – her unhealthy relationship with Fayne ("You and she would have been burned in Salem for witches" [92]) – is abruptly followed by a climactic scene between Hermione and Fayne (93–100). Fayne insists upon returning to the States with her mother while Hermione begs Fayne to stay in London with her. Sister-love must replace mother-love, Hermione pleads: "we can't creep back into our mothers, be born again that way. We must be born again in another way. You must, cut, as it were the cord" (94).[28] The two women will write poems in London, be poets, Hermione insists, inspired by their special and "different" love for each other. To quote in part from Hermione's lengthy speech, her most coherent and uninterrupted utterance in the novel:

> "I, Hermione, tell you I love you Fayne Rabb. Men and women will come and say I love you. I love you Hermione, you Fayne. Men will say I love you Hermione but will anyone ever say I love you Fayne as I say it? . . . Do people say it's indecent? Maybe it is. . . . But I'm something different. It's nothing to do with them. I'm something else. Different. You Fayne know that. . . . You aren't going to stay because you're afraid simply. You urge me to defy my mother, poor soft dear and sentimental Eugenia. Eugenia is as beautiful as Clara. Even more so. Soft and holding tight to her convention. But not rigid. Clara is rigid. But her love for you is incest. Mothers and daughters don't sleep in the same bed. It's horrible."
>
> "Peter Piper picked a peck of pickled peppers –" "Yes, it appears so. But I'll go on talking. We are legitimate children. We are children of the Rossettis, of Burne Jones, of Swinburne. We were in the thoughts of Wilde. . . . I don't know Fayne Rabb but your silliness is unworth[y] of you. . . . You are Hyacinth mired with horror. Hyacinth was a strong boy not a pimp. . . . You are the youth of the god Hermes, but you have neither wand nor wings nor sandals." (I 96–100)

At a metafictional level, Hermione's plea for Fayne to stay in London is a plea for the narrative itself (and the reader) to resist the "thralldom" and, as DuPlessis would say, write beyond the ending of the marriage plot. Just as Hermione loses her battle for Fayne, so the narrative of Part I capitulates to the compulsion of heterosexual courtship and marriage. Fayne marries and Hermione gradually disengages from George and engages with Darrington. However, even this narrative capitulation is subject to repeated disruptions that resist heterosexual romance as the desire that forwards the plot. The story of women – of women's relationships with other women constituted within and in spite of the patriarchal social order – keeps inserting itself into the marriage plot to prevent the narrative from becoming what convention would have it be: a love story.

Fayne's fulfillment of the marriage plot is completely undermined by her odd display of marital transformation and by the illicit subtext of desire that underlies her triumphant return to London with her prestigious new husband. At her hotel, she keeps her friends waiting for her dramatic appearance in wedding gown and veil. "Fayne looking odd in a fashion-plate veil and a fashion-plate bride-train" stands before them looking "right and proper," a "married woman," as Hermione keeps thinking (I 158). Her new mother-in-law, fussing happily about the veil and the white glove with its ring finger cut out for the ceremony of wedlock, heightens the scene of metamorphosis with images suggesting hymenal rupture (veil) as woman's castration (cut glove) in patriarchy. As in Woolf's *Orlando,* the clothes make the woman, signifying metonymically her transformation from Fayne Rabb into Mrs. Maurice Morrison, a figure with status in the social order. Still single, Hermione is fixated by the sight of Fayne, somehow objectified in her new role as wife – "odd curious stone like, marble lift of flawless feature . . . in the right setting . . . in the right place. Fayne with fair skin, with magnolia white skin but looking right" (I 157). If Fayne is "right" to marry, then Hermione must be "wrong" to refuse.

Fayne's "rightness" takes another twist that further undermines the romance plot she ostensibly fulfills. Occupying the "right" position as wife, she suggests, gives a woman the freedom to fulfill "wrong" desires. Fayne has convinced Maurice to bring Hermione on their honeymoon to the continent. Has she arranged the respectable screen for forbidden desire that Hermione failed to provide in her gallant, but impractical speech? Although Hermione (and the reader) doesn't know if she can trust him, George smashes such a hope by insisting that Fayne has schemed to take Hermione as a cover for her affair with the poet John Llewyn (the Powys figure).[29] Shocked and shaken by this revelation, Hermione allows George to prevent her trip with Fayne, Maurice, and John. With Fayne "grown up now in your bride things" and "carrying on a 'vulgar intrigue,' " the loss of "little Fay rather wistful with her hatred (her then hatred) of all men" seems final (I 170). As wife, Fayne becomes in Hermione's eyes a role player, a circus performer: "Fayne Rabb pirouetting in white face and white frilled petticoats, Fayne turned from Pygmalion with strong sturdy thighs and staunch young shoulders into a parody of womanhood. Doing her little prize stunt for the world to see" (I 181).

Whatever the nature of Fayne's desire, her marriage has nothing to do with love; rather, it signifies the cultural construction of femininity through what Adrienne Rich has called the ideology of "compulsory heterosexuality." As such, it foreshadows the denouement of Part 1, Hermione's own capitulation to the marriage plot. Like Volume 1 of *Portrait of a Lady*, Part 1 of *Asphodel* ends with Hermione's impending marriage to the poet Darrington. But it is fear, not love, that draws her into the courtship – fear of abandonment, of difference, of being an "old maid" in a world of married couples. In *Madrigal*, Julia's memories of courtship are pastoral idylls, shimmering memory beads to be worn as talismans against the dissolutions of war. *Asphodel*, in contrast, suggests that the compulsion to marry led Hermione to notice Darrington's persistent attentions, his letters pushed daily under her door, "taken with her tooth-brush, with her morning chocolate" (I 177). Once again, the story of women dominates the narrative discourse, preventing the story of romance from taking shape. The key events are Hermione's visits to Verené and Shirley, each of which teaches her that she must do what women do, marry. Herself now a triumphant "housewife" married to Walter, Verené pointedly tells Hermione that George is engaged and that Shirley, now thirty, is devastated because she had been led by George's kisses to believe that she would marry George herself. Recognizing herself in Shirley, Hermione is both repulsed and frightened. George had been kissing her as well as Shirley, who takes on the status of her double:

> Had George then deceived her? You don't kiss people like that, you don't kiss them at all if you are "engaged" elsewhere. Engaged, what an odd idea. The whole place was mad, obsessed. . . . Was she a spectator then? Was she to be always looking, watching, seeing other people's lives work out right? Hermione seemed to herself suddenly forgotten. As old maids must feel turning out lavender letters, letters gone dim and smelling of sweet lavender. Was she then lost? It seemed suddenly that she must clutch, find something. Herself was it? "I don't seem to understand this sudden fury of engagements." "O it's natural." "I suppose so –" But it wasn't. It was somehow queer and twisted...
>
> No, no. It wasn't twisted. Walter wasn't twisted. What had gone wrong, gone wrong with everything? (I 174–5)

The marriage plot is *cultural*, not *natural*, somehow "queer and twisted" in its insistence that "untwisted" individuals couple. Verené's pity for "poor Shirley," the aging woman without a man, leads Hermione to reassess the meaning of Darrington's letters: "She didn't want to be married, all satin like Fayne Rabb, all a snare. . . . Was marriage always a sham, a pretence like this was? . . . Letters were different now, might mean something. Letters in the light of Shirley just turned thirty might mean something. Must mean something" (I 177). Hermione's visit to Shirley decodes the meaning of those letters –" 'Darrington to the rescue' " (I 189). Hermione arrives for tea at Shirley's invitation only to be told abruptly by the maid that Shirley has just committed suicide, leaving a note stating her love for Walter.[30] Hermione's chaotic interior monologue in the closing pages of Part 1 both resists and capitulates to Shirley's example:

> Virgins. Shirley was a virgin. That was what made them laugh, asking why she didn't marry George Lowndes. Soon they would laugh at Hermione who hadn't married George Lowndes. "But of course you can't *marry* him." Marry. No. Dress up and parade like a vulgar midinette in a bride's veil and let your mother-in-law (by proxy) hold up the long gloves with the severed finger. "But it's for the *bride's ring*."
> (I 187)

The only alternative to the "castration" of marriage seems to be madness and suicide. Verené tells Hermione that Shirley "should have married – someone," and Hermione repeats "She should have married. Then it would have been all right. Then she wouldn't have been a virgin, gone mad, simply, like Cassandra" (I 190).

The story of Shirley's suicide and its impact on Hermione completely overwhelms the wedlock plot – not only in sheer textual space (Darrington is scarcely present except in his formulaic manifestation, " 'Darrington to the rescue' "), not only in providing the motivation for marriage, but even more fundamentally in the final twist of Hermione's distress. Her despair for herself, which the reader knows will lead to her marriage, becomes anguish for the "murder" of Shirley. Instead of being treated to a satisfying scene of "Darrington to the rescue," in which his love displaces her sorrow, the reader overhears Hermione become aware that everyone, including herself, is complicitous in Shirley's death. "They had all killed her," Hermione thinks. "George must be blamed, scapegoat. He was a scape-goat. Kissing them all. Let all the sins of all the kisses be upon him. For this was a sin. Kisses that had killed Shirley" (I 190). The structure of desire within the social order had "murdered" Shirley, the "old maid" who had no place. She, Hermione, had participated in that murder by not reaching out to Shirley – woman to woman:

> Love could kill people. It was Hermione who had killed her. Hermione on May-day might have reached her. Shirley looking wan and odd, seeing that Hermione was unhappy. Shirley had seen this. Hermione might have reached across, said simply, "I am so unhappy." Hermione hadn't done this. Hermione had killed her.... Myself had wound round myself so that I was like a white spider shut in by my own hideous selfishness.... Intuition and fine feeling had not been fine enough

to sense this. The very proximity of this other spirit. The very nearness of this authentic sister, tangled in a worse web than she was. Herself had wound about herself blinding herself to the soul's unhappiness about her. (I 190–3)

Anticipating the moment in *Madrigal* when Julia recognizes what she shares as a woman with her rival, Bella, the end of Part 1 in *Asphodel* stresses Hermione's awareness that her impending marriage represents a retreat from "this authentic sister," a capitulation to the social order which will legitimate and privilege her as a married woman. The wedlock plot is both affirmed and undermined as Hermione imagines "Fayne on a white horse lead[ing] the fantastic circus. Parade round and round a room, parade round and round a world. The whole world was girded by this fantastic procession" (I 193–4). Like "Henry James lost in Sussex marshes," Hermione thinks, she is an "innocent" American craving "the wilderness" who has been caught up in the mad processions of the social order epitomized by European culture (I 194).

Like Part 1 of *Asphodel,* Part 2 presents a conventional narrative repeatedly subject to rupture by an unexpected, usually repressed story. The ostensible subject is marriage and its dissolution through the triangulation of desire instigated by the war. Darrington's affairs – first with Merry Dalton (the Brigit Patmore figure), then with Louise Blake (the Dorothy Yorke figure) – are betrayals that propel Hermione into an affair with Cyril Vane (the Cecil Gray figure). The subtext that overwhelms the text in Part 2 is the story of procreation – pregnancy, childbirth, and motherhood. Structurally, this story of the mother (nine chapters) implodes onto the story of lovers (six chapters). Chapters 1 and 2 center on Hermione's stillbirth in 1915. Chapters 8 through 13 and 15 focus on her pregnancy in 1918 and the miraculous birth of her baby in 1919. Restricted to Chapters 3 through 7 and 14, the story of the lovers is nearly smothered by its frame, the unusual exploration of a woman's feelings about pregnancy and childbirth. The tradition of the novel abounds with plots of adultery, betrayal, and erotic rivalries, but the subject of procreation has been largely absent from literary discourse until the recent wave of feminism has extended women's writing into such tabooed areas of the female body as menstruation, conception, abortion, miscarriage, pregnancy, birth, and lactation. Part 2 of *Asphodel* anticipates this contemporary breakthrough not only in its portrait of a pregnant woman, but also in its structural overthrow of the conventional marriage plot.

Asphodel's disruption of the marriage story represents the return of the repressed in relationship to *Madrigal,* as well as to literary discourse in general. As a whole, Part 2 of *Asphodel* erupts into the gaps of *Madrigal* itself as if the earlier text contained the repressed memories of the final text. Although *Madrigal* obscures the story of pregnancy in 1918 and *Asphodel* erases the story of Lawrence, Part 2 of *Asphodel* is more closely related to *Madrigal* than any of H.D.'s texts about the war years. They share some of the same episodes and many of the same motifs, so much so that the term "draft" has some cogency as a description of the connection between the two texts. However, decoded with the grammar of the dream-work, Part 2 of *Asphodel* can also be read as the textual and political unconscious of *Madrigal*. Revealing what *Madrigal* conceals, *Asphodel* presents scenes that are fully repressed, partially obscured, or painfully remembered in *Madrigal*. Further, *Asphodel,* as the private text, presents a different and in some ways more radical version of the *political* unconscious of history than does *Madrigal*, the public text.

The marriage stories of *Madrigal* and Part 2 of *Asphodel* share memories of a courtship idyll centered in Italy and signaled by lines from Robert Browning that resonate through both texts. Browning's " 'De Gustibus –' " ends with a refrain that H.D. quoted in both novels: "Open my heart and you will see / Graved inside of it, 'Italy.' "[31] But where *Asphodel* identifies the lines as Browning's, *Madrigal* does not. They simply appear without attribution or even quotation marks in an ironic statement Rafe makes to Julia when she tells him she was "thinking of Italy" (25). Extensively quoted in *Asphodel,* Browning's "The Englishman in Italy" is even further suppressed in *Madrigal*, although important, unidentified traces remain. *Asphodel* opens in the middle of a bombing raid shortly after Hermione has returned from the nursing home where her baby was born dead during a prior raid. Darrington is reading "The Englishman in Italy" to his bedridden wife as a talisman against death that brings their past moments of "paradise" into the present inferno. This scene partially recapitulates the setting of the poem itself, which begins: *"Fortù, Fortù, my beloved one, / sit here by my side"* (*Poetical Works* 260; *Asphodel* II 4). The poem's speaker is a young man who tells his young beloved about his travels in Italy with her brother, "telling my memories over / As you tell your beads" (*Poetical Works* 260). His vivid memories of the sea and the "Pomegranates . . . chapping and splitting / In halves on the tree" are surrogates for those of Jerrold and Hermione. Browning's image of "great butterflies fighting, / Some five for one cup" is a comforting pastoral analogue to the deadly war outside their flat (*Poetical Works* 260; *Asphodel* II 4–5). Browning's Italy is an emblem for their own Italy, a stimulant to the "telling" of their own memory beads.

Browning's "The Englishman in Italy" disappears as overt intertext in *Madrigal,* but his image of "telling beads" reappears in the novel's central metaphor for memory – "the frail spider-web of a silver-cord that might so soon be broken" – presented in a section that quotes from Browning's " 'De Gustibus –,' " without attribution (24–5). Echoing,

without naming "The Englishman in Italy," Julia thinks of Italian cities
– "Capri, Verona, Venice" – as "words that she did not speak [that] held
old cities together; on this fine strand, this silver-cord, Venice was a
bright glass-bead" (24).

Browning remains in *Madrigal* only as an imagistic residue ultimately
overshadowed by resonating lines from Keats and Herrick. *Madrigal's*
Keatsian motif, the "mellow fruitfulness" of the "season of mists," replaces *Asphodel's* repetition of "gaudy melon flower," an image from
Browning's "Home-Thoughts from Abroad."[32] Keats's "To Autumn"
provides the images of harvest instead of Browning's autumn in "The
Englishman in Italy." Herrick's vow of eternal love in "To Anthea"
appears instead of the related final lines from Browning's " 'De Gustibus
–' ": "Such lovers old are I and she: / So it always was, so shall ever
be!" (*Poetical Works* 179). These lines, which do not appear in either
Madrigal or *Asphodel,* may nonetheless hover beneath the surface of Herrick's "Bid me to love, and I will give / A loving heart to thee / . . . /
Or bid me die, and I will dare / E'en Death, to die for thee." The lines
from " 'De Gustibus –' " that immediately precede the declaration of
love reveal the beloved to be "Italy" in lines that appear in both *Madrigal*
and *Asphodel:* "Open my heart and you will see / Graved inside of it,
'Italy' " (179). But in *Madrigal,* Browning's name, fully present in *Asphodel,* has vanished. Curiously, poetry continues to mediate the Italian
memories of idyllic love in the minds of both Hermione and Julia, but
Keats and Herrick replace Browning as the overt intertexts signifying
love.

The dissolution and remembered bliss of marriage undergo significant
change in the revision process from *Asphodel* to *Madrigal*. While *Madrigal*
measures the disintegration of the marriage in a succession of increasingly
disastrous leaves, *Asphodel* focuses on one leave, in which a series of
painful events occur that appear as displaced trace memories in *Madrigal*.
Chapter 3, 4, and 5 of *Asphodel* – the core of the marriage story – center
on a party Hermione arranges for Darrington, an event that becomes a
hedonistic orgy of alcohol and kisses, an "over the top" on the home
front. The beautifully enticing Merry Dalton returns after the party for
shelter, which she gets in full measure as Darrington leaves his wife's
bed and makes love to Merry on the nearby couch. The morning after,
Hermione represses her sorrow, insists to Darrington that it is all right,
and achieves a moment of bliss with him before he leaves for the front.
Nonetheless, she refuses to be Penelope and leaves home for a friend's,
where she meets Vane (Chapter 6). During a subsequent leave, narrated
in Chapter 7, Darrington turns to another beautiful woman, Louise
Blake, for whom he later leaves Hermione in Chapter 14.

This constellation of betrayal, reconciliation, and betrayal is reformulated in *Madrigal* – as if the dream-work had subjected the "draft" to the processes of condensation, displacement, and secondary revision. *Asphodel*'s extended, hedonistic, nihilist party reappears briefly in *Madrigal* in the "wild people at the party" for whom Rafe "shows off" by kicking "the books across the floor" (48).[33] Darrington's explicitly rendered fling with Merry appears cryptically in *Madrigal* as part of Julia's silent thoughts: "She could not tell Rafe that it was the casual taking-for-granted of Morgan coming in and spending the night, of her way of throwing her arms about Rafe that had started the whole thing [the succession of affairs]" (67). The painful process of Hermione's morning-after forgiveness for Darrington's pleasure with Merry is projected into Julia's tortured thoughts about Bella, whose care for Rafe's body frees him to be with Julia without pressuring her for sex. The moment of perfection between Hermione and Darrington is replayed in moments of "paradise" ("there was only now" [73]) that Julia and Rafe share in Chapters 2, 4, and 5. Bella in *Madrigal* is a conflation of Merry and Louise in *Asphodel*. Julia in *Madrigal* is pitted against one femme fatale, unlike Hermione who confronts a range of conventionally feminine women. In contrast to the condensed, concentrated marriage story of *Madrigal*, *Asphodel* is diffuse, an excess.

Madrigal's repression of Browning and condensation of *Asphodel*'s affairs signal an underlying shift in the marriage story from the earlier text to the later one, a change that embeds a different kind of social critique. Where *Madrigal* stresses Rafe's conflict between his love for Julia and his desire for Bella, *Asphodel* emphasizes Darrington's abandonment of his own difference from the masculinist norm. In *Madrigal*, Rafe betrays Julia with and for another woman. In *Asphodel*, Darrington betrays Hermione by betraying himself. The dominant erotic structure in *Madrigal* is triadic, consistent with the conventional narratives of courtship and adultery. The diffused affairs in *Asphodel* leave a dyadic structure in place. What dominates the marriage story is not a triangle, but rather a *couple* from which Darrington gradually withdraws because of the war.

The replacement of Browning with Keats and Herrick reinforces the move from a dyadic to a triadic narrative. Browning's marriage to a poet whose work he revered made him "different" as a man from poets like Keats and Herrick, whose work fixed WOMAN in the position of muse and lover, never poet. Browning's belief in and support of Elizabeth Barrett freed her from her father's jealous tyranny, a liberation symbolized by their residence in Italy, where Barrett Browning could work *and* love in an erotic and aesthetic companionship with her husband. *Asphodel*'s emphasis on "The Englishman in Italy" and the poem's erasure from *Madrigal* may be connected to Browning's difference. The "Englishman" expresses his love by *telling* stories, not by demanding sex

("Fortù, Fortù, my beloved one / Sit here by my side"); the Italian idyll he reports centers on the companionate travels of himself and a young man. Hermione recalls her Italian travels with Darrington as just such companionship, and her pleasure in remembering them also centers in the telling. Darrington sits on the bed at her side reading the poem just as Browning's speaker sat at his beloved's side talking.

Like Browning, Darrington was "different," even in Part 1. His voice was "different," Hermione keeps noticing. His presence after the loss of Fayne and George is comforting; his daily letters under her door break her isolation; his support after Shirley's suicide is nurturing. Above all, he encourages her to write. While George "wants to – to – somehow suppress me," Darrington wants her to write (*Asphodel* I 115, 137, 140, 182, 194). "Darrington had given her words and the ability to cope with words, to write words," Hermione reflects after the war starts; "People had been asking her (just before the war) for poems, had written saying her things had power, individuality, genius. Darrington had done this" (II 13). In Part 1, Hermione had scarcely noticed the importance of Darrington's nurturance, and she became engaged out of fear, not love. But in the time gap between Part 1 and Part 2 (1912–15), which included their travels in Italy, love "happens" as a feeling fed by the love and work they shared in Italy. In Part 2, Hermione repeatedly associates this love with Amalfi, a reference to "The Englishman in Italy" and to one of Aldington's best known imagist poems, "Amalfi."[34] The "guns, guns, guns" of the air raid that drown out Darrington's voice as he reads about Amalfi shatter Amalfi itself, kill the part of Darrington that is different: "Amalfi's gone with that crash. . . . Amalfi. They've got Amalfi this time. The zeppelins and the anti-aircraft guns are both shattering Amalfi" (II 4). H.D.'s intensely personal poem "Evny," written during Aldington's military training and affair(s) in 1916, expresses the loss of Darrington's difference from a masculine norm that Hermione laments in *Asphodel*. The speaker is betrayed by the destructive transformation of her beloved into a man "more male than the sun-god":

> Could I have known
> you were more male than the sun-god,
> more hot, more intense,
> could I have known?
> for your glance all-enfolding,
> sympathetic, was selfless
> as a girl's glance.
>
> (*Collected Poems* 321)

Madrigal also laments the metamorphosis of Rafe from poet to soldier. "She had married him when he was another person," Julia thinks (16). But we learn far more about what that prewar "person" was not, than we do about what he had been. *Asphodel* highlights what is more muted in *Madrigal*, that the man Hermione had loved was boyish and tender until the war "made a man of him." In its critique of the masculine ethos, *Asphodel* anticipates Woolf's *Mrs. Dalloway*, in which Septimus, the sensitive poet, learns how not to feel as he becomes a successful soldier. *Asphodel*'s emphasis on Darrington's original difference and capitulation to "normal" masculinity anticipates as well the reverse process that Achilles undergoes as the "new mortal" in *Helen in Egypt*.[35] Instead of foregrounding the story of romantic rivalry, *Asphodel* focuses on the loss of difference. "I had liked you, loved you. That you were different," Hermione tells Darrington as they part (II 77). The sexual politics unveiled in *Madrigal* center on the home as battlefront as the war permeates love and shapes male representations of WOMAN into the binaries of muse and mistress, mother and lover. *Asphodel*, on the other hand, stresses the loss of the androgynous male companion in the mad procession of war, history's theft of what Adrienne Rich has called "the man-who-would-understand, / the lost brother, the twin" (*Dream* 62).

As significant as the marriage story is in Part 2 of *Asphodel*, the story of procreation overshadows the narrative of love and its discontents. As such, it serves even more dramatically as the textual unconscious for *Madrigal*, a relationship apparent in the resonance of the opening chapters of *Madrigal* and Part 2 of *Asphodel*. Both openings present Hermione/Julia in bed being cared for by Darrington/Rafe, whose tenderness (embodied in lines from Browning) turns to the desire for sex. Both center Hermione/Julia's thoughts on the stillbirth – recent for Hermione, two years earlier for Julia. Julia can remember the stillbirth only as "the gap in her consciousness, a sort of black hollow, a cave, a pit of blackness; black nebula . . . not yet concentrated out into clear thought" (12–13). Hermione's memory of delivery in *Asphodel* fills this gap, takes on the status of Julia's repressed memory in *Madrigal*. Julia's "pit of blackness" is a "gap in consciousness" filled by Hermione's memory of the cellar to which she was moved when the baby's birth was interrupted by bombs: "I know they took me into the cellar. I know the baby was dead. . . . Khaki killed it" (II 2, 3). Love and war, birth and death, are intertwined in both scenes, one of which serves as the repressed memory of the other.

Madrigal suppresses entirely the story of the second pregnancy, refusing even to specify directly that Vane is Julia's lover. But read intertextually with its "draft," the overt story of *creation* in *Madrigal* is unveiled as a covert story of *procreation* as well. In setting and spirit, *Madrigal*'s Chapter 9 directly parallels *Asphodel*'s Chapter 8. Both chapters present Hermione/Julia wandering over the rocks on the Cornwall coast, spiritually restored by her escape from the unreality of wartime London. Druidic,

even animistic, the rocks and gulls and flowers and trees near the sea
heal the battered spirit of both Hermione and Julia. Vane is an impresario
of freedom – in *Asphodel*, he is a tender lover; in *Madrigal*, he offers
solitude and a room of her own. The difference is instructive, for in
Asphodel, Hermione gets pregnant; in *Madrigal*, Julia starts to write again.

Images for pregnancy, fully developed in *Asphodel*, reappear in *Madrigal*
without a clue to their procreative origins, suggesting in their new context the (re)birth of the writer. Hermione, for example, was a "cocoon
for the enfolding of a spirit," a "cocoon . . . that had trapped a butterfly,
that had trapped a thing that would soon be a butterfly" (II 91, 131).[36]
Julia "hugged her old coat tight, hugging herself tight, rejoicing in herself, butterfly in cocoon" (151). Rejecting Vane as her baby's "real"
father, Hermione identifies with a syncretist tradition of "wise virgins"
impregnated by a god: "Mystery had stooped, had embraced, had wel-
comed her" (II 95). She is "like Madonna was (like a charwoman was,
like the mother of Caesarion was) alone" (II 150). In a parallel passage,
Julia thinks "the very Holy Spirit had breathed on this. . . . She was filled
literally now with that divine Spirit" (145, 147). The divine "enters"
Hermione through the agency of the bright sun on the rockscape; for
Julia, it is a "healing mist" that breathes into her (145). Near term,
Hermione is "flowering in a crystal globe," while Julia is "enclosed in
crystal" (II 119; *Madrigal* 141). Both women see themselves as witches,
seers, and priestesses – all regenerative figures of power. "Morgan le
Fay," Hermione thinks. "I am witch. I have made this thing. . . . I am
priestess, infallible, inviolate. I am chosen" (II 100, 86). Julia echoes: "She
was Medea of some blessed incarnation, a witch with power. A wise
woman. She was seer, see-er . . . wise-woman with her witch-ball, the
world" (147). The switch to Medea from Morgan le Fay, the mother of
an illicit babe, is significant. Abandoned by her husband, Medea killed
her children, prefiguring *Madrigal*'s "killing" of the pregnancy through
repression and sublimation. Morgan in *Madrigal* is the name H.D. gave
the Brigit Patmore figure, a Circe who initiates the theft of Rafe by the
femme fatale. In *Asphodel*, Morgan is an identity Hermione claims to
affirm her power as mother.

Asphodel's introduction of the mother-story into *Madrigal*'s lover-story
alters the critique of history. *Asphodel* reveals that *Madrigal* has not only
a textual unconscious centered in pregnancy, but also a political unconscious focused on the meaning of procreation in and for the social order,
specifically for the societal structures of violence. *Asphodel*'s narrative of
pregnancy and birth is inseparable from its story of the war, in two
seemingly contradictory ways. First, H.D. paralleled war and pregnancy
as public and private versions of an underlying patriarchal structure.
Second, she proposed women's procreative power as a counterweight

to men's violence, as a regenerative force in the (re)birth of both individual and society. Ultimately, these contradictory perspectives on procreation complement each other by showing how war externalizes sexual
politics, how women as the repressed of history return again and again
to participate in and disrupt its (re)production.

The parallels between birth and war pervade the novel's structure and
imagery. Like H.D., Hermione becomes pregnant at the same time the
war begins, in August of 1914, a coincidence given symbolic weight in
the novel. The death of the baby is linked literally and figuratively with
the war. "Men and guns, women and babies," Hermione thinks; "she
had had a baby in an air raid just like Daily Mail atrocities" (II 16, 17).[37]
The baby's stillbirth in an air raid functions as oracle and emblem for
civilization itself, caught in a "waste land," a "no man's land" of sterility
and violence. Hermione's metonymic statement "Khaki killed it" applies
directly to the child and more figuratively to what the child represents,
the lost renewal of civilization (II 2–4).

Inscribing the analogy, images of entrapment and "splitting" appear
repeatedly for both the war and Hermione's pregnancies. "The world
was caught as she had been caught," Hermione reflects during the air
raid (II 13). "I feel Europe is splitting like that [Browning's] pomegranate
in halves on the tree, Europe, all of it that I so love," she tells Darrington
(II 5). Pregnant again, she becomes the pomegranate whose splitting
open sealed Koré's doom in the Underworld. "She had been Dryad in
the old days," Hermione thinks, "before the earth opened and left part
on one side, part on the other" (II 18). Near the end of her pregnancy,
Beryl's piercing eyes are "splitting open a chrysalis, now so soon itself
to be split . . . for now the chrysalis was so near, only a little while" (II
135). The weary waiting in the last few weeks makes Hermione feel like
a soldier waiting for battle or sitting dazed on a park bench. Both are
"wounded," pounded by "beat, beat, beat of pulse, that was beat, beat
of guns that was going on" (II 141). Both are forgotten: "We never hear
about Madonna and her weary waiting and all that and we never hear
about blue soldiers on the bench" (II 143). Childbirth itself is going "over
the top," an expression borrowed from the suicidal charges soldiers had
to make in leaping out of the relative safety of the trenches into the
attempt to take a few more feet of territory (II 32, 37, 153, 159, 160).
Like death, the actual birth of the baby in 1919 is represented as a gap
in the text, a silent and blank space that cannot be filled with words (II
166).

Pregnancy and birth as violence to the mother's body, as a confrontation with death analogous to a soldier's going over the top, helps to
explain the parallel H.D. made in *Asphodel.* But as Nancy Huston's
probing psychohistory in "The Matrix of War: Mothers and Heroes"

argues, "the social contract requires" the "symbolic equivalence between childbirth and war," that "every member of each sex pay his or her tithe of suffering: women are required to breed, just as men are required to brawl" (127, 134). Huston's notion of reciprocal metaphorization suggests that the fundamental binary of civilization is not men and women, but heroes and mothers. Men express their virility through aggression while women express their power through birth. Did men first make war, Huston asked, out of womb envy, to find an arena of their own to express the awesome power of the birthing woman?

Asphodel anticipates Huston's provocative questions. In H.D.'s "symbolic equivalence between childbirth and war" lies a critique of the social organization of sexual difference. Women's (re)production of babies is part of the larger symbiotic system in which men produce wars. In choosing not to abort, Hermione thinks that "it was a mangy sort of choice for she couldn't help it. It was like 'yes I joined the army as a volunteer' " (II 111). Both mother and soldier are caught in a web they cannot control. Moreover, in producing sons that they send to war, mothers are complicitous in the production of war itself. Hermione regards with horror how everyone, including mothers, is caught in making war:

> We are in it. Killing and being killed. Obscene rows of suppressed women, not women, but some of them have lost sons. . . . and being sorry that they had lost sons and the other half saying but damn, damn, damn, why did you let them go, why did you let them go? You have lost sons but what have they lost, what have *we* lost? . . . O but you gave them life. I know, mothers, mothers, mothers. But I am a mother. I mean I am not, was not. (II 22, 30)

Asphodel, however, explores the opposition between procreation and war as well as its correspondence. Indeed, what moves the linear narrative of Part 2 is an agonistic struggle between the war and a pregnant woman, which she eventually "wins." The woman whose stillbirth in 1915 symbolizes the power and sterility of war defiantly and successfully gives birth in 1919. Rejecting both Darrington and Vane as the "father" of her child, she recasts herself as a mortal woman impregnated by the Divine. She legitimates her illegitimate child by affirming a parthenogenic conception − "God had swept across her white clean body" as the sun embraces her where she sits on the rocks (93). She refuses the role of the faithful Penelope and denies the image of "faithless wife" who cheated on her soldier husband (II 62, 81). Instead, she claims the position and power of the witch − the witch as Maid in Part 1 (Joan of Arc) becomes the witch as Mother in Part 2 (Morgan le Fay). Her "morganlefayish" smile is the dominant motif of her pregnancy and sign of her magic in the Druidic landscape of Cornwall. As Morgan le Fay, Hermione sees men as a danger and her pregnancy as her protection:

> God has told you some of his little secrets [the pregnancy] but you are in a world of men and men can blight you, men can ruin you. . . . Men, men, men, men. There were thousands of men. War dripped its rose-red petals, life upon life and love upon love and lilies rose up across the broken trenches. . . . Must she go back to men, men, men? Men could mar or make her. Men could not. Men could do nothing to her for a butterfly, a soft and luminous moth larvae was keeping her safe. She was stronger than men, men, men – she was stronger than guns, guns, guns. (II 105–8)

The repetitions of Hermione's discourse are linguistic reflections of the web Morgan is weaving to protect both her child and herself against the war. The discourse of pregnancy in *Asphodel* is consistently lyric and rhythmic, repetitious and hypnotic, an eruption of the Kristevan Semiotic into the Symbolic – in H.D.'s text, not only inscribing the daughter's longing for the maternal body, but also representing the mother speaking. Pregnancy is represented as a textual labyrinth, a spell that counters both the power of war and the discourse of men in which the speech of a pregnant woman has no place. Hermione had tried to talk to Darrington about the stillbirth in associative, near-delirious terms. He told her repeatedly, "Hush," "Don't talk." Hermione was unable to utter a direct announcement of her second pregnancy to Beryl. The conventions of dominant discourse provide no language in which to speak as pregnant subject. But Hermione's interior monologues about pregnancy create an alternative discourse, one characterized by a linguistic and rhythmic experimentation that deconstructs the opposition of subject and object and anticipates contemporary theories of *écriture féminine*.

A mirror stage of sorts sets in motion the affair with Vane that leads to pregnancy and procreative discourse. Hermione decides to join Vane in Cornwall at the moment when she contemplates her image in the mirror: "Then staring in the mirror she saw herself, saw herself, yes, she was somehow dehumanized. . . . Who was Mrs. Darrington? Mrs. Darrington was a bit of earth and someone, someone else had stepped out of Mrs. Darrington. Mrs. Darrington was a trench, wide and deep and someone else had stepped out and was out and wasn't Mrs. Darrington" (II 67). But instead of identifying with her image in the Lacanian sense, Hermione recognizes "Mrs. Darrington" as the false imago, as the socially constructed self out of which the woman who will be the mother steps. Tasting wine signals this woman's abandonment of the alienating imago and initiates the procreative discourse that prefigures her coming pregnancy:

> You tasted grape and grape and gold grape (can you imagine it?) and gold on gold and gold filled your palate, pushed against your mouth, pushed down your throat, filled you with some divine web, a spider, gold web and you wove with it, wove with it, wove with the web inside you, wove outward images and saw yourself opposite smiling with eyes uptilted, smiling at something that had crept out of Mrs. Darrington, small, not very good, looking at you in a glass, tall, very tall, not very good, divine like a great lily. Someone, something was looking at something and someone, something was smiling at someone. Wine went to your brain and you knew there was no division now and there was someone, one left, just one left like yourself who was dead and not dead who was alone and not alone. (68–9)

The absence of division between self and other, the presence of an indeterminate "you" and split subject, the "something that had crept out of Mrs. Darrington, small," and the one "like yourself who was dead and not dead" foreshadow pregnancy to come. The spider, web, weaving, gold, and lily reappear interwoven with gulls, swallows, bees, frogs, butterflies, and rings to signify a pregnancy that can only be indirectly imaged, not directly articulated. The repetitive, hypnotic weave of words initiates the discourse of pregnancy that punctuates the nine months of gestation. Near term, Hermione moves to a "little hut," itself a womb:

> Weave, that is your metier, Morgan le Fay, weave subtly, weave grape-green by grape-silver and let your voice weave songs, songs in the little hut that gets so blithely cold, cold with such clarity that you are like a flower of green-grape flowering in a crystal globe, in an ice globe for the air that you breathe into your lungs makes you too part of the crystal, you are part of the air, part of the crystal.... (II 119)

Weaving both song and baby out of her own body, Hermione is a "spider" who is container and contained. Confined by the pregnancy, she is also the cocoon that births a butterfly: "Hermione was a cocoon, a blur of gold and gilt, a gauze net that had trapped a butterfly, that had trapped a thing that would soon be a butterfly.... Herself had woven herself an aura, a net, a soft and luminous cocoon" (II 136, 146). Boundaries and distinctions of the Symbolic order vanish in the fluid oscillations of pregnancy:

> There is God in one and God out of one and now that God is in me. I feel no difference between in and out. Something had happened to me, whatever the oracle may say, I know already something has happened to me. But I'll ask it, for inside and outside are the same, God in and out, all gold, gorse, pollen–dust, gold and gold of rayed light slanting across the low spikes of white orchid and fragrance in and out. ... (II 87–8)

The symptoms of pregnancy not only disorient, but also induce a discourse without Symbolic signification. Words as sound, sight, color,

rhythm, and smell flood the words as signifiers of meaning. The play
on "in and out," "inside and outside," is a startling anticipation of and
variation on Derrida's concept of "hymenal" discourse, the inscription
of a simultaneous enfolding and enfolded, inside and outside that deconstructs the difference upon which phallogocentrism depends.[38] The
uterus in H.D.'s text displaces the hymen in Derrida's text as a literal
and figurative site of deconstructive power. The woman as speaking
mother, not the woman as silent virgin, disrupts the binary system of
patriarchy. Pregnancy makes Hermione both mother and babe, inside
and outside:

> The symptoms made her realize that she was not so neatly a painted
> box, a neat coffin for its keeping. She was being disorganized as the
> parchment-like plain substance of the germ that holds the butterfly
> becomes fluid, inchoate, as the very tight bond of her germination
> became inchoate, frog-shaped small greedy domineering monster. The
> thing within her made her one with frogs, with eels. She was animal,
> reptile. . . . eel-Hermione . . . alligator-Hermione . . . sea-gull Hermione
> . . . She wanted what an animal wants, what an eel wants, what even a
> bird must have. She didn't want the letter of the covenant. (II 100)

As container, Hermione shelters the developing babe who is and is
not her own body. As contained, she is confined by the fetal ambush on
her body. She is also nourished by feeding the "thing" that is and is not
herself. The birth of the baby births the mother as well, not only because
the child gives her a new identity, but also because she is pregnant with
herself. The baby mothers the self that is healed in the act of procreation.
She is both cocoon and butterfly. Images for the baby become images
for the self – the self reborn out of the destruction of the war. She is a
fetus "trying to get out, trying to get away, worse than having a baby
a real one, herself in herself trying to be born, pain that tore and wracked
and what was there to do? . . . Soul beating and tearing, why don't you
get born?" (II 75–6). The baby is a "lily bud," and so is its mother: "In
a vision, I saw myself grow up against myself and knew in a few days
the white lily bud would strike the top of my head which is my brain,
which is my skull. . . . the lily of me grew up and up and up" (II 85–6).
Before the birth, Hermione thinks, "Self is a lotus bud slimed over in
mud" (II 136). The birth narrative of *Asphodel* reveals the (re)birth of
the "dead" mother through the agency of her own procreation.

The procreative politics of *Asphodel* is not a valorization of motherhood, but rather the basis for a pacifist critique of the patriarchal order,
one that anticipates the kind of pacifism later promoted by Woolf in
Three Guineas and developed by H.D. herself in *Trilogy* and *Helen in
Egypt*. This pacifism did not advocate an absolutist refusal to fight under
any circumstances – although she never got caught up in the war fever

of World War I, H.D. certainly supported the war effort to defeat Hitler. Instead, H.D. suggested that the structure of the social order makes war inevitable. The analogue between childbearing and fighting, as well as Hermione's anguish about mothers sending sons to war, critiques the sexual division of labor that leads to both women and men playing their symbiotic parts in the cycles of violence. Even a "just war," H.D. was to say in *Trilogy* and *Helen in Egypt,* makes victims and victimizers of everyone. Conversely, Hermione's pregnant birth opposes the sterility of war with the fertility of peace, the power of men with the witchcraft of women: "she was stronger than men, men, men – she was stronger than guns, guns, guns" (II 114, 111). At the same time H.D. was writing *Asphodel,* Lawrence was formulating his phallic politics of salvation – regeneration through the return of the repressed phallus.[39] H.D., in contrast, envisioned the rebirth of civilization and the self through the return of the repressed womb.

Madrigal and *Asphodel* can be read as a layered inscription of the psyche whose creation emerges in the (pro)creation of its texts. *Asphodel*'s private story of the scandalous mother is repressed and sublimated into the public story of the acclaimed poet in *Madrigal.* But the stories of *creation* and *procreation* are complementary, not contradictory. Together, they establish a (pro)creative poetic akin to the one promoted in *Notes on Thought and Vision* and pervasively present in *Trilogy* and *Hermetic Definition.* In *Trilogy,* the Lady who brings visions of (re)birth in the midst of war incarnates the Mother Goddess whose Child is the poet's book. In *Hermetic Definition,* a poem about its own creation, the poet (pro)creates the poem in which she is "pregnant" with both her self and her child/poem.[40] As parts of a composite, (pro)creative text, *Asphodel* and *Madrigal* paved the way for the mother/muse and poet/mother figures of H.D.'s later poetry.

III. PAINT IT TO-DAY: *ARTEMISIAN DESIRE AND DISCOURSE*

Herself is that dart.

H.D., "The Master"
(*Collected Poems* 456)

Asphodel restores the story of the mother to *Madrigal* from which it was censored for both personal and literary reasons. Representing an even more forbidden layer of the psyche, *Paint It To-Day* restores to both *Asphodel* and *Madrigal* the story of the sister–lover that is marginally present in the former and absent almost without trace from the latter. Like *Madrigal, Asphodel* has a "black hole" into which *Paint It To-Day* disappeared: Hermione in *Asphodel* "realized now in a moment a great gap. There was a gap. A gap that must be filled" (II 153). The "gap" in *Asphodel* that *Paint It To-Day* fills is the narrative of lesbian love posed as a viable alternative to heterosexual desire and marriage. This sister-love does exist in *Asphodel,* but only as the novel's frame, its beginning and end. *Asphodel* opens with the unit of a mother and two "daughters," Fayne and Hermione, whose sister-love Hermione tries unsuccessfully to perpetuate. *Asphodel* closes with the unit of two mothers and a daughter, Hermione and Beryl, whose commitment to the baby is their hold on life. But the narrative movement of both Part 1 and Part 2 centers on the interrelated, heterosexual stories of courtship, marriage, and motherhood. The lesbian love that frames *Asphodel* is the dominant subject of narration in *Paint It To-Day.* The point of narrative stasis in *Asphodel* is the process of narrative kinesis in *Paint It To-Day.* The story of Midget's love for "the friend," Josepha, flows almost without break into the narrative of Midget's relationship with "the white Althea." Midget's connection to "the erstwhile fiancé," Raymond, and marriage to "the companion," Basil, enter the story in muted form, as accessories to the dominant lesbian plot. Consequently, *Paint It To-Day* challenges the sexual politics of the heterosexual family from outside, instead of from within, as the later novels do. As the repressed political unconscious of *Asphodel* and *Madrigal, Paint It To-Day*'s critique of the social order, of history, focuses on what Rich has called compulsory heterosexuality – the institutionalization of the heterosexual family essential to patriarchy. Countering an androcentric social construction of desire, *Paint It To-Day* proposes a lesbian matrix of sister-love that implies an alternative reality to a world caught up in unending cycles of violence.

Artemis is the ruling presence in *Paint It To-Day,* the liminal spirit hovering on the textual threshold who governs its authorial, narrative, and symbolic structures. Her importance in the novel reflects her larger significance in a cluster of texts and in a network of relationships with women that H.D. developed in the 1910s and 1920s.[41] By the time she wrote *Paint It To-Day,* H.D. had already translated choruses from two Euripidean tragedies in which Artemis features centrally. She had also written the sequence of related Phaedra poems about Artemis and Aphrodite that served as the initial core for her verse drama, *Hippolytus Temporizes,* an adaptation of Euripides's *Hippolytus* that she began as early as 1923 and published in 1927. In all of these texts, H.D.'s Artemis is a figure of female independence and rebellion against the desire of men. Her inviolate chastity represents a female desire for freedom, the escape from the sheltered garden of domesticated love for the wilderness of space without men. H.D.'s Artemis is a *presence* in her texts that crystallizes a lesbian refusal to accept an androcentric construction of desire.

The Artemis of *Hippolytus Temporizes* directly states what is more implicit in *Paint It To-Day*.[42] She laments Hippolytus's reverent fervor, his worship and pursuit: "Alas, / alas, / alas, / I would escape from all men's songs / and praying" (17). He announces that he is "Hot on the trail, / hot, / hot, in my desire / to trace you in the forest /. . . . / I follow and I share abandonment / with Artemis" (20–21). But she responds, "None share / but womankind" (21). When he counters that his Amazon mother Hippolyta still lives within him ("Hippolyta is my arrow-point, / my spear"), Artemis rejects his plea, tells him "You desecrate," and mourns that "Hippolyta, / my friend, / chaste queen and ally, / valiant and fervid amazon / is dead" (24, 28). Even more than the Euripidean or traditional Artemis, H.D.'s Artemis yearns for a wild space outside the circle of man's desire, look, and touch.[43]

This wilderness in which H.D.'s Artemis roams in a series of her texts is pastoral in nature, a specifically lesbian pastoral based in the desire for a space outside culture, beyond the power of men and the compulsion to marry.[44] Such an idealized pastoral scene exists as one pole within a binary system that contains its opposite, the realm of culture in which men hold sway. The landscape of H.D.'s 1915 poem "Huntress" is the wilderness of Artemisian desire that negates the world in which it was composed: "Come, blunt your spear with us, / our pace is hot / and our bare heels / in the heel-prints – /. . . / our feet cut into the crust / as with spears" (*Collected Poems* 23–4). In "Hymen," H.D.'s Epithalamian, the maidens of Artemis mournfully prepare their sister for the rites of marriage as if for death. "Never more will the wind / Cherish you again, / Never more will the rain," they lament in choral union. The prose voice continues their "wistful notes":

> *Free and wild, like the wood-maidens of Artemis, is this last group of four – very straight with heads tossed back. They sing in rich, free, swift notes. They move swiftly. . . . Their hair is loose and rayed out like that of the sun-god. They are boyish in shape and gesture. They carry hyacinths in baskets, strapped like quivers to their backs. They reach to draw the flower sprays from the baskets as the Huntress her arrows. . . . they dart swiftly to and fro. . . .*
> *(Collected Poems* 104)[45]

The rhetoric of H.D.'s Artemisian pastorals was part of a "common language" (to echo Rich) she developed with other women – to some extent with Gregg and Marianne Moore, to a great degree with Bryher. Gregg's few published poems often have a generalized animistic landscape with ritualized flowers and an archaic sacred presence. "Iris," published in *Others* in 1915, begins "Ah, / bow your head, white sword flower, / Lest you pierce the thing you would save, / Lest your white beauty slay me."[46] Much more distinct from H.D.'s than Gregg's, Moore's early poetic discourse shared a fascination for untamed landscapes concretely observed. The language of an Artemisian spear-play pervades the letters and reviews Moore and H.D. wrote back and forth to and for each other. As Alicia Ostriker has argued, this rhetoric of battle demonstrates the necessity they felt as women poets to fight for a place in the world of letters ("What Do Women [Poets] Want?" 481–2). Privately, H.D. invited Moore to stay with her (and Aldington) in England:

> I know, more or less, what you are up against, though I escaped some five years ago! – There are terrible difficulties and discouragements to be met on this side, too – But at least, it is a fight – there is something definite To fight! I felt so terribly when I was in U.S.A., the putty that met my whet[t]ed lance! (21 August 1915)

Publicly, she wrote of Moore's poems in *The Egoist:*

> And if Miss Moore is laughing at us, it is laughter that catches us, that holds, fascinates and half-paralyses us, as light flashed from a very fine steel blade, wielded playfully, ironically, with all the fine shades of thrust and counter-thrust, with absolute surety and with absolute disdain. Yet with all the assurance [sic] of the perfect swordsman. . . ." ("Marianne Moore" 118)

In her review of *Hymen,* Moore responded in kind:

> Talk of weapons and the tendency to match one's intellectual and emotional vigor with the violence of nature, give a martial, an apparently masculine tone to such writing as H.D.'s, the more so that women are regarded as belonging necessarily to either of two classes – that of the intellectual freelance or that of the eternally sleeping beauty. . . . preeminently in the case of H.D., we have the intellectual, social woman, nonpublic and "feminine." There is, however, a connection between weapons and beauty. Cowardice and beauty are at swords' points and in H.D.'s work . . . we have heroics which do not confuse transcendence with domination. . . . (*Complete Prose* 82)

A shared Artemisian discourse is more extensively evident in the case of H.D. and Bryher, especially during the early 1920s, the period of their most intense intimacy. Bryher's *Two Selves* (1923) climaxes with an account of her persona Nancy's first meeting with her beloved poet in Cornwall: "A tall figure opened the door. Young. A spear flower if a spear could bloom. She looked up into eyes that had the sea in them, the fire and colour and the splendour of it. A voice all wind and gull notes said: 'I was waiting for you to come' " (126). Anticipating the title of her memoir *The Heart to Artemis* (1963), Bryher published a volume of poems entitled *Arrow Music* at about the same time H.D. wrote *Paint It To-Day.* "Amazon" is a love lyric written in H.D.'s Artemisian discourse:

> The closed bud of dawn opens on your face.
> The thong of my javelin

is not as supple as your arm.
You have torn your limbs
with spines of gorse-flower, bramble and cytisus.
I remember
wind, April, the black rain.

(12)

"Eos," a poem almost certainly written for H.D., also features the fierce
beauty of the Huntress, but is less chaste, more openly erotic than H.D.'s
Artemisian language:

Your face is the flush of Eos:
You are dawn.
Your face is Greece.

Under your lifted arm
There is lavender to kiss;
Sea-lavender, spiced with salt.

Before the fierce cyclamen wine has burnt my lips
I kiss your limbs, wild followers of Artemis.

Your eyes break sleep!
I touch the pansy set below your heart;
Each kiss a star
That fades upon your body, which is dawn.

April scene of your throat,
O spiced flowers of your shoulders,
Will you shrink from the lion, my heart?

(16)[47]

H.D. probably began *Paint It To-Day* shortly after or even during her
visit to the States with Bryher, where the two women became intimate
friends with Moore before they went to California. In the Carmel Highlands in the winter of 1920–1, as Diana Collecott has described, H.D.
and Bryher played out their fantasy of a lesbian pastoral. They wore
"trousers" and explored the rocky and mountainous seascape. They
bathed nude and took photos of each other in the woods, rock pools,
and cliffs of the coast. Greece was still vividly in their minds, since they
had traveled there together in the spring of 1920. The Carmel Highlands
was a healing Arcadian landscape, a wilderness in the modern world still
recovering from the war.[48] By April of 1921, H.D. wrote to Moore
about *Paint It To-Day*, clearly connecting its landscape with her trip to
the States and placing Moore firmly in its world: "I am busy on a sort
of prose-poem novel. . . . *You* are one of the tribe to which these two
girls, Josepha and Midget, belong" (11 April 1921).

Paint It To-Day, then, emerged out of an Artemisian matrix of female
companionship, poetic affinities, and love, which in turn helped shape

the discourse of the novel. Artemis is invoked directly in *Paint It To-Day* at several key points in the narrative. She first appears in Chapter 1 ("Morning and Evening Star") as guardian, along with Hera, of Midget's girlhood. The goddesses take human form in the "wonderful and goddess-like" shapes of Midget's neighbors, "Olive and Cornelia, like a young Hera and Artemis, the one mothering, the other championing the games and hunts and expeditions" (445). Hera, the mothering force, largely drops out of *Paint It To-Day* to resurface later in *Asphodel*. Artemis dominates the unfolding story of Midget in *Paint It To-Day*. She is the "maid of Delos," the goddess of "weed and shells that clung to the amber weed-stems" in the "sea-wafted mist" and sand, the one to whom Midget alludes in her letter to the pregnant Josepha: "Has the maid of Delos departed from you now that you have your baby?" (V 18). In the final chapter, she inspires "a living prayer of the passion of swift feet, of the passion of struggling tall white young bodies, of the passion of intense young faces, uplifted to the dash of rain and the more cruel interpiercing of rare hail stones . . . that most passionate of passions, the innate chastity of the young, the living spirits of the untouched, sacred virgins of Artemis" (VIII 5). At the conclusion of the story, she is "the deity, the goddess of shaft and bow, standing in bronze . . . in the basin from which rises the pedestal she stands on," the one to whom Midget ultimately directs Althea in the novel's climactic moment (VIII 10).[49]

Less directly, Artemis is present in the authorial signature of *Paint It To-Day*. Helga Dart is the nom de plume on the novel's typescript, a choice that not only fleshes out "H.D." into a female body, but also suggests the attributes of power H.D. associated with Artemis. Echoing Hilda, which means battle maiden, Helga is also a Teutonic name, one that means holy. Dart suggests both a sharp, pointed object and a sudden, swift movement – the darting arrow of Artemis, the flash of her running feet. Dart is also a play on the French *d'art*. Hilda Doolittle, who became the poet H.D., is transformed into the novelist Helga Dart, – a holy, battle maiden *d'art*; a sacred virgin whose battle is art, whose spear is a pen or paintbrush. The impotence of Do-little has become the potency of Dart. Although H.D. abandoned the name Helga Dart for *Asphodel*, which has no name on the title page, and for *HER*, whose author has been softened into Helga Doorn, Dart remains as trace in the name Hermione Gart for the protagonist in both novels. Later, in "The Master," a poem written in direct response to Freud's concept of penis envy, H.D. affirmed that "*woman is perfect*," even without the phallus, for she "herself / is that dart and pulse of the male, / hands, feet, thighs, / herself perfect" (*Collected Poems* 456).

The Artemisian discourse of Helga Dart appropriates the martial language of the phallus to forge and defend a linguistic space outside the

gaze of men. Claire Buck has read this appropriation as evidence for the
Lacanian feminist view that women's difference and desire is unrepre-
sentable in language because of the inherently phallogocentric nature of
signification. Captured by what she tries to escape, the poet of "The
Master," according to Buck, can only reproduce her confinement within
an androcentric system of representation. However, we can read H.D.'s
Artemisian discourse within the context of Cixous's triple notion of *voler:*
to steal, to fly, to love. "Stealing" the martial language of men and
placing it within an exclusively female space and time potentially transforms the images into a source of flight – flight from man's power to
define woman, flight toward the expression of woman's desire. As H.D.
later wrote in *Trilogy* about the special bond between "thieves and poets,"
who share the patronage of Hermes, "steal then, O orator, / plunder,
O poet" (*Collected Poems* 547). Like Woolf in *To the Lighthouse,* H.D.'s
Artemisian discourse "steals" the language of the Father to defeat its own
representation of WOMAN.[50]

As an Artemisian force in the modern landscape, Helga Dart asserts
considerable authority in her text as a narrator distinct from the woman
whose story she tells. Unlike *Asphodel,* which lacks not only an authorial
signature, but also an identifiable narrator, *Paint It To-Day* has a self-
reflexive narrator who continually inserts herself into the narrative flow
to reflect on the act of writing and to posit abstract theories for which
the story serves as exemplum. The result is something of a textual anom-
aly, a hybrid that is, as DuPlessis has argued, part essay, part novel, part
poem.[51] The first two pages of the novel, for example, speculate on what
it means to "paint a portrait" in time, that is, create a narrative. At the
same time, the narrator initiates the narrative by introducing the protagonist in a discourse reminiscent of H.D.'s condensed imagist lyric.
To quote in part:

> A portrait, a painting? You can not paint to-day as you painted yes-
> terday. You cannot paint to-morrow as you paint to-day. A portrait,
> a painting? Do not paint it of yesterday's rapt and rigid formula nor of
> yesterday's day-after-tomorrow's criss-cross – jagged, geometric, pris-
> matic. . . .
>   The child itself, I would make dark cypress-wood, rounded head,
> claw-like hands, an archaic, small Hermione, a nameless foundling sister
> of princess Minne-ha-ha, a bird of intermediate, of a lost reptile race,
> clawing its way into the pear and wisteria tangle, to cling, to be lost,
> to defy worlds from there. . . .
>   A portrait? Paint it yesterday on porcelain, in print pinafore and
> leghorn wreathed with corn-flowers. Paint it to-day; colt-knees crawl-
> ing into the rabbit-hutch, scent of old straw and this morning's lettuce
> leaves and yesterday's half-gnawed carrot-tops and sprinklings of oats
> and stiff straws to print little, half perceived pricklings on the grimed
> knees and length of half-leg. . . .

> I find it a cold and perhaps thin and lifeless picture, this etching of a spirit. . . . But at the moment, I am attempting, not so much, to reproduce an atmosphere, a medley of conditions and circumstances and surroundings. . . . I am trying rather to give a picture of that being, that spider, that small hatched bird, that flawless shell that once contained an unborn being. (444–7)[52]

A portrait in time and space (narrative) comes from a point in time and space (narrator) – a today, not a yesterday or a tomorrow. That is, the narrator exists as a distinct voice at a moment in history that shapes her interpretation of the past. *Paint It To-Day* intensifies the split that is present to some degree in all autobiographical texts. Helga Dart, the "I now," paints a portrait of Midget, the "I then," one that reflects the historical moment of its composition, the immediate postwar world of H.D., Bryher, and Perdita. From this stance in time – the novel's "today" – Helga Dart pronounces, summarizes, interprets, exhorts, and interrupts her story with self-reflections. She delays all identification between herself and Midget until the third chapter. Throughout the text, she emphasizes the distance between the "I now" and the "I then" through a manipulation of tone that oscillates from heuristic and hortatory to lyric and hypnotic. As she records how Midget loved to sit in the Louvre looking at statues, for example, she interrupts Midget's gaze in a long, italicized discourse on art and desire, part of which reads:

> *We measure, or should measure, our capacity for life, (the depth in us for living) should be measured not by our power of attracting but by our power or possibilities of being attracted. The two, though, no doubt, like positive and negative electricities, are interdependent one on another. . . .*
> *A work of art is the materialization of the electric force of the artist, electric force plus the directing impetus of the intellect.* (VI 6)

An imperative exhortation, for another example, serves as the novel's hypnotically repeated refrain, one version of which reads in its fractured syntax: "– *quique amavit* – Whoever has loved. Whoever, whoever has loved. Has loved. In all the past has loved. Who was it that had loved?" (451). Helga Dart answers her own question authoritatively at a later point, clearly setting her Latin source against itself in privileging lesbian love:

> Cras amet qui numquam amavit,
> quique amavit, cras amet.
>
> To-morrow, let him love who never has guessed the meaning of love; whoever has loved, or in someway apprehended what love might be or become, let him to love, let him love to-morrow.
> The fiancé had shown Midget what love might be or become if one, in desperation, should accept the shadow of an understanding for an understanding itself. Josepha had shown her or she had shown Josepha what love was or could be or become if the earth, by some incautious

legerdemain should be swept from beneath our feet, and we were left ungravitated between the stars. (458)

Whatever the shifts in tone, the common denominator of *Paint It To-Day*'s Artemisian discourse is its self-authorizing insistence on how we should regard the past, the story Helga Dart narrates. This interpretive authority pervades the highly selective, controlled narrative as well. The story is indeed visualized as in a painting. A span of some thirty years is covered by fragmentary tableaux that suggest, rather than plot, movement in time. Some of these are moments that appear briefly as memories in *Asphodel* – such as the scene where Midget/Hermione bids Josepha/Fayne goodbye in Liverpool in 1911, or the Italian countryside where Midget/Hermione and Basil/Jerrold fall in love in 1913. Some directly parallel scenes in *Asphodel* – such as the taxi ride where "the finacé"/George convinces Midget/Hermione that she must not accompany Josepha/Fayne on her honeymoon trip. In toto, however, the tight narrative control of *Paint It To-Day* contrasts with the narrative excess of *Asphodel* in its more extreme denial of the marriage plot.

The spirit of H.D.'s Artemis governs the process of narrative selection, which in turn constructs the novel's lesbian hermeneutic of history. First, the novel's narrative frame – extended, authoritative commentary by Helga Dart – establishes a cyclical structure that disrupts the linear plot of the conventional *Bildungsroman*. Helga Dart initiates her "portrait" by imaging a child with "rounded head, claw-like hands...a bird or intermediate, of a lost reptile race" (445). This infant becomes, in Helga Dart's next tableau, the young Midget, who experiences her first epiphany, a moment of fecund revelation, when on "colt-knees crawling into the rabbit-hutch," she sees "a vision of eight pink bodies, eight unexpectedly furless and rigid bodies, to be lifted, one by one from the nest of tight packed straw, and cherished against a quivering cheek" (445). As child, she herself is cherished by "Olive and Cornelia, like a young Hera and Artemis" (445). Helga Dart finishes her portrait with a figurative and structural recapitulation of her first strokes. There are two women – Midget, newly (re)born and Althea – themselves in the position of Hera and Artemis. And there is a babe with clawlike hands whom Midget tenderly holds as she had once held the baby rabbits:

> A small amber coloured being crept into Midget's life, . . . a creature, white as a camelia, amber as a honey-bee, black as a gipsy's baby. . . . not to be believed yet easily proved as existent by cupping its firm black head in the hollow of a hand and watching it laugh, clutching with its humming-bird's claw. I have seen it with my own eyes the creature. I know that it exists. (VIII 13)

Circular narrative structures are by no means all lesbian in their construction of desire, nor, I would argue, are linear narratives all heterosexual. But *Paint It To-Day*'s spiral narrative, like that of *HER*, represents a lesbian critique of the androcentric and heterocentric structure of Oedipal narrative patterns.[53] Midget's *Bildung* moves from a wild and fertile female world, in which those who nurture are nurtured, to another wild and fertile female world, in which those who are born also give birth. It is a gynocentric world in which men are irrelevant.

Second, the story that Helga Dart tells is itself Artemisian. Midget's relationships with women form the emotional center and narrative movement of the novel, which highlights events in H.D.'s life from approximately 1911 to 1919. Chapters 1 and 2 focus entirely on Midget's relationship with Josepha, first in the States, then in Europe. "Morning and Evening Star," Chapter 1, builds to an epiphanic climax celebrating the women's love for each other. "Below Etaples," Chapter 2, takes the women to the avant-garde circles of France and England. There, "something in themselves" made "she and Josepha . . . separated, from the great mass of the people of the nations of the world," "separated from the separated too," different even from the artists "of the mid-layers of so called bohemia" (457). The final two chapters – 7 and 8 – also focus entirely on two women – Midget and Althea, alone in an unnamed landscape during Midget's recovery from the war years. Two men have some part to play in Chapters 3–6. They make their first appearances in generic form, stressing their role as *men,* delaying and repressing identification of their individuality. The Pound figure is "the youth" and "the erstwhile finacé" in Chapter 1, "the fiancé" in Chapter 3, and finally "the Raymond person," "the Raymond," "the erstwhile," and "Raymond" in Chapter 4. The Aldington figure is first "my companion" in Chapter 3 and then "Basil" in 4, 5, and 6. The other men portrayed in *Asphodel* and *Madrigal* are simply gone: Rummel, Cournos, Lawrence, Gray.

In spite of their evident importance as fiancé and husband, Raymond and Basil remain tangential to the main story of Midget and Josepha. Chapter 3 – *Cras Amet* – is set in the lush gardenscapes of Italy during the wanderings of Midget and Basil before their marriage. It is the scene repeatedly remembered, but not directly narrated in *Asphodel* and *Madrigal.* But the focus of their Italian idyll in *Paint It To-Day* is not their own romance, but rather Midget's grief for the loss of Josepha, who had returned to the States with her mother. The "love" of the Latin "whoever has loved" is lesbian, not heterosexual, in the "courtship" chapter. Chapter 4 ("Vulgar Details"), which culminates in Midget's engagement to Basil, similarly focuses on Midget's lost love for Josepha. The tripartite chapter opens with the taxi scene, Raymond's most extended "part" in the novel, in which he convinces Midget not to go to Germany with Josepha and her new husband because Josepha is really in love with someone else, a male poet. The second tableau features a moment of intimacy between Midget and Basil, the only one in the novel between a man and a woman. But their bond centers on Basil's intuitive understanding of what Midget was thinking about Josepha. Loving his "delicacy," Midget thinks, "I had never met anyone in my life before who understood the other half or the explanatory quarter of the part of the sentence I left unsaid" (469). The final scene is Midget's confrontation with her mother, her murderous desire to "kill" the woman who would stifle her daughter's spirit by imposing conventionality upon her. Her inability to hurt her mother by refusing to return to the States as her mother requests precipitates her engagement. In *Madrigal*, the marriage results from idyllic love; in *Asphodel*, the marriage follows the suicide of the aging Shirley, Hermione's double as an "old maid"; in *Paint It To-Day*, marriage to an Englishman is presented as a compromise between the mother's demand for a normative femininity in the States and the daughter's desire for lesbian freedom in Europe.

Even the two chapters covering the war years and the dissolution of the marriage – 5 and 6 – displace Basil and the story of triangulated desire to the periphery. The loss of Basil comes not from his defection to other women (no lovers are mentioned), but rather to patriotism and the fever of battle. Chapter 5 touches briefly on Basil's transformation from faun to soldier, but then focuses extensively on an exchange of hurtful and defensive letters between the pregnant Josepha and Midget about their meaning to each other. The "story" of Chapters 1–5 has been the love affair between the women. Chapter 6 – the only chapter that does not center on lesbian desire – serves as a transition between lesbian couples and, even more subversively, transforms Basil's significance to Midget into ultimate insignificance. Reflecting on the loss of his companionship, Midget recalls Basil reading to her Oscar Wilde's poem "Charmides" about a Greek boy who "fell in love with a statue" of Athena. She, Basil told her, was "sister of Charmides," a designation suggesting that she loved him without human passion, as if he were a statue: "She knew that she did not feel as he wanted her to feel with warmth and depth and warm intensity. She knew that if she felt at all it was not with warm but with cold intensity. She did not feel for Basil with that intensity. She was forever conscious of the fact. But the companionship was perfect" (VII 2). As in many of H.D.'s texts, heat is associated with heterosexual passion, while cool is connected to its opposite, a lesbian intensity in *Paint It To-Day*.[54]

The reference to Wilde's "Charmides," a homoerotic poem awash in the speaker's love for the boy whose story he tells, returns the "heterosexual" chapter about Midget and Basil back to a homosexual foundation of desire – especially when we recall Midget's first gaze at Josepha: "It was her eyes, set in the unwholesome face; it was the shoulders, a marble splendour, unspoiled by the severe draping of straight cut rainproof; it was her hand, small, unbending, stiff with archaic grandeur; it was her eyes, an unholy splendour" (448). The rest of the chapter repeats this move even more directly. Midget recalls loving a succession of statues in the Louvre and a museum in Rome: first the Venus de Milo; then statues of Jason and a discus thrower; and finally the Hermaphroditus in Paris, then Rome. Revising both the myth of Pygmalion and the story of Charmides, Midget's love for Hermaphroditus brings the statue to life: "This was a gentle breathing image, modelled in strange, soft, honey coloured stone. The small head lay on the perfect child like arm. It was a child, here in Rome, no monster. This was no 'double rose of love's' it was no rose at all. This was a spray of honey-flower caught in the shadow of a dark wall" (VI 12). This "child" recalls the child of Chapter 1 and the child of Chapter 8.[55] The statue is Midget herself as well as Josepha and Althea, signifying a love based on sameness, not difference.

A third man of great significance plays a key role in Chapter 5, but his importance depends greatly on the fact that he does not exist "in what, we might call real life" (VII 9). He is the unnamed poet/lover about whom Midget writes in her response to Josepha's cruel letter in Chapter 5, the one chapter devoted to the war years. Never appearing in the same textual plane of action with Basil or Raymond, he exists only in a narrative within a narrative – Helga Gart telling Midget's story of telling Josepha about her "distinguished" lover. Additionally, Midget's telling and its intertextual resonances call into question his reality and ultimately turn the heterosexual text back into a lesbian plot. Although she never names her lover, Midget hints that he is pure spirit, a visitation identified with Edgar Allan Poe whom she conjures as her "trick" to survive the onslaught of history.[56] War makes this visionary experience outside the body a spiritual necessity for Midget. Helga Dart's repetitive, staccato fragments set the scene:

> There was a war. A cloud. Five years. . . . Time had them by the throat. Time had the world by the throat, shaking and shaking, evil and vicious. Shaking the world till its head was numb and its heart wrenched from its body. Shaking and shaking and never letting it go. Until the world seemed mercifully past its agony, about to perish, and there was peace.
> A cloud. Five years. (V 1)

Trapped in and by history, Midget "found a new trick of seeing," a kind of visionary "dreaming" that Helga Dart likens to riding the crest of a tidal wave or existing as a "volcano, blazing and roaring beneath, but all the surface covered with snow and ash" (V 5–6) – as if Midget had become a visual text of Hokusai, the artist who appears emblematically in *HER*.

Just what Midget sees when she leaves her body, Helga Dart does not say. But Josepha's letter leads Midget to specify what Helga Dart had alluded to. The pregnant Josepha, after years of silence, writes to Midget to mock their former love – to say it wasn't real. As evidence, she taunts Midget's gullibility in believing Josepha's reports of "seeing" things: "Why did you always believe in all the lies I told you? . . . I never saw any of the things I pretended to see. . . . I liked you because I could tell you the most lies" (V 8–10). As an unhappy child, Josepha reminds Midget, she had learned to get attention and love by lying about "seeing" things. Midget's response is to say that "Now . . . I see things for myself," and she gives a lengthy account of her visions of her poet/lover that clearly indicates that he exists on a different plane, one to which she escapes to remove herself from the terrible war:

> I have a lover – not Basil.
> I don't see him very often, but I know he is there. He is a distinguished poet.
> I suppose you might say I was a spiritual prostitute, but I don't think so; no, I don't think so, because I have only one lover and he is a great poet.
> You might say that he is one of those evil things you read about in great tomes, who come and seduce women, those ghouls or whatever. You know what I mean, from Anatole France we read on the boat crossing. But he is not a ghoul. He is a spirit. He is a great poet. (V 12–13)

Midget's game with her reader, Josepha – and by extension all readers – is to reveal and conceal the identity of her lover, to play with our curiosity by deploying clues as she multiplies the mystery. She meets him in a forest, we learn, in a small Roman house with white columns on the porch, white stone floors, and a room with "a whortle-berry crimson blanket on the floor" (V 13). She is coy with him, as she is with us: "If my lover asks me to come into the room beyond, I run away at once" (V 13). She most prefers the house when he is not there, "then I sit in the sunlight in the porch and lean my head against a pillar and sleep. That is queer, isn't it? To sleep in one's sleep" (V 14). The mysteries abound: a lover from whom she flees, a dream within a dream. To tantalize, she describes him as "very like a cheap steel engraving of an idealized eighteenth century portrait of Catullus . . . (though I don't think my lover is Catullus)" (V 14). Doesn't she know for sure, we wonder?

To further the mystery, Midget suggests that her lover is her muse, a nameless projection of her mind that fosters her creative work:

> We simply meet by accident in the woods, or in the little house in the woods. We usually look and look at one another. Sometimes he says a poem. Sometimes it grows dark and my ecstasy becomes so great that I leave him there alone and come back to myself to my room and try to read and try to work. Sometimes, I write a poem. Of course, none as beautiful as his poems. (V 13)

But this description of their trysts abounds with contradictions that cannot be explained as a simple reversal of a male poet seeking inspiration of a female muse. The careful parallelisms of accidental meeting, looking, and poem-making stress a mutuality absent from the muse tradition. Intensified by her repetitive syntax, Midget appears to assert equivalences in the erotics of poetic inspiration. She is his muse; he is hers. As lovers, they are both poets and muses. But, the final fragment drops like a bombshell to reassert a masculine hierarchy, to remind us that the double subjects in this heterosexual affair inevitably fall back into (male) subject and (female) object. *He* is the "distinguished poet," she the satellite. Even as her imaginative creation, *he* has an identity more powerful than her own, one that crystallizes in her own mind the presence of male writers named in the text: Plato, Meleager, Theocritus, Catullus, Virgil, Shelley, Heine, Swinburne, Wilde, and Anatole France.

As the letter continues, Midget finally lets her poet's own words in "To Helen" unmask and name him: Poe, "the great" *poe(t)*, a successor of Catullus in the long line of love lyricists.[57] However, anticipating H.D.'s rescription of Pound's lyrics in *HER*, Midget re-places Poe's lines from a heterosexual into a lesbian scene of desire. Midget's Artemis supplants Poe's Aphrodite in the very words of his poem:

> When my lover wrote, "thy hyacinth hair, thy classic face," he was thinking of you when, that day, the morning and evening star sang. When he wrote, "Ah Psyche, from the regions which," he was thinking of me when I stand with my clothes off and admire myself, turned half side ways in the glass.
>
> Did my soul get transmuted here by some chance and does my body wait for it there with my lover? Will they come together some day, my soul and my body? . . .
>
> Do you remember the very first hyacinths were out that day your train left? Your arms were full of them and your eyes hated me above them and you seemed to say, " . . . you see there are other hyacinths than the ones you bring me."
>
> Yes, you tell lies, Josepha. There were never other hyacinths. Midget (V 15–16)

Poe's lines to his beloved in the image of Helen are split and redeployed to define first Josepha and then Midget herself. A supreme statement of heterosexual erotics serves the memory of lesbian love – first, the epiphany of their desire when "the morning and evening star sang" in Chapter

1 and then the moment of separation that led both to marriage. Poe's image of the hyacinths provides the occasion for dialectical transformation; for the hyacinth sprang from the blood of the beautiful youth Hyacinthus whom Apollo loved and accidentally killed. In the language of H.D.'s flowers, hyacinths often signal homoerotic desire, particularly of Artemisian maids who run wild in the fields and forests.[58] The association of her poe(t)/lover with Catullus also encodes a secret reference to lesbian desire. Catullus is most famous for a sequence of love lyrics he wrote charting his disastrous affair with a woman he called "Lesbia." While his poems to Lesbia are central to the tradition of the male love lyric in which the beloved is trapped as object of the poet's desire, Lesbia's name suggests her ultimate escape. There is no evidence to suggest that the woman Catullus loved was lesbian, or even bisexual; but the linguistic disguise he gives her evokes the lesbian poet Sappho, a resonance Aldington himself developed in his well-known imagist poem "Lesbia."[59]

Midget's transformation of Poe extends to his fusion of desire for Helen with the myth of Psyche to celebrate the return "home" to an imaginative Greece of the spirit. Psyche has frequently been equated with the soul, who must quest for the body (Eros, son of Aphrodite) she has lost. The union of the two has often been allegorized into a sacred, ecstatic, and mystical passion. Poe adapts the story to the erotics of the (male) love lyric in which the poet's desire for the untouchable and sacred muse – Helen, the most unattainable of women – fuels his poem. In related poems, such as "Annabel Lee" and "Ulalame," the death of the beloved intensifies the object status of WOMAN within this system of desire. The lady is unattainable because she is dead, a state beyond the poet's control that guarantees the perpetuation of desire and its by-product, poetic inspiration. The erotization of death reaches a fever pitch of sadomasochism in Poe's story "Ligeia," in which the narrator's desire conjures the spirit of his dead first wife (whom he loves) into the body of his dying second wife (whom he hates).[60]

Midget's play on Poe's Psyche signals her deconstruction of the male economy of desire, epitomized by his necromancy, and her reconstruction of a lesbian eros. The binaries of body and soul, conjurer and conjured, poet and muse, death and life are invoked only to be dismantled, with Midget reaching to occupy both positions in a world of hyacinthian desire. As conjurer, Midget raises the spirit of Poe, bringing him out of his age into her own. Her love draws him to her, much as the narrator in "Ligeia" conjures his dead wife, much as Helen draws the soul of the dead Achilles to her in *Helen in Egypt*. But, as conjurer, she is also conjured. Her "visits" to the house in the woods are a kind of astral projection into a dimension beyond death. Anticipating H.D.'s account in *The Gift* of her "trick" for surviving air raids in World War II, Midget's soul leaves her body for a dreamscape similar to that in Poe's own

"Dream-land."[61] But Midget also reverses this form of the Psyche myth to say that she has left her *soul* "here" (in ordinary space and time) and sends her *body* "there" to meet her lover in a spirit world: "I think it is my body that lives there and my soul here" (V 15). As the "real" world, "here" is also the land of the dead: "The present was dead. They were all dead" (V 2). As a fourth-dimensional world, "there" is a spirit world of living bodies who love. Will the two – body and soul, here and there – unite *in her,* she asks? As Psyche, she would also be Eros. The spirit world is material; the body is the soul.

The transformation of this deconstruction into an Artemisian Eros is completed in Chapters 7 and 8, in which the meetings of Midget and Althea recapitulate and supplant the meetings of Midget and her poet/ lover/muse. During "the period of recovery" after the war, Midget continues her "trick" of "seeing things" (VII 1). "A Zola or a de Goncourt," Helga Dart tells us, "would not have found her altogether a heroine, however, for a realistic novel. . . . Sometimes her thoughts in order to escape the battle of realities went, as I have tried to show you, far to[o?] far. In order to escape judging one way or the other, Midget went perilously far out of the track of realities" (VII 4–5). This time, however, she meets not Poe, but "the white Althea," who seems to reincarnate the spirit of a little Roman girl perfectly preserved and discovered in the Renaissance, or even "Heliodora, the girl Meleager of Alexandra loved" (VII 5). She "meets" with Althea in a "small temple" in the woods near the shore. Recalling the little "Roman" house in the woods where she "visited" her Poe(t), this has a "marble floor," a "porch set with white pillars," a "little hall," and an inner room with the same "whortle-berry coloured blanket" that appeared in the earlier scene (VIII 1–3).

But rather than sitting sleepily in the sun, Midget and Althea are very active. Dressed in "tunics," with "bare upper legs," the two women battle a fierce storm in their canoe, strip off their wet clothes, and stand on the whortle-berry blanket to warm their naked bodies before the "smouldering brazier" (VIII). Like maids of Artemis, the women are strong, athletic, chaste. Eroticism is covertly present, sublimated into their battle against the storm, their undressing before the fire, the pastoral landscape where the wind catches "the branches of the white rose-tree," where the "plumes of the wild willow . . . drift across Midget's shoulder" (VII 8). The connection of love to poetry made in Chapter 5 resurfaces in Midget's debate with Althea about the nature of beauty and the role of the "creative intellect" in Chapter 8. Like Poe, Althea is a muse figure whose power to inspire is inseparable from the erotic.

Althea is unnamed at first, as the men were. She is called simply, "the friend," a generic term that invokes the code common in lesbian literature for lover. The name Althea means healing, which reflects the function she plays in lifting the "cloud" of suffering from the war years.[62] But, in substituting for the heterosexual poet/lover and the companion/husband, Althea also plays a healing role in replacing the lost Josepha in an ideal landscape whose rhetoric recalls the earlier Artemisian discourse of H.D.'s lesbian pastoral. The wind and storm that Althea and Midget battle in their canoe recapitulate "that wind" which was a "rush of swords that cut the sand stretches into snow and ice pattern," "the sting and dash of spray, in the rains and wind," "the white sand that lived, the wind, the stainless rout of stars" of the wild terrain Midget and Josepha had shared (452–3). Josepha and Midget and "such as she and Josepha" belonged to "the roughness and the power of that wilderness" associated with America. They were alien to the "civilized," lush vineyards of Europe (455). Midget is a "white sword-flower," with a mind that is "steel-white javelin" – resonating with lines from Gregg's "Iris" and Bryher's "Amazon." With their eyes of "slate-grey, or a rain-gray" and "sky-blue of the water and the cold," Midget and Josepha are "different" (455, 457). The harshness of their landscape contrasts with the ripe, warm beauty of Basil's Italy, "the thousand, thousand roses," the "roses of Paestum" – a direct quote from Aldington's poem "Reflections" (*Complete Poems* 40–1). Like Midget and Josepha, Midget and Althea are at home where "the sea grass and the marsh grass seemed to blend," in "the scrub pine and small cornel and decidous oak and young sassafras that edged the forest" (VII 11, 14).

But, in recalling the earlier pastoral scene, the later one also surpasses it. As a projection of Midget's desire, Althea fulfills the unfilled promise of Josepha. Standing naked in front of Althea, Midget recalls how she and Josepha had undressed in a boat to take pictures of one another, a moment interrupted by the approach of a man. In the realm beyond the "visible world," "the conditions of what we might call real life" did not interrupt (VIII, VII 8). With Josepha, Midget had experienced a revelation as transformative as the light Paul of Tarsus saw on the road to Damascus (447). It was a moment out of space, out of time: "The past and the future, morning and evening star, hung there, a beacon in the darkness between this world and the future. . . . the present which was dead melted away and they were together in the past and in the future" (451). With Josepha's departure from England and subsequent marriage, that moment was broken. "Wee witches grow up," Josepha had written her.[63] But with Althea, Midget could return to her maidenhood. Althea lived entirely in a timeless realm, beyond the imperfections of "the world of what we call, real life" (VII 12). The lesbian scene of Chapters 7 and 8 echoes, but replaces, the lost desire of Chapters 1 and 2, as well as the heterosexual love of Chapter 5. Althea brings to fruition the wild spirit of Artemis in the dreamscape of Midget's imagination.

Helga Dart, however, is curiously disturbed by the story she tells. Split off from her younger self by time and the authority of hindsight, she is terribly worried about Midget's idyll with Althea – as if she were not fully in control of the history she narrates, which so clearly privileges Midget's healing "visits" with Althea as a Neo-Platonic ideal and Artemisian pastoral. She authoritatively and ominously comments that Midget's trick of seeing is dangerous:

> The trick was not altogether a good trick. I have my reasons for saying this. It shut her out from life. You might argue that life had or was trying to shut her out from it. But life is not a thing you can argue about. A cloud. Five years. It came. It lifted. You do not argue about a tidal wave. You escape it if you can. . . .
> Snow and ash, you might have said this trick was. Not the pearl reflecting all minute and vivid landscapes, tiny, tiny surfaces, colour of purple bean-flower or faint tint of thistle. Not the pearl; sanity, life, salvation. It was not a good trick of dreaming. (V 5–6)

From her vantage point in the future, Helga Dart warns us before we even hear about them that the very visitations to the spirit world the narrative valorizes can sever all ties to life, that is, to life anchored in ordinary space and time. Helga Dart, in other words, undermines the Artemisian pastoral she celebrates by suggesting that its Neo-Platonic ideal cannot exist in the real. Althea, the "healer," can take Midget off the deep end – into madness or even suicide.

Their erotically charged battle against the storm is followed by a struggle between Althea and Midget over the relevance of the visible world, that is, material existence in ordinary space and time. Their debate functions both as a contest between two characters and as a psychodrama within a single, split psyche.[64] As a "visitor" from the visible world, Midget defends it, feeling in fact quite "patriotic":

> She was not patriotic as you or I should use or understand the term. But she had a sense of loyalty to the world of what we call, real life, at large. When her friend began abusing the real world, Midget became warm about the jaw bone. . . . She was feeling patriotic. The world is a country, she thought, and I do no[t] wish to see the world perish. I do not wish to see the world knocked out by another world. Yes, I am very patriotic. This is the way my landlady in Bloomsbury used to feel about England and Germany. "And about modernity." (VII 12–13)

Althea responds to Midget's "little tirade on the beauties of the visible world" by saying

> I have not yet heard a plea, or a defence, as you seem to have made it, of the visible world. If you must argue about, and defend your so called visible world, I do not think it can be a very pleasant, satisfying nor convincing place to live in. In fact, I do not understand you at all. You

seem to be talking in a cloud, about a cloud,[.] Is your world a cloud, that you must make these curious distinctions between past, present, visible and invisible?" (VIII 1)

Althea's image of the cloud repeats Helga Dart's term for the war years – a cloud. As healer, she offers Midget a lyric Artemisian landscape outside the cloud – that is, outside ordinary space and time, the coordinates of culture and narrative. The rhetoric of patriotism in Midget's apologia for the visible world emphasizes her refusal of transcendental escapism as a solution to the problems of history, even in its most terrible manifestation – war. As defender of the visible world, Midget takes on the role of "rescuer" in relationship to Althea. Because she has no existance in the visible world, Althea is "yet unborn" and seems to step out of a frieze like a statue come to life (VII 15; VIII 3). Midget, in contrast, asks "Why not live?" and asserts "I am alive" (VII 6; VIII 4). It is only through her living companion that Althea comes into being: Midget "had rescued her friend from the forest, at least so she said. Her friend was duly grateful. . . . Said Midget, 'Who would remember you, if it were not for me? Remember yourself the beauty of your playmates, what good does that do you? Sleep in the forest or get lost in a half dream what good does that do you? You are dead' " (VII 7–8).

To make Althea "live," Midget must conjure her back into the visible world, must mediate between Althea, the transcendental signifier, and the world of history, the signified. Midget tells Althea:

> The visible world exists; I have found since I have outgrown the period of war convalescence, that the visible world exists as poignantly, as etherially as the invisible. There is another world, or a combining of two worlds. When we can get the visible and the invisible together that makes another world. I used to believe in the past and in what I called the future; when you get the past and the future together, you get what I call, now for the sake of argument, the present. . . . There is a present which is dead, there is also the living present. (VII 22)

Midget's image for the "living present" is Hyde Park, a garden set in the heart of London that translates the wild gardens of her imagined pastorals into the manifest world of history. It is both of the city/society and a pastoral space within it. Like all translations, it is a compromise. As the park where London's high society displayed itself for centuries, Hyde Park is hardly outside culture. Midget describes the iron railings around it, as well as the streams of riders within it, especially the English ladies who are so intimidating in their rightness. The flow of the crowd in the park represents the dominant currents of the social order. But the park also grants a measure of "surety" and "privacy," the right to be different: "I can wear any kind of clothes I want, good ones or old ones. I can sit on one of the little green chairs for an hour alone, just ruminating and no one speaks to me . . . or seems to be saying . . . 'it's too bad her admirer has deserted her.' Alone or with an escort, one is equally shielded and apart" (VII 21). Moreover, the park has room for traces of hyacinthian wildness: "The sward beyond the rail is close and green save under the far trees where it has been left wild and free in homage to the tall blue hyacinths that grow there. These patches of wild grass and spikes of hyacinth rise like islands in the short grass" (VIII 9–10). The hyacinths in Hyde Park represent the presence of the invisible in the visible, the Artemisian in the social order.

Midget's desire to link the visible and invisible in history is the task of the writer as H.D. defined it in *Paint It To-Day*.[65] Her speech to Althea recalls earlier discourses on creativity – one in Chapter 1, where the young Midget "painstakingly" translates lines from Heine that anticipate her "visits" with Althea: "I have come again away from the dead, / Drawn by strange powers to thee / Quicken me now nor fear to give, / Too much of yourself to me." This is the kind of "poetry and the beat and the swallow-wings" that Midget aspires to write (450). Aesthetic discussion continues in Chapter 6, where Helga Dart tells us that a statue materializes "the electric force of the artist" and shows us how Midget's passion for the statues gives the lifeless a form of life – the invisible, a form of visibility. Finally, in Chapter 8, Midget answers Althea's aesthetic question on the nature of beauty by saying, " 'All things become beautiful if we, through the creative use of the intellect, transform them by a process of resetting them or reconsidering them in relation to what they have been or more important still, to what they may become. Nothing is static. All things change.' . . . 'You and I change,' said Midget, 'but the creative mind in us does not alter' " (VIII 6).[66] As a poet, Midget will fulfill the promise of the Heine poem she had translated, by resetting the Artemisian world of Althea into the discourses of the visible world.

Midget's debate with Althea recapitulates the split between imagist poet and novelist about which H.D. wrote to Cournos in 1919. The poet's "sea garden" was her "escape" from the tidal wave of history; the poet's drive to fiction and narrative represents her need to anchor the self in history. *Paint It To-Day*, as an imagist novel, relies on a complex, split-subject narrative to work through this conflict between the real and the ideal, the personal and the transcendental. The first split is in Midget, by which her loss of Josepha and Basil leads to her development of a male muse/lover, then a female muse/lover. The second split is in H.D. herself, whereby the pressures of the war and the conditions of her healing led her to create Helga Dart, who was herself split into the narrating subject and narrated object of the novel.

H.D. emphasized these splits in Helga Dart by having her lose control of her narrative, by having her character usurp the authoritative tone she herself exhibits in the novel's frame and in the selection of narrative tableau. In her debate with Althea, Midget pronounces on aesthetics, instructing her muse and, by extension, Helga Dart herself. Helga Dart's occasional interventions in the conversation undermine instead of assert her authority – as, for example, when she comments parenthetically "(I do not know that the child's name was Althea but Midget called her that.)" (VII 13). Helga Dart diffuses herself as the "I now" even further by becoming a generalized and various "we now" at the opening of Chapter 7: "So it was over, not only the peril, the suffering, the agonizing, we called the war, but the years [of] the (to some of us) even more painful period of convalescence. . . . We have all different invalid charts for this time. Some of us jumped up to a hectic fever heat. . . . Some of us went limp. . . . Some of us were snuffed quietly out, many of us, in the wave of fever that caught us from the battle fields" (VII 1). Destabilizing the narrative voice once again, Helga Dart then inserts a personal history of her past that seems distinct from Midget's. Continuing for several pages, it begins: "I loved Europe with such intensity and with such baffling counter currents of pain during all the years of waiting. I trust you do not consider me 'pro-German' since I make my little heroine of such a curious blend. I cannot say that I am. But I was singularly unhappy through the war. I have never, I regret yet visited the great fatherland. But my clearest memories are of an old nurse who read me brothers Grimm . . . " (VII 2).

Helga Dart recovers some authority by interrupting the conversation between Midget and Althea to pose the closing frame: "I must leave them there; their worlds, I think are not so very many worlds apart" (VIII 10). But the impact of this oscillating narrative authority is to undermine the Artemisian discourse that the novel eloquently asserts. It reminds us that the text is "*a* portrait," not "*the*" portrait of the narrator's younger self; it is, further, a portrait painted from the perspective of "*today*," not of all time. Helga Dart lives in the visible world, caught in the imperfections of the real through which she can gain only glimpses of the ideal in the hidden recesses of London. Althea exists as a trace, to be inscribed, of a free and wild Artemisian terrain outside the confines of conventional femininity. Helga Dart – and behind this screen, H.D. – exists as the point of mediation between history and a sacred space and time. The difficulty of her task is nowhere more evident than at the very moment when Helga Dart cuts off her narration of Midget's debate with Althea:

> "Where there is a garden, where there is a patch of untrod grass, there is a god[dess]. . . . "
> "Who is this goddess?"
> Midget answered, "Artemis."

Althea yawned. She asked, "and Aphrodite?"
Midget knew she was defeated. She said, "there is no Aphrodite." (VIII
10)

Midget's defeat is also Helga Dart's. In telling the story of Artemis in
the visible world, *Paint It To-Day* has repressed the story of Aphrodite,
the tale, that is, of heterosexual passion and suffering – the very subject
that H.D. worked through in her subsequent portraits in the Madrigal
cycle, *Asphodel* and *Madrigal*.

IV. RETURN OF THE REPRESSED TEXT IN
THE MADRIGAL CYCLE

The presence of Artemis and the absence of Aphrodite in *Paint
It To-Day* signifies both the autonomy and incompleteness of the novel
as a single text in itself. Within the cluster of works H.D. wrote about
her first decade in Europe, *Paint It To-Day* represents the textual and
political unconscious of *Asphodel* and *Madrigal*. Its vision of an Artemisian
domain – however incompletely realizable – is the most forbidden of
H.D.'s discourses on the Great War. For, like Monique Wittig's separatist
utopian fantasy, *Les Guérillères, Paint It To-Day* imagines a world in
which a lesbian erotic and poetic replaces an androcentric and heterocentric one. In a world in which men control the engines of the state
and its extension onto the battlefield, such an inscription of a wilderness
of hyacinthian desire outside history is blasphemous. In the repressed
narratives of history and the history of repressed narratives, the story of
women without men is perhaps the most taboo. The "unholy splendour"
of Midget and Josepha in *Paint It-Day* is like the "torch in that vast
chamber where nobody has been" in Mary Carmichael's *Life's Adventures,*
which breaks the "expected sequence" by narrating how "Chloe liked
Olivia" (*Room* 85–8). Woolf emphasized the heresy of such narrative acts
by breaking off her "lecture" "abruptly" to ask her audience if there are
"no men present," and urge them not "to start" or "blush" as she
continued: "For I wanted to see how Mary Carmichael set to work to
catch those unrecorded gestures, those unsaid or half-said words, which
form themselves, no more palpably than the shadows of moths on the
ceiling, when women are alone, unlit by the capricious and coloured
light of the other sex" (88).

Woolf's coy wit and fanciful fictions screen the forbidden. H.D. veiled
her vision of women without men by suppressing her more direct, iden-
tifiably autobiographical "life's adventures." Instead of publishing *Paint
It To-Day*, she rewrote it. The less heretical *Asphodel* contains many
traces of *Paint It To-Day* – most notably the story of Fayne and Hermione
before the war and the narrative of gynocentric healing after the war.

Paint It To-Day is hidden almost without trace in *Madrigal,* whose story of triangulated desire is least threatening to the Oedipal history of narrative and to the narrative histories of love and war. Midget's deconstruction of her imaginary poet/lover's dominance within the economy of male desire is extended dramatically into Julia's transformations of Rafe's and Rico's real power in the visible world. Additionally, *Paint It To-Day's* authoritative narrator, the Artemisian Helga Dart, exists within Delia ("she of Delos") Alton, who pronounces on "the times . . . the customs," "the cosmic, comic, crucifying times of history" in *Madrigal.* Mediating between the lesbian Helga Dart and the heterosexual Delia Alton is the unnamed, bisexual author of *Asphodel* whose central story becomes the narrative of the mother in a world at war. Hermione's transformative pregnancy and childbirth, with its distinctive discourse of regeneration, shadows the rebirth of Julia's creative power.

The three texts of the Madrigal cycle stand alone and together. As a unit, they form a palimpsest, an inscription in three parts constituting three layers of the same psyche. Rather than contradicting each other, the three novels are superimposed on each other, interdependent and interpenetrating. Never the equivalent of the historical writer, they nonetheless all refer back to her. Their difference demonstrates not a contradictory self-image, but rather a recognition of different selves created at different points in time, from different heuristic perspectives. The lesbian layer, *Paint It To-Day,* suffers the most erasure in the processes of rewriting because, within the context of history, its narrative is the most forbidden. The mother layer, *Asphodel,* challenges the dominant narratives of history by posing birth and fusion instead of death and separation as its principle of sequence. The wife layer, *Madrigal,* tells the familiar story of triangular desire in an unfamiliar way, transposing the conventional interplay of love and war into an unconventional exposé of sexual politics on the home front. Each novel has its own challenge to pose, its own hermeneutic of history. Gender is central to each work's interpretive self-creation. But each novel genders history differently, highlighting different aspects of the gender system. Consequently, each text poses its particular critique of the position of women in history; each plays out its own story of women's agency within that history.

In the context of the dominant narratives of history, the earliest and least public novel – *Paint It To-Day* – tells the most repressed, politically forbidden story. Each time H.D. rewrote her "life's adventures" of the war decade, she brought her saga closer to the surface of conscious history. But within the context of her evolution as a writer, each textual (re)creation of the war decade represented a repetition of those events, one that worked through the past in order to bring repressed memories to consciousness (to echo Freud once again). The writing self – the "I now" as autobiographical analyst – is caught in the round of repetitions that signal the transference. Instead of remembering the past – gaining control over it by making an orderly story about it – the writing self gets swallowed up by the narrated self and is compelled to repeat the past. However, the revision of the story in each successive text also represents the writing self's attempt to gain more hermeneutic power by restoring to consciousness what has been repressed. From this psychoanalytic perspective, we could expect that the later texts might include material that had been repressed in the earlier ones.

This is indeed the case with H.D.'s Madrigal cycle. Her suffering during the war years made the stories of her self as mother and wife more painful to remember than the tabooed story of her lesbian love. The more historically acceptable story of the wife and mother, in other words, was the story she initially repressed. The death of her first-born child, Aldington's abandonment of their different marriage based in poetic companionship, the loss of Lawrence's cerebral friendship so important to her art, her consoling dalliance with Gray that left her pregnant, and the birth of her illegitimate and fatherless child were more immediately conflictual and unresolved experiences for H.D. than Gregg's desertion and the arrival of Bryher. These events from 1915 to 1918 destroyed her self-esteem and left her feeling intensely guilty, even sinful – a failure as a woman. Consequently, *Paint It To-Day* avoids these episodes, which exist as mere traces, or not at all, in the surface of this celebration of Artemisian maidenhood. The first child is missing completely, as are Lawrence and Gray; the second child is present only as a hint of humming bird claw. Basil and Raymond are on the fringes of Midget's emotional life, whereas Aldington and Pound remained intensely important to H.D. until her death. Her first attempt to write the story of the war decade, in other words, left out Aphrodite, as the last line of the narrative ominously suggests. If nothing else, H.D.'s own translation and adaptation of Euripides's *Hippolytus* taught her that Aphrodite retaliates swiftly when her power is denied – a mythological version of psychoanalytic theory. As with the progression of so many of Lawrence's novels, *Asphodel* takes off at the point *Paint It To-Day* begins to unravel. It explores the significance of Pound, Aldington, and Gray, as well as that of Patmore and Margaret Cravens. It confronts head-on the pain of the stillbirth and the trauma of the second pregnancy. But it does not touch the loss of Lawrence, and it only begins to suggest the artistic crisis that is central to *Madrigal*. In 1933, Freud advised H.D. to write her story "straight," without any Greek frills (H.D., Letters to Bryher, 15 and 18 May 1933). While *Madrigal* is as much a slant on "truth" as the prior texts, it does account for Aphrodite, and it does directly explore the interlocking systems of patriarchal erotics and poetics. More directly than the earlier novels, *Madrigal* is both an effect of and about the "searing" "Hell" of Love and War, "this flame" that "is my very Daemon driving me to write," as she wrote to Cournos in a letter quoted in one of the epigraphs for this chapter. *Madrigal* is, as she reflected in *Thorn Thicket*, "the Child of War I," the Child of "that marriage," the Child of that "original 'primal scene,' the consciousness or actual 'picture' of father–mother in the act of creating – creating 'us' or a replica or repetition of 'us' " (34, 19).

We need to read the Madrigal cycle both ways, resisting the temptation to locate "truth" in any one text. In both senses, *Paint It To-Day* is paradoxically the most repressed of the three novels. As the earliest and most private text, it represents the most radical critique of history in its Artemisian gynocentrism. It serves as the textual unconscious of the later novels and the political unconscious of history. But it is also a repressive text with its own unconscious in which it has buried the painful stories of H.D.'s heterosexual side. Conversely, in both senses, *Madrigal* is the most repressed of the three novels. As the latest and most public text, it attacks the patriarchal structures of love and war from within the family romance. The lesbian alternative to that social and literary script has vanished, and the story of the mother as a critique of history has been sublimated into the story of the poet. But it is also a text that directly remembers the heterosexual trauma of the war years. As stylistically most experimental of the three texts, *Asphodel* stands in the middle between the lesbian Helga Dart and the heterosexual Delia Alton. Without authorial signature, without narrator, in a discourse of the speaking mother awash in the maternal body – in a Kristevan Semiotic – *Asphodel* is the living present that absorbs what came before, what comes after. In its linguistic excesses and its contradictory selves, it anticipates the fictions H.D. wrote about the poet who drifted through the lost generations of the 1920s – the subject of the next chapter.

4

Borderlines: Diaspora in the History Novels and the Dijon Series

I can't write unless I am an outcast.

H.D., Letter to Marianne
Moore (17 January 1921)

She was no longer a stray, a waif wandering, a stranger, in heavy sodden cities. . . . an outcast.

H.D., *Palimpsest* (37)

. . . after my years of exile and wandering, I greet the Sea. The Sea encompasses me, encompasses my Book. The Sea envelopes me.

H.D., *Thorn Thicket* (24)

In the postwar wasteland of modern Europe, H.D. was perpetually the stranger longing for home, but recognizing that exile was the precondition of her art. To write, she had to be "different" – cut off from mother, motherland, and the womanhood both represented to her. Yet the devastations of the Great War left H.D. "dynamited to bits," as she wrote about her persona in *Nights* (73). Like the dismembered Orpheus and Osiris, she was in need of healing. But instead of being mothered, she was mother to a fatherless child, herself "a stray, a waif wandering" rootless on geographic and spiritual borderlines. The autobiographical fictions H.D. wrote to (re)construct the poet's broken psyche of the 1920s and early 1930s embody the contradictions of her exile, dismemberment, and search for divine healing. Taken as a group, they represent a dialectic between the Scylla of home and Charybdis of homelessness. The role of Astrid she played as Helga Doorn in *Borderline* crystallizes her personae in these fictions. She was one of those "borderline social cases, not out of life, not in life. . . . [She] is and is not outcast, is and is not a social alien, is and is not a normal human being, she is borderline" (*Borderline* 5).

H.D.'s narratives constituting her selves in the postwar years – some

215

four novels, five novellas, and several stories – fall generally into two generic clusters: the historical novels set in the ancient world and the novellas set in contemporary time. The historical novels – *Palimpsest, Hedylus,* and *Pilate's Wife* – "ghost" for her state of mind in the early to middle 1920s, when she was particularly preoccupied with a conflicted desire to forget and remember the events of the war years. These texts, all of which she published (or tried to publish) with established presses, disguise their autobiographical content to a great degree through the manipulations of their historical settings. Two sketches – "Pontikonisi (Mouse Island)" and "Ear-Ring" – are exceptions. Set in contemporary time, they narrate different parts of her trip to Greece with Bryher and Peter Rodeck. Their protective coloration is not a historical disguise, but rather the pseudonyms, Rhoda Peter and D. A. Hill; in any case, they were not published until the 1930s.[1] Taken as separate texts, the last two stories of *Palimpsest* are also exceptions. Like the sketches, they are set in modern times, but basic biographical events, such as the birth of Perdita or H.D.'s unconsummated shipboard romance with Rodeck, are suppressed or displaced so as to be unrecognizable.

The contemporary novellas – H.D. called them "booklets" in *Compassionate Friendship* – focus not on memory of the past, but on H.D.'s immediate present, namely the conflicted web of her ménage à trois with Bryher and Macpherson. *Narthex,* the first of these, appeared in *The American Caravan,* but Bryher used the Dijon printer to publish the rest, in limited editions of 100 copies "for the author's friends," as the flyleaves proclaim. In *Compassionate Friendship,* H.D. called the group, including *Narthex,* "the Dijon series" and noted that their composition was framed by her mother's death in 1927 and her psychoanalysis with Freud in 1933–4 (88–9).[2] Written more in the manner of her romans à clef, these texts mask their autobiographical content with an elusive narrative or a surrealist dreamscape. The more public the text, the greater the disguise, facilitated by the historical genre. The more private the text, the greater the direct revelation of its autobiographical basis.

Although her narrative method shifted from historical to contemporary settings, both kinds of texts split, displaced and distorted the autobiographical subject. The division between the autobiographical "I now" and "I then" pervades all the texts, as does the dissonance between conscious and unconscious selves. Additionally, however, the fragmentation of the self became increasingly the central focus of the text – thematically and formalistically. H.D. regularly projected parts of herself into separate personae – as in *Hedylus,* where she is both mother and son, or in *Nights,* where she is both prosaic male narrator and lyric female suicide. Gender is the mediating factor in all these splits – between woman and poet, male and female, heterosexual and homosexual, mad and sane, old and young, sacred and profane, in time and out of time.

The search to heal these splits provides narrative momentum in self-consciously experimental texts that often seem otherwise plotless. The lyric invocations of the sacred in *Sea Garden* reappear in these fictions with an even greater personal urgency and religious intensity. Re-union of fragmented selves will come, the texts suggest, through a divine agency that takes paternal and maternal forms. Helios–Apollo, the god of light and poetic inspiration, and Isis, the deity of Mystery and (re)birth, are the mythicparental figures to whom the texts most regularly appeal. Akin to the Fisher King in *The Waste Land,* the presence and absence of these deities in H.D.'s texts is sign and symptom of sterility and religious longing for rebirth in the modern period. Throughout, however, the mother – both the historical woman, Helen Doolittle, and the longed-for primal Mother of the daughter's fantasy – is the textual matrix. Taking precedence over the father, she is the site of the daughter's desire and rebellion, of matricide and suicide, of the longing for the healing touch of the sacred.[3]

About the Dijon series, H.D. observed: "They are subtle stories, difficult to re-read" (*Compassionate Friendship* 87). We might apply her comment to the historical novels as well, although these more conventionally plotted novels are "easier" to read than the Dijon series. But, with some variation, all these texts *are* difficult to read, perhaps even more difficult to like, because they are claustrophobic texts that threaten to drown both author and reader in a sea of rhythmic repetitions. Their sheer intensity, what H.D. herself called that "high-vibration-to-the-breaking-point level," suck the reader into a transferential repeating of and resistance to their author's dismemberment and religious longing for divine/parental intervention (Letter to McAlmon, 18 August 1933). Highly performative texts, their very experimentalism as avant-garde prose increasingly acts out anguish in various distressed and fragmented discourses that repress and resist the desires that seek expression. Awash in the Kristevan Semiotic, the ordered plot of the Symbolic is muted, sometimes barely a trace for the reader to track.

Reflecting the intensification of H.D.'s spiritual diaspora during the decade, these fictions became increasingly despairing as the divisions within grew worse. "Helios and Athena," an experimental prose-poem written in 1920, celebrated the divine power and authority of androgyny. *Nights,* written in the summer of 1931, demonstrated its danger – the disintegration of identity into incompatible male and female parts in which the female is driven to suicide. The Artemisian sisterhood dreamed of in *Paint It To-Day* and *Asphodel* dissolves into the claustrophobic twinning of *Narthex* and *The Usual Star,* written some seven years later. The celebratory gynopoetic of *Notes on Thought and Vision* from 1919 is followed at the end of the next decade by the gloomier *Borderline,* which offers a modernist poetics of the outcast. The general drift of H.D.'s works about her self in the 1920s shows a descent into the borderline between sanity and madness. On the threshold between the two, she emerged into the 1930s as a woman who projected a death wish into her autobiographical writings. In the textual world of *Nights,* she committed suicide. In the volume of poetry she drew together in the 1930s, she was "the dead priestess" who speaks.

Fortunately, these sublimated suicides took the place of actual attempts; and, for the most part, Perdita remembered, H.D.'s sense of humor, capacity for friendship, and delight in everyday life and people anchored her dangerous cerebralism.[4] But, like Woolf, and later Sylvia Plath, these textual encounters with paralysis, madness, and death were part of the psychodynamics of her creativity. However successful these fictional "speeches" from the borderlands are – and some of them are not – they were essential to the making of the modernism that informed her great works of the 1940s. In Section 1, this chapter will examine the roots of H.D.'s diaspora in the exhilarations of her prewar expatriatism and in the entangling web of what she called "the family problem." Sections 2 and 3 will explore her articulations of that exile and search for home in the historical novels and the Dijon series.

I. FROM EXPATRIATISM TO DIASPORA IN THE 1920S

> and there had been war,
> and that thing (my soul)
> was a lost star
> or a lost boat
> adrift, without rudder
> or sail or sternsman. . . .
>   H.D., "Child Poems"
>   (*Collected Poems* 341)

The rootless despair that H.D. inscribed in her fictions about the 1920s emerged dialectically out of the early exhilaration of her escape from America. Her expatriatism was a spatial metaphor of interior difference, itself a geographic enactment of an inner alienation that was the precondition of her modernism. Like Stephen Dedalus at the end of *Portrait of the Artist,* H.D. fled from the *communitas* of family, religion, and nation for the sake of her art. As an American in Europe, she could remain forever alien; as a woman required to adopt her husband's citi-

zenship with his name, she could be both British and not-British, in-
habiting a netherland that left her symbolically free to pursue her
difference as a woman poet. As she wrote Marianne Moore on 17 January
1921: "I am beginning to feel as if the world approved of me and I can't
write unless I am an outcast." To feel fully at home, to be harmoniously
integrated into family and nation was to be domesticated and tamed. For
women in particular, home meant a web of feminine obligation, a conventional domesticity that was incompatible with creativity. "Can you
see," she once asked Bryher, "how London at least left me *free?*" (23
August 1924). Being an American in Europe was both sign and symptom
of the differences that fueled H.D.'s writing.[5]

To borrow Susan Howe's characterization of Emily Dickinson,
H.D. "built a new poetic form from her fractured sense of being eter-
nally on intellectual borders" (Howe 21). She had made her mark on
modern poetry by situating her voice neither here, nor there – on the
borderline between land and sea in "Hermes of the Ways," between
repression and desire in "Orchard," between confinement and freedom in "Sheltered Garden," between polarity and transcendence in
"Oread," between the ordinary and divine, the archaic and modern in
Sea Garden as a whole.[6] For H.D., Janus, the two-faced god of
thresholds, and Hermes, the mercurial patron of crossroads, were
presences that crystallized her sense of difference. She had always felt
"different," as she reflected throughout *Tribute to Freud* and *The Gift:*
different as the only girl to survive in a family of five brothers; as an
"ugly duckling" daughter nearly six feet tall, pleasing neither mother
nor father; as a Moravian in a predominantly Christian world for
whom the Moravians were an exotic sect; as an American who carried a British passport, visiting her homeland only six times until her
death; as a woman who "had two loves separate," desire for both
women and men; as a mother of a child whose parentage she felt she
had to hide; as an artist devoted to the spirit in a materialist world; as
a woman born with a powerful gift, driven by a daemon that compelled her to write within a tradition dominated by male masters.

Pound had promoted prewar London as the culture capital of the
world, the hub of an internationalist modernism.[7] But London meant
freedom to H.D. in the prewar days not only because of its artistic
ferment, but more fundamentally because it represented the scene of her
break from home. It was the absence of America, not just the presence
of London, where she wasn't, not where she was, that mattered. "I had
to GET AWAY to make good," she once explained to Bryher; "London
was MY OWN, just as Berlin is your own" (24 June 1931). In 1918, she
had urged Bryher to go to the States with the warning that it was the
break from her family, not the place itself that would free her:

Don't go with the false idea that America will give you *anything* that
you don't already possess. But the break from England may give you
a spiritual impulse that will carry you on. . . . *Go to America!* . . . Forgive
my preach – but your mind and your surroundings, and your problems
(though in some ways so different) are also very similar to my own
early ones. There is no help for it! You must have freedom of mind
and spirit soon, or things will close over you & it will be too late." (31
December 1918)

Freedom of mind and spirit, for H.D. and Bryher, centered on escape
from the family pressure to conform, to do the respectable, the proper,
the expected for women. Expatriatism was above all a flight from femininity, not from womanhood, but from the norms of Victorian femininity that clashed with the demands of creativity. In this respect, H.D.'s
flight to London functioned much like Dickinson's "self-imposed exile"
to reclusivity (Howe 13) or Woolf's move from fashionable Hyde Park
Gate, under the control of her socially ambitious half-brother, to the less
reputable Bloomsbury with her sister Vanessa. Woolf's parents left her
"free" to be different from them by dying. H.D.'s expatriatism accomplished for her what the death of the Stephens had done for Woolf. The
flight from home was a psychological matricide and patricide, a "killing"
of the motherland and fatherland embedded in the psyche of the fleeing
artist, for which she felt perpetually guilty. Matricidal expatriatism is a
central theme in *Paint It To-Day,* where Midget tries to accomplish the
separation from her mother through an imagined identification with
Orestes: " 'Your mother, your mother, your mother,' the present said
to Midget, 'has betrayed, or would betray, through the clutch and tyranny of the emotion, the mind in you. . . . Look,' said the present, 'and
choose. Here is a knife, slay your mother. She has betrayed or would
betray your gift' " (473). To break free means – terrifyingly – to "kill"
the mother.[8]

The Great War transformed what had begun as a liberating expatriatism into a geographic and spiritual diaspora. Escape from home
became a loss of homeland, and endless exile, a perpetual absence of
divine presence. H.D. directly identified with the diaspora of the Jews
to articulate the significance of her postwar exile. "Perhaps dispersion
is the key-word," she wrote in *H.D. by Delia Alton.* "We were dispersed and scattered after War I" (184). Like the destruction of the
temple that initiated the diaspora of the Jews, World War I was the
event that created a "lost generation," specifically, those permanently
cut off from the *communitas* of exiled artists who had made up the
core of the prewar modernist movement. Aware of Stein's characterization of young writers of the 1920s like Ernest Hemingway as the
Lost Generation, H.D. was quick to say that she meant something

different – she belonged to the generation who had known a world
before the war and consequently lived with the knowledge of loss.[9]
"What was left of them," she wrote in *Madrigal* about the survivors,
"was the war-generation, not the lost generation, but lost actually in
fact, doomed by the stars in their courses, an actuality, holocaust to
Mars, not blighted, not anaemic, but wounded, but dying, but dead"
(8). Separated from their prewar past by an impenetrable "asbestos
curtain," they were a generation "drifting" without direction into the
future (*Advent* 153; *Tribute to Freud* 13).

The words of Isaiah addressed for H.D. the meaning of modernity's
holocaust. "Your country *is* desolate, your cities *are* burned with fire,"
the prophet told his people. But a "very small remnant" would return
and prosper after long wanderings (Is 1:9; 10:20–2). "If you are consoled
or integrated," H.D. later wrote, "you help console and integrate the
scattered remnant" (*Sword* 41). Largely unconsoled and disintegrated
during the 1920s, H.D. wandered from place to place, never setting up
a permanent home for herself and her baby daughter – as if her spiritual
exile mandated a corresponding geographical homelessness.

In search of healing, H.D. traveled widely in the 1920s and early 1930s
– first to Greece in the spring of 1920, along with Bryher and Havelock
Ellis. By the fall of 1920, she agreed to go to the States with Bryher,
who believed her liberation from family obligations could be accomplished in the New World. With Bryher's discovery that she was no
more free in America than she had been in England, the two women
returned to London – Bryher to her parents' mansion at 1 South Audley
Street with her new husband, Robert McAlmon, and H.D. to a flat too
small to set up a household for Perdita, who stayed at the nearby Norland
Nursery. In 1922, along with Helen Doolittle, H.D. and Bryher went
again to Greece, then on to Constantinople. In February of 1923, the
three women were present at the dramatic opening of King Tut's tomb
in Egypt. With side trips to Paris, Berlin, and Italy, H.D. spent the rest
of the 1920s moving back and forth between the alpine solitude of rooms
in a pension in Territet, Switzerland, and the intensely peopled milieu
of London, where she stayed in a room at the Hotel Washington until
she finally furnished a small flat on Sloane Street in 1925. These exterior
wanderings acted out an interior quest for direction, for a revelation of
the sacred that would signify a healing "return," like the Israelites longing
for Jerusalem, or Odysseus yearning for Ithaca. The very intensity of
H.D.'s search, however, attested to the absence of integration, of a centered identity, and to the failure of the desired *nostos*.

H.D.'s web of personal relationships during this period provided essential support during this decade of wandering. But they also constituted
a "social-texture" that entangled H.D. in a mesh of ambivalence (*Com-*

passionate Friendship 87). The most intimate of these were her ties to her mother, her daughter, Bryher, and Macpherson – the people, in other words, who formed the core of what she called her ménage. Her personal network was considerably wider; like Woolf, H.D. loved the excitement of London, where she saw an endless stream of writers, artists, and friends, including people like Dorothy Richardson, May Sinclair, Norman Douglas, Nancy Cunard, Mary Butts, Brigit Patmore, H. P. Collins, Havelock Ellis, Frances Gregg, and Robert Herring. But it was the intimate relationships within her ménage that were the most significant. While the intense love and loyalty pervading these relationships proved essential to her survival, the tensions inherent in them also intensified her alienation. Each had a profound impact on the fictions H.D. constructed out of her wanderings in the 1920s and is consequently worth a brief review.

The Artemisian companionship of two women that *Paint It To-Day* and *Asphodel* suggest did not come to pass as a postwar household. Even if they had wanted to, H.D. and Bryher could not set up an establishment like Stein and Toklas (for example) without a complete break from their families, which neither was willing to make. Bryher was often with her parents, and, for nearly five years, Helen Doolittle spent most of her time with H.D. She accompanied the women to California in 1920, and then later went with them on their cruise to the Greek islands and Constantinople in 1922, and their trip to Egypt in 1923. Often in the company of her sister Laura, she lived with or near H.D., Bryher, and Perdita in London and Territet, although one or another of the group was often off traveling. She returned to the States in the fall of 1925 and died on March 21, 1927.[10]

Helen's presence was both comforting and oppressive to her daughter. Ultimately, it led H.D. to repeat the ambivalent feelings that had led to her escape in 1913. On the one hand, Helen provided plenty of loving support to her war-shattered, high-strung daughter. She strongly identified with H.D. against Aldington's desertion, worried greatly about Bryher's unhappiness with McAlmon, showed enormous pride at the appearance of H.D.'s books, and was enchanted with Perdita. Delighting in the use of intimate code names, she often addressed her letters to "H. and Boy [Bryher]," signed them "Beaver," and tried to collect local "dirt" (gossip) that would interest the two women. As her totem name suggests, she exuded a kind of bustling energy that created a certain stability, a household of sorts, with a predictable routine that was especially beneficial for Perdita. Not that she was a tower of calm strength – H.D. wrote Bryher at one point that her mother had at least one "*crise*" per day and was as phobic about traveling as H.D. herself (26 August 1924). "She is more & more helpless," H.D. wrote before one trip, "though she has been very helpful & good in other ways. I could not have got on without her.""[11]

At the same time, however, H.D. found her mother's busy interest in her life a "tyranny" that she felt compelled to overthrow. As she wrote to Bryher, "I am not fighting Bvr. I get her flowers etc. – occasionally manage to shed a few tears, about 'dear baby's future' and *so* on! But it is a *constant* Prussian tyranny – a constant wearing away of every power of resistance" (23 August 1924). Helen did not appear to criticize H.D., but her very presence seemed to make her daughter feel guilty, as if her mother personified the parental superego of conventional feminine respectability. H.D. never told her mother that Aldington was not Perdita's father, and it is not clear that Helen understood the nature of her daughter's relationship with Bryher. These silences necessitated that H.D. keep up a certain front as the victimized wife and abandoned mother, cultural formulas with which she was profoundly uncomfortable.[12] By 1924, H.D. wrote desperately to Bryher:

> Forgive me, dear Fido, for my rage of just now about the general atmosphere of the flat. I feel so grateful to you for your sweetness but always remember that a very wild horse has been trimmed down and kept pretty close in its paddock for some five years. Not that it wanted to kick up its heels and have twenty stallions at it, but after all, it needs a certain amount of free roaming and these old Flanders mares [Helen and Aunt Laura] and this very, very, fat COLT [Perdita] sometimes make it feel it has lost itself in a strange field. I don't want to run amuck but if the gates clang too, too tight, I shall one day, in spite of myself, simply jump the fence and perhaps never come back.
>
> You have of course, been too, too good and in some ways spoiled me. But I can't stand more than just so much domesticity and I have had TOO MUCH. I will have a good chew with Henriette [Helen] and then things MUST be arranged. They simply must. Or I will BUST. (22 April 1924)

As good as she was with Perdita, Helen's mere presence led H.D. to feel she had to reenact her initial rebellion against her mother in her flight to Europe and marriage to Aldington. This time, however, she, as the expatriate, had to send her mother home to the States. Feeling trapped in Territet with her mother and daughter, H.D. wrote to Bryher in London about her hopes for getting her mother to leave:

> No – I am not *really* bored – only last night Bvr. & I had a long "talk," one of those awful affairs, all about Cuth [Aldington] etc. etc. & I felt so unprotected after it. You know! But I will soon see you. It may be better even *not* to attempt baby for present in London. But I won't do anything too decided until I have seen you & had a good talk. Don't worry. It won't *kill* me not to have a flat in London. Only I must shake-off poor old Bvr. as she really at times with all the good will in the

world, oppresses me as if the Matterhorn were sitting on my chest. I will write you later about the 'talk' we had – there's no time to go into it. Nothing *special* but sentiment & so on. She says if we take a flat, she will return U.S.A. in spring!! So perhaps we'll *have* to take a flat! One screams with rage at this insistence on never *facing* anything straigh[t]. All sentiment – *bursting* to go yet acting almost as if we had let her down like Los Angeles! (22 August 1924)

The expulsion of "poor old Bvr." and the domesticity she represented from H.D.'s "spirit and mind" reopened the issue of expatriatism. "She is driven mad with me," H.D. wrote Bryher, "unless I am *constantly* telling her how I *really* like U.S.A. – really am so interested etc. . . . I *am*. But I want to be interested in *my own way*" (23 August 1924). It is this observation that led H.D. to continue with her already-quoted explosion: "Can you see how London at least left me *free?*" (23 August 1924). Superimposed on the matricidal break in 1913, London was once again to be the agent of her freedom – this time in the form of a flat where her mother would or could not live. But H.D. was also haunted by memories of her mother's gifts and the image of their final parting: her mother's lap filled with "a swathe of red aenemones" in the train station.[13] Separation from her mother was the precondition of (re)birth, but she imaged her expatriatism as a "caesarian" whose wounds could never heal. In the 1920 sketch "Pontikonisi," Madelon is pulled both ways, anguished by the pain of necessary separation from mother and motherland: "was that break toward re-birth, artificial psychic caesarian, America–Europe, beginning to tell now? The place where the graft was, rubbed raw. She hadn't felt it till this letting go London, where her graft-bandages still were" (4).

Breaking out of the mother–daughter dyad, however incompletely, H.D. was not about to reproduce it generationally in her own mothering of her daughter. The ambivalence she felt as the daughter replicated what she felt as the mother. At issue in both dyads was the threat posed to her creativity. To feel free enough to write, H.D. fled a restrictive domesticity symbolized by the mother–daughter bond and enforced in a household where mother and daughter lived together. In *The Reproduction of Mothering,* Nancy Chodorow has argued that, in Western patriarchy, girls are socialized to become mothers in a psychosexual development characterized by fluid ego boundaries in which the identities of mothers and daughters intermingle and never fully separate. In refusing to mother Perdita as she herself had been mothered by Helen, H.D. was attempting – whether consciously or unconsciously – to break the cycle that has traditionally confined women.

H.D.'s conflicted mothering of Perdita reproduced the interplay of love and the need for some distance enacted with her mother. Although she loved Perdita intensely, she did not set up a home in which she bore the primary responsibility for her daughter – not for financial, but rather for psychological, reasons.[14] In first announcing her pregnancy to Bryher, H.D. asserted her intention to be a "modern" mother: "Do not take this too seriously, as you know my views on the average parent, and if arrangements can be made, an old nurse of Mrs. Patmore's children, will take at times, entire charge, so that I may continue my work, and make whatever arrangements I wish for being in London" (23 December 1923). But, after Perdita's birth, H.D. felt very conflicted about leaving her at Norland Nursery. "Perdita is so very good," she told Bryher; "She stays with me most of the day" (19 April 1919). Then later on the same day,

> I *will* be so glad when tomorrow is over. I grow weaker as the parting comes – but I *know* it is best to leave Perdita for the time. She gets more charming & that is the trouble.... We must have some fun – some great adventures – I am torn between a desire for any little place with Perdita & fairy-books & Noah's arks and dolls, and a wild adventure. Perhaps in time, I will have both. (19 April 1919)

Bryher was even more worried than H.D. about the seductive attractions of the infant to the poet, for she responded:

> "I hope you will be sensible over Perdita and remember you were not given poetry to sit and worry over an infant in a solitary cottage. I am very jealous for your poetry and I will even fight Perdita about it. She will be much healthier and happier for the next year or two in the home and when she is older we will take her to California and the Greek Islands and teach her to adventure." (22 April 1919)

Ten years later, after Bryher and Macpherson had officially adopted Perdita in the fall of 1928, H.D. explained to Pound the threat the child had posed: "I was quite unprepared for the experience [of motherhood], I mean the terror of feeling that that wadge [?] of bird-feathers and petticoats HAD to be protected. The freedom of my spirit...went. I was no longer free. Now almost for the first time in ten years I am FREE" (February 1929[?]).

H.D. never had a "little place with Perdita & fairy-books & Noah's arks and dolls," whether because Bryher succeeded in dividing mother and daughter or because H.D.'s fears of her own maternal desire intervened. From April of 1919 until the summer of 1921, Perdita lived at the Norland Nursery in London, while H.D. lived nearby at Bullingham Mansions and visited her daily. When Helen and Aunt Laura arrived in the summer of 1921, Perdita left Norland with a nurse to join her "two grandmothers" and "two mothers" at Riant Chateau, the pension in which each had her own room. In the spring of 1925, H.D. briefly rented a furnished flat and then, in the fall of 1925, she finally took out a seven-year lease on an apartment on Sloane Street. Perdita probably lived there, but she spent a great deal of time at the Ellerman mansion at 1 South Audley Street, and a nurse was engaged to keep the child away from her "nervous" mother.[15] By early 1927, H.D., Bryher, and Perdita had returned to Territet with Macpherson. As Perdita has written: "H.D. was hardly an archetypal mother.... She was intensely maternal – on an esoteric plane. She venerated the concept of motherhood, but was unprepared for its disruptions. She flinched at sudden noise, and fled from chaos. Mercifully for her, she was well-buffered" ("The Egyptian Cat" 143).

H.D.'s "well-buffered" motherhood reflects her fear of domesticity, the threat a conventional home posed to her creative identity. As *Notes on Thought and Vision* and *Asphodel* suggest, H.D. linked her second pregnancy and childbirth with the rebirth of her creative drive. But, unlike motherhood, pregnancy ends. Not a self-contained experience, motherhood is a new state of being, one with perpetual demands on time and energy, one that changes forever a woman's concept of her own identity. Motherhood is also a social construction whose normative boundaries shift over time and across culture and class. For H.D., being a mother suggested that she should be like her own mother – become, in other words, the angel in the house that Coventry Patmore had idealized and Woolf renounced in order to write. H.D. probably had enough money to insulate herself against the demands of a child on her time, but money could not buy freedom from internalized norms of what a good mother should be.

A defensive distance from Perdita did not mean indifference, however. A fragmentary memory recorded in "Autobiographical Notes" reveals the attachment and profound identification beneath the surface: "P. riding in row, trouble with getting her into her riding-clothes. One evening P. 'knots' or 'weaves' velvet ribbons of a frock that Br and mother got me material for, in Paris. I feel rather isolated but this 'weave' recalls the Greek sequence and my place in the pattern with Br and P, and the two grandmothers" (15). "Maternal love was true, but she showed it sporadically, in sudden impulsive rushes," Perdita recalled ("Pandora's Box" *viii*). H.D. wanted motherhood on her own terms, in her own time and place, ones that did not include the primary responsibility for caretaking and discipline. The sequence of six lyrics entitled "Child Poems" attests to the fantasies mother and daughter shared, the special moments of imaginative flight and intimacy that Perdita has described (*Collected Poems* 341–8). The bond H.D. felt with Perdita is curiously inscribed in *The Hedgehog,* ostensibly a children's story dedicated to Perdita and featuring the child's naughty spirit of adventure. Disobeying her mother, the child climbs down a cliff and feels touched by the gods in the form of a swooping eagle. H.D. made Perdita into a persona for her own quest for the divine. Further, she gifted her fatherless daughter not only with permission to roam "wild and free" in the mountains like Artemis, but also with a divine "father in heaven" and a successful *nostos*, a return home to mother.

What these fragments of H.D.'s mothering in the 1920s and early 1930s add up to is a portrait of motherhood on the borderlines. H.D. was both mother and not-mother, there and not-there for Perdita. In 1919, H.D. had promised to let Bryher help raise Perdita as a way of preventing the suicide Bryher apparently threatened. Damaged by her own upbringing, Bryher was passionate about educational reform and eagerly responded to the chance to "experiment."[16] H.D. also allowed her own mother to take on the role of Perdita's care-giving parent, while she played the part of visitor who could retreat at will. Although her motive for the adoption was to remove Perdita forever from Aldington's reach, the legal proceedings also signified H.D.'s difference as a mother.[17] In the eyes of the law, Bryher became Perdita's mother and bore ultimate responsibility for her. H.D. could be the mother behind the mother – there for Perdita on her own terms, in a heterodox rather than orthodox way.

The Macphersons' adoption of Perdita was bound up as well in the ambivalence of H.D.'s relationships with both Bryher and Macpherson. During the 1920s, neither lesbian nor heterosexual love could fully "console" or "integrate" H.D.'s shattered identity, although each played a significant part in her survival. If H.D. had ever hoped that she and Bryher could unite against the world in an Artemisian sisterhood as she had once begged Gregg to do, Bryher's entanglement with her family made such a desire unrealistic. The fact that they were never able to live together in the 1920s is symptomatic of the constant interventions in their relationship. Bryher probably stayed with H.D. at 16 Bullingham Mansions frequently during 1919 and 1920. But, as an unmarried daughter, she had to come at parental demand to stuffy South Audley Street, where H.D. was called "That Woman" and made to feel unwelcome.[18] Given her own inhibitions and need for the appearance of respectability, the only way Bryher could free herself from her parents was to marry – hence her abrupt proposal and marriage to McAlmon on Valentine's Day, 1921. However much it was a marriage of convenience, the existence of a McAlmon "couple" in residence first at South Audley Street and then at Herbert Mansions – as well as the presence of H.D.'s mother – interrupted the formation of a lesbian family – if such indeed had even been in the making. The women were deeply devoted to each other, mutually interdependent, as their poetry and prose about each other and their daily correspondence whenever they were apart demonstrate. The most intensely intimate period of their relationship appears to have been from about April of 1919 until 1924, at least as far as their sporadic letters

reveal. Perdita's assessment that her "two mothers" were "platonic lesbians" may well be right on the mark. By the mid-1920s, they were
profoundly attached and loyal to each other, bonded in a primary relationship, probably not (or no longer) sexually engaged with each other,
and open to other erotic attachments.[19]

These other erotic ties, especially H.D.'s, no doubt contributed to the
companionate nature of their relationship. H.D.'s brief, unconsummated
fling with Peter Rodeck on the way to Athens in the spring of 1920 had
a profound influence on her feelings for Bryher and the sense of loss that
characterized her diaspora. An ex-officer and the adoptive son of a Dutch
painter, Rodeck used a nom de guerre, Peter Van Eck, the name H.D.
used for him in *Advent* (133, 154–64). Van Eck had lived in Greece and
worked on archeological excavations in Crete and Egypt, and was on
his way to India when H.D. met him on the *Borodino,* where they had
"a conventional meeting or voyage-out romance" (*Advent* 164). He apparently asked her to go to Egypt, then India with him, but she refused
and abruptly broke off with him in Athens. For years, she carried with
her the consoling memory of his offer, as well as the uncanny experience
she thought she had shared with him one moonlit night on deck.[20] His
appearance was doubly significant. He had "a startling heavy scar above
his left eyebrow," and "he stood a good military height, with broad
shoulders, rather square in build" (*Advent* 154, 156). He was, in short,
an early avatar of what she later called the "heros fatal," the wounded
soldier/lover like Aldington and Sir Hugh Dowding, a prototype of
Achilles in *Helen in Egypt*.[21] The wound was gone, the body perfected,
in the strange moment she stood with him on the deck and watched a
school of dolphins swimming in an absolutely "quiet sea . . . that is level
yet broken in a thousand perfectly peaked wavelets like the waves in the
background of a Botticelli" (*Advent* 160). The mysteries of the moment
convinced her that this "Man on the boat" was a visitation outside ordinary space and time. He looked like Van Eck, but was taller and had
no scar. Further, the captain said there were no dolphins, the stillness
was uncanny, and Van Eck did not confirm later that they had been
together on the deck. Like the writing on the wall she experienced in
Corfu a month later with Bryher, this moment with Van Eck became
for her the mute speech of the unconscious whose translation might signal
healing. In 1935, she wrote in a burst of intimacy to George Plank about
Rodeck, specifically how Bryher played out the fantasy of an affair in
her relationship with H.D. As yet another textual reconstruction of the
key events in her life, her letter to Plank is worth quoting without ellipsis:

> I met him on the boat that we took spring 1920, her father's boat. I
> don't know if he really cared as much for me as he thought – it was
> one of those dynamic "pockets." He was just ten years older, an ar-

chitect, ex-officer, on his way to a job in India. He wanted to stay with us in Athens, or have us come part way, to Egypt, or for me to go right on with him. I took this partly as a sort of "joke," you know these things, when we are not too old, on boats. He had a very dynamic manner and rather got what Br[yher] felt for me – it was with him, a sort of "marriage by prozy [sic]" that I had, a very lovely relationship with Br in Greece. It did not last long, as she was utterly unresponsive and those things, you know MUST inter-act. Still there HAD been the contact and the sort of "marriage in heaven" with the architect (we will call him.) He became a symbol of everything I had not had, the perfect balance in my life, and the support and the father for Perdita. We parted very abruptly in Athens – because I had[n]'t any strength, had been too battered. I have held to his image all these years, in spite of the side-tracks, that were really almost necessary. I found out, by accident, that he had married later in India – and I never saw him till seven years after. He was the same, but then seemed ill and his wife was an invalid. She died about four years ago.

He had some kind of break-down or crise and went into the church. I see him, now occasionally, in fact, he seems to be filling out – you know how it is – bits in the waste-land of the pattern. I left him, I had to of course, but I DID leave him, because of Br and P[erdita]. You see, I couldn't risk anything. Richard had begged me to come back. I had left the other man almost at once, lived alone in Buckingshire. When I went back to R., he simply said, "now you will register this child as 'Vane's' (we will call him) I will just take that slip of paper to the courts, and there will be no difficulty about divorce." Just like that. He had of course, started the trouble by living in that same house in M. Square with Arabella. The doctor and lawyer said the only thing was to consider it shell-shock, and get on with my life. Well...that was all right. Out of the frying pan into the fire. There was Br to look after and Perdita.

All that about R. was "fate"; without it, I would not have met this "architect," this one man, the only person, and the one I have lived for. I have made up that Holy Family, myself, the architect, P. and Br.; K[enneth]. came into it, like that – he was all along a sort of younger lover–son, if you will. I have had the greatest tenderness for K. And in a way, I felt at a moment I might atrophy. He was a perfect lover – beautifully young-male, and absolutely. This is the tragedy of his perversity.

Br of course, knows of this "architect," in many ways she was exquisite. She used to send me flowers in his name, identified herself with him. But you see, I needed above all, my feet on *the ground* and everything has driven me off. (1 May 1935)[22]

H.D. let go of Rodeck so as to retain the sensation of his perfection in a moment outside ordinary space and time. But after her mother left, H.D. kicked up her heels as she had threatened to do. The reappearance of Gregg and the men she sent to H.D. in 1926 – first Andrew Gibson and then Macpherson – placed a great strain on her relationship with Bryher. By the fall of 1926, H.D. was deeply in love with Macpherson, which distressed Bryher at first, according to "Autobiographical Notes" (15). After Macpherson joined them at the Riant Chateau in Territet, Bryher became more accommodating, if no less hurt. But H.D. remembered "quarrels" between Bryher and Macpherson, then long walks in the woods, then their engagement. By September 1, 1927, Bryher had divorced McAlmon, married Macpherson, and taken a London flat at Park Mansions, not far from H.D. As Perdita explained: "They had a *ménage à trois* with the status divided down the middle. Bryher was Mrs. Macpherson in name only; H.D. the romantic attachment" ("Profound Animal" 190). Many years later, Bryher explained to Pearson that she had married Macpherson to protect H.D.'s affair. Macpherson's mother was upset by her son's liaison with an older woman and wanted him to marry an heiress.[23] As the daughter of England's richest man, Bryher fit the bill. Her marriage gave her the position of a married woman, provided a screen for H.D., and bound H.D. to her at a time when Macpherson had taken her place.

At first, the ménage à trois with Perdita in tow seemed ideal – H.D. playfully echoed Shakespeare's more ominous "beast with two backs" in describing her unusual family situation to Havelock Ellis: "The Macphersons are almost MYSELF, we seem to be a composite beast with three faces" (1928?). But, by 1928, the tensions inherent in the threesome initiated the disintegration that was complete by 1931. The very intensity of H.D.'s bond to Macpherson left Bryher out, which probably contributed to Bryher's later assessment that these years were among her most unhappy.[24] Like Lawrence, Macpherson was a twin soul in spirit and creative sensibility. But, unlike Lawrence, Macpherson was not purely cerebral; their relationship was intensely erotic, however much desire was sublimated into the specular erotics of film, fashion, and photomontage. As Macpherson's *Poolreflection* anticipates, however, he became restive in a heterosexual relationship with an older woman and turned increasingly to younger men. Fascinated by black culture in both Harlem and expatriate communities like Capri, Macpherson fell in love with a black café singer, Toni Slocum, and later a black tubercular youth whom he (with Bryher's money) cared for. The crisis came in December of 1930 with "the Toni drama in Monte Carlo – and the charm of the original spell of K is broken, though there are periods, occasional talks that bring back the echo of the original" ("Autobiographical Notes" 19). Enthralled by Toni, Macpherson forgot to meet H.D. at the train and to keep "arrangements" with her.[25]

H.D. felt abandoned and betrayed. Although the cast was different,

the end of the 1920s repeated the end of the 1910s. A heterosexual relationship that had promised a perfect companionship of love and creative
work ended in what H.D. experienced as desertion. This time, Bryher
could not pick up the emotional pieces. H.D. wrote that at her return
from Monte Carlo, "I am very unhappy, almost estranged from Bryher
and worried terribly about Kenneth's state of mind and his future. . . .
Bryher is much with Perdita, will not talk with me about the Monte
Carlo problems" ("Autobiographical Notes" 21). Having contracted a
venereal disease with Slocum, Macpherson was ill, "strange and contradictory, reserved and then flighty with Norman Douglas" (22). On "the
day before anniversary of mother's death," he "makes an appalling re-
mark to me...I am stricken and not only for myself; he seems a moral
and psychic wreak" (22). As if to externalize their inner plight, the
threesome traveled incessantly in the spring of 1931. Macpherson had a
breakdown on the train during one of these trips, and Bryher finally
convinced H.D. to try psychoanalysis with Mary Chadwick.

H.D.'s abortion in November of 1928 may have acquired a related
symbolic significance.[26] She had associated her successful pregnancy of
1918 with the rebirth of her creative powers; it is possible that she connected her aborted pregnancy ten years later with what she called "the
sterility" of her creative efforts in this period. Guest's speculation that
H.D. handled the abortion with surprising calm is essentially correct, I
believe. Without any sign of breakdown, she stayed on in Berlin by
herself, seeing films, and writing a review for *Close Up*. At forty-two,
she seems to have had no regrets about ending this pregnancy. But there
is a complete gap in her writings on the abortion, an astonishing silence
for someone who went over and over the significant events of her life
in a variety of texts. Like the "gap in consciousness" representing the
stillbirth in *Madrigal,* the absence of the abortion in autobiographical
writings, even "Autobiographical Notes," which was not written for
publication, may signify its very importance to H.D.'s psychic state at
the end of the decade.[27]

By the beginning of the 1930s, H.D.'s ménage had essentially fallen
apart, fragmented into relationships that were broken across by ambivalence, however much support they provided. With Helen Doolittle's
death in 1927, H.D. was unmoored from mother and motherland. Yet
she felt shaken by her mother's death and more American than ever as
she crisscrossed the face of Europe. Macpherson had begun to go in his
own direction by 1930, in spite of the triumph they all felt at the opening
of *Borderline* in October of that year. He was erratically there and not
there in their lives for the next five years. Needing Bryher as usual, H.D.
nonetheless felt estranged from the woman who would continue to be
her most intimate companion until her death. She inhabited an erotic

borderline, living in a ménage à trois where no one slept with anyone, where everyone clung together and flung themselves apart. In sum, the decade ended with H.D. exiled from the two adults with whom she was most intensely involved – more "unconsoled" and "disintegrated" than she had been at the end of World War I.

Odysseus reached Ithaca after his ten years of wandering; Bloom even found comfort in his second-best bed after his epic journey on June 16th. But H.D.'s wandering intensified her sense of exile. The expatriatism that had been so exhilarating in prewar days had become a spiritual diaspora. This decade of wandering – parallel in many ways to the expatriate rootlessness of Lawrence, Aldington, Pound, and (to a lesser extent) Joyce, Nancy Cunard, and Mina Loy – led to fictions of an increasingly dispersed and scattered self. Each text itself examined her sense of dislocation and search for centeredness. Taken together, the fictions of the 1920s additionally show an intensification of desolation and dislocation. As a group and individually, these fictions operate on the premise common to many of the modernists: that the story of inner, personal conflict mirrored the outer, impersonal patterns of history; the dis-ease within reproduced the general cultural malaise without. It is this correspondence that motivates *The Waste Land* and "Hugh Selwyn Mauberley," that pervades *Mrs. Dalloway, Between the Acts, Lady Chatterley's Lover,* and *Nightwood.* Wandering in the wilderness of the postwar world, the modernist writer often split and displaced the public voice of the prophet into the shattered and fragmentary private voices of those whose personal search articulates against all odds and without the sure authority of God the despair and hope of a people.

II. GHOST STORIES: (UN)MASKING THE SELF IN PALIMPSEST *AND* HEDYLUS

The notion of traveling through space is integral to the unfolding of history and the development of the individual's consciousness with regard to the past. The voyage over geographic space is an expanded metaphor for the process of one person's coming to know who she is.

Susan Willis, "Black
Women Writers" (220)

In *Advent,* H.D. referred to *Hedylus* and *Pilate's Wife* as "historical or classic reconstructions" that "ghosted" for her own life story (*Advent* 148). To these "ghost stories," we might add "Hipparchia," the first panel in *Palimpsest*'s triptych. However, the historical novel is not an auspicious genre for autobiography. Indeed, essential conventions for each conflict radically and may account for the strain that characterizes a novel like *Hedylus*. Readers expect the historical novel to be about a past whose very difference from the present fuels its fascinations. Even when that past illuminates the present or demonstrates continuities, the historical novel removes the reader from the here and now to a distant time and place imaginatively re-created and reinterpreted by the author. Autobiography, on the other hand, is about the recent past, particularly as it created the present voice of its narrator, who is the teleological endpoint of the life story he or she tells. The subject may be split into the "I now" and the "I then," but the reader is continuously aware of the identification of the two within a single lifespan. What motivates the narrative in the historical novel and autobiography also differs. Where the historical novelist imaginatively reconstructs the lives of others, the autobiographer narcissistically examines the self. Where the historical novel attempts to bring to life the forces of history as they impinge on individual lives at a different moment in time, autobiography centers on the story of the author's self in his or her own time and place. To attempt autobiography within the conventions of the historical novel seems perverse and doomed to irreconcilable contradiction.

For H.D., the very difficulty of integrating autobiography and the historical novel may have contributed to its attraction. As romans à clef, *Paint It To-Day* and *Asphodel* disclosed too much for the intensely private H.D., who made no effort to publish them. Still feeling compelled to narrate her way out of her personal tangle and ambitious to make her mark as a prose writer, H.D. chose the historical novel as a sufficiently distanced and different discourse to tell her story publicly. In 1923, she began *Palimpsest,* which adapts the historical novel into its tripartite structure. And, in 1924, she began two full-blown historical novels, *Hedylus* and *Pilate's Wife.* Each uses a historical setting in the ancient world to screen its autobiographical content. Each displaces and distorts the events of her own life so as to hide what it expresses. Feeling safe enough behind her generic disguise, she published *Palimpsest* and *Hedylus,* whose reviews she watched with an intensity akin to Woolf's, and tried to publish *Pilate's Wife.* Unlike her romans à clef, her historical novels were written for public consumption.

The historical novel proved serviceable, not only as a disguise, but also as a form particularly suited to H.D.'s concerns during the 1920s. First, the classical settings of the novels replicated that of her post–*Sea Garden* lyrics. As she reflected in *H.D. by Delia Alton,* "The Greek, or the Greek and Roman scenes and sequences of these prose studies are related to the early poems" (184). In *Hymen* and *Heliodora,* place names and deities anchored her lyric cris de coeur in the ancient world. Adding the full coordinates of narrative space and time, the historical novels told the stories left implicit in the poems. *Hedylus*, for example, is set on Samos, one of the islands talismanically named in one of her favorite poems, "The Islands"; the concluding question of the poem could serve as coda to the novel: "what is Greece if you draw back / from the terror / and cold splendour of song / and its bleak sacrifice?" (*Collected Poems* 127). In *Palimpsest*, "Hipparchia" resonates with the lush eroticism of poems like "Leda," "Evadne," and "At Baia"; but, unlike the poems, "Hipparchia" narrates the conflicted course of love in the social world.

Second, the narrativization of her classical lyrics in the historical novels reflected H.D.'s preoccupation with the autobiographical and historical world out of which the poems had been distilled. Her sense of prose narrative as a discourse that could examine the realm of history fostered her use of the historical novel as a vehicle for autobiography. As genres, the historical novel and autobiography share a relationship to historical "fact" that is distinct from the conventions of "fiction." Readers expect fiction to tell the "truth" by lying, that is by making up "facts" that are not literally "real." Fiction is understood to deal with the "real" and the "true" at the level of symbol and representation. Like history itself, the historical novel and autobiography are assumed to be grounded in the literally "real." More of a generic hybrid than autobiography, the historical novel might well feature fictional characters against a backdrop of factual events and persons who actually lived. But readers generally expect that the historical novelist will have done extensive research to ensure a kind of historical accuracy not demanded of the purely fictional novel. Readers of autobiography have even more stringent expectations for accuracy in autobiographies. They can feel cheated or betrayed by an autobiography that deviates from the events in the author's life. In adapting the historical novel to the needs of autobiography, H.D. was attuned to these related generic expectations for historical accuracy. It was, after all, the need for a discourse anchored in "real" space and time that had drawn her to narrative in the first place.

Third, the conflation of autobiography and the historical novel was reinforced by the Einsteinian concepts of space and time that H.D. was developing in the 1920s. "Einstein was right," H.D. repeated several times in "Murex," the middle story of *Palimpsest*, in a telling refrain that gestures toward her view of the interdependence of space and time. *Palimpsest*'s matching refrain is "Joyce was right," an allusion to his prototypical status as a master of modernist subjectivities. Freud himself had argued that psychoanalysis was adding new depth to "the Kantian theorem that time and space are 'necessary forms of thought' " (*Beyond the Pleasure Principle* 22). Adapting an Einsteinian worldview, H.D. regarded space and time as coordinates of consciousness that exist relative to each other. No longer absolutes in a Newtonian universe, space and time were inseparable constructs of the mind. Popularly called the fourth dimension, time was conceived as a plane intersecting with the first three spatial dimensions and incorporating past, present, and future.[28] For H.D., this meant that a horizontal journey through space could be a vertical descent back in time. The ancient Greece, Rome, Egypt, and Palestine of her novels represent a textual fourth dimension of Einsteinian time/space. Not the netherworld of her early imagist pastoral, this fourth dimension exists in history, as narrative time. Each space represents a moment in time with its special ambiance; each time in turn recapitulates the symbolic significance of its geographic setting. What establishes the interplay of the two is their coexistence in the writer's mind as entities within, not outside of, consciousness.

Einsteinian relativity facilitated H.D.'s displacement of her own story into the time/space of the ancient past. Her expatriate wanderings across Europe in the 1920s represent a spatialization of a historical impulse. Her trip to Egypt in 1923, for example, enacted the relativity of space and time. Horizontal movement through space became an archeological dig into time, undoubtedly heightened by her presence at the opening of King Tut's tomb. Conversely, a period in the past could become a setting for her own movement through space. Hipparchia's exile in Rome after the defeat of her native Corinth recapitulates H.D.'s own dispersion after the war. This geographical and archeological fluidity contributes to the erasure of difference between individual and collective history. Time, Einstein's fourth dimension, is experienced through memory, the stories of a people about its collective past and the stories of a person about her individual past. As Raymonde thinks in "Murex": "The present and the actual past and the future were (Einstein was right) one. All planes were going, on, on, on together" (166). Likewise Susan Willis, in the epigraph to this section, superimposed the autobiographical search into the personal past onto a journey through space and time.

This superimposition of times and spaces in H.D.'s autobiographical/historical novels contributed to the development of her view of history as repetition rather than linear progression. As she observed, in *H.D. by Delia Alton,* her historical novels were set in eras with which she felt an affinity: "the thought of the first *Palimpsest* story, 'Hipparchia,' *Hedylus* and *Pilate's Wife* unnerves me. They are all set in antiquity, not strictly of the classic period but of the so-called dispersion. Perhaps dispersion is the key-word. We were dispersed and scattered after War I" (184). Each text features a persona who is alien, like H.D. herself, living far from home at a time of historical turmoil and transition. " 'Hipparchia,'" she recalled, "deals with a Greek girl in Rome, a stranger or half-stranger, like Veronica. [In] *Pilate's Wife,* Veronica is an Etruscan, 'a little out of step with the procession she was, of necessity, part of' " (184). Hedyle, abandoned years ago by her lover and left with a child to raise, lives far from her beloved Athens on the island of Samos as the mistress of the tyrant Douris. Veronica, exiled from the rich culture of Tuscany, lives as the wife of Pontius Pilate in the tumultuous times after the crucifixion of Jesus in Jerusalem. Hipparchia, after the defeat of Greece, is an exotic and learned curiosity in wartime Rome, about 75 B.C. The women can be superimposed because history repeats itself – the pattern of destruction, dispersion, and alienation structures the processus of time. Modernity – with its matrix of rebellion and dislocation – has happened before and will happen again, as Raymonde observes in "Murex," as H.D. reflected in *Notes on Euripides, Pausanius, and Greek Lyric Poets* and *By Avon River.*[29] Perversely, H.D. used the historical novel to define modernity.

In displacing her own story into a period of antiquity analogous to postwar Europe, H.D.'s autobiographical–historical novels foreground an often obscured aspect of the historical novel – that is, its interpretive, even heuristic narrative function as a commentary on the present. Ostensibly about a previous era, a historical novel nonetheless represents the interpretive lens and needs of the present. "The historical novelist," Avrom Fleishman noted, "writes trans-temporally: he is rooted in the history of his own time and yet can conceive another. In ranging back into history, he discovers not merely his own origins but his historicity, his existence as a historical being. What makes a historical novel is the active presence of a concept of history as a shaping force – acting not only upon the characters in the novel but on the author and readers outside it" (15).[30] H.D.'s historical novels personify this interplay of past and present by having the author exist in both time frames, a superimposition aimed at inscribing "not merely [her] own origins but [her] historicity, [her] existence as a historical being."

The experimental structure of *Palimpsest,* glossed as it is by the metaphor of a palimpsest itself, embodies both the contradictions and continuities between autobiography and the historical novel. A palimpsest, as H.D.'s own epigraph to the novel explains, is "a parchment from which one writing has been erased to make room for another." Erasure, however, is never complete. Traces of the earlier text erupt into the gaps of the more recent one; conversely, the surface text invites the reader to scrape away the top layer to discover the hidden and forgotten texts beneath. As Deborah Kelly Kloepfer wrote, a palimpsest "creates a strange, marginal writing that is both intentional and accidental; it must be excavated, sought after, at the very moment it is seeping through unbidden" ("Fishing the Murex" 553).[31] For H.D., the palimpsest served as a metaphor for the layering of both personal and collective histories. As an image for the psyche, palimpsest suggests the psychodynamics of conscious and unconscious memory and repression. As an image for history, it signifies the cyclical repetitions that structure the seemingly linear march of time. As an autobiographical/historical novel, *Palimpsest* collapses the personal and the historical into a single text whose layers "bleed" backward and forward into each cther, as Kloepfer has demonstrated ("Fishing" 561).

Palimpsest is a novel written backward. Composed of three distinct novellas, each is set in its own time and place with its own cast of characters. The narratives appear to have nothing in common; even the narrative styles of the three differ substantially.[32] A Table of Contents clearly separates the three:

    1. Hipparchia: War Rome (*circa* 75 B.C.)
    2. Murex: War and Postwar London (*circa* A.D. 1916–1926)
    3. Secret Name: Excavator's Egypt (*circa* A.D. 1925)

"Secret Name" was most likely the first of the three to be written; H.D. drafted it immediately after her trip to Egypt in February of 1923. "Hipparchia" might well have been the last; for, in "Autobiographical Notes" and *Compassionate Friendship,* H.D. referred to *Palimpsest* and *Hedylus* as "Greek reconstructions" on which she was working in Territet in 1924.[33] In both *Advent* and *H.D. by Delia Alton,* she described *Palimpsest* as a "rather loosely written long-short-story volume" (148, 183) and alluded to its haphazard assemblage when she reminded McAlmon of his visits to Territet in 1924 – "you suggested three stories, instead of the two I had offered, as it was in the Henry James tradition to have three long-short in a volume" (28 May 1949).

Nonetheless, the title, *Palimpsest,* invites us to read it as a single, layered text whose parts are unconventionally joined. Traditionally, a novel charts the narrative movement of selected major characters from one point in time to another. Anticipating experimental forms like Faulkner's *Go Down, Moses,* H.D. broke narrative sequence and disconnected the stories of the protagonists. But, as Kloepfer has demonstrated, H.D. linked the three long short stories both structurally and linguistically. All three protagonists, Kloepfer noted, are women who write and feel caught in a vise between past and present. Further, she argued:

> ...images...form the connective tissue of the text, images that will be retrieved in the actual Egypt section and then wash backwards to redetermine "Hipparchia" and "Murex" like a sea that is both eroding and increasing the shoreline. This is the functioning of the palimpsest which simultaneously erases and glosses the earlier texts.
>
> Once H.D. has set this tide into motion, it works in both directions; images initially engendered in "Hipparchia" resurface in "Murex" and "Secret Name." ("Fishing the Murex" 558–9)

The three stories acquire the status of novel as they are read backward and forward or viewed like a triptych in any and every direction. Repetitive images create a textual mesh that tenuously holds the three times and places in a single time/space of the author's and reader's consciousness.

Read in the context of her other work, *Palimpsest* also becomes a single text through its origin in and reference to H.D.'s own life. The autobiographical motive of *Palimpsest*, in other words, makes three stories one. Unlike the unpublished *Paint It To-Day* and *Asphodel*, *Palimpsest* does not signal that it should be read as autobiography. But an intertextual reading of *Palimpsest* transforms the triptych into a palimpsest of its author's psyche. Taken together, the stories represent a psychodynamic splitting and projection of identity into three different directions. Each woman acts out fully a partial aspect of H.D. All are writers, for example, but each does only one type of creative work – Hipparchia is a translator and compiler of Greek manuscripts; Raymonde is a poet of neo-Greek lyrics; Helen is a scholar of Graeco-Roman texts. As a further example of splitting, each story is an exercise in memory, an archeological dig into a different layer of H.D.'s war and postwar experience. Highlighting the role of repression in all efforts to remember, each story suppresses, condenses, and displaces various pieces of H.D.'s life story.

Repeating Part 2 of *Asphodel* and anticipating *Madrigal*, "Hipparchia" presents yet another version of the years between 1917 and 1919 – H.D.'s marriage to Aldington, affair with Gray, life-threatening illness, and Bryher's life-saving promise of a trip to Greece. As a screen for H.D., Hipparchia is the war-weary Greek "companion" of Marius, an oversexed Roman soldier, who pressures her for sex, then turns to the voluptuous Olivia for satisfaction. She leaves his Roman villa for the "perfection" of the Villa Capua, with the gentle grace of the aesthete, Verrus, who ultimately bores her. Returning to her work as a translator of Greek manuscripts, she becomes deliriously ill and begins recovering with the appearance of Julia Augusta, a young writer who has memorized all her poems and promises to take her to Greece. As in *Madrigal*, pregnancy and the birth of Perdita are missing; as in *Asphodel*, the Bryher figure appears at the end, but Lawrence does not exist in "Hipparchia."

"Murex," set in postwar London, focuses on the poet Raymonde Ransome who is forced to remember what she thought she had successfully forgotten – her wartime stillbirth and her soldier/husband's betrayal with the seductively beautiful Mavis, a composite version of Brigit Patmore and Dorothy Yorke. Awash in painful memories that culminate in the healing composition of a poem, Raymonde is a textual exemplar for H.D. herself, immersed in the process of writing *Palimpsest*. The story of "Hipparchia" is a displaced version of what Raymonde remembers in "Murex," much as *Palimpsest* represents what H.D. remembered as she engaged with her past. Like "Hipparchia," "Murex" erases the birth of Perdita and the relationship with Lawrence; like *Madrigal,* it deletes the story of Bryher.

"Secret Name" conflates H.D.'s visionary experience and spiritualized, shipboard romance with Peter Rodeck on the way to Greece in 1920 with her visit to Luxor and King Tut's tomb in February of 1923. Its protagonist, Helen Fairwood, is an author of esoteric articles on Graeco-Roman texts who has suffered in some unspecified way during the war. With Captain Rafton at her side, she experiences the occult Mystery of ancient Egypt as they stand before the Birth House in the moonlit Valley of the Dead. When they return the next day, the Birth House has vanished into the "fourth dimension" into which they had momentarily entered in the moonlight.

The names of the three women are like dream codes that lead back to their namer, H.D. Literally translated, the name "Hipparchia" means ruler of horses, a regal form for the familiar "Horse," one of H.D.'s pet names with Bryher during the early 1920s. Along with her nom de guerre, Ray Bart, the name Raymonde Ransome resonates with autobiographical associations. Ray was Pound's nickname as a young boy and code name in *Paint It To-Day,* here appropriated for the French-feminine Raymonde and the masculine-poet Ray. Ray is also metonymically related to Helios–Apollo, the major deity H.D. associated with poetry during the 1920s. Bart rhymes with Gart, Hermione's family name in *Asphodel* and *HER.* It also recalls Helga Dart, the pen name for H.D.'s Artemisian fantasy, *Paint It To-Day.* Broken into component parts, Raymonde Ransome invokes H.D.'s diaspora: the "rays" wandering over the world (*"monde"*); the "handsome" poet held hostage for some unnamed "ransom" for some unknown "reason." Raymonde's rootless alienation and exile is already present in her last name – "Ran some." Countering Raymonde is the name Helen Fairwood, whose archetypal resonance signals the story's focus on rebirth. Helen incarnates not only Helen of Troy, invoked all through "Murex" with the lines from Poe's "To Helen," but also of course H.D.'s own mother. Like Sylvia Plath's "Greenwood" in *The Bell Jar,* Fairwood is an organic name with a Druidic resonance. It alludes to H.D.'s name Dryad and anticipates the Helen Dendritis of "Leuké" in *Helen in Egypt.* With such name games, H.D. wove the "texts" of her life into the life of her text, very possibly modeling her punning on Freud's autobiographical wordplay in his decoding of his own dreams in *The Interpretation of Dreams.*[34]

Narrative repetitions also unify the disconnected stories. Like the manifest content of different dreams, the plots are completely distinct. But the latent content from which the manifest content was constructed is the same – essentially, the story of H.D.'s exile and search for healing in the 1920s. Although the specific autobiographical referents in the three stories point to different events in H.D.'s life, all three are united in narrating the structure of her diaspora in the 1920s. Superimposed on each other, the three tell the story of an exiled woman whose psyche is split by sexual politics at a time of vast societal disruption. The narrative pattern is linear – it opens with a presentation of the woman's fragmented identity, moves to her search for healing, and concludes with the process of self-creation affirmed. This repeated plot (re)enacts the biographical movement that brings the text itself into being. Exiled and alienated after the war, H.D. attempted to reunite her shattered psyche through the act of inscribing its division and reunification. Believing in the magic and mystery of the Word, H.D. played God to her own becoming.

Like that of H.D., the geographic exile of Hipparchia, Raymonde, and Helen is an externalization of an inner rootlessness produced by war. For both the victors and the vanquished, war has meant a fundamental loss, a separation from a past that consequently comes to represent an idealized, prelapsarian world. In "Hipparchia," Greece before Rome's conquest exists in Hipparchia's memory as a beacon of light flickering in the darkness of brutal Rome. To Romans like Marius and Verrus, Hipparchia incarnates the brilliant culture they have destroyed in attempting to possess it. She is "some exiled Muse," a "phantom wraith," a "homesick" woman, "favoured among the lost rabble, the sweepings of the broken states and cities of dispersed Hellas" (42, 15, 10).

In the "post-war Limbo" of London, Raymonde embodies a "battered generation" without hope (166). Unlike Hipparchia, Raymonde belongs with the victors of war. But she and her "still-born generation" are just as lost (117). As the story opens, only forgetting makes existence possible – like "Lethe," a lyric version of "Murex's" narrative opening (*Collected Poems* 190).[35] London's "delicious over-blur of autumn mist" is a "lotus-drug," a "cocoon-blur of not-thinking" that blocks out the war years (96, 98). Ermy, a young Jewish woman, disrupts Raymonde's London "Nirvana" by forcing her to see that history repeats itself, particularly when the past is repressed. Mavis, the woman who "took" Raymonde's husband during the war, has now claimed Ermy's lover. Raymonde, a "transplanted American [in a] pays lointain," relives her past in listening to "Ermy, odd exile like herself, with caution of a transplanted race" (132, 125). Ermy, a link to the ancient Semitic and Egyptian civilizations, "was not of this milieu. She would always be a misfit, but it didn't do to betray them. Not Jews. It was lacking in taste to betray one of the East. An Arab, a Jew. One didn't. One just couldn't. Respect for learning" (160–1). In hearing her own story transposed into Ermy's narrative, Raymonde learns that she too will always be "a misfit": "What anyhow was Ermy, odd Eastern Jewess? Ermy was outside. . . . [was] of a captive, of a lost race. Feet, feet, feet, feet, feet. Raymonde was like that. She was of a lost race" (114).[36]

Like Hipparchia and Raymonde, Helen appears cut off from her roots. She is an American who has lived in London and suffered in some unspecified way during the war. Although she is "Mrs. Helen Fairwood," no husband seems to exist – even in memory. Her past remains veiled, but her sensibility as an exile is heightened by reverberations from the previous two stories. During the story, she is a scholar in hiding, posing as a tourist at the Hotel Luxor. Exiled from her status as an authoritative expert on the ancient world, she plays the role of an ignorant woman enchanted with the expertise of the handsome, "war-battered" "ex-captain of the Great War," who wants her to join him on his trip to Assuan for the department of Public Works (192, 176). When he asks her "are you New York or London," she "answered 'both' " (183). Like H.D., she is both American and British, both with and without a husband, most at home in an ancient world reconstituted in her imagination.

The exile of the three women is an externalization of inner conflict rooted in sexual politics. Anticipating the portraits of Hermione in *HER* and Julia in *Madrigal,* all three women are writers whose work and womanhood, mind and body, are at odds. The result is an interior civil war "of self against self, the self of intellect, the self of the drift and dream of anodyne, the intermediate self, that slender balancing pole that held the two together, joined the two, keeping them strictly separate" (*Palimpsest* 208). "Hipparchia" introduces this fragmentation of female identity as the result of male desire acted out in the intersecting, brutal politics of empire and bedroom. The only story to use male centers of consciousness, "Hipparchia" opens with and often returns to Marius's obsessive thoughts about Hipparchia, who both fascinates and repels him. He is drawn to her because she epitomizes the Greek intellect that Rome has vanquished; he rejects her because that intellect makes her appear to him as "cold alabaster" (25, 16). "I slept not with a woman but a phantom," he keeps thinking, and gossip has it that Hipparchia is "frigid" (11, 20, 9, 26). In taking her sexually for the "one hundred and fifty-second time," he reenacts Rome's conquest of Greece: "He breathed in some relic of a vanished and vanquished loveliness. A vanished and vanquished body of reality. Vanquished. Rome the invincible. He felt, withdrawing from her, in one moment, the overpowering beauty of this conquest" (29). As the embodiment of a dying Greece, she is the "death-hyacinth," to which he is drawn like a Roman "drone" (21, 14). She personifies as well the "body" of Corinth, "the lost city" of "charm incarnate" (29). His desire for her ever-elusive body is the longing to possess the Other, a desire for conquest presented as inherently sadistic.

As Marius "Mars-like" "plunge[d] dagger into a gold lily" (6), public and private spheres collapse into a analogic series – Victor:Vanquished :: Roman Empire:Greece :: Rome:Corinth :: Man:Woman :: Marius:Hipparchia.

Just as Rome could conquer, but never possess Greece, Marius takes, but cannot hold Hipparchia. Popping the balloon of masculine fantasy, H.D. shifts the center of consciousness from Marius to Hipparchia with dramatic effect – in its full autobiographical context, Hipparchia's resistance unveils the institution of marriage as a form of prostitution and suggests that the phallic power upon which it rests is a sham. In expressing her reluctant willingness to have sex, Hipparchia unromantically alludes to the raw exchange of sex for security that structures their relationship: "A bargain is a bargain Marius. I do not give you satisfaction" (12). Then, feeling violated by his "smothering" kisses, she eludes him by refusing the erotic response he craves. Unlike Europa, to whom he compares her, she does not enjoy rape, here radically defined as intercourse without (female) desire (15). Instead of being swept away by the invincible Roman in his naked splendour, she compares him to a "bulbous vegetable": "But when one has slept perhaps on a rough estimate, one hundred and fifty times with one man, it is, can you not see, somewhat of a shock, at the end, to find it has not been a man at all, merely, a rather bulbous vegetable. No, I apologise, no cabbage but a turnip" (11). The sexual innuendo is shocking, not for its vulgarity, but rather for its mock-heroic reduction of a man to a vegetable shaped like a penis.[37]

Hipparchia's verbal transformation of Marius's "dagger" into a "turnip" spoils his conquest, but it cannot prevent her ultimate victimization by the system he represents. For all her sexual reluctance and biting scorn, she loves his warmth and yearns for the comfort and stability he can provide, symbolized by his "brazier," a precursor of Achilles's brazier in *Helen in Egypt* (12, 61). Although she eludes his desire, she is unable to resist his view of her as a cold and frigid "phantom." Her "intellect," she believes, is a tyranny that separates her from her body, specifically her womanhood. Her mind, she thinks, is masculine, her link with Philip, her "first love," companion, and half-uncle, the botanist who was killed by Roman soldiers (10). Helios-Apollo is her divine inspiration; his twin, Artemis, is her counterpart, the goddess who stands "hesitant between girl and boyhood" (67).

Like Julia in *Madrigal*, Hipparchia has internalized the system of representation Marius (like Rafe in *Madrigal*) perpetuates – namely, the division of WOMAN into angel and whore – one denied a body, the other a mind. While Hipparchia feeds his spirit, Olivia satisfies his body. Olivia, he thinks, "has no brain for anything," but "she was so simply, so whole-heartedly a woman" (26, 24). In retaliation, Hipparchia goes off with Verrus, with whom "it was apparent that some Aphrodite had recalled her, called her to the realm of womankind" (38). "Her body recalled her to herself," she discovers; "Verrus had given her a body that beat with rhythm to near sea" (38, 43). Her liberation from Marius's view of her is evident when she notes "with a faint shiver of astonishment that she was not altogether 'heartless' " (36). Verrus cannot, however, reconcile her divided self because he bores her intellectually (51). With Marius, she feels all intellect; with Verrus, all body. Hipparchia's descent into delirium centers in the continued interior war of "self against self," the split between mind and body, intellect and sex.

Raymonde experiences a related, but more severe, split inscribed in her two names and intensified by the continuing reverberations of Hipparchia's story in her own. The erotics of empire are muted, but still present in "Murex," in the form of the soldier/husband Freddie, who fell in love with Mavis after the stillbirth of Raymonde's baby. Raymonde repeatedly thinks of Ray Bart in the third person, much as H.D. referred to her pseudonymous identities: "Beyond Raymonde there was another Raymonde. She called it Ray Bart. Freddie called it Ray Bart (as if it were Robert or Norbert). Raybart. . . . " (149). "Raymonde" is the mother whose baby was stillborn, the woman whose husband left her for another, the aging face in the mirror. As "Raymonde's" double, "Ray Bart" is the male nom de guerre for the poet, who is distinct from the deserted wife who drifts in the anodyne of forgetting (127, 123). Where Raymonde is passive and listless, Ray Bart is hard like steel. Raymonde would drift forever, repressing both past and poetry. Ray Bart insists fiercely on remembering and on continued dedication to art, under the aegis of Helios for whom "Poetry was to remember" (151, 155). Like Hipparchia, Raymonde–Ray feels split between a mind and art she images in masculine terms and a body and heart that is feminine; her repetitive discourse heightens the sense of paralysis:

> It was Ray Bart who always checkmated her. It was Ray Bart who caught her open-handed. . . . It was the poet, the young spearman who was Raymonde's genius. Ray Bart held a sword of pure steel. . . . Ray Bart was a flaming white sword of the spirit. . . . Raymonde was tenuous, Raymonde was obliterated. . . .
>
> The icy glamour of the thing she knew was Ray Bart's helmet closed above her. Above Raymonde's forehead (where she would have worn some slight and fragrant but soon withering little crown of field flowers) Ray Bart's helmet rested. The helmet of Ray Bart weighed heavy on her. (127–8, 148)

With the inner conflicts of Hipparchia and Raymonde informing her own, Helen reenacts their psychic split between mind and body, head and heart. Less schizophrenic than Raymonde, Helen nonetheless resorts to disguise to hide "her brain, that dart and pulse of steel that was her brain, almost mechanical in its trained daring" (205). A few days away from her work with the famous Egyptologist who is opening King Tut's tomb allows her a respite from intellectual work and the chance to play out the role of an ordinary woman on holiday at the Hotel Luxor. Incognito, she accompanies the American mother and daughter, Mrs. and Mary Wharton, with whom she meets Captain Rafton. Assuming that she, too, is a tourist, Rafton explains the tombs to her. Like many brilliant women, Helen hides her own knowledge to feed the male ego:

> She meant to tell him about her work, to make him know what this had meant, this morning's freedom, even this few hours' evening escape. She didn't tell him. She let him go on explaining the difference between Isis and Hathor, Osiris and Nut. . . . She let him go on in his soft London voice, let him go on, saying things that were the very primer of myth and saying them to her, of all people, with conviction. He must never, never know of that round half-dozen terrible little articles that had got her here. Terrible, intense, erudite and in their limited way, illuminating and terribly right. (188–9)

Helen's disguise of ignorance is a veil of femininity that obscures her own ambivalence toward her "brain," the intellect that she (like Hipparchia and Raymonde) associates repeatedly with Greece, Helios, and blades of steel. These masculine motifs suggest that Helen exhibits a twentieth-century version of what George Eliot experienced in saying that she had a man's mind in a female body. Disguise of this "masculine" genius is a relief, a vacation from the strain of a divided self. Anticipating Woolf's use of clothing as a metaphor for the cultural construction of gender in *Orlando,* Helen's elaborate ritual of dressing in a shimmering blue dress for a romantic, moonlit evening with Rafton signals her assumption of femininity and repression of her "masculine" intellect. "Her thin arm" held in "the straight vise" of the Captain's grip, Helen "was for the moment free from the insistent tyranny of brain, like any other servant" (209, 211). Echoing the touch of Marius and Freddie, Rafton's hand is the "conqueror's bracelet" on her arm (210). Although the moment of pure femininity is only temporary, Helen revels in it, asking "Of what use was ambition and achievement? Of what possible meaning that dart and pulse of steel, of measured light, that was the very apt and prevalent image of her thought?" (208). The very question, however, attests to the continued interior strife of "self against self" that mirrors the exterior structure of patriarchy. The mark of the "conqueror's bracelet" on woman's mind and body recapitulates the erotics of empire laid out in "Hipparchia."

The search of the three women to unify the divided self is a quest plot that gives the narrative of each story its linear direction and tenuous resolution. Healing, for all three, centers on (pro) creativity – that is, on the entanglement of motherhood and authorhood, which is itself split and displaced in different ways to suggest the significance of the absent Mother for the daughter/writer's self-creation. With increasing intensity, each story presents a longing for the powerful Mother who is not there, whose presence must be reconstituted to heal and (re)birth the daughter as a whole woman. As subtext for this longing is a desire for the sister, a muted homoerotic layer linked in each story to the narrative search for the Mother – just as Freud posited in his general theory of lesbian desire and in his specific diagnosis of H.D.'s need.[38] Like the composite text made up of *Paint It To-Day*, *Asphodel*, and *Madrigal*, *Palimpsest* disperses the components of (pro) creativity into the different layers of the text. In the full palimpsestic text, creativity and procreativity, motherhood and authorhood, mothers and daughters "bleed" into each other (to echo Kloepfer again) to signify a re-union of body and brain. This synchronic palimpsest coexists alongside a diachronic progression from story to story. As historical time moves forward from antiquity to modernity, the quest plot of the whole text regresses back to the womb of psychic time, the Birth House of the Mother in which the daughter can be (re)born.

"Hipparchia" introduces this maternal quest plot by connecting Hipparchia's divided self to her ambivalence toward her dead mother, the first Hipparchia.[39] One of the historical personages mixed with the fictional in "Hipparchia," the mother lives on in the text of Antipater's poem that Marius and Hipparchia keep reciting: "*I cast my lot with cynics, not / with women seated at the distaff, / weighted with silk and ornament!*" (8). Against the pleas of her family, the first Hipparchia had married and shared a beggar's life with the philosopher Crates, the Cynic who preached worldly denial. To her daughter, this gesture signified the renunciation of her womanhood for the sake of her intellect. The Greeks, the daughter says, "got my mother through appeal to intellect. She went off, putting aside her patterned robes, her bracelets, her beautiful saffron and dyed shoes, her lovely woman's sandals" (62). To the daughter, this abandonment of ornamental femininity pointed to a deeper and more threatening renunciation of womanhood itself. Dedication to philosophy precluded maternal love for her daughter. Still resentful of her father's influence, the daughter remembers feeling "He might have left her to us," that is, to nurture the young Hipparchia and her companion Philip (14). As mother, Hipparchia was absent to her daughter because she was committed to the life of the intellect.

Unmothered, Hipparchia's greatest fear is that she has become her own mother – cut off by her intellect from giving and receiving love. Hurt by Marius's view that she is cold, she at first fights against the haunting image of her mother: "more than ever she repudiated her mother and her mother's intellectual decision" (34–5). In a telling reversal of Chodorow's theory of the reproduction of mothering, Hipparchia thinks she cannot respond to Marius as a woman because her mother's "intellectual decision" denied her the maternal love she needed. The awakening of her body with the gentler advances of Verrus, however, leads Hipparchia to imagine that she has laid her mother's ghost to rest. Having rejected her mother's choice of pure intellect, she feels like "a giant Thetis," a mother to herself, "like a moth from a split chrysalis" (41).

This resolution is short lived, perhaps because it is founded in a matriphobia that leaves the split self intact. Hipparchia cannot give up her mind any more than she can repudiate her mother. Her decision to leave Verrus is inseparable from her search for reconciliation with the haunting maternal presence. Staring into the mirrored goblet, she sees "Hipparchia" – herself as her mother, the boundaries between mother and daughter dissolved: "Hipparchia no longer repudiated her mother and her mother's intellectual decision. . . . The image [in the goblet] remained silver, detached and alone and Hipparchia, gazing at Hipparchia, saw that Hipparchia was some abstraction, no warm honey-coloured goddess. . . . She saw Hipparchia and she loved Hipparchia" (53–5). No longer hating her mother and her mother in her self, she repeats her mother's intellectual decision. Phaenna, the servant woman who is "a mythical presence, a freed woman, a type almost vanished, devoted in adversity," oversees the process, like a Demeter who has found her daughter (68). Leaving behind her fancy clothes, Hipparchia packs all her manuscripts for a journey to Tusculum, an Etruscan city settled by Greeks, where she plans to finish Philip's book, "a fervid compilation of poetry, religion and ethics" (71).

In Tusculum, however, she is not healed. Rather, her initial conflict with her mother is heightened to the point of delirium. The more she tries to write, the more split she feels: "She was back with the family problem, treading round and round" (78). Replicating her mother's intellectual decision takes her into the heady realm of "intoxicating intellect," a kind of pure cerebralism that still leaves her cut off from her self as woman. As "devoté" of Helios, she is "drunk" with poetry, bringing the dead Philip back to life in her work: "Philip asked other things of her. Philip said better, better, better, work, work, work. But she had worked. Philip was a sword, Philip was her mind but mind was pure god. . . . The mind was Philip who stood like a sword over me" (80–1). Phaenna's efforts to nurse and nurture fail as Hipparchia is once again haunted by a demonic ghost of the intellectual mother from whom she cannot separate: "Hipparchia her mother, rose most frequently to plague

her. Hipparchia faced Hipparchia, her mother who rose to plague her.
. . . Round and round and round. It went round and round and round"
(78). The sudden appearance of Julia Augusta at the height of Hipparchia's
illness offers the possibility of a healing break from "the family problem"
and thereby gives the narrative a linear direction. The lesbian eroticism
of *Paint It To-Day* and *Asphodel* has been suppressed in "Hipparchia,"
but Julia's devotion and promise of a trip to Greece invoke Bryher and
recall the more explicitly lesbian love of the Bryher figures in the earlier
texts. "Hipparchia" ends on a note of hope, that Hipparchia's return to
her motherland with a "sister" will release her from the repetitions of
the past.

"Murex" advances the maternal quest plot without fully resolving
what haunts Hipparchia. Whereas Hipparchia's conflict centers on her
mother, Raymonde's suppressed crisis focuses on her self as mother.
Forced by Ermy to remember what she chose to forget, Raymonde
relives the dissolution of her marriage, in which Freddie's preference
for Mavis repeats Marius's choice of Olivia. Like Hipparchia, Raymonde's defense against rejection of her womanhood is to return to
her work – in this case, a poem whose lines keep coming as persistently as a child being born. The poem does not begin to come,
however, until she can recall what pained her the most – that Freddie's affair with Mavis began right after the stillbirth of her baby.
Her "failure" as mother led to her "failure" as wife, thereby intensifying the split she felt between Raymonde and Ray Bart. Remembering that failed birth, however, allows her to birth a poem, to mother
words the way she might have nurtured a baby. The (re)production
of memory precedes and continues to be interwoven with the production of the poem. Raymonde and Ray Bart temporarily unite in a
creativity made possible by procreativity.

Raymonde's poem not only comes after the memory of her stillbirth,
but it comes like an extended birth – haltingly, laboriously, with pain
and exhilaration (146–72). Like contractions and the respite between, the
text alternates between intense poetic lines and reflective prose interludes.
The verse comes just a few lines at a time, followed by Raymonde's
interior monologue, which situates the pure lyric into its originating
narrative context. Like labor, the movement is ultimately linear – a babe
is born, a poem is completed; but, also like labor, the rhythm is ragged,
not steadily progressive. Sometimes nine lines pop out, sometimes only
one. Other times, the poem gets stuck in one place, where Raymonde
repeats the same lines over like a woman whose labor halts on a plateau
of partial cervical dilation. The constant repetition of "feet, feet, feet,
feet" conflates the soldier's feet she heard in the nursing home, the poetic
feet of her coming poem, and the heartbeat of mother and babe, poet

and poem. At first, she resists the coming poem – "that pain and that sound and that rhythm of pain. . . . I don't want to write it" (145–56); but, by the end, she is overjoyed by the birth and rebirth the poem represents. She decides that she must leave the drift of London for the clairvoyant Swiss air of Cret-d'y-Vau, where she can write out "the memories shut up in one small spherical surface, her own head, to be watched going round and round and round" (172). Raymonde's sense of renewed direction as a poet and the (pro)creative aesthetic that its production embodies represent a clear advance over Hipparchia's hope for a return to her motherland.

The homoerotic subtext of the maternal plot in "Murex" also intensifies the suggestion of female bonding at the end of "Hipparchia." Raymonde's poem, with its persistently erotic undertone, is written to and for Ermy about Mavis. Remembering her loss of Freddie to Mavis is the ostensible occasion for the poem, but love and hate among the three women (the "I," "you," and "she") overwhelms the initially heterosexual motive for the poem. "She," the unnamed Mavis, is a "Circe" whom the speaker has hated for her *"treachery"* and *"invidious lies"* (149, 150). "You," the poem's addressée, is a *"gold and amber"* *"queen"* of the East, the Jewess Ermy, whose appeal to Raymonde has restored her buried self to consciousness and helped her to forgive Mavis. As an alter ego for herself, Ermy is a sister figure *"with fair / Tyrian-blue hyacinths / against hyacinth hair"* (151). Ermy's association with hyacinths picks up on the motif of homoerotic love in the myth of Hyacinthus alluded to elsewhere in *Palimpsest* and throughout the Artemisian imagery of H.D.'s other texts. Initially resentful of Ermy's presence, Raymonde comes in the course of the poem to beg *"speak on, speak on; / . . . / so I may treasure (yet no thief) / your name, / may build in exquisite loneliness / your shrine"* (157). *"Let me take your hand,"* she says, *"who know not Love's / illegal rapture / and his withering fire"* (164). Further, her reverence and desire for Ermy transforms her hatred of Mavis into a bond of love: *"this woman, O my sweet, / finds worshipper / in me who fled her often –"* (169). *"See –,"* Raymonde tells Ermy in the last line, *"I worship, / more, more, more – I love her / who has sent you to my door"* (172). Loving Ermy brings Raymonde a healing self-love; seeing Ermy as stately queen empowers – much as Her's love for Fayne was to do in *HER.*[40]

The maternal plot of "Secret Name" represents a progression through regression in relation to "Murex" and "Hipparchia." Hipparchia fought feelings of love and hate for her mother. Raymonde's memory of an aborted motherhood allows for her procreation of a poem. But Helen is actually borne to the Birth House, washed in the natal waters of the mystically present, powerful Mother in a transcendent time/space of the psyche. She experiences the healing re-union with the Mother that Hipparchia and Raymonde desired. This movement forward and backward gives *Palimpsest* a simultaneously linear and circular structure. Helen, whose name combines woman as lover and (H.D.'s) mother, brings the past back into the present so that story's moment is both ancient and modern. Historical and personal pasts collapse into a single psychic space, a fourth dimension ruled by the maternal presence. "The Greeks came to Egypt to learn," Helen thinks repeatedly as she comes face to face with the maternal Mystery of Egypt that underlies the paternal intellect of Greece in both her own and Western culture's past (217, 218). Helen's split selves are healed, at least temporarily, as she and the soldier/ lover stand before the Birth House bathed in moonlight in the Valley of the Kings. It is both the womb and the tomb of time, the cyclic image of life and death, origins and ends that anticipates what Kristeva called women's time ("Women's Time"). Standing in the light of the Birth House, Helen hears the mystic "laughter" of Isis that "merged and made one all the selves, the self of the slave locked into the silver barred and shimmering intellect, the slave more languorous, yet still locked into the pleasure terraces of some Asiatic or Egyptian city, the other, the slave that held, a sold link, her everyday self, enslaved to both these others" (212). Helen's own "laugh" is the daughter's echo of the healing Mother: "Like the light, fourth dimensional, a bird, something with gold feathers swept across the silver strings of an Egyptian's throat, across the thin and tenuous strings of a Greek throat" (210). In the geographical axes of Helen's psyche, Greece represents the Law of the Father, the Symbolic and Intellectual, while Egypt signifies the Laugh of the Mother, the Semiotic and Mystical. Anticipating texts like *The Gift, Trilogy,* and *Hermetic Definition,* Isis (maternal deity) is the divine presence upon which Helios (paternal deity) rests.

Like the two preceding stories, the maternal quest narrative in "Secret Name" has a homoerotic subtext. Beneath her twinship with Rafton, Helen identifies even more deeply with Mary, a pretty, young American girl who is caught up in her courtship with Jerry Cope, the handsome, mindless chap on his way back to England from Bengal. Nonetheless, Helen feels a strong bond with the girl: "For weren't she and Mary in their outlook singularly ... alike? The same gaunt frames, thin with that underlayer of reserve power. ... Thin and virile, the two were temperamentally matched and physically" (231). Both act out the heterosexual plot appropriate to their age, but Helen "rejoiced" in Mary's "tribute" to her transformation in the blue dress as she realizes that "it was the girl Mary she was, in all conscience, after" (198). Echoing the erotic mirror motifs of "Hipparchia" and "Murex," Helen and Mary regard each other in the mirror – the blue of Helen's dress meeting the "blue, blue eyes" of Mary – in an emotionally charged scene (198–9). Later,

Helen yearns to tell Mary not to marry Jerry: " 'don't marry him, Mary-land,' but she had no courage to voice the words while her heart tapped on invidious, 'don't marry, marry, marry – him – Mary – land.' She had no courage whatever to voice the words, to face the girl with her doubts, her increasing doubts and intimations, her very serious ideas on the subject of these foreign marriages" (202).

After the Birth House experience with Rafton, Helen returns to the tombs with Mary the next day to have a different kind of ecstatic experience marked by their touch. Together, the women exclaim over the beautiful colors that had been invisible in the wash of moonlight. The language is lyrically repetitive, hypnotic, erotically charged – dominated by the discourse of the Kristevan Semiotic:

> Blue, green, Nile green, the green of wet apple leaves. Blue, cobalt, blue again, the burning blue fire of the iris. Isis, iris, wasn't it almost the same, Mary had said. Hot, burning, a blue that had no ice and shale of Attic promontories. . . . Would this sun-pool of light melt even Delphic Helios? . . . She felt under her hand, beneath the cool thick linen of the dust-coat, bones of the girl's thin shoulders and the fibre of her being alike intent, enthralled, almost in some flame of enthusiasm at her side. . . . Iris blue, iris green, iris bright-blue, iris wet-blue altogether different, a blue brighter than the brightest that can ever be named. (232–3)

The maternal/lesbian eroticism that supplants the heterosexual plot in "Secret Name" appears to fulfill the desires for the divine Mother expressed in the two earlier stories. But *Palimpsest*'s linear structure is undermined in a number of ways that ultimately call into question the resolution the text proposes. First, the repetitions of *Palimpsest* – linguistic and structural – disrupt narrative progression in the text as a whole. While each story ends with a tentative resolution of the protagonist's conflict, the next story begins with the same conflict manifesting in a different form. This structural repetition contradicts the linear direction of the text as a whole and sets up an expectation in the reader for yet another layer in the palimpsest. What guarantee is there, we wonder, that the vision of the Mother at the Birth House can cure "the compulsion to repeat" that *Palimpsest* structurally inscribes? Freud's concept of the repetition compulsion in *Beyond the Pleasure Principle* suggests that repetitive patterns – what H.D. calls "going round and round and round" throughout *Palimpsest* – are based in an infantile anxiety about the Mother's presence and absence, alternations of pleasure and pain that the child cannot control. Repetitive games (like "*fort-da*") parallel other repetitive symbolic structures (like a text) that represent the fantasy of controlling the uncontrollable presence of the all-powerful Mother of the child's desire. Helen's re-union with Isis may represent just such a textual fantasy. It exists in a fourth-dimensional time/space of psychic reality. It fulfills the desire for the Mother's presence that originated in her absence in the first two stories. Who is to say that this rhythm of absence and presence will not be repeated?

Secondly, each woman's resolution of a split identity exists as epiphany, as a lyric moment of wholeness temporarily outside ordinary time and space. But for all three the moments of lyric intensity end with a fall back into narrative time and space, where the cultural constructions of history hold sway. Nothing in the epiphanies of the three women changes the external structures of society that initiated their interior conflicts. Epitomized by war, the politics of empire and bedroom are unchanged. The androcentric economy of desire and sexual exchange leaves intact the construction of gender that splits woman's mind off from her body, that separates creativity and procreativity. The homoerotic subtext of each story – the bonding between women – poses the only threat to patriarchy. But, like *Mrs. Dalloway,* there is no suggestion in these stories that moments of bliss between women can provide the narrative structure of a woman's life in the "real" world. Instead, the constant bisexual pull between the dominant heterosexual plot and the muted lesbian subtext implies that there is no realizable resolution. Each of the women loves and continues to love a soldier caught up in the sadomasochist dynamics of empire; each woman's resistance to playing the role of masochist in that system is inseparable from her homoerotic desire. The textual seesaw of bisexual desires inscribes the problem, not a solution. Furthermore, like Julia at the end of *Madrigal,* none of the women can change the way their soldier/lovers see them. The women's momentary experiences of wholeness have no impact on the men's continued need to see women as "masculine" intellects or "feminine" objects of desire.

Thirdly, "Secret Name," the penultimate end point of the linear quest plot, itself explores the problematics of progression in *Palimpsest.* As a fourth-dimensional presence, Helen's Birth House is both there and not there – like the powerful Mother of the daughter's desire. Helen's epiphany of the Mother in the moonlight cannot be replicated in the sunlight, that is, in the bright rays of Helios, who is throughout *Palimpsest* associated with the paternal law, intellect, and language. When she returns the next day with her notepad and camera to record the beautiful little temple with the tools of science, the Birth House has vanished. Its absence convinces Helen that she had indeed been initiated into the Mystery of Egypt, of the primal Mother. But its disappearance also confronts her with the basic problem H.D. later addressed in *Trilogy, Helen in Egypt,* and *Hermetic Definition:* How does one relate the out-of-time to the in-time, the eternal to history, the spiritual to the material, the lyric to the narrative? *Palimpsest* suggests that this question, fundamental to religion, has a basis in desire, in the dynamics of what Hipparchia calls the family problem: How does the daughter relate the Mother to the Father in a world dominated by the intellectual "law" of the Father that represses the mystic "laugh" of the Mother? In such a world, the narrative time/ space of *Palimpsest,* the Mother is materially absent and mystically present. Exiled on the borderline between presence and absence, the daughter must mother herself with the pregnant Word.

The instability of linearity in *Palimpsest* causes its beginning and end to collapse into the middle. The novel's undermining of its own progression invites us to read the stories as a triptych, where the central panel is the dominant one. "Hipparchia" represents Raymonde's past – the events of the war years; "Secret Name" is her future – the revelation of the divine. In "Murex," Raymonde is thoroughly grounded in present time, haunted by memories she has tried to forget and hoping for spiritual renewal through their recovery. Raymonde's "reading" and "writing" of her past replicates H.D.'s production of *Palimpsest* itself, and suggests how we in turn should read her writing. The alternation of prose and poetry in the final section of "Murex" parallels the dialectical movement of H.D.'s lyric and narrative discourses. Like H.D.'s poems of the period, Raymonde's lyric is depersonalized, its biographical origins distilled out. The poem's place in the prose narrative, however, recontextualizes the lyric, much as H.D.'s prose foregrounds the autobiographical narrative muted in her poems. Finally, Raymonde's labored creation of a poem made possible by her memory of procreation suggests the (pro)creative aesthetic that H.D. had articulated in *Notes on Thought and Vision.* It highlights as well her belief that the split identity of the woman poet achieves momentary wholeness in the (re)production of language.

Raymonde's problems, resolved only in the time/space of her poem, resurface as the motive in H.D.'s other classical reconstructions, *Hedylus* and *Pilate's Wife,* both of which she began writing at the same time she was hard at work on *Palimpsest.* Like "Secret Name," *Pilate's Wife* presents the protagonist's quest for divinity as a search to heal a fragmented, alienated female identity. Veronica in *Pilate's Wife* is an exiled Etruscan, caught in the empty roles of conqueror's wife and man's mistress. She reaches for wholeness through her love for Mnevis, the priestess who brings her to Isis. Like the Goddess in "Secret Name," Isis in *Pilate's Wife* unites in women the qualities culture splits and displaces:

> Isis was a magician and goddess of wisdom. The Greeks, for all their immense pragmatism and logical philosophy, had to split the perfect image of the perfect Woman, say here is Love, faithless and here is Wisdom, loveless. Yet even Aphrodite and Athené, re-modelled, flung into some blasting furnace, to return, one perfectly welded figure,

would yet lack something – something of the magic that Isis held in Egypt. (25)"

Veronica's lover Fabius (a portrait of Lawrence) tries to convert her to the "ideal brother-love" in the cult for Mithra, but she refuses because "it leaves . . . out, women" (64). Paralleling his pursuit of brother-love, she seeks "an ideal sister," whom she finds in Mnevis, the earthly incarnation of Isis. Artemisian sister-love is the route to recovery of the Mother and rebirth of the self:

> She had recognized a high sort of loving, dangerous maybe, but the sort of clear white-passion that deified the earlier nymphs of Arcadian Artemis. Sister to sister, lover to lover, Veronica had loved Mnevis, as one grown satiated with too much admiration, turns to view a familiar face, washed clear as in spring water, and realizes with no vanity that face is one's own. (88)

When Mnevis tells Veronica that Jesus "is good for women," Veronica learns that Wholeness can take a male as well as a female form. Jesus is the new Osiris, twin to Isis. For Veronica, the two are Mother and Father in whom she can be reborn as "a person" (167).[42]

Where *Pilate's Wife* ends in a celebration of androgynous rebirth cradled in the lap of the divine Mother/Father, *Hedylus* shows the split growing worse. *Hedylus*'s gloomier forecast is closer in spirit to the autobiographical fictions of the late 1920s. It also intensifies the tendency in *Palimpsest* to identify the intellect and creativity with the masculine and, consequently, helps to explain the kind of inner conflict that pervades the later Dijon fiction. Even more than *Palimpsest* and *Pilate's Wife*, *Hedylus* adapts the distortions of the dream-work to repeat and work through the patterns of H.D.'s spiritual diaspora. *Hedylus* can be read as a story of male adolescence – the son's break from his mother; the mother's loss of the son. It can also be read as the story of the artist's quest for inspiration – from deity and the magic inherent in the word. But within the intertextual grid of her autobiographical fictions, *Hedylus* can also be decoded as a textual psychodrama in which the people and events in H.D.'s life have been split, doubled, and displaced so as to conceal the conflicts and desires that are indirectly expressed.[43]

Hedylus takes place on the island of Samos some years after the Macedonians sacked Athens. Its epigraph from *The Garland of Meleager* links it to history. Hedylus, H.D. wrote later in *Advent*, was "the Alexandrian poet who is mentioned in *The Garland of Meleager*, and Hedyle his mother" (133). The novel fills out this lyric fragment by narrating two climactic days in the life of mother and son, who are divided by generation and sex, but united in image and spirit. Hedyle is an exiled Athenian, once famous for her wit, intellect, and beauty, but now the weary and aging mistress of the kindly, but matter-of-fact Douris, the tyrant of Samos. As the novel opens, she gazes in the mirror, which confronts her with the truth of her faded beauty, like the mirror in "Snow White." Imagist clusters hypnotically repeated in a lyric technique that anticipates Woolf's *The Waves* associate her with both Aphrodite and Athena. Like the women in *Palimpsest,* her "intellect" is a "steel blade" that binds her to Pallas Athena (97). As the daughter of an atheistic mathematician, Hedyle is also like Athena in having no mother, as we are repeatedly reminded (14, 27–8). But mirrors, veils, iridescent robes, and jewelry signify her femininity and bond with Aphrodite. Brutally betrayed by Clarix years before, she had become pregnant by "this other," a man she will not or cannot name. Sitting on a rock in the sun like Hermione in *Asphodel,* she decided to have the baby if the gods gave her a sign. Paralleling the swallow in *Asphodel,* a snake "out of ordinary time" appeared as "a signet of the god of Delphi" ordering her to have "the sun's child" (126). A year later, Helios-Apollo seems to have taken on human form in the mysterious appearance of the godlike Demion. She rejected his request that she accompany him to India so that, in refusing an ordinary affair with the man, she could keep the presence of the god. On the way to Alexandria with her son, she met Douris, who gave them both security on the island of Samos. Here, Hedyle lives for her son and is haunted by the image of a dead woman in a coffin, a symbol of her former self and missing mother.

Hedylus, however, is a rebellious youth who resists what she offers and resents his namelessness. Marked by a searing wound to his forehead when he was five, Hedylus aspires to be a poet, to which he connects his search for a father and his desire for a muse. Radiant words continuously wash through him, appearing as opaque objects much as they do for Stephen Dedalus in *Portrait.* "Words were his preoccupation, his plague," just as they were for Hermione in *HER* (17). During the two-day period of the novel, he asserts his manhood by deciding to leave his mother and emigrate with Irene and two other friends to join the circle of academic poets in Alexandria. Irene is his muse, a delicate, yet boylike child-woman whose motifs are tiny hands, the sea, shells, and fish. What permits Hedylus to break from his mother is the mysterious appearance of Demion, who comes like a hallucination to the rock ledge where Hedylus is declaiming his poetry over the crashing waves of the sea. Demion's presence, like a visitation from Helios himself, is a "revelation" of the sacred to the would-be poet and fatherless child, as John Walsh has argued (Afterward 148). After their meeting, Hedylus completes his break from his mother and leaves home with Irene.

The formulaic people and events of H.D.'s life are reassembled in *Hedylus* in classical disguise. Papa, Hedyle's intellectual father who died in the plague after Clarix left her, is a portrait of Professor Doolittle, who died just after the Great War. Clio, Hedyle's beloved sister who suddenly marries, is a version of Gregg. Clarix is a scarcely developed version of Aldington, while "the other" is an allusion to Gray. Demion represents an interpretation of H.D.'s unconsummated, uncanny "affair" or "shipboard romance" with Rodeck in 1920. The matricidal break from home, the loss of "sister" and husband, the omen blessing illegitimate pregnancy, the revelation of divine presence, are all elements we have met in H.D.'s other life stories. But, unlike the earlier novels, the central characters in *Hedylus* do not correspond on a one-to-one basis with real people. Instead, the story of Hedyle, Hedylus, Irene, and Douris is a psychodrama in which H.D. and Bryher have been split, then doubled. Analogous to distortions of the dream-work, these displacements conceal the intimate autobiographical core, but reveal the conflicts that plagued their author in the 1920s.

As psychodrama, *Hedylus* presents the two sides of H.D. and Bryher. H.D. split, then doubled, her own self into Hedyle (woman, mother) and Hedylus (poet, son). She did the same for Bryher, whom she split and projected into Irene (lover-muse) and Douris (pragmatic caretaker). Like Clarissa and Septimus in *Mrs. Dalloway,* Hedyle and Hedylus are textual projections of H.D.'s divided self. The opposition of mother and son, woman and poet in *Hedylus* carries the split between Raymonde Ransome and Ray Bart in *Palimpsest* one step further. Like the women in *Palimpsest,* Hedyle personifies H.D.'s woman-self, the heterosexual woman and mother trapped in the dynamics of the romance plot. Hedylus is the projection of H.D.'s poet-self, the "crystallized" youth whose inspiration comes from his status as the *son* of the *sun,* Helios/Apollo, and from his lover/muse, the boyish girl Irene. One persona embodies H.D.'s heterosexual self, identified as female; the other encodes her lesbian self, projected into a male body. One is the woman. The other is the poet. The split self, doubled into two characters bonded by name and blood, but separated by sex and age, seems irrevocable.

The changing nature of H.D.'s relationship with Bryher in the 1920s is transposed into the other generational couple – Douris and Irene. Imagist motifs for Irene repeat the associations H.D. connected with the intense early period of her love for Bryher – the sea, shells, fish, the color blue, delicate hands, smallness, and a childlike manner. Taking the place of the lost sister Clio, as Bryher "take[s] the place of Frances" (*Advent* 152), Irene "says now she is just a boy. . . . she thinks she is some wild sea-creature. Fishing. Pulling in nets. Always with the men about the islets. She fancies she is violently masculine. . . . The tiny childlike hands, so unfitting to the brave sea-faring mentality of the child. She is so tiny. And her mind, violent, instructive, deep and plausible. She seems to be always a sort of Muse, rather than any goddess, or any god's child. Clio" (91, 93). These motifs resonate with the small hands of the childlike Bryher figure in *Asphodel,* who is also associated with the sea, flowers, and blueness. The image of hands reappears centrally in the poem "Hyacinth," where the myth of Apollo's love for Hyacinth screens H.D.'s early love for Bryher: "Your anger charms me, / and yet all the time / I think of chaste, slight hands, / veined snow" (*Collected Poems* 201). Again, in a tribute to their love in "Halcyon," Bryher appears in a cluster of images associated with Irene, especially the sea, shells and "those small, small hands, / funny little gestures, / ways no one understands, / a figure under-small" (*Collected Poems* 271).[44]

On the other hand, the faithful, sheerly intellectual, and ultimately stolid qualities of Douris evoke the "Fido" aspect of Bryher that H.D. highlighted in works such as *Narthex* and the dedicatory poem to Bryher that opens *Palimpsest,* "*Stars wheel in purple.*" Douris, Hedyle explains to Demion, "was the highest type of sheer intellectual mortal, without perception" (140). In *Narthex,* Gareth (the Bryher figure) is "the intellectual almost-twin" whose "metallic" thought cannot follow the "spiral-thoughts of swallow curves" of Raymonde and Daniel (the Macpherson figure) (243, 236, 228). Douris is, however, the soul of "loyalty," like the "steel-set" star that "*keeps lone and frigid trist*" in *Palimpsest*'s dedicatory poem. Like Fido, who gave H.D. expensive clothes and loved to see her in feminine finery, "Douris accepted the mirage, dresses and adores it like an image" (140).

The final transposition in *Hedylus* centers on Perdita, to whom the novel is dedicated. Nine years old when the book appeared, Perdita was also fatherless and, by her own accounts, pressing to know how and why. On one level, the novel is an apologia, a defense of the mother for the daughter – a confession of the child's holy "father," an explanation of her diaspora, and a dispensation for the daughter's own future break from home. But why does Perdita become a son? What does this displacement from daughter to son tell us about the novel? Or H.D.? Read in the context of Freud's theory of female psychosexual desire proposed in the 1920s, the transformation of a female to a male child could represent an unconscious desire for a son, the son who takes the place of the missing penis. But, read in the context of Freud's hermeneutic decoding in *The Interpretation of Dreams,* the child's appearance as a son is a screen that protects both writer and reader from the forbidden desire inscribed in the text.

Hedylus can be decoded as the daughter in drag – the one who both adores and denies the mother, who feels compelled to repeat the mother and therefore must separate from her. He is, in short, a self-portrait of H.D., who made the break from her mother's "tyranny" in 1913 and then again in the mid-1920s for the sake of her art. Like *Palimpsest* and *Pilate's Wife*, *Hedylus* is deeply bound up in the matrix of mother–daughter relations. But unlike these texts, *Hedylus*'s matricidal plot must be screened under the guise of the less-forbidden Oedipal narrative. Hedylus's role as the daughter lies hidden beneath the part he plays as son. As the son, Hedylus acts out the prototypical Oedipal narrative of the male *Bildungsroman* – the young man who abandons his love for his mother, identifies with his powerful father, and goes out into the world as a man who replaces his mother with a lover. His final repudiation of Hedyle and love for Irene assures his normalcy as a man who will take his father's place in the world. Hedyle's open jealousy of Irene and manipulations to keep him in Samos simply emphasize that Hedylus is doing what any "normal" boy must do make himself a man – cut the apron strings and leave. The mark of his genius – the wound on his forehead – symbolically separates him from his mother and signifies his future as a poet.

But for Hedylus-as-daughter, the wound is a mark of difference, of "castration." Repeatedly described, Hedylus's "gash" is his most important motif, one whose images invite comparison to Freud's concept of female castration. At five, he acquired the gash by falling on the marble steps in Athens, and he is haunted by the image of blood as a field of red poppies. Its aftermath is a "flaming" scar Hedylus calls a "cleft" or "fissure" (85, 100). The wound is "his obvious defect," a sign of "some intellectual deficiency," "apparent at all times," "there whatever he might do, might want to do about it," "branding him primitive, disobedient" (20). For Hedyle, the wound signifies his intellectual inferiority – "If you hadn't broken your head that day, you'd be another Sophocles," she jokes (20, 39). "To make up for the mark on his forehead," Hedylus worked hard searching "through manuscripts, reading and compiling," ostensibly for Douris, but really for Hedyle (20). Additionally, the wound is the site of his difference, his calling to be a poet, the fissure into which the god enters and out of which the words of "ice and fire" emerge (74). It is also the sign of his split self:

> Hedylus knew now, seated calmly by this stranger [Demion], that he had always been striving self with self, the two distinct halves, reft (he visualized it) that day when at five he had flung forward, clinging to scrub-root of dwarf-cypress to find his brow wreathed with poppy-scarlet. That scarlet, field-flower purple, had been always in his mind, the direct physical manifestation of his spiritual cleavage. (78)

As the daughter's wound, however, the gash on Hedylus's brow is not the sign of lack, but rather of plenitude. It signifies not the "castration" of all women, but instead the fullness of difference – not only sexual difference, but also the daughter's difference from her mother. As the site of woman's split identity, it is the source of her poetry. Hedyle reads the wound as the sign of inferiority, but Hedylus knows it as the mark of his genius, a searing touch from the gods. Rejection of Hedyle (the victimized Mother) and identification with Demion (the powerful Father) heals the "fissure" and allows Hedylus to sail for Alexandria. With Demion at his side, Hedylus "seemed now to have been made, by the mere physical or spiritual emanation of the man beside him, one entire and concrete entity. Self met self as two waves, for long chafing at some fragile barrier, finally join, white with white crest; irradiating a fine spray that told, in an exact moment, that the tiny demarcation of dividing sand (dividing self) was merged. . . . Hedylus recognized the exact moment when the old cleft was healed and each self satisfied" (85).

The price of the father's healing presence is the absence of the mother. For the daughter, this preference for the father is matricidal. Instead of identifying with the mother (as Freud's theory of "normal" femininity prescribes), Hedylus-as-daughter is erasing the mother. A simple Oedipal reading might suggest that the "daughter" (Hedylus) rejects the mother (Hedyle) so as to have the father (Demion) to herself. But interpretation of the need to screen the daughter's desire with the son suggests that something even more taboo is at stake. Hedylus-as-daughter "kills" the mother, not to take her place, but to ensure that "she" will never have to be a woman at all. To be a poet, to be healed, the daughter must repudiate the mother, must "kill" the woman she would become if she were to identify with the figure that represents conventional femininity. She must, in short, identify with her father, make herself into a "man" by playing the part of the son. As the daughter, Hedylus's separation from Hedyle enacts the aspiring woman poet's need to make herself different from her conventional mother. To succeed, she must "kill" not only her mother, but her self-as-woman. In this sense, the matricidal plot is also a suicidal one.

With its highly coded, forbidden longing to kill the mother, *Hedylus* appears to reverse the desire for re-union with the mother in *Palimpsest* and *Pilate's Wife*. We might indeed read *Hedylus* as an entirely suicidal, woman-hating text if the novel had ended with Hedylus's departure. But it doesn't. Chapter 18 ends with a curiously disoriented Hedylus being led off to the boats by Irene, who has the final word: "Tell me about your work – and Helios" (116). The remaining four chapters show Hedyle anything but "dead." In fact, she talks almost nonstop, telling her story to Demion – explaining to him why she refused to go to India with him ten years before, reviewing the loss of Clio and Clarix, the brief affair with "the other," the pregnancy and omen from Helios, her love for him as a woman, and her desire to protect what he meant to her by refusing an ordinary affair. Hedyle, in other words, supplants the

Bildungsroman of her son by narrating a woman's story in a man's world
– a resistance in prose to the fate the poet Hedylus had imagined for his
mother. Hedyle's long speech, which recapitulates H.D.'s fictionalizing
prose in the 1920s, is an affirmation of a woman's voice, not the repudiation Hedylus represented. We recall that her serpent bracelet, the
ouroboros removed from the mummy of the dead woman, is a feminine
symbol of rebirth. The mother – the woman – is not dead. She has the
last word.

III. PSYCHODRAMA IN THE DIJON SERIES

> She never got away from that past, she went on repeating that past.
>
> H.D., *Nights* (9)

The romans à clef in which H.D. moved through the web of
her tangled relationships in the late 1920s "went on repeating that past"
articulated in the history novels about her self in the early 1920s. Whatever
textual resolution might have been achieved in the writing unraveled in
the living. She could not bring the timeless visionary moments in the
fourth-dimensional time/space of the historical novels back into contemporary time and space. The interior struggle of "self against self," of
going "round and round," reasserted itself severely. Perhaps in consequence, H.D. went back to the present time of "Murex" to extend the
story of Raymonde into the future. Three texts feature expanded versions
of the dramatis personae of "Murex" – *Narthex* (written and published
in 1928); *The Usual Star* (written in 1930, published in 1934); and "Two
Americans" (written in 1930, published in 1934). But instead of exploring
the meaning of the war years, H.D. attempted to break the pattern of
repetition by writing about Raymonde's current personal tangles and
spiritual paralysis. Once more, however, the resolution reached in each
text dissolved in the aftermath, setting the cycle in motion again. Like
Hedylus, the last three prose texts H.D. wrote about herself in the 1920s
intensified psychic fragmentation through surrealistically rendered splitting, doubling, and displacement: *Kora and Ka* (written in 1930, published
in 1934); *Mira-Mare* (written in 1930, published in 1934); and *Nights*
(written in 1931 and 1934, published in 1935). Although they differ in
significant ways, the romans à clef repeat the essential pattern of the
historical novels: Exile externalizes an inner division between woman
and poet; the search for healing involves the daughter in a quest for the
divine maternal presence and in initiation into the mysteries of rebirth.
Like *Hedylus, Nights* presents this quest, only to suggest its ultimate
failure. On the cusp between decades, *Nights* is alarmingly schizophrenic
and suicidal, brilliantly prefiguring the battered soul who knocked on

Freud's door in 1933, who drew together a projected volume of poems from the 1930s called *The Dead Priestess Speaks.*

The Raymonde Ransome texts exaggerate the textual disguise of "Murex" by further altering the facts of H.D.'s life. In *Narthex,* for example, Raymonde's husband Freddie was killed in the war; there have been no pregnancies or births; and Raymonde and Gareth (the Bryher figure) were separated for five years after the war. In the public forum of *Second America Caravan: A Yearbook of American Literature,* where *Narthex* appeared, H.D. may have felt the need to hide her adultery, the illegitimacy of her child, and her bisexuality. Fear of disclosure no doubt contributed to the elusive plot of the Raymonde texts, especially *Narthex.* Modernist experimentalism – with its deemphasis on plot and heightened stream of consciousness – provided a convenient screen behind which H.D. could write through the tangles of her ménage à trois. But the desire for secrecy led to texts that ultimately depend on the reader's knowledge of her life to be comprehensible – unlike other romans à clef such as *HER, Asphodel, Paint It To-Day,* or *Madrigal. Narthex,* for example, is based on the "honeymoon" trip H.D., Bryher, and Macpherson made to Venice in May of 1927 shortly before Bryher divorced McAlmon in June and married Macpherson in September of 1927.[45] *Narthex* examines the violent ambivalences among the three, but never indicates the key "facts" that clarify the origin of the characters' emotion – namely, that H.D.'s companion Bryher was about to marry H.D.'s lover, ostensibly to protect the affair. In the context of tense realignments in the ménage, *Narthex* makes sense. Without that information, which the text does not provide, *Narthex* frustrates and confuses the reader, who is compelled to piece together narrative fragments without knowing that the author has withheld the key pieces of the puzzle. Reading becomes a contest between the reader who wants to know and the author who wants to hide – a scene ripe for transference, the reader's entrapment in the compulsion to repeat.

Read in the context of H.D.'s other fictions, however, the Raymonde texts contribute to the familiar patterns of spiritual diaspora. In "Two Americans," for example, Raymonde comes to terms with her expatriation by identifying with Saul Howard, the Paul Robeson figure, a black man exiled because of his race. She imagines this "bronze" man of song and passion as a Nietzschean Dionysus, to which she counters her self as a "marble" "Nietzschian Apollo, though where he was complete, she was strikingly deficient. She was deficient, even, you might say, crippled in some psychic song-wing" by "that very so-Great War" which had left "herself entirely defeated" (94, 93). Raymonde's Apollonian cerebralism is a sign of her rootless Europeanization. But a moment of intimacy with Saul's Dionysian "in-rooted power of his gigantic Being" makes her feel American again (94).[46]

Raymonde's homelessness in "Two Americans" takes the form of paralyzing alienation in *Narthex* and *The Usual Star*. Frustration, hostility, and hurt pervade Raymonde's relationships with Gareth, Daniel, and Katherine (representations of Bryher, Macpherson, and Gregg). The idealization of an Artemisian sisterhood in *HER* and *Paint It To-Day* is completely missing in the claustrophobic tangle of love and hate of *Narthex* and *The Usual Star*. *Narthex* opens with Raymonde, Gareth, and Daniel quietly drinking tea in Florian's Café near St. Mark's Cathedral in Venice. Outwardly calm, Raymonde is internally raging against both Gareth and Katherine, whom she later sees as nightmare exaggerations of Artemis: "Katherine, Gareth, they were two antique coin sides, Katherine one side, towered head, some Asiatic goddess, many breasted, something monstrous, that yet holds authenticity, Gareth, the other side, boy Emperor . . . short hair and the boy-turn of the chin and that frightening intensity" (262). Like a demonic version of Irene, Gareth "sat ridiculous and exquisite, her small hands struggling . . . as a child" (228). Raymonde is furious with "Garry's exquisite pedantry and letters after her ridiculous distinguished little name" with her "ridiculous way of putting too much dynamic energy into everything, whether it was some ridiculous little thesis signed with her ridiculous little distinguished name, or the collecting of rugs from refractory cab or motor" (228). Katherine, on the other hand, "was an Hellenistic monster," who "ripped souls from bodies" like a "spiritual gynecologist" (231). Like the "psychic vamp" H.D. described in a letter about Gregg, Katherine "tampers" with people's souls, "blights" and "withers" them in their "spiritual flowering" (231). With a "predilection for destruction," Katherine has "the instinct of a Harpy. She would gouge the soul out of any body" (231–2).

Raymonde is caught in the middle between Gareth and Katherine, both of whom she hates – and deeply loves. This ambivalence is fueled not only by Gareth's jealousy of Katherine, but more fundamentally by the way each woman acts out one aspect of Raymonde's split self. Katherine is a muse figure, a riddling "Sphinx" whose magnetism and mystery attract both men and women. No longer the Lacedaemonian girl/twin of *HER*, the Gregg figure of *Narthex* has grown up into Artemis of Ephesus, the many-breasted mystery of fecundity whose name suggests a link to the Arcadian Artemis, sister of Apollo. Desiring them for herself, Katherine nonetheless sends two men to Raymonde – the ex-soldier/ poet Alex Mordant, who wants Raymonde to be the mother of his children; and Daniel, the "neophyte narthex" who "wa: Florence, Tuscan fidelity, intellectual subtlety, clairvoyant physical intuition" (235, 241).[47] Gareth, on the other hand, is her "intellectual almost-twin," a "symbol of intellectual vistas [who] was silver bars and claustrophobia," a "metallic" mind made of "gun-metal" (243, 235–6). The "steel blue recorder of her conscience, the sort of needle to her intellectual compass," Gareth ties Raymonde to the "Greek vibration," the intensely shattering "white lightning across daylight skies," "the inhumanity of spirit" (230, 240). In short, Raymonde sees Katherine as a projection of her own "feminine" and heterosexual self; Gareth, of her "masculine" and lesbian self. Internalizing patriarchal constructions of gender and sexuality, Raymonde regards the clear light of intellect as masculine and the dark mystery of sexuality as feminine.[48]

The split between "masculine" and "feminine" within Raymonde is even more paralyzing in Narthex than it was in "Murex." Twinship is a trap, not a liberation, as it was in HER. "Let Daniel see," Raymonde thinks, "that she and Gareth were a sort of composite person she and Gareth, Raymondegareth or Garethraymonde, a person that had existed (Raymondegareth) before ever there was a Daniel" (244). But, "She was sick of Garethraymonde. She would have been done long long since with Garethraymonde if it weren't for Daniel" (263). On the one hand, Raymonde "wouldn't play false to her loyalty to Gareth" (243); they are twins, held to the memory of "hyacinth-blue years before the war cloud" (229). On the other hand, Gareth has separated her from both Katherine and Mordant, and Raymonde thinks, "I'm tired of Gareth's phobia. Gareth's phobia is a python rising in the loveliest surroundings to terrify me, to drag me back, back to my own forgotten terrors. Gareth has no right to terrorize" (270). "Let Gareth stay a stranger, not come too close," Raymonde wishes; but she knows that "People, things, net work of places, people, she and Gareth were linked, nothing could interfere, not even Daniel who was so terribly part of it, webbed into it treasonably, silver web of exquisite silk texture that shelters problematic twin grubs" (245).

Where twinship with Fayne had nurtured Her's writing in HER, it stifles Raymonde's creativity in Narthex. "I'm tired of writing," Raymonde tells Daniel and Gareth in the café; "I'm through burning in a vacuum" (234). The bisexuality – psychic and sexual – that had proved such a tantalizing escape from the conventions of femininity appears to Raymonde as the mark of sterility. "Man–woman, a temptation," she thinks; "The intellect grows sterile being bi-sexual...or a-sexual" (233). As she has done for years, she keeps on writing in the attempt to break the "round and round" of "self against self." But all she has are "pages and pages re-written, over-worked, scrawled and re-typed and copied. Writing was no inspiration...it was pages and pages" (266). Raymonde's state of mind and body is summed up in her despairing thought: "I am nothing, a sort of lens at the end of a sort of telescopic, cannon-like, useless tube. Iron and metallic burnt out residue...of Freddie. Of Katherine. Of Mordant. I am nothing" (265–6). The reader, drawn into the vortex of Raymonde's vacuum, begins to drown in the repetitions of textual compulsion. In *Narthex,* one of the most hateful texts H.D. wrote, the medium is the message.

Author and text attempt to break out of this demonic cycle by invoking the familiar pattern of the maternal quest plot. Florian's, the name of the café in which the three sit, suggests the goddess Flora, mistress of springtime renewal, as does the nearby café called the Aurora. The woman selling flowers in the square is "the old Sibyl hag" come back, moving against time, "counter-clockwise" (251). Moving with time are the "Fascisti," the "black shirts" who march past the Cathedral to make "St. Mark's Square alien to Italy" (237). For Raymonde, however, it is the cathedral whose presence dominates Venice. After Daniel and Gareth leave, she feels its "aura" "pull[ing]" her in. Invoking the holy enclosures that Freud associated with the maternal body in *The Interpretation of Dreams,* the cathedral is womblike, the scene of gestation, a "sort of bee-hive" (276).[49] "This *is* a temple," Raymonde thinks; "Light across light in her tired brain. The cool slightly fragrant corridor rose, flooding her like water. 'We float like water, into water, float into some luminous state...' " (270).

Gareth "hates Cathedrals," as she hates Venice, but Raymonde finds her moment in the cathedral healing. It makes the "gift of Venice" a "loss of identity," the "power to crawl, snail self up the surface of high window and creep half-hatched moth in among tenuous rootlets and dynamic deep earth feelers" (271). In the womb/tomb of the dimly lit cathedral, Raymonde travels back in time to another honeymoon, her mother's, to (re)experience her own gestation: "Venice was in her, before she was yet born, my mother loved it; dial hand swiftly backward, my mother came to Venice on her honeymoon" (281). In this place "out of time, out of space," Raymonde feels reborn – "her mind a lily, rising out of hysteria, saw things clearly" (276, 279). This image of her mind as lily is repeated several times, as if to intensify the lily's traditional associations with purity, the Annunciation, and female genitalia. *Narthex* ends with Daniel coming to the cathedral to bring Raymonde back to Gareth. Raymonde experiences this gesture as the completion of the circle in which she is "mother" to a trinity, the Three who have become One, the ménage à trois sanctified in the maternal body of the cathedral (280–4).

The Usual Star and *Mira-Mare* unravel the One back into Three to repeat the pattern of fragmented identities and suppressed hostility. The entity tenuously achieved in the shadow of the cathedral in *Narthex* has disintegrated in these stories about a later stage of the ménage. In *The Usual Star*, Raymonde feels the split between Ray Bart the writer and Raymonde the woman with all the intensity of Raymonde in "Murex": "Daniel called her Ray Bart when he was being different, distant. Gareth called her Ray Bart when she particularly loved her. People called her Ray Bart, to distinguish the things she wrote from the things they found wanting in her" (73). As in *Narthex,* we are denied direct knowledge of Gareth's marriage to Daniel, or Raymonde's affair with him. But Raymonde's alienation within the threesome is symbolically evident when Raymonde refuses to join them at dinner in the family mansion of Gareth's "octopus" mother. For Raymonde, Gareth is "a sort of robot," "a quaint ironic comment on the thing that life was," while Daniel is "a sort of spirit-brother" (28–9). Together, they were "Danielraymonde," "burning with their cerebral intensity" that "couldn't be born forever, it must go out" (21). Raymonde momentarily breaks out of these "intolerable" bonds with Gareth and Daniel when Katherine suddenly appears at Raymonde's flat to spend the evening. After a tense beginning, the two women achieve a momentary intimacy based on their mutual desire for Daniel. Raymonde's acceptance of Katherine as a sort of surrogate mother supplants her earlier rejection of Gareth's mother.

In *Mira-Mare,* H.D. abandoned the names Raymonde and Daniel, but the story represents a continuation of the family saga. Based on the first of two trips H.D. and Macpherson made in 1930 to Monte Carlo at Bryher's urging, *Mira-Mare* is a mood piece attached to Macpherson's desertion, which it never narrates. By the summer of 1930, their affair was over, with Macpherson's attentions thoroughly directed toward the young men attached to casino life. In the plotless story, however, the relationship between Alex and Chris is never named – they could be brother and sister or lovers. With their androgynous names, they are twinlike; but we see only the emotional effects of their relationship, never its narratable events. Conflict between them is symbolically embedded in their different use of space and time on the last afternoon of their vacation. Chris is fascinated with the casino, which Alex says is "full of maggots" patriotically singing the "Marseillaise" (81). She in contrast turns to the sea, associated with the maternal fragrance of their hotel, the "Mira-Mare," whose name prefigures the Lady of *Trilogy*: "mer, mere, mère, mater, Maia, Mary // Star of the Sea [Stella Maris] / Mother" (552). The word Mira-Mare heals, like the mysterious word " 'Aloe' remembered from nowhere, a word forgotten stirred memory-in-forgetting": "Mira-Mare. She said Mira-Mare. It was a charm" (91). Like Raymonde and Hedyle in the prior texts, Alex has a mind like steel, from which she wants to escape into the wash of the sea: "Thought was

steel, was platinum, was silver-coloured sluice-gates. Those gates stood
wide open. Through her mind, sensation poured, drowning" (62). A
French pun identifies Alex's desire to crawl back into the watery domain
of maternal space: " 'I am écrivan' (I almost said écrivisse) I almost said,
'I am a crawfish' " (81). While Chris spends his time in the casino, Alex
loses herself in the sensations of "Mnemoseyne, the Mother of the
Muses," of "sub-aqueous memory" (70, 79). The imagery is amniotic
and prenatal, invoking Isis, for whom the Phoenicians had built a temple
on this spot. The water's blue is the blue of Isis: "Blue. She gathered
the blue-impression, like a cloak, about her" (71). Alex's trancelike fusion
with the maternal sea is broken when the clock strikes, which "recalled
space, time" and broke "mythopoetic" sensation (92–3). *Mira-Mare* is an
extended lyric sketch of pain and longing for a restorative amniotic bliss.
Like the lyrics of the "early H.D.," *Mira-Mare* represses the narrative
origins of the emotions distilled into image.

In its refusal to narrate the specific events that gave rise to its existence,
Mira-Mare bridges the gap between the Raymonde Ransome romans à
clef and the texts in which H.D. abandoned one-to-one correspondence
between protagonists and living people, between plot and the events in
her own life. Like *Hedylus, Kora and Ka* and *Nights* are highly displaced
autobiographical texts in which H.D. split and doubled herself into different personae. Her description of these texts as hallucinated writing
emphasizes their kinship with a dreamworld which distorts, condenses,
projects, and symbolically represents the waking world of ordinary space
and time. In particular, *Kora and Ka* and *Nights* are surrealist, nightmarish
– with a sparse prose style more like Djuna Barnes's *Nightwood* than the
"weedy" repetitions of *Palimpsest* or *Narthex*. As poetic psychodrama,
Kora and Ka and *Nights* could explore what the less-disguised Raymonde
Ransome narratives suppressed: the intersections of madness and creativity, death and desire in a bisexual psyche.

Written in 1930 shortly after the trip to Monte Carlo described in *Mira-
Mare, Kora and Ka* has two protagonists, John Helforth and Kora, who
represent not only the twinship of H.D. and Macpherson, but also the
split inside H.D. herself. Members of the "lost generation," their names
suggest the mythic dimension of their hellish existence. Helforth is a
"forth"-right British accountant, a veteran of the Great War caught in
the "hell" of a nervous breakdown. He takes on the role of Adonis/
Dionysus, the dying god who is cradled and reborn in the lap of the
Eleusinian Great Mother. Kora is the daughter-as-mother, "captured"
by a soldier/husband who left her lost in an unregenerated modern world.
Like Demeter, she is a maternal figure who grieves for her two sons and
nurtures John's broken spirit. Together, their names evoke Williams's
Kora in Hell (1920) to suggest that this text answers his despairing prose

improvisations of the modern wasteland.[50] The spiritual devastation wrought by the war is the text's *donée*, what sets in motion the journey of Kora and John to some unspecified southern resort for escape and healing some ten years after the war ended.

John and Kora may be lovers – we are not really told. But they are more fundamentally bound together by the Ka. The Ka is the text's first speaker, narrating the first of three parts in the first person. Immediately identifying itself as "that sort of shadow they used to call a Ka, in Egypt," the Ka tells the reader that it is Helforth's Ka, the part of him that "lives after the body is dead" (9). In Egyptian religion, the Ka is "a spiritual double" akin to "Paracelsus's theory of astral bodies," according to a passage H.D. marked in a reference book. E. A. Wallis Budge described the Ka as "an image, genius, double" attached to, but independent of a living person. Similar to a Greek *eidolon* (image, phantom), the Ka "could move freely from place to place, separating itself from, or uniting itself to, the body at will."[51] After death, the Ka survives as a kind of soul that accompanies the mummy on its journey to the afterworld, where it is judged by Thoth and reborn, if found virtuous, under the aegis of the twin lovers Isis and Osiris. Akin to the butterfly iconography of the Greeks, the Ka was often imaged as a bird that hovered near the body. Similarly, the Ka in *Kora and Ka* describes itself as "a glow-worm or just hatched moth" that could be crushed by the "old tread wheel and the iron ferris-wheel of Helforth's fatigue" (15).

H.D. extends the Egyptian Ka considerably to examine the psychodynamics of dissociation and schizophrenic madness. In the three sections of Part 1 it narrates, the Ka "shadows" Helforth, watching and recording his every move, "remembering" his trip to the doctor that led to the journey with Kora, detailing the physical symptoms of his nerve strain – particularly the heightened perception of color and dissociated fragmentation of his observations of people and things. Curiously detached, and yet inside the man he possesses, the Ka's description of Helforth's suffering is clinical, meticulously detailed, and rational. The style is short, choppy, and factual – almost a parody of Hemingway's laconic prose:

> I, this Ka, cannot see the face of Helforth.
> I feel Helforth's eyes. They are glass-gray eyes. I feel his contempt. It is the contempt of integrity, he has worked too hard. I tear, as it were, the curtain that shuts me from Helforth and I feel Helforth's eyes widen. When his eyes have sufficiently stared at that wall opposite, I will look out. At the moment, the eyes of Helforth see in detail, wooden images placed on a shelf, two cows, one painted red, the other black. His eyes are focussed there, they are not wide enough for me yet. He smiles as he notes the red cow has a bell exactly matching in its minute disproportion, those the others wear on the far hill. He sees the red

> cow, placed at the shuttered window, like a cuckoo out of its clock. (10–11)

In the sections it narrates, the Ka appears to personify one portion of a split subject, the sane voice of reason that comments on the mad self. But when Helforth takes over the narration for the remaining two parts of the three-part text, he describes the Ka as an irrational enemy, a Dionysian force from the unconscious that invades the conscious mind to inspire and destroy. As an accountant trying to forget the war, Helforth resists the voice of the Ka as the onset of neurosis.

> I am John Helforth, I say, yawning and I endeavour to banish, in that yawn's exaggeration the monster I call, for lazy lack of definition, "Ka." Ka is far off now; Ka partook of symptom, was neurotic breakdown; Ka, it is true, led me, made me, having made me, preserved me – but yawning, I say, for what? If I, Helforth, get rapt back into this Ka thing, contemplating vine-green leaf, Helforth will be good for nothing. (25–6)

Banishing his Ka, Helforth tries to be "hail-fellow-well-met," a regular bloke who feels and sees nothing beyond the ordinary: "I will to be John Helforth, an Englishman and a normal brutal one. I will strength into my body, into my loins" (27). Helforth without his Ka is stereotypically masculine, a man of numbers, an ex-soldier who has survived the war intact. From this perspective, the Ka resembles a Jungian anima – the feminine soul that Western man has repressed. But, like Woolf's Septimus in *Mrs. Dalloway,* Helforth (who also walks up Bond Street in London) cannot deny his Ka. The more he tries, the more it returns like "a jelly fish, who is a microbe, who is (a specialist all but told me) a disease" (26, 29). To echo Freud, the Ka personifies the irresistible return of the repressed. "Ka weeps, wails for attention," Helforth complains, "and then must be put to sleep like any tired infant. . . . Ka wears me to a shred. It is I who am bone-thin. Soul is, I have proved it, octopus" (26).

As his repressed soul, the Ka is linked to creativity and heightened states of transrational consciousness. The jellyfish and octopus imagery echo H.D.'s private code word – Fish – for supernormal states of mind, as well as her images for "the over-mind" in *Notes on Thought and Vision.* In its three narrated sections, the Ka makes Helforth see and feel the intense green of the vine, the shimmering rose of the clematis in the bowl – almost as if he were in a drug-induced state of mind, almost as if he were about to declaim an imagist poem of "the early H.D."

The Ka, however, does not belong to Helforth alone. It ties Helforth irrevocably and mysteriously to Kora, as if it were the soul for two bodies, one male and one female. Helforth thinks:

> Kora is everything. Without Kora, Ka would have got me. Sometimes
> I call Kora, Ka, or reverse the process and call Ka, Kora. I am on
> familiar terms with Kora, with Ka, likewise. We are, it is evident, some
> integral triple alliance, primordial Three-in-One. I am Kora, Kora is
> Helforth and Ka is shared between us. Though she repudiates affiliation
> with Ka, and refuses to discuss it, yet the fact remains. Ka is Kora,
> Kora is Ka. The waif must be shared between us. (26)

Kora is both Helforth's protection against the Ka as disease and the
projection of the Ka as soul into a female body. Kora is the female side
of Helforth's bisexual identity. Conversely, the Ka shadows Kora and
links her to Helforth as her twin, the masculine side of her psyche.
Together, the three represent a psychic ménage à trois, a "primordial
Three-in-One" that echoes Aristophanes's myth of the Androgyne, re-
counted in Plato's *Symposium* (30–2). The Ka represents as well H.D.'s
surrealist version of the mysterious bond between Clarissa and Septimus
in *Mrs. Dalloway*. Like Kora and Helforth, Clarissa and Septimus act out
a stereotypically masculine and feminine destiny – he, as a soldier and
veteran; she as a wife and hostess. Like H.D., Woolf split herself in two
and projected her own symptoms of madness into a male character,
whose fate is mystically bound up with that of a female character.

But where Septimus's suicide makes possible Clarissa's survival in *Mrs.
Dalloway*, *Kora and Ka* narrates the healing of both Kora and Helforth
through a transference–countertransference exchange mediated by their
shared Ka. The Ka forces a return to consciousness of what each has
repressed. Like Septimus, Helforth's breakdown is related to his repressed
grief, guilt, and anger about the war. "If I had said this ten years ago, I
might now be all right," Helforth realizes (30–1). Kora forces him to
talk about his beloved brother Larry, who died in the war: "Larry was
of course vicious to have told me, in precise detail, all that he did. It was
a perverse sort of sadism. I loved Larry. I would have gone on, loving
men and women if it hadn't been for Larry. How could I love anyone
after Larry? . . . We were virgin, though Larry saw to it that I was not.
Larry" (32). As for Septimus, homoerotic desire forms the undercurrent
of Helforth's grief. But, unlike Septimus, Helforth is entangled in an
incestuous family web that reads like a psychoanalytic case study. Not
only did Larry initiate his younger brother John into some unnameable
knowledge of love, but Helforth is convinced that his mother deliberately
sent Larry to his death because her favorite oldest son, Bob ("the young
'father' "), had already died in the war. Helforth's grief for Larry screens
a covert hatred for his mother: "Larry was sent to avenge Bob, I was to
be sent to avenge Larry. . . . *It was our Mother*. . . . I blamed mother for
the death of Larry" (32, 35). Helforth sees his mother and "a row of

aunts" as a "choros out of Hades" that sends young men to their death in battle: "the 'family' was only another name for warfare and sacrifice of the young" (38–9).

With another turn of the screw, however, Kora insists that beneath his hatred lay a forbidden desire for his mother: "Kora declares that I was in love with madre and that Bob taking the place of father, was my rival" (35). Having identified Helforth's "mother-complex," an explanation that he resists as "fantastic," Kora becomes the mother, in a transference situation. Helforth alternately loves and hates Kora, thereby repeating with her the ambivalent feelings he has had toward his mother. Helforth's "cure" follows the pattern Freud laid out in his papers on transference: By repeating the past with Kora, he is able to remember what he had forgotten, a working through that reconciles him to his mother and to Larry's death.

Conversely, Kora is drawn into the vortex of Helforth's desire to the point of her own collapse. As she becomes the mother in transference, Helforth becomes the son in her countertransference. Once Helforth has worked through his mother complex, Kora's calm nurturance splits open into a mother complex of a different sort. Events related to her dissolved marriage remain unclear, but Kora's love for her sons has made her suffer. When Helforth says that he might have avoided "these great volcanic break-downs" if he had been able to express his anger all along, Kora's own volcanic anger with her husband Stamford erupts (44). Somehow, her rage at Stamford is linked to her anguish about her children: "If I could have hated Stamford, known what he was, if I could have loathed him, I might have loathed his children" (44). Helforth responds to this admission by slipping the chiffon from her shoulder, kissing her and saying, "I hate the children, not because they are your children, not even because they are Stamford's. I hate them because they made you suffer" (44–5). Beneath Kora's anger at her husband lies a forbidden rage against her own motherhood. Loving her children so intensely forged a kind of trap that inhibited her own life as the daughter – as the lover, as the writer.

To feel free, Kora needs to loathe her sons. But this she cannot do. She responds to Helforth's caresses by telling him that she must return to her children and by making him see that she has never been able to love him (47, 49). Grasping him with an "octopus-like clutch," she suddenly slips to the floor in a deathlike faint, taking on the role of Koré in the Underworld. The mother becomes the daughter:

> She slips from me, lies on the floor; the print-poppies make poppy and corn-flower pattern on her back. I am amazed to see poppies and corn-flowers convulsed, shaken like field flowers under high wind or down

sweep of sharp scythe. Something has been cut down, it lies gasping among those silver and rose-fish from a Japanese aquarium. "Kora." It is Kora lying there, gasping in her agony. . . . (47)

As mother of sons, Kora is daughter and bride of Hades. As mother, Kora is herself motherless, in need of Demeter. Where Helforth finds his Demeter in Kora, Kora remains motherless. Kora's collapse inspires Helforth to mythologize them both: "We were Kora of the Underworld and Dionysus, not yet risen. I was then Larry and those others, had no place then in any living landscape. Now we are Kore and the slain God...risen" (53). Within this context, the shimmering bowl of flowers Kora had arranged is "the Grail" (53). The cows and "speckled eggs" upon which the Ka had led him to fixate were the symbols of the maternal mysteries into which he was being initiated through neurotic breakdown. Helforth is Dionysus, "the slain God...risen."

The psychoanalytic/religious cure in *Kora and Ka,* however, is ultimately one sided. The triumph of the mysteries at the end is Helforth's rebirth, not Kora's. She is silent, never the narrator, not even the center of consciousness. The story belongs to Helforth, for whom Kora serves as mother/muse: "I could see through the wall behind Kora and I saw Kora sitting in a Florentine frame, her head encompassed with an aura of lilies" (52). Framed in Helforth's vision of her as virgin mother, Kora is mute, unborn, unhealed. This unsymmetrical symbiosis is critically evident in the face the couple presents to the outside world. Kora explains to the maid who sees the "profusion of books and notebooks" that "Monsieur is tired out, . . . writing" (49). But Helforth admits to the reader that it is really Kora who writes, not himself: "My writing has been a symbol and a myth. We hold to it; I am writing. I will not have invalidism thrust on me but it is Kora does the writing" (49). Kora – the woman – writes, but Helforth – the man – is her mask. As autobiographical psychodrama, *Kora and Ka* indicates a radical split in the writer's psyche, one in which the "masculine" side is restored to speech and sanity, while the "feminine" side remains unreconciled and mad, impervious to the psychoanalytic cure.

Nights intensifies this demonic fragmentation of identity to suggest that the writing woman can survive only in the persona of a man. As psychodrama, *Nights* represents the erasure of the feminine through suicide. It suggests as well that the matricidal plot of split identity in *Hedylus* became, a few years later, a dangerously suicidal one in *Nights*. For *Nights*, H.D. generated two authors who were also characters in their own stories – a female one who kills herself after completing her tale and a male one who survives to introduce the female author to the world. H.D. privately printed 100 copies of *Nights* in 1935 under the name John Helforth, a screen which particularly delighted her, even though it surely couldn't have deceived the friends to whom she sent copies of the book. The text is split in two, with the composition of its parts divided by three years. The first part, entitled "Part 1: Prologue," was written in August and December of 1934, sandwiching H.D.'s brief, but severe, breakdown in August and her return to Freud for analysis from October 30th to December 2nd. Entitled "Part 2: Nights," the second part was written in the summer of 1931, not long after she finished unsatisfactory psychoanalytic sessions with Mary Chadwick. Narrated by Natalia Saunderson, Part 2 records twelve nights of passionate lovemaking between Natalia and the beautiful young stranger David, just after her husband Neil has left her to fulfill his desire for boys. "Part 1: Prologue," narrated by Helforth, serves as ostensible introduction to Natalia's story, a fiction that covers his attempt to understand Natalia's recent suicide.

Both as authors and characters, Natalia and Helforth represent exaggerated "masculine" and "feminine" fragments of H.D. herself. They are doubles for each other and for H.D.'s own life story. Like Kora and Helforth in *Kora and Ka,* Natalia and Helforth are specially bonded psychic twins whose difference is anchored in gender. As Helforth says in his Prologue, "I knew enough about Natalia, to know that her problems would have been my problems, but for my somewhat tantalising scientific habits" (6). Renne Saunderson, Neil's sister and the novel's Bryher figure, has brought Natalia's manuscript "Nights" to Helforth to publish precisely because "you are a half-and-half sort of person yourself," as Helforth reports in the Prologue (5).

Their affinity, however, ultimately takes the form of a stereotypically masculine and feminine opposition. As if to demarcate his safe distance from the woman whose problems are like his own, Helforth systematically presents himself and Natalia in binary terms. Both are writers, but he stresses that she has no audience, while he strives to write popular fiction. Her writing is "fervid stream-of-consciousness," "prose experiments" that are "radium and electricity" "bleed[ing] fire and ice" – qualities that resonate with the reviews of H.D.'s work (4, 5, 21, 22). He, on the other hand, has to support himself as a "reader, travelling-salesman, and general, under-paid, overworked utility-man, to a publishing firm of semi-popular scientific brochures" (5–6). On the side, he writes novels, hoping for the big break, but always hampered by his "scientific training" that doesn't allow him "to let go" (5). He has been psychoanalyzed by the great Dr. Frank of Vienna, a mask for "frank" Freud that is both reverential and ironic. Reflecting her desire to live at the "peak or nothing," Natalia's prose is lyric, intense (6–7). As his introduction demonstrates, his prose is like his life – inhibited, cautious, prosaic, rational, journalistic. Content with the possible, Helforth sees Natalia's suicide as a Promethean gesture affirming the impossible. She

killed herself by skating into a hole on the Swiss Lac de Brey, so deep
that it was as yet "un-plumbed" by science: "The two lines ran straight
out, two parallel lines – they met in a dark gash of the luminous ice-
surface. . . . Only Natalia had the courage to cut two straight lines, on a
flat surface of an Alpine lake, running to infinity. Infinity? I think, she
found that" (5, 10).

One piece of the puzzle does not fit Helforth's neat binary schemati-
zation, however. Natalia had borrowed Renne's sturdy watch, and before
she skated to her Icarian death, she carefully laid the watch on her muff.
Reading this sign psychoanalytically, he rationalizes her act by saying
that her borrowing and returning of the watch showed her desire to take
Renne's place, to be like Renne – sensible, loyal, practical. This desire
was also incestuous; she wanted to be Neil's sister, as well as his wife.
In spite of her death, Helforth concludes, Natalia wanted to accept the
limits of ordinary time and space, just as he did. Helforth's introduction
to Natalia's text is ultimately self-serving. He undermines what he seems
to praise and rationalizes what he cannot understand. We in turn are left
wondering if Natalia represents Helforth's Ka, the inspired, intense, mad,
"feminine" side of himself that he is repressing – the side that disrupts
the finite and scientific to reach for the infinite and transcendental.

Natalia's narrative of twelve nights both confirms and undermines the
Prologue that introduces it. The prose *is* electric, experimentally a cross
between a surrealist stream of consciousness and imagist lyric. Natalia's
self-portrait "fits" Helforth's image of the woman who would cut parallel
lines into "a dark gash of the luminous ice-surface." Shared images of
fire, ice, radium, electricity, lightning, platinum resonate back and forth
between Helforth's Prologue and Natalia's "Nights" to weave the two
texts into one. The prosaic style of the first and the lyric style of the
latter reaffirm the opposition that Helforth establishes to rationalize her
suicide and his survival.

But Natalia's text provides a vastly different explanation of her suicide,
which, though unnarrated, is nonetheless implied and interpreted. Echoing the twelve sections of the Prologue, "Nights" has twelve chapters,
successively called "Night I," "Night II," "Night III," and so forth.
Natalia's Tarot meditation on "Death," the thirteenth card of the Major
Arcana, suggests that the next chapter, "Night XIII," would have told
the story of her suicide. The "Nights" Natalia narrates are thereby given
a teleological direction as an interpretation of what cannot be narrated –
the "dark gash" in the ice, the black hole of the text.

Where Helforth explains Natalia's suicide in terms of her failure as a
writer, Natalia presents her impending death in terms of her failure as a
woman. Reading Helforth, we are only minimally aware that Natalia is
a lover, a wife; reading Natalia, we would never know that she is a

writer. For Helforth, Natalia is the Romantic artist-as-woman who was burned like Semele and Icarus by the sheer intensity of Promethean daring (27). "Her writing," he tells us, "did not satisfy her, it was too luminous, too cerebral altogether" (26). Its "dazzling" "intricacy and daring," he believes, was a sign of her "unquestionable talent" (21). But "her battery was surcharged," and she chose the wrong medium for self-presentation. Helforth writes that he

> would have suggested a complete re-casting of her whole theme, to make it, not so much saleable, as merely presentable. . . . She was presenting truth, or what she saw as truth, in other words, not as a photographer, a journalist, or even a portrait-painter or a dramatist, but in some other medium. She seemed to work actually in radium or electricity. Is that, I ask you, the medium for a novel?" (21–2)

Such writing, he believes, feeds on neurosis: "If Natalia had resolved her problem, she wouldn't have gone on writing" (9–10). In imagining her death, he does not see her "swirling and whirling like that ice-Pavlova," but rather "upright, swaying, swinging out. She was nothing. A sort of pencil" (14).

Natalia explains her impending death in terms of the sterility of desire – heterosexual, homosexual, bisexual – in the limbo of the postwar world. If Helforth represents the rationalist impulse in psychoanalysis to neutralize the unconscious by knowing it, Natalia reflects the Freud of *Beyond the Pleasure Principle,* the theorist of repetition, of *Eros* and the death instinct, of sadism and masochism, of the unconscious resistant to interpretation. Two types of events punctuate Natalia's text – wounding discourse from Neil and compensatory intercourse with David. Neil has gone to Capri with his boy lover, to the very hotel, Saint Angelo, where he had honeymooned with Natalia. From there, he sends her three missives – two cards ("Nights I and X") and a wire announcing his return ("Night XII"). Wounding like knives, each in its own way mocks the special love and twinship Natalia thought she had shared with Neil. Each stirs up "her own black-phobia of approaching guilt" (35). Young David is her "Angelo Titan," a "torso" as beautiful as Michelangelo's David, whom she uses to counter Neil's Saint Angelo: "The boy, her new lover, would be antidote, cure, heal-all" (40, 35). David's twelve visits to her room at night, where they make love, are the major structural repetition of Natalia's text. But rather than healing, his passion is an "opiate" that obliterates her, drowns her in the rising "blackness" (34).

"Nights" pierces the veil before desire to expose its sterility in startlingly blunt terms – as explicit as Joyce in *Ulysses* or Lawrence in *Lady Chatterley's Lover,* but more despairing. As Perdita Schaffner observed in her Introduction, Natalia's "bed is the epicenter" of "Nights" (*xiii*). Much of the text is narrated from beneath David's heavy body: "She is with him, under him; he is dead weight" (41). Natalia is brutally frank about their sexual exchanges – "clumsy" on his part, distant and ambivalent on hers. His kisses cover her nose and mouth so that she can't breathe: "His lips had enclosed her nostrils, so that she fainted into blackness. His mouth, closed over her mouth. He breathed into her, his breath had to be caught; strangling, she cried, 'you must let me breathe' " (49). At least twice, David experiences premature ejaculation, for which he is terribly embarrassed. Natalia must comfort him – "it's all right, I love all that, don't worry, lie down now" and "one must learn. You didn't realise – we have been only these few times together. . . . the most beautiful dream is remembered sometimes, because of the moment of its breaking" (50). To reassure him, she would lie about or explain away her need to masturbate after his early orgasm by saying, "you see you excite me and, after you left, I excited myself more" (89, 63). Orgasm, which Natalia experiences through masturbation, is an onanistic, "sexless" eroticism: "She was sexless, being one chord, drawn out, waiting the high-powered rush of the electric fervour. It crept up the left side, she held it, timed it, let it gather momentum, let it gather force. . . . " (51).

Sex offered them all, Natalia writes, the chance to be "experimentalists in this very-vibrant power, this holy radium" (52). But her generation committed the "sin" of "damning of this force until it ate back into the fibre of existence, turned foul, in spite and suppression of maniacal repudiation" (52). Their bisexual ménage enacts this "sin" and reads increasingly to Natalia like a parody of the family structure they had sought to escape – brothers, sisters, mothers, fathers, all exist in a tangle of incestuous desire that is neither fertile nor fecund. Renne, Natalia recalls, had been her "half-lover but frightened, 'I don't really satisfy you,' and at a sort of psychological débâcle of a moment, flung Neil at her. Natalia hadn't wanted a husband but. . . . Neil was a sort of incarnation of Renne . . . half of the tenderness, left out in Renne, had been expended on Neil, so that the half-woman made for strength" (92). Natalia, Renne believes, suffers from a "father-fixation" and needs a "good stiff spot of psychoanalysis," while Neil has a "mother-fixation" and "mother[s]" his boys (52, 35, 46). Renne's current flame is not Natalia, but Una, the waiflike actress who moves in and out of the text with her lover, Felice Barton.[52] But both Una and Felice want Natalia, who wonders "Why did Renne's girl-lovers turn, as inevitably to her, as Neil's boys?" (77). Rejecting Una and Felice, Natalia thinks "Women were mad to go on that way, about women" (67). But David accuses her of loving only women, and she wonders, "Was this homosexuality at fault, then? Had Nat really loved the tall girl in Neil?" (69). Perhaps, she thinks, if she had had Neil's baby, he would not have left. But Renne says, "that would spoil

everything. If you have his child then *you* are woman, *he* is man, that's
smashed" (46). As in *Narthex,* bisexuality is "sterile negativism" (71).
"Of course, it was all a muddle," Natalia concludes (78).

Natalia's affair with David represents her attempt to leave the bisexual
muddle behind and return to a conventional heterosexuality. In contrast
to Neil, David is stereotypically masculine, "one of these smug, athletic,
Empire-building Englishmen" with a "bull-sensuous" mouth (37, 71).
Where Nat and Neil were "this terrible Siamese-twin" whose love was
too "cerebral," David was literally and figuratively "on top" in a love
that was oppressively physical (37). But Natalia discovers another form
of sterility with David, one bound up in desire as a death wish, the
entanglement of *L'Amour* and *La Mort* H.D. explored later in *Helen in
Egypt* and *Madrigal.* Where Nat and Neil momentarily achieved a star-
equilibrium akin to Ursula and Birkin in *Women in Love,* Natalia and
David echo the sadomasochism of Gudrun and Gerald. Images of violence, dominance, and submission pervade the lovemaking of Natalia
and David. "Night I" opens, for example, with the repetition of her pet
name Neith: " 'Neith' and she felt rhymes go with the word; sheathe,
unsheathe – claws certainly. He says, 'you have no need to be so cruel.
You bully me' " (33). In a later reversal, "she lay under boulders. Over
his left shoulder, wind howled and she dragged feet in, out of the cold.
His feet found and pinned hers, rape out of stone-age. He was stone,
out of stone-age" (74).

In *Beyond the Pleasure Principle,* Freud described sadism as the diversion
of the death instinct into eros, and masochism as sadism "turned round
upon the subject's own ego" (48). This erotically charged wish to overpower and be overpowered in a sadomasochistic economy of desire explains why Natalia is not healed in her affair with David, but brought
ever closer to death. Although "Nights" begins with her in the position
of master, intercourse reverses the roles so that she is swept up in a
sadistic destruction of her self. Underneath his body, "she felt herself go
cold, static, electrocuted, dead corpse. She felt death creep in" (73). Night
after night, erotic arousal for Natalia means being swallowed into "blackness," a mystical/erotic void akin to a Lawrentian *jouissance,* with its
anticerebral, racialist rhetoric. In "Night VI," for example, Natalia
writes:

> She believed that David's kiss was death because there was only black-
> ness as she dropped under it and it spread (when she stopped breathing)
> a black canopy over her head. The kiss was, in that sense, authentic.
> They were out of European, modern computation, white thoughts.
> Their thoughts were Egyptian, Indian, Hindoo, American Indian. They
> met in the Greater Arcana, there was no separating of body and spirit.
> (79)[53]

Both Natalia's pleasure in and resistance to David's embrace screens a deeper longing for the maternal presence, for a return to prenatal bliss. "Was bed tomb; womb?" she wonders (71). Obliteration with David restores the blackness of the womb, for the absence of cerebralism is the presence of the maternal body. This conflation of death wish and desire for the primal Mother produces a dream vision that prefigures Natalia's suicide. In "Night III," Natalia sits alone wrapped in a silk shawl, staring into an abalone shell. The tense shifts from standard past into the timeless, continuous present; the repetitive, lyric rhythm of sensation signals the Semiotic discourse of the Kristevan *chora*:

> The coat is soft against her shoulder, her sleeves and the silk fringe of the shawl are dull rose. The shell in her hand is pearl. Out of the hollow of the shell (held, reflecting the blurred edge of the upper inset line of concealed wall-lights) her world begins. It will begin. Her shell will begin. When the shell is focussed at the required angle, it will begin. She waits; the stream makes background. . . . Out of the shell...out of the shell.
>
> The flat, Pacific abalone shell, gives back patterns. This pattern is assembled in her mind, it glows out, then her heart stops and her breathing. There is a crude shaped statue, seated on a ledge of stone. The columns are not Greek, they are not Egyptian. Nat's breath holds, her sharp sense goes out, she feels the shell is living. . . . She finds the columns are carved with no known hieroglyph. There is an intensified, tall, slight statue. This woman must turn.
>
> There is a door and a purple hill-slope, cut into layers, purple, green. There is a hill-slope that intensifies itself and the door of this temple is set on a ledge of water . . . the small statue is upright, delicate, unclassified. Nat will hold this. It will, she knows, turn under her vision, a butterfly wing under microscope, turn and fling out Protean syllable. (54–6)

This mysterious woman – pre-Greek, pre-Egyptian – prefigures the Lady of *Trilogy* who carries the book of the yet-unwritten. Her temple echoes the Birth House of "Secret Name." She condenses into a single figure an image of Aphrodite rising out of the sea on a shell, the paintings of the Madonna with shells, and the second Tarot card of the Major Arcana, the High Priestess whose book of the mysteries is partially veiled. Further, she parallels the enigmatic motif in Woolf's *The Waves* (1931), the silent fairy woman of Elvedon who sits writing in a garden in the story Bernard tells to comfort Susan.

Natalia's lady of the shell is mistress of the unknown hieroglyph, spinner of "Protean syllable." As primal Mother, she represents the origins of life and language as mystery, the perpetually unknown. If only she will turn, Natalia's vision suggests, Natalia will be saved. But "the woman, will not turn round. Her heart leaps out towards the woman who will not turn round. . . . The woman became pre-Ionic, gross, with large breasts, she looked out, over another stretch of water" (56). Natalia's vision ends with her longing unsatisfied. David substitutes for the lady in the shell; when he arrives, Natalia murmurs "*You are out of this shell*" (57). Like Rhoda in *The Waves* who broke off her affair with Louis and later threw herself in the river, Natalia separates from David in "Night XII." The sea imagery of her anguish not only recalls her desire for the watery womb/tomb of the maternal body, but also prefigures her return into the "dark gash" of the earth's body, the black hole of the Lac de Brey:

> . . . something was drawing to an end, that was all. The great billow that had lifted her out of her stagnant misery had broken, flung her high on the dry sand, then curving about her feet, it kissed her, curved into her body, impregnated her with all the sea. The sea of life was there in reality, she was part of that great rhythm. She had not been lost. A billow had detached itself, from all the ocean, for one moment, impersonated "David." . . . She was hovering over a stagnant pond, while the sea was waiting, while it had only to draw her – out – (104, 106)

As Rhoda did for Woolf, Natalia represents a projection of one part of H.D.'s psyche as she constructed it in a psychodramatic text. Anchoring both Woolf and H.D. to the ordinary time/space of survivors, Bernard in *The Waves* and Helforth in *Nights* represent another part. For both Woolf and H.D. in their 1931 texts, the feminine fragment of the self is lyric, poetic, and tragic, living intensely in a visionary time/space of moments. It is also suicidal, as if the price of creativity is a flirtation with madness and death. Bernard and Helforth are ironic personae, masculine figures of fun who nonetheless represent the comedic principle of survival. They are sane precisely because they can accept the prosaic sequence of time within the existing social order. The price of their compromise, however, is the absence of mystery. In Nietzschean terms, the masculine is the harmonious Apollonian, while the feminine is the disruptive Dionysian. As psychodramatic texts, both *Nights* and *The Waves* represent a reassuring murder of the "madwoman in the attic" (to echo Gilbert and Gubar) and an affirmation of the ordinary that is ultimately a disturbing erasure of the feminine.

As the final text in a series of autobiographical fictions about her life in the 1920s and early 1930s, *Nights* is the nadir of a downward spiral. Longing for the primal Mother in *Palimpsest* produces the healing time/space of the divine Birth House; the same desire in *Nights* leads to a vision of the maternal figure who "will not turn" to nourish her daughter and leads ultimately to the daughter's re-union with the mother through suicide. The psychodrama of *Nights* is similarly more bleak than that in

Hedylus or *Kora and Ka*. Hedyle survives the abandonment of her son to tell her story; but it is the son, not the mother, who is the poet. In playing the role of Persephone in the mysteries of death and rebirth, Kora experiences some reconciliation with her past, even though she does not herself speak in the text. But, like his narrating voice, Helforth's "cure" is dominant; Kora's is muted. Natalia's speech in "Nights" signals her death in *Nights,* the volume John Helforth introduces and naturalizes. In all three texts, the male fragment of the author's split psyche is the survivor. The female voice is left behind, silent, or silenced through death – unmothered and unhealed.

IV. EXILE FROM THE MATERNAL BODY

> . . . and she was flung on a shore that had no end, no beginning; all time converged from that shore, that river.
>
> H.D., *Nights* (105)

The patterns of H.D.'s fictions about her decade of wandering reveal her caught in a series of contradictions that she could articulate but not transcend either in her living or writing. Every text, in one form or another, focuses on the fundamental conflict she felt as a woman and a writer – what critics have called the "double bind of the woman writer." The form this split takes in her fiction about herself in the 1920s includes a dangerous identification of her creativity with Helios-Apollo – with the piercing light and steel blade of the masculine mind, epitomized by one of her noms de plume, Ray Bart. Within this binary system, her female body is the vessel of the mind, the vestal prophetess through whom Helios-Apollo speaks. Two cinematic poems of the period – "Projector and Projector II" – are lyric manifestations of what she narrates in prose: The magical light of the (male) god passes through the (female) body of the projector to create the (child) art on the cinematic screen (*Collected Poems* 349–59).

This conflict between masculine mind and feminine body can be read as a symptom of ambivalent desires centered on the mother, the kind of longing for the primal Mother and denial of the "real" mother that characterizes the relationship of so many women writers with their mothers. For women like H.D. and Woolf, whose mothers were powerful figures of conventional femininity, identification with the mother threatens the death of the writer. Both felt they had to "kill" the "angel in the house" most forcefully personified in the figure of the mother they also desired. But this matricidal plot against the mother left the daughter/ writer adrift in a male sea. Mothered, the daughter can't write; unmothered, she is paralyzed. The way out seems to be the daughter's

desire for a primal Mother, a fictionalizing fantasy for a Demeter who
has not yet lost her beloved daughter to the clutch of Hades, for a mother
who will nurture, not deny, her daughter's difference. In H.D.'s case,
this oscillation between desire and denial of the mother is inscribed in
her texts about exile and loss. To write, she had to wander homeless,
an outcast from the feminine norm. But, as outcast, she felt a perpetual
sense of loss, diaspora from the maternal body of the motherland.

This diaspora, the (pre)condition of her writing, channeled her longing
in heterodox religious directions. At the very time that Eliot found his
home in the patriarchal bosom of the Church of England, H.D. was
defining the boundaries of her alienation from the Establishment and
mapping her search for the sacred. Like Eliot, the Word – the text –
represented a linguistic mediation between the divine and the mortal,
the out-of-time and the in-time. The Word invites the incarnation of the
sacred in a textual medium that is simultaneously elusive and fixed. But
in contrast to Eliot, the Word was not the product of an exchange between
Father and poet-Son, but rather the (re)production of the poet-daughter's
negotiation with the Father and the Mother, whose powers are different.
"What is this mother–father duality / to tear at our entrails?" the poet
asks in *Trilogy* (552). She had already asked this question for a decade in
prose. Helios/Apollo and Isis/Demeter are the paternal and maternal
manifestations of the divine whose presence she seeks, whose absence
she laments, whose duality "Splintered the crystal of identity, / shattered
the vessel of integrity" (526). Beneath the brilliance of Helios/Apollo lies
the (pro)creative, generative warmth of Isis, who knows, after all, the
"secret name" of Amen-Ra. A decade or more before she wrote *The
Walls Do Not Fall,* H.D.'s Ray Bart/Raymonde Ransome and Nat/Na-
talia had taken on the paternal–maternal masks of the poet who says in
Trilogy: "here am I, Amen-Ra whispers, / *Amen,* Aries, the Ram, // be
cocoon, smothered in wool, / be Lamb, mothered again" (*Collected Poems*
527).[54]

The image of the poet-daughter (s)mothered in the maternal body
conflates birth and death, just as the Birth House in "Secret Name" is
simultaneously a "womb, tomb." The daughter's desire for the maternal
throughout this fiction about the 1920s and early 1930s is entangled with
a longing for death, ultimately so strong that Natalia vanishes into the
black hole of a watery womb/tomb. As Sylvia Plath probably came to
believe some thirty years later, (re)birth depends on a death that replicates
the cycles of the mystery religions. You must "die" to be "reborn," dismembered to be re-membered. By the beginning of the 1930s, the text
became for H.D. a site of surrogate death, as well as a scene of birth.

As the nadir of this contradiction, *Nights* also gestures toward "resurrection," what the poet of *Trilogy* calls "a sense of direction," a "bee-

line, // straight to the horde and plunder, // the treasure, the store-room, // the honeycomb" (*Collected Poems* 583). If the womb is the tomb, then the tomb is the womb – the "store-room" of the maternal body out of which the writer will emerge from her textual suicide. *Nights* testifies to the severity of H.D.'s split psyche – only the male persona survives to encase the female voice in his mystified and moralistic prose. But *Nights* also signifies a shift in the binary poles of the split subject, one that started in *Kora and Ka* and finds full flowering in the reborn poet of the 1940s and 1950s. In contrast to *Palimpsest* and *Hedylus,* where the poet wears a male mask, *Kora and Ka* and *Nights* unveil the woman as the "real" writer, as the figure of genius. John Helforth is the speaker and survivor in both texts, but he is dull. Where Helios/Apollo is the source of poetic inspiration in *Palimpsest,* where Hedylus spouts lyrics suspiciously like H.D.'s own, Helforth's only claim to fame is his survival. Kora, we mysteriously learn, does the "real" writing in spite of appearances. And Natalia, not Helforth, is the writer of lyric brilliance. Even though these women are silenced at the end of each text, they – in their female bodies – are the writers. This re-vision of the poet as *female* replaces the gender-free "early H.D.," reverses the masculine mind of Ray Bart, and pre-figures the mother/muses that inspire the daughter/poet to write in *Trilogy* and *Hermetic Definition.*

As the "bee-line" toward "resurrection," *Nights* thus suggests without yet narrating that a woman – in her very femaleness – can be a writer. As "outcast" of conventional femininity, she inhabits a perpetual borderline. But, to write, she does not have to cast out her womanhood and pretend to inhabit a male body or male space. Raymonde Ransome doesn't need Ray Bart to be a poet in her own right; Hedyle doesn't need Hedylus. She can speak, in other words, from the position of outcast. In *Nights,* H.D. began to apply to herself what she had articulated for others in *Borderline* and "Two Americans," where she had formulated a vision of modernism based on racial Otherness. What the "entire deep in-rooted power" of Saul Howard's "gigantic Being" represents to Raymonde is his capacity as an outcast to "sing" nonetheless, and to sing the songs of his African-American people. Identification with Saul, the uncrowned king and fellow exiled American, restores Raymonde's sense of artistic direction. But before H.D. could speak, like Robeson, from the position of her Otherness, she had to enter the "bee-hive" of the "blameless physician," where she could die and be reborn in the body of psychoanalysis.[55]

5

Rebirths: Re/Membering the Father and Mother

> I must drown completely and come out on the other side, or rise to
> the surface after the third time down, not dead to this life but with a
> new set of values, my treasure dredged from the depth. I must be born
> again or break utterly.
>
> H.D., *Tribute to Freud* (54)

Preoccupation with death often represents a desire to return to origins,
a longing to start again, to reinstitute beginnings and reaffirm becoming.
By the early 1930s, H.D. had written her textual self into the death by
drowning that concludes *Nights,* threatens Woolf's despairing horizon,
and hovers over Eliot's modernist waste land. H.D.'s sublimated suicide
represented the death of the writer and the onset of her creative block.
But it also left the living woman open to self-creation through psychoanalysis, an autobiographical process in which the "text" is dialogic talk.
Give and take between analyst and analysand in the talking cure returns
the latter to beginnings so that the past does not have to be repeated. As
H.D. wrote about her collaboration with Freud, "We had come together
in order to substantiate something. I did not know what. There was
something that was beating in my brain; I do not say my heart – my
brain. I wanted it to be let out. I wanted to free myself of repetitive
thoughts and experiences – my own and those of many of my contemporaries" (*Tribute to Freud* 13).

Caught in the "round and round" of "repetitive thoughts and experiences," H.D. finally agreed in 1931 to Bryher's insistence that she
undergo the experience of analysis. Among other things, psychoanalysis
would, she believed, enact the death of the repetitive textual selves she
had created and the (re)birth of a new self through talk. During the Great
War, she had turned away from poetry and toward prose to work
"through a weed, a tangle of bushes and bracken out to a clearing," as
she wrote to Cournos (9 July 1919). Some thirteen years later, she turned

away from (monologic) writing toward (dialogic) talking to clear "away a bit of rubbish, so that at least a small section of the river should run clear . . . [where] it ran muddy . . . blocked by fallen logs, some petrified – and an accumulation of decaying leaves and branches" (*Tribute to Freud* 83). To paraphrase the epigraph for this chapter, she had to drown in the unknown depths of the unconscious, recover its treasures through psychoanalytic decoding, and rise to the surface reborn. The process of psychoanalysis was to be a pedagogical experience akin to the rites of the Eleusinian mysteries – a death of the old self and a rebirth of the new through an initiation into secret wisdom.

Just as initiation ritual wove the individual into the communal in the Eleusinian mysteries, psychoanalysis as H.D. understood it would construct a narrative that explained the intersections of the personal and the societal. The repetitive thoughts and experiences in which she and her contemporaries had been caught were not the expressions of idiosyncratic neuroses, but rather the product of civilization and its discontents, to borrow the title from Freud's speculative work on the implicit social contract that requires repression as the price of civilization. It was the repetitions of history – particularly its compulsion to cycles of violence – that initiated the repetitions of individuals. The erotics of empire and the interlocking economies of war and motherhood that H.D. had already articulated in *Asphodel* and *Palimpsest* laid the framework for her understanding of psychoanalysis as a theory of history.[1] As she wrote in *Tribute to Freud,* she went to Freud partially because she "wanted to fight in the open, war, its cause and effect, with its inevitable aftermath of neurotic breakdown and related nerve disorders" (94). Reading the "preliminary signs and symbols of the approaching ordeal," she knew that she and her whole "lost generation" of survivors from the Great War were "drifting" down the clogged river of history toward another catastrophic war (94, 13). Psychoanalysis was "a new form of healing" that might allow her to confront "my own personal Phobia, my own personal little Dragon of war-terror" so as to "fortify and equip myself to face war when it came, and to help in some subsidiary way, if my training were sufficient and my aptitudes suitable, with war-shocked and war-shattered people" (81, 93–4).

Unlike Bryher, H.D. never sought an official status within the psychoanalytic community, but she did consider herself Freud's "student" in a training analysis that would allow her to give informal sessions, especially to "war-shattered" people. But both she and Freud understood that their collaboration was to produce the rebirth of the writer, rather than the birth of an analyst. When McAlmon wrote that she was wasting her time in analysis, she defended her work with Freud by writing back, "But you yourself have been pointing out – and rightly – that my writing had reached a vanishing point of sterility and finesse" (18 August 1933). Near the end of her scheduled sessions with Freud, he pronounced her analysis "finished" and gave his "blessing" for her to give "private" hours. But his parting gift – a branch of orange leaves – at their last session had a weightier symbolic message. Like Virgil's gift to Dante, his "golden bough" signaled his belief that their work together would bear fruit. Freud's letters to H.D. frequently and gently inquire about her writing. "I confidently expected to hear from you that you are writing," he wrote at one point, "but such matter should never be forced" (*Tribute to Freud* 191). H.D. was well aware of his desire. "Freud however wants me to write," she had confided earlier to Conrad Aiken. "Well – its a horrible responsibility" (20 August 1933).

What began as talk became writing in a series of texts that (re)create the self-creation H.D. experienced in analysis with Freud. In an endless chain of *mise en abyme,* the talk aimed at (re)producing the writer led to the writer who produced a text about the (re)creation of the writer who wrote the texts. The most public of these is the memoir *Tribute to Freud,* written in 1944, first printed in serial form under the title "Writing on the Wall" in *Life and Letters Today* (1945–6), and then published with only minor changes as a volume with its present title in 1956. The most private of these are the letters H.D. wrote to Bryher on a daily basis detailing fragments of the analysis, adding and subtracting to what she explored with Freud. As a kind of composite text, these letters are written in a discourse that creates its own, distinctive self-portrait.[2] More intimate than *Tribute to Freud,* but less private than her letters to Bryher, is *Advent,* a text in journal form that was "assembled" for publication late in 1948 from the notes she kept during the first three weeks of analysis with Freud and later destroyed. In more disguised and mythologized forms, H.D.'s collaboration with Freud appears in a poem she suppressed, "The Master," probably written in 1935 (*Collected Poems* 451–61), in the confrontation between Kaspar and Mary Magdalene in *The Flowering of the Rod* (*Collected Poems* 586–612), and in the Theseus sequence in *Helen in Egypt* (147–92). Finally, her memoir *The Gift,* written from 1941–3, represents a continuation of her analysis, both in its review of her early childhood and in its examination of the war phobia she wanted, but was unable, to discuss directly with Freud.

As different as these texts are, they all reflect an interplay between the discourses of repetition and recollection as Freud distinguished the two in "Further Recommendations in the Technique of Psychoanalysis: Recollection, Repetition and Working Through" (1914). As a discourse of repetition, each text reproduces the scene of analysis and also reenacts the drama of transference. As a discourse of recollection, each text re-members the scene of analysis and also works through the conflicts it repeats to express new interpretations of what was unknown. The free-associational structure that pervades the discourse of all these texts embodies this interplay between repetition and recollection. Free association invokes Freud's first rule of analysis – his requirement that the analysand's talk flow freely by association, rather than by linear modes of thought. At the same time, free association recalls the controlled techniques of the modernist novel – the stream of consciousness in which past, present, future, and fantasy are woven together; the broken sequences in which narrative reaches for the simultaneities of subjective time and lyric epiphany.

As modernist texts, these repetitions/recollections of analysis both record and reproduce the psychodynamics of analysis. They represent a transferential discourse built on the foundations of repression and resistance. Freud called the transference an "artificial illness" in the hermetically sealed womb of analysis – one that signified the presence of the analysand's "resistance" to a "cure," but one that was essential to the dynamics of healing ("Further Recommendations" 165). Transference, he argued, is a form of *repeating* that in an analytic situation ideally leads to *recollection*. As repetition, transference serves the psyche's desire to continue the repression of forbidden desires ("Further Recommendations"). In this sense, "the transference provides the *strongest resistance* to the cure" ("Dynamics of the Transference" 107). In what Freud termed the "art" of interpretation, the analyst's task is to use the transference against itself. Analysis thus comes to focus on the dynamics of the analysis itself. As itself the contested site, analysis is a scene in which the analysand's resistance to the analyst repeated her or his repression of childhood memories. Working through the analysand's resistance to analysis would accomplish a parallel working through of repressed memories so that ultimately recollection would replace repetition. The self-reflexivity of the analytic situation was essential, Freud believed, to its success. Similarly, the self-reflexivity of H.D.'s texts reproduces the psychodynamics of repression, transference, resistance, and working through.

The differences among the texts relate to their respective genres, particularly as the conventions of the various genres intersect with H.D.'s negotiations of the related binaries of prose and poetry, and of public and private speech. The opposition that H.D. articulated to Cournos in her first defense of her prose – between the personal novelist and the clairvoyant poet – resonates throughout the prophetic constructions of her analysis in poetry and the more intimate accounts in prose. Mediated by gender, the conflict between public and private, speech and silence, that characterized H.D.'s publication and suppression of books in the Madrigal cycle is reenacted in her discourses about Freud, which are layered like the palimpsest of the psyche. The more public the text, the less H.D. revealed; the more private the text, the less she concealed. Texts like her letters to Bryher do not contradict *Tribute to Freud* so much as they erupt into the formal tribute's gaps, at times disrupting the harmonious surface of the polished text with a racy Rabelaisian glee.

Out of the various discourses replicating the scene of analysis emerged a new prose form for H.D. – the personal essay that integrates autobiography and meditation, dream and history, the self and the other, poetics and psychology, lyric and narrative. *Tribute to Freud* and *The Gift*, as well as the later *Compassionate Friendship* and *End to Torment*, are generic hybrids that influenced or foreshadowed more contemporary works such as Robert Duncan's *H.D. Book*, Adrienne Rich's "When We Dead Awaken: Writing as Re-Vision," Alice Walker's "In Search of Our Mothers' Gardens," and DuPlessis's "For the Etruscans."[3] They are openly autobiographical, without the usual disguises of name changes, distortions, condensations, and displacements that we have seen in her fiction. The "I" is of course no less textually constructed than the personae of her novels. But the self projected in *Tribute to Freud* and *The Gift* has a different directness and authority, a public voice that moves widely and deeply across the landscape of culture. Like many of Lawrence's essays, Pound's critical dictates, or Williams's *Kora in Hell: Improvisations,* H.D.'s texts present a personal and prophetic commentary on aesthetics, history, religion, and the modern condition. Like Woolf's voice of the "common reader" in her critical essays, H.D.'s persona invites the reader into the process of discovering meanings that are at once personal and general in significance. Also like the Woolf of *A Room of One's Own* and "Professions for Women," H.D. adapted techniques of the modernist novel – broken narratives, interior monologue, associational structures, lyrical clusters of motif and metaphor – to forge a fictionalized essay. Like Colette's *Sido* and *My Mother's House* or Woolf's "A Sketch of the Past," they focus intensely on memories of the lost world of childhood revolving around a powerful figure of nurturance – the goddess-like mother of the daughter's first love. Like Havelock Ellis's ongoing series *Impressions and Comments,* commentaries on art and literature are woven into confessional intimacies. But above all, like Freud's *Interpretation of Dreams,* H.D.'s texts are performative – they enact a self-analysis in which the (re)constructed self is presented as exemplum for general principles.[4]

What particularly distinguishes H.D.'s personal essays from those of her fellow modernists is that they are written as tributes to another, gifts that enact an ambivalence of reverence and resistance. As Adalaide Morris has pointed out, "Each 'tribute' partakes of the doubleness of the word, for it is both a payment levied and a gift rendered" ("Relay of Power" 513). Morris went on to connect H.D.'s double-edged tributes to the "gift economy" whereby her "final tribute" is a "gift rendered" that releases her from thralldom to the person she honors (513). We might also extend this argument to see H.D.'s tributes as transferential texts in which she repeats the love–hate she felt for maternal–paternal figures and works through that ambivalence in a textual self-analysis. This working through transforms the text into a scene of recollection instead of repetition, the place where she escapes infantilization and moves toward independence.

   This chapter will review in the first section the biographical outlines of H.D.'s various engagements with psychoanalysis in the 1920s and 1930s. Sections 2 and 3 will examine how H.D.'s various texts about her analysis with Freud reflect upon, repeat, and work through first the paternal transference, then the maternal transference. Section 4 will read *The Gift* as a continuation of the specific analysis she began with Freud, one undertaken under the pressure of Nazi bombs. In Section 5, *The Gift*, read intertextually with *Trilogy*, will be explored as the personal discourse of prose that clears away the "rubbish" to make possible the prophetic discourse of poetry. Throughout, the chapter will examine how H.D.'s texts about analysis rearticulate and move beyond the paralyzing repetitions of the Dijon series – especially the ambivalent longing for mother and motherland, the desire for a "home" that would nurture, not deny, her special gift.

I. ANALYSIS: TERMINABLE AND INTERMINABLE

It is a long and slimy process, this of un-UNKing the UNK or debunking the junk.

H.D., Letter to Bryher
(2 May 1936)

   Freud was the only analyst H.D. called her "guardian of all beginnings," but he was neither her first nor her last analyst before she wrote *Tribute to Freud* and *The Gift*. Although she was never a patient of Havelock Ellis, her friendship with him paved the way for her analysis with Freud. H.D. resisted Bryher's passionate advocacy for undergoing an analysis until 1931. But the aftershocks of her disastrous trip to Monte Carlo with Macpherson in December of 1930 and his breakdown on the train at Easter time in 1931 led her to agree to a series of twenty-four sessions from April 13 to July 6, 1931 with British analyst Mary Chadwick, the author of numerous books and articles in applied psychoanalysis and a member of the iconoclastic Tavistock Clinic in Bloomsbury.[5] "Chaddie," as they called her, was an intimate member of H.D.'s circle during this period and frequently attended parties with them. The sessions made H.D. "happy" at first, but she quickly became "distressed" with this "mixing" of "ps-a with ordinary affairs," but "could not openly criticize" Chaddie's breaking the "rules" ("Autobiographical Notes" 22). Later references to these sessions suggest as well that H.D. associated Chaddie with the nasty "War home Matron," who had chastised her after the stillbirth of her child in 1915 for having a husband out of uniform and for taking the doctor's time away from wounded soldiers.[6] H.D.'s generally unsatisfactory analysis was followed by Chaddie's extended visit to Riant Chateau in July and August of 1931, which in turn led to the composition of "Nights" (Part 2 of *Nights*) in September. Natalia's final, wordless "..." at the conclusion of "Nights," as well as her impending suicide, are thoroughly entangled with Chaddie's visit. Dan Burt, Chaddie's nephew and the primary referent for Natalia's lover David in *Nights,* came with her. In "Autobiographical Notes," H.D. wrote that Chaddie "follows K everywhere and tries to keep us apart. Dan and I are flung together" (23). Instead of initiating a rebirth experience, Chaddie seemed to have intensified the drive toward death.

Analysis with Hanns Sachs, Bryher's analyst since 1928, followed, in late November and December of 1931. A longstanding and loyal member of Freud's innermost circle of disciples, Sachs was a lay analyst who did numerous training analyses at the Berlin Psychoanalytic Institute, co-edited the psychoanalytic journal *Imago,* and wrote widely on psycho-analysis, especially in relation to creativity, aesthetics, film, literature, and the arts. This brief analysis made her "happy," but she resisted Bryher's pressure to continue with Sachs in the spring. When the rise of Nazism in Berlin led Sachs to emigrate to Boston shortly thereafter, H.D. toyed with the idea of continuing analysis with him in the States. Like Chadwick, Sachs had been a frequent visitor and was very close to Bryher, for whom he tried to arrange membership in a psychoanalytic society so that she could practice officially as a lay analyst. Moreover, H.D. was extremely fond of the rotund enthusiast, whom they called by the pet name Turtle. But she did not, as she later wrote Macpherson, establish a transference with him, and she decided against the move to Boston.

When Sachs and Bryher suggested that she might be able to see Freud, she eagerly agreed and began exhaustive preparation in August of 1932. She had already read widely in the psychoanalytical journals to which Bryher had subscribed since the early 1920s. She had also attended psychoanalytic lectures in Berlin. But, with the possibility of analysis with Freud, she began "intensive reading of psycho-analytical journals, books and study Sigmund Freud" ("Autobiographical Notes" 25). A cryptic entry in "Autobiographical Notes" suggests that she even began her own analysis before Freud finally sent word in December that he would accept her as an analysand: "Begin record of Dreams. Analytical Note Books, Aug. 1932." Unfortunately, these notebooks were either destroyed or misplaced. But the reference to them in "Autobiographical Notes" glosses H.D.'s statement in *Tribute to Freud:* "I was a student, working under the direction of the greatest mind of this and of perhaps many succeeding generations" (18). "He wants me to go back," she wrote Aiken on August 20, 1933, "– for the 'discipleship.' He considered it a question of that."

As a student, however, H.D. also went in search of healing – to learn firsthand "the science of the unravelling of the tangled skeins of the unconscious mind and the healing implicit in the process" (*Tribute to Freud* 16). Her analysis began on March 1, 1933 and was to continue through June, but was broken off on June 12, 1933 during the week of Nazi terror in the streets of Vienna. The tram she was riding was stopped by a bomb on the tracks; passengers had to remain still on board for twenty terrifying minutes while the bomb was disassembled. H.D.'s war phobia returned in full force, and Bryher took her back to Switzerland. Freud wanted her to return in the fall of 1933, but she didn't go back to analysis until a brief, but intense breakdown in August of 1934 led her to agree.[7] Dr. J. J. van der Leeuw, the theosophist and educator who had had the hour with Freud just before hers in 1933, died in a reckless crash of the airplane he was piloting. Identifying deeply with van der Leeuw, whom she called "the Flying Dutchman," the man without a home, H.D. was shattered. She recovered quickly, determined to resume analysis with Freud. He was delighted to have her again to "listen to the working of your mind," as he wrote (24 September 1934). In making the arrangements for a five-week analysis from October 31–December 2, Freud confessed to H.D. that he felt "the catastrophe of vd [van der] Leeuw's" death "as a personal loss" because "Too late I conceived the idea I could have prevented him risking his life in so dangerous a way having found out the intimate connection of his reckless flying with his intimate phantasies" (24 September 1934). When she arrived in Vienna to tell Freud "how sorry I am," he told her, "You have come to take his place" (*Tribute to Freud* 6).

H.D. often compared analysis to a cocoon that hatched the soul, with Freud as its midwife. But in no sense was her analysis removed from the anguish of the times – for either of them. Hitler had just come to power in February of 1933. "Already in Vienna," she wrote in *Tribute to Freud,* "the shadows were lengthening or the tide was rising" (58). The Austrian Nazi movement, already strong in the provinces, was making serious inroads in Vienna itself, where the Social Democratic Party led the resistance to both Nazism and the rightist regime of the Christian Socialist Chancellor, Engelbert Dollfuss. H.D. sometimes walked from the Hotel Regina to 19 Bergasse Street amidst strange "confetti-like showers from the air, glided paper swastikas," that looked like Christmas bonbons, like "Dannae's legendary shower," but ominously presaged the "grim coming events" (*Tribute to Freud* 58).

H.D.'s letters are filled with cryptic references to the "troubles" from "the north," while Bryher responded with elaborate and terrifying plans for rapid escape from Vienna should her father signal an imminent German takeover of Austria. Freud himself appeared outwardly calm about the situation for the most part, insisting for example that H.D. ignore Bryher's warning because he would surely know from his own sources of any immediate danger. Moreover, he retained his faith that the Austrian people were essentially "kind," that the League of Nations would never allow Hitler to impose the *anchluss*. But, H.D. wrote Bryher, during one of their sessions, he broke down and sobbed about the fate awaiting his grandchildren (12 May 1933). While he refused the requests of many friends that he leave Vienna immediately, his letters illustrate his deep pessimism about Nazi power and his recognition that Dollfuss's pro-Italian, anti-Hitler stance spelled the end of social democracy in Austria and offered only minimal hope for the Jews.[8]

May and June of 1933 were particularly frightening times in Vienna. In its attempt to smash the socialists in the Social Democratic Party, the Dollfuss regime heavily censored the press and forbade the workers' traditional May Day celebration. On May 1st, with the streets empty of civilians, H.D. stubbornly made her way through barricades made of machine guns, soldiers, and barbed wire, first to Freud's home and later to the opera. Freud was stunned; Bryher was frantic; and H.D. was defiantly proud, determined to make her private, symbolic stand against the coming madness (*Tribute to Freud* 59–62). Street violence erupted frequently in May, and news of a possible Italian takeover of Austria came in mid-May. At the same time, Freud's books were burned in Berlin and the largely pro-Nazi Heimwehr guards staged a massive street demonstration in Vienna. The death of Freud's once-close friend, Sandor Ferenczi, on May 24th must have added personal angst to the larger maelstrom of events. This tense spring provided the context for the bomb threat that finally drove H.D. out of Vienna on June 12th.

The streets of Vienna were strangely quiet during H.D.'s second analysis with Freud. The Nazi presence was everywhere, the Social Democrats had been completely suppressed in the brutal fighting and mass arrests in the spring of 1934, and Dollfuss had been assassinated by the Nazis in the summer. But the mood of the city, H.D. kept noting in her letters, was surreally playful as the opera was jammed and the student cafés she loved to frequent hummed with talk.

During this chaotic period, Bryher became one of Freud's main sources of news. She regularly sent newspapers and magazines to H.D., who brought them to Freud. He was so grateful, she wrote, that one day "Freud broke his great analytical rule of not noticing mags. and papers, yesterday when I took him the pamphlet. He said, '*what* – in English? Have the English DONE THIS?' He almost wept. Then he got up, shuffled to his sacred desk with the paper, turned and said most solemnly 'thank you' as if I had presented him with the keys to the city" (16 May 33). When Bryher visited Vienna in April and June of 1933, she contacted the Friends organization and began her seven-year effort to help refugees escape from Germany. At first, she helped the psychoanalytic community, providing funds, papers, jobs, and new analysands in London and America. By the outbreak of the war, she had helped some 105 people escape (*Heart to Artemis* 275–6). With Bryher, H.D. remained intensely concerned about these refugees and the impending war.

Above all, H.D. was worried about Freud. "With the death-head swastika chalked on the pavement, leading to the Professor's very door," she could not "in all decency" bring herself to discuss "my own personal little Dragon of war-terror" (*Tribute to Freud* 59, 94). During her second analysis, they did address her suppressed fears of violence, particularly of male violence against women, rooted, they agreed, in the primal scene. But, to spare his feelings, she censored her fear of Nazism out of their sessions. Freud's frailty intensified her desire to protect him. Pessimistic, even fatalistic about the future, Freud was very old and sick by the time H.D. went to Vienna. Even before his first cancer operation in 1923, Freud had talked continuously and obsessively about his own death. But at age seventy-seven, he suffered not only from cancer and an ill-fitting mouthpiece, but also heart failure, deafness, and bouts with pneumonia. He was so certain of immanent death that he commonly didn't allow analysands to pay in advance in case he died before the contracted sessions were complete.[9] Even before her analysis began, H.D. was frightened, with justification, that he might die at any moment.

His frailty and "obsession" with his own death (to quote Ernest Jones) does not mean, however, that the 1930s was an insignificant, twilight period for Freud. His writing shows as much mastery and vigor as ever, and his particular interests at this period dovetailed with H.D.'s own to such a degree that they help explain the special rapport they obviously achieved immediately. Not long before he saw H.D., he had published "Femininity" (1933), the final essay in a series of three beginning in 1925 in which he argued that psychoanalysis needed to shift its emphasis from the Oedipal to the pre-Oedipal period in its theory of female psychosexual development. He apparently communicated a sense of being on the frontiers of a new psychology of women to H.D., who wrote to Bryher "Papa has a complete new theory but he says he does not dare write it, because he does not want to make enemies of women. Apparently, we have all stirred him up frightfully" (3 May 1933). *New Introductory Lectures,* in which "Femininity" appeared, also included his "lecture" on "Dreams and Occultism," which attested to his ongoing fascination with mysticism and occult phenomena. H.D.'s first analysis centered heavily on the "writing on the wall" she experienced in Corfu in 1920, as well as her jellyfish and bell-jar experiences with Bryher in the Scilly Isles in 1919, and the vision of Van Eck on the *Borodino* in 1920. Freud was apparently intrigued, for H.D. wrote to Bryher: "Papa has nearly chewed off his right whisker with excitement over Corfu" (18 March 1933).

The late 1920s and 1930s were also the period of his most speculative and philosophical writings, especially as he explored the interplay between psyche and civilization and postulated a psychoanalytic theory of social contract in works such as *The Future of an Illusion* and *Civilization and Its Discontents.* The rise of Nazism further stimulated this direction in his work. During H.D.'s analyses, the ideas for *Moses and Monotheism* (1937–8) were percolating, no doubt entangling his own fantasies about Moses with those embodied in her dreams. One of the major dreams they discussed was her dream of the Princess descending the stairs to discover the baby in the bulrushes; they debated whether he or she was baby Moses in the symbolism of the dream (*Tribute to Freud* 119–20). About another dream, he was "purring and snorting," H.D. wrote to Bryher, "as he comes 'out big' of course, the heavy-sun god in exile" (27 April 1933).

With his death around the corner, Freud was also deeply concerned about the future of psychoanalysis, about his legacy to history. The 1930s was a key decade in the battle over the medicalization of psychoanalysis, with the American analysts pushing hard for requiring all analysts to have a medical degree. As he wrote in *The Question of Lay Analysis,* Freud was deeply opposed to this requirement. He saw psychoanalysis at a crossroads. In one direction lay the reduction of psychoanalysis to serving as the "handmaid of Psychiatry." In the other lay the broad application of psychoanalytic principles to all aspects of humanistic endeavor. During the 1930s, Freud took only analysands whom he considered "students" of one kind of another (Blanton 5, 35). Most likely, he assessed the potential of an analysand not only in terms of personal neurosis, but also in connection with what he or she might contribute to the future of psychoanalysis. "The chief aim of psychoanalysis," Freud told Smiley Blanton, "is to contribute to the science of psychology and to the world of literature and life in general" (Blanton 116). Similarly, H.D. reported that Freud told her: "My discoveries are a basis for a very grave philosophy. There are very few who understand this, *there are very few who are capable of understanding this*" (*Tribute to Freud* 18). As a gifted writer, H.D.

must have seemed to Freud as one of those capable few, as one whose future writings might help to prevent the reduction of psychoanalysis to medicine. In George Moraitis's words, H.D. and Freud engaged in "a pact for the future," for posterity, with each of the actors in the drama of analysis aware that their work together might well affect the shape of their legacy in history.[10]

H.D. described her analysis with Freud as a "most luscious sort of *vers libre* relationship" and summarized its effect as "a bar of radium at the back of my head" (Letters to Macpherson, 1 April 1933, and Aiken, 20 August 1933). She further believed that this "mixed analysis" with three different analysts represented a smooth progression, giving her "an added sense of values – as if one had been having music lessons, first with a good teacher, then with a master, then with a genius," as she wrote to Aiken ([September/October?] 1933). But the progression did not end with the gifts of the awesome genius. Instead, with Freud's permission, H.D. began analysis in October of 1935 with Walter Schmideberg, a more comfortable, homey friend, whom H.D. and Bryher nicknamed Polar Bear, or simply Bear. Comparing him to Freud, H.D. wrote Bryher that Schmideberg "is really so nice and reliable, more like a feather-bed than gem-like flame, but for that, cozy and always helpful, and makes us all laugh so."[11] If, with Freud, H.D. had sketched in the framework, with Schmideberg she filled in the gaps. Freud's radium bar had brought cerebral intensity, a searing penetration into the deepest layers of memory and experience. The Bear, "so good at re-threading and re-stitching," made H.D. feel "well knitted," she wrote Bryher (9 May 1936). By May of 1937, H.D. reported to Bryher that Schmideberg considered her "graduated," that she could always return for an "occasional 'hour' " if "something out-of-the-way crops up," but that formal psychoanalysis was no longer necessary. That "something" soon cropped up, in the form of Aldington's sudden demand for a divorce. He had been living with Brigit Patmore since 1928. But, in 1937, he ran away with Brigit's daughter-in-law Netta, who soon became pregnant. Apparently insensitive to the irony of the situation, Aldington pressured H.D. for a rapid divorce so that his child would be born legitimate. Unable to pay the court fees, he applied to H.D. for help, which she gave him. Occasional talks with the comforting Bear helped H.D. through the period of crisis until the divorce became final on July 22, 1938.[12]

"It is a long and slimy process, this of un-UNKing the UNK or de-bunking the junk," H.D. concluded from her near-decade of experience in psychoanalysis (Letter to Bryher, 2 May 1936). In one of his final essays, "Analysis Terminable and Interminable" (1937), Freud himself wondered if any analysis could be complete (237). H.D. believed that "the UNK is never finished," nor is the process of "un-UNKing," but she felt by the end of the decade that she had learned how to continue the process by herself, to do what Freud himself had done in *The Interpretation of Dreams* – that is, a self-analysis that extends the talking cure into writing. While the Bear provided essential support during the second half of the 1930s, H.D. credited her collaboration with Freud for breaking her writer's block. After leaving Freud in December of 1934, she returned with renewed spirit to work begun on Euripides's *Ion* during her pregnancy at the end of World War I. She wrote Bryher that "if I can get this Ion done, it will break the back-bone of my H.D. repression. Its funny how the ps-a helped," and she said repeatedly, "I consider the ION as the Freud contribution."[13] H.D. considered her translation of *Ion,* with its experimental prose insets in her own voice, as central to her renewed artistic drive. Freud had helped her to reunite spiritual with "physical creative force." "Last night," she concluded after finishing *Ion,*

> I had a complete series of the most emphatic sort of Greek dreams, mixed up with the sea, swimming, I sang in this dream, the sea was near, my mother appeared, I talked to her of Ion and said I was probably re-creating "mysteries," all very odd and birds in my bed and bedroom. Well – this is part ps-a, part literary, part Eleusinian." (Letter to Bryher, 25 August 1935)

In the Eleusinian mysteries of analysis with Freud, H.D. had been reborn, initiated into an interminable self-creative process that she would continue in her texts for the rest of her life.

II. RESISTANCE: WORKING THROUGH THE PATERNAL TRANSFERENCE

> Freud says you can't be helped unless you have a real resistance.
> H.D., Letter to Bryher
> (11 March 1933)

H.D.'s texts about her analysis with Freud split the autobiographical subject, to construct an "I then" who was engaged in the talking cure with Freud and an "I now" who repeats that initial experience as a writing cure.[14] Each text doubles the analysis by recreating the primary scene of analysis in the past and then establishing a secondary scene of analysis constituted in and through the act of writing. The transference, the temporary "illness" that Freud regarded as a form of resistance to analysis, consequently appears doubly in these texts: first, in the writing *about* transference (primary scene of analysis); second, in the writing *as* transference (secondary scene). As accounts of analysis, the texts reveal H.D.'s transferential projection of ambivalent feelings about her father and mother onto Freud; and, as continuations of analysis, they repeat that drama. Each text, in other words, (re)constructs in its own way the repressed longing for and resistance to the father and mother upon which the adult events of H.D.'s life had been superimposed. Her return to her parents in primary and secondary scenes of analysis enacts a creative regression out of which Psyche is reborn, with Freud as both midwife and surrogate parents. This (re)engagement with her parents through the agency of Freud in turn reflects and recapitulates the larger emergence of women out of the dominant cultural scripts enforced by the institution of the patriarchal family.

H.D.'s paternal transference with Freud was well established long before she went to Vienna, continued during both series of sessions, and repeated itself in all the texts she wrote about him. In her private letters to Bryher, even before her analysis began, H.D. regularly called Freud "papa." In *Advent,* she explained, "I think of Sigmund Freud as this little-papa, Papalie, the grandfather" – alluding to her maternal grandfather, the master of the microscope who taught biology in the Moravian Seminary (124). Her more public autobiographical accounts refer formally to Freud as "the Professor," superimposing him onto her own distinguished professor father. As she later wrote in *Compassionate Friendship,* "I found the perfect father-image in the Professor himself" (83). Freud's characterization of psychoanalysis as an empirical science in the great tradition of Copernicus and Darwin helped trigger the transference. Like her father, the astronomer, and her grandfather, the biologist, Freud was a "specular" scientist with a special "lens" that allowed him to probe the secrets of an unknown landscape: "my father's telescope, my grandfather's microscope. If I let go (I, this one drop, this one ego under the microscope–telescope of Sigmund Freud) I fear to be dissolved utterly" (*Advent* 116). The ancient treasures set carefully on Freud's desk and shelves "repeated" the sacred objects in her father's study into which she had been admitted as his favorite.[15]

Early in her analysis, Freud shocked H.D. by suddenly "beating with his hand, with his fist, on the head-piece of the old-fashioned horsehair sofa" and saying, "The trouble is – I am an old man – *you do not think it worth your while to love me*" (*Tribute to Freud* 16). Freud's pounding demand that she love him more repeated the implicit desire in her father's jealousy of Pound and the explicit complaints of Pound, Aldington, and Lawrence.[16] Her father, she recalled in *End to Torment,* had been shocked to find his daughter and Pound "caught 'in the very act,' " kissing on a couch in the "first *demi-vierge* embraces" of " 'first love' " (17–18, 54). "To recall Ezra is to recall my father," she further wrote (48). In turn, Pound's visit in the maternity home just before the birth of Perdita led to more "beating," more demands: "He seemed to beat with the ebony stick like a baton. . . . there is a sense of his pounding, pounding (*Pound-*

ing) with the stick against the wall. He had banged that way, with a stick once before, in a taxi, at a grave crisis in my life [when he demanded that she not accompany Gregg on her honeymoon]. This was a grave crisis in my life. It was happening here. 'But,' he said, 'my only real criticism is that this is not my child' " (*End to Torment* 8). Aldington, then Lawrence, repeated these pounding complaints – the one, by telling her she was a phantom, not a woman; the other, by demanding that she kick over her "frozen altars," then rejecting her erotic overtures. To adapt the language of Lacanian psychoanalysis, the Law of the Father beats on woman's desiring to mold her into man's object of desire. In the domain of the Maestro (as H.D. sometimes called Freud), the demands of the father/analyst repeated the patriarchal system of desire.

Resistance – all kinds of resistance – was essential to the psychodynamics of H.D.'s transference. She frequently referred to the various signs of her resistance to analysis, particularly to Freud's authority as the father in transference. In *Advent,* for example, H.D. noted that "Sigmund Freud said at our next session that he saw 'from signs' that I did not want to be analyzed" (139). One such sign was her looking at her watch in the middle of the hour. H.D. reported Freud's authoritative interpretation to Bryher as a near-castration of "Kat's tail":

> Papa bit my tail almost off, O so very, very delicately, like a scorpion-flea yesterday. He did not like me looking at my watch. . . . One is not to see the time, one is not to look at one's watch, it meant all sorts of dire and diabolic things, on my part...that I was really not happy on his couch, that I really wanted him to die, that I really wanted to die myself, that I really did not believe the analysis would help me and so on, and so on...my dear, I was a wreck. (9 March 1933)

For Freud, resistance to analysis was preeminently evident with the blockage of free association, a "refusal to speak" which announced that the analysand "is now possessed by a thought which concerns the person of the physician," as he wrote in "Dynamics of the Transference" (107). That blocked thought, Freud believed, was the clue to the analysand's repression. The "refusal to speak" about the analyst in the transference signals resistance to knowing what has been repressed (107–8). H.D.'s "refusal to speak" to Freud about the Nazi atrocities was the "sign" of resistance to analysis that Freud saw and could not penetrate. As H.D. wrote in *Advent,* "I have been leafing over papers in the café, there are fresh atrocity stories. I cannot talk about the thing that actually concerns me, I cannot talk to Sigmund Freud in Vienna, 1933, about Jewish atrocities in Berlin" (134). These stories recall for her the repressed memory of her father's head wound when she was about ten – the night she answered the door to find her limp father pale as a ghost and bleeding from a cut on the head. She spoke cryptically with Freud about the accident, but then wrote in her journal, "How can I tell him of my constant pre-vision of disaster? It is better to have an unsuccessful or 'delayed' analysis than to bring my actual terror of the lurking Nazi menace into the open" (*Advent* 139). Freud told her that she was "impatient" with him, a wish for his death so that she could avoid analysis (*Advent* 144). But she wrote, "I cannot be disappointed in Sigmund Freud, only I have this constant obsession that the analysis will be broken by death. I cannot discuss this with the Professor" (*Advent* 141).

What did H.D.'s "refusal to speak" signify? What forbidden thought did her resistance repress? On the one hand, her sensitivity to his vulnerability as a Jew drove her own war phobia ever deeper into the unconscious, as she noted in *Tribute to Freud*. But if we apply Freud's concept of the transference-resistance, her silence can be read as a wish for his symbolic castration – the desire to see him in the position of her father, wounded in the head, no longer the authoritative figure of the Oedipal daughter's dream. Like Hedylus, the wounded Father/Freud occupies the position of woman, of daughter, the one who does not wield the Sword. H.D.'s resistance to Freud can be interpreted as a resistance to the Law of the Father that results in wars. The forbidden thought, in other words, is a kind of feminist, antifascist fantasy akin to Woolf's *Three Guineas,* one that identifies the rise of Nazism with the authority of the father in the patriarchal family and state. Repressed in analysis, this forbidden thought pervades H.D.'s portrait of Achilles in *Helen in Egypt* – in which the wounding of the fascist hero ultimately restores him to the forces of *Eros* embodied in Helen.

With another turn of the interpretive screw, H.D.'s resistance can be read as the conflation of the categories "woman" and "Jew." In relation to the dominant anti-Semitic order, Freud-as-Jew fills the position of woman in relation to man. Freud's "wound," superimposed on her father's wound, is a frightening prevision of "the final solution." In multiple senses, then, H.D.'s resistance claims Freud as an exile, an outsider to the patriarchal, anti-Semitic social order.

I am deliberately eliding, of course, different meanings of the word resistance – specifically, the resistance to conscious knowledge of repressed desire that Freud identified as a component of neurosis and the resistance to the structures of oppression or repression or suppression by which the social order is organized. Freud himself invited such an elision in *Civilization and Its Discontents.* But, for women, resistance in the talking cure – particularly where the analyst is a man – is overdetermined, with multiple layers of psychopolitical meanings in the interlocking domains of desire, language, and history. These layered resistances are startlingly evident in H.D.'s texts when we read them intertextually as a secondary scene of analysis, a contested site that itself performs the psychodynamics of paternal transference. Here, the forbidden thought the texts resist is the daughter's resistance to the Law of the Father.

The resistance in the secondary analysis takes the form of the creation of different discourses, each one of which represents a different negotiation of the need to repress and the desire to express forbidden thoughts. The different generic discourses of H.D.'s accounts of analysis form a palimpsest in which each layer represents a different negotiation of the resistance. These layers do not contradict each other so much as they complement one another by filling in each other's gaps. The more public the text about Freud, the greater the resistance to revealing forbidden thoughts and the greater the reverence toward Freud-as-Father. The more private the text, the greater the resistance to Freud's paternal authority and the greater the revelation of that resistance.

This equation works somewhat differently for the prose texts about Freud than it does in the poetic texts, none of which specifically identifies him. *Tribute to Freud, Advent,* and the composite "text" of H.D.'s letters to Bryher about analysis form a spectrum of discourses, with the most public text – *Tribute to Freud* – forming one pole and the most private "text" – the letters – constituting the other. This opposition inscribes the conflict between speech and silence that conditions women's status as exile in a landscape mapped by patriarchal discourse. Public discourse allows women to claim the Word, assert a voice and presence in the public domain, defy the injunctions to silence in Paul's epistles, and by extension, in the institutions of culture. But this speech often imposes a silence of its own on women, whether because the language itself is phallocentric or because the public nature of that discourse leads the woman writer to censor herself. Private discourse, on the other hand, has allowed women to utter forbidden thoughts in the silent speech of secret expression. In the privacy of unpublished diaries and letters, women have often inscribed the desire and anger they did not dare write for public speech. Father/Freud exists transferentially in H.D.'s prose texts as personification of the patriarchal Word that the daughter/writer resists in the dialectics of speech and silence.

As the most public and polished text, *Tribute to Freud* reveals the least about her analysis, particularly about the nature of her rebellion against Freud. Written as the bombs fell on London in the fall of 1944, just after she had completed the second volume of her *Trilogy,* just before she would begin the third, *Tribute to Freud* reflects the pressing needs of the moment. Its narrative of analysis focuses on the (re)construction of the poet H.D. as the prophet immersed in historical apocalypse and searching for the inner voice of her muse. In *H.D. by Delia Alton,* H.D. described the tribute as "the very superficial account that I give of some of our sessions at *Bergasse,* in Vienna, [where] I touch on the family-scene" (190). As a modernist reflection on psyche and society, *Tribute to Freud* is not a superficial text, but as a reconstruction of the analysis, it is a *surface* text – that is, it represses certain kinds of forbidden thoughts, which exist only as vestigial traces in the carefully woven texture of the public discourse. Reading *Tribute to Freud* intertextually with her private discourses on analysis, we can interpret those traces and reconstruct what H.D. has resisted telling us. *Tribute to Freud* in particular represses the extent of her conflict with Freud, as well as the frank discussions they had about gender and sexuality. *Tribute to Freud,* in other words, replicates the "refusal to speak" that Freud identified with the resistance.

As the most private and spontaneous "text," H.D.'s letters to Bryher speak openly and repeatedly about the very things *Tribute to Freud* obscures and represses. Written in a style she entirely disassociated from her published work, H.D.'s daily letters are breezy, witty, and intimate – dashed off with a morning cigarette or afternoon tea, sometimes moments before or after she saw Freud at her five o'clock hour. Not at all exclusively about psychoanalysis, they are free-associational tapestries woven of disparate threads – the hieratic dream juxtaposed to racy psychoanalytic gossip; lyric portraits of Freud interspersed with partial accounts of what he said and did; descriptions of street violence jumbled on top of reports on food and sleep, operas and the latest film, or café life and the lesbian porn shop she frequented to buy photos of Bryher's latest flame, the actress Elizabeth Bergner. As much a textual composition as *Tribute to Freud,* these letters cannot be said to represent "the truth" about analysis. As Wendy Deutelbaum has written about correspondence in general, H.D.'s letters to Bryher exist within the implicit boundaries of what they would say to each other, what they expected of each other. But nonetheless, the discourse of the letters is stylistically less controlled, more free associational than *Tribute to Freud.* As John Walsh said (Letter to author), "The slackness of the letters is the other side of the tautness of the poetry," a tautness and condensed perfection that *Tribute to Freud* exhibits as well.

Content, as well as style, suggests the usefulness of regarding the letters as the textual unconscious of *Tribute to Freud.* To Bryher, H.D. delightedly revealed fragments – some more extended than others – of her frank discussions with Freud about sexuality and gender, topics present only in coded form in *Tribute to Freud.* In a discourse replete with the technical psychoanalytic terminology erased from *Tribute to Freud,* H.D. reported on their analysis of her erotic fantasies, dreams, and experiences with masturbation, lesbianism, bisexuality, penis envy, the primal scene, and the Oedipal and pre-Oedipal stages of psychosexual development. Where *Tribute to Freud* drew fine portraits of an etherealized "family romance" of mother, father, and child, the letters explicitly describe conversations about mother fixation and fear of castration. Where *Tribute to Freud* encoded discussion of gender in a report of Freud's statue of Athena without her spear, the letters comment directly on the relationship between her bisexuality and her writer's block, between her love for women and longing for her mother, between her phobias and fears of male violence against women.[17] And where *Tribute to Freud* identified the "argument implicit in our very bones" as their views on "transcendental issues," the letters explore the multilayered dimensions of her resistance to Freud's paternal authority. With their explicit discussions of sexuality and conflict, the letters fill in the gaps in *Tribute to Freud* and often clarify the gender issues that lie beneath the brilliant surface of the memoir. They also testify to the existence of the resistance, to H.D.'s "refusal to speak," in the largely reverential public tribute to Freud's genius.

As a text written in journal form, prepared for publication, but left in manuscript until 1974, *Advent* represents a compromise between the "refusal to speak" in public (*Tribute to Freud*) and the willingness to speak in private (the letters). At first glance, *Advent* appears to reproduce the notes H.D. wrote during her first analysis with Freud. There are almost daily entries dated from March 2, 1933 to March 25, 1933, and then two cryptic entries dated June 12 and June 15, 1933 that "explain" the abrupt break in her journal (done at Freud's request) and the abrupt break in her analysis (necessitated by the bomb) (*Advent* 187). But, for all its studied appearance of an actual journal, *Advent* is *not* the notes H.D. kept in school copybooks in Vienna in March of 1933. Those originals have unfortunately been destroyed or lost. As the title page of her heavily revised typescript for *Advent* clarifies, she "assembled" the new text from the original notebooks: "ADVENT, the continuation of *Writing on the Wall* [*Tribute to Freud*'s original title], or its prelude, was taken direct from the old note-books of 1933, though it was not assembled until December 1948, *Lausanne*."[18] *Tribute to Freud,* in contrast, had been written during the war without access to the notebooks (*Tribute to Freud* 14). "Taken direct" from the notebooks, *Advent* was more closely anchored in her original record. The extremely high correlation between conversations reported in *Advent* and her letters to Bryher confirms *Advent*'s close tie to the daily progression of her analysis in March of 1933. But *Advent* was, nonetheless, "assembled"; it was what she called a "reworking of old notes" in a letter to Pearson (14 August 1953). In 1949, H.D. sent the manuscript of *Advent* to Pearson and asked whether he thought *Advent* should be published with the new edition of *Tribute to Freud* (27 March 1949; 4 August 1949). Clearly, she considered *Advent* a "composed," text, for she explained to him that "It is called *Advent.* . . . This *Advent* is the notes I did on Sigmund Freud. It would follow or be prelude to the L & L Writing. I explain this. It is not very long. I repeat incidents that I later bring into the child-story, *The Gift,* but I felt they should be assembled in their order as they first manifested with the dream-work with Freud in Vienna, in 1933." Pearson himself described *Tribute to Freud* as a "meditation" and the more personal *Advent* as "its gloss" when he published *Advent* for the first time in 1974 (Foreword *viii*).

Advent's status as a text self-consciously composed in journal form for possible publication is evident in a number of ways. First, its discourse is generally more formal than H.D.'s other diaries, such as the scribbled blue copybooks labeled at Beinecke Library as the "Paris 1912 Diary," "Lionel Durand Diary," and *Hirslanden Notebooks.* Second, its expanded explanations of people and events she would not have to identify in a private journal implies an audience, as do the later personal essays she wrote in journal form, such as *H.D. by Delia Alton, End to Torment,* and *Thorn Thicket.* Third, the absence of code names, like Papa for Freud and Turtle for Sachs, suggests its preparation for a wider audience. And fourth, *Advent* includes a number of "slips of the text" that clue a careful reader into its later, self-conscious composition. For example, her first "journal entry," dated March 2nd, refers to "my last sessions" with Freud, the plural in this case belying the beginning of her analysis the day before, on March 1st (119).

These traces of subsequent composition, however, are overshadowed by the sense of immediacy the journal form brings to the text. H.D. used the journal form for *Advent* not because the text was in fact the journal she kept, but rather because the form itself suggested a greater license to reveal intimate detail than the more formal genre of the memoir. The more formal and public the discourse, the less appropriate are the intrusions of the specifically female self. The more private the genre, the more suitable the form for an exploration of gender. *Advent* stands between the public, partially censored *Tribute* and the private, more revealing letters to Bryher. For example, *Advent* refers to H.D.'s "infatuation" with Gregg in 1910 and the way in which Bryher appeared to "take the place of Frances" (*Advent* 152). The letters, in contrast, openly use the word "lesbian," while *Tribute to Freud* simply refers to Bryher as a "friend." *Advent* notes that Freud raised the subject of "the mother-layer of fixation" in general terms. But in her letters, she wrote jauntily and openly about her own "mother-fix," while in *Tribute to Freud,* she more euphemistically reported on her desire for "re-union" with her mother. *Advent*'s accounts of her dreams also stand between the public tribute and the private letters. Important dreams about being chosen for special gifts *because* she is a girl (120) or being terrified by the pecking beaks of giant blackbirds appear in *Advent,* more direct in their evocation of gender issues than the mythologized Princess dream in

Tribute to Freud, but less direct than the sexual dreams about masturbation and lesbian desire that she reported to Bryher. Her feelings about Lawrence and Rodeck, very close to the questions of sexual identity dealt with in her letters, are explored in *Advent* and scarcely mentioned in *Tribute to Freud.* Similarly, in *Advent,* she expressed anger at Freud for "one of his volumes. He said (as I remember) that women did not creatively amount to anything or amount to much, unless they had a male counterpart or a male companion from whom they drew their inspiration" (149). *Tribute to Freud* defuses the anger over women's creativity by alluding cryptically to the superiority of her "intuition," while her private letters frankly record the ups and downs of her anger and resistance.

As the most private of genres, the journal H.D. kept in Vienna was undoubtedly the least-censored account she wrote. But this discourse was literally forbidden. Freud did not like his analysands to write about their sessions. In general, he considered "diary keeping" to be "a neurotic trait" (Roazen 170). More specifically, he regarded note taking by analysands to be a form of "preparation." Preparation inhibited the flow of free association, thereby indicating resistance. Preparation would ensure that "the most valuable part of the communication escapes," he wrote in "Further Recommendations on Technique" (149). Before her analysis began, Freud wrote to H.D.: "I would like to ask you to refrain from dr[eam] analysis and anything else analytical for the time being" (2 February 1933). In *Advent,* H.D. reported that Freud repeatedly asked her not to "prepare" or take notes (125–6, 165, 184, 185, 187). But, for a time, she resisted him – "He does not, apparently, want me to take notes, but I must do that" (*Advent* 165). She defended herself by calling her journal a form of "reverie." She liked to sit in a café or lie in bed and "dream over my note-book." "I am not preparing for tomorrow's session," she wrote; "I am simply going on with today's." However, Freud sensed "some sort of 'resistance' " and asked her to stop taking notes, which she apparently did at the end of March (184–5).[19]

But she did not stop writing to Bryher. "There are moments," she confessed to Bryher, "when I feel I shall scream not to have you to throw off on . . . I am SICK in heart for you to talk to" (16 November 1934). Her letters became the forbidden discourse that took the place of the journal. Freud had written that he didn't allow his analysands to talk over their sessions with intimate friends. This too was a form of "preparation," and therefore resistance, that interfered with the free flow of associations. "The treatment," he wrote in his recommendations, "then suffers from a *leak* which lets through just what is most valuable" (emphasis added; "Further Recommendations" 149).[20]

Freud was right. Like *Advent,* the letters are full of references to things she did not dare bring up with Freud – from her terror of the Nazis to her humorous resentment of fleabites from Freud's precious chow, Yo-fi. Poking fun at the concept of resistance, she wrote Bryher: "I have at the moment a tame flea, called Cincinnatus. He just won't go. I don't dare tell Freud about this trauma, as I think I caught C. off Yo-fi" (23 March 1933). More seriously, she reported near the end of her first analysis: "Freud says I have such clear and vivid dreams and they seem to have told everything, yet there is some block and connecting link missing that he can't get at. I suppose it is the 'father' vibration, for we can't, no matter how we idealize the mother-idea, get rid of the father. I think that is it" (28 May 1933). Whatever the specific thought she communicated to Bryher instead of Freud, the letters to Bryher represented a "leak" in the analysis, a form of textual resistance to Freud's paternal authority.

Freud may have been right that note taking, letters, and conversations with friends were forms of resistance to analysis. But his silencing of his analysands also served as a authoritative mechanism of control that, for his female analysands, was overdetermined by male dominance in the larger social order. It meant that he set the terms of discourse. It meant that all defiance must be channeled through his analysis of resistance and transference. It gave him a power that, for his female analysands, replicated patriarchal control of the Word and interpretation of the Word. Dora's resistance came in her sudden and irreversible decision to quit analysis. H.D.'s resistance involved the reclamation of the Word – the letters that leaked what Freud would have contained in the hermetically sealed enclosure of his study. Her letters to Bryher represent just the kind of leak Freud feared – a discourse between two women forbidden by the Father, a discourse that fueled the resistance, all kinds of resistance.

H.D.'s poetic texts about her analysis with Freud repeat the dynamics of paternal transference and resistance in a related, but somewhat different, way. Like the prose texts, the poetic ones vary in relationship to how much direct resistance to Freud they reveal. But, unlike the prose texts, H.D. adapted the impersonal discourse she had developed for "the early H.D." to screen her resistance. "The Master," *Trilogy*, and *Helen in Egypt* all mythologize Freud by distilling the impersonal out of the personal, the universal out of the particular. The more public and recognizable the text, the more reverential it was toward Freud. The more private and encoded the text, the more it expressed H.D.'s resistance. The three poetic texts can be superimposed on top of the prose texts in a sort of spectrum of resistances.

Like *Tribute to Freud*, the Theseus sequence in *Helen in Egypt* reproduces a clearly identifiable therapeutic situation. Time and place have been mythologized; wind and snow are objective correlatives for the inner anguish of Helen's spirit. Freud is in no sense directly named here, nor is psychoanalysis explicitly portrayed. Removed from the historical moment that is so carefully depicted in *Tribute to Freud,* Helen's exchange with Theseus takes place in the realm of "all myth, the one reality." Nonetheless, *Helen in Egypt,* as a psychoanalytic narrative that reconstitutes Helen's past, replicates the healing recovery of repressed memories in *Tribute to Freud.* Like the H.D. of *Tribute to Freud,* Helen tells Theseus about her past suffering, especially during the war, with only traces of the resistance explored more fully in private accounts. Like the Freud of her tribute, Theseus helps Helen retrieve what she has forgotten and reunite the fragmented selves of Helen in Sparta, Helen in Troy, Helen in Egypt. *Helen in Egypt* is a public text, prophetic and hieratic in tone; *Tribute to Freud* is relatively more personal and historical. But both texts reenact the paternal transference in their public expressions of love and reverence.

Trilogy is equally public and prophetic, but its repetition of paternal transference demonstrates more resistance to the Law of the Father than *Tribute to Freud.* Consequently, Freud's presence is more thoroughly disguised behind the mythological screen.[21] As Kaspar, Freud is a Mage, one of the wise men who knows the esoteric lore of the spirit. He possesses an alabaster jar of myrrh, an herb associated not only with the bitterness of woman, but also with resurrection and rebirth. Like the fragments of a dream, each detail of H.D.'s "tale of the jar" in *The Flowering of the Rod* can be decoded as a mythological transformation of analysis with Freud. Freud, too, was a wise man who possessed the secrets of the soul and the process of rebirth. Mary Magdalene, the fallen woman, appears suddenly before Kaspar to acquire the jar of myrrh, that "heal-all, / everlasting" (*Trilogy* 585). Their brief moment together takes on an archetypal significance as a confrontation between patriarch and goddess. His ironic dismissal of the unveiled, "unseemly" woman repeats the fundamental gesture of patriarchy in the face of female desire. But Mary's defiant refusal to be dismissed allows Kaspar an epiphanic glimpse of "the whole secret of the mystery" in the "fleck of light" in her "unseemly" hair (*Trilogy* 600). His refrain – *"it is unseemly that a woman / appear disordered, dishevelled, // it is unseemly that a woman / appear at all"* – is transformed into ecstatic worship "through spiral upon spiral of the shell / of memory that yet connects us // with the drowned cities" of Atlantis (*Trilogy* 601–3). The poem ends with a vision of nativity – the archetype of (re)birth. But Kaspar worships Mary in the stable – not as mother of God, but as God the Mother.[22]

The overthrow of paternal authority in *The Flowering of the Rod* is relatively "safe" as a textual resistance because Freud is unrecognizable in H.D.'s retelling of Biblical narrative without *Trilogy*'s analytic inter-

texts. But in "The Master," the disguise is so thin and the resistance so
direct that H.D. suppressed the poem. In spite of its mythological content, "The Master" is more like the history novels and the romans à clef
than it is like *Trilogy* or *Helen in Egypt*. Vienna becomes Miletus, with
a generalized mythic setting; the "beautiful" old man so near death is
unnamed. But as "he taught / 'nothing is lost,' " as "we wrought philosophy on the dream content," the translation is crystal clear (*Collected
Poems* 451). The "Master" is Freud; his Miletian oracle is the hermeneutics
of psychoanalysis. Bryher and Herring wanted to publish the poem in
Life and Letters Today, but H.D. adamantly refused, reporting to Bryher:
"he argued, as for [i.e., like] you, for Master and I screamed and said I
will not   , NOT   , N O T   have my analysis spoiled again
...and that is about Freud and I will never write again...etc." (1 November 1935).

In what sense would "The Master" "spoil" H.D.'s analysis? What is
the weight of the word "again?" There are many possible explanations,
but one would surely be that publication of the poem would make public
her dramatic resistance in the midst of a powerful paternal transference.
The Nazi bomb on the track in June of 1933 "spoiled" her first analysis
because she could not discuss her war phobia. Now she did not want to
"spoil" her second analysis by a public revelation of her anger at Freud-
as-Father. Suppression of the poem repeated the "refusal to speak" that
characterizes the resistance. During H.D.'s lifetime, the poem remained
in limbo – public poetic discourse encased in the safety of silence.

As resistance to patriarchal authority, "The Master" is a narrative poem
that moves from worship of the wise old man so near to God to a rejection
of his "man strength," and to a substitution of her own vision of woman's
erotic perfection and divinity. Its celebration of woman's body directly
counters Freud's theory of penis envy, a theory so subtly alluded to in
Tribute to Freud when Freud hands her his favorite statue of Athena and
says, "She is perfect . . . *only she has lost her spear*" (68–9). In fact, "The
Master" functions as the textual unconscious of the cryptic scene in the
public tribute when Freud hands her the statue of a woman who is
"perfect" in her castration. In *Tribute to Freud*, H.D. resisted Freud's
interpretation of female castration only by "reading" the statue as an
allusion to Niké, the avatar of Athena as Wingless Victory, the Protectress
of Athens.[23] But in "The Master," she directly resisted Freud-as-Father
by celebrating the divinity of woman.

In the opening sections of the poem, the poet reverences the Master
as a God, much as a daughter might worship the idealized father/pro-
tector of fantasy. But then the poet writes that "his tyranny was absolute"
and finally explodes with anger, which begins innocently enough at his
refusal to give her a "neat answer," but moves suddenly to challenge

the cornerstone of his theory of female psychology – penis envy and the girl's castration complex:

> I was angry at the old man,
> I wanted an answer,
> a neat answer,
> . . . .
> I was angry with the old man
> with his talk of the man-strength,
> I was angry with his mystery, his mysteries,
> I argued till day-break;
>
> (*Collected Poems* 455)

She replaces his image of female castration with her vision of female perfection – "*woman is perfect.*" To resist Freud, H.D. resurrects the wild landscape of her erotic Artemisian sisterhood, the "white world" of *Paint It To-Day* and "Huntress," where "she needs no man," where she is "herself perfect":

> She is a woman,
> yet beyond woman,
> yet in woman,
> her feet are the delicate pulse of the narcissus bud,
> pushing from earth
> (ah, where is your man-strength?)
> . . . .
> she is woman,
> her thighs are frail yet strong,
> she leaps from rock to rock
> (it was only a small circle for her dance)
> and the hills dance,
> . . . .
> there is purple flower
> between her marble, her birch-tree white
> thighs,
> or there is a red flower,
> there is a rose flower
> parted wide,
> . . . .
> . . . O God, what is it,
> this flower
> that in itself had power over the whole earth?
>
> (*Collected Poems* 455–6)

This lesbian eroticism of H.D.'s resistance in "The Master" explicitly challenges the patriarchal Law of the Father. This woman – the goddess Rhodocleia – brings men to their knees in worship, like Kaspar before Mary, like Achilles before Helen.[24] But in this most resistant of all texts, the one she refused to publish, H.D. played directly with images of impotence and castration, by which she meant the defeat of patriarchal authority in the interlocking domains of language, sexuality, and religion:

> no man will be present in those mysteries,
> yet all men will kneel,
> no man will be potent,
> important,
> yet all men will feel
> what it is to be a woman,
> will yearn,
> burn,
> turn from easy pleasure
> to hardship
> of the spirit,
>
> men will see how long they have been blind,
> poor men
> poor man-kind
> how long
> how long
> this thought of the man-pulse has tricked them,
> has weakened them,
> shall see woman,
> perfect.
>
> (*Collected Poems* 460)

H.D.'s prose and poetic texts not only repeat her multilayered resistance to Freud, but they also work through the paternal transference into the discourse of recollection. The art of analysis, as Freud articulated it, is a paradox. Analyst and analysand conspire to use the transferential resistance against analysis on behalf of analysis. H.D.'s resistance to Freud – her refusal to speak only within the confines of his control, her capacity to disagree with the Master – is precisely what allowed their collaboration to move forward. In contrast to his treatment of his male colleagues, Freud did not impose a suffocating discipleship upon her – perhaps because of his age, or his sense of a poet's freedom, or his inability to see women as genuine rivals.[25] As she wrote in "The Master" itself:

> And it was he himself, he who set me free
> to prophesy,
>
> he did not say
> "stay,
> my disciple,"
> he did not say,
> "write,
> each word I say is sacred,"
> he did not say, "teach"

he did not say,
heal
or seal
documents in my name,"

no,
he was rather casual,
"we won't argue about that"
(he said)
"you are a poet."
                                        (*Collected Poems* 458)

Working through the paternal transference "set" her "free to prophesy" by nurturing her poetic authority, by inviting her to love and
identify with the father. In H.D.'s (re)constructed scenes of analysis (both
primary and secondary), Freud's resistance to the tyranny of his own
rules for psychoanalytic technique was essential to their collaborative
working through. The analyst, Freud wrote in 1912, should maintain
"the same measure of calm, quiet attentiveness – of 'evenly hovering
attention' " ("Recommendations for Physicians" 118). Condemning intimacy between analyst and analysand, Freud said that "the physician
should be impenetrable to the patient, and, like a mirror, reflect nothing
but what is shown to him" ("Psychoanalytic Method" 124). Relying on
a hierarchical medical model with striking phallic overtones, Freud rec-
ommended that analysts "take as a model in psychoanalytic treatment
the surgeon who puts aside all his own feelings, including that of human
sympathy, and concentrates his mind on one single purpose, that of
performing the operation as skillfully as possible" ("Psychoanalytic
Method" 121). As mirror, the analyst represses his own desire in order
to clear the way for the psychodynamics of transference and resistance.
As surgeon, the analyst uses his theory like a knife to penetrate the virgin
psyche of the analysand.

As an analyst, however, Freud seldom followed his own rules. As he
once told Jung, "psychoanalysis is in essence a cure through love" (Bet-
tleheim *v*). Anything *but* an "evenly hovering attention," a blank "mirror" or a cold surgeon, Freud was often garrulous, gossipy, and
emotional in analysis – at least when an analysand engaged his interest.
Hardly disengaged, he analyzed his own daughter, fed the Rat Man,
ordered Alix and James Strachey to do translations of his work while
they were his analysands, and advised Ruth Brunswick to divorce her
first husband and marry Mark Brunswick, whom he then advised to
have an affair.[26] With H.D., he was equally engaged, talkative, and warm
– dispensing "forgiveness," praising her poetic mind and keen interpretations, and giving her gifts. H.D.'s resistance to Freud existed within
an atmosphere of intimacy and love. Her own father, Freud told her,

had been cold and distant, which had inhibited her from making "the conventional transference from mother to father" (*Advent* 136). In the transferential scene of analysis, he would become the idealized warm father she never had.

Freud's refusal to establish the inflexible boundaries between the analytic and the nonanalytic that have come to characterize "psychoanalytic formalism" fostered H.D.'s working through of the paternal transference. He seemed to recognize that an intimate, personal conversation could stimulate a rich vein of free association, transference, or resistance. His virtuosity centered particularly on a brilliant ability to transform a personal moment into an analytic one. Human exchanges, based in real warmth and respect, could at a moment's notice become grist for the analytic mill. Or they could remain, just a human exchange, one of the components of rapport.

The role of Freud's chows in H.D.'s analysis is a case in point. In March of 1933, Yo-fi's daughter (little Yo-fi) was pregnant, and he was quite concerned about the coming birth and disposition of the pups. "I had a shock yesterday," H.D. wrote Bryher,

> as Yo-fi (pronounced to rhyme with Queen So-fi) went and drank water under a table, then walked away to a corner and went to sleep and moaned and sobbed in her sleep. Papa had to stop my long tale . . . to tell me that Yo-fi was now having strange dreams, as little Yo-fi was pregnant. I screamed, "what?" at him and he told me the sad story of Yo-fi's last litter which consisted of ONE delicate and lovely little yo-fi bear and it died. (15 March 1933)

Shortly thereafter, H.D. reported that "Papa is now getting worried lest maybe, after all, Yo-fi is only getting fat and lazy and is not actually pregnant" (17 March 1933). When the chow actually gave birth to a huge, healthy litter, Freud broke off all sessions and personally took H.D., Bryher, and Perdita on an excursion to view the pups. Perhaps unaware that Perdita's nickname from birth was Pup, Freud asked H.D. during one of their sessions if he could give one of the pups to Perdita. Surely these discussions and the proffered gift break all the rules of "pure analysis."

Rules aside, Freud and H.D. were able to use the dreams and fantasies the chows initiated in her analysis to play out the father–daughter–lover–child eroticism in the transference/countertransference situation. The chow's pregnancy served as a trigger to the repressed pain surrounding the stillbirth of her first child in 1915 and the birth of Perdita in 1919. H.D. was distressed by Freud's wavering reports of possible pregnancies and dying pups. She was both exhilarated and terrified of the possible responsibility of owning a dog of Freud's, then utterly confused about how to handle the adamant refusals of Bryher and Macpherson. Her dreams and distress began to link the pups with her own childbirths, associations she brought to Freud. "Evidently I was afraid of becoming pregnant by papa Freud; funny?????," she reported to Bryher (25 April 1933). And she humorously promised not to dump another "pup" on Bryher's doorstep, as she had done in 1919. Clearly, the birth of the chows and Freud's gift entered the saga of transference and resistance. Clearly, Freud and H.D. were able to capitalize on that in the analysis, constituted as it was in such a fluid way.

Given Freud's general disinterest in countertransference, however, he may not have seen how his own feelings were implicated in the discussions of the chows.[27] In 1920, Freud's favorite daughter Sophie (whose name rhymes with Yo-fi) died of the same influenza that nearly killed H.D. and Perdita. Freud usually responded to the deaths of close friends and family members with a detached fatalism, but Sophie's death had such an impact on him that it may have changed his formulation of the death instinct in *Beyond the Pleasure Principle*.[28] In September of 1919, just months after Perdita's birth, Sophie had given birth to Heinerle, the grandson of whom Freud was most fond. Heinerle's death in 1923 not long after his own first cancer operation had devastated Freud, causing him to shed tears for the first time in his adult life, according to Ernest Jones (381–2, 429–30).

H.D. believed that Freud (counter)transferred onto her his own unresolved feelings about his daughter, her child, and their deaths. To Bryher, she begged that they not refuse the pup "while I am on the operating table": "But while this idea of his is at work, ..., I must, must, MUST feel that he has our sympathy about the doglet. It may date to the fact of his daughter dying with the trouble I had, in 1919. Papa was most concerned for my 'pregnancy symptoms,' and I think DOES link me up in some way with that daughter, who not only died like that but who also lost a child. You see?????" (3 May 1933).[29] Certainly, one of Freud's final statements about the chows to H.D. in 1933 suggests that the drama of the pups enacted procreative fantasies for both of them. "Evidently," H.D. wrote Bryher, "the Frau Professor finds the dogs very disintegrating, so he told me. Poor Frau ... she had, he told me, the six children in eight years. He says he thinks the five dogs remind her in the uc-n [unconscious] of those days though 'of course, I would not tell HER.' It must be a pretty big job being the Frau Professor" (20 May 1933). In their "most luscious" interplay of words and warmth, dreams and desire, H.D. and Freud created a "child" that was no mere "pup," but rather their multifaceted gifts to posterity.

H.D. worked through her resistance to Freud-as-Father not only by having his "child," but also by identifying with his power, as she had once tried to do with Paul Robeson in "Two Americans." He set her "free to prophesy" by authorizing her to do what he did – to interpret the dreams of humankind in the discourses of her own work. As H.D. reconstructed the primary scene of analysis, Freud repeatedly communicated his belief in her, particularly in her future as a writer. *Tribute to Freud* reports on how their translation of the "writing on the wall," the mysterious light pictures projected onto her hotel wall in Corfu, represented a special call to destiny, an invitation to don the voice of the prophet who would reunite what the modern world has sundered – science, religion, and poetry.[30] Her Princess dream, he told her, meant that she wanted to be the "founder of a new religion" (*Tribute to Freud* 37). H.D.'s letters and journals articulate the power of Freud's authorizing acts more personally. His validation sometimes came in the form of praise, evident in H.D.'s report to Bryher: "He also complimented me on the astuteness of some dream analysis I did again for him yesterday" (3 March 1933). At other times, he made her feel special, as she recalled in her later reflection in the *Hirslanden Notebooks*: "Of course, as the Prof. said, 'There is always something new to find out.' I felt that he was speaking for himself (an informal moment, as I was about to leave). It was almost as if something I had said was *new*, that he even felt that I was a *new* experience. He must have thought the same of everyone, but I felt his personal delight, I was *new*, every dream & dream-association was *new*. After the years & years of patient plodding research, it was all *new*" (II, 15). The intimacy of Freud's gossip implicitly invited H.D. into an inner circle of his psychoanalytic elite: "Then he told," H.D. wrote Bryher, "about a new patient that Dr. Ellis had sent – who has been most disappointing – and *how* was he to have known that Dr. Ellis would send such a dud?" (30 October 1934).[31] Above all, he did not separate the woman from the poet. "He says," H.D. wrote to Bryher, "I have the sort of dreams he would expect from a 'woman poet' " (19 November 1934).

One of the most significant of Freud's authorizations, however, was his praise for her bisexuality. As discussed in Chapter 4, bisexuality had become a sign of erotic and linguistic sterility for H.D. by the early 1930s. Androgyny, twinship, and bisexual desire were key components of the borderline existence she articulated in *Narthex, Kora and Ka, Mire-Mare,* and *Nights*. Being (erotically) bisexual meant being cast out of a "home" category – whether heterosexual or lesbian. Being (psychically) androgynous meant living in limbo – neither man nor woman. "I had two loves separate," H.D. wrote in "The Master – "God who loves all mountains, / alone knew why / and understood / and told the old man / to explain // the impossible, // which he did" (*Collected Poems* 453).[32] What he did was to link her bisexuality to her creativity – both to its block and to its flowering. H.D. wrote Bryher: "I have gone terribly deep with papa. He says, 'you had two things to hide, one that you were a girl, the other that you were a boy.' It appears I am that all-but extinct phenomena, the perfect bi-. Well, this is terribly exciting, but for the moment, PLEASE do not speak of my own MSS, for it seems the conflict consists partly that what I write commits me – to one sex, or to the other, I no longer HIDE. It is not quite so obvious as that – and no doubt, before I leave, we will come to some balance" (24 November 1934). What Freud's interpretation freed H.D. to do was stop hiding that she was "girl–boy," the nearly extinct bisexual in a sexually polarized world. As androgyne, she was *perfect*. Instead of feeling split, she could be whole. Then, he seemed to say, her writer's block would vanish. Freud-as-Father gave her permission to be "different."

As the secondary scene of analysis, H.D.'s texts take on Freud's authority by repeating his paternal gestures. *Tribute to Freud,* for example, works through the paternal transference by repeating *The Interpretation of Dreams* – its self-relexivity, its megalomania, its narcissism, its contradictory (dis)association from neurosis. As Freud explained in his first preface, *The Interpretation of Dreams* relies on and continues his self-analysis to demonstrate the principles of his new science of healing. The book is both about psychoanalysis and a demonstration of it – with himself as primary subject and object of interpretation. It was a bold stroke: to conflate theory and autobiography. He justified it by explaining that he wanted to use the dreams of a "normal" person, instead of an hysteric, because he regarded his theory of dreams as universal, not particular to neurosis (*xxiii–xxvi*). But at the same time, the theory he propounded ultimately erased the distance between the normal and the neurotic.

His first dream analysis – the interpretation of the dream of Irma's injection – is emblematic. The dream, one of his own, is the inaugural dream of psychoanalysis – in a double sense. First, his extended interpretation displays the essential principles of psychoanalytic decoding. Second, the dream itself, as he translated its latent wish, is about his desire for recognition as the brilliant founder of a new science, one whose implications for human knowledge are as profound and far reaching as the Copernican Revolution. With the self-reflexivity that is the cornerstone of psychoanalysis, *The Interpretation of Dreams* repeats its inaugural dream analysis many times over. The dreams from his self-analysis that Freud chose to feature as exemplary interpretations are overwhelmingly translated as dreams about his desire to be recognized as a great man.[33]

In the voice of the daughter, *Tribute to Freud* repeats the discourse of the father of psychoanalysis in *The Interpretation of Dreams*. *Tribute to Freud* is both about psychoanalysis and a demonstration of its textual continuation – with H.D. as primary subject and object of interpretation.

Its conflation of theory and autobiography (the universal and the personal) was also bold – even more than Freud's, because it challenged the prevailing exclusion of woman (the cultural sign of difference) from the universal and the theoretical. Where Freud's narcissism was designed to demonstrate the applicability of psychoanalysis to everyone, H.D.'s parallel narcissism threatened the dismissal of her text because it invoked the association of narcissism with femininity. But, like Freud, she aligned her dreams and visions with those of everyone, everywhere, everytime – thereby removing them, as Freud did his own, from the domain of mere symptom of mental disease. At the same time, however, this insistence on her own sanity (as Freud's *student*, not patient) is undermined like his own normality (as *physician*, not patient) by the shared language of the unconscious.

Like Freud's, H.D.'s first dream analysis – the interpretation of the Princess dream – inaugurates her own hermeneutics and locates her authority to do so in the dream itself. As she told Freud on the second day of her analysis, she had dreamed of a Princess who descended the steps to find a baby in a basket, floating in the river, while "I, the dreamer, wait at the foot of the steps" (*Tribute to Freud* 37–9, *Advent* 119–20). Who is she in the dream, Freud wanted to know – the mother? Miriam? or the baby Moses? He "insisted I myself wanted to be Moses; not only did I want to be a boy but I wanted to be a hero" (*Advent* 120). Her first response is to disagree – Freud was "the baby, the 'founder of a new religion' " (*Advent* 119). But then she wondered, "Do I wish myself in the deepest unconscious or subconscious layers of my being, to be the founder of a new religion?" (*Tribute to Freud* 37). The conflation of H.D. and Freud into the figure of the baby Moses highlights the daughter's identification with the father. The interpretation of her dream makes her a hero, "the founder of a new religion," whose theology *Tribute to Freud* itself articulates. For the texts in which they are embedded, Freud's interpretation of the Irma dream and H.D.'s reading of the Princess dream accomplish the same authorization to speak to a world in need of healing.

In repeating the Father's self-begetting text, the daughter takes on the mantle of his authority. Transference leads to identification, the daughter occupying the textual space of the father, even re-placing the father's science with her own religion. Like the son in Freud's "savage horde," she challenges the father's authority by imitating and ultimately supplanting him. In *The Interpretation of Dreams*, Freud portrayed himself standing alone against the scientific establishment in his affirmation that all fragments of unconscious speech mean something. Like Father, like daughter, in *Tribute to Freud* – H.D. stood against all experts, including Freud, to assert her place as "hero." *Trilogy*, the text whose composition frames *Tribute to Freud*, articulates the "new religion" she founds, one that is based in, but not limited to the interpretation of dreams as Freud defined it. This identification with (male) authority in order to subvert it is the psychodynamic principle that structures H.D.'s other tributes to great men.[34]

III. DESIRE: WORKING THROUGH THE MATERNAL TRANSFERENCE

> F. says mine is absolutely FIRST layer, I got stuck at the earliest pre-OE stage, and "back to the womb" seems to be my only solution.
>
> H.D., Letter to Bryher,
> 23 March 1933

Occupying the space of the son, H.D. nonetheless spoke as the daughter in a woman's voice. The "new religion" she sought to found might have been authorized by identification with Freud-as-Father, but it emerged out of her desire for Freud-as-Mother. Indeed, the capacity of analysis to unify the split identity of Ray Bart and Raymonde Ransome depended fundamentally on the maternal transference. For H.D., the deepest layers of analysis returned her to the re-creative womb of the maternal body, the death that precedes rebirth. "You can go round and round in circles like the ants under that log that Eric pried up for us," she wrote, "Or your psyche, your soul, can curl up and sleep like those white slugs" (*Tribute to Freud* 31). Through the maternal transference, analysis was the chrysalis in which her soul, as "worm," would metamorphosize into "Psyche, the butterfly, / out of the cocoon" (*Collected Poems* 569).[35] Freud-as-Mother brought back to the daughter what had been lost under the Law of the Father: the primal Mother of the daughter's pre-Oedipal desire.

H.D. was the first to point out in her analysis that Freud was also the mother in her transference, a fact that helped initiate her ultimate subversion of the Law of the Father. She announced this "discovery" to Freud after confiding that Ellis was aroused by watching women urinate, a secret that delighted Freud as evidence of his own superiority. In the breezy discourse of her letters to Bryher, replete with code names (Chiron = Ellis; Beaver = Helen Doolittle; Cat = H.D.; small dog = Bryher), H.D. wrote that Ellis, the man who had rejected her *Notes on Thought and Vision,* had become the father figure, while Freud was the mother in transference:

> I gave him a terrible shock; this is funny. My TRANSFERENCE seems to have taken place and what is it? This – Chiron, big and remote and dumb is father-symbol and papa is a sort of Old Beaver. Isn't that odd? Well, there is the language of course, and his being small and delicate

(woman) and having lots of friends and relatives (family, analysands) and so on. But papa was too sweet, when I told him of my constatation, he beat the pillow and said, "*but you are very clever.*" (Cat tail waving, cat purring its whiskers off.) He said he suspected it, then he said, in the best small-dog manner, "but – to be perfectly frank with YOU – I do not like it – I feel so very, very, very MASCULINE." He says he always feels hurt when his analysands have a maternal transference. I asked if it happened often, he said sadly, "O, very often." (10 March 1933)

Vienna, they both noted, was the city where Helen Doolittle went for her honeymoon, and her family had originally come from Moravia, Freud's birthplace. In explaining her association of her mother's Vienna with Freud in *Tribute to Freud*, H.D. did not use the technical term "transference," as she had in her letter. Instead, she conflated the original scene of analysis with its textual repetition to (re)enact the maternal transference:

> Vienna? Venice? My mother had come here on her honeymoon, tired, having 'done' Italy as a bride. Maybe my mother was already sheltering the child, a girl, that first child that lived such a very short time. It was the bread she talked of, Vienna and how she loved the different rolls and the shapes of them and ones with poppy-seeds and Oh – the coffee! Why had I come to Vienna? The Professor had said in the very beginning that I had come to Vienna hoping to find my mother. Mother? Mamma. But my mother was dead. I was dead; that is, the child in me that had called her mamma was dead. (16–17)

In analysis – and in the texts that repeat that analysis – the maternal transference resurrected "the child in me that had called her mama" as the first step in the healing process. But like an embryo in the womb, this maternal transference was embedded inside the paternal transference. Layered like the psyche, the maternal transference represented a deeper layer – like the pre-Oedipal desire of the Kristevan Semiotic that underlies the Oedipal realm of the Symbolic governed by the Law of the Father.

In contrast to the paternal transference, the maternal transference was characterized by desire, not resistance. All the longing expressed for the all-powerful, all-(for)giving primal Mother in the borderline fiction of the 1920s and early 1930s was projected onto Freud, a psychodynamic for which he was probably prepared because he had read *Palimpsest* and perhaps some of the others.[36] In finding Freud-as-Mother, H.D. "had come home" to what Freud called "the phallic mother," the mother of the pre-Oedipal daughter's desire.

Taken together, *Tribute to Freud, Advent,* and H.D.'s letters to Bryher represent a layered palimpsest of maternal transference in prose, one whose revelations and concealments reproduce the contradictions of women's public and private speech. As with the paternal transference, the more public the speech, the more it conceals; the more private the speech, the more it reveals of the daughter's desire for the mother. In turn, "The Master," *Trilogy,* and *Helen in Egypt* depersonalize the maternal transference into mythic forms that ultimately articulate a gynopoetic centered in a hermetic chrysalis of mother–daughter love.

As the most public and direct account of analysis, *Tribute to Freud* does not use the term "transference," but instead gestures toward it by indicating Freud's repeated interpretations of H.D.'s desire for "reunion" with her mother (17, 30, 33, 37, 41, 44, 49). The text's dream interpretations and free associations – some of which record what H.D. discussed with Freud, others of which continue that process in the textual scene of analysis – move back toward the pre-Oedipal mother by working through feelings about the Oedipal mother. That is, *Tribute to Freud* reconstructs the daughter as she stands on the cusp of past longing for and future hostility toward her mother. Her mother, H.D. recalled, had always preferred her older brother Gilbert, while the daughter had been her father's favorite. Instead of accepting this Oedipal constellation, she had yearned to get close to her mother through identification with the favored brother. The ambiguities of the Princess dream capture this moment of transition. The Princess is an "obvious mother-symbol," Freud said, but who is the baby? Is Miriam in the dream? Is H.D. the sidelined sister, watching the adoring mother save the preferred son? Or is H.D., in the dream, the beloved "son," reunited with the pre-Oedipal mother?

Tribute to Freud uncovers an implicit hostility toward the mother who preferred the son to the daughter, an anger that serves as a public badge of respectability because it associates H.D. with the prevailing route to "normal" femininity. As a more private account, however, *Advent* openly recovers the repressed longing for the pre-Oedipal mother that fueled her maternal transference. Even *Tribute to Freud* hints that beneath the anger lay jealousy and desire: "The trouble is, she knows so many people and they come and interrupt. And besides that, she likes my brother better. If I stay with my brother, become part almost of my brother, perhaps I can get nearer to *her.* But one can never get near enough. . . . *If* one could stay near her always, there would be no break in consciousness" (33). But *Advent* is even more explicitly about this desire, as well as a textual repetition of it. Where *Tribute to Freud* moves elegantly from one portrait of Freud to another (a *moving* portrait), *Advent* is structured on a series of seemingly more disjointed free associations, many of which revolve centrally about her mother. Dreams, memories, interpretations that feature the powerful, pre-Oedipal mother of the daughter's desire rhythmically mark the chaotic flow as if to inscribe a textual (re)union with the primal Mother, in which "there would be no break in consciousness."

Each maternal cluster centers on dream images that can be read according to the principles laid out in *The Interpretation of Dreams* as condensed and symbolic representations of the maternal body. The series begins with the dream or fantasy of the Madonna-lily growing in a beautiful garden in the town of Bethlehem. An old man – Freud reads him as God (the Father) – chooses the "shy, but bold" young Hilda out of a crowd of children and offers to make her alone a special gift from the garden. "Overwhelmed by her audacity," she selects the Madonna-lily, which he cuts with his knife (120–21). Her grandmother directs her to place the "Easter-lily or Madonna-lily" – the traditional symbol of Christ's passion – onto her grandfather's grave. Only *she* is "chosen," Hilda stresses; only *she* can choose her gift. She selects what Freud called the "phallic" Mother, but in choosing a gift from the Father, she must see the powerful become powerless. As flower of the Annunciation and the Resurrection, as representation of female genitalia in the town of Mary (the Mother), the Madonna-lily cut by the Father signifies both the Mother's power and castration. The gardener's act both gives and takes away the primal Mother to the daughter; it both attests to and denies her power for the daughter.

The Madonna-lily initiates a series of maternal representations which encode the daughter's longing for the powerful mother from whom she is somehow separated. Next, H.D. reported on her dream of the "red-velvet-lined box" which Bryher had given her in Florence. In the dream, this beautiful jewel box is the gift of her mother to the daughter. But two other women – "rivals for my mother's love" – are claiming it as their own (135, 137). "I say," H.D. wrote, "Can't you understand? My *mother* gave me this box" (135). This dream symbol of the maternal womb is followed by a dream of the old mirror whose velvet setting her mother had painted with delicate narcissa, evoking for Hilda the "myth of Narcissus falling in love with his reflection in a pool" (151), invoking for us the narcissism of the daughter mirrored in her mother's eyes.

The maternal rhythm of the text continues by (re)producing another dream – the "familiar nightmare" of returning to her hotel room, only to discover that she has been shut out, with all her belongings removed: "The landlady glares at me, 'But we have *no* room here; you must get right out' " (162). This negative mother figure, who enforces Hilda's homelessness under the Law of the Father, vanishes in the dream as she finally locates her mother, who is with Bryher in Florence: "My mother says, 'You are only safe on *this* side of the river' " (163). Florence, the city of "Flora," flowers, is a female space, an idealized home where she can be safe. As a dreamscape of the maternal body, it contrasts with the waking world where "I am still overburdened and lost. My mother died just six years ago, in March." In this, the "real" world, she had been sick unto death awaiting the birth of Perdita, when another landlady had shocked Bryher by asking, "who is to see to the funeral if she dies?" (163).

Within the context of this separation from and longing for the primal Mother, Freud translated H.D.'s visionary episode with Peter Van Eck as a "fixation that was to be referred back to my mother. The maternal uncle, church, art" (184). Van Eck, Freud revealed, was a Dutch version of the Austrian name Vaneck; Fred Wolle, H.D.'s maternal uncle, was the famous Bach musician and organist for the Moravian Church. Further, as the adopted son of a Victorian painter, Van Eck linked up to H.D.'s mother: "I said painting reminded me of my mother. I told him how as children we had admired her painting and boasted to visitors, 'My mother *painted* that.' My mother was morbidly self-effacing" (164). As a maternal figure in a man's body, Van Eck embodies the pre-Oedipal mother, the "uncastrated" woman who paints and would *not* be "morbidly self-effacing," unlike the Oedipal mother, who wanders "castrated" in the world of the Father.

Advent's lengthy account of discussions about Van Eck is sandwiched between the hotel nightmare and H.D.'s reporting of the bell-jar experience in the Scilly Isles in July of 1919 and the writing on the wall in Corfu in 1920, both of which took place in Bryher's presence. The sensation of being suspended in a watery bell-jar "was some sort of prenatal fantasy," she told Freud. "Yes, obviously;" he answered, "you found the answer, good – good" (168). The writing on the wall also recalls her mother; the room where the light pictures materialize is in the "Hotel Belle Venise" – the "*room*" of the beautiful Venus, or Venice, the maternal city.

These prenatal fantasies bring back the primal Mother, who next takes form in the text in another nightmare. In this dream, H.D. has once again been shut out from her rooms, this time at her flat in Sloane Street. Feeling "a little lost," she tries to go home, but she is barred at the door by threats of a "rough boy," representing in the dream the "fresh Nazi atrocities" H.D. had read about in the paper that day. The nightmare resolves into the figure of the primal Mother, whose power – symbolized by the flaming candle she holds – protects her daughter who has been cast out by the might of the Nazis:

> As I stood threatened and terrified I call, loudly, "Mother." I am out on the pavement now. I look up at the window of my flat. It has different

curtains or a suggestion of Venetian blinds [Venus, Venice]. A figure
is standing there, holding a lighted candle. It is my mother.
  I was overpowered with happiness and all trace of terror vanished.
(174–5)

In this dream, H.D. is still outside the uterine room of the maternal
body, but the dream of the "phallic" Mother nonetheless vanquishes
terror. Anticipating the coming war, H.D. linked the matriarchal deities
of the past with the maternal desire repressed in her own unconscious.
The Mother of her dreams had materialized centuries before and survived
still in the priceless statues of the rare Cretan Snake Goddess that she
and Freud discussed as they pored through the volumes of Sir Arthur
Evans that Bryher had sent.

  Demonstrating the gift economy of giving and receiving that Adalaide
Morris called a central paradigm in H.D.'s life and work, she wanted to
locate a statue of the Cretan Goddess to give Freud. Through the agency
of the maternal transference, Freud had given her back her repressed
desires for the primal Mother. Now empowered herself, she would return
the gift by giving him back what she had desired and received. Bryher
was apparently unable to fulfill H.D.'s request. But in 1936, H.D. sent
Freud a birthday gift of "white cattle," which he read as a sign of "af-
fection," "not praise": "Life at my age is not easy, but spring is beautiful
and so is love" (Letter to H.D., 24 May 1936, in *Tribute to Freud* 194).
These cows are themselves a maternal symbol, recalling the cows John
Helforth saw in moments of mad intensity. They also allude to what
H.D. described to Bryher as the "epic-dream" that broke "the back of
the analysis" (27 April 1933). In this important dream, which makes no
appearance in *Tribute to Freud* or *Advent,* Freud "comes 'out big' " as
"the heavy sun-god in exile," and a central episode features the arrival
of "numerous white steers, bulls or oxen" out of the river. H.D. told
Freud that the river was "the Milky Way, as I insist that the Bulls are
'mother-bulls' to his great amusement" (27 April 1933). Her gift of the
"mother-bulls" functioned as symbolic substitute for the Cretan Snake
Goddess.

  As Morris pointed out, H.D. continued the gift exchange by sending
Freud an anonymous gift of gardenias to greet his flight from the Nazis
in November of 1938 ("Relay of Power" 500–2). Gardenias, Freud had
told her, were his favorite flowers, not orchids, as everyone believed.
Correctly reading the flowers as her signature, he wrote immediately to
thank her and to puzzle about the mysterious note that accompanied
them: "*To greet the return of the Gods,*" to which he added "*(other people
read Goods).*"[37] Gardenias suggest "gardens," the dream symbol of the
primal Mother. H.D.'s gift represents the "return of the God(des)s" that
Freud had returned to her.

As a textual repetition of the maternal transference, *Advent* focuses on the mother–daughter dyad and links the "return of the Goddess" to consciousness with a working through of maternal desire. But H.D.'s maternal transference had a deeper level, one that exists not at all in the public *Tribute to Freud* and only as trace in the semiprivate "journal," *Advent*. This layer, thoroughly discussed in her private letters to Bryher, connects the longing for the primal Mother to lesbian desire and masturbation. Clues exist in *Advent* – especially in Bryher's repeated presence in the maternal clusters and in the introduction of the term "mother-fixation." But in *Advent,* H.D. did not translate the meaning of the technical psychoanalytic term or the conflation of Bryher and Helen Doolittle in her dreams and visions. Her letters to Bryher are explicit where the more public texts repress the desire for which H.D. would have been censured by a heterocentric culture. For example, she wrote to Bryher one day in great excitement about the collaborative analysis of the maternal transference:

> F. says I have sketched in, in the large, all the chief points of importance, he thinks, and the fun comes in the details. The "transference" was of course, the all-important thing. He also cheered me up one day by saying that my special kind of "fixation" was not known till three years ago, so perhaps it is as well, that I was not analysed some ten years back. . . . F. says mine is the absolutely FIRST layer, I got stuck at the earliest pre-OE stage, and "back to the womb" seems to be my only solution. Hence islands, sea, Greek primitives and so on. Its all too, too wonder-making. Even T[urtle, i.e., Sachs] said I was deeply attached to my father which I suppose I was and am, but I always felt there was a catch somewhere. My triangle is mother–brother–self. That is, early phallic-mother, baby brother or smaller brother and self. I have worked in and around that, I have HAD the baby with my mother, and been the phallic-baby, hence Moses in the bull-rushes [the Princess dream], I have HAD the baby with the brother, hence Cuthbert [Aldington], Cecil Grey [Gray], Kenneth etc. I have HAD the "illumination" or the back to womb WITH, the brother, hence you and me in Corfu (island = mother), with Rodeck always as a phallic-mother. . . . well, well, well, I could go on and on and on, demonstrating but once you get the first idea, all the other, later diverse-looking manifestations fit in somehow. Savvy?????? Its all too queer and at first, I felt life had been wasted in all this repetition etc., but somehow F. seems to find it amusing, sometimes, and apparently I am of a good "life" vibration as I went on and on, repeating, wanting to give life or save life, never in that sense, to destroy life (except self-rat to get back to the island-womb phase, all most natural). (23 March 1933)

This extraordinary letter suggests that H.D.'s maternal transference unleashed the desire that had fueled all the repetitions in her life and work: the longing to return to the womb. Heterosexual as well as lesbian eroticism represented her desire for the lost "phallic mother" – to be her baby, to have her baby, or to be unborn inside her body. Suicidal desire ("self-rat to get back to the island-womb") represents the ultimate longing for (re)union with the mother. Heterosexual desire repeats the love of the brother, who exists as her twin in the maternal triad of mother–daughter–son. Lesbian desire ("you and me in Corfu [island = mother]") represents the return to the "phallic mother," the mother whom the daughter still desires and still sees as all-powerful. As H.D. had written to Bryher more briefly a few days before:

> Evidently ALL the gents linked on, in one way or another with beaver [Helen Doolittle] and with Ida that old nurse we had. Funny. Shows what a mess one can make of choosing 'masculine' types. Alas...it is all however, very helpful though last night had most god-awful nightmares, guilt, I suppose in supplanting mother-object with second mother-object, Pieter R. [Peter Rodeck]. You, are very likely the Kangaroo, the younger *BROTHER*. Trust this does not, offend your masculinity. Anyhow, you are something plus mother-object, must be small boy." (14 March 1933)

According to these translations, Peter Rodeck represented the "phallic mother" and Bryher the phallus ("small boy") on the "phallic mother." Heterosexual and lesbian desire were, for Freud, substitutions for the repressed longing for the pre-Oedipal mother.

Such equations are linked to the theoretical connections Freud made between lesbianism and mother fixation. Lesbian women, he argued in "Psychogenesis of a Case of Homosexuality in a Woman," refuse to accept their own or their mother's "castration" and love other women as a way of returning to the pre-Oedipal stage of desire. Penis envy in lesbian women represents a psychic regression to the Edenic period of a young girl's love for her mother before the Fall – before, that is, she has become aware of women's "castration." Similarly, masturbation reflects a return to the little girl's "phallic" phase, the pre-Oedipal period when she gets sexual pleasure through clitoral manipulation.

Another major dream H.D. suppressed in *Advent* and *Tribute to Freud,* but reported in her letters to Bryher illustrates how working through the maternal transference with Freud reinforced the daughter's search for the empowering presence of the primal Mother/Lover:

> I feel cleared as if I had had a baby, and very weak. I told you I had dream.... [in which] you and Joan and I had left a theatre, a Noel Coward play, in which Noel C. had a mistress and a wife and so on. I got that to mean that I was watching now from without, the "play" of the literary people, that is N. C. was probably Lawrence or R. A. [Aldington]. Anyhow, I had none of the usual p[enis]-envy reactions,

was just amused, and you and Joan and I went off in car or carriage. We got to the country. I looked up. There was a giant moon, bigger than the sun. It was rainbow coloured and like a pool of rainbow in the sky. Enormous. As I looked, there was a dim figure of a woman in the moon. She was clothed with "samite, mystic, wonderful," if you know what I mean, draped in flowing rainbow robes, seated like a madonna in a curved frame. Artemis, yet she was pregnant. A perfect renaissance idea...VIRGIN but pregnant. "O moon of my delight that knows no wane." I shouted to you and Joan to look. A bird crossed the surface, a dark pigeon, a dove. Freud tells me it is an almost perfect mythological state, I was in. The moon, of course, equated mother, but it was "mother in heaven." You and Joan (Cole) and I were a sort of band of sisters, the Graces or Fates.

Well, I give this just in outline, but evidently it meant that I had, in the uc-n [unconscious], completely turned about to a homo layer. . . . not L[esbian] exactly, but just that, the three sisters, the "band of sisters" with the "mother in heaven." . . . In the "play," I seemed to mean that these men and all their little vagaries were only a "play," a performance, something to enjoy, not envy, but to keep out of Savvy ??????? All very neat.

The dove or pigeon across the moon was the "holy Ghost," or the pregnancy agent. . . . The "band of sisters" of course, can not contemplate the "father" as fertilizing element, in the pure state of homosexuality. So its as neat as a pin. . . .

I was apparently hanging on to Kex [Macpherson] in some way, as one does, as the phallic-mother was a layer before the final moon-mother. This was no phallic mother, the bird was phallus. So now I am in this pure spirit-mother state, and very happy. (26 May 1933)

This dream about the pregnant Artemis and the band of sisters may have been stimulated by Freud's own direction and blessing the day before. H.D. wrote to Bryher on March 25, 1933: "papa says now I have gone over all the historical war and post-war matter and he wants me to stick back in the child-period of pure mother-fix. He more or less gave me his blessing and forgiveness and dispensation for all past 'sins,' said it was not really necessary to dwell on all that, only as an indication of guilt toward mother, that otherwise, there was nothing 'wrong,' or words to that effect. [sentence cut from letter] The result was that I came home with a ghastly cramp and could hardly eat." The sentence removed from H.D.'s letter with scissors is a gap in the text that we can fill only with conjecture. Someone, probably not H.D. and most likely Bryher, here and elsewhere surgically removed phrases, sentences, and even paragraphs whose contents cannot be identified with certainty. I believe, however, that these cuts read in context suggest that Bryher suppressed H.D.'s references to orgasm, most often her own orgasm produced by masturbation.[38]

There are scattered references in H.D.'s letters about analysis to dis-cussions about masturbation. For example, H.D. wrote Bryher on March 10, 1933: "Over-slept this morning...have to tell papa to-day that I [half line cut out]. I follow my dream-trail...I don't like telling this to papa." On the next day, she was probably alluding to what she told Freud about this episode when she wrote Bryher: "I mean it goes on and on and on, but very slunk-ful and Sargasso-sea like, you have to wallow. I am afraid Berlin and N.Y. are too high-powered for me, I need taking down into the weed slime depth. Papa was most sweet and 'sophisticated' yesterday as I began to" (11 March 1933). Here the letter breaks off at the end of the page, and its follow-up page is missing. For posterity, Bryher may well have preferred that H.D.'s desire for the Mother/Lover remain in the "pure mythological state" of the textual dream, with its erotic con-sequences in "real" orgasm erased. H.D. had no such need to censure explicit representations of orgasm, even from masturbation – *Nights* echoed and countered Lawrence's *Lady Chatterley's Lover* in its openness about the body. Although she did not like to tell either Freud-as-Father or Freud-as-Mother about masturbation, she did not at all mind telling Bryher in the privacy of her letters.

Held simultaneously suspended in our minds as a composite text, H.D.'s prose discourses about working through the maternal transference chart the development of a gynopoetic empowered by the Mother/Muse. Each layer of the palimpsest connects the maternal transference to H.D.'s creativity with an explicitness related to its status as a public, semiprivate, or private text. *Tribute to Freud* never directly mentions her writing block, but instead refers generally to "repetitive experiences" and "rubbish" cluttering the stream of her consciousness. Freud's references to her writ-ing block in the letters she included in the 1956 edition of *Tribute to Freud* constitute the major textual trace of their discussions on these issues (191–4). *Advent* comments more directly on her dissatisfaction with her work, particularly the "narcissistic" prose of her historical novels and the Dijon fiction. It also, unlike *Tribute to Freud,* reveals the rivalry she felt as a woman writer up against the genius of men like Lawrence. But it does not report what she and Freud discussed about her own insecurity as a woman poet in a male-dominated literary tradition (148–51). Her letters to Bryher are the most frank about what she and Freud worked out on her writing "inhibitions," her loss of creative drive, and the wrenching difficulty she experienced in writing at all. Read intertextually, all three texts attest to the centrality of the maternal transference for the analytic regeneration of creative inspiration.

H.D. did not raise the subject of her creative work until the third week of April, some seven weeks into her analysis and well after the maternal transference was established. Freud told her he was astonished to see such "modesty" in a poet, but she warned him that the reasons for her silence were "deeper" (21 April 1933). The signs had probably been present in her analysis right from the beginning, as *Advent* demonstrates, but apparently they did not decode the implications of her dreams for her creativity until April and May of 1933, when it was a regular subject of discussion. Nonetheless, the maternal clusters in *Advent* inscribe a connection between her longing for the lost primal Mother and her creative block. Often, the link is made by sharp juxtaposition – like a textual montage. Embedded in the lengthy account of the dream of the Madonna-lily, for example, is a seemingly unconnected paragraph assessing her heritage. Recalling the child's act at her father's grave, one paragraph ends: "She 'plants' the lily" (121). The next paragraph abruptly begins: "Obviously, this is my inheritance. I derive my imaginative faculties through my musician-mother. . . . " (121). The subsequent paragraph returns to the garden of the dream.

Similarly, the dreams of her mother's jewel box and painted mirror are woven in and between dreams about Lawrence, in which she resists his authority and genius. The mirror, with its narcissa painted on velvet, produces a sharp judgment of her own texts and then a longing for the domestic art that her mother represents: "Perhaps the books I last wrote of were too self-centered or 'narcissistic' to satisfy my heart. I want a fusion or a transfusion of my mother's art. Though she discarded the velvet with the realistic sprays of goldenrod and other treasures of the same period, there is nothing of De Vinci's nor of Durer's that can now fire my very entrails with adoration as did those apple-blossoms, daisies, hare-bells, wild roses on her set of 'wedding plates' " (151). The connection between maternal longing and art is explicit with Van Eck. Freud decoded his link to the pre-Oedipal mother through painting (164). The Mother is the daughter's lifeblood. Within the transferential text, these maternal clusters function as a "transfusion" of the "mother's art" that restores the daughter's text to life.

In H.D.'s letters to Bryher, the importance of the maternal transference for her creativity is even more explicitly articulated, particularly in a series of dreams and discussions that feature literary men. Not long after she first talked to Freud about being a poet, she reported a dream in which Bryher appeared as the substitute for the Mother/Lover:

> I had more dream of the "house" sequence [i.e., "houses" in astrology], you and me gathering roses from enormous trees in an old garden. "House of pleasure"??? We climb on a wall as we near a wing of the house, and you jump down. I cling to my roses and stay ON THE WALL. There are two elderly gents, Bernard Shaw and Cunninghame Grahame...and I am afraid they will scold me for stealing the roses. You say they won't mind. Evidently the gents are fathers, the roses

> [word(s) cut out] the big house set back in the enchanted garden,
> "mother" in general. Its all like that now...it has boiled down to the
> sun [Father] and moon [Mother] and myself a wandering planet....
> terribly exciting and keeps papa purring like mad. (28 April 1933)

The "roses" the literary men possess are female genitalia, erased from
H.D.'s text, no doubt by Bryher; the "big house" is the maternal body,
the womb walled up by the power of men. Bryher and the dreamer have
been gathering roses in the astrological House of Pleasure – in the dream,
a garden of lesbian delight near the "enchanted garden" and house of
the primal Mother. The dreamer is afraid of the Law of the Father, the
gents who control "the roses," but in the Artemisian sisterhood of the
dream, Bryher leads her on. The dream equation links creative power
with the mystic rose of the Mother/Lover's body.

H.D.'s fear of Shaw and Grahame was a screen for her feelings about
Lawrence, anxieties stimulated by reading the volume of his letters and
another memoir that had recently been published. She and Freud linked
these feelings to her writing block. On May 12, 1933, H.D. wrote briefly
to Bryher about her "creative work": "I think I will finally get this idea
out of my head of being a back-number." Then on May 15, 1933, she
continued her report:

> I have been soaking in D.H. L. letters, not too good for me, but Freud
> seems to agree with me for once. Evidently I blocked the whole of the
> "period" and if I can skeleton-in a vol. about it, it will break the clutch.
> . . . But the "cure" will be, I fear me, writing that damn vol. straight,
> as history, no frills as in Narthex, Palimp. and so on, just a straight
> narrative, then later, changing names and so on. I keep dreaming of
> literary men, Shaw, Cunninghame Grahame, now Noel Coward and
> Lawrence himself, over and over. It is important as book means *penis*
> evidently and as a "writer," only, am I an equal in uc-n, in the right
> way, with men. Most odd. (15 May 1933)

The dream of the pregnant Artemis – the moon lady and the band of
sisters – represents a continuation of these discussions about her writing
"clutch." As she reported to Bryher on May 26, 1933, this dream presents
a ritualizing longing for the Mother/Lover framed by anxiety about
literary men. It begins with the "band of sisters" leaving a Noel Coward
play, which H.D. significantly translated as her acceptance of her position
outside masculine literary space (the theater). She is not envious, she
stressed, but rather happy that male "play" is something "to keep out
of." After all, the dreamer has her Mother (the Virgin Mother, about to
give birth) and her "band of sisters" with whom she creates her own
community. This fantasy of Artemisian sisterhood can be read as an
answer to these discussions about her writing block at two levels. First,
it shows her defiant refusal – at least in the dream – to consider herself

a "back-number" as a writer, and her empowering insistence of the band of lesbian sisters who need "no man," themselves "that dart and pulse of the male, / hands, feet, thighs, / ... perfect" (*Collected Poems* 456). In this sense, the dream offers her gynocentric guidance and support in her resistance to the patriarchal world of letters.

But secondarily, the dream also counters Freud's equation of "book means *penis*," which H.D. seemed to have accepted a few days before. If books means penis in the language of the unconscious, then penis envy motivates the dreamer's conscious desire to write. Within the framework of this symbolism, H.D.'s male writing personae (Hedylus, Ray Bart, John Helforth, etc.) inscribe her unconscious desire to possess through writing what men possess through birth. The Artemis dream, however, poses the powerful ritual of women who (pro)create as virgins, who "can not contemplate the 'father' as fertilizing element, in the pure state of homosexuality." The dream's frame *in the letter* repeats this (pro)creative power. H.D. began and closed her account of the dream by saying she felt like she had just given birth. As one of the "band of sisters" worshiping the Mother, she has herself become the pregnant Artemis, giving birth to herself and, by extension, her books.[39]

This parthenogenic (pro)creativity, envisioned through the agency of the maternal transference, suggests a poetic in which the primal Mother and daughter are reunited in a textual (trans)fusion. Writing repeats the transferential repetition of the daughter's desire. This kind of pre-Oedipal gynopoetic is evident in Freud's translation of the "poem-series" H.D. acted out for a depressed Bryher at the Hotel Belle Venise in Corfu. Typically, *Advent* sketches the outline, while H.D.'s letters to Bryher go into depth. Describing the various female and male parts she dramatized for Bryher, H.D. wrote that "The Professor said, 'It was a poem-series the acting was drama, half-motivated by desire to comfort Bryher' " (*Advent* 172–3). A few days later Freud linked these performances to Peter Van Eck, both of which he "referred back to my mother" (*Advent* 184). He wanted also to know if she "had ever wanted to go on the stage," a question that dredged up memories of "dressing up" and acting for her mother (*Advent* 184). In her letters to Bryher, H.D. connected these performances – child and adult – directly to her mother fixation and her writing block. In the letter about Freud wanting her to "stick back in the child-period of pure mother-fix," H.D. also wrote: "Final dirt: stop press; papa seems to imply that I wanted all along in uc-n to be an actress, and that is one reason I am never satisfied with writing. Its made me feel like hell. . . . my dance and song turn in Corfu, was final and complete indication of what I wanted" (25 March 1933). The next day, she added: "yesterday we were supposed to have turned a corner, going back FROM the Greek trip and picking up strands of acting, in way of charades, school shows, dressing up and so on and so on. He evidently considers this an important thing and a clue to a lot of my inhibitions about my writing" (26 March 1933).

Writing, in other words, was a performative display of desire for the lost Mother. As a substitute for the young daughter's dance for the pre-Oedipal Mother, writing was Koré's call for Demeter. The transferential text became the scene of "call and response," to borrow a phrase from Afro-American culture – the daughter's call as writer, the mother's response as muse. "The Mother is the Muse," H.D. reflected much later in *End to Torment* (41). This gynopoetic, articulated by working through the maternal transference with Freud, anticipates aspects of *écriture féminine* proposed by Cixous in "The Laugh of the Medusa," which explicitly links women's masturbation and creativity. More implicitly, she proposes a pre-Oedipal poetic in advocating that women "write the body," write in "white ink." Irigaray extends Cixous's poetics of the erotic body by conflating speaking, masturbating, and lesbian lovemaking in "When Our Lips Speak Together" (*This Sex* 205–18).

For H.D. in particular, the (re)construction of the Mother/Lover/Muse feminized the process and product of writing. Helios, who had been the dominant inspirational figure in her writing of the 1920s, had been decoded as "Helen." Greece was no longer the land of metallic intellect, as it was in *Hedylus* and *Narthex*. In the language of her unconscious, Greece was now "Hellas, Helen" (*Tribute to Freud* 49). The Greece of H.D.'s *Ion,* a text whose completion she credited to Freud, is quite different from the Greece of *Hedylus*. By decoding her love of Greece and the Greek islands as a desire for the pre-Oedipal Mother, Freud had facilitated the feminization of her most potent symbol of creative inspiration.

In the "relay of power and of peace" that governed the gift exchange between H.D. and Freud (to echo Morris once more), she passed along to the readers of her poetry the gift of the primal Mother that Freud had given (back to) her. Although the lesbian/masturbatory/erotic layer has been distilled out of the relatively impersonal discourse of the poems, H.D.'s major poetic texts after analysis with Freud repeat the scene of maternal transference in "the pure mythological state" of her dreams. The pregnant Artemis in her dream of the "band of sisters" reappears as the Lady of *Tribute to the Angels*. She too is associated with the Moon and with the rainbow of promise. As the poet's muse, she comes not with the Child, but with the Book-as-Child – the book whose "pages, I imagine, are the blank pages / of the unwritten volume of the new" (*Trilogy* 569). In *Helen in Egypt,* the primal Mother of H.D.'s dreams transfuses the protean goddesses of Eros with her power. *Sagesse* materializes the mother of dreams in the figure of the *Grande Mer* who whispers through the sea shell "listen, my child, it is enough, // the echo of the sea, our secret // and our simple mystery" (*Hermetic Definition* 75). And in *Hermetic Definition*, Isis "unbinds my eyes, / commands, / write, write or die" (7). These Mother/Muse figures inspire and authorize the daughter/poet who no longer imagines her writing self as masculine. The erotics of this gynopoetic do not appear on the surface of these mythologized texts. But read intertextually, these poems have a textual unconscious that can be interpreted through the successively hidden layers of H.D.'s maternal discourses about Freud.[40]

Ultimately, however, we must read the discourses of the maternal and paternal transference together as a doubly layered palimpsest. The interplay between the two transferences is significant in the texts as both reconstructions and repetitions of analysis. This interaction takes two basic forms – the first, dialectical and the second, developmental. On the one hand, H.D.'s texts reproduce the double transference by first inscribing them as polarities and then deconstructing the binary so as to move toward a new integration. On the other hand, these texts also connect the double transference to the psychosexual stages of individual and cultural development, as these are posited by psychoanalytic theory. Both the Oedipal and the pre-Oedipal layers of the psyche and of human history are reproduced in the layers of transference. These dialectical and developmental patterns contribute to the ultimate integration that H.D. sought in both the primary and secondary scenes of analysis. Analysis, Freud told H.D., was like the cathedral of her dream, the "house" or "home" in which she found "regeneration or reintegration" (*Advent* 146). Freud's "room" was the cathedral, which "in some indescribable way depends on father–mother. At the point of integration or regeneration, there is no conflict over rival loyalties" (*Advent* 146). Freud was father/mother, and she was the child in the chrysalis of analysis. "He said," she remembered, "he wanted me to feel at home here" (*Advent* 146).

The dialectical pattern of paternal and maternal interaction explores the "rival loyalties" that precede "regeneration or reintegration." H.D.'s maternal transference fueled her resistance to Freud-as-Father – it not only made him feel uncomfortable, but it also proposed representations of desire and power that revolved around Mother, not Father. H.D.'s letters to Bryher, revealing the full extent of the maternal transference, were themselves a textual resistance to Freud's paternal authority. But this conflict between the paternal and maternal transference accomplishes a deconstruction of its own polarity. Working through both transferences transforms Freud into the parental figures she did not in actuality have – a powerful mother who was not "morbidly self-effacing" and a nurturing father who was not forbidding and austere. The primal Mother produced through the maternal transference is a figure of power with whom the daughter/writer can identify. The Father constructed in the paternal transference is the "wounded" and all-(for)giving man who heals the split psyche of the daughter. Moreover, the daughter's resistance to Freud-as-Father lays the necessary groundwork for her identification with his authority, for her textual repetitions of his "megalomania." The daughter's desire for Freud-as-Mother transforms that authority she occupies from a patriarchal to a gynocentric one.

The developmental pattern of the double transference suggests "regeneration or reintegration" through successive regressions back through the layers of the psyche. The paternal transference repeats the psychodynamics of the Oedipal daughter, while the maternal transference tunnels deeper into the psyche to reach the desire of the pre-Oedipal daughter. Freud was always "the Professor" and "Papa" for H.D., but just as she believed that an esoteric mystery lay hidden within the cold abstraction of her father's numbers, so she burrowed deep inside Freud-as-Father to find Freud-as-Mother. As Albert Gelpi emphasized in "Remembering the Mother: A Reading of H.D.'s *Trilogy*," the poet asks God, the "Lord *Amen*," "the Ram," in *The Walls Do Not Fall*: "Hide me in your fleece, / . . . / let me be warm in your belly" (*Trilogy* 527). Finding the Mother in the Father is a movement back in time – personal time and mythological time. "*The childhood of the individual is the childhood of the race*," H.D. remembered Freud writing (*Tribute to Freud* 12). Her transferential movement from the Oedipal Father back to the pre-Oedipal Mother recapitulates the passage in the history of mythological time from God-the-Father to God-the-Mother.

What H.D. called her special "feeling" for the shrine of Delphi encodes this developmental progression through regression. The room of analysis is a modern shrine of Delphi, where the entrance to the cave bore the carved message "Know thyself": "*Know thyself,* said the ironic Delphic oracle, and the sage or priest who framed the utterance knew that to know thyself in the full sense was to know everybody. *Know thyself,* said the Professor, and plunging time and again, he amassed that store of intimate revelation contained in his impressive volumes" (*Tribute to Freud* 72–3). Delphi – and by analogy, analysis – "was the shrine of the Prophet and Musician, the inspiration of artists and the patron of physicians" (*Tribute to Freud* 50). But the shrine of Apollo, the sun god and twin of Artemis, was superimposed – geographically and symbolically – onto the shrine of the maternal chthonic deities of the pre-Olympian pantheon. Suspended on a tripod over the cleft in the earth from which trance-inducing vapors issued, the Pythia uttered the enigmatic oracles of Delphi that the priests would interpret. The Pythia's dark cave also contained the *omphalos,* the stone that marked the navel of the universe. Snakes were sacred to the shrine, symbolic of Apollo's power. To win the shrine for his own, Apollo had slain the great Python, a female serpent who guarded the holy site of the Earth Goddess. The sun god's coup over the chthonic deities is one of the many mythological signs. J. J. Bachofen and Jane Ellen Harrison read in proposing the theory of a patriarchal overthrow of a matriarchal period in human history.[41]

Much like Freud, who longed to go to Rome and waited years before his wish could be fulfilled, H.D. yearned to go to Delphi. When Bryher promised the barely living H.D. in 1919 that she would take her to Greece, it was to Delphi that H.D. most wanted to go. "If I could only feel that I could walk the sacred way to Delphi, I know I would get well," she had answered (*Tribute to Freud* 50). But Delphi was blocked by mines in the harbor left over by war. It was too dangerous to go. H.D. did not get to Delphi until the spring of 1932, when a peasant woman sitting like one of the Fates in a field of daisies pointed to Perdita and said "helios." She probably meant "sun-burnt," H.D. wrote home to Macpherson, but the healing touch of Helios on mother and daughter, as well as H.D.'s general experience of the sacred city, no doubt paved the way for her analysis with Freud one year later (18 April 1932).

In Vienna, H.D. found Delphi once again. Through the paternal transference, H.D. felt in touch with Helios/Apollo, the light of reason that Freud brought to the interpretation of the unconscious. But through the maternal transference, H.D. plunged back in time to the shrine beneath the shrine, to the Mother below the Father, to the layer of individual and human history that the Law of the Father has repressed. The reintegration or regeneration produced by this regression does not represent an androgynous fusion or even interplay of the masculine and feminine. Rather, it is profoundly gynocentric. The maternal is the omphalos of the psyche, the foundation from which the self emerges, the base to which it must return to be healed, and the origin of its own speech. As H.D. wrote during a bombing raid in *The Gift*:

> Mary, Maia, Miriam, Mut, Madre, Mère, Mother, pray for us. . . . This is Gaia, this is the beginning. This is the end. Under every shrine to Zeus, to Jupiter, to Zeu[s?]-pater or Theus-pater or God-the-Father . . . there is an earlier altar. There is, beneath the carved super-structure of every temple to God-the-Father, the dark cave or grotto or inner hall or cella[r] to Mary, mère, Mut, mutter, pray for us. (MSS IV, 10)

IV. THE WRITING CURE IN THE GIFT

Certainly *The Gift*, the story of the Child, synthesizes or harmonizes with the Sigmund Freud notes. I assembled *The Gift* during the early war-years, but without the analysis and the illuminating doctrine or philosophy of Sigmund Freud, I would hardly have found the clue or

the bridge between the child-life, the memories of peaceful
Bethlehem, and the orgy of destruction, later to be witnessed and
lived through in London.

H.D., *H.D. by Delia
Alton* (192)

The Gift is a self-analysis, undertaken not in the semidark cave
of Freud's safe room, but rather in a flat under constant bombardment
from Nazi bombs. It was not the threat of war, but its very materiality
that impelled H.D. to continue what she had begun with Freud. His
absence from the textual scene of analysis allowed her to articulate what
she had repressed or displaced during her sessions in 1933 and 1934 –
namely, her war phobia, with its conflation of violence, fascism, and
patriarchal power in the family. *The Gift* is the closest H.D. came to a
formal autobiography of her formative years in her family. It is a direct
re-creation of her roots – her childhood in Bethlehem, her mother's
Moravian heritage, her father's and grandfather's science, the family's
move from Bethlehem to Upper Darby when she was about ten. But
more than in most conventional autobiographies, H.D. reproduced the
analytic scene in her text by foregrounding the "I now," the present time
and space of the narrator caught in the Nazi terror. Bombing raids punctuate the flow of memories like the narrative march of soldier's "feet,
feet, feet" in *Asphodel* and *Palimpsest*. Anchored in the time/space of
history, the "I now" travels to the time/space of memory and fantasy,
both as an escape from war and as an attempt to understand the roots
of violence and the promise of peace.

Consequently, *The Gift* is doubly autobiographical. It (re)constructs
the formation of the child Hilda in the late nineteenth century and the
survival of the adult H.D. in the midst of World War II. Like the analysis
with Freud it extends, *The Gift* repeats and works through the paternal
and maternal transference – the powerful Father whom she must resist
and feminize; the primal Mother whom she must resurrect and revere.
The Gift is a self-analysis that protects and heals by bringing the exiled
daughter back "home," by redefining that home so that it empowers
instead of suffocates. And like Freud's analysis of his own dreams in *The
Interpretation of Dreams*, *The Gift* also reads the fragments of the unconscious as signs for the origin and meaning of what H.D. calls "the gift"
– specifically, *her* gift to bring the message of peace to a world perpetually
at war.

As an autobiography that textually reproduces the scene of analysis,
the structure of *The Gift* is experimental, as is its texture, in which strands
of childlike and adult discourses are alternately woven. The text has seven
chapters, a number that signals its spiritual message. But, in a way that

recalls Woolf's preoccupation with "facts" in the notes for *Three Guineas*, *The Gift* also contains some ninety pages of Notes that provide historical context, source material, and further commentary on each chapter.[42] Chapter 1, entitled "Dark Room," begins in medias res in the voice of a child, as if the narrator were lying on Freud's proverbial couch, cinematically reproducing the seemingly disconnected associations of a bewildered young Hilda, who is witness to fragments she cannot connect or interpret. The distinction between the "I now" and the "I then" repeatedly collapses as we watch what is clearly a flow of fragmented memories nonetheless narrated in the voice of the child who is living them.[43] This "child's" prose is at times Steinian in its simplicity, repetitiveness, and attention to externalities that serve as signifiers of a veiled signified. For example, the child's repetitive visualization of the Moravian Mortuary as "the Dead-house" functions textually as a "screen memory," revealing and concealing a repressed and uninterpreted terror of death:

> Florence said one of the Sisters was lying in the Dead-house, but we could not see her. The dead-house had little windows, too high up but Florence said Melinda had said that Nettie had said, there was a Sister in the Dead-house. She would lie there until they carried her to the old grave-yard or more likely to Nisky Hill, as the old grave-yard was very crowded. Along the fence of the old grave-yard, there were mounds without stones, which were the soldiers, grey and blue, who had died in the old Seminary, when Papalie was there, during the Civil War. (MSS I, 5–6)

However, the flow of the child's consciousness not only records what she sees and cannot understand, but also introduces her innocent attempts at interpretation. Her questions punctuate the flow of the first chapter and initiate the central themes of the adult text. Why was the little girl in the Seminary "burnt to death in a crinoline" when her dress caught fire from the Christmas tree? Why had Mamalie laughed to discover little Helen huddled inside Papalie's grandfather clock and crying about the death of her long-dead half-sister Fanny? Why had all of Hilda's little sisters and half-sisters died while all the brothers survived? Why did Bluebeard murder his wives, and was his beard really blue? Why did Papa pick the name Hilda out of a book? Why did Mama praise Gilbert's misspelled word "d-a-g" and pass over Hilda's clever "c-a-t"? Did "spelling" make a *"spell?"* Why did the audience laugh at Eva's fate in the local performance of *Uncle Tom's Cabin?* Was the play "real," or was it "play"? Above all, what was the "gift" and why did Mama believe that none of her children had "it"?

The child's unfulfilled desire to "read" the mysterious signs all about her invites the reader into a similar process of interpretation and suggests the presence of the adult narrator who is displacing her own desire to understand onto the figure of the child. The child's tortured connection of herself with the heritage of the dead Fanny demonstrates this hermeneutic and introduces the theme of "the gift," its connection to her status as "girl," and the omnipresence of death:

> I was the inheritor. The boys, of whom there were so many, the two brothers and later, the baby-brother, the two half-brothers, the five grown Howard cousins, not to mention the small-fry, Tottie, Dick and Laddie . . . could not really care about Fanny. . . . I cared about Fanny. And she died. I inherited Fanny from Mama, from Mamalie, if you will, but I inherited Fanny. Was I indeed, Frances come back? Then I would be Papalie's own child for Papalie's name was Francis; I would be like Mama; in a sense, I would be Mama. . . . Why was it always a girl who had died? Why did Alice die and not Alfred? Why did Edith die and not Gilbert? I did not cry because Fanny died, but I had inherited Fanny. Mama cried (although I had seldom seen her cry) because Fanny died, so Mama had cried. I did not cry. The crying was frozen in me but it was my own, it was my own crying. There was Alice, my own half-sister, Edith, my own sister and I was the third of this trio, these three Fates, or maybe Fanny was the third. The gift was there but the expression of the gift was somewhere else.
> It lay buried in the ground. (MSS I, 4–5)

From time to time, the "I now" narrator abruptly inserts herself into the discontinuous jumble of the child's associations to comment on the process we are witnessing. She doesn't yet interpret these signs, or answer the child's questions for us, although we cannot help noticing that they revolve around the mysteries of violence, time, death, language, and "the gift." Rather, she explains in the abstract discourse of a detached analyst how the mind works, how the fabric of the text comes to reproduce the naïve discourse of the child. The mind – and the text as the representation of the mind – is a darkroom in which memories are developed into photographic images that flow like film through a projector. "It would not always be like that," that narrator comments on the preceding picture/memory:

> But because it once had been like that, it would be possible with time and with the curious chemical constituents of biological or psychic thought-processes – whatever thought is, nobody yet knows – to develop single photographs or to develop long strips of continuous photographs, stored in the dark-room of memory, and again to watch people enter a room, leave a room, to watch, not only those people enter and leave a room, but to watch the child watching them. (MSS I, 27–8)

In this *"camera obscura,"* "a word opens a door," and "these flashes of flash-backs" are "film [that] unrolls in my head" (MSS I, 31, 30, 15, 35). The montage of this "film" parallels the "dark-room" of cinematic creation with the "dark room" of Freudian analysis.

Chapters 2 and 3 continue unrolling the film with scarcely a hint of the narrator's time/space setting in the present. There is one ominous but enigmatic reference to the "fever and turmoil of present-day events" (MSS I, 35). But the narrator's presence is mainly registered through her essayistic commentary on the processes of mind and memory. Chapter 2, entitled "The Dream," opens with a discourse on the dream as "the un-walled province of the fourth-dimensional," and moves to her "dream" of Helen's premarriage love for the mysterious South American musician, courtship by the austere professor of astronomy, and visit to the fortune teller, who predicted that she would have a "gifted" child. Chapter 3 projects young Hilda's impressions of three different Christmases in Bethlehem and Upper Darby centered on Papalie and Papa. The narrator delays telling us until Chapter 4 that the film unrolling before her and our eyes is the product of Nazi air raids.

Chapter 4, entitled "Because One Is Happy," finally explains why we have been viewing these prior pictographs of the past. Recording the present, the narrator sets the wartime scene of violence with self-reflexive meditations that clarify the status of the text as analytic scene.[44] "There was a time-bomb that had neatly nosed its way under the pavement edge, less than two minutes' walk from my door," she informs us. The bomb, with its "fins like a little submarine, like a little shark," signifies how "the silt of time is dynamited to powder, along with the walls of the house on the corner" (MSS IV, 1). The sediments of time are "wiped away" in seconds, faster than any "amount of critical research or analytical probing could give us" (MSS IV, 2). As H.D. later wrote in *Hirslanden Notebooks,* "the past is literally blasted into consciousness with the Blitz in London" (III 2). The memories structurally preceding these observations in Chapter 4 have been a direct result of the war. Somehow, war has forced a repetition and working through of the past. It has instigated and propelled the darkroom of memory and interpretation. In turn, the flowing pictographs from childhood hold the key to a commentary on the present, the secret to the enigma of death and violence.

The narrator's deliberate withholding of the text's present context until Chapter 4 represents a kind of resistance to analysis, a block in the path of interpretation embodied in the structure of the autobiography. Chapters 1–3, in other words, have a textual unconscious that is not brought to light until Chapter 4. But the flow of memories finally allows the narrator's current terror to surface. Abandoning her essayistic theorizing about the mind, the narrator projects her stream of consciousness, which now replaces that of the child:

> The noise is not loud enough, the planes follow one another singly, so the mind is still held in the grip of vital terror. Tonight there may be fire, how will we get out? Is it better to stay in bed or crawl out to the hall in the dark, open the flat-door and wait in the entrance, even run down the four flights of stairs and crouch in the air-raid shelter? . . . I listen to hurried footsteps on the pavement outside my window, the clang of fire-engines making off from a near-by station. . . .
>
> When the noise becomes intolerable, when the planes swoop low, there is a moment when indecision passes, I can not move now, anyway. I am paralyzed, "frozen" rather, like the rabbit in the woods when it senses the leaves moving with that special uncanny rustling, that means the final, the almost abstract enemy is near.
>
> My body is "frozen." (MSS IV, 3)

The imagery of fire and ice in this passage replicates the imagery of the child's pictographs in Chapter 1. The child opens the text with the horrible tableau of the girl who is "burnt to death in a crinoline," who "is shrieking and they can not tear off her clothes because of the hoop" (MSS I, 1, 2). The adult begins her first personal narration with the terror of being burnt to death by a bomb. The child likens the "crying" that is "frozen in me" for the dead sister to "the gift that was somewhere else. . . . buried in the ground" (MSS I, 5). The adult images herself as a rabbit "frozen" in fear of the "uncanny." The child in turn is like that rabbit – caught in a forest of images that she cannot interpret, of signs that seem uncanny. The world of both child and adult is "uncanny," in the psychoanalytic sense of the term. Hilda and H.D. are like the Wolf Man, who is frozen in his dream by the uncanny stare of the wolves outside his window.[45] The adult, paralyzed by war phobia, acts out the repressed terror of the child.

As scene of analysis, the text brings to consciousness the past terror that has been repressed. Conversely, however, the child's fear is a displaced version of the adult's war phobia. Too "frozen" to narrate the air raids directly, the narrator first presents them indirectly, mediated by a textual artifice that replicates the distortions, condensations, and representations of the dream-work. In the darkroom of the text, she begins to work through her current fear by repeating it in the discourse of the child – by displacing the fire of war onto the fire in the Seminary, the death by bombs onto deaths of the sisters, and the fallen walls in London onto the "Dead-house" of Bethlehem. Lying frozen in her bed, she *is* the girl "burnt to death in a crinoline," shrieking to get out.

The narrator explains this displacement as "a trick" of "psychical projection" that allows her to feel "safe" (MSS IV, 4, 25): "I can not move now. Like the rabbit, like the wild-deer, a sort of protective 'invisibility' seems to surround me. My body is paralysed, 'frozen.' But the mind, has its wings. The trick works again. It works every time now. . . . I am safe. Now exaltation rises like sap in a tree. I am happy" (MSS IV, 4). The narrator delays full explanation of "the trick" until Chapter 7, which is also historically anchored in a bombing raid:

> I had learned a trick, lying on my bed. . . . the roar of the wings and the slight trembling of the walls were like the vibration set up in a great ocean-liner, and I was on a great ocean-liner and the ship might or might not go down. And then there would come that moment when I had left myself lying secure and it did not matter what happened to the frozen image of myself, lying on the bed, because there was a stronger image of myself, at least I did not see myself but I was myself, whether with attributes or pure abstraction or of days and in places that had been the surroundings of my childhood. . . . (MSS VII, 6)

As Morris has argued, the trick is a form of astral projection by which she leaves her body, caught in the time/space of war, for the fourth-dimensional time/space of dream and memory ("Trans-Actions"). The scenes of her childhood are "safe," not because they represent a pre-lapsarian Eden, but rather because she can work through her terror of the bombs by seeing them reshaped into the images of childhood. Linking the two scenes, she writes: "here the forces of evil and the forces of good are struggling; the whole structure of civilisation may go down at any moment like the Christmas-tree in the Seminary that caught fire when the girl in the crinoline was burnt to death" (MSS IV, 25).

In the relatively safe textual space of childhood, H.D. worked through the war phobia she could not directly discuss with Freud. Analysis in this darkroom triggered a double transference of Father and Mother patterned much like the transferences she worked through in Freud's "dark room." As the site of paternal transference, *The Gift* centers on the meaning of Papalie and Papa for the child Hilda and their connection to war. Papalie and Papa are figures of patriarchal authority who inspire both fear and reverence in young Hilda, an ambivalence that the adult narrator must work through by textually repeating the feelings of the child. Both men are scientists whose mysterious microscope and tele-scope penetrate the dark unknown to make visible what cannot be seen in the drop of water or the nighttime sky. Their tools, phallic metonyms for their (masculine) knowledge, are inseparable from their status as professors in society and patriarchs in the family.

To the child, Papalie and Papa are godlike, divinely authorized to create and protect, as Chapter 3 ("The Dream") makes clear. The fragments of the chapter cohere around the child's Christmas images of the Three Wise Men – Papalie, Papa, and the Old Man in the garden. Papalie, Hilda remembers, exercised the magic power every Christmas of carving the traditional Moravian *putz* out of clay, the rams, sheep, and figures that he nestled in snowy wool for the sacred crèche to celebrate the birth of God's Son. The narrator names this a "mysterious occult ceremony" and connects the goatlike Papalie to "Ammon, *Amen* from time immemorial, later Aries, our gold-fleeced Ram," the same protective Amen-Ra of *Trilogy* (MSS III, 4–5).

After Papalie's death, Papa, who was not Moravian and had never had a Christmas tree as a child, takes his children through the snowy night before Christmas to a toy store where he bought them twelve carved animals to place beneath the tree. For the child, their dark walk through the storm takes on special meaning – her father's firm, protective figure in the "round circle" of the lamplight ahead is reassuring to the little girl. Four times the narrator circles back to narrate that epiphanic moment when "Our-father" – like All-Father – moves into the lamplight (MSS IV, 15). As All-Father, Papa wraps his large hand around the little fingers of his only daughter, calls her his *Töcterlein* (little one), and tells everyone that "his one girl was worth all his five boys put together" (MSS III, 24, 27). To her, he is "different," "outside" the Moravian circle in Bethlehem. He is "a pathfinder, an explorer," the "gifted" one around whom "everything revolved" (MSS III, 26–8). And yet, he has selected her, the daughter, out of all the others, as his chosen child, the one he names Hilda.

The dream of the Old Man, narrated in the child's discourse, repeats and mythologizes the powerful and protective figures of Papalie and Papa. He is the same "old man" H.D. described in *Advent,* the God in the Garden who specially chooses the only girl in the bunch of children to whom he will give a gift. As in *Advent,* he cuts a beautiful lily for the child and later promises everyone a ride in the sleigh "because the girl asks" (MSS III, 37). His presence in the text represents the paternal transference, the daughter's love for the all-(for)giving Father inscribed in *Tribute to Freud, Advent,* and H.D.'s letters to Bryher. The sacred *putz* return to their "maker" and "giver" in H.D.'s dream of the white oxen and her gift of the cattle on Freud's birthday.

But just as Freud's paternal authority had to be resisted in analysis and in texts about analysis, the paternal constellation in *The Gift* has its negative side. The child's terror of the all-powerful Father is a textual repetition of H.D.'s resistance to Freud. To Hilda, both Papalie and Papa are associated with time, which inevitably brings death – Papalie, through his emblematic grandfather's clock in which little Helen sits crying about the dead sister; Papa, through his watch and proverbial comment, "*tempus fugit.*" They serve as motifs to which both child and narrator return. In the child's mind, Papalie, as professor of the Seminary, is somehow implicated in the death of the girl "burnt to death in a crinoline." Papa, in turn, is like Bluebeard, who "murdered his wives"; for "our kind father" also has a black beard and "Edith and Alice and the Lady (the mother of Alfred and Eric [Papa's first wife, Martha]) all belonged to Papa and were there in the grave-yard" (MSS I, 9).

Most importantly, Papalie and Papa are linked in the child's mind with nightmares through a picture entitled "Nightmare" in a book called *Simple Science*. Hilda is fixated on the image, which is both there and not there after her mother cuts the page out of the book. "Mama cut it out," she thinks. "Because Mama cut it out, it was there always," like the world inside Papalie's drop of water, "where there is nothing, there is something" (MSS III, 37; I, 14).[46] Embedded in the book of Science, "Nightmare" recapitulates all the child's fears of dead girls and dead sisters:

> the picture was a girl lying on her back, she was asleep, she might be dead but no, Ida said she was asleep. She had a white dress on like the dress the baby wore in the photograph, Aunt Rosa sent Mama that Mama tried to hide from us, of Aunt Rosa's baby in a long white dress in a box, lying on a pillow. The baby looked as if it were asleep, the girl in the picture looked as if she were dead but the baby was dead and the girl was asleep and the picture was called Nightmare. (MSS III, 38)

The child's image of "Nightmare" in the Father's book is superimposed in Chapter 4 on the reality of the adult's world, which is reported in the child's voice: "I know that Gilbert has been resting for a very long time, in a place called Thiacourt in France, and that Mama went to sleep too . . . and did not wake up again" (MSS IV, 9).

The "I now," the "I then," and the dead girl in the book fuse as the child has a nightmare of her own, one that prefigures the adult's "nightmare" of Nazi attack and links the war with the sadomasochism of the primal scene. Hilda dreams of a horrible snake sitting in her parents' bed and drinking water from a tumbler with paintbrushes in it. Another snake suddenly rears up from the floor "like a thick terrible length of fire-hose" encircling the bedpost in a deathgrip. Suddenly, "he strikes at me," at which point the dream veers off into her questions for Gilbert and Ida about Aladdin in *Arabian Nights*. He looks like a girl with his long braid, but Ida tells her firmly that Aladdin is a boy, and Hilda wonders "Is it only a boy who may rub the wishing-lamp. . . . maybe it is only a boy who may have the wish" (MSS IV, 9). With this thought:

> The snake has sprung at me . . . I shout through the snake-face, that it is fastened at the side of my mouth, "Gilbert; Mama, Mama, Mama."
> The snake falls off. His great head, as he falls away, is close to my eyes and his teeth are long, like the teeth of a horse. He has bitten the side of my mouth. I will never get well, I will die soon of the poison of this horrible snake. I pull at Ida's apron. . . . She looks at the scar on

my mouth. How ugly my mouth is with a scar, and the side of my
face seems stung to death. (MSS IV, 9–10)

The text contains no interpretation of this nightmare, as if the child's
frozen terror is transposed to the adult narrator who resists the pursuit
of analysis. But the dream is resonant within the system of Freud's
hermeneutics, particularly when it is read in the context of H.D.'s letters
to Bryher about her second analysis with Freud. Like the Wolf Man's
dream of the uncanny wolves, this dream can be read as a representation
of the primal scene, Freud's term for the young child's observation of
his or her parents having intercourse. In H.D.'s dream, the child is caught
in the act of watching her parents caught in the act, which in the pre-
Oedipal mind of the daughter is an act of violence performed by the
father on the body of her beloved mother. The snake on the bed, the
water, the paintbrushes – all have sexual referents in the language of the
dream. The dream's sudden swerve into the story of Aladdin represents
the psychoanalytic parable of "castration" – the girl's discovery that only
boys have magic "lamps" they can rub to get their wishes. The second
snake rears erect to accomplish what the story has predicted – the wound
which leaves an ugly scar that can never be healed. Female genitals and
mouth conflate in a scene of "castration" – the theft of both erotic pleasure
and speech – which is the destiny of both mother and daughter in the
primal scene and its repetition.[47] "What I wanted to know," the dreamer
reflects, "was, what was a Nightmare, was the Nightmare real?" (MSS
III, 39).

H.D.'s letters to Bryher about her second analysis with Freud supply
the explicit analysis of nightmares that is only implied in *The Gift*.
Whereas her first analysis in 1933 centered on a recovery of the pre-
Oedipal mother, the second in 1934 broke through her initial "terrific
resistance" to discussing the "father vibration" and centered on the father
figure, particularly "the father who terrifies."[48] Her paternal transference
in November of 1934 placed Freud in the position of the fearful and
violent father of the primal scene, which, in turn, she linked to her war
phobia. She reported to Bryher, for example:

> I have had terrible amount of dream material over week-end. A long
> dream that R. A. [Aldington] and you are in bed together, evidently
> married and that R. A. shoots you. Then shoots himself. . . . I am sure,
> but will take it to papa, that it is primal scene, the father or husband,
> R. A., "kills" the mother by shooting her in the head in bed. If so, it
> is an immense discouvery and would tap my war phobia and so on.
> . . . Papa is most kind and helpful since he discouvered I had linked him
> up with blackmailing father-symbol. . . . [and] with the usual text-book,
> Zoo primal scene. (18 or 19 November 1934)

In their subsequent discussion of this and other nightmares, H.D. and
Freud concluded that her war phobia was rooted in repressed memories

of the primal scene, whose psychic scar was the perpetual entanglement of *Eros* and *Thanatos*. "Evident," H.D. reflected to Bryher, "it is DEATH, at the last that I feared or wanted. Having see[n] the parents and thought it was 'death,' love and death got tangled" (10 December 1934). In another nightmare, "I end by going into deep black and have a horrible nightmare loss and desolate feeling. So it is perfectly clear I did LOOSE [*sic*] both parents at the age of 3 or 4 and built up my whole love-life on that love and terror mixed, and violence as of war etc." (29 November 1934). In the unconscious, sex meant war to H.D.: "I was to be another 'victim'. . . . I wanted to be victimized in the Zoo [sexual] way, but felt or knew it would mean death. . . . But child meant primal scene, meant being 'killed' by a man, the father. Odd" (18 or 19 November 1934). Heterosexuality and motherhood, in other words, triggered a repressed sadomasochistic psychodynamic.

Like the Freud of *Civilization and Its Discontents,* H.D. used this psychodynamic to link events in the public and private sphere: to analyze personal and societal history as extensions of each other, as interlocking expressions of eros and the death instinct. In *The Gift,* the nightmares of the child are inseparable from the nightmare of history. The politics of fascism are superimposed onto the psychodynamics of the patriarchal family, a psychopolitical analysis that evokes Woolf's critique of the patriarchal origins of war in *Three Guineas.* The nightmare of the snake is a displaced account of the Nazi bombing raids. H.D.'s terror of the erect snake who bites her mouth is a symbolic representation of her paralyzing fear of the roaring planes overhead. Snake and planes merge in Chapter 4 in the image of "the vilest Python whom Apollo, the light, slew with his burning arrows" (MSS IV, 12). Significantly changing the traditional sex of Delphi's sacred serpent, H.D. depicts Python as distinctly male: "Can one look into the jaws of the Python and live? Can one be stung on the mouth by the Python and utter words other than poisonous? . . . The Python took shape, his wings whirred overhead, he dropped his sulphur and his fire on us" (MSS IV 12). The all-powerful Father who is a figure of terror in the daughter's nightmare finds "real" expression in Hitler. Nazism is an extension of the politics implicit in the primal scene into the domain of history. Yes, the "Nightmare" *is* "real."

But, like *Three Guineas,* the radical feminist pacifism of *The Gift* resides in its refusal to regard the rise of fascism in purely nationalist terms. As the narrator reflects on her essayistic prologue to Chapter 4:

> There are no national boundaries, I do not think, "that is a German who dropped that bomb." . . . Though I know that this host flies to incarcerate us or incinerate us, from Germany, I do not think in journalists truisms, in terms of nation against nation. Light and Darkness have unfurled their banners, and though we take our place beside the

legions of Light, we must never forget how each one of us (through inertia, through indifference, through ignorance) is, in part, responsible for the world-calamity. (MSS IV, 2)

During World War II, H.D. believed that civilization was at stake, as she stated in *The Gift,* and she was every bit as antifascist as Bryher. But *The Gift* argues that "Germany," per se, was not the enemy, but rather the psychodynamics of sadomasochistic desire played out in the power relations of the public and private spheres. The Father Who Terrifies occupies a position of real power through the institutions of the state and the family – both abroad and at home. In spite of her play on Light and Dark, H.D. refused a reductionist, Manichaean politics that explained war in terms of good nations against bad nations. Like Freud, H.D. believed that both sides were complicit in war. Like Woolf, H.D. connected aggression with patriarchy.

Herein lay H.D.'s difficulty with the paternal transference. In connecting Freud with the "Bad Father" during her second analysis, she was able to articulate the links between the primal scene and her terror during the *past* war, but not in the war to come. To discuss her fear of Nazi atrocities in 1934 would require her to do the unmentionable – link Freud, the potential victim, with the Nazi victimizers. In awakening the terrors associated with the primal scene, the Nazis played the part of the Father Who Terrifies – the one who kills and maims the mother and daughter in a sadomasochistic scene of violence and desire. H.D. could not tell Freud that, in being a potent/important man, in occupying the position of the all-powerful father, he was participating in that economy of power. In *The Gift,* however, she makes that association between her own father and the Nazis, and therefore, implicitly, between Freud-as-Father and Hitler, the ultimate Father of the Fatherland.

The Gift works through the transferential construction of the Father Who Terrifies by (re)constructing an ideal father who redeems. Like Christ, the power of this re-visioned father figure depends upon his wounds. The Bad Father must be disarmed, symbolically "castrated" so that he occupies the position of women in history. The poet prophecies this process in the hieratic language of "The Master": "yet all men will kneel, / no man will be potent / important, / yet all men will feel / what it is to be a woman" (*Collected Poems* 460). *The Gift* narrates a related "lesson" in the personal discourse of autobiography. Within the psychoanalytic structure of *The Gift,* the memory of her father's accident is the last – and most forbidden – to be recovered. Chapter 6 returns to the discourse of the child to repeat the story that has been repressed – the night Hilda answered a late knock at the door and found her father slumped like a wan ghost at the door with blood dripping down his forehead.

On one level, the accident represents the daughter's terrible loss of the all-powerful Father who protects his daughter. In the repetitive discourse of the terrified and bewildered child, Hilda thinks:

> I took his hand and I said, "O, Papa," and he didn't say anything. He did not hold my hand tight in his hand, he did not take my hand the way he did, his fingers did not close tight round my hand the way they always did. It had never happened before that his fingers did not close round my hand. His hand did not seem to belong to him, his arm seemed like the arm of a scare-crow or a rag-doll. (MSS VI, 7)

Paralleling the three times she told the story of her protective father in the lamplight, Hilda narrates finding her father wounded at the door three times. Images of powerlessness replace those of power. He is not tall and straight, but limp and weak. He does not hold her hand or call her *Töchterlein*. He cannot speak, but only stares in an uncanny scene of speechless "looking." No adult will explain the mystery to the child – was he robbed by a thief, did he fall off the tram, will he live or die? The terror of the unprotected child in Chapter 6 introduces the paralysis of the adult during the three waves of the bombing raid in Chapter 7. In recovering the repressed memory of her father's accident, H.D. has interpreted its unconscious presence in her terrified response to the Nazi planes. Like the child, she is exposed to the full force of death, with no all-powerful Father to hold her hand.

On a second, more forbidden level, however, the repressed story of her father's accident also represents a desire for his victimization and resurrection as the wounded Christ "three" days later. Before his accident, his beard was "black," like Bluebeard; after the accident, it turned white. Formerly, the child heard her father compared to a "thief in the night" who works in the dark; now he was perhaps wounded by a "thief in the night" who might have robbed and beaten him.[49] In his new role, the dethroned Father may not be all-powerful against the forces of death, but his wound links him with the mystery of the pacifist Moravian Jesus, "a liturgy, the litany of the wounds":

> *Wound of Christ,*
> *Wound of God,*
> *Wound of Beauty,*
> *Wound of Blessing,*
> *Wound of Poverty,*
> *Wound of Peace*
> (MSS VII, 25–6)

In her nightmare, she is wounded. In her reading of his "reality," he is wounded. Father and daughter meet in the world of their wounds – on different and more equal terms. A symbolic castration of patriarchal power is a precondition of this new relationship, one that presents a pacifist message for the wars of nations and sexes alike. This re-vision of the father/lover in *The Gift* resonates with other men in women's writing who take on the position of WOMAN through some symbolic wounding – like Rochester in *Jane Eyre* and Romney in *Aurora Leigh*, even Septimus Smith in *Mrs. Dalloway*. It prefigures as well H.D.'s Achilles in *Helen in Egypt*, the "New Mortal" who limps across the sand toward Helen.[50] To be loved, the father and male lover must become what H.D. called a *hero fatal*, a man who has passed beyond his position of privilege into a companionship with a woman who is his full equal.

No wonder, then, that H.D. resisted discussing her nightmares about Nazi atrocities with Freud. They not only prefigured the terror to come from which there was no protection, but they also contained a wish for Freud to occupy the position of victim as the precondition of rebirth – the killing of the Father Who Terrifies and the "birth" of the wounded son who would be her equal.[51] In analysis, Freud was a surrogate father in transference. In *The Gift*, her father stood in for Freud through the agency of the transferential text. What she wished for her father is what she wished for Freud. Both *Advent* and her letters confirm this connection by linking Freud with Lawrence and Christ. *Advent* explores the likeness she saw between Freud and Lawrence in the context of Lawrence's *The Man Who Died*, his last novel, about the wounded Christ who is healed by the priestess of Isis, apparently modeled on H.D. And, to Macpherson, H.D. wrote: "Freud is simply Jesus-Christ after the resurrection, he has that wistful ghost look of someone who has been right past the door of the tomb, and such tenderness with such humour, he just IS all that. I am sure he IS the absolute inheritor of all that eastern mystery and majic, just IS, in spite of his monumental work and all that, he is the real, the final healer" (15 March 1933). H.D.'s portrait of Freud as Christ represents a resistance to his authority in multiple ways – certainly to his status as a Jew in anti-Semitic times, also to his stand against religion as "mass delusion" in *Civilization and Its Discontents*. But, on another level, this association of Freud with Jesus places him within the mystery religions of the ancient Near East that featured the rituals of the dying god under the aegis of the Great Mother.

The wounded father of *The Gift* similarly exists within the context of the daughter's recovery of the primal Mother. In its exploration of her maternal heritage, *The Gift* repeats H.D.'s maternal transference with Freud and extends it into a healing gynopoetic that opposes the Law of the Father embodied in the Nazi attacks. This process requires, however, that she confront the "Bad Mother," the mother who rejects the daughter in favor of the son, as a precondition to recovering the empowering mother/muse who nourishes the daughter's art. The primal Mother of the daughter's desire is split in two in *The Gift*. Mamalie, her mother's

mother, takes on the qualities of the pre-Oedipal mother, while Helen
plays the part of the Oedipal mother who accepts her role as "castrated"
woman in the Symbolic order. Regressing back through the developmental layers of the psyche, the daughter works through her repressed
feelings about the mother who betrayed her and the grandmother who
fulfilled her needs.

At issue in the relationship between Helen and Hilda is the status of
"the gift." As a young woman, Helen has been told by the fortune teller
that she will have a "gifted" child, a scene so important that the narrator
centers a whole chapter around it. Chapter 2, "The Fortune Teller,"
invents the history of the mother whose denial of the daughter's gift has
already been introduced in Chapter 1. The narrator reflects: "I do not
remember when she first told me about it [encounter with fortune teller],
yet I remember the strange gap in consciousness, the sort of emptiness
there, which I soon covered over with my childish philosophy or logic,
when she said, 'it's funny, the fortune-teller told me, I would have a
child who was in some way especially gifted' " (MSS I, 32). Hilda's
"childish philosophy" explains what she lacks by imagining that her
mother must have given away the "gift" to Uncle Fred, the famous Bach
musician:

> But where did he get the Gift, just like that? Why didn't Mama wait
> and teach us music like she did Uncle Fred when he was a little boy?
> Mama gave all her music to Uncle Fred, that is what she did. That is
> why we hadn't the Gift, because it was Mama who started being the
> musician and then she said she taught Uncle Fred; she gave it away,
> she gave the Gift to Uncle Fred, she should have waited and given the
> Gift to us. (MSS I, 15–16)

The child's explanation screens the adult's repressed anger with her
mother. As a psychoanalytic parable, it suggests that Helen created a
"gap" in her daughter's consciousness by pointing to Hilda's "lack" –
that is, her lack of a penis and, by extension, talent. The "gift" that the
Oedipal mother takes away from her daughter to give to her brother is
the phallus that signifies creative authority. Hilda's "gift" is "frozen,"
"buried in the ground" because her mother collaborates with the Symbolic order that confers it on men. This mother who denies the daughter's
power is the same mother who appeared in the unedited manuscripts of
Paint It To-Day and *HER,* the conventional mother that the daughter
fantasized killing in order to save her talent.

In *The Gift,* however, H.D. works through the rage expressed in (and
excised from) the earlier novels by reflecting on the patriarchal origins
of her mother's betrayal. The passage about her gap in consciousness is
abruptly juxtaposed to a pictograph of Mama as a little girl. She is singing
in the Seminary when her father, Papalie, bellows "who is making this

dreadful noise in here?" (MSS I, 32). The conversation between father and daughter fades cinematically into Helen telling her daughter Hilda "I was so hurt, I never sang any more, not even in church" (MSS I, 33). "How could I know," the narrator reflects, "that this apparent disappointment that her children were not 'gifted,' was itself her own sense of inadequacy and frustration, carried a step further?" (MSS I, 32). Chapter 2 explores the roots of Helen's sense of inadequacy even further by showing how she had not had the courage to be unconventional. Madame Rinaldo, the eccentric voice teacher and former opera singer, had told her that her voice was "a gift from heaven." But Helen was silenced by her father. The exotic Spanish student whom she loved adored her and wanted to whisk her away, but she was afraid to go. To her daughter, Helen represented women's fear of being different, women's silence and invisibility in the domain of the all-powerful Father. Helen's betrayal of her daughter was not her inability to give her a penis, but rather her failure to rebel against patriarchal authority.

Mamalie becomes the model of difference that Helen is not. Chapter 5, "The Secret," narrates the scene in Bethlehem in which Mamalie awakens the buried "gift" in Hilda by passing down the secret of her esoteric Moravian heritage. The setting is significant, loaded with signs of a women's culture and domestic art rich in meaning. On a hot summer night when Helen and her friends sit outside watching shooting stars, nine-year-old Hilda snuggles deep into a quilt with pink rose-buds Mamalie made out of her dead daughter Agnes's wedding dress. Listening to the murmur of female voices outside, Hilda thinks of a Kate Greenaway poem, the one she recited in her first school performance, "Under the Window." Somewhat befuddled and senile, the kindly Mamalie imagines that Hilda is her daughter Agnes (her "lamb") and begins to tell a story she has never told anyone. "The story was like the quilt," the narrator tells us. "Bits of it came clear, as I say, in patches" (MSS V, 38).[52]

A long time ago, Mamalie and her first husband Henry Seidel found a secret copy of a book inscribed 100 years before by the Moravian linguist John Christopher Pyrlaeus and the Indian priest Shooting Star. Written in scraps of Greek, Hebrew, and an American Indian sign language, the book told about a secret meeting of Moravians and Indians held on *Wunden Eiland* (The Island of Wounds) in the Monacacy Creek just below the Seminary. There, David Zeisberger, well known for his fairness with native tribes, and Chief Paxnous of the Shawanese, who did not want war with the whites, recognized their common bond in worshiping the Moravian *Sanctus Spiritus* and the Indian Great Spirit. The European Anna von Pahlen and the native woman Morning Star exchanged names to symbolize the promise of peace. Henry and Mamalie deciphered the

pages, a task not complete until she transcribed the musical notations of
Indian music at the spinet. As she played the notes, suddenly "the Gift"
descended upon her, and, in the telling, upon Hilda:

> ... in trying over and putting together the indicated rhythms, she herself
> became one with the *Wunden Eiland* initiates and herself spoke with
> tongues, hymns of the spirits in the air, or spirits at sun-rise and sun-
> setting, of the deer and the wild squirrel, the beaver, the otter, the king-
> fisher and the hawk and eagle. She laughed when she told me about it.
> ... "It was laughing, laughing all the time. ... it was the laughter of
> leaves of winds, of snow swirling, it was the laughter of the water. ...
> it poured from the sky or from the inner realm of the Spirit, this laughter
> that ran over us." (MSS V, 42–3)

Like the laughter of Aphrodite and Isis in *Palimpsest,* the mystic laughter
of Mamalie empowers Hilda. The "Gift," she learns, is her legacy from
the Hidden Church, from the Moravians who sang the "Liturgy of
Wounds" on *Wunden Eiland* with the American Indians in the promise
of peace.

Mamalie's gift fills the gap in consciousness left by Helen's inability
to read the signs of her daughter's talent. In the textual transference, she
represents the daughter's return to the all-powerful Mother, the same
mother who holds the flaming candle for the daughter caught in the Nazi
atrocities in *Advent*. She embodies as well the Great Mother to whom
the little girl appeals in the snake dream. "Our much-beloved Mary," it
will be remembered, looked at the scar on the little girl's mouth: "But
no, 'you are not stung to death,' says dark Mary, who is enormous and
very kind. 'You must drink milk,' she says" (MSS IV, 10). This "dark
Mary," who gives the nourishment the mother denied the daughter, is
the Great Mother to whom the narrator prays during the bombing raid:
"Mary, Maia, Miriam, Mut, Madre, Mère, Mother" (MSS IV, 10). As
the pre-Oedipal maternal presence that predates the daughter's entrance
into the Symbolic order, Mamalie is bedrock – "the dark cave or grotto
or inner hall or cella[r] to Mary, mère, Mut" that lies "beneath the carved
super-structure of every temple to God-the-Father" (MSS IV, 10).

The mark of Mamalie's difference is not only her sex, but also her
Moravianism. Her power to feed the hungry spirit of the narrator resides
in a femaleness that is inseparable from her roots in the esoteric current
of Moravian history and doctrine. Mamalie is a precursor of the "saints"
Alice Walker recovered and revered from Afro-American tradition in
"In Search of Our Mothers' Gardens." By the time H.D. was born in
Bethlehem, the Moravians had for the most part lost touch with their
origin as a mystical and egalitarian sect. Certain distinguishing customs
remained – the ritual love feasts, the kiss of peace, the pacifism, the flat
gravestones, the missions around the world. But the esoteric roots of

those traditions, going back to at least the fifteenth century, had been lost to most Moravians. Mamalie's "Gift" to Hilda initiated H.D.'s researches as an adult into the Hidden Church of the *Unitas Fratrum,* as the Moravians were known. *The Gift* documents that search and finds a parable of war and peace that gave meaning to the contemporary "holocaust to Mars."

As an expatriate wandering on the psychic borderlines of Europe, H.D. "came home" through her identification with the exiled and persecuted Moravians who had founded Bethlehem. "I have felt all along a deep gratitude for the place of my birth and for my people," she wrote in the Notes for *The Gift,* "but my people . . . are not parochial, not conditioned by small boundaries, not shut-in by provincial barriers" (MSS Notes, 51–2). She found that her own expatriatism mirrored that of her persecuted ancestors – to fulfill the promise of her gift, she had to wander as they had wandered. Like them, she would not be parochial. The Moravians who founded Bethlehem came from all over Europe, brought a love for learning and music with them, and looked even to the cultures of Asia, Africa, and Arabia, as well as to the native Americans, she recorded in the Notes. Like Pound, she found the healing qualities she admired in a great leader – Count Zinzendorf, who offered safe haven for Moravians all over Europe on his estate in Bohemia before he helped them journey to the New World. But unlike Pound's leaders, patriarchs and protofascists, H.D.'s Zinzendorf represented the outcast and the marginal. She wrote: "He was a dreamer, a poet, a reformer, a man-of-the-world, a mystic, a great gentleman and an intimate friend of carpenters, wood-cutters, farmers, itinerant preachers and all women" (MSS Notes, 92). While his enemies believed his great Plan was a conspiracy for world dictatorship, she learned that his Plan was for the peaceful organization of democratic communities wherever the persecuted could find freedom.[53]

The internationalism of the Moravians was also syncretist. Sensitive to persecution, tolerant of difference, themselves a heterodox sect of Christianity, the early Moravians were not fundamentalist in their religion. This is the great Secret that Mamalie passes on to Hilda, who cannot interpret it until she herself is persecuted during World War II. Respecting the Great Spirit of the American Indians as another name for their own *Sanctus Spiritus,* the peace-loving Moravians had an unusual relationship with nearby native tribes. They founded biracial communities, celebrated rituals of peace, and negotiated fair treaties that they upheld. They were also among the first to document American Indian languages and culture. When an unfriendly Indian tribe burned Gnadenhuetten, one of the biracial Moravian villages, Zeisberger helped some Indians establish New Gnadenhuetten, which became a peaceful and prosperous village in the Midwest. With horror, H.D. discovered that a "band of 'soldiers,' gangsters of the then new west, toughs, flotsam and jetsam, washed up on the shores of the Indian continent," had massacred every Indian in the village. This white betrayal of the peace made between Indians and Moravians was emblematic for H.D. of America's heritage, a mix of peace and violence, gift and theft, freedom and oppression.

The lesson of Mamalie's Moravian story, however, goes deeper than the discovery of non-Moravian barbarity. Just as H.D. refused to explain the rise of Nazism in strictly nationalist terms, so she interpreted Mamalie's tale for signs of Moravian complicity in history's compulsion to repeat its cycles of violence. Mamalie's tale ended not with her epiphany, but with its aftermath in madness. Not long after she and Henry found "the secret," he died, and she fell sick with "brain fever," convinced that Shooting Star had cursed the world because the Promise of *Wunden Eiland* was broken. After the meeting between Paxnous and Zeisberger, more-fundamentalist Moravians accused them of scandalous witchcraft with the devil and burned the original copy of the sacred book. Eventually, the syncretist and esoteric current of Moravianism was forced underground by the more-conventional and literal-minded Brothers and Sisters. To the adult narrator, Mamalie's madness and guilt signified that the Moravians had betrayed their special "Gift" of peace to the world and were therefore complicitous in the larger cycles of violence.

In the transferential logic of *The Gift*, what H.D. learned about the past is superimposed on the mysteries of the present. The "curse" of Shooting Star reappears not only in the child's fear of the "shooting stars" Helen watches outside Mamalie's window, but also in the Nazi bombs. The fire that burns the sacred book symbolizing the promise of peace is the fire in the Seminary that burns the little girl, which in turn is the fire of Mamalie's candle that Hilda is afraid will ignite the house. All these fires resurface in the firebombs of the narrator's current war. Similarly, the snake as resurrection symbol for the group on *Wunden Eiland* reappears as the terrifying Python of the snake dream, in itself a displaced representation of the bombing raid. Violence and death, terror and paralysis, are inscribed in the signs of history, in the layers of the palimpsest. Not until she is an adult who has recovered the repressed memories of her personal history and Moravian heritage can she interpret "the whistling of evil wings, the falling of poisonous arrows, the deadly signature of a sign of evil-magic in the sky" (MSS V, 37).

What has been repressed in her own past recapitulates what has been repressed in history. *The Gift* represents the return of the repressed – the narratives of war that lie buried in the personal and political unconscious of history. The religious persecution of the Moravians, the white ex-

ploitation of the American Indians, the Nazi aggression against civilization itself exist as layers of violence in the palimpsest of history. These
in turn are linked to the patriarchal politics of the family in which the
all-powerful Father symbolically silences and "castrates" the daughter.
Working through the paternal and maternal transferences, however,
H.D. turned to her Moravian matrilineage, embodied in Mamalie, to re-
awaken her frozen "Gift" and to re-vision the Father as a force for peace
instead of war. In the Moravian "Liturgy of Wounds," man – through
the image of the crucified Christ – has "died" in order to be reborn as
a "New Mortal" cradled in the lap of the Great Mother. "Morning Star,"
the final chapter, signals this rebirth. The morning star is not only a
conventional sign of resurrection, associated with Jesus, but also the
planet Venus, the name of the Indian princess at *Wunden Eiland,* the root
word of Astarte (a star), and the star Sirius, sacred to Isis. The shooting
star of war has been transformed into a syncretist star of promise, one
that integrates Jewish, Christian, Greek, Egyptian, Mesopotamian, and
American Indian traditions.

The legacy of Mamalie's "gift" to the child is aesthetic as well as
religious, a connection embedded in the double meaning of the word
"gift" as present and talent. Mamalie was an accomplished musician who
brought to life the magic buried in the runic script by playing music.
She passed that "gift" down to her daughter Helen, but, being silenced
by Papalie's judgment and "giving" her musical gift to her brother Fred,
Helen denies her inheritance and suppresses her own talent, which she
then cannot recognize in her daughter. But she does serve as the conduit
of that "gift" to H.D., whose reconciliation with her mother is evidenced
in her dedication of *The Gift* "To Helen, who brought me home."

Like Eugenia in *HER,* Mamalie's creative "gift" was rooted in the
"little tradition" and domestic crafts within which the narrator situates
her own creativity. Mamalie's favorite music was ballads, especially the
song called "The Four Marys," the same song that Woolf used in her
delineation of a female literary tradition in *A Room of One's Own.* Sung
in the voice of Mary Hamilton, one of the queen's ladies, the song is a
traditional lament of woman's position in a man's world. Desired by the
king, Mary Hamilton gives birth to his babe, whom she kills to protect
herself from the queen. Hung for her crime, Mary Hamilton emblemizes
women's punishment for sexuality and reproduction within an androcentric economy of desire. In the Notes, H.D. made this song, in turn,
a sign of women's "almost voiceless" presence within the dominant
masculine tradition:

> *The Four Marys* was my grandmother's personal preference.
> Jedediah's mighty bass and the "surge and thunder" of his trombone
> had not stilled in her a delicate Celtic lyric that ran alongside the mighty
> torrent of German classic tradition.

> It had threaded its way into her heart and into mine; it was an un-
> spoken tradition, breathless, almost voiceless; this was something we
> understood together and perhaps we two only. If Jedediah gave Uncle
> Fred the whole ocean of musical-consciousness called Haydn or called
> Bach, well, it was something over which we had no control, we could
> not argue about it. . . . yet she was firm and adamant on one point, *now*
> *Fred...to finish, Four Marys.* (MSS Notes, 8–9)

Mamalie defies the "mighty torrent of German classic tradition" by
preferring a ballad, a woman's lament, with which she makes Fred finish
the singing. This choice, which "was something we understood together," provides the code that allows us to decipher all the scattered
allusions to other "almost voiceless" traditions that have been drowned
out by the "mighty torrent" of male voices. Mamalie's quilt functions
as a motif throughout Chapter 5, "The Secret," as the major metaphor
for the creativity that the grandmother is passing down to her granddaughter. Greenaway's sentimental little verse, "Under My Window,"
reappears at several key points in the chapter to remind the narrator of
her first "artistic" performance, when she recited the poem in school.
The "early H.D." had fled just the kind of feminine flower language that
Greenaway epitomized for a generation of Victorians. But in *The Gift,*
H.D. "came back home," not only to Greenaway's verse, but also to
the fairy tales Ida and Miss Helen (Hilda's teacher) used to read, to little
hand-crafted carved animals, to quilts and all the other domestic arts
with which women made a "home."

In this context, we can interpret the prominence that Chapter 1 gives
to a school performance of *Uncle Tom's Cabin* in awakening the child's
creative gift. In the montage of cinematic memory, the play unfolds
before us to answer the questions raised in two immediately preceding
pictographs. Hilda's thoughts on how her mother must have given away
the "gift" to Uncle Fred fade into a conversation with her Uncle Hartley
in which she asks, "can ladies be just the same as men . . . about writing
a book?" "Why, yes," he answers, "ladies write books of course, lots
of ladies write very good books. . . . like Louisa Alcott and like Harriet
Beecher Stowe" (MSS I, 16). This affirmation, in turn, produces the
memory of the school play. The performance is a bad one, so unprofes-
sional that the audience laughs when Eliza, terrorized by the blood-
hounds, dashes around the stage clutching her baby. But, like Huck Finn
at the circus, Hilda believes what she sees. The chase is "real" – it "comes
true" in the enchantment of the theater. In a gesture radically at odds
with male modernists like Pound and Eliot, H.D. founded her artistic
origins in Harriet Beecher Stowe – a woman, a radical, an American,
whose popular, didactic, and sentimental novel inspired the outrage
against slavery that helped ignite the Civil War. Hilda's naïve empathy
for the suffering of the black mother and child awakens her creative

"Gift" and lays the foundation for the adult writer's identification with
all the outcasts of the mainstream:

> ...everything came true – that is what it was. Everything came true.
> ...O well, I know it was only Little Eva in a jerry built, gold chariot,
> and yet it was the very dawn of art, it was the sun, the drama, the
> theatre, it was poetry, why, it was music, it was folk-lore and folk-
> song, it was history.... It was art or many of the arts, concentrated
> and maybe consecrated by the fixed game of these same American
> children, who in the intensity of their naif yet inherent or inherited
> perception... became one with their visionary mid-European ances-
> tors.... (MSS I, 24–5)

Awakened and consecrated by the "little" traditions at the margins of
male culture and the center of women's culture, the child Hilda revitalizes
the adult narrator and provides her with "a sense of direction," defined
in *Trilogy* as "resurrection" (*Collected Poems* 583). As a transferential scene
continuing her analysis, *The Gift* completes the process that Freud initiated: the restoration of H.D.'s creative drive and inspiration.

V. INTIMACY AND CLAIRVOYANCE IN THE GIFT AND TRILOGY

> *The Walls Do Not Fall* is, in a sense, like certain passages of *The Gift*,
> runic, divinatory. This is not the "crystalline" poetry that my early
> critics would insist on. It is no pillar of salt nor yet of hewn rock-
> crystal. It is the pillar of fire by night, the pillar of cloud by day.
>
> H.D., *H.D. by Delia Alton* (192–3)

H.D.'s writing cure in *The Gift* was in no sense a permanent
"cure," a fixed end point to analysis. Like Freud, H.D. believed that
self-analysis was an interminable process. But working through, in *The
Gift,* the paternal and maternal transference that she had resisted revealing
fully to Freud was healing. Self-analysis in *The Gift* accomplished the
(re)creation of the poet who writes *Trilogy*. *The Gift* and *Trilogy* are
paired texts that fulfill the apologia H.D. made to Cournos in 1919 to
explain why she wanted to write prose in the letter with which I began
in Chapter 1. Read intertextually, they dramatize the split between impersonalism and personalism, lyric and narrative. *The Gift* is personal,
clearing up the tangles of brushwood in the forests of memory so that
she could step into the clearing as the clairvoyant poet of *Trilogy* who
mediates between the sacred and the profane. Although the discourses
of *The Gift* and *Trilogy* are different, they are, however, also interlocking.
Taken together, they deconstruct the binary of poetry and prose that
they inscribe. The prose writer in *The Gift* discovers her roots in a

prophetic tradition, while the poet's meditations in *Trilogy* reach for a conversational intimacy with the reader as participant in a quest narrative. H.D.'s self-creations in the early 1940s bridge the gap, the splits in consciousness, that had impelled her to write for decades.

Both texts are testaments to survival, textual talismans against the bombs. In the midst of war, she would think of peace; in the midst of death, she would think of birth. Facing the possibility of annihilation, she would "bear witness to this truth" through her art (MSS IV, 5). But where *The Gift* is intimate, personal, *Trilogy* is hieratic, mythic. The prose writer is a frightened woman, her mind caught in the "vital terror" of history. The poet is a depersonalized bard, a prophet crying in the wilderness of all-time, all-space. Using real names and places, the autobiographer splits herself into the "I now" and the "I then" to untangle the skeins of what has been repressed in the personal and historical unconscious. Ranging over the mythic landscape of hermetic traditions, the poet is an authoritative voice clairvoyantly reading the runic remains through the partial erasures of time.

The image of self as mollusc in both texts is emblematic of their difference and commonality. In *The Gift*, the narrator says during the final bombing raid: "I had no mother-of-pearl shell around me. I was broken open, the mollusc or oyster or clam that was my perceptive abstract self or soul, had neither the super-human reasoning nor the human habitation. . . . I would be burned to death . . . [like] one girl in a crinoline" (MSS VII, 13). In *Trilogy*, the poet says: "I sense my own limit, / my shell-jaws snap shut // at invasion of the limitless, / ocean weight; infinite water // can not crack me, egg in egg-shell; / . . . / be indigestible, hard, ungiving, // so that, living within, / you beget, self-out-of-self, // selfless, / that pearl-of-great-price" (513–14). The poet in *Trilogy* is reborn as "complete, immortal" because the writer of *The Gift* has been vulnerable, split, open to defeat. But even though *The Gift* birthed the poet of *Trilogy*, the prose text is no handmaiden to the epic poem. Instead, it is a complete text in its own right that addresses the same issues as *Trilogy*, but in its own discourse.

Shaped as a self-analysis that works through the personal to reach the mythic, the discourse of *The Gift* is fundamentally and defiantly rooted in female space at the margins of the Great Tradition mapped by men of the dominant Eurocentric culture. The Moravian gynopoetic forged in *The Gift* serves as the bedrock for *Trilogy*, even as its personal roots in H.D.'s matrilineage have been distilled out and mythologized. Mamalie both is and is not the hieratic Lady of *Tribute to the Angels*. Like the Lady, she is a Mother/Muse who emerges out of the daughter's desire for the primal Mother. But where the Lady with the Book seems to step out of the male representations of her that the poet revises, Mamalie sits in her dark room lit by a candle – evocations of a womb. Cozy and senile, Mamalie is an intimate muse whom the world would regard as a silly old lady who can't even call her granddaughter by the right name. But like the regal Grand Mer of *Sagesse,* Mamalie knows the "secret": Hilda-as-Agnes is God's "lamb," the Moravian "Christ" who will bring the message of peace to the world at war. Speaking in disconnected fragments of old memories, Mamalie is like the quilt that she tucks up under the chin of her granddaughter – full of bits and pieces of the past that the child Hilda must grow up to piece together for herself. When H.D. later wrote that "my Muse is an old doll" that "I hug . . . to my heart," she might well have had Mamalie in mind (*Compassionate Friendship* 62).

The intimate muse and Moravian gynopoetics of *The Gift* fulfill the narrator's warning: "we must not step right over into the transcendental, we must crouch near the grass and near to the earth that made us. And the people who created us" (MSS I, 29–30). At first glance, it seems as if the poet/prophet of *Trilogy* does not have her feet on the ground. The Lady performs the function of Mamalie, but is clearly a transcendental figure. The poet is not a "naïf" child reciting Greenaway. She defiantly occupies the masculine position and voice to utter her gynocentric message of peace and rebirth: "*I John saw,*" she authoritatively states to introduce her revelation of the Lady and the rainbow span of heaven.[54] However, read intertextually with *The Gift, Trilogy* reveals the presence of the personal in the mythic, the earth in the transcendental, the "little tradition" in the Great Tradition of the epic. Like the Kristevan Semiotic that erupts into the discourse of the Symbolic, *The Gift* exists inside *Trilogy* as a major force feminizing the masculine epic tradition within which *Trilogy* situates itself.

The intimacy of autobiography colors the prosody of *Trilogy,* which, as Alicia Ostriker has argued, is boldly light, conversational, and open ended, sharply at odds with the weightier rhythms and lines of epic or meditative long poems by men ("The Open Poetics of H.D."). Many of the image clusters and repetitive motifs in *The Gift* resonate with those that establish the major lyric units of *Trilogy.* The worm on the grass blade in *The Walls Do Not Fall,* for example, is a major persona for the poet, one that recalls the warning in *The Gift* to "crouch near the grass" before moving into the transcendental. The spare meeting house of the poet's dream of the Christos in *The Walls Do Not Fall* universalizes the stark sanctum of the Moravian Church in Bethlehem. The figures of Mamalie and Papalie, Mama and Papa are personal versions of the divine figures that people *Trilogy.* Even the Lady, who is so much more formal than Mamalie, appears in *Tribute to the Angels* as an interruption, a disruption of the poet's mediations on the angels around God's throne – as if to insist that the gynocentric vision articulated in *The Gift* must insert its presence in the discourse of the Symbolic in which the poet had been engaged. The narrator's free-associational movement from the in-time of history – specifically, the Nazi bombs and their aftermath – to the out-of-time of memory and myth provides the narrative shape of the poet/prophet's quest to read the ruins and runes in *Trilogy*. In short, everything in *The Gift* and *Trilogy* has both a personal and a transcendental form, one of which dominates the prose, the other the poetry. Both, however, are present in each. "Everything is the same, yet in the great tide-wave of moving everything is different," the narrator comments in *The Gift* (MSS III, 15). "The same – different – the same attributes, / different yet the same as before," the poet says in *Trilogy* (*Collected Poems* 570).

As a poem that bears witness to the Nazi holocaust and celebrates the rebirth of civilization, *Trilogy* acts out on the stage of history what *The Gift* performed in relation to the family. In its structure, *Trilogy* repeats the transferential scene of self-analysis in *The Gift*, which itself repeated and extended the transference H.D. worked through with Freud. As in *The Gift*, the developmental movement of *Trilogy* moves forward by moving backward from the Oedipal to the pre-Oedipal, from the paternal transference to the maternal.[55] *The Walls Do Not Fall* works through the attachment to the All-Father, the Amen-Ra or Ram who is the transcendental incarnation of Papalie, nicknamed the Goat. After dreaming of the amber-eyed Christos, the poet enters the mystery of the dying god, the Osiris ("O-Sire-is") who mythologizes her wounded father and the wandering tribes of persecuted Moravians and American Indians under the leadership of Zinzendorf, the man who loved outcasts. *Tribute to the Angels* tunnels more deeply into the psyche of the poet to produce three manifestations of the primal Mother, each of whom repeats some aspect of Mamalie's presence to Hilda in *The Gift:* first, the "bitter, bitter jewel" in the crucible that fused into "mer, mere, mère, mater, Maia, Mary, // Star of the Sea, / Mother," recalling the dark Mary of Hilda's snake dream; second, the sign of resurrection sent by the goddess in the half-burnt out, blossoming may-apple tree, at the sight of which the poet hears the mystic music of the spheres, like Mamalie's musical epiphany; and third, the dream of the Lady who carries the blank book of the new, a hieratic avatar of Mamalie herself as the child's muse. *The Flowering of the Rod* crowns the uncrowned Queen by unveiling Mary Magdalene, the epitome of despised womanhood, as a vision of the lost Atlantis, the land where the promise of peace is kept. *Trilogy* ends its backward–forward movement in the lap of the Great Mother, whose "shy and simple" presence flowers in the fragrance "from the bundle of myrrh / she held in her arms" (*Collected Poems* 612). She holds not the

Son, but the power of her own (pro)creativity, her "gift" to the poet, and the poet's "gift" to the world. Mamalie's "gift" to her "gifted" granddaughter returns in *Trilogy* in the form of the poet's gyno-vision of (re)birth for a world caught in the death spiral of war.

Coda: Bridging the Double Discourse in H.D.'s Oeuvre

> There is a bridge needed, but possibly if there had been the bridge, I would have worked at neither.
>
> H.D., *Compassionate Friendship* (28)

> the same – different – the same attributes,
> different yet the same as before.
>
> H.D., *Trilogy* (571)

The bridge between H.D.'s poetry and prose was always there to be endlessly sought and resisted, as the clairvoyant memoir and intimate epic, *The Gift* and *Trilogy*, demonstrate. In *Compassionate Friendship*, H.D. contrasted the self ("an octave above my ordinary self") represented in her verse drama *Hippolytus Temporizes* with the prosaic self inscribed in *Palimpsest*, written at the same time. But her assessment of the symbiotic (dis)connection between her poetry and prose applies to her entire oeuvre. Some tenuous and fluid bridge was necessary to keep the prose and poetry selves from spinning schizophrenically out of the psyche in which they originated, to which they referred. But this bridge, like all bridges, separated as well as connected the two. The link between them depended on their difference.

The polarities between H.D.'s poetry and prose existed to be continuously broken and reconstituted like the pattern of Penelope's weaving. *Penelope's Web* has variously explored their difference, the prose *as* difference, and the difference the prose makes for H.D.'s poetry and modernism in general. The authoritative, yet conversational and intimate persona of *Trilogy* was first made in the wordshop of *The Gift* before it was reconstituted in the narrative poem. The layered psyche resisting and recovering the past in *Helen in Egypt* first unraveled in the self-reflecting writing cures of texts like *Palimpsest* and *Tribute to Freud*. The (pro)creative poet of *Hermetic Definition* reconfigured the personae of *Notes on Thought and Vision, Asphodel,* and *Madrigal.* Initially occupying the position of "woman" in relationship to H.D.'s poetry, the prose, as a discourse of difference, fundamentally changed "the early H.D." Moreover, like women in the fabric of patriarchy, H.D.'s prose disrupts the Symbolic order of modernism, with its language of excess, its repetitions, its reweavings of self and society from the position of Other.

Yet I would like to conclude by suggesting briefly what the discourse of difference suppresses: namely, the discourse of the same. The difference between H.D.'s early prose and poetry ultimately brought the two voices closer together in the production of increasingly personal poetry and hermetic prose. Initially constructed as opposites, the impersonal poet and the personal prose writer did not remain in fixed opposition. Each was necessary to the other, and, for that, each retained its distinctness in fluid interplay. The poet remained more clairvoyant and prophetic, concerned with all-time and the mythic out-of-time; the poems continued to be "bridges to the sacred," to quote Morris again. The prose writer remained more personal and autobiographical, concerned with the historical in-time; novels and memoirs continued to work through the intimate "tangles" of the poet who is therapeutically reconstituted in the prose text. Distinct as they were, they nonetheless changed each other dramatically. The poet became increasingly more personal and narrative, while the prose writer, especially the novelist, was lyric and increasingly clairvoyant.

H.D. both wanted the bridge between poetry and prose, between the impersonal and the personal, and did not want it, for fear that integration would preclude the need to write. Her writing, she believed, depended on the pain of splittings, divisions, separations: the diaspora of her Otherness. This retreat from and advance toward a bridge between poetry and prose took two major forms throughout her writing career: first, the existence of paired prose and poetic texts, two discourses shaping the same material in different ways, the one largely historical, the other generally mythological; and second, the creation of hybrid texts that oscillate unendingly among prose and poetic forms both affirmed and subverted.

Penelope's Web has mentioned the existence of paired texts in H.D.'s writing through World War II – such nonidentical twins as *The Gift* and *Trilogy;* "Murex" and "Lethe"; *HER* and poems like "Oread," "Heat," and "Huntress"; *Madrigal* and the trio of "Eros," "Amaranth," and "Envy"; "Two Americans" and "Red Roses for Bronze"; *Nights* and *The Dead Priestess Speaks; Tribute to Freud* and *The Flowering of the Rod.* Read intertextually with the poetry, the prose provides the narrative and historical reference that has been largely distilled out of the lyric and

mythic poems. After the war, this pattern of repetition of paired discourses continued unabated. The writing cure accomplished in *The Gift*
led directly to *Trilogy*, but it in no sense represented a position of fixity.
H.D.'s severe physical and mental breakdown in 1946 set the pattern in
motion once again, leading as the events of World War I had done to
another decade or so of extraordinary creative production. In historical
novels, romans à clef, and memoirs, H.D. once again used prose to
reconstitute the poet who then reappeared in her poems of the 1950s.

Through acts of interpretation and inscription, *Helen in Egypt* repeats
the fluid (re)constructions of identity narrated in the Madrigal cycle, but
the epic is most immediately paired with the "prose trilogy" of Delia
Alton: *The Sword Went Out to Sea* (1946–7), *White Rose and the Red* (1948),
and *The Mystery* (1949, 1951). H.D. considered them necessary preparation for the writing of *Helen in Egypt,* which she began in the fall of
1952 "after my first summer of freedom from the overwhelming drive
that had forced me through, yet sustained me in the writing of the three
novels" (*Compassionate Friendship* 94). "The prose phase," she continued,
"was finished, you might say, the story was recorded. But there was
still the poetry, I discovered to my surprise," "the final epitome of the
novel or the novels in the *Helen* poems. I am alive in the *Helen* sequence"
(94, 65). At the same time, she resisted any suggestion that the novels,
so close in spirit to the epic, could not stand on their own. To Pearson,
she expressed her annoyance at someone who told her, "I feel really that
you should keep this theme [in *The Sword,* of hearing spirits from the
dead warn about the third World War] under your cloak and make a
poem of it" (28 December 1958). These novels are among the least
successful of H.D.'s prose texts. *White Rose and the Red,* about the Pre-
Raphaelites, and the Moravian novel, *The Mystery,* work neither as autobiography nor as history novels. *The Sword Went Out to Sea,* as spir-
itualist séance, moves uneasily from journalistic reportage to hermetic
dreamscapes. In the symbiosis of paired texts, *Helen in Egypt* explodes
vibrantly out of these relatively dead novels.

End to Torment, which rescripts the much earlier *HER,* stands more
successfully alone and with its twin, *Winter Love,* a mythologized reconstruction of H.D.'s renewed relationship with Pound in the 1950s
after his release from St. Elizabeth's. *Thorn Thicket,* her last memoir,
and *Hermetic Definition,* her final poem, are also interlocking texts. Both
are summations – "definitions" – of the personal and impersonal, the
intimate and the hieratic, in the interpenetrating spaces of her life and
writing. Distinct as a prose journal and a hieratic poem, they are nonetheless overlapping texts. About a vulnerable, aging woman poet who
falls in love with a young man whom she (re)births in the esoteric region
of the poem, *Hermetic Definition* is the most singularly hermetic *and*

personal poem she ever wrote. *Thorn Thicket*, as a meta-commentary on her oeuvre, relooks at the dynamics of *Eros* and *Thanatos* as they structured her heterosexual relationships and inscriptions of them in texts like *Madrigal*, whose story in particular is unwoven and rewoven.

The symbiosis of prose and poetry also existed in the hybrid texts H.D. began writing as early as *Notes on Thought and Vision*. Sometimes this hybridization took the form of texts with double discourses. "Hymen," the opening poem of the first volume after *Sea Garden*, experimentally alternates prose and poetic voices; the issues of the marriage masque are then explored further in the explicitly gendered, often narrative, myth poems that follow. H.D. wrote with enthusiasm to Bryher about this new form and was delighted with Bryher's praise: "I am really made very happy over your acceptance of *Hymen* [the poem] as a form. I have already planned four or five others – would you call them masques? . . . poems, with prose-intervals and music" (14 February 1919). Her translation of *Ion*, begun during World War I and completed in 1935, continues the practice of alternating prose and poetry. Freely rendered translations of Euripides are interwoven with extended, interpretive "stage directions" in prose. *By Avon River*, whose composition framed H.D.'s 1946 breakdown, opens with a narrative poem in tribute to Shakespeare written before her illness and concludes with an essay on Shakespeare and the Elizabethan Age written just after her recovery. *Helen in Egypt* is a lengthy sequence of lyric poems organized on the narrative principle of reflective self-analysis. Each lyric is introduced by a prose voice which comments on the poetry, much as H.D. reflected upon her own work in *H.D. by Delia Alton*, *Compassionate Friendship*, and *Thorn Thicket*. The prose insets in *Helen in Egypt*, written after the lyrics were completed, do not provide authoritative readings of the lyrics, but rather, in their rhetoric of indeterminacy, emphasize the Penelopean endlessness of (re)interpretation and inscription.

Conversely, much of H.D.'s prose is highly lyrical, the Semiotic register of language repeatedly bursting the confines of the Symbolic, narrative modality – so much so that many commentators on her work stressed the hybrid nature of her texts, particularly her fiction, which belongs, like Woolf's, in the tradition of the lyric novel. She herself told Cournos in reference to *Asphodel* that she was "neck deep in a novel – I mean a prose-poem the length of a novel" (4 July 1922). Publishing *Palimpsest* in the United States, Ferris Greenslet compared it to her "crystallized" poems (Letter to H.D., 25 May 1926). One review of *Hedylus* was titled "An Imagist Novel," a phrase which could have served equally for *Paint It To-Day* and *HER*, had H.D. published them. Much later, the lawyer who reviewed *Madrigal* for possible libel wrote: "The book has the fascination of a powerful dream, now glorious, now nightmarish.

It is really a poem, a tremendous poem" (Pearson, Letter to H.D., 2 November 1959). Not only lyrical, these prose texts often record the process of producing a poem, much like Joyce showed the making of Stephen's villanelle in the final chapter of *Portrait of the Artist as a Young Man*. The prose narrative encases a lyric poem, in fact provides the narrative reference that the poems of "the early H.D." denied in their impersonalism.

Hybridization is paradoxical, on the borders of oxymoron, of taint and taboo. Breaking what Derrida called the "law of genre" against linguistic miscegenation, a hybrid is a new species in which the strands of its component parts are still distinctively present ("Law"). As a synthesis, it retains a split reference to its origin in difference and is constantly threatened with regression. H.D.'s prose-poems, lyrical novels, and paired texts simultaneously gesture at the bridge that connects the oppositional discourses of her poetry and prose and at the gap between that kept her writing. It was the difference that made all the difference.

> Frail is the thread and long,
> pale is the hand and fragile,
> busy upon the loom,
> day and night, night and day,
> re-weaving with threads of gold,
> cyclamen, purple and blue,
> the pattern, the history,
> the legend;
>
> H.D., *Winter Love* (94)

Chronology: Dating H.D.'s Writing

The chart below[1] provides dates for the composition and publication of H.D.'s work, including volumes of poetry and translation, book-length poems, novels and novellas, shorter prose fiction assembled into volumes, short stories published in periodicals after 1913, film essays, volumes of personal/meditative essays, and memoirs. It includes published and unpublished work, as well as texts that have been destroyed. It does not include the stories H.D. wrote and partially published between 1907 to 1913; her reading notebooks (e.g., for *Helen in Egypt;* on Dante); her brief diaries not prepared for publication (e.g., Paris 1912 diary; Lionel Durand 1960–1 diary); her signed and unsigned book reviews; periodical publication of individual poems; and foreign editions or translations of her work.[2] Republication dates and partial publication information may be incomplete because of the numerous reprintings of H.D.'s work by small, avant-garde presses.

I have determined or estimated dates for the composition, destruction, submission, and rejection of manuscripts from the following sources: (1) dates recorded on manuscripts and published volumes; (2) H.D.'s dating of her own writing in texts like "Autobiographical Notes," *H.D. by Delia Alton, Advent, End to Torment, Thorn Thicket, Compassionate Friendship,* and *Hirslanden Notebooks;* (3) correspondence, especially letters to and/or from H.D., Bryher, Norman Holmes Pearson, Richard Aldington, John Cournos, Marianne Moore, George Plank, Robert McAlmon, Robert Herring, Viola Jordan, or Silvia Dobson; (4) Louis Silverstein's remarkable *H.D. Chronology,* a work in progress. I have included information about manuscripts destroyed, submitted for publication, and rejected where I have come across such references, but I suspect that more information will come to light in the future. Question marks indicate uncertainty of dating. The chart reflects my best knowledge and estimates as of November 1989 and will undoubtedly need revision as more about H.D.'s life becomes known.

By the 1940s, H.D. regularly dated her manuscripts and published volumes. But, as a note of caution, I would emphasize that she may have fictionalized some dates to give the work a favorable "natal" horoscope. She wrote in *Thorn Thicket,* for example, "I have dated the *Rose* 1948, and to *The Sword went out to Sea* that preceeded [*sic*] in [it?], 1947. I gave *The Sword* dates, Part I (Kusnacht, Lausanne), May 6, Professor Freud's birthday, and to Part II (Lausanne, Lugano), July 17, the annivery [*sic*] of the day that I met Bryher in Cornwall" (28).

The various noms de plume that appeared on H.D.'s manuscripts and publications are an important part of the composition of her texts because each name crystallized a different identity for the writer as she both made and was (re)made by each text. She used the name H.D. for almost all her published works, with the exceptions of her pre–1913 stories, published under the name Edith Gray; "Pontikonisi (Mouse Island)," by Rhoda Peter; *Nights,* by John Helforth; and "Ear-Ring," by D. A. Hill. A number of manuscripts carried other names on the title page: *Paint It To-Day,* by Helga Dart; *HER,* by Helga Doorn (H.D.'s film name); *Bid Me to Live (A Madrigal), Majic Ring, The Sword Went Out to Sea (Synthesis of a Dream), White Rose and the Red, H.D.* by Delia Alton, *The Mystery,* and *Magic Mirror,* by Delia Alton. Other manuscripts had no names on the title page, such as *Asphodel* and *Pilate's Wife.* H.D. was dissuaded from using the name D. A. Hill for *The Hedgehog* and Delia Alton for *Bid Me to Live.*

Title	Composition	Publication
Sea Garden (poems)	1912–15 or 1916	1916, 1983
Choruses from Iphigeneia in Aulis (translation)	1913?	1916, 1919, 1925, 1983
Choruses from Iphigeneia in Aulis *and the* Hippolytus *of Euripides* (translation)	1913?	1919, 1925, 1983
Notes on Euripides, Pausanius, and Greek Lyric Poets (essays, translation)	1916?–18?; fall 1919; fall 1920	Portions: "People of Sparta," 1924; "Choruses from the Bacchae," 1931; prose in *Ion,* 1937; "The Wise Sappho," 1982
Notes on Thought and Vision (essay)	July 1919	1982

Hymen (poetry, with prose insets in "Hymen")	1916, 1918?–21	1921, 1925, 1983
Paint It To-Day (novel)	1921	Chapters 1–4, 1986
Asphodel (novel)	1921–2	In press
Untitled ("prose work": three "long short stories" planned as a volume) to include: "Floriel," "Behind Me a Sword," "Beryl"	1922	Destroyed
Heliodora (poetry)	1916, 192[?]–4	1924, 1925, 1983
Collected Poems (poetry and translation)	1912–24	1925
Hippolytus Temporizes (verse drama)	1920, 1922, 1924, 1925	Portion: 1925. Whole, 1927, 1985
Palimpsest (story sequence/novel): "Secret Name," "Hipparchia," "Murex"	Spring 1923 1924–?	1926, 1968
"Pontikonisi (Mouse Island)" (story)	1924	1932
Niké (novel)	1924–?	Destroyed
Hedylus (novel)	1924–?	Portion: 1925 Whole: 1928, 1980
Pilate's Wife (novel)	1924, 1929, July–August 1934	Submitted and rejected
The Hedgehog ("children's" novel)	1924, 1926–7, 193[?]	1936
HER (novel)	1926, 1927?, 1930	1981
Close Up reviews (11 film-review essays)	1927–9	4: 1927; 5: 1928; 2: 1929
Narthex (novella)	1927 or 1928	1928
The Usual Star (includes 2 stories): "The Usual Star," "Two Americans"	Augumn 1928 1930	1934
Borderline (essay)	1929 or 1930	1930
"Low Tide" (story or novella)	1931 or 1932	Destroyed

Red Roses for Bronze (poetry and translation)	1924–?	1931, 1983
Kora and Ka (includes 2 novellas):	July–August 1930	Whole: 1934
Kora and Ka, Mira-Mare		Without *Mira-Mare*: 1978
Nights (novella in two parts):		1935, 1986
"Prologue,"	Summer, December 1934	
"Nights"	August–September 1931	
Euripides' Ion (translation with prose insets)	1916, 1919, Summer 1934, August 1935	1937, 1986
"Ear-Ring" (story)	?	1936
The Dead Priestess Speaks (poetry)	1931–8 (?)	Portions: 1931, 1933, 1937 Whole: 1983
The Moment (short-story volume):	January 1950	—
"The Moment,"	1926	
"Jubilee,"	1935	
"The Last Time,"	1936	
"Hesperia,"	1923, 1934, 1948	
"AEgina,"	1933	
"The Guardians"	1945	
The Seven or *Seven Stories*[3] (short-story volume):	1960	—
"Hesperia,"	1924, 1934, 1948	
"AEgina,"	1932	
"The Moment,"	1926	
"Jubilee,"	1935	
"The Last Time,"	1935	
"The Death of Martin Presser,"	194?	1965
"The Guardians"	1945–6	

Bid Me to Live (A Madrigal) (novel)	February 5–March 30, July 27–November 8, 1939; autumn/winter 1947; November 1948; December 1949–June 1950	1960, 1983
Within the Walls (14 sketches)	Summer 1940–Spring 1941	1990
The Gift (autobiography)	1941; 1943; 1944	Portions: Chapter 3, 1969; Chapter 1, 1981; Chapter 2, 1986 Abridged edition: 1982
Chapters 1–6	1941?	
Chapter 7	1943	
Notes	June, July 1944	
The Walls Do Not Fall (poetry, Volume 1 of *Trilogy*)	1942	1944, 1973, 1983
Majic Ring (novel)	1943, 1944, April 1954	—
What Do I Love? (poetry)	1941, 1943, 1944	1944, 1983
Tribute to the Angels (poetry, Volume 2 of *Trilogy*)	May 17–31, 1944	1945, 1973, 1983
Writing on the Wall (essay/memoir, later titled *Tribute to Freud*)	September 19–November 2, 1944	1945–6, 1956, 1974, 1985
The Flowering of the Rod (poetry, Volume 3 of *Trilogy*)	December 18–31, 1944	1946, 1973, 1983
By Avon River		1949, 1990
(poetry): "Good Frend"	April 23, 1945?	
(essay): "The Guest"	September 19–November 1, 1946	

The Sword Went Out to Sea (Synthesis of a Dream) (novel)	Part 1: December 1946–May 6, 1947; Part 2: May–July 17, 1947	Submitted and rejected
White Rose and the Red (novel)	1947?, summer 1948	Submitted and probably rejected
Advent (journal/essay, later published in *Tribute to Freud*)	December 1948	1974, 1985
H.D. by Delia Alton (journal/essay, titled *Notes on Recent Writing* by Norman Holmes Pearson)	December 12, 1949–June 5, 1950	Portion: 1983. Whole: 1986
"Autobiographical Notes" (3 chronologies and notes)	1949?	—
The Mystery (novel)	Part 1: 1949; Part 2: 1951	Portion: Chapters 3 and 14–19, 1976
Helen in Egypt (poetry with prose captions)		1961, 1974
"Pallinode"	September 1952–Winter 1952–3	
"Leuké"	August 1953–?	
"Eidolon"	January 1954, September–October 1954	
Prose captions	1955	
Magic Mirror (novel)	January 1, 1955[6?]–1956	—
Compassionate Friendship (journal/essay)	February 18, 1955–September 21, 1955	—
Selected Poems (poetry)	Selection and correction, 1956	1957
Hirslanden Notebooks (4 journals)		—
I	January 26–February 3, 1957	

II	n.d.	
III	February 4–11, 1957	
IV	October 1958; February 1959; April 1959	
Vale Ave (poetry)	Spring 1957	Sections 5, 37: 1958; Section 18: 1958 Whole: 1982
Sagesse (poetry, in *Hermetic Definition*)	June 9, 1957– Winter 1957	Sections 1–10, 1958 Whole: 1972
End to Torment (essay/memoir)	March 7–July 13, 1958	1979
Winter Love (Espérance) (poetry, in *Hermetic Definition*)	January 3– April 15, 1959	Portion: 1969 Whole: 1972
Thorn Thicket (journal/essay)	January 1– October 27, 1960	—
Hermetic Definition (poetry, in *Hermetic Definition*)		Pirated edition, 1971
I	August 17– September 24, 1960	Authorized edition, 1972
II	November 1– December 24, 1960	
III	January 24– February 19, 1961	

Notes

Introduction

1 For other readings of Penelope, see Marcus, "Still Practice"; Kamuf, *Signature Pieces;* and Karen Lawrence, *Penelope Voyages.* In these deconstructions, Marcus defined Penelope's aesthetic as "a poetics of commitment" (84); Kamuf read Penelope "as a shuttling figure in power's household" who succeeds in deferral and represents how "a woman's text plots the place of its own undoing" (147–8); Lawrence, adapting Michel Serres's *Hermes,* saw in Penelope how "woman, both inside and outside the narrative, destabilizes the geography of narrative theorizing and the journey plots as well" (13). For a cross-cultural discussion of weaving and spinning in relation to feminism, see Weigle, *Spiders.*

2 Although Jardine noted that she wanted to determine the possibility of the female subject within the context of post-structuralist theories of the feminine, she in fact scarcely addressed the issue of women as writers in *Gynesis.* By modernity, Jardine clarified, she was not referring to modernism, but rather to post-structuralist thought emanating primarily from France (22–3). But many of the French writers Jardine discussed find their exempla in avant-garde writers and thinkers associated with Continental and Anglo-American "modernism." The "modernity" she identified is, I believe, a "post"-modernist matrix, one that intensifies currents already present in modernism. Consequently, I think her analysis is relevant to modernism.

3 For other recent literary histories that ignore, trivialize, or tokenize women, see Schwartz, *The Matrix of Modernism* and Levenson, *The Genealogy of Modernism.* Kiely's *Modernism Reconsidered* is an important exception.

4 See also Barthes, "From Work to Text" (*Rustle* 56–64), and my discussion of anonymous intertextuality in Barthes (and Kristeva) and of Miller's reinsertion of the author into a concept of "political intertextuality" in "Weavings."

5 See also the gender narrative for modernism that Gilbert and Gubar propose in *The War of the Words* – namely, the ongoing battle between the sexes in which women's growing literary powers led to anxiety, hostility, and violent fantasies in male writers, which in turn led to increased anxiety and fear in women writers. As I have argued in my review of the book, I value their insistence that we confront the violence of and in discourses of modernism; but I find their iden-

367

tification of a single "meta-narrative" for modernism ultimately reductive. I have found the dialogic interplay of *gynesis* and *arachnology* more flexible and useful for a reading of gender in modernism and in H.D.'s work. *Penelope's Web* was completed before Volumes 2 and 3 of *No Man's Land* became available.

6 See Boughn, "Bibliographic Record." He listed one piece published in 1909; six in 1910; two in 1911; four in 1912; and one in 1913. These short short stories mainly appeared in the *Boston Globe*, syndicated by the Associated Literary Press. Four more unpublished early stories exist in manuscript at Beinecke. H.D. described her early writing in letters to Pearson as some "Sunday stories," signed Edith Gray, and a few "child-astronomical articles" she did "as Hilda Doolittle for the Sunday Pres.[byterian] paper" (20 April 1949; 22 June 1949[?]).

7 For titles, see the Chronology, Dating H.D.'s Writing, in this volume. H.D. also left some of her poetry unpublished, though not nearly as much as her prose. A carefully ordered volume of poems from the 1930s entitled *The Dead Priestess Speaks* composes the bulk of the unpublished poetry that Martz included in *Collected Poems, 1912–1944*. A number of major poems from the 1950s H.D. prepared for publication and sent to Pearson, who arranged for the publication of selections in various poetry journals and for the appearance of *Helen in Egypt* just before her death. *Hermetic Definition, Sagesse, Winter Love,* and *Vale Ave* – all written in the late 1950s and early 1960s – appeared in the 1970s and 1980s.

8 See Gilbert, *Acts of Attention* for the relation between prose and poetry in Lawrence's oeuvre. Many modernists, of course, wrote prose and poetry, but either one discourse took precedence over the other (Joyce, Williams, Langston Hughes); one discourse preceded the other (William Faulkner, Richard Wright); or the poets who wrote prose (Eliot, Pound, and Moore) mainly did so as critics, not as fiction writers.

9 Barthes's sweeping generalizations about the difference between "classical" and "modern" poetry and prose do not, in my opinion, hold up under careful scrutiny, but I find them suggestive for reading H.D.'s gendered modernism.

10 See also Hanscombe and Smyers, *Writing for Their Lives* for an extended account of Marsden's relationship with early modernism (141–50, 161–9).

11 The review of Mew's *The Farmer's Bride* does not allude to the war, but the long selection H.D. chose to quote presents a daughter gazing at a radiant portrait of her mother, a passage that anticipates the figure of the mother in *Trilogy*.

12 See *Advent* (129–30) for a description of this visit. Winifred Bryher (1894–1983), daughter of Britain's wealthiest shipowner (Sir John Ellerman), was a writer H.D. met in July of 1918, and lived with off and on until 1946. They remained intimate in an intense, companionate relationship until H.D.'s death in 1961. See Guest, *Herself Defined* for a vivid portrait of Bryher.

13 See also DuPlessis's discussion of *Notes* in relation to the authority of the woman writer to speak her Otherness (*Career* 39–41); see Gelpi's analysis of the epiphanal "spots of time" in his introduction to *Notes* (9–12).

14 This image of the poet as doubly child and mother anticipates the psycho-dynamics of mother–daughter desire described by Nancy Chodorow, who hypothesized that mothers relive the pleasure of their infancy in nurturing their babies (*Reproduction* 201). In using the term *maternal body*, I am of course echoing Kristeva's psycholinguistic category for the pre-Oedipal register in language (see *Desire* 210–36; "Women's Time"). For a discussion of H.D.'s procreative imagery in the context of the childbirth metaphor for creativity, see my "Creativity"; for childbirth and motherhood in H.D.'s writing, see Hollenberg, "Nursing the Muse."

15 See especially Woolf's "A Sketch of the Past" in *Moments of Being*.

16 See for example Cixous, "The Laugh of the Medusa," Irigaray, "When Our Lips Speak Together" (*This Sex* 205–18), and Yaeger's discussion of how the "feminine" as defined in French feminist theory has already been inscribed by many women poets (*Honey-Mad Women*).

17 City Lights, which published *Notes* for the first time, inserted highly suggestive "Os" (perfect spheres/empty ciphers) for the two-inch line H.D. used throughout the text to separate the brief sections.

18 For discussions of H.D.'s involvement in cinema and its impact on her writing, see especially Friedberg; Morris, "Projection"; Guest, *Herself Defined* 189–201; Mandel; Peck; Diepeveen; and Brown.

19 See H.D.'s account of a dream catalyzed by Dietrich, in *Advent* (180–1), and Mandel's discussion of her identification with Garbo ("Helen/Garbo").

20 For extended discussion of the impact of the Harlem Renaissance on the formation of H.D.'s modernism, see my "Modernism of the 'Scattered Remnant.' " Copies of the film *Borderline,* which has been shown a number of times in recent years, are at the George Eastman House in Rochester, New York, and the Museum of Modern Art in New York City. Friedberg has pieced together some fragments of film from *Wing Beat* and *Foothills,* which are now housed at the Museum of Modern Art (Friedberg, "The POOL Films"). For discussion of the making and reception of *Borderline,* see Friedberg, "Approaching *Borderline.*"

21 This is the same film that Adrienne Rich featured quite differently in "Cartographies of Silence" in *The Dream* (16–20).

22 H.D.'s view of Russian films may well have been influenced by Bryher, who thoroughly researched and passionately advocated Russian cinema. See her *Film Problems of the Soviet Union* (1929).

23 H.D.'s descriptions of the Elizabethan period in "The Guest" (the prose portion of *By Avon River*) and of Euripides in the mostly unpublished *Notes on Euripides, Pausanius, and Greek Lyric Poets* (1916–20) also screen an account of modernity. See de Man's association of modernity with all historical moments of great rupture (166–77).

24 As I discuss in Chapter 4, the borderline metaphor also signifies the increasingly intense sense of homelessness H.D. felt in the late 1920s and early 1930s.

25 For discussion of the care H.D. took not to collapse important differences between racial oppression and other forms of alienation, see my "Modernism of the 'Scattered Remnant.' "

26 See also Friedberg's discussion of the role of H.D. and Bryher in editing the 1,000 shots of *Borderline* ("Approaching *Borderline*").

27 For the use of such terms, which threaten to reinscribe traditional periodization and literary history, I certainly include my own readings here, in works like *Psyche Reborn*. My earlier efforts to place H.D.'s poetry in the "mainstream" of modernism have been usefully critiqued by Benstock, "Beyond the Reaches," and Schenck, "Exiled by Genre," who raise important questions about the ideological bases of categories such as "mainstream" and "margins." Terminology aside, many critics now place H.D.'s poetic achievement alongside that of Pound,

Eliot, Moore, and Williams; but many others still consider her a "minor" poet. For discussion of her reputation, see Bryer and Roblyer; and my "Hilda Doolittle."

28 See Showalter, "Feminist Criticism in the Wilderness," and Irigaray, "The Looking Glass" (*This Sex* 9–22).

29 See *Tribute to Freud* for H.D.'s extensive identification with the Delphic Pythoness. Definitive statements on H.D.'s poetic process are impossible to make because of the destruction and/or loss of poetic manuscripts prior to *Trilogy*, written in the 1940s. Aldington did note that H.D.'s earliest poems were the result of endless revision driven by perfectionism (*Life* 138–9). Productions of imagist poems are narrated in "Murex" (*Palimpsest*), *Hedylus*, and *Bid Me to Live (A Madrigal)*, in all of which the poet's initial inspired production is lineated and/ or cut and shaped at a later point. H.D. herself in a letter to Pearson about how she wrote her early poems noted that she would begin with "pseudo-automatic writing" done in school copybooks from which she would later "select the few lines that satisfied me" ("A Note on Poetry" 73). Her later composition of poetry may well have involved less revision. The school copybooks in which she penciled the lines of *Trilogy* and *Helen in Egypt* contain few changes, with an occasional line drawn through whole stanzas that she deleted. Diana Collecott has suggested to me that these copybooks may be revisions of earlier, now-lost manuscripts. Because H.D. by the 1940s had begun to save and date everything; however, I believe these manuscripts are the originals of poems that just "came as they came." Eric Walter White described H.D.'s astounding capacity to compose complete poems, in a trancelike state, on the spot, like the Pythoness (*Images of H.D.* 17).

30 See Rowbotham (67–80) for an analysis of women's work as repetitive. In "Still Practice," Marcus advocated a socialist/feminist aesthetic based on art as women's repetitive and daily work: "Penelope's art is work, as women cook food that is eaten, weave cloth that is worn, clean houses that are dirtied. Transformation, rather than permanence, is at the heart of this aesthetic" (84). For H.D.'s prose composition, I would emphasize the endlessness of women's work rather than its transformative power.

31 For H.D.'s references to prose submissions to and/or rejections from publishers (including Houghton Mifflin, Viking, Pantheon, Macmillan, Oxford, Unwin, Rupert Hart-Davis), see the following: for *The Hedgehog*, see *Thorn Thicket* (26); for *Pilate's Wife*, see *Compassionate Friendship* (61); for *The Sword Went Out to Sea*, see Letters to Pearson, 24 March, 18 April, 8 May, 17 June of 1951, 4 June 1954 and see Letters to Aldington, 16 September 1949, 2 June 19??, 6 June 19??; for *The Mystery*, see Letter to Pearson 18 April 1951; for "Hesperia," see Letter to McAlmon, 6 November 194?; for *White Rose and the Red*, see Letters to Aldington, 16 September 1949, 28 November 19??, see Letter to Pearson, 18 April 1951), and see Letter to Viola Jordan, 5 September 1947. See also Guest, *Herself Defined* (319) for a discussion of Aldington's attempt to get Hart-Davis to publish *Bid Me to Live*. I have come across only one reference to a rejection of poetry, although there are probably more in Pearson's papers: Karl Shapiro rejected a portion of *Helen in Egypt* submitted by Pearson to *Poetry* (Letter from Shapiro to Pearson, 28 May 1953).

32 See Pondrom, "Marianne Moore and H.D.," and the H.D.–Moore correspondence in general (e.g., Moore to H.D., 10 November 1916, 11 January 1921, 3 September 1922; H.D. to Moore, 3 September 1916, 17 January 1921, 22 June 1925).

33 See June Wayne's discussion of how male and female artists of the modern period have been forced to occupy the position of the feminine in relation to the social order; she partially attributed the extreme machismo of some male artists to their compensatory need to (re)establish their masculinity in a feminized cultural endeavor.

34 Several other men had played the role of buffer/agent before Pearson appeared: Pound, Aldington, and H. P. Collins (a critic with whom H.D. exchanged numerous letters in the 1920s; he arranged for her many unsigned reviews to appear in *The Adelphi;* see his unpublished memoir of H.D., probably written in the 1960s). But H.D. did some of her own negotiations with presses, especially in the 1920s and 1930s, with Ferris Greenslet at Houghton Mifflin and John McDougall of Chatto and Windus. To varying degrees, H.D.'s exchanges with the men who helped her into print carried erotic undertones (with the exception of Greenslet), which gives credence to Schmideberg's reading of the "family romance" in H.D.'s publishing history.

35 See Guest, *Herself Defined,* for allusions to resentment against Pearson as a power-hungry manuscript grabber (267). Whatever the truth of these underground allegations, the H.D.–Pearson correspondence establishes to my satisfaction Pearson's extraordinary importance to H.D. and the enormous amount of time he gave to the preservation and promotion of her work. "Your spiritual help and understanding of the MSS has meant everything to me," she wrote him (8 August 1949).

36 Caroline Zilboorg quoted Aldington's account of how H.D. destroyed a long poem that she wrote during the period when he was having an affair with Flo Fallas in the late summer and fall of 1916. But I have not seen a single other reference to H.D.'s destruction of poetry.

37 This is probably the manuscript H.D. identified as the "two or three story-sequences, as for the war experience in London and Cornwall" that she destroyed ("Autobiographical Notes" 11).

38 See Friedman and DuPlessis, "Two Loves Separate" for a discussion of the suppression of *HER.* H.D. also suppressed several autobiographical poems: "The Master," about her analysis with Freud (see DuPlessis and Friedman, " 'Woman Is Perfect' "); "Amaranth," "Eros," and "Envy," a trilogy of poems about her marriage that she published only years later in disguised form (see Martz, Introduction, *Collected Poems*); and *Winter Love,* about her renewed relationship with Pound in the 1950s, scheduled for publication as a coda for *Helen in Egypt,* but withdrawn by H.D. at the last moment because it was too personal to be included with the more impersonal *Helen* (see Pearson, Foreword, *Hermetic Definition viii*). As highly confessional poems about feelings and events H.D. did not want to disclose, these poems are the exception that proves the rule. On the whole, H.D. did not suppress her poems the way she did some of her sensitive prose texts.

39 See Breuer and Freud, *Studies in Hysteria* for discussion of the talking cure. The term, which has come to be associated with Freud's psychoanalytic therapy in general, originated with Bertha Pappenheim, the woman whom Breuer treated for hysteria from 1880–2 and about whom he wrote in his case history of Anna O. (*Studies* 14–31). Freud did not introduce the term "superego" into psycho-analysis until the 1920s, but the concept was present in his work as early as his contributions to *Studies in Hysteria*. For Freud's concepts of resistance, repetition, and working through in relation to his therapeutic technique, see especially "Further Recommendations: Repetition, Recollection, and Working Through." Throughout *Penelope's Web*, I will use these terms in accordance with Freud's basic definitions.

40   See Gilbert and Gubar's pathbreaking analysis of Woolf's essay for feminist poetics in *Madwoman* (16–23, *passim*).

41   In spite of Cixous's privileging of poetry in "The Laugh of the Medusa," she identified past signs of *écriture féminine* in the novelists Colette and Marguerite Duras, and in the playwright Jean Genêt (879). Joyce and the Brazilian novelist Clarice Lispector are also writers with whom Cixous has associated *écriture féminine*. See "Reaching the Point of Wheat."

42   See especially DuPlessis, *Career*, and Hirsh.

43   In her self-reflections, the only dissatisfaction she expressed about her poetry was about *Red Roses for Bronze* (*Advent* 148); negative assessments of her prose are, on the other hand, quite common.

44   See also Gubar's discussion of ambivalence in women writers invoked by the conflation of woman and textual body in " 'The Blank Page.' "

45   Aiken placed H.D. in the company of James and Joyce. See Mark Van Doren's review of *Palimpsest*, which links the novel with James, Woolf, and Joyce. Walter Kohn's "Con Amore," a review of *Hedylus*, praised her second published novel as "more intimate than Dorothy Richardson; more moving, more authentic, and more profound" than Woolf; "nowhere in contemporary English prose fiction is there any prose more exquisite than that of H.D.; and nowhere in English prose fiction are human emotions and experiences more immaculately reproduced" (200). *Palimpsest* received eight reviews, only two of which were negative (see Shanks, "Snootness," and Storm, "H.D.'s 'Palimpsest,' Limited to 700 Copies, Is Decipherable Only by a Very Few Clairvoyant Readers").

46   For some unknown reason, McAlmon's preface did not appear with *Palimpsest* until the 1968 revised edition.

47   For his letters soliciting her prose for Contact Editions, which he edited with Williams, see 1 October 1931 and 11 October 1932.

48   As always, Moore's praise meant a great deal to H.D. Before receiving Moore's letter, H.D. had written to George Plank about her discouragement at the negative responses of women, particularly several "devoted women friends" (unnamed, but not Bryher), who did not like this prose. She wondered if her work offended women by dealing with men or if it "doesn't just ring a bell," but was greatly relieved by Moore's enthusiasm, which proved that she could still reach women readers (16 October 1934; November[?] 1934). H.D.'s respect for Moore made her value her friend's praise even more; after Moore's review of *Heliodora* in *The Dial*, H.D. wrote her: "I value a word from you more than pages from others ... you know how much real intelligence does to prod one onwards" (8 January 1925[?]).

49   In "Autobiographical Notes," H.D. said "Ezra had written me most brutally about a section of *Hedylus* that had appeared in Paris magazine" (16); see also Guest, who called it clumsy (*Herself Defined* 165); like Moore and Dorothy Richardson, Sitwell frequently wrote admiring letters to H.D. about her work, especially about *Trilogy*.

50 Engel also objected to H.D.'s "longer poems" for their inability to "write narrative"; would he level this criticism at the long poems of Pound, Williams, and Eliot? Meyers also rejected H.D.'s poetry as "always narcissistic and ultimately self-reductive."

51 For discussions of women's experimental writing in the twentieth century, see Friedman and Fuchs, editors, *Breaking the Sequence*.

Chapter 1

1 The year of this key letter is uncertain. Like other letters to Cournos from Cornwall, this letter explicitly refers to her pleasure in the "sun, sea, wind, hills, birds, work both mental and physical." On July 9, 1918, H.D. was with Cecil Gray at Bosigran, near St. Ives, in Cornwall. In July of 1919, H.D. was in the Scilly Isles, Cornwall, with Bryher. The sequence of the letters in the files at Houghton Library places the July 9th letter with a group of 1918 letters (from April through August, when the letters essentially break off until the early 1920s). But both the undated 1918 letter from Cornwall and the letter of 17 July 1918 (both of which refer to her novel) suggest that the July 9th letter could have been written in the following year, after she would have sent him a draft. See Hollenberg's "Art and Ardor" for a selection of H.D.'s letters to Cournos; she dated the July 9th letter as "[c. 1920–1921]." The intimate tone of the July 9th letter is consistent with others written in 1916–19, but not consistent with the more distant letters from the early 1920s. Cournos's *The Mask,* which H.D. must have seen in manuscript, was published in 1919.

2 See Elliot (1–32) for a discussion of the concept and term "persona," and of Pound's important role in introducing the term into literary criticism. As Elliot pointed out, the Latin word *persona,* which refers to the mask an actor wore on stage, serves as the root for our words person and persona. Literary persona encodes a double reference to identity and mask (19–32).

3 See for example Kristeva, *Desire* (74–6, 124–47), *Revolution* (21–4), as well as Jardine's discussion of the death of the Cartesian subject in the discourses of modernity in *Gynesis*.

4 See Boughn, "Bibliographic Record" and note 5 in Introduction. For the significance of authorial names, see also Cohen.

5 The typescript for the unpublished *Asphodel* is divided into two volumes; citations will indicate the volume and page numbers. Edited by Robert Spoo, *Asphodel* is forthcoming from Duke University Press.

6 20 February 1932, quoted in White (18). See also H.D.'s concern about her name reflected in Cournos's roman à clef *Miranda Masters* (1–2).

7 Citations from Chapters 1–4 of *Paint It To-Day* are from the *Contemporary Literature* edition; citations from the remaining unpublished four chapters will be to the typescript at Beinecke and will be identified by chapter and page. Edited by Cassandra Laity, the full text of *Paint It To-Day* is in press, New York University Press.

8 Aldington has yet another version in *Life for Life's Sake*. He recalled being present at this inaugural scene, which he said took place in a Kensington bun shop and remembered that "I didn't like his insistence that the poems should be signed: 'H.D. Imagist,' because it sounded a little ridiculous. And I think H.D. disliked it too" (135). Pearson's undated notes from his interview were probably made some time in the late 1940s or early 1950s after he visited H.D. in Lugano. They are part of a file at Beinecke containing Pearson's extensive notes for a biography that he never wrote. All further citations from this file will be cited in the text as "Notes."

9 See also DuPlessis, *Career* (6–7) and Gilbert and Gubar, "Ceremonies" for discussions of the significance of H.D.'s names. Janice Robinson is correct in her identification of H.D.'s ambivalence toward Pound's role in launching her career. But I have seen no evidence that would support her undocumented assertions that H.D. was traumatized by Pound's "betrayal of trust," that Pound "robbed" her of the right to make a decision about the publication of her own work, or that she did not write the poems for "public exhibition" (36, 58). *End to Torment*, Aldington's recollections about their eagerness for Pound's help in getting published (*Life*), and Pearson's "Notes" suggest the opposite.

10 See for example Sinclair, "Two Notes" (88); Nardi (266); Lowell, *Tendencies* (279); Kreymborg, *Singing Strength* (347); Untermeyer, *American Poetry* (309).

11 For a contemporary parallel, see Goodman's discussion of Doris Lessing's publication of a novel under a pseudonym designed to fool her publisher, reviewers, and readers.

12 H.D. did not regard her literary names as "false" personae masking a "real" self; even the "real" person, Hilda Doolittle Aldington, was a persona, inseparable from her various names. In *Thorn Thicket*, H.D. reflected: "The *name?* The 'Poet,' yes, H.D. But the matrix of the gem, the human, suffering person or persona or mixed personalities, still 'share your name,' Aldington" (19).

13 Perhaps Gray's connection to her early nom de plume explains why H.D. regularly misspelled his name as "Grey."

14 Bryher in *West* and Bright Patmore in *No Tomorrow* also used the name Helga for their H.D. figures; both autobiographical texts explore the authors' love for H.D.

15 In *Tribute to Freud* and *Advent*, H.D. wrote extensively about Rodeck, using his own nom de guerre, Peter Van Eck. The Rhoda may also reflect the importance of rhododendron in H.D.'s poetry, particularly for the figure of Rhodocleia, the daemon of "The Dancer" and the deity of "The Master," poems written between 1933 and 1935 (*Collected Poems* 440–61). Rhoda Peter may also represent a double feminization – of Rhodes (the Greek island after which the male Rhodes fellowships were named) and Peter, the disciple who founded Roman Catholicism. My thanks to C. Carter for these associations.

16 See, for example, her letters to Pearson of 31 July 1948 and 1 April 1949. For the phrase "nom de paix," see Pearson's letter to H.D., 28 September 1958.

17 H.D. probably anticipated problems with getting Delia Alton on the cover page because she wrote to Aldington, "I sign it, Delia Alton, though I don't know yet, how any of that will work out" (23 February 195[9?]).

18   See letters from H.D. to Pearson, 17 September 1959, 26 September 1959, 28 September 1959.

19   See, for example, Kenner, *The Invisible Poet*.

20   For Eliot's complaint to Woolf about the accusations of coldness, see Ackroyd (107). For useful discussions of impersonalism and modernism, see, for example, de Man (166–76), Ellmann, Levenson, Albright, Menard, Hoffman, Moody, and Farwell.

21   See Eliot, "Hamlet" (*Selected Prose* 48) and "The Metaphysical Poets" (*Selected Prose* 65–6). Like the imagists, Eliot did not see the objective correlative as an innovation of modern poetry, but rather as a technique of transmutation present in "good" poetry.

22   Discussion of modernist impersonalism frequently centers on Eliot and Pound; with the exception of Farwell, critics have ignored the issue of gender and the role of women like H.D. and Moore in the formation of an aesthetic of impersonality. But see also Menard, who suggested that Eliot may have taken the concept of impersonality from an essay in *The Egoist* by Dora Marsden (142).

23   See Lowell's letter to H.D., 2 January 1917, in which she said that she had finally written to H.D.'s mother, who had supplied "merely the barest facts, as, she said, you were always so reticent about yourself."

24   The conversation is reported at third hand in Wolle's useful, but frequently inaccurate, chapter on H.D. in *A Moravian Heritage* (55–60). In a letter to H.D., Helen Doolittle was possibly showing some concern about H.D.'s response to another photo by pointing to Perdita's pride: "Gretchen sent me a cutting from the N. Y. Times Book Review on H.D. which I do not think you will object to – written by Herman S. Gorman & your picture taken at Montreux. Perdita saw it – greatly impressed – 'why is Mother's picture in the paper' & 'why do people read what Mother writes?' " (12 September 1924).

25   See Farwell's discussion of the interconnections between concepts of androgyny, modernist impersonalism, and New Criticism.

26   I am indebted to Alicia Ostriker for pointing out the revisionist aspect of H.D.'s pastorals. For a related, but different, discussion of H.D.'s imagist landscape which emphasizes its connection to Romanticism, see Laity's "H.D.'s Romantic Landscapes."

27   See *New Larousse* (170–1, 122, 130). Euripides's *Iphigenia in Tauris* centers on the shrine to Artemis of Tauris where all the shipwrecked were sacrificed to the goddess. Aphrodite Pelagia or Pontia was the goddess in her aspect of protector of sailors.

28   See for example, W. R. Johnson (1–3, 30–1, 35); James Johnson; Brooks (20–1); in spite of important differences, all stressed the lyric's emphasis on feeling, sensibility, or state of mind at the expense of narrative. See also my discussion of lyric convention in "Gender and Genre Anxiety" and "Lyric Subversion."

29   Untermeyer's review "Fire and Ice" begins with Robert Frost's poem of that title, which he used to characterize the poetry of Aline Kilmer, Elinor Wylie, and H.D., all of whom he compared to Dickinson. He described Kilmer as "sentimental" and Wylie as a poet of "frigid ecstasy," with "passion frozen at its source." For others who commented on the sculptural quality of H.D.'s lyric, see Harriet Monroe, *Poets and Their Art* (98); Aldington, "Modern Poetry" (201); Nardi; Marianne Moore, "Review of *Heliodora*." See also H.D.'s "Pygmalion" (1917) and "Red Roses for Bronze" (1929) in which the persona for the poet is a sculptor (*Collected Poems* 48, 211).

30 See DuPlessis's discussion of how the "demand for her perfection returns her covertly to the status of Muse" and canonizes her as "imagist saint (miracle worker and icon)" (*Career* 8, 31). For a related Irigarayan reading of H.D.'s capture into the fetishistic Image of imagism, see Hirsh, "Imaginary Images." For other discussions of H.D.'s "coldness" and "passion," see for example Troy; Bryher, "Spear-shaft"; Sinclair, "Poems," "Two Notes" (88); Lowell, *Tendencies* (275–6, 279); MacLeish; Aiken, "Review of *Palimpsest*"; Harriet Monroe, *Poets* (95–6); Flint, "Poetry"; Engel; Collins, *Modern Poetry*.

31 H.D.'s concept of the matrix bears an uncanny resemblance to the matrix jewels of contemporary science fiction writer Marion Zimmer Bradley, whose planet Darkover features powerful crystals that intensify psychic powers. H.D., often a reader of popular fiction and fantasy (such as Tolkein), would probably have been fascinated by Bradley's Darkover novels, as well as her *Mists of Avalon*.

32 See also Gregory, "Rose Cut in Rock."

33 For extended discussion of H.D.'s expatriation, see my "Exile"; for discussion of exile and expatriation in modernism, see Benstock, "Expatriate Modernism."

34 See especially Freud, *Interpretation of Dreams* (312–546). For discussions of the parallels between the dream-work and literary production, see for example Trilling; Rieff, *Freud* (140); Lacan, *Ecrits* (30–114, 146–79); and my *Psyche Reborn* (52–9, 304) and "Return." For other formulations of H.D.'s imagist encoding, see Benstock, *Left Bank* (327–8) and Jackson.

35 For discussion of the impact of this stereotype on women poets, see Ostriker, "What Do Women [Poets] Want?" and my "Gender and Genre Anxiety."

36 See also Untermeyer, *American Poetry* (311–12); Sinclair, "Poems"; Troy; Marianne Moore, Review of *Heliodora*; Bryher, "Spear-shaft (334, 337); Flint, "Poetry" (73); Nardi; MacLeish (587). See Greenwood for a discussion of "escapism" in H.D., and DuPlessis for H.D.'s use of the "Greek" as part of a strategy of self-authorization (*Career* 1–31).

37 H.D., Letter to Pearson, 12 December 1937, published as "A Note on Poetry," and reprinted in *Agenda*, the text from which I quote. See Collecott's discussion of this letter in "Memory and Desire."

38 I want to emphasize that I view this outline as a reconstruction, not a definitive account of "the facts." As Fredric Jameson argued in *The Political Unconscious*, "History" is "the Real," but we can only know it through its textualizations. Particularly sensitive to the problem of textualization and subjective fictionalizations, I have built this outline mainly from H.D.'s accounts in letters, journals, memoirs, and, with special care, her divorce papers and autobiographical novels. Aldington's letters from the front in 1918 provide important corroboration of H.D.'s versions of the events in this critical year. I have also found other memoirs, letters, and fictionalizations useful, especially those by Aldington, Bryher, Schaffner, McAlmon, Lawrence, Pound, Cournos, and Patmore. Silverstein's *H.D.: A Chronological Account* has been invaluable, as have the annotations of Pondrom and Hollenberg for H.D.'s letters to Flint and Cournos. Events related to H.D.'s prose will be documented in subsequent chapters. For other reconstructions, see Guest, Robinson, Crawford, and Satterthwaite.

39 Through the 1930s, H.D. wrote only three more poems and one sequence in this confessional mode. Two poems about Bryher, "We Two" and "Halcyon," appeared in *Heliodora* and *Red Rose for Bronze* (*Collected Poems* 164–5, 270–7), but, while autobiographical, neither addresses the intensities of anguish or erotic love. Perhaps because of their greater intimacy, she did not publish "I Said," also about Bryher, and "Child Poems," about herself, Peter Rodeck, and Perdita (*Collected Poems* 322–5, 341–8).

40 See especially Watt; Richetti; and Scholes and Kellog.

41 For discussions of women in the history of the novel, see for example Watt (43, 47, 137–8, 151–4, 193–4, 245–57); Richetti; Davidson; and Spencer. For discussions of the novel as a more-inviting genre for women than poetry, see especially Gilbert and Gubar, *Madwoman*.

42 See for example Foucault's "What Is an Author?"; Barthes's "The Death of the Author" (*Image*); Nancy K. Miller's "Arachnology" (*Subject*); Greenblatt's *Renaissance Self-Fashioning,* from which I have borrowed the title of this section.

43 For narrow definitions of autobiography, see for example Pascal and Gusdorf. For representative critiques of how concepts of the unitary, coherent, and singular self are inappropriate for women and therefore for women's autobiography, see Kolodny; Stanton, "Autogynography"; Mason; Jelinek, Introduction; Sidone Smith; and my "Autobiographical Selves." Some women have, of course, written autobiographies that narrate a coherent, ordered self in linear form; conversely, some men have written autobiographies in which the self is fragmentary and decentered.

44 See H.D., Letter to Aldington, 8 June 1951, and H.D., Letter to Pearson, 18 April 1951.

45 For related discussion of self-reflexivity in fiction and autobiography, see Hutcheon, Kellman, Waugh, and Elliot.

46 While Pascal's 1960 book has been very influential in the development of autobiography studies, many critics have abandoned his narrow definition of autobiography, one that even excludes diaries and journals. See Spengemann for a discussion of the debate about definitions (*xii–xiii*). See also Olney, *Metaphors and Autobiography* (3–25). In *Metaphors* Olney goes even further than Spengemann to say "a man's life work is his fullest autobiography" (3–4). For discussion of how narrow definitions have excluded women's life-writing, see Stanton, "Autogynography"; my "Autobiographical Selves"; Jelinek, Introduction; Mason; Mason and Green; Benstock, Introduction to *Private Self;* and Schenck, "All of a Piece."

47 For discussion of the roman à clef, see Richetti (120–6); for the historical novel, see Lukacs, Fleishman, and Manzoni.

48 For a discussion of *The Hedgehog* as a text exploring H.D.'s anxiety of authorship and prefiguring *Trilogy,* see Gubar, "The Echoing Spell."

49 Colette's life-writing (especially *Sido and My Mother's House*) and Ethel Smyth's multivolume memoirs may also have been important models. The

Beinecke collection also includes a number of important autobiographical prose manuscripts that H.D. did not prepare for publication: the "Paris Diary" (1912), her divorce papers (1937–8), "Autobiographical Notes" (1949?), *Hirslanden Notebooks* (1957–9), the "Lionel Durand Diary" (1960–1), the Dante notes (1948), the notes for *Helen in Egypt,* and the Zinzendorf notes. In addition, her vast correspondence, appointment diaries, and various other miscellaneous items should be regarded as self-creating "texts" of great importance. In subsequent chapters, I will draw on them where relevant.

50 See also Mason's brief discussion of H.D. (232) and Mason and Green.

51 For an extended application of Chodorow and Mason in relation to women's autobiography, see my "Autobiographical Selves."

52 See also Gusdorf (36–41). The debate over the definition of autobiography has important implications for the exclusion or inclusion of women's autobiographical writings. In general, narrow definitions of autobiography foster a predominantly male tradition, as the many recent books on autobiography without a single reference to a female text attest. More inclusive definitions, especially those that recognize diaries and letters as a form of life-writing, are potentially more useful for women's writing because women more commonly used these private discourses than they did the self-assertive "autobiography proper."

53 For a discussion of referentiality and conventions of mimesis in the novel, see for example Foley; for early discussions of fictionality in autobiography see Pascal and Gusdorf (43). See also the distinction Scholes and Kellog made between "empirical" and "fictional" forms of narrative and the blurring of this distinction in both the novel and autobiography (13–15, 151).

54 Barthes's statements are quoted and translated in Kennedy. See also Barthes, "From Work to Text," "The Rustle of Language," and "The Discourse of History" (*Rustle* 56–64, 76–82, 127–40). For theorists of autobiography influenced by Barthes and later post-structuralist theories of the subject, see for example Kennedy, Mehlman, Willis Buck, Ulmer, Paul Jay, Ryan, and Sidonie Smith.

55 For feminist critics who argue for such an interplay, see especially Nancy K. Miller; Stanton, "Autogynography"; Yaeger; and Sidonie Smith. See also Paul Smith's critique of post-structuralist theory of the subject and Bruss's advocacy of a post-Lacanian "identification" of the "speaking subject and the subject of the sentence" in the "autobiographical project" (301).

56 See Kennedy and Ulmer.

57 Unlike Katherine Anne Porter and Isak Dinesen, for example, H.D. did not deliberately misrepresent basic "facts" in her writings to make up a persona she knew to be false. While she recognized the fictional nature of identity and the interpretive nature of life-writing, she strove for accuracy in her portraits of self and others.

58 For an astute reading of gendered subjectivity in *Sea Garden,* see, for example, Thomas Foster.

59 See for example Kristeva, *Revolution* (21–31, 214–16) and *Desire* (6–7, 18–19, 97–8, 124–47, 237–43); Carroll; Jardine (especially 105–17); Derrida, "Signature Event Context"; Nancy K. Miller; Paul Smith; and DeKoven. See Claire Buck's Lacanian/feminist critique of what she identified as American feminist perspectives on identity, as represented in DuPlessis and Friedman, " 'Woman Is Perfect.' "

60 See for example Martz, Introduction to *Collected Poems;* Pondrom, "The Origins"; Morris, "Projection."

61 See also Freud's argument that patients initially can only produce incoherent, gap-filled "stories" of their lives; the goal of analysis is for them to be able to produce an "ordered history" (*Dora* 30–1). For a discussion of the implications of analysis for the theory of autobiography, see Gregory Jay. For a psychoanalytic view of writing autobiography as therapeutic, see also Loughman's discussion of the Wolf Man's memoirs.

62 For theoretical discussions of this position, see for example de Beauvoir, Rowbotham, and de Lauretis, whose *Alice Doesn't* is an extended examination of "the relation between women as historical subjects and the notion of woman as it is produced by hegemonic discourses" (5–6).

63 Kristeva's concept of intertextuality does not, of course, include an analysis of the writer's agency; see Nancy K. Miller's reformulation of a "political intertextuality" in reading women's writing (*Subject* 102–21) and my discussion of "the author" in debates about intertextuality in "Weavings."

64 For extended discussion of theories of the self/subject and autobiographical writings of women and minorities, see my "Autobiographical Selves" and "Theories of Autobiography"; see also Stanton; Sidonie Smith; Brodzki and Schenck; Benstock, *The Private Self.*

65 For the term *Penelopean,* I am greatly indebted to DuPlessis, who used it to describe the "textual weave of inscribed associative memory in personal essays" like *Tribute to Freud* and *End to Torment* (*Career* 117). I am using the term somewhat differently, in relationship to the repetitive discourse of her autobiographical prose in general and her prose fiction in particular.

66 H.D. also described the endless rereading and reviewing she liked to do as a tapestry. To Pound, she wrote: "I am afraid I am only picking up threads in my ragged intellectual tapestry – going back, re-reading classics, Bible, folklore, the old series of Lang fairy-tales, Thomas Mann Joseph in Egypt series and so on – nothing 'original' or startling" (11 August 1939).

67 The word "shape" is the one trope that she regularly used about both her prose and poetry, significantly a word that is appropriate for sculpting as well as sewing or housecleaning. *Helen in Egypt* is the one poem to which I have seen as occasional reference to it as a fabric. She wrote to Pearson, for example, "I will look into 'caravel;' I wanted to weave in the thread, as to first *Helen*" (25 November 1953). The manuscript of *Helen in Egypt* shows little revision, but this poem is the most "novelistic" of her poetry, and she did occasionally resort to the weaving trope to describe all the different strands that went into the text.

68 The definition of this pervasive metaphor in H.D.'s poetry and prose comes from the title page of *Palimpsest.* For discussions of the image in H.D.'s work, see Chapter 4, particularly note 31.

69 See Nancy K. Miller's critique of J. Hillis Miller in which she showed how "Ariadne's Thread" collapses the distinct myths of Arachne and Ariadne and consequently erases the "spider," the woman weaver as agent of and in her own text (*Subject* 90–4).

70 Pound's review of *Portrait* directly echoes the phrases he used to praise H.D.'s three poems to Harriet Monroe in 1912; it appeared in the February 1917 issue of *The Egoist* immediately following H.D.'s poem "Pygmalion." As assistant editor for *The Egoist* from May 1916 until June 1917, H.D. may have placed the poem and review together.

71 For important novelists in the United States similarly experimenting with repetition, I would include Jean Toomer in *Cane* and William Faulkner, both of whom H.D. read.

72 See DuPlessis's "Language Acquisition," which connects the style of H.D.'s personal essays with Kristeva's theory of the Semiotic. For the first sustained reading of H.D.'s maternal desire in the context of Kristeva's theory of language, see Kloepfer, "Flesh Made Word." See also Lucas's reading of the Kristevan Semiotic in *Trilogy* and *Helen in Egypt* and Travis's use of Kristeva and Irigaray for reading *HER*. Although I agree with DuPlessis and Lucas, I think that the Semiotic modality is much more pronounced in H.D.'s prose fiction of the 1920s and 1930s than it is in her memoirs and poems. I have capitalized *Semiotic* and *Symbolic* throughout to indicate reference to Kristeva's specific terminology, including her adaptation of the Lacanian Symbolic.

73 See also her essay on Céline, "From One Identity to an Other," in *Desire* (124–47); Kristeva's examples of avant-garde writing that highlights the Semiotic are taken from male texts.

74 Repetition was also important in her poetry, but in a different way. The repetitions of her imagist verse tend to introduce syntactic structure and stability. Many of the poems in *Red Rose for Bronze* and *The Dead Priestess Speaks,* particularly the least successful ones, experiment with a hypnotic repetition analogous to that in her prose. For the conflation of modernism and feminism in Woolf, see DuPlessis, *Writing* (31–46). For a discussion of H.D.'s prose in relation to Otherness, see DuPlessis, *Career* (31–69).

75 For earlier formulations of this argument, see my "Against Discipleship," "The Writing Cure," and "Return of the Repressed."

76 See for example, Kristeva, *Revolution* (208–13); Felman, "Turning the Screw of Interpretation"; Culler, *On Deconstruction* (215, 261, 270–1) and "Textual Self-Consciousness"; Gallop, "Lacan and Literature."

77 She continued analysis with Walter Schmideberg, with Freud's approval, from 1935 until her divorce was finalized in the summer of 1938. *Bid Me to Live,* first drafted in 1939, is stylistically much less repetitive than *Palimpsest* and *HER*.

Chapter 2

1 The novel, whose typescript carries the title *HER,* was published by New Directions with the title *HERmione.* I have reverted to H.D.'s title, but all citations are from the New Directions edition.

2 See Friedman and DuPlessis, "Two Loves Separate." This chapter's analysis of the bisexual narrative in *HER* is greatly indebted to the ideas we worked out together. For earlier formulations of other readings in this chapter, see my "Palimpsest of Origins," "Portrait of the Artist as a Young Woman," and "Lyric Subversion."

3   When asked if H.D. and Bryher were worried about Hall's trial, Silvia Dobson, a close friend of H.D.'s from 1934 until 1961, remarked: "Oh yes, very much so. We didn't call ourselves homosexuals in those days. We had to be very, very careful" (Interview, 1980).

4   See DuPlessis, "Family"; Robinson (34ff); Paul Smith, *Pound Revised* (110–32); Gilbert and Gubar, "Ceremonies of the Alphabet"; and Hirsh.

5   The second account in "Autobiographical Notes" is: "Sept. 1912. 26. [her age]. – In London in fall, mist and fog, E. P. in B. M. tea shops says, Hermes, Orchard, Acon will 'do.' Poetry, H.D. Imagiste" (3).

6   Typical lines include "I have heard the pipings of Pan, – / The confused sweet music of his memories" and "Ah, there is bleeding and I am bent down, / I that was swaying and lissome and strong, – / I, that stood up from the earth, from the water, / I am bent down" (681–3). Gregg also published a poem entitled "Dreams" in two parts in the October 1912 issue of *Forum*. Omar Pound and Robert Spoo noted that Pound called Gregg "the she-poet" and that early poems by Gregg also appeared in the *Cerebralist* (86). In *Asphodel*, the H.D. figure tells the Gregg figure that "George took your poems to send to the Lyre, not mine" (I 96). Gregg's decadent, Poe-esque prose sketch, "Contes Macabres," appeared in the January 1913 issue of *The New Freewoman*, the same month H.D.'s three poems appeared in *Poetry*. I am indebted to Robert Spoo for help in locating Gregg's early poems.

7   For discussions of the woman artist's double bind in the *Kunstlerroman*, see DuPlessis, *Writing;* Huf; Stewart; Gilbert and Gubar, *Madwoman* (3–104).

8   For the erotic fountain imagery associated with both Lily's painting and Mrs. Ramsay's creative power, see *To the Lighthouse* (58, 238). See also my discussion of this connection in "Lyric Subversion."

9   Not a personal friend of Joyce, H.D. knew his work well and was close to his female supporters – Adrienne Monnier, Sylvia Beach, and Harriet Shaw Weaver. Aldington was assistant editor of *The Egoist* when *Portrait* appeared in serial form (February 1914–September 1915); she was assistant editor when the Egoist Press published the novel in book form. Several episodes of *Ulysses* appeared in *The Egoist* in 1919 after Eliot replaced H.D. as assistant editor. See also Dembo, "Norman Holmes Pearson on H.D." (438). For H.D.'s portraits of Lawrence, see especially *Tribute to Freud* (116, 128, 131–5, 140–2, 140–5, 149–50); *Compassionate Friendship; Bid Me to Live*. Except for *The Man Who Died*, H.D. did not like Lawrence's novels after *The Rainbow* (see Chapter 3 for extended discussion). But she wrote to Amy Lowell: "Did you read 'Rainbow' ? – Magnificent – And he has had such stupid reviews" (4 October 1916). Much later, she wrote Aldington: "I am reading *Rainbow* carefully, from quite a different angle. It is better than lots that came after. . . . Have you the pre-Rainbow in paperbacks? I prefer them" (27 February 195[6?]).

10 H.D. wrote about Pound reading Swinburne to her in *End to Torment*. For other Swinburne poems from *Poems and Ballads, First Series* that prefigure *Hilda's Book,* see especially "Fragoletta" (82–5), "Félise" (188–98), and "Madonna Mia"

(273–5). *A Lume Spento,* Pound's first book of poems, includes "Salve O Pontifex," dedicated to Swinburne (63).

11 See also poems in *A Lume Spento* that associated the poet's Lady with a tree, such as "La Fraisne" and "La Regina Avrillouse" ("your arms are long like boughs of ash," 74–5) and Pound's prose gloss of "La Frainse," which refers to the "faun and the dryad, a woodland-dweller amid the rocks and streams" (14).

12 For feminist discussions of "the male gaze" in film, see Ann Kaplan and Mulvey. See also Homans, " 'Syllables' " and Irigaray's *Speculum* and *This Sex Which Is Not One* (23–33, 205–18), which associate touch with feminine eroticism and specularity with masculine desire.

13 See Joyce, *Portrait* (7, 14); Stephen's socialization into the "tribe" of boys at school centers on his learning to deny that he kisses his mother before he goes to bed.

14 The silence of Stephen's muse is highlighted by a comparison between Emma Cleary in *Stephen Hero* and E. C. in *Portrait.* In the earlier version, Joyce fleshed out the character of Stephen's first love into what Bonnie Kime Scott described as "a central, sustained, individualized portrait of a modern, urban, intelligent young woman who is permitted to some extent to speak her mind and direct her affairs" (*Joyce and Feminism* 133); in the later version, however, E. C. exists merely as an etherial presence in Stephen's life, signaled by her silence and the barrenness of her initials.

15 For discussions of narrative as inherently Oedipal, see Barthes, *Pleasure* (10, 44–5, 47); Brooks (92–110). For critiques of this view, see de Lauretis (103–57) and my "Lyric Subversion."

16 In a reversal typical of Lawrence, the colors red and black associated with Miriam's appearance link her to Paul's father, who is also described with imagery of red and black. Conversely, the colors yellow, gold, and white appear in the descriptions of both Gertrude and Clara. In essential spirit, however, Miriam is allied with Paul's mother, while Clara's physicality connects her with Paul's father. Lawrence suggests that behind Paul's desire for both Miriam and Clara lies his tabooed desire for his mother and his even more forbidden homoerotic desire for his father.

17 The voicing of the muse in *HER* paved the way for the potent mother/muse figures in H.D.'s later poetry, especially *Trilogy* and *Hermetic Definition.* For discussions of the muse in H.D.'s poetry, see my "Psyche Reborn"; DuPlessis, "Family"; DeShazer; Kloepfer, "Mother as Muse."

18 This phrase, to which Hermione repeatedly returns, may echo Swinburne's "Choriambics," a poem in which the poet's muse is a beautiful dead woman whose silence and absence is a presence that makes the poem possible (*Poems and Ballads, Second Series* 141–3). Like Poe's "Ligeia," "Choriambics" may be part of an intertextual grid for H.D.'s "Helen," in which male worship transforms a living woman into a dead statue (*Collected Poems* 154).

19 This phrase comes from the final stanza of the first poem in Robert Browning's "Transcendentalism: A Poem in Twelve Books" (*Poetical Works* 335–63). I am indebted to Emily Wallace and James Nelson for identification of the quotation. Both Pound and H.D. altered the function of Browning's line. In Browning's text (which is perhaps a variation on the pastoral convention of a contest between two male poets), an older male poet addresses a younger male poet who has been trying to impress male readers by eliminating figurative language and music from his verse in favor of a more discursive discourse. The older poet calls on the younger poet to return "the harp back to your heart again!" and concludes with a homoerotic tableau: "you are a poem, though your poem's naught. / The best of all you showed before, believe, / Was your own boy-face o'er the finer chords / Bent, following the cherub at the top / That points to God with his paired half-moon wings" (336). In addressing the line to H.D., Pound altered it to serve the "story of looking" in a heterosexual scene of writing; H.D., in turn, critiqued Pound's appropriation and ultimately returned to Browning's homoeroticism.

20 Contemporary feminist theorists often argue that the "gaze" is inherently masculine and patriarchal (see Irigaray, Mulvey, Ann Kaplan). But, for H.D., *sight* and *seeing* could be appropriated (like language itself) for female desire; the *context* of both sight and touch (rather than some "inherent" qualities) would determine its impact on the story of female desire. The importance of the specular for cinema and visionary experience may have influenced her view. See also my "Lyric Subversion." For a discussion of the imagery of perception in *HER,* see Dembo, "H.D. *Imagiste.*"

21 For a discussion of humor in *HER,* see also Dembo, "H.D. *Imagiste.*" For an Irigarayan reading of H.D.'s *Helen in Egypt* based on "mimicry," see Hirsh.

22 See for example, Friedman and DuPlessis, "Two Loves"; DuPlessis, *Writing* (72–3); Friedman, "Palimpsest of Origins"; Laity, "H.D. and Swinburne"; and Travis, who related disrupted syntax to Kristeva's theory of Semiotic "irruption" into the Symbolic (126).

23 See also Pound's "Nel Biancheggiar" in *A Lume Spento,* in which the poet feels "the dusky softness whirr / Of color, as upon a dulcimer / 'Her' dreaming fingers lay . . . " (109).

24 For a different reading of this narcissism, see Travis, who argued that the lesbian relationship of Fayne and Her in this scene is "not 'woman-centered' " because its mirroring is like the alienation of the Lacanian mirror stage. Using Irigaray's re-vision of Lacan's mirror stage, Travis read the mirroring moments between the women as a stage that is superceded by Her's final moments on the ice ("*la glace*" as both ice and mirror) and a more equitable relationship between the women in the final lines of the novel in which "neither woman will be frozen into the static image of the other" (139).

25 Several poems by Gregg also play on the interplay of hands. See for example "Dreams," published in 1912 with the lines "The hand you lay upon me is too heavy with dreams," in reference to the lover as lute who is played upon "until I quiver and grow dumb" (390); the untitled poem Gregg wrote inside the cover of her copy of *Sea Garden,* with "So, as you touch me, I dream my Hilda / . . . / Your hands in my hands / And the life in me leaps / to the sound of your dreams" (Hanscombe and Smyers 20).

26 See Laity's extended discussion of H.D.'s transformative use of Swinburne, contrasted with the male modernists' repudiation of him, in "H.D. and Swinburne" and "H.D.'s Romantic Landscapes."

27 See also Wagner-Martin's discussion of *The Winter's Tale* and *HER.*

28 There is a startling resonance here between the novel and Adrienne Rich's "Sibling Mysteries," a poem written before *HER* was published, a portion of which reads: "Remind me / how her touch melted childgrief // how she floated great and tender in our dark / . . . // and how we thought she loved / the strange male body first / that took, that took, whose taking seemed a law // and how she sent us weeping / into that law / how we remet her in our childbirth visions // erect, enthroned, above / a spiral stair" (*Dream* 48). For discussion of Rich and H.D., see my " 'I go where I love.' "

29 As DuPlessis and I have argued, the relationship between Fayne and Hermione has troubling undertones, even before Fayne's betrayal with George, particularly in the scene where Her passively mimics what Fayne tells her ("Two Loves" 177). But, in contrast to Travis's reading, I believe that this lyric fusion between the women is presented as an idyllic moment that cannot fully manifest in the narrative of ordinary space and time.

30 For a discussion of the intersecting racial and gender dynamics in *HER*, see my "Modernism of the 'Scattered Remnant.' "

31 See Friedman and DuPlessis, "Two Loves" for a discussion of how Freud's theory of lesbian love as "maternal fixation" may have contributed to H.D.'s sublimation of lesbian sister-love into the story of the daughter's desire for the lost mother.

32 See Pearson's "Notes," which record several interviews with H.D. in the late 1940s and 1950s. She did not at first want to allow him to include any imagist poems in the *Selected Poems*, published in 1956.

33 Both poems, along with the novel, may echo Pound's "La Fraisne," the opening poem in *A Lume Spento*, which includes the lines "my bride / Is a pool of the wood" (16). Gregg's "Trees by the Water," the third poem in "La Mendiante," also connects trees and water: "To lie close in the clasp of your moss-hung long arms, / Your branches above me – / How you would laugh, you wild rippling water" (682-3).

34 The repeated images of moss may echo Pound's "La Regina Avrillouse," in which "Moss and the mold of earth, / These be thy couch of mirth, / Long arms thy boughs of shade / April-alluring" (*Lume* 75).

35 For discussion of the cinematic gaze in relation to H.D. and Macpherson, see Collecott, "Images."

36 See Guest, *Herself Defined* (179-87). According to Guest, Macpherson's novel *Gaunt Island*, published by Bryher in 1927, portrays Macpherson's affairs with Gregg and Brigit Patmore (who had been in love with both H.D. and Aldington during the war years). See "The Apartment House" (published in the same issue of *The American Caravan* as *Narthex*) for Gregg's account of Macpherson. See also "Autobiographical Notes" (15-16); Schaffner's account of how H.D. described Gregg to her as "A very dear friend," "beautiful and good, that's why I named you Frances Perdita" and how Bryher told her "Don't mention Frances Gregg, ever again. She is very dangerous" ("Pandora's Box" ix-x); Penny Smith; Collins, *H.D.*

37 "Autobiographical Notes," for the year 1926, reports on the beginnings of H.D.'s relationship with Macpherson, notes that he read the proofs of *Palimpsest* with excitement ("this is a great help as Ezra had written me most brutally about a section of *Hedylus*"), says that "Kenneth writes *Poolreflection*, which fascinates me," and concludes with "Unpublished writing; *Her* and *Asphodel*" (16). Guest's undocumented date for *HER* is 1922, but I have seen no evidence that contradicts the 1926−7 dates provided by H.D.

38 Heavily influenced by *Palimpsest*, the style of Macpherson's novel is strikingly "H.D.-ian" in its technique of lyric interior monologue and characterization. Repetition of motifs − especially of flowers, colors, butterflies, land and water, light and dark, classical and pastoral deities − are very reminiscent of *Palimpsest*, as well as of *HER* and *Asphodel*, which H.D. might have shown him.

39 Macpherson's language often resonates with Pound's and H.D.'s − for example, the scene with Lex and Moreen at poolside: "Swaying, she smiled on him. His hand with epileptic striving traversed the bark of a tree. Burnished air was hot of friction, drone of bees was friction generating impossible heat. Hamadryads have ye fled this place, the trees are dumb?" (64−5); and, of Moreen, "Why couldn't she, like Thessalian Daphne, for her prayer be changed here, in Picadilly, to a laurel tree?" (128−9). The portrait of Moreen partially echoes the imagery of Pound's *Hilda's Book* (which Gregg, who had the manuscript, might have shown him) as well as H.D.'s own self-portraits. For example, Peter thinks: "Your voice.....polished marble slashed with holy water. . . . Your body is hard and vicious and unkind. . . . You are crystal laid upon plate glass. Your arms are long and cool. . . . Moreen moved, high priestess, in a temple of strange ritual. . . . She towered to his vision like some fatigued Persephone gazing down upon her dead, light hiding over her shoulders. Her neck rose stark from it, − tall rock in a waterfall. Light lay along the edges of her hair, gilded the hands she now laid on his head" (38−40).

40 See Gubar's discussion of H.D.'s re-vision of the Echo myth in *The Hedgehog* in "The Echoing Spell."

Chapter 3

1 I disagree with Hayden White's contention in "The Burden of History" that the modernists had no "historical consciousness" (*Tropics* 27−50). Some may have yearned, like Stephen Dedalus, to awaken from the nightmare of history. But even Joyce's famous line signifies not the lack of a historical consciousness, but the inevitability of it.

2 I will use H.D.'s original title *Madrigal* for *Bid Me to Live (A Madrigal)* hereafter. H.D. did not identify the novels of the "Madrigal cycle" by name, but rather attached the phrase in *Thorn Thicket* to her life during the time frame of World War I (including its prelude and postlude). In "Autobiographical Notes," she identified *Paint It To-Day*, *Asphodel*, *Madrigal*, and a two- or three-story sequence that she later destroyed as part of "the novel" about the war period (11). DuPlessis and I originally included *HER* in the Madrigal cycle because the characters have the same names as those in *Asphodel* ("Two Loves"). But, because of how H.D. used the term "Madrigal" in *Thorn Thicket*, I would now not include *HER* in "the Madrigal cycle." "Murex," in *Palimpsest*, and *Hedylus* also retell the events of the war years, but only indirectly, through memory. "Hipparchia," in *Palimpsest*, narrates the Madrigal events directly, but its version is part of a three-part novel, two parts of which focus on re-creations of H.D.'s self in the 1920s. I have therefore included analysis of *Palimpsest* and *Hedylus* in the following chapter. Additionally, *Thorn Thicket*, written in 1960 when *Madrigal* was in press, is a layered reflection on World War I, her efforts to write about those events (particularly in *Madrigal*), and the superimposition of the events in World War II (especially with Sir Hugh Dowding) on the earlier war. Of great significance in *Thorn Thicket* is H.D.'s application of Freud's concept of "the primal scene" (which had been the focus of her second analysis with Freud in 1934) to the *Kunstler* theme (17–19).

3 For analysis of Woolf, see Marcus, *Languages;* DuPlessis, *Writing;* Edwards, "Bread and Roses." For contemporary feminist theory on the personal as political, see for example Rowbotham.

4 See Ernest Jones (395–7). By the time she drafted *Madrigal* in 1939, H.D. had read *Beyond the Pleasure Principle* and *Civilization and Its Discontents* (*Tribute to Freud* 103–4); Freud's analysis of eros and the death instinct became important for *Helen in Egypt,* but her revision of his ideas was first worked out in her prose.

5 *Paint It To-Day,* or a closely related text, may have been begun as early as 1916, when H.D.'s letter to Cournos noted that she wanted to write a "Created Legends" in prose, like his (Wed. [October?] 1916), or in July of 1918, when she described a novel she was writing that resembled his *The Mask* (see Note 1, Chapter 1). For the story sequence she destroyed, see "Autobiographical Notes" (11). The typescript of *Asphodel* has two title pages, one with "*Fields of Asphodel* London 1921–1922?"; the other "*Asphodel.*" Both titles probably allude to Odysseus's descent to the Underworld, where he sees the shade of Achilles stride off into "fields of asphodel," in *The Odyssey,* Pound's "Canto I," and Aldington's "Reflections" and "Captive" (*Complete Poems* 40, 68) and satiric "Synthetic Sonnets, I" (Gates 245). *Asphodel* may have had a sequel in progress (later destroyed) about "Beryl and Margaret at Bullingham flat [H.D.–Bryher residence in 1919–20] – very sub-c. modern stuff" (H.D., Letters to Bryher, 14 and 17 June 1923).

6 Various sources suggest that H.D. drafted the novel in 1939, revised it late in 1947 and 1948, and completed all corrections on the typescript by 1950 ("Autobiographical Notes" 28, 34; *H.D. by Delia Alton* 201). In *Thorn Thicket,* H.D. reflected about the 1939 draft: "Somewhere about the middle of Chapter 10, 'it' stopped. I could not say what 'it' was but the last third or even half of the MS wavered, trembled and wandered, indeed to quote my daughter again, it simply didn't 'jell.' It was easy to see where 'it' stopped. ('It' stopped exactly where Julia thought, 'I'll get some fresh flowers for that jug.' [see 166]) It was almost as if 'it' were a sort of 'control' and had gone away. I bundled up the last third or it might even have been half of the MS, and put it aside. I would destroy it later. It was easy to see where 'it' stopped. The room grew colder as 'it' compelled my pencil. It was a letter that I (Julia) was writing to Lorenzo, Rico or Frederico" (27–8). The 1947–50 draft thus added the concluding reflections on, and letter to, Rico. No version of the 1939 end has survived, but in a letter to Aldington she noted that she "scrapped" the "last chapters" because "they did not ring quite true and brought in 'others,' if you know what I mean," a possible allusion to Bryher and/or Perdita (27 December 195?).

7 I am indebted to Tilottama Rajan for directing me to De Quincey's chapter, "The Palimpsest of the Human Brain," in which the male persona patronizingly explains the Greek term to an imagined female reader because "our sex enjoys the office and privilege of standing counsel to yours in all questions of Greek"

and "if, by accident, you know the meaning... you will always seem *not* to know it" (*Collected Writings* 341). H.D. may have seen Huntley Cater's "A Palimpsest" in *The New Freewoman*, which describes an artist whose concept of "Space" is characterized as a "mental" quality. Freud also used the term "palimpsest" to describe the layers of the dream (*Interpretation of Dreams* 169).

8 H.D. was aware of the significance of the frame for *Madrigal*; in *Thorn Thicket*, she reflected: "Bryher came into the *Madrigal* cycle, July 17, 1918, but I do not bring her into the story. The story ends with the letter that Julia writes to Frederico or Lorenzo" (28).

9 For the term "textual unconscious," see Culler, "Textual Self-Consciousness"; for work that presumes a textual unconscious, see especially Felman, *Lacan* and "Turning the Screw"; Riffaterre; Jameson. For theoretical presentations of the psycho/political, intertextual hermeneutic I use in this chapter, see my "Return of the Repressed" and "Weavings."

10 For Aldington's closely related version of this transformation, see "The Faun Captive" and "Captive" (*Complete Poems* 68–9); see also H.D.'s letters to Cournos in 1916 for accounts of the "faun's" suffering during military training (Hollenberg, "Art and Ardor"). For other accounts of H.D.'s relationship with Aldington during the war, see Crawford and Guest, *Herself Defined* (72–101).

11 See Aldington's "Leave-taking" (*Complete Poems* 75). *Madrigal*'s portrait of a marriage has its most intense counterpart in Aldington's letters to H.D. from France (April–November 1918). On the whole, these letters confirm many aspects of H.D.'s account. He wrote, for example, "The truth is: I love you & I desire – l'autre" (20 May 1918); "there is a side of me which, as you know, goes hankering after unredeemed sensualism; and there is a part of you which is always seeking something purer and more spiritual than me.... you didn't see that I *loved* you and *desired* the other" (14 August 1918); "To you I have under-estimated my passion for A[rabella].; to A. I have underestimated my tenacious devotion to you" (31 August 1918); "You are not a wife; you are a dryad" (10 October 1918). He spoke openly in his letters of his great passion for the earthy body of Yorke, but he also wrote about his desire for "the touch of your chaste mouth upon my over-heavy, over-eager lips" (14 August) and her fear of not being desirable to him: "You speak of not having a body – you are wrong; you have a beautiful and passionate body. I knew that the last times we were together" (2 July).

12 "Anthea" echoes "Astraea," Aldington's name for H.D., frequently used in his letters from the front and in *Asphodel*. See his "Sestina; For Astraea" (Gates 211–12). "Astraea" may allude to the virgin Astraea, who heralds the return of the Golden Age in Virgil's 4th Eclogue, or to one of the poetic terms used for the virgin queen, Elizabeth I. H.D.'s use of Herrick's "To Anthea" also echoes Pound's early "Fistulae": " 'To make her madrigal / Who shall the rose sprays bring; / To make her madrigal / And bid my heart to sing?' " (*Lume* 71).

13 For other discussions of the motif of letters in *Madrigal* and war literature, see Schweik and also Milicia, "*Bid Me*."

14 See Harry T. Moore (282).

15 Brigit Patmore also wrote a roman à clef featuring H.D. as "Julia." Stephen Guest told H.D. that it was set up for publishing in the States and then withdrawn (*Compassionate Friendship* 60–1). The name Julia also echoes the names Julia and

Juliet used interchangeably in *By Avon River* in reference to *Romeo and Juliet* and focalizing, I suspect, H.D.'s heterosexual self.

16 H.D.'s letter to Cournos about Aldington's passion for Flo refers to its beginning in the spring in Devonshire (5 September 1916). Aldington and Patmore had been lovers before he met H.D. (Hanscombe and Smyers 23), and they may have resumed the affair in 1915. Collins noted "Brigit acted disastrously in telling Hilda of her 'consoling' Richard at the time of Hilda's stillbirth and his compassionate leave in 1916 and was rebuked for this, I believe, by no less a person than T. S. Eliot" (*H.D.*). To Cournos, H.D. later wrote that Patmore "did not need or ask my sanction in the old days for any relationship she wanted with R." (26 November 1922[?]). For other accounts of these events and Lawrence's part in them, see Satterthwaite; Firchow; Meyers; and Robinson (132–228).

17 See especially his letters to H.D., 3, 4, 5, 11, 12, 14, 21, 31 August 1918; 1, 17 September 1918; 1 December 1918; 26 March 1919. Aldington alternately promised to support H.D., cut himself off from her, restore the marriage, accept the baby as his, and refuse to accept or care for the baby.

18 Lawrence had also worried about H.D. in a letter to Lowell dated 23 March 1917: "Hilda Aldington is very sad and suppressed, everything is wrong" (Harry T. Moore 276).

19 *Madrigal* does not suggest that Rico's refusal might relate to homosexuality, but H.D. was certainly aware of the possibility. First, *Kangaroo* portrays the homoerotic "friendship" Lawrence enjoyed with William Henry Hocking, which Frieda believed to be a consummated affair; Hocking was still on Lawrence's "list" for Rananim in December 1917 (Harry T. Moore 278, 282). Second, in *Compassionate Friendship*, H.D. filled out the scene in *Madrigal* with an allusion to homosexuality: "There had been the scene the night before or shortly before, in which Lawrence said that Frieda was there for ever on his right hand, I was *there* forever – on his left. Frieda said when we were alone, 'but Lawrence does not really care for women. He only cares for men. Hilda, *you have no idea of what he is like*'" (58). Third, H.D. had read John Middleton Murry's *Son of Woman* (1932), the first book to assert Lawrence's homoeroticism. For discussion of Lawrence's *noli me tangere* motif in relation to war poetry, including *Trilogy*, see Schweik.

20 See *Madrigal* (84) for development of the "Satyr" image; see *St. Mawr* (53–5) for Lawrence's connection of "The Great Goat Pan" with the "dark god" the novella resurrects. H.D. may also have had in mind a sequence of *Pansies* poems, "Ego-Bound" and "Ego-Bound Women" (*Collected Poems* 474–5). Her image of the plant possibly echoes "Ego-Bound," which begins "As a plant becomes pot-bound / man becomes ego-bound / enclosed in his own limited mental consciousness" and ends with the image of man as a "sturdy plant" that can "burst the pot." "Ego-Bound Women" condemns female egoism as lesbian: "Ego-bound women are often lesbian, / perhaps always. // Perhaps the ego-bound can only love their own kind, / if they can love at all. // And of all passions / the lesbian passion is the most appalling, / a frenzy of tortured possession" (*Collected Poems* 475).

21 It is a mistake, I believe, to read Lawrence's fiction after *Sons and Lovers* as romans à clef. But Lawrence regularly used people and events from his own experience as the basis for his fiction. Frieda told Murry that he and Katherine Mansfield formed the basis for Birkin and Gudrun; Max Gertler was the model for Loerke. For other identifications and the problems they caused for Lawrence, see Harry T. Moore (259–71).

22 H.D. alluded to reading *A Room of One's Own* and another, unspecified Woolf book in a letter to Patmore (12 July 192?). According to Perdita Schaffner, H.D. never met Woolf, but owned (with Bryher) and read all her books (Interview, May 1978). After reading the manuscript of *Madrigal*, Aldington wrote H.D.: "It seems to me just as well written as Virginia Woolf, much more interesting and 'human' and truly poetical" (Guest, *Herself Defined* 288).

23 Julia's defiant love of the wind and wildness of St. Ives (159) might well be an answer to Woolf's more ambivalent representation of nature in *To the Lighthouse*. For a discussion of parallels between the "room" in *Madrigal* and *A Room of One's Own*, see Milicia, *"Bid Me."*

24 See also DuPlessis's reading of H.D.'s *gloire* as transcendence of gender polarity; Milicia, *"Bid Me."*

25 Since no manuscript versions of "Eurydice" have survived, we cannot know for certain if H.D. originally wrote an Orpheus sequence and then removed it under pressure from Lawrence. For discussion of this poem, see DuPlessis, *Writing* (70–1, 109–10). It is worth noting that H.D. wrote *Advent*, which extensively explores her feelings for Lawrence, at about the same time she rewrote the ending of *Madrigal*'s 1939 draft to focus on Lawrence. In the period following her postwar breakdown (May–October 1946), Lawrence was much on H.D.'s mind, fueled in part by correspondence with Aldington about his book on Lawrence and Harry T. Moore's biography. She wrote Aldington, for example, that *Madrigal* pays "tribute" to "that particular Bloomsbury scene"; "it ends with a sort of good-bye to Frederico, old Rico; I never wrote anything of Lawrence, though I was asked to. I do think I have a very authentic Frederico, and that pleases me as I did not want to let all that go, without a sort of hail and farewell" (24 February 195?).

26 In *H.D.,* Collins wrote that "H.D. always regarded her involved, introspective prose fiction as 'Henry James.' It was largely interior monologue in nature and manner; but I am fairly sure she did not feel any specific filiation to Dorothy Richardson" (n.p.). H.D. wrote Cournos: "I have written two long short stories – a little in the manner (I am told) of the late Henry James" (15 September 1922), and she mentioned the James connection in letters to Collins (e.g., 4 March 1925). In the late 1940s, H.D. returned to reread James (Letter to Pearson, 19 March 1947), and in a letter to McAlmon she compared *Palimpsest*'s three-part form to James (28 May 1949 or 50?). It is possible that she adapted the elaborate structures of "Books" and "Chapters" in his novels in *Helen in Egypt,* which has three sections, each of which has six or seven "Books."

27 *Asphodel*'s opening may also echo Woolf's *The Voyage Out.* For discussions of the marriage plot and women's writing, see DuPlessis, *Writing;* Nancy K. Miller, "Emphasis Added" (*Subject* 25–46); Boone; Heinz; and D. A. Miller.

28 H.D.'s representation (through Hermione) of an intense mother–daughter bond as perverse and distinct from the sister–lover bond shifts dramatically by

1926–7 when *HER* was written. *HER*'s connection between sister-love and mother–daughter love shows the influence of Freud; see Chapter 2 and Friedman and DuPlessis, "Two Loves."

29 John Llewyn is a composite figure for the Powys brothers, both of whom were in love with Gregg. See also Hopkins (34); Penny Smith.

30 For an account of Margaret Cravens's suicide and its effect on H.D., Pound, and Aldington, see Pound and Spoo, *Ezra Pound and Margaret Cravens.*

31 See Browning, *Poetical Works* (178–9); *Madrigal* (25); *Asphodel* (II 4).

32 See Keats, *Poetical Works* (179). Other Browning lyrics about Italy or love also resonate with *Asphodel* and *Madrigal;* see especially "In the Gondola," "Two in the Campagna," "A Serenade at the Villa," "My Star," "By the Fireside," and "Women and Roses" (*Poetical Works* 184–7, 189–90, 193, 262–4).

33 See H.D.'s "A Note on Poetry" for an account of this scene and quotations from Browning.

34 Echoing Browning's imagery in "The Englishman in Italy," "Amalfi" begins: "We will come down to you, / O very deep sea, / And drift upon your pale green waves / Like scattered petals" (*Complete Poems* 35).

35 See my "Gender and Genre Anxiety" for an analysis of the demasculinization of male heroes in women's writing, especially *Helen in Egypt* and Barrett Browning's *Aurora Leigh.*

36 Cocoon and butterfly imagery pervades the chapters on pregnancy in *Asphodel* and prefigures the related imagery in *Palimpsest, HER, Trilogy, Tribute to Freud,* and *Advent.*

37 No other reference to the stillbirth taking place in the basement because of an air raid exists in H.D.'s papers. She may have introduced this setting into *Asphodel* to highlight the connection between guns and babies.

38 See for example Derrida, *Disseminations* (212–16).

39 See for example, *Aaron's Rod, The Plumed Serpent,* "The Woman Who Rode Away," and ultimately *Lady Chatterley's Lover.*

40 For discussions of these poems as (pro)creative, see my "Creativity and the Childbirth Metaphor"; Hollenberg, "Nursing the Muse"; and Quinn, "H.D.'s 'Hermetic Definition.' "

41 See Gregory's discussion of Sappho's (and Aphrodite's) liminal presence in *Sea Garden* ("Rose Cut in Rock"). Midget, the nickname of H.D.'s persona in *Paint It To-Day,* encodes H.D.'s bond with Bryher at the time she wrote the novel by alluding to the pet name Bryher's father liked to call her (*Heart to Artemis* 35).

42 Imagery associated with Artemis in *Paint It To-Day* reappears in *Hippolytus Temporizes* – especially stars, flowers, forest, sea, and shore. Artemis's speech in the play about "The broken weed, / the scattered broken shell –" (12), for example, directly echoes *Paint It To-Day* (V 18).

43 For variants in Artemis worship, see *New Larousse Encyclopedia* (120–3); Farnall, *Cults of the Greeks States* (volumes that H.D. owned and marked); Euripides's *Hippolytus.* Some variants suggest Artemis's pleasure in male worship as long as she was not touched or seen bathing; others have Artemsis falling in love with Orion and avenging his death. Euripides's Artemis in *Hippolytus* enjoys Hippolytus's worship; the tragedy unfolds with Arphodite's jealousy. H.D.'s variant emphasizes the tradition of Artemis as an Arcadian moon goddess of the hunt who frequented the wild mountain country with her virgin maidens in short tunic, leather buskins, and simple headband.

44 See Gregory's discussion of virginity in *Hippolytus Temporizes* in "Virginity." See also Marks, "Lesbian Intertextuality," and Gubar, "Sapphistries" for discussions of other poetic constitutions of a lesbian space in the early twentieth century. H.D.'s emphasis on a wild, erotically charged, but chaste Artemisian landscape reverses the tradition of Swinburne and the decadents for whom lesbianism's association with "evil" made it titillating. It also differs from the sensual Sapphism of Renée Vivien or the privileged "perversity" of Djuna Barnes's *Nightwood* and Colette's *The Pure and the Impure*.

45 For discussions of "Hymen," see Schenck, "Songs"; Gubar, "Sapphistries"; and Gregory, "Scarlet Experience." In *Selected Poems,* the lyric beginning "Never more will the wind" was published as a separate poem; as such, with no hint that it refers to a coming marriage, the lament becomes an elegy without consolation, a poem about death. Other poems that partially or entirely develop this kind of Artemisian landscape are "The Helmsman," "The Shrine," "White World," "She Contrasts with Herself Hippolyta," "She Rebukes Hippolyta," "Prayer," "*wash of cold river,*" "Hyacinth," "Triplex," "Sigil," "The Master" (*Collected Poems* 5–10, 134, 136–40, 141–2, 147–8, 201–6, 294–9, 451–61).

46 See also Gregg's "Quest," Perché," "Les Ombres de la Mer," "Pageant," and "To H.D." But Gregg also published prose in 1915–16 in a non-Artemisian discourse. See "The Two Brothers" (based on her relationship with the Powys brothers), "Within Tuscan Walls," and "Whose Dog?" (a dialect sketch about a drunk), the first two of which extend Gregg's interest in decadence.

47 *Arrow Music* was probably privately printed, for it lists no city, publisher, or date. The volume Bryher inscribed for Moore on 8 July 1922 suggests that the book came out some time after Bryher and H.D. left New York in February, 1921 – that is, the spring of 1921 when H.D. was writing *Paint It To-Day*. "Eos" also appeared in *Poetry*. Bryher's poetry is imagist, much like H.D.'s in image and tone. But *Arrow Music* is more overtly erotic than the poetry of H.D., Gregg, Moore, or Lowell.

48 See Collecott, "Images at the Crossroads," for an account of their California visit and the photomontage Macpherson made with the photos. On 24 September 1920, H.D. wrote to Moore that she and Bryher did not like Santa Barbara because it was too rich and "civilized": "we have been advised to go north to Carmel where I am told I can wear my trousers and where we can have more roughness and freedom. Since the war in England most girls go about in riding breeches and old coats in the country and I thought out here I could get into them again all the time. . . . " She probably showed Moore the nude photos upon their return to New York in February of 1921 because Moore wrote H.D. on 27 March 1921: "William's [*sic*] cavorting about naked for the fun of the thing is a different matter and speaking of liberty, I must tell you what Mother said when I tried to describe to her, some of your snap-shots in the woods. She said: 'I'd adore to run through the hedges at Matthew Arnold's, under the big trees, in the deep snow – alone – or with just a few.' I said, 'With Mary, perhaps?'

(My neice.) 'No,' said Mother, 'she wouldn't enjoy it as much as if she were my age.' I meant to tell you this one day while you were in town but I forgot."

49 H.D. alluded to Artemis as one aspect of her self in *Thorn Thicket:* "Mr. Thomas Burnett Swann of Gain[e]sville, Florida is writing an essay on me, or rather an essay on the 'poet' H.D. I gather it is the *Madrigal* H.D. that he is featuring, or even the pre-*Madrigal,* as he calls this 'thesis,' *The Ivory Artemis.* We have gone far from ivory, far from Artemis since those days" (25). The "Madrigal H.D." is linked to Julia Ashton and Delia Alton, the heterosexual personae tied up with love and war. The "ivory Artemis" is the woman who has refused or withdrawn from the plot of heterosexual romance, the same spirit of female independence to which Bryher alluded in naming her memoir *The Heart to Artemis.*

50 See also Ostriker, *Stealing the Language;* DuPlessis and Friedman, " 'Woman Is Perfect.' " Buck's Lacanian reading of women's position in relationship to language ignores how Lacan's theory is itself phallogocentric. See Homans's *Bearing the Word,* in which she argued that Lacan's theory of language is useful not as a "true" idea, but as an example of the androcentric view of language within which women have had to write. See also Yaeger, *Honey-Mad Women* for analysis of how women poets have already been practicing *écriture féminine* from their position of Otherness.

51 See Friedman and DuPlessis, Foreword.

52 For a discussion of H.D.'s prose containing sections that could be type-set as an imagist poem, see Dembo.

53 For example, Kate Chopin's *The Awakening, Ulysses,* and *To the Lighthouse* are all at least partially circular in structure; none is explicitly or implicitly lesbian. Kristeva's concept of *women's time* based on seasonal and bodily cycles is relevant to the narrative structure of *Paint It To-Day* ("Women's Time"). See also my "Lyric Subversion."

54 The play on loving statues foreshadows the treatment of this theme in *HER* and also reflects H.D.'s experimental prose-poem "Helios and Athene" (1920), in which she wrote: "The statue is a link between the beauty of our human lovers and the gods" (*Extended Outlooks* 151).

55 The statue of Hermaphroditus also recalls Gregg's poem "Hermaphroditus."

56 Robinson identified this poet/lover with Lawrence and argued on this basis that he and H.D. had an affair, that Lawrence was probably Perdita's father, and that H.D. was the model for Lady Chatterley. This biographical reading is reductionist and ignores the textual evidence in the novel that this poet/lover is Poe and does not occupy a physical plane of existence. For Schaffner's identification of her father as Cecil Gray, see "Profound Animal." For a refutation of Robinson's claims, based on H.D.'s papers, see my " 'Remembering Shakespeare always.' "

57 See Poe's "To Helen," from which Midget directly quotes (*Selected Writings* 23); Poe's poem also figures prominently in *Tribute to Freud* (97) and "Egypt (To E. A. Poe)" (*Collected Poems* 140). See also Wallace's discussion of the problems H.D. had in school for defending Poe as a great American poet ("Athene's Owl").

58 See for example "Hymen," where the maidens of Artemis wistfully lay hyacinths at the feet of the bride (*Collected Poems* 104), and *End to Torment,* in which

H.D. said she wrote a poem for Frances after Theocritus that begins "O hyacinth of the swamp-lands" (36). Hyacinths are also associated with Fayne in *Asphodel* and *HER*.

59 Aldington's "Lesbia" (*Complete Poems* 28) was first published in *Des Imagistes* (1914); its evocation of a lost classical world is not simply biographical, but the Lesbia to whom the poem is addressed was almost certainly inspired by H.D. Catullus, a favorite of the imagists, was singled out, along with Sappho and Villon, as an example of poetry "in the best tradition" by F. S. Flint in "Imagisme."

60 The story is ambivalent on whether it is the narrator or Ligeia herself that causes the possession of Lady Rowena's resurrected body. As a story about male desire, however, the two wives represent a split in the narrator's representation of WOMAN into the woman he adores and the woman he abuses. For Poe's poems that eroticize death, see "Lenore," "The Sleeper," "To One in Paradise," "The Raven," "Ulalume," "Annabel Lee" (*Selected Writings* 23–4, 27–8, 31–3, 36–42, 46–7).

61 See Poe, "Dream-Land" (*Selected Writings* 35), in which the poet wanders "Out of SPACE – out of TIME" to see an "Eidolon, named Night." See Morris's discussion of H.D.'s astral projection in "Trans-Actions."

62 The name Althea sounds like Astraea, Rafe's name for Julia in *Madrigal* and Aldington's name for H.D. H.D.'s Althea may reverse the myth of the Meleagan boar hunt, retold in Swinburne's *Atalanta*, in which Meleager's mother Althea is jealous of the swift huntress Atalanta, whose arrow is the first to strike the boar. For the motif of "the friend," see Stimpson, "Zero Degree." Bryher in *Two Selves* (1923) portrayed her persona's quest for "the friend," even though "If she found a friend they might shut her up. . . . Because if she had a friend something would burst and she would shoot ahead, be the thing she wanted and disgrace them by her knowledge. Because she would care for no laws, only for happiness" (124). The novel concludes with a scene in which she finds "the friend," based on Bryher's first meeting with H.D. and described in H.D.'s Artemisian discourse.

63 This anticipates *HER*, in which H.D. changed Swinburne's lament in "Itylus" ("the heart's division divideth us") to "the world's division divideth us" (179), thus suggesting that the social order – with its prescription of an androcentric heterosexuality – makes the fulfillment of a lesbian love both desirable and impossible.

64 It is a mistake, I believe, to attempt to identify direct biographical analogues for Chapters 7 and 8. No one character in the novel corresponds to Bryher in the same way that Raymond and Basil serve as personae for Pound and Aldington (or Beryl in *Asphodel*, for Bryher). Rather, Althea is a "character" in the novel who lives in a nonphysical plane; she is also a projection of one aspect of Midget's psyche. Anticipating the splitting and doubling characteristic of works like *Hedylus* and *Nights*, Althea (the healer and Artemisian companion) and Brindel (the practical minded mystery friend mentioned briefly) represent different aspects of Bryher split into two characters.

65 The poetics of *Paint It To-Day* anticipate *Helen in Egypt*, in which Helen works to relate the "out-of-time" to the "in-time," the eternal world of spirits to the changing world of history. Like the novel, the epic's narrative turns on the heroine's conjuration of a spirit from a nonmaterial plane of existence.

66 Midget's statement on the nature of beauty echoes Shelley's "Hymn to Intellectual Beauty" (229–31) and may also respond to the aesthetic discussions in Joyce's *Portrait of the Artist*.

Chapter 4

1 H.D. also worked "feverishly" in 1924 on a novel called *Niké* about the trip to Greece, but later destroyed it ("Autobiographical Notes" 14, 30).

2 In *Compassionate Friendship*, H.D. made much of the fact that the Dijon series was made up of seven stories. But there are only six that deal with the *ménage*: *Narthex, The Usual Star*, "Two Americans," *Kora and Ka, Mira-Mare*, and *Nights*. She may have been including "Low Tide," a story about Macpherson that she destroyed, according to "Autobiographical Notes" (21). She may also have included *The Hedgehog*, set in Vaud, or "The Moment," a story about Gregg written in 1926 and later included in an unpublished collection of stories she variously titled *The Moment* (*H.D. by Delia Alton* 208), *The Seven*, and *Seven Stories* (*Thorn Thicket* 35–7).

3 See Kloepfer's discussion of desire for the maternal presence in *Palimpsest* ("Fishing the Murex") and *HER* ("Flesh Made Word").

4 See "The Egyptian Cat" and her Introduction to *Nights*.

5 I have coined the term "expatriatism" to suggest more than the fact of expatriation in the commitment to and necessity of a self-imposed exile in the lives of H.D. and many other modernists. For extended discussion, particularly of how H.D.'s expatriatism combined aspects of Pound's internationalism and Williams's nationalism, see my "Exile."

6 See Martz's Introduction to *Collected Poems* for a discussion of "borderline" in *Sea Garden*.

7 See for example Pound, "Patria Mia" (1913) and "Provincialism the Enemy" (1917) in *Selected Prose*. See also Kenner ("Origins") for whom internationalism is a defining characteristic of modernism.

8 The draft of *HER* also contains a matricidal fantasy that is crossed out in H.D.'s penciled revision.

9 H.D. may have known Malcolm Cowley's *Exile's Return* (1934), which discussed Stein's statement to Hemingway, Hemingway's use of the phrase in his first novel, and the widespread currency of the term in reference to writers born after about 1900 (3–12).

10 The precise location of Helen Doolittle and her sister Laura from 1921–5 is not fully clear. Perdita wrote "My grandmother and her sister came over from the States every year" ("Profound Animal" 188). "Autobiographical Notes" provides no dates for comings and goings except the arrival in 1921 and the departure in 1925. There is no correspondence from Helen to her daughter from 1921–5, and no indication of travel to and from the States in H.D.'s correspondence to Bryher.

11 See Perdita Schaffner's description of her grandmother's influence in "Pandora's Box." I am also summarizing the contents and tone of some forty-three letters from Helen Doolittle to H.D. from 1924–7 in the Beinecke Collection. Full of family news and accounts of weather, food, and activities, the letters show great warmth for H.D., Bryher, and Perdita and a special desire to participate in their special language – not only with the use of code names, but also with their private slang. She also reported repeatedly on what she was reading, including Joseph Conrad, Stephen Crane, and *Palimpsest*. But, remaining on the surface of things, these letters do not address the deeper currents of H.D.'s (or her own) life. They are far livelier and more tolerant than we might expect from H.D.'s portraits of her mother in *Paint It To-Day* and *HER*. But Gretchen Baker's letter to Pearson about her Aunt Helen suggests an underlying disappointment: She "always wished that Hilda could be more congenial & more of a daughter to her. . . . However, it did not work out that way & so Aunt Helen was greatly disappointed" (6 March 196?).

12 See for example *Madrigal* and H.D.'s 10 April 1919 letter to Bryher: "I fear I shall be forced to shout the truth at everyone: I can't stand this virtuous & abused wife business. I really can't." Although Helen participated in Bryher's fantasy of being a "boy," she once wrote that she didn't like to call Bryher Boy and would use Fido instead (2 October 1924). I doubt that she was familiar with Ellis's formulation of lesbians as "trapped souls" (so comforting to Bryher in 1919); it is more likely, I believe, that Helen regarded the two women as friends within the context of nineteenth-century female-friendship norms described by Carol Smith-Rosenberg. See Pearson's Notes for a biography, for an account of secrecy about Gray.

13 See *Thorn Thicket* (29) and 1925 entries in "Autobiographical Notes." The anemones may have been a deliberate choice. H.D. always remembered the anemones Bryher brought her at Perdita's birth ("Autobiographical Notes" 7); in Greenaway's language of flowers, anemones mean "forsaken" (77).

14 H.D. may have felt financially pressed in 1922 since she indirectly approached Gray for child support, which he refused (Guest, *Herself Defined* 154–5). But I think it is safe to say that H.D. had access to enough funds in the 1920s to establish a small household for herself, Perdita, and a nursemaid, and that she chose not to because of her ambivalence toward the domesticity that a home represented. H.D. had regular income from her father's legacy and her work; her letters to Bryher show her scrupulous need to pay her own bills, to feel that she was financially independent. Bryher provided frequent gifts, from checks to books and clothing, from cruises to major medical bills. Bryher also gave a great deal of money to other writers – including Richardson, Moore, Douglas, and Joyce (Guest 141; 154; 156; 264). H.D.'s ambivalence continued well into the 1950s when she clearly had plenty of money to establish a household, but preferred to live in a room at Küsnacht, her "magic mountain" retreat; yet she told Pearson to send no presents because she had a "phobia" about not having a "home" in which to keep them (3 August 1954). See Morris, "Relay of Power" for a discussion of H.D.'s "eccentric" attitude toward money within the context of "the gift exchange."

15 See Schaffner, "The Egyptian Cat" (143) and "Autobiographical Notes" for 1925.

16 For Bryher's psychological distress, see H.D.'s letters to Bryher, 10 April 1919; Monday, 1919; 19 May 1919; H.D.'s letter to Pearson 26 September 1946. For Bryher's ideas about educational reform, see especially *Development* (1920) and *Heart to Artemis;* and Schaffner, "Pandora's Box," in which Perdita recalled that Bryher confusingly combined "free-wheeling experimentation and old-world discipline. 'Hippo, hippo,' she would yell, pursuing me with a hippo hide whip. And I was stood in corners, and deprived of desert like any bad Victorian child" (*viii–xi*).

17 See Pearson's notes on an interview with Bryher in August of 1966. Bryher's statement may not be reliable. In the same interview, she told Pearson that Aldington had threatened to shoot H.D. and Perdita in April of 1919, an incident that appears nowhere in H.D.'s writings. H.D.'s renewed correspondence with Pound in the spring of 1929 indirectly corroborates Bryher's assertion that the adoption was connected to H.D.'s fears of Aldington. Pound must have been acting as go-between on behalf of Aldington, who had dropped Yorke and taken up with Patmore in December of 1928. H.D. wrote Pound that she was willing to pursue a divorce if Aldington wanted it, now that she was "free" – an allusion to the adoption, I believe. On February 20, [1929?], she wrote: "He [Aldington] can get a divource [*sic*] any time if he will do it in the right way. I don't know what I do mean. I mean he could have had it ten years ago if it hadn't been for Perdita." Soon after, she wrote:

> I mean I am very old and very, very tired. I put down a lot of myself after Perdita's birth. I loved Richard very much and you know he threatened to use Perdita to divource me [*sic*] and to have me locked up if I registered her as legitimate. This you see, was after he had said he would look after us, up to the point at least, of seeing me on my feet again. I was "not on my feet" was literally "dying." . . . I seem to remember always the indignity of being unsheltered and then the treachery of betrayal. It doesn't make any difference to my LOVE and I will always love Richard. But you see it built up a wall...and this side and that side of the wall are so very different. R. and A[rabella – that is, Yorke] had told me they didn't want to marry and I suppose their turning on me afterwards when I was actually crippled, has put me out of touch with my own integrity. I mean I do NOT care, only suddenly they were howling at me, screaming illegitimacy and what not, and they started it. I mean I wanted A. and R. to be "happy," as R. was too forceful for me and too éxig[e]ant and I knew all the time he did not get enough of the sort of thing he wanted. (Friday [February or March 1929?])

In May of 1929, H.D. saw Aldington and Patmore in Paris, where Brigit told her that her husband would never divorce her; the subject of divorce came up again briefly in 1931 (see H.D.'s Divorce File, letters to Collier). H.D.'s divorce papers refer repeatedly to Aldington's threat (e.g., "I left Richard because he terrorized me in regard to my child and my own position. His actual words were: 'you know, of course that you are to register the child as Vane's. If you do otherwise, it is perjury and five years penal servitude.' Those were his words . . .").

18 See Schaffner, "Running," in which Perdita recalled that Bryher, even after her marriage to McAlmon, had to lie to her mother in order to sneak off for a brief visit with H.D. (8).

19 See for example Bryher's *Two Selves, West,* and *Arrow Music;* H.D.'s *Asphodel,* "We Two," and "Halcyon" (*Collected Poems*). From 1919 until 1928, H.D. and Bryher were not often apart; their correspondence for these years is not as extensive, and many letters to which they refer seem to be lost. By 1925, H.D.'s intense, intimate endearments had dropped out of her letters to Bryher. Perdita's comment about her mothers was made to me in an interview in May, 1978. For an important perspective on the varieties of lesbian bonds, see Rich's concept of a *lesbian continuum* in "Compulsory Heterosexuality."

20 See for example the first lyric, entitled "Dedication," from "Child Poems," from which the epigraph to this section is taken (*Collected Poems* 341–2). H.D. wrote variously about Rodeck in *Palimpsest, Hedylus,* and *Advent.*

21 *Compassionate Friendship* (72). See also *The Sword Went Out to Sea, Hirslanden Notebooks,* and Gelpi's discussion of the biographical roots of the heros fatal in "Hilda in Egypt." Robinson contended in *H.D.* (238*ff*) that H.D. superimposed Rodeck on Lawrence. This misses, I believe, the real importance Rodeck had for H.D. and misunderstands the significance of H.D.'s soldier/lovers. H.D. was attracted to two different types of men – first, strongly heterosexual types whom she associated with father figures and war, as well as with a hidden esoteric/poetic core (like Aldington and Rodeck); and second, bisexual or homosexual types whom she associated with brother figures, twinship, and pacifism (Gray, Lawrence, Macpherson). Like all of H.D.'s dialectical binaries, these types became implicated in each other, a process most especially represented by Pound in *End to Torment.*

22 H.D. wrote a series of intense letters to Plank in May of 1935, many of which centered on her frustrations with Bryher, whom she dubbed "S. R." for Steamroller. It would be a mistake, I believe, to take these letters as "the truth" about Rodeck, H.D., and Bryher in 1920; they represent instead H.D.'s construction of those years, from the needs and perspectives of 1935, and Plank as her reader.

23 See Pearson's Notes on his 1963 interview with Bryher at Beinecke. Bryher may not be a thoroughly reliable source, even on her own motivations. By the late 1960s Bryher made many factually inaccurate statements to cover up things she considered embarrassing, a pattern that may have begun earlier.

24 See Pearson's Notes on his 1963 interview with Bryher. See also Collecott, "Images," for a discussion of the ménage.

25 H.D. was probably severely depressed – if not suicidal – by Macpherson's behavior, for she wrote in "Autobiographical Notes": "I return from walk in rain, down by old Reserve promenade; K is alarmed. (Later, I write of this, Low Tide)" (21). A note in Pearson's hand indicates that "Low Tide" was destroyed.

26 See Pearson's Notes for interview of Bryher in 1963 at which she mentioned that Sachs arranged for the abortion in Berlin.

27 H.D.'s entry in "Autobiographical Notes" records the trip, without mentioning its purpose: "November 19, I am in Berlin. . . . I stay at the first Russian pension; they, Br and K are both very kind. Dr. Sachs had helped me. They return as usual, to London for Christmas. There are trees in the street and snow. Krasa Kraus wants to take me out but I do not see anyone" (17–18). *Nights* alludes elusively to an abortion in a fictionalized context (71). I have found no other reference to the abortion.

28 Einstein's theory of relativity was generally part of the intellectual crosscurrents of modernism; but, in addition, H.D. most likely read Sullivan's "A Sketch of Einstein's Theory," an article printed just a few pages from one of her poems in *The Adelphi* (1924). See also Morris, "Science and the Mythopoeic Mind" about H.D. and Einsteinian concepts.

29 See H.D.'s discussions of Euripides in the ferment of wartime Athens and Shakespeare in the disruptions of Elizabethan England (*Notes on Euripides; By Avon River*). H.D.'s concept of history as repetition in her novels anticipates recent theoretical formulations of narrative and temporality. See, for example, Ricoeur, "Narrative Time" and J. Hillis Miller in *Fiction and Repetition*. Kristeva, in contrast, associated repetition with what she called women's time and the lyric Semiotic, while she connected linearity with history and narrative ("Women's Time").

30 See also Berman, Introduction in Manzoni, *On the Historical Novel* (37).

31 Much else has been written on H.D.'s use of palimpsest as an image; see for example, Riddel, "Spiritual Realism"; Guest, *Herself Defined* (171); DuPlessis, " 'While these letters' " (60), *Career* (55-7); Benstock, *Women* (349-50); and my *Psyche Reborn* (109-15, 146-8, 245-7) and "Return."

32 In its handling of narrative point of view, "Hipparchia" is akin to both James and Lawrence – with shifts between two centers of consciousness and a heavy reliance on symbolically weighted motifs such as flowers and colors. "Murex" presents a single stream of consciousness seemingly without a narrator, much like *Asphodel* or sections of *Ulysses*. "Secret Name" has a distinct narrator who stays in one center of consciousness; unlike "Murex," the style is direct, almost factual and journalistic, in part to lend credence to its report of an occult experience, a technique H.D. later used in *Sword*.

33 See *H.D. by Delia Alton* (181) for dating of "Secret Name"; "Autobiographical Notes" (14) and *Compassionate Friendship* (28) for references to *Palimpsest* and *Hedylus*.

34 Play on the men's names is also evident, though to a lesser extent. The unmarried Marius stands in for H.D.'s *mari*, husband, linked as a soldier to Mars. Verrus is a Latinized version of Vane, in *Asphodel* and *Madrigal*, that also means "true." Rafton anticipates Rafe Alton of *Madrigal*; Rafe may have been connected for her to the RAF (Royal Air Force). Curiously, in *H.D. by Delia Alton*, H.D. misremembered Helen Fairwood's name as Margaret Fairwood. Margaret is the name of her persona in the story "Hesperia," which is a continuation of "Secret Name," first drafted in 1923, revised in the mid-1930s, and completed in 1948 (184-5).

35 Like her imagist lyrics in general, "Lethe" depersonalizes the desire to forget and distills out of its pure lyric statement the narrative process of repression. "Murex" restores what "Lethe" (first published in 1920) has eliminated. For another reference to Lethe, see H.D., *End to Torment* (55), in which she also (mis)quotes Keats's "Ode to a Nightingale."

36 H.D.'s heavy emphasis on Ermy's Jewishness picks up on and then separates itself from the kind of anti-Semitism of Lawrence's *The Virgin and the Gipsy* and Hemingway's *The Sun Also Rises*. Based on H.D.'s friend Oppie (the British writer Doris Leslie, later Lady Hannay), Ermy is a symbol of marginality (Guest, *Herself Defined* 171-3). "Murex" anticipates later texts in which H.D.'s identification with marginalized peoples helps her to understand her own alienation. See my "Modernism of the 'Scattered Remnant' "; DuPlessis and Friedman, " 'Woman Is Perfect.' "

37 Hipparchia's shift from "cabbage" to "turnip" can be read as a play on Freudian dream symbols, in which the move from (vaginal) cabbage to (phallic) turnip reinforces psychoanalytic symbolism and then undermines through ridicule the related theory of female penis envy (who could want a turnip, after all?).

38 See Chapter 5. A letter from her American publisher, Ferris Greenslet of Houghton Mifflin, demonstrates H.D.'s fear of exposure and need to disguise homoerotic desire in her published prose: "I have your letter about Palimpsest which greatly surprises me. We have certainly never advertised PALIMPSEST as a 'homo-erotic' novel and I have seen no such advertising elsewhere nor heard of any pirated edition. . . . 'Homo-erotic' is indeed a quaint coining! It is easy to see in it the hand of some purveyor of pornographic literature, though any consumer of such buying PAL. in the hope of sexual excitement, would certainly be in for a disappointment" (3 December 1932). H.D. had apparently written that her brother had seen such an ad. H.D. wrote "Destroy!" across the top of Greenslet's letter; the word is crossed out three times.

39 Kloepfer ("Flesh Made Word") and DuPlessis (*Career* 46–7) also discussed Hipparchia's ambivalence toward her mother.

40 See Guest's discussion of this poem in the context of Patmore's and H.D.'s attraction for each other and competition for Aldington (*Herself Defined* 171–3).

41 This passage, set in its narrative context in the novel, is the prose version of the lyric "Triplex, A Prayer" (1928), in which the poet asks "Let them not war in me, / these three" – namely, Artemis, Athena, and Aphrodite (*Collected Poems* 291).

42 In *Advent*, H.D. paired *Pilate's Wife* with Lawrence's *The Man Who Died*, published in the year she completed the novel. Since she revised the novel again in 1934, it is difficult to determine to what extent *Pilate's Wife* is an answer to *The Man Who Died*, in which a Lawrentian Christ/Osiris is healed by the priestess of Isis in the act of impregnation, after which he leaves her to bear the child alone. Stephen Guest brought Lawrence's book to H.D. and told her that she was the priestess of Isis in the book (*Advent* 141–2). She believed that Lawrence had been told about *Pilate's Wife*, first drafted in 1924, and that *The Man Who Died* was both a theft and a peace offering. The texts should be read in tandem as gendered retellings of Egyptian and Christian resurrection myths. For further discussion of *Pilate's Wife*, see my *Psyche Reborn* (180–2).

43 For such readings, see Milicia, "H.D.'s 'Athenians' " and Walsh, Afterword; for an earlier reading of *Hedylus* as psychodrama, see my Review of *Hedylus*.

44 For H.D.'s association of the early Bryher with Frances, see *Advent* (152). The description of tiny Irene who loves the sea and thinks she is a boy directly parallels Bryher's self-portrait in *Two Selves* (1923).

45 See "Autobiographical Notes": "K & Bryher: *Vienna. May 1* – Venice. *Narthex*" (31), and *H.D. by Delia Alton* (219); see also the discussion of this trip in Guest, *Herself Defined* (186–7).

46 For extended discussion of "Two Americans" in the context of the Harlem Renaissance, see my "Modernism of the 'Scattered Remnant.' "

47 Mordant may be a portrait of Andrew Gibson, whom Gregg sent to H.D. in 1926 before she sent Macpherson ("Autobiographical Notes" 15).

48 Katherine in *Narthex* represents the "feminine" and heterosexual, as she draws Raymonde away from Gareth into relationships with Mordant and Daniel. But, at another level, Raymonde's relationship with Katherine is also erotically charged, with the men acting as displaced substitutes for Katherine herself.

49 See Freud, *Interpretation* (389, 401). H.D. elsewhere associated cathedrals with the mother and "regeneration or reintegration," as for example in *Advent* (146). The bee imagery that pervades *Narthex* evokes the bees sacred to Isis and other Near Eastern goddesses; see King-Smyth.

50 *Kora in Hell: Improvisations* opens with the line "Fools have big wombs," oscillates between images of sterility and faith, and frequently resorts to woman's historical body to represent disease and man's imagination of pure woman to represent hope, however tenuous. See my "Exile" for a discussion of H.D. and Williams's "Prologue" for *Kora in Hell*. Williams may have intended a private allusion to H.D. in one fragment of *Kora,* as well as in the "Prologue": "*The Poet transforms himself into a satyr and goes in pursuit of a white skinned dryad. The gaiety of his mood full of lustihood, even so, turns back with a mocking jibe*" (60).

51 See Broderick and Morton, *A Concise Dictionary of Egyptian Archeology* (82), a book Bryher gave to H.D. and inscribed "Luxor 1923 From Bryher." See also Budge, *The Egyptian Book of the Dead* (lxi–lxii).

52 As Schaffner explained in her Introduction, Una is based on the film star Elizabeth Bergner, about whom Bryher wrote in *Manchester*.

53 Alicia Ostriker suggested another reading of the relationship between Natalia and David: "I see her as using him, not only as compensating young lover but to get herself into a visionary state – for which the near-suffocation of his kisses is essential. She sees his kisses as a new sexual (mystical) technique which she learns to use to get herself out of time, into Egypt. . . . I found myself comparing these sexual episodes with things in Lawrence – especially the masturbatory sex–death conjunction with "The Rocking Horse Winner" and the idea of 'getting there' sexually with getting to another space-time. Also, maybe there is some kind of response here to Lawrence's dread of women 'getting there' on their own" (Letter to author 15 February 1990).

54 See Gelpi's discussion of the maternal desire in *Trilogy*'s Amen-Ra in "Remembering the Mother."

55 The phrases come from H.D.'s dedication to Freud in *Tribute to Freud* and her description of her six-month stay at Küsnacht during her 1946 breakdown: "I didn't stay long in the bee-hive. I got well there" (*Sword* 110).

Chapter 5

1 For a contemporary discussion of Freud's theory of the individual as a theory of history, see Roth, *Psycho-analysis as History*.

2 For theoretical discussions of letters as "texts" functioning within an implied or constructed system of communication, see Deutelbaum, Porter, and the special issue of *Yale French Studies* entitled *Men/Women of Letters*. I will treat H.D.'s letters to Bryher from Vienna in 1933–4 throughout this chapter as a composite "text." For a comparison of these historically important letters to the other accounts of analysis with Freud, see my *"Vers Libre* Relationship."

3 See DuPlessis, *Career* for a discussion of the associative "Penelopean depiction" of H.D.'s interpretive personal essays (117–22), and "Language Acquisition" for a post-structuralist reading of these strategies.

4 H.D. was familiar with the essays of her contemporaries mentioned. Bryher was devoted to Colette's work, and no doubt had *Sido* and *My Mother's House* in her library (*Heart to Artemis* 128–9). Woolf's "A Sketch of the Past" was not published until 1976, but H.D. may have seen "Professions for Women," which appeared in *The Death of the Moth and Other Essays* (1942).

5 See "Autobiographical Notes" (22,32). Psychoanalytic reviews of Chadwick's work frequently criticized the weight she placed on the parents' behavior and general social circumstances in the etiology of neurosis. The "independent" and "eclectic" psychoanalysts of Tavistock Clinic were regarded with disapproval by more orthodox members of the British Society such as Ernest Jones and Barbara Low (Roazen 350).

6 See H.D.'s letter to Macpherson where she makes this connection (28 December 1932). Other scattered references allude to Chadwick's sadism and some unspecified incidence of cruelty, possibly in a hospital, which abruptly ended the analysis.

7 See Bryher, Letter to Conrad Aiken, 29 August 1933; Freud, Letter to Bryher, 29 August 1933; and *Tribute to Freud* (93–4).

8 For an account of the street battles, civil war, and rise of Nazism in Vienna during 1933–4, see Gulick, *Austria from Hapsburg to Hitler* (1,057–91). For a discussion of Freud's response to the Nazi threat, see Ernest Jones (484).

9 See for example Blanton, *My Analysis with Freud* (61); Freud's letter to H.D., 24 September 1934; Ernest Jones (402, 415, 446–85); and Choisy, *Sigmund Freud.*

10 Moraitis, Letter to author (25 February 1985). See also my "Against Discipleship." For a discussion of the debate about lay analysis, see Fine, *A History of Psychoanalysis* (68–9, 96–7).

11 H.D., Letter to Bryher, 24 March 1936. Schmideberg was married to Melitta Klein, who sided against her mother (Melanie Klein) in the disputes in the British psychoanalytic circles.

12 See H.D., Letters to Bryher, 21 October 1937; 25 May, 10 June, 11 June, 12 June 1938. H.D. resumed analysis when she suffered first a physical, then a mental, breakdown at the end of World War II. In May of 1946, Schmideberg and Bryher arranged for H.D. to fly to Klinik Brunner in Küsnacht, Switzerland, where she recovered by October, 1946. She returned to Küsnacht in 1953 for an operation and began informal "tea sessions" in 1954 with the existential analyst Erich Heydt, who regarded her as a "colleague." Their sessions continued off and on until her death in September of 1961. Heydt figures prominently in *End to Torment,* in fictional form in *Magic Mirror* (her roman à clef about Küsnacht), and in *Sagesse* (as Germain).

13 H.D., Letters to Bryher, 14 August 1935, 5 April 1937; see also all her letters in August 1935.

14 For other discussions of writing as a scene of analysis, see my "Writing Cure"; DuPlessis, *Career* (117–21); Riddel, "H.D.'s Scene of Writing"; Jaffe,

" 'She herself is the writing' "; and Knapp, "Women's Freud(e)." For other readings of the talking cure in relationship to literature, see for example McCabe and Felman, "Turning the Screw." For discussions of analysis as pedagogical, see Romig and Felman, *Lacan*. For Freud and H.D., see also Arthur; Eder; and my *Psyche Reborn*.

15 For the significance of her father's telescope and her grandfather's microscope, see Mandel, "Magical Lenses" (301–18); Morris, "Science and the Mythopoeic Mind." See also *Tribute to Freud* (25, 34) and *Advent* (118).

16 H.D. referred to Freud's action as "uncanonical," which it certainly was in relationship to the rules of an "evenly hovering attention" that Freud prescribed for analysts ("Recommendations for Physicians" 118). But in fact, he often beat on his famous couch for emphasis. See for example Blanton (16), Ruitenbeek (182).

17 The striking silence of *Tribute to Freud* on issues of sexuality may account for the relative absence of H.D. from the psychoanalytic literature on Freud. For exceptions, see Freeman and Stream, *Freud and Women* (117–22); Rosenberg, *Why Freud Fainted* (42–3, 58–9, 62–3, 74–7, 90–3, 175–6, 179); Romm, *Unwelcome Intruder* (104–7).

18 H.D. wrote in *Thorn Thicket*: "I remember that I assembled the *Advent* notes from a mass of material, most of which I tore up, in that cold, alien room at *La Paix* where I finished *Madrigal*" (38). The typescript is not the usual clean copy prepared by a typist. It is unmistakably H.D.'s typed draft, filled with Xed out phrases, penciled-in stylistic changes, and a note to her typist.

19 Freud's request is typical for his clinical practice. He allowed Marie Bonaparte to keep a journal about her analysis for three months, but then told her to stop so that they could reach "the deeper layers of herself" (Bertin 166, Roazen 449). He discouraged Smiley Blanton from writing a public revelation of his analysis, gave permission for a general autobiographical account, but repeatedly warned him not to prepare for the sessions and not to write down any dreams (Blanton 23, 26, 29–30, 68–9, 98). After Kardiner's first session, Freud asked, " 'Did you prepare this hour?' I replied, 'No! But why do you ask?' 'Because it was a perfect presentation' " (Kardiner 37).

20 Bryher's visit to Vienna for about three weeks undoubtedly expanded "the leak." H.D. later wrote Bryher: "I think now, I have had time to think that papa smelt with the whisker that you and I had been chewing things too much. . . . I do hope papa won't be nasty and say we talked too much...but it can NOT be helped" (n.d. April 1933). For further discussion of this "leak," see my "Against Discipleship."

21 I am indebted to Adrienne Rich for pointing out this identification (letter to author). See also Ostriker, *Writing* (34).

22 For extended discussion, see Friedman, " 'I go where I love' "; Gelpi, "Remembering the Mother"; Schweik.

23 For extended discussion of H.D.'s rebellion encoded in this episode of *Tribute to Freud*, see DuPlessis and Friedman, " 'Woman Is Perfect.' "

24 For the name Rhodocleia, H.D. may have borrowed from one of Aldington's earliest published poems, "Greek Epigram," which links Rhodocleia with Narcissus (Gates 231).

25 For extended discussion of how and why H.D. escaped the "dire mastery" of psychoanalytic discipleship that Roustang described, see my "Against Discipleship."

26   See for example, Ruitenbeek; Wortis; Blanton; Choisy; Kardiner; Gardener; Helene Deutsch.

27   See Lacan, "Intervention on Transference"; Langs, *The Psychotherapeutic Conspiracy*, which argues that Freud's fear of acknowledging his own feelings about his patients in the 1890s led to his concept of a detached technique and his relative lack of interest in countertransference. For a historical survey of ideas on transference/countertransference, see Orr. For Freud's intense feelings about his dogs and tendency to associate them with children, see Blanton (24); Roazen (499); Clark (483–4); and Martin Freud.

28   See Ernest Jones (392); Clark (432).

29   See also *Advent* (128).

30   See *Tribute to Freud* (39–56) and my *Psyche Reborn* (70–86).

31   The "patient" was the analyst-in-training Joseph Wortis, who admired Ellis more than he did Freud. See his *Fragments of an Analysis with Freud*. Because of his tie to Ellis, Wortis's failed analysis became a significant aspect of H.D.'s successful analysis in 1934. H.D.'s letters to Bryher frequently report on the psychoanalytic gossip Freud passed on to her "*entre nous.*"

32   For extended discussion of H.D.'s bisexuality, see Friedman and DuPlessis, "Two Loves" and DuPlessis and Friedman, " 'Woman Is Perfect.' "

33   Although Freud wrote in his preface to the first edition that he would use only his own dreams for interpretation, he made liberal use of his patients' dreams in the text. These dreams, mostly those of female hysterics, were used to demonstrate his theories of repressed erotic desires. His own dreams, in contrast, tended to be about his desires and anxieties about himself as the founder of psychoanalysis. He often blocked interpretation of the sexual content of his dreams by intervening in the analysis to state that his desire for privacy would allow him to go no further on the pages of a public text.

34   See my " 'Remembering Shakespeare' "; DuPlessis, *Career;* Baccolini.

35   The "worm" is a dominant metaphor for the psyche in *Tribute to Freud, Advent,* and *The Walls Do Not Fall*. For its hermetic association with the serpent as symbol of rebirth, see my *Psyche Reborn* (216–18).

36   In a letter to Bryher, Freud asked for copies of H.D.'s books to increase his "empathy" (27 November 1932); a letter to H.D. refers specifically to *Palimpsest,* brought to him by an American friend (18 December 1932; in *Tribute to Freud* 190).

37   Letter to H.D., 28 November 1938, reprinted and discussed in *Tribute to Freud* (10–12).

38   Also excised was a reference to Ellis's arousal by viewing women (including H.D.) urinate (10 March 1933). When he was curator of the American Collection at Beinecke Library, Donald Gallup told me that he believed Bryher had cut sections out of H.D.'s letters to her. H.D. had not sent these letters to Pearson in her lifetime. But some time before Pearson's death in 1976, Bryher went through the lot and then gave them to Beinecke. The cuts almost always deal with explicit discussions of sexuality.

39   For another example of H.D.'s initial acceptance of Freudian penis envy and then retreat from it in favor of a primal female erotic, compare her letter to

Bryher (3 May 1933) with "The Master." This important letter expresses great
excitement at his "complete new theory" about women: "*all* women are deeply
rooted in penis-envy, not only the bi-sexual or homo-sexual women. . . . *the homo
woman is simply frank and truthful* but that the whole of domestic womanhood *is
exactly the same.*" H.D.'s line, "Woman is perfect," in "The Master" demonstrates
a withdrawal of her initial agreement. For Freud's formulations of femininity,
see "Femininity"; "Psychosexual Consequences"; "Female Sexuality"; "Psychogenesis."

40 For extended discussions of H.D.'s Mother/Muse in her poetry, see my
Psyche Reborn (148–51, 229–72); DuPlessis, *Writing* (117–22); Gubar, "The Echoing Spell"; Kloepfer, "Flesh Made Word"; DeShazer, *Inspiring Women* (67–110);
Gelpi, "Re-membering the Mother"; Baccolini. For a discussion of lesbian encoding in H.D.'s poetic goddesses, see Friedman and DuPlessis, "Two Loves."

41 See for example Bachofen, *Myth, Religion, and Mother Right* (63–5, 114–15).
The opening speech by Pythia in Aeschylus's *Eumenides* charts the succession of
deities at the shrine as Earth, Themis, Phoebe, then Apollo (135). See also *Advent*,
where H.D.'s chain of associations – "Delphi, Delhi?" – links Delphi to her
"mother-fixation" through New Delhi, where Van Eck proposed to take her
(161).

42 All quotations from and references to *The Gift* have been made to the
manuscript version. The edition of *The Gift* published by New Directions is
not the text that H.D. corrected and sent to Pearson for publication. Chapter
2, "The Fortune Teller," and the Notes have been cut entirely; whole sentences, paragraphs, and pages have been deleted from the remaining chapters;
and many sentences have undergone stylistic editing. An unabridged, unedited text of *The Gift* should be published as H.D. wanted it to be. See
DuPlessis, "A Note." H.D. probably wrote *The Gift* in clearly defined seg-
ments in 1941 (Chapters 1–6), in January of 1943 (Chapter 7), and June–July
of 1944 (Notes).

43 As H.D. explained her narrative method in the notes for Chapter 4: "In
assembling these chapters of *The Gift* during, before and after the worst days
of the 1941 London Blitz, I let the story tell itself or the child tell it for me.
Things that I thought I had forgotten came to light in the course of the narrative. . . . Yet I tried to keep 'myself' out of this, and if the subconscious bubbled
up with some unexpected finding from the depth, I accepted this finding as part
of the texture of the narrative and have so far, in going over these chapters (to-
day is July 22nd 1944) changed very little. Instead of tidying up the body of the
narrative, I thought it better to let things stand as they were (as the story was
written under stress of danger and great emotion) and where indicated, confirm
certain statements or enlarge on them in these Notes" (MSS *The Gift*, Notes
56).

44 The first six manuscript pages of Chapter 4, set in the narrator's London,
have been excised from the New Directions edition. This cut severely distorts
the text's play between present and past, between the voice of the narrator and
that of the child.

45 See Freud, "An Infantile Neurosis" in *Three Case Studies* and "The
Uncanny."

46 H.D.'s play with the presence/absence in the water drop resonates with contemporary Lacanian theory of the word or signifier as a material presence that signifies the absence of the phallus.

47 Chapter 4 contains other motifs of female "castration" – namely, the alligators and crabs that bite girls. As with the snake dream, these images of "castration" do not portray girls and women as born castrated, but rather fantasize a man, boy, or male figure as a castrator. In H.D.'s dream language, men castrate women – that is, take away their power. In this respect, H.D. read castration symbols differently from Freud, who argued that the girl's castration complex centered on her recognition of the "fact" of her castration.

48 See H.D.'s letters to Bryher, 28 May 1933; 1 November 1934; 15 November 1934.

49 For an account of the accident that happened shortly after the Doolittles moved to Upper Darby, see H.D., Letter to Havelock Ellis, 17 January 1933; Guest, *Herself Defined* (19). The adults apparently concluded that the Professor had slipped in getting off the tram, but neglected to inform the children of their conclusions.

50 For a discussion of such symbolic castrations as a structural component in women's heterosexual narratives, see my "Gender and Genre Anxiety."

51 See DuPlessis's discussion in *Writing beyond the Ending* of how women writers often reconfigure the family as a narrative strategy of "writing beyond the ending" and of how H.D. in particular reconstituted the lover as the son in *Helen in Egypt*.

52 Whether or nor such an exchange took place is unclear. H.D. mentioned it nowhere else in her writings. If Mamalie's secret "gift" to her granddaughter is fictional, then its role as fantasy in the maternal transference is even more clearly evident.

53 After doing extensive reading on Moravian history and theology, H.D. wrote about the eighteenth-century European Moravians in *The Mystery* (1949, 1951), an unpublished novel at Beinecke Library. See Robinson, *H.D.* (3–10); Augustine.

54 For discussion of H.D.'s revisionist mythmaking, see my *Psyche Reborn* (207–72); Gubar, "The Echoing Spell"; DuPlessis, *Writing* (66–83, 105–22); Ostriker, "Thieves"; Baccolini.

55 See Gelpi's discussion of the move from father to mother in *Trilogy* ("Remembering the Mother"). The same narrative progression structures *Helen in Egypt*. Helen moves from prayers to All-Father Zeus to (re)discovery of the protean Goddess whom she herself incarnates.

Dating H.D.'s Writing

1 This chronology is an updated version of "H.D. Chronology: Composition and Publication of Volumes," first published in the *H.D. Newsletter* 1 (Spring 1987): 12–15, and reprinted in *Sagetrieb* 6 (Fall 1987): 51–6.

2 For H.D.'s periodical publications, see Boughn; Bryer and Roblyer. The following texts, not yet published, are forthcoming: *Notes on Euripides, Pausanius, and Greek Lyric Poets*, edited by Robert Babock; *Paint It To-Day*, edited by

Cassandra Laity (New York University Press); *Asphodel,* edited by Robert Spoo (Duke University Press); and *Within the Walls* (Windover Press).

3   *The Moment* and *The Seven* (or *Seven Stories*) are basically the same collection, but they were conceived as volumes at different times. *The Moment,* with six stories, was drawn together in 1950 (*H.D. by Delia Alton* 208). *The Seven,* with the addition of "The Death of Martin Presser" to the same six stories, was formulated in 1960 (*Thorn Thicket* 35–7). The dates H.D. provided for the stories differ slightly (see also *H.D. by Delia Alton* 181, 183).

Works Cited

Ackroyd, Peter. *T. S. Eliot: A Life*. New York: Simon and Schuster, 1984.

Adorno, Theodor. "Lyric Poetry and Society." *Telos* 20 (Spring 1974): 56–71.

Aeschylus. *Eumenides. Oresteia.* Translator, Richard Lattimore. Chicago: University of Chicago Press, 1953.

Aiken, Conrad. Review of *Palimpsest. The New Republic* 49 (2 February 1927): 309.

Albright, Daniel. *Personality and Impersonality: Lawrence, Woolf, and Mann.* Chicago: University of Chicago Press, 1978.

Aldington, Richard. *The Complete Poems.* London: Allan Wingate, 1948.

Death of a Hero. London: Hogarth Press, (1929) 1984.

Letters to H.D. H.D. Papers. Beinecke Library, Yale University, New Haven, CT.

Life for Life's Sake: A Book of Reminiscences. New York: Viking, 1941.

"Madrigal." *Poetry* 22 (June 1923): 117.

"Modern Poetry and the Imagists." *The Egoist* 1 (1 June 1914): 201–3.

Arthur, Marilyn. "Psycho-Mythology: The Case of H.D." *Bucknell Review* 28 (1983): 65–79.

Augustine, Jane. "*The Mystery:* H.D.'s Unpublished Moravian Novel Edited and Annotated. Towards a Study in the Sources of a Poet's Religious Thinking (Hilda Doolittle)." Doctoral dissertation, City University of New York, 1988.

Baccolina, Raffaella. "Tradition, Identity, Desire: H.D.'s Revisionist Strategies in *By Avon River, Winter Love,* and *Hermetic Definition.*" Doctoral dissertation, University of Wisconsin at Madison, 1989.

Bachofen, J. J. *Myth, Religion, and Mother Right: Selected Writings.* Translator, Ralph Manheim. Princeton: Princeton University Press, 1967.

Barnes, Djuna. *Ladies' Almanack.* New York: Harper & Row, (1928) 1972.

Nightwood. New York: New Directions, (1936) 1937.

Barthes, Roland. *Camera Lucida: Reflections on Photography.* Translator, Richard Howard. New York: Hill and Wang, 1981.

Image–Music–Text. Translator, Stephen Heath. New York: Hill and Wang, 1977.

The Pleasure of the Text. Translator, Richard Miller. New York: Hill and Wang, 1975.

The Rustle of Language. Translator, Richard Howard. New York: Hill and Wang, 1986.

Writing Degree Zero. Translators, Annette Lavers and Colin Smith. New York: Hill and Wang, 1967.

Beauvoir, Simone de. *The Second Sex.* Translator, H. M. Parshley. New York: Bantam, 1961.

Bell, Quentin. *Virginia Woolf: A Biography.* New York: Harcourt Brace Jovanovich, 1972.

Benstock, Shari. "Beyond the Readers of Feminist Criticism: A Letter from Paris." In *Feminist Issues,* edited by Benstock, pp. 7–29.

"Expatriate Modernism: Writing on the Cultural Rim." In *Women Writers in Exile,* edited by Mary Lynn Broe and Angela Ingram, pp. 19–40. Chapel Hill, NC: University of North Carolina Press, 1989.

ed. *Feminist Issues in Literary Scholarship.* Bloomington: University of Indiana Press, 1987.

ed. *The Private Self: Theory and Practice in Women's Autobiographical Writings.* Durham: University of North Carolina Press, 1988.

Women of the Left Bank, Paris, 1900–1940. Austin: University of Texas Press, 1986.

Bertin, Celia. *Marie Bonaparte: A Life.* New York: Harcourt Brace Jovanovich, 1982.

Bettelheim, Bruno. *Freud and Man's Soul.* New York: Knopf, 1983.

Blanton, Smiley. *Diary of My Analysis with Sigmund Freud,* M. G. Blanton, editor. New York: Hawthorn Books, 1971.

Bloom, Harold. *The Anxiety of Influence.* New York: Oxford University Press, 1973.

A Map of Misreading. New York: Oxford University Press, 1975.

Boone, Joseph Allen. *Tradition Counter-Tradition: Love and the Form of Fiction.* Chicago: University of Chicago Press, 1987.

Boughn, Michael. "The Bibliographic Record of H.D.'s Contributions to Periodicals." *Sagetrieb* 6 (Fall 1987): 171–94.

Bradley, Marian Zimmer. *Mists of Avalon.* New York: Knopf, 1982.

Breuer, Josef, and Sigmund Freud. *Studies on Hysteria.* New York: Avon, 1966.

Broderick, M., and A. A. Morton. *A Concise Dictionary of Egyptian Archaeology.* London, 1922.

Brodzki, Bella, and Celeste Schenck, eds. *Life/Lines: Theorizing Women's Autobiography.* Ithaca, NY: Cornell University Press, 1988.

Brooks, Peter. *Reading for the Plot: Design and Intention in Narrative.* New York: Vintage, 1984.

Brown, Chris. "A Filmography for H.D." *H.D. Newsletter* 2 (Spring 1988): 19–24.

Browning, Robert. *The Poetical Works,* G. Robert Stange, editor. Boston: Houghton Mifflin, 1974.

Bruss, Elizabeth. "Eye for I: Making and Unmaking Autobiography in Film." In *Autobiography,* edited by Olney, pp. 296–320.

Bryer, Jackson R., and Pamela Roblyer. "H.D.: A Preliminary Checklist." *Contemporary Literature* 10 (Autumn 1969): 632–75.

Bryher, Winifred. *Arrow Music.* N.c.: n.p., c. 1922.

Development, A Novel. London: Constable, 1920. ·

Film Problems in the Soviet Russia. Territet, Switzerland: Pool, 1929.

The Heart to Artemis: A Writer's Memoirs. New York: Harcourt, Brace & World, 1962.

Letters to H.D. H.D. Papers. Beinecke Library, Yale University, New Haven, CT.

Letters to Conrad Aiken. Huntington Library, Los Angeles.

Manchester. Life and Letters Today 13 (December 1935): 89–112; 14 (Spring 1936): 94–114; 14 (Summer 1936): 74–98.

"Spear-Shaft and Cyclamen-Flower." *Poetry* 19 (March 1922): 333–7.

Two Selves. Paris: Contact, 1923.

West. London: Jonathan Cape, 1925.

Buck, Claire. "Freud and H.D. – Bisexuality and a Feminine Discourse." *M/F* 8 (1983): 53–65.

Buck, Willis R. "Reading Autobiography." *Genre* 13 (Winter 1980): 477–98.

Burnett, Gary. "H.D.'s Responses to the First World War." *Agenda* 25 (Autumn/Winter 1987–8): 54–63.

Bush, Douglas. *Mythology and the Romantic Tradition in English Poetry.* Cambridge, MA: Harvard University Press, 1937.

Cameron, Sharon. *Lyric Time: Dickinson and the Limits of Genre.* Baltimore, MD: Johns Hopkins University Press, 1979.

Carroll, David. *The Subject in Question: The Languages of Theory and the Strategies of Fiction.* Chicago: University of Chicago Press, 1982.

Cater, Huntley. "A Palimpsest." *The New Freewoman* 1 (15 July 1913): 53–4.

Catullus. *The Complete Poetry.* Translator, Frank O. Copley. Ann Arbor: University of Michigan Press, 1957.

Chodorow, Nancy. *The Reproduction of Mothering: Psychoanalysis and the Sociology of Gender.* Berkeley: University of California Press, 1978.

Chopin, Kate. *The Awakening.* New York: Avon, (1899) 1972.

Choisy, Marie. *Sigmund Freud: A New Appraisal.* London: Peter Owen, 1963.

Cixous, Hélène. "The Laugh of the Medusa." Translators, Keith Cohen and Paula Cohen. *Signs* 1 (Winter 1974): 875–93.

"Reaching the Point of Wheat, or A Portrait of the Artist as a Maturing Woman." *New Literary History* 19 (Autumn 1987): 1–23.

Clark, Ronald W. *Freud: The Man and the Cause.* London: Jonathan Cape, 1980.

Cohen, Susan D. "An Onanistic Bind: Colette's *Gigi* and the Politics of Naming." *PMLA* 100 (October 1985): 793–809.

Colette. *My Mother's House* and *Sido.* Translators, Una Vicenzo Troubridge and Enid McLeod. New York: Farrar, Straus, and Giroux, (1929) 1953.

The Pure and the Impure. Translator, Herma Briffault. New York: Farrar, Strauss, and Giroux, (1932) 1966.

Collecott, Diana. "Images at the Crossroads: The 'H.D. Scrapbook.'" In *H.D.,* edited by King, pp. 319–68.

"Memory and Desire: H.D.'s Note on Poetry." *Agenda* 25 (1988): 64–70.

Collins, H. P.   *H.D.* [196?] Ts. H.D. Papers. Beinecke Library, Yale University,
    New Haven, CT.
    Modern Poetry. London: Jonathan Cape, 1925.
Cournos, John.   *The Mask*. New York: George H. Doran, 1919.
    Miranda Masters. London: Knopf, 1926.
    Autobiography. New York: Putnam, 1935.
Cowley, Malcolm.   *Exile's Return: A Literary Odyssey of the 1920s*. New York:
    Viking, 1956.
Crawford, Fred D.   "Misleading Accounts of Aldington and H.D." *English
    Literature in Transition, 1880–1920* 30 (1987): 48–67.
    "Approaches to Biography: Two Studies of H.D." *Review* 7 (1985): 215–38.
Culler, Jonathan.   *On Deconstruction: Theory and Criticism after Structuralism*. Ith-
    aca, NY: Cornell University Press, 1982.
    Structuralist Poetics: Structuralism, Linguistics, and the Study of Literature. Ithaca,
    NY: Cornell University Press, 1975.
    "Textual Self-Consciousness and the Textual Unconscious." *Style* 18 (Sum-
    mer 1984): 369–76.
Davidson, Cathy N.   *Revolution and the Word: The Rise of the Novel in America*.
    New York: Oxford University Press, 1986.
DeKoven, Marianne.   *A Different Language: Gertrude Stein's Experimental Writing*.
    Madison: University of Wisconsin Press, 1983.
De Lauretis, Teresa.   *Alice Doesn't: Feminism, Semiotics, Cinema*. Bloomington:
    Indiana University Press, 1984.
Dembo, L. S.   "H.D. *Imagiste* and Her Octopus Intelligence." In *H.D.*, by
    King, pp. 209–26.
    "Norman Holmes Pearson on H.D.: An Interview." *Contemporary Literature*
    10 (Autumn 1969): 435–46.
De Quincey, Thomas.   *The Collected Writings*, David Masoon, editor. Edin-
    burgh: Adam and Charles Black, 1890.
Derrida, Jacques.   *Disseminations*. Translator, Barbara Johnson. Chicago: Uni-
    versity of Chicago Press, 1981.
    "The Law of Genre." *Critical Inquiry* 7 (Autumn 1980): 55–79.
    "Signature Event Context" (1971). *Margins of Philosophy*. Translator, Alan
    Bass. Chicago: University of Chicago Press, 1982, pp. 309–30.
DeShazer, Mary K.   *Inspiring Women: Reimagining the Muse*. New York: Per-
    gamon Press, 1986.
    " 'A Primary Intensity between Women': H.D. and the Female Muse." In
    H.D., edited by King, pp. 157–72.
Deutelbaum, Wendy.   "Epistolary Systems: A Study of Five Correspondences."
    Introduction for a work in progress.
    "Desolation and Consolation: The Correspondence of Gustave Flaubert and
    George Sand." *Genre* 15 (Fall 1982): 281–302.
Deutsch, Babette.   "Rapunzel, Rapunzel, Let Down Thy Long Hair." *New York
    Herald Tribune* 3 (28 November 1926): 2.
Deutsch, Helene.   *Confrontations with Myself: An Epilogue*. New York: Norton,
    1973.

Diepeveen, Leonard. "H.D. and the Film Arts." *Journal of Aesthetic Education* 18 (Winter 1984): 57–65.

Doolittle, Helen. Letters to H.D. H.D. Papers. Beinecke Library, Yale University, New Haven, CT.

DuBois, W. E. B. *The Souls of Black Folk*. New York: Signet, (1903) 1969.

DuPlessis, Rachel Blau. *H.D.: The Career of That Struggle*. Brighton, England: Harvester, 1986.

"Family, Sexes, Psyche: An Essay on H.D. and the Muse of the Woman Writer." *Montemora* 6 (1979): 137–56.

"For the Etruscans." In *The New Feminist Criticism*, edited by Elaine Showalter, pp. 271–91.

"Language Acquisition." *Iowa Review* 16 (Fall 1986): 252–83.

"Modernism: Agendas and Genders." Paper delivered at Modern Language Association, December 1984.

"A Note on the State of H.D.'s *The Gift*." *Sulfur* 9 (1984): 178–82.

" 'While these letters were a-reading': An Essay on Beverly Dahlen's *A Reading*." *Ironwood* 27 (Spring 1986): 159–69.

Writing beyond the Ending: Narrative Strategies of Twentieth-Century Women Writers. Bloomington: Indiana University Press, 1985.

DuPlessis, Rachel Blau and Susan Stanford Friedman. " 'Woman Is Perfect': H.D.'s Debate with Freud." *Feminist Studies* 7 (Fall 1981): 417–30.

Duncan, Robert. "H.D.'s Challenge." *Poesis* 6 (1985): 21–34.

Eagleton, Terry. *Literary Theory: An Introduction*. Minneapolis: University of Minnesota Press, 1983.

Eder, Doris. "Freud and H.D." *Book Form: An International Transdisciplinary Quarterly* 1 (1975): 365–9.

Edwards, Lee. "War and Roses: The Politics of *Mrs. Dalloway*." In *The Authority of Experience,* edited by Arlyn Diamond and Lee R. Edwards. Amherst: University of Massachusetts Press, 1977, pp. 160–77.

Eliot, T. S. *The Complete Poems and Plays, 1909–1950*. New York: Harcourt, Brace & World, 1971.

Selected Essays: 1917–1932. London: Faber and Faber, 1932.

Selected Prose, Frank Kermode, editor. New York: Harcourt Brace Jovanovich, 1975.

Elliot, Robert C. *The Literary Persona*. Chicago: University of Chicago Press, 1982.

Ellis, Havelock. *Fountain of Life: Impressions and Comments*. Boston: Houghton Mifflin, 1930.

Ellmann, Maud. *The Poetics of Impersonality: T. S. Eliot and Ezra Pound*. Brighton, England: Harvester, 1987.

Engel, Bernard. "H.D.: Poems That Matter and Dilutions." *Contemporary Literature* 10 (Autumn 1969): 507–22.

Farnell, Lewis Richard. *The Cults of the Greek States*. Oxford: Oxford University Press, 1896.

Farwell, Marilyn R. "Feminist Criticism and the Concept of the Poetic Persona." *Bucknell Review* 24 (Spring 1978): 139–56.

Felman, Shoshana. *Lacan and the Adventure of Insight: Psychoanalysis in Contemporary Culture.* Cambridge, MA: Harvard University Press, 1987.
"Turning the Screw of Interpretation." In *Psychoanalysis and Literature: The Question of Reading: Otherwise,* edited by Shoshana Felman. Baltimore: Johns Hopkins University Press, 1980, pp. 94–207.
Fine, Reuben. *A History of Psychoanalysis.* New York: Columbia University Press, 1979.
Firchow, Peter E. "Rico and Julia: The Hilda Doolittle–D. H. Lawrence Affair Reconsidered." *Journal of Modern Literature* 8 (1980): 51–76.
Fleishman, Avrom. *The English Historical Novel: Walter Scott to Virginia Woolf.* Baltimore: Johns Hopkins University Press, 1971.
Flint, F. S. "Imagisme." *Poetry* 1 (March 1913): 198–200.
"The Poetry of H.D." *The Egoist* 2 (1 May 1915): 72–3.
Foley, Barbara. *Telling the Truth: The Theory and Practice of Documentary Fiction.* Ithaca, NY: Cornell University Press, 1986.
Foster, R. Thomas. "Oppositional Practices and Modern Women's Writing." Doctoral dissertation, University of Wisconsin, 1990.
Foucault, Michel. "What Is an Author?" In *Textual Strategies: Perspective in Post-Structuralist Criticism,* edited by Josué V. Herari. Ithaca, NY: Cornell University Press, 1979, pp. 141–60.
Freeman, Lucy, and Herbert Stream. *Freud and Women.* New York: Ungar, 1981.
Freud, Martin. *Sigmund Freud: Man and Father.* New York: Vanguard Press, 1958.
Freud, Sigmund. "Analysis Terminable and Interminable" (1937). In *Therapy and Technique,* edited by Rieff, pp. 233–72.
Beyond the Pleasure Principle. Translator, James Strachey. New York: Norton, (1920) 1961.
Civilization and Its Discontents. Translator, James Strachey. New York: Norton, (1930) 1961.
Dora: An Analysis of a Case of Hysteria, Philip Rieff, editor. New York: Collier, 1963.
"The Dynamics of the Transference" (1912). In *Therapy and Technique,* edited by Rieff, pp. 105–16.
"Female Sexuality" (1931). In *Sexuality,* edited by Rieff, pp. 194–211.
"Femininity." In *New Introductory Lectures on Psychoanalysis,* translated by James Strachey. New York: Norton, (1933) 1965, pp. 112–35.
"Further Recommendations in the Technique of Psychoanalysis: Recollection, Repetition, and Working Through" (1914). In *Therapy and Technique,* edited by Rieff, pp. 157–66.
General Psychological Theory, Philip Rieff, editor. New York: Collier, 1963.
The Interpretation of Dreams. Translator, James Strachey. New York: Avon, (1900) 1965.
Letters to H.D., Bryher (unpublished). H.D. Papers. Beinecke Library, Yale University.
Letters to H.D. (published). In *Tribute to Freud,* H.D., pp. 189–94.
Moses and Monotheism. Translator, Katherine Jones. New York: Vintage, 1939.

"On Narcissism: An Introduction." In *General Psychological Theory*, edited by Rieff, pp. 56–62.

An Outline of Psychoanalysis. Translator, James Strachey. New York: Norton, (1940) 1949.

"Recommendations for Physicians on the Psychoanalytic Method of Treatment" (1912). In *Therapy and Technique*, edited by Rieff, pp. 117–26.

"The Psychogenesis of a Case of Homosexuality in a Woman" (1920). In *Sexuality*, edited by Rieff, pp. 133–59.

The Question of Lay Analysis; Conversations with an Impartial Person. Translator, James Strachey. New York: Anchor, 1964.

Sexuality and the Psychology of Love, Philip Rieff, editor. New York: Collier, 1963.

"Some Psychological Consequences of the Anatomical Distinction between the Sexes" (1925). In *Sexuality*, edited by Rieff, pp. 183–93.

"The 'Uncanny' " (1919). *The Standard Edition of the Complete Psychological Works*, Vol. 17. Translator, James Strachey. London: Hogarth Press, 1957, pp. 219–52.

Therapy and Technique, Philip Rieff, editor. New York: Collier, 1963.

Three Case Histories, Philip Rieff, editor. New York: Collier, 1963.

Three Contributions to the Theory of Sex. Translator, A. A. Brill. New York: Dutton, (1905), 1962.

"Turnings in the Ways of Psychoanalytic Therapy" (1919). In *Therapy and Technique*, edited by Rieff, pp. 181–90.

Friedberg, Ann. "Approaching *Borderline*." In *H.D.*, edited by King, pp. 369–90.

"On H.D., Woman, History, Recognition." *Wide Angle: A Film Quarterly of Theory, Criticism, and Practice* 5 (1982): 26–31.

"The POOL Films: What They Are, Where They Are, How to See Them." *H.D. Newsletter* 1 (Spring 1987): 10–11.

Friedman, Ellen G., and Miriam Fuchs, eds. *Breaking the Sequence: Women's Experimental Writing*. Princeton, NJ: Princeton University Press, 1989.

Friedman, Susan Stanford. "Against Discipleship: Intimacy and Collaboration in H.D.'s Analysis with Freud." *Literature and Psychology* 33 (1987): 89–108.

"Creativity and the Childbirth Metaphor: Gender Difference in Literary Discourse." *Feminist Studies* 13 (1986): 49–82.

"Exile in the American Grain: H.D.'s Diaspora." *Agenda* 25 (1988): 27–50.

"Gender and Genre Anxiety: Elizabeth Barrett Browning and H.D. as Epic Poets." *Tulsa Studies in Women's Literature* 5 (Fall 1986): 203–29.

"Hilda Doolittle (H.D.)." In *Dictionary of Literary Biography: American Poets, First Series, 1880–1945*, Vol. 45, Peter Quartermain, editor. Detroit, MI: Gale, 1986, pp. 115–49.

" 'I go where I love': An Intertextual Study of H.D. and Adrienne Rich." *Signs* 9 (Winter 1983): 228–46.

"Lyric Subversion of Narrative in Women's Writing: Virginia Woolf and the Tyranny of Plot." In *Narrative: Ethics, Form, Ideology*, edited by James Phelan, pp. 162–85. Columbus: Ohio State University Press, 1989.

"Modernism of the 'Scattered Remnant': Race and Politics in H.D.'s Development." In *Feminist Issues,* edited by Benstock, pp. 208–32.

"A Most Luscious Vers Libre Relationship: H.D. and Freud." In *The Annual of Psychoanalysis,* Vol. 14. Madison, CT: International Universities Press, 1986, pp. 319–44.

"Palimpsest of Origins in H.D.'s Career." *Poesis* 6 (1985): 56–73.

"Portrait of the Artist as a Young Woman: H.D.'s Rescriptions of Joyce, Lawrence, and Pound." In *Writing the Woman Artist,* edited by Suzanne Jones. Philadelphia: University of Pennsylvania Press, in press.

Psyche Reborn: The Emergence of H.D. Bloomington: Indiana University Press, 1981.

"Psyche Reborn: Tradition, Re-Vision, and the Goddess as Mother-Symbol in H.D.'s Epic Poetry." *Women's Studies* 6 (1979): 147–60.

" 'Remembering Shakespeare always, but remembering him differently': H.D.'s *By Avon River.*" *Sagetrieb* 2 (Summer–Fall 1983): 45–70.

"The Return of the Repressed in Women's Narratives." *Journal of Narrative Technique* 19 (January 1989): 141–56.

"Theories of Autobiography and H.D.'s Canon." In *Figuring the Self: Modernism and Autobiographical Writing,* edited by Thomas R. Smith. University Park, PA: Penn State University, in press.

Review of *Hedylus,* by H.D. *Sagetrieb* 4 (Fall–Winter 1985): 325–34.

Review of *The War of the Words,* by Sandra M. Gilbert and Susan Gubar. *The Women's Review of Books* 5 (July 1988): 14.

"Weavings: Intertextuality and the (Re)Birth of the Author." In *Influence and Intertextuality in Literary History,* edited by Jay Clayton and Eric Rothstein. Madison: University of Wisconsin Press, in press.

"Women's Autobiographical Selves: Theory and Practice." In *Private Self,* edited by Benstock, pp. 34–62.

"The Writing Cure: Transference and Resistance in a Dialogic Analysis." *H.D. Newsletter* 2 (Winter 1988): 25–35.

Friedman, Susan Stanford, and Rachel Blau DuPlessis. " 'I had two loves separate': The Sexualities of H.D.'s *Her.*" *Monetmora* 8 (1981): 3–30.

Foreword to *Paint It To-Day. Contemporary Literature* 27 (Winter 1986): 440–3.

Gallop, Jane. "Lacan and Literature: A Case for Transference." *Poetics* 13 (1984): 301–308.

Gardiner, Muriel, ed. *The Wolf-Man by the Wolf-Man.* New York: Basic Books, 1971.

Gates, Norman T. *The Poetry of Richard Aldington: A Critical Evaluation and an Anthology of Uncollected Poems.* University Park, PA: Pennsylvania State University Press, 1974.

Gelpi, Albert. "Hilda in Egypt." *The Southern Review* 18 (Spring 1982): 233–50.

Introduction to *Notes on Thought and Vision and The Wise Sappho,* by H.D., pp. 7–16. San Francisco: City Lights, 1982.

"Re-membering the Mother: A Reading of H.D.'s *Trilogy.*" In *H.D.,* edited by King, pp. 173–90.

Gilbert, Sandra M.   *Acts of Attention: The Poems of D. H. Lawrence.* Ithaca, NY: Cornell University Press, 1972.

Gilbert, Sandra M., and Susan Gubar.   "Ceremonies of the Alphabet: Female Grandmatologies and the Female Autograph." In *The Female Autograph,* edited by Stanton, pp. 21–48.

The Madwoman in the Attic: The Woman Writer and the Nineteenth-Century Literary Imagination. New Haven, CT: Yale University Press, 1979.

No Man's Land: The Place of the Woman Writer in the Twentieth Century. Vol. 1, *The War of the Words.* New Haven, CT: Yale University Press, 1988.

Goodman, Ellen.   "Taking Risks to Find Your Own Identity." *The Capital Times* (29 September 1984): 6.

Greenaway, Kate.   *The Kate Greenaway Book,* Byran Holme, editor. New York: Gallery, 1976.

Greenwood, E. B.   "H.D. and the Problem of Escapism." *Essays in Criticism* 21 (October 1971): 365–76.

Gregg, Frances.   "The Apartment House"; "The Unknown Face." In *The Second American Caravan,* edited by Alfred Kreymborg, pp. 285–301. New York: Macaulay, 1928.

"Contes Macabres." *The New Freewoman* 1 (December 1913): 234–6.

"Dreams" [I: The Lute; II: Fallow]. *Forum* 48 (October 1912): 390.

"The Hunch-Back." *The Dial* 79 (July–December 1925): 31–3.

"La Mendiante." *Forum* 46 (December 1911): 680–3.

"The Nun." *The Adelphi* 4 (July 1926): 116–17.

"Pageant"; "To H.D." *Poetry* (October–March 1914–15): 165–6.

"Quest"; "Perché"; "Les Ombres de la Mer"; "Hermaphroditus." *Others* 1 (November 1915): 75–7.

"The Two Brothers." *Forum* 54 (August 1914): 165–71.

"White Kaffir." *The New Adelphi* 2 (December 1928): 150–3.

"Whose Dog – ?" *Forum* 54 (December 1915): 704–5.

"Within Tuscan Walls." *Forum* 55 (June 1916): 415–18.

Gregory, Eileen.   "Rose Cut in Rock: Sappho and H.D.'s *Sea Garden.*" *Contemporary Literature* 27 (Winter 1986): 525–52.

"Scarlet Experience: H.D.'s *Hymen.*" *Sagetrieb* 6 (Fall 1987): 77–100.

"Virginity and Erotic Liminality: H.D.'s *Hippolytus Temporizes.*" *Contemporary Literature* 31 (1990): 133–60.

Greenblatt, Stephen.   *Renaissance Self-Fashioning: From More to Shakespeare.* Chicago: University of Chicago Press, 1980.

Greenslet, Ferris.   Letter to H.D. H.D. Papers. Beinecke Library, Yale University, New Haven, CT.

Gubar, Susan.   " 'The Blank Page' and the Issues of Female Creativity." In *The New Feminist Criticism,* edited by Showalter, pp. 292–313.

"The Echoing Spell of H.D.'s *Trilogy.*" *Contemporary Literature* 19 (Spring 1978): 196–218.

"Sapphistries." *Signs* 10 (Autumn 1984): 43–62.

Gulick, Charles A.   *Austria from Hapsburg to Hitler.* Berkeley: University of California Press, 1948.

Gusdorf, Georges. "Conditions and Limits of Autobiography." In *Autobiography*, edited by Olney, pp. 28–48.

H.D. (Hilda Doolittle). *Advent*. In *Tribute to Freud*, pp. 115–87.

"An Appreciation." *Close Up* 4 (March 1929): 56–68.

Asphodel. Ts. H.D. Papers. Beinecke Library, Yale University, New Haven, CT.

"Autobiographical Notes." Ts. H.D. Papers. Beinecke Library, Yale University, New Haven, CT.

Bid Me to Live (A Madrigal). Redding Ridge, CT: Black Swan Books, (1960) 1983.

By Avon River. New York: Macmillan, 1949.

Borderline – A Pool Film with Paul Robeson (1930). Reprinted in *Sagetrieb* 7 (Fall 1987): 29–50.

"The Cinema and the Classics I." *Close Up* 1 (July 1927): 22–33.

"The Cinema and the Classics II." *Close Up* 1 (August 1927): 30–39.

Compassionate Friendship. Ts. H.D. Papers. Beinecke Library, Yale University, New Haven, CT.

The Collected Poems, 1912–1944, Louis L. Martz, editor. New York: New Directions, 1983.

"Conrad Veidt." *Close Up* 1 (September 1927): 34–44.

Divorce Papers. Ts. 1937–8. H.D. Papers. Beinecke Library, Yale University, New Haven, CT.

"Ear-Ring." (D. A. Hill pseudonym) *Life and Letters Today* 14 (Summer 1936): 116–28.

End to Torment: A Memoir of Ezra Pound; with *Hilda's Book,* by Ezra Pound; Norman Holmes Pearson and Michael King, editors. New York: New Directions, 1979.

Euripides's Ion. Redding Ridge, CT: Black Swan Books, (1937) 1986.

"A Friendship Traced: H.D.'s Letters to Silvia Dobson" (Editor, Carol T. Tinker). *Conjunctions* 2 (Spring/Summer 1982): 115–57.

The Gift [abridged]. New York: New Directions, 1982.

The Gift. Ts. H.D. Papers. Beinecke Library, Yale University, New Haven, CT.

H.D. by Delia Alton. The *Iowa Review* 16 (Fall 1986): 174–221.

The Hedgehog. New York: New Directions, (1936), 1988.

Hedylus. Revised edition. Redding Ridge, CT: Black Swan Books, (1928) 1980.

Helen in Egypt. New York: New Directions, (1961) 1974.

"Helios and Athene." In *Extended Outlooks,* edited by Jane Cooper, Given Head, Adalaide Morris, and Marcia Southwick, pp. 150–4. New York: Collier, 1982.

HERmione [HER]. New York: New Directions, 1981.

Hermetic Definition. Foreword by Norman Holmes Pearson. New York: New Directions, 1972.

Hippolytus Temporizes. Redding Ridge, CT: Black Swan Books, (1927) 1985.

Hirslanden Notebooks. Ms. H.D. Papers. Beinecke Library, Yale University, New Haven, CT.

"Joan of Arc." *Close Up* 3 (July 1928): 15–23.

Kora and Ka [*Kora and Ka; Mira-Mare*]. Dijon: Darantière, 1934.

Letters to Conrad Aiken. Huntington Library, Los Angeles.

Letters to Richard Aldington. Carbondale: University of Southern Illinois.

Letters to Winifred Bryher, H. P. Collins, Havelock Ellis, Robert Herring, Viola Jordon, Robert McAlmon, John McDougall, Kenneth Macpherson, Norman Holmes Pearson, George Plank, and Ezra Pound. Beinecke Library, Yale University, New Haven, CT.

Letters to John Cournos and Ferris Greenslet. Houghton Library, Harvard University, Cambridge, MA.

Letters to Marianne Moore. Rosenbach Foundation, Philadelphia, PA.

Lionel Durand Diary. Ms. 1960–1. H.D. Papers. Beinecke Library, Yale University, New Haven, CT.

Magic Mirror. Ts. H.D. Papers. Beinecke Library, Yale University, New Haven, CT.

Majic Ring. Ts. H.D. Papers. Beinecke Library, Yale University, New Haven, CT.

"Marianne Moore" *The Egoist* 3 (August 1916): 118–19.

Mira-Mare. In *Kora and Ka*, by H.D., pp. 57–101.

The Moment [Seven Stories]. Ts. H.D. Papers. Beinecke Library, Yale University, New Haven, CT.

The Mystery [Chapters 3, 14–19]. In *Images of H.D.*, Eric W. White. London: Enitharmon Press, 1976.

Ts. H.D. Papers. Beinecke Library, Yale University, New Haven, CT.

Narthex. In *The Second American Caravan*, edited by Alfred Kreymborg, Lewis Mumford, and Paul Rosenfeld, pp. 225–84. New York: Macaulay, 1928.

Nights. (John Helforth pseudonym) New York: New Directions, (1935) 1986.

"A Note on Poetry." Letter to Norman Holmes Pearson of 12 December 1937. In *The Oxford Anthology of American Literature*, edited by William Rose Benét and Norman Holmes Pearson, pp. 1,287–8. New York: Oxford University Press, 1938. Reprinted in *Agenda* 25 (1988): 71–6.

Notes on Euripides, Pausanius, and Greek Lyric Poets. Ts. H.D. Papers. Beinecke Library, Yale University, New Haven, CT.

Notes on Thought and Vision & The Wise Sappho. San Francisco: City Lights Books, 1982.

Paint It To-Day [Chapters 1–4.] Edited by Susan Stanford Friedman and Rachel Blau DuPlessis. *Contemporary Literature* 27 (Winter 1986): 444–74.

Ts. H.D. Papers. Beinecke Library, Yale University, New Haven, CT.

Palimpsest. Revised edition. Carbondale, IL: Southern Illinois University Press, (1926) 1968.

Paris Diary. Ms. 1912. H.D. Papers. Beinecke Library, Yale University, New Haven, CT.

Pilate's Wife. Ts. Beinecke Library, Yale University, New Haven, CT.

"Pontikonisi (Mouse Island)" (Rhoda Peter pseudonym). *Pagany* 3 (July–September 1932): 1–9.

Review of *Goblins and Pagodas*, by John Gould Fletcher. *The Egoist* 3 (December 1916): 183–4.

Review of *The Farmer's Bride*, by Charlotte Mew. *The Egoist* 3 (September 1916): 135.

Review of *Responsibilities and Other Poems*, by W. B. Yeats. *Agenda* 25 (Autumn–Winter 1987–8): 51–3.

"Russian Films." *Close Up* 3 (September 1928): 18–29.

Sagesse. In *Hermetic Definition*, pp. 57–84.

"The Suffragette." Ts. H.D. Papers. Beinecke Library, Yale University, New Haven, CT.

The Sword Went Out to Sea (Synthesis of a Dream). Ts. H.D. Papers. Beinecke Library, Yale University, New Haven, CT.

Thorn Thicket. Ts. H.D. Papers. Beinecke Library, Yale University, New Haven, CT.

Tribute to Freud [*Tribute to Freud* and *Advent*]. Boston: David R. Godine, (1956) 1974.

Trilogy [*The Walls Do Not Fall; Tribute to the Angels; The Flowering of the Rod*]. 1973. In *Collected Poems*, pp. 505–612.

"Two Americans." In *The Usual Star*, pp. 93–116.

The Usual Star. ["Two Americans"; *The Usual Star*]. Dijon: Darantière, 1934.

Vale Ave. In *New Directions: An International Anthology of Poetry and Prose*, 44, edited by James Laughlin, pp. 18–166. New York: New Directions, 1982.

White Rose and the Red. Ts. H.D. Papers. Beinecke Library, Yale University, New Haven, CT.

Winter Love. In *Hermetic Definition*, pp. 85–117.

Writing on the Wall. Life and Letters Today 45 (April–June 1945): 67, 137–54; 46 (July–September 1945): 72, 136–51; 48 (January–March 1946): 33–118.

Halbert, Stephen, with Richard Johns, eds. *A Return to Pagany: The History, Correspondence, and Selections from a Little Magazine, 1929–1932.* Boston: Beacon, 1969.

Hanscombe, Gillian, and Virginia L. Smyers. *Writing for Their Lives: The Modernist Women, 1910–1940.* London: The Women's Press, 1987.

Heilbrun, Carolyn G. *Writing a Woman's Life.* New York: Norton, 1988.

Herrick, Robert. *The Complete Poetry,* J. Max Patrick, editor. New York: New York University Press, 1963.

Herring, Robert. Letters to H.D. H.D. Papers. Beinecke Library. Yale University, New Haven, CT.

Hinz, Evelyn. "Hierogamy versus Wedlock: Types of Marriage Plots and Their Relationship to Genres of Prose Fiction." *PMLA* 91 (October 1976): 900–13.

Hirsh, Elizabeth A. "Imaginary Images: 'H.D.,' Modernism, and the Psychoanalysis of Seeing." In *Discontented Discourses: Feminism and Psychoanalysis*, edited by Richard Feldstein and Marlene Barr, pp. 141–59. Champaign and Urbana: University of Illinois Press, 1989.

Hoffman, Steven K. "Impersonal Personalism: The Making of a Confessional Poetic." *English Literary History* 45 (Winter 1978): 687–709.

Hollenberg, Donna Krolik, ed. "Art and Ardor in World War One: Selected Letters from H.D. to John Cournos." *The Iowa Review* 16 (Fall 1986): 126–55.

"Nursing the Muse: The Childbirth Metaphor in H.D.'s Poetry." Doctoral dissertation, Tufts University, 1986.

Homans, Margaret. *Bearing the Word: Language and Female Experience in Nineteenth-Century Women's Writing*. Chicago: University of Chicago Press, 1986.

——— " 'Her Very Own Howl': The Ambiguities of Representation in Recent Women's Fiction." *Signs* 9 (1983): 186–205.

——— " 'Syllables of Velvet': Dickinson, Rossetti, and the Rhetorics of Sexuality." *Feminist Studies* 11 (Fall 1985): 569–93.

Hopkins, Kenneth. *The Powys Brothers: A Biographical Appreciation*. London: Phoenix House, 1967.

Howe, Susan. *My Emily Dickinson*. Berkeley: North Atlantic Books, 1985.

Huf, Linda. *A Portrait of the Artist as a Young Woman: The Writer as Heroine in American Literature*. New York: Ungar, 1983.

Huston, Nancy. "The Matrix of War: Mothers and Heroes." In *The Female Body in Western Culture: Contemporary Perspectives,* edited by Susan Rubin Suleiman, pp. 119–38. Cambridge, MA: Harvard University Press, 1986.

Hutcheon, Linda. *Narcissistic Narrative: The Metafictional Paradox*. London: Methuen, 1984.

Irigaray, Luce. *Speculum*. Translator, Gillian C. Gill. Ithaca, NY: Cornell University Press, 1985.

——— *This Sex Which Is Not One*. Translators, Catherine Porter with Carolyn Burke. Ithaca, NY: Cornell University Press, 1985.

Jackson, Brendan. " 'The Fulsomeness of Her Prolixity': Reflections on 'H.D., Imagiste.' " *The South Atlantic Quarterly* 83 (Winter 1984): 91–102.

Jaffe, Nora Crow. " 'She herself is the writing': Language and Sexual Identity in H.D." *Literature and Medicine* 4 (Fall 1985): 86–111.

Jameson, Fredric. *The Political Unconscious: Narrative as a Socially Symbolic Act*. Ithaca, NY: Cornell University Press, 1981.

Jardine, Alice A. *Gynesis: Configurations of Woman and Modernity*. Ithaca, NY: Cornell University Press, 1985.

Jay, Gregory S. "Freud: The Death of Autobiography." *Genre* 19 (Summer 1986): 103–28.

Jay, Paul. *Being in the Text: Self-Representations from Wordsworth to Roland Barthes*. Ithaca, NY: Cornell University Press, 1984.

Jehlen, Myra. "Archimedes and the Paradox of Feminist Criticism." *Sings* 6 (Winter 1981): 575–601.

Jelinek, Estelle C., ed. *Women's Autobiography: Essays in Criticism*. Bloomington: Indiana University Press, 1980.

Johnson, Barbara. "The Frame of Reference: Poe, Lacan, Derrida." In *The Purloined Poe: Lacan, Derrida, and Psychoanalytic Reading,* edited by John P. Muller and William J. Richardson, pp. 213–51. Baltimore, MD: Johns Hopkins University Press, 1988.

Johnson, James William. "Lyric." In *Princeton Encyclopedia of Poetry and Poetics,* edited by Alex Preminger, pp. 460–70. Princeton, NJ: Princeton University Press, 1974.

Johnson, W. R.   *The Idea of Lyric: Lyric Modes in Ancient and Modern Poetry.*
Berkeley: University of California Press, 1982.
Jones, Ernest.   *The Life and Work of Sigmund Freud.* Abridged and edited by
Lionel Trilling and Steven Marcus. New York: Anchor, 1963.
Joyce, James.   *A Portrait of the Artist as a Young Man.* New York: Viking, (1916)
1964.
  Ulysses. New York: The Modern Library, (1922) 1961.
Kamuf, Peggy.   *Signature Pieces: On the Institution of Authorship.* Ithaca, NY:
Cornell University Press, 1988.
Kaplan, E. Ann.   *Women and Film: Both Sides of the Camera.* London: Methuen,
1983.
Kaplan, Justin.   "The Naked Self and Other Problems." In *Telling Lives: The
Biographer's Art,* edited by Marc Pachter, pp. 37–55. Philadelphia: University of Pennsylvania Press, 1981.
Kardiner, A.   *My Analysis with Freud: Reminiscences.* New York: Norton,
1977.
Karl, Frederick R.   *Modern and Modernism: The Sovereignty of the Artist, 1885–
1925.* New York: Atheneum, 1985.
Keats, John.   *Selected Poems and Letters,* Douglas Bush, editor. Boston: Houghton Mifflin, 1959.
Kellman, Steven G.   *The Self-Begetting Novel.* New York: Macmillan, 1980.
Kennedy, J. Gerald.   "Roland Barthes, Autobiography, and the End of Writing." *The Georgia Review* 35 (Summer 1981): 381–400.
Kenner, Hugh.   *The Invisible Poet: T. S. Eliot.* New York: Citadel, 1959.
  "The Making of the Modernist Canon." In *Canons,* edited by Robert von
Hallberg, pp, 363–76. Chicago: University of Chicago Press, 1984.
  The Pound Era. Berkeley: University of California Press, 1972.
Kermode, Frank.   Introduction to *Selected Prose,* by Eliot, pp. 11–22.
Kiely, Robert, ed.   *Modernism Reconsidered.* Cambridge, MA: Harvard University Press, 1983.
King, Michael, ed.   *H.D.: Woman and Poet.* Orono, ME: National Poetry Foundation, 1986.
King-Smyth, Rosie.   "The Spell of the Luxor Bee." *San Jose Studies* 13 (Fall
1987): 77–87.
Kloepfer, Deborah Kelly.   "Fishing the Murex Up: Sense and Resonance in
H.D.'s *Palimpsest.*" *Contemporary Literature* 27 (Winter 1986): 553–73.
  "Flesh Made Word: Maternal Inscription in H.D." *Sagetrieb* 3 (Spring 1984):
27–48.
  "Mother as Muse and Desire: The Sexual Politics of H.D.'s *Trilogy.*" In *H.D.,*
by King, pp. 191–208.
Knapp, Peggy A.   "Women's Freud(e): H.D.'s *Tribute to Freud* and Gladys
Schmitt's *Sonnets for an Analyst.*" *Massachusetts Review* 24 (Summer 1983):
338–52.
Kohn, Walter F.   "Con Amore." *New Republic* 57 (2 January 1929): 200.
Kolodny, Annette.   "The Lady's Not for Spurning." In *Women's Autobiography,*
by Jelinek, pp. 221–60.

Kreymborg, Alfred. *Our Singing Self: An Outline of American Poetry (1620–1930)*. New York: Coward-McCann, 1929.

Kristeva, Julia. *Desire in Language: A Semiotic Approach to Literature and Art*. Translator, Leon S. Roudiez. New York: Columbia University Press, 1980.

    Revolution in Poetic Language. Translator, Margaret Waller. New York: Columbia University Press, 1984.

    "Women's Time." Translated by Alice Jardine and Harry Blake. *Signs* 7 (Autumn 1981): 13–35.

Lacan, Jacques. *Ecrits: A Selection*. Translator, Alan Sheridan. New York: Norton, 1977.

    "Intervention on Transference" (1951). In *In Dora's Case: Freud – Hysteria – Feminism*, edited by Charles Bernheimer and Claire Kahane, pp. 92–104. New York: Columbia University Press, 1985.

Laity, Cassandra. "H.D. and A. C. Swinburne: Decadence and Modernist Women's Writing." *Feminist Studies* 15 (Fall 1989): 461–84

    "H.D.'s Romantic Landscape: The Sexual Politics of the Garden." *Sagetrieb* 6 (Fall 1987): 57–76.

Langbaum, Robert. *The Mysteries of Identity: A Theme in Modern Literature*. New York: Oxford University Press, 1977.

Langs, Richard. *The Psychotherapeutic Conspiracy*. New York: Jason Aronson, 1982.

Lawrence, D. H. *Aaron's Rod*. New York: Viking, (1922) 1950.

    The Complete Poems, Vivian De Sola Pinto and F. Warren Roberts, editors. New York: Penguin, (1964) 1977.

    The Crown. Phoenix II: Uncollected Writings, Edward D. McDonald, editor. New York: Viking, 1970, 365–415.

    Kangaroo. New York: Penguin, (1923) 1951.

    Lady Chatterley's Lover. New York: Grove Press, (1928) 1957.

    The Plumed Serpent. New York: Penguin, (1926) 1950.

    The Rainbow. New York: Penguin, (1915) 1976.

    Sons and Lovers. New York: Penguin, (1913) 1976.

    St. Mawr & The Man Who Died. New York: Vintage, (1925, 1928) 1953.

    Study of Thomas Hardy. Phoenix: The Posthumous Papers, Edward D. McDonald, editor. New York: Viking, 1936, pp. 398–516.

    The Virgin and the Gipsy. New York: Bantam, (1930) 1970.

    The Woman Who Rode Away and Other Stories. New York: Penguin, (1928) 1950.

    Women in Love. New York: Penguin, (1920) 1976.

Lawrence, Karen. *Penelope Voyages: Representations of Female Travel in British Literary Tradition*, in progress.

Levenson, Michael H. *A Genealogy of Modernism*. Cambridge, England: Cambridge University Press, 1984.

Levertov, Denise. *To Stay Alive*. New York: New Directions, 1971.

Lewis, C. Day. *The Lyric Impulse*. Cambridge, MA: Harvard University Press, 1965.

Lorde, Audre. "Uses of the Erotic: The Erotic as Power." In *Sister Outsider: Essays and Speeches,* edited by Lorde, pp. 53–9. Trumansburg, NY: The Crossing Press, 1984.

Loughman, Celeste. "Voices of the Wolf Man: The Wolf Man as Autobiographer." *Psychoanalytic Review* 71 (Summer 1984): 211–25.

Lowell, Amy. Letters to H.D. Houghton Library, Harvard University, Cambridge, MA.

   Tendencies in Modern American Poetry. New York: Macmillin, 1917, pp. 235–43.

Lukacs, Georg. *The Historical Novel.* Translators, Hannah and Stanley Mitchell. Boston: Beacon, (1937) 1962.

McAlmon, Robert. Letters to H.D. H.D. Papers. Beinecke Library, Yale University, New Haven, CT.

   Some Have Their Moments. (193?) Ts. Beinecke Library, Yale University, New Haven, CT.

McCabe, Colin, ed. *The Talking Cure: Essays in Psychoanalysis and Language.* London: Macmillan, 1981.

MacLeish, Archibald. "Four Poets." *Yale Review* 14 (April 1925): 590–1.

Macpherson, Kenneth. *Gaunt Island.* Dijon: Darantière, 1927[?].

   Poolreflection. Territet, Switzerland: POOL, 1927.

Man, Paul de. *Blindness and Insight.* London: Oxford University Press, 1971.

Mandel, Charlotte. "Garbo/Helen: The Self-Projection of Beauty by H.D." *Women's Studies* 7 (1980):127–35.

   "Magical Lenses: Poet's Vision beyond the Naked Eye." In *H.D.,* by King, pp. 301–18.

   "The Redirected Image: Cinematic Dynamics in the Style of H.D. (Hilda Doolittle)." *Literature/Film Quarterly* 11 (1983): 35–45.

Manzoni, Alessandro. *On the Historical Novel.* Translator, Sandra Bermann. Lincoln: University of Nebraska Press, (1850) 1984.

Marcus, Jane. " 'Still Practice,' A/Wrested Alphabet." In *Feminist Issues,* edited by Benstock, pp. 79–97.

   Virginia Wolf and the Languages of Patriarchy. Bloomington: Indiana University Press, 1987.

Marks, Elaine. "Lesbian Intertextuality." In *Homosexualities and French Literature,* edited by Elaine Marks and George Stambolian, pp. 353–77. Ithaca, NY: Cornell University Press, 1979.

Martz, Louis L. Introduction to *H.D.: Collected Poems, 1912–1944,* pp. xi–xxxvi. New York: New Directions, 1983.

   "Voices of the Prophet." Paper delivered at Centennial Exhibition for H.D., Yale University, September 1986.

Mason, Mary G. "The Other Voice: Autobiographies of Women Writers." In *Autobiography,* edited by Olney, pp. 207–35.

Mason, Mary G., and Carol Hurd Green, eds. *Journeys: Autobiographical Writings by Women.* Boston: G. K. Hall, 1979.

Mehlman, Jeffrey. *A Structural Study of Autobiography: Proust, Leiris, Sartre, Levi-Strauss.* Ithaca, NY: Cornell University Press, 1974.

Mellow, James. "Gertrude Stein." In *Dictionary of Literary Biography: Volume 4, American Writers in Paris, 1870–1939,* edited by Karen Lane Rood, pp. 36–73. Detroit, MI: Gale, 1980.

Menand, Louis. *Discovering Modernism: T. S. Eliot and His Context.* New York: Oxford University Press, 1987.

Meyers, Jeffrey. "H.D. and D. H." *Hudson Review* 35 (Winter 1982–3): 628–32.

Milicia, Joseph. "*Bid Me to Live:* Within the Storm." In *H.D.,* edited by King, pp. 279–300.

——— "H.D.'s 'Athenians': Son and Mother in *Hedylus.*" *Contemporary Literature* 27 (Winter 1986): 574–94.

Miller, D. A. *Narrative and Its Discontents: Problems of Closure in the Traditional Novel.* New Haven: Yale University Press, 1981.

J. Hillis Miller. "Ariadne's Thread: Repetition and the Narrative Line." *Critical Inquiry* 3 (Autumn 1976): 57–78.

——— *Fiction and Repetition: Seven British Novels.* Cambridge, MA: Harvard University Press, 1982.

Miller, Nancy K. *Subject to Change: Reading Feminist Writing.* New York: Columbia University Press, 1988.

Monro, Harold. "The Imagists Discussed." *Egoist* 5 (May 1915): 77–80.

Monroe, Harriet. *Poets and Their Art.* Revised edition. New York: Macmillan, 1932, pp. 92–9.

——— Review of *Some Imagist Poets. Poetry* 16 (April–September 1915): 150–3.

Moody, A. D. *Thomas Sterns Eliot: Poet.* Cambridge, England: Cambridge University Press, 1979.

Moore, Harry T. *The Priest of Love: A Life of D. H. Lawrence.* Revised edition. New York: Penguin, (1954) 1981.

Moore, Marianne. *Complete Prose,* Patricia C. Willis, editor. New York: Viking, 1986.

——— Letters to H.D., at Beinecke Library, Yale University, New Haven, CT.

——— Review of *Heliodora. The Dial* 77 (July–December 1924): 348.

Morris, Adalaide. "The Concept of Projection: H.D.'s Visionary Powers." *Contemporary Literature* 25 (Winter 1984): 411–36.

——— "Reading H.D.'s 'Helios and Athene.' " *The Iowa Review* 12 (Spring–Summer 1981): 155–63.

——— "A Relay of Power and of Peace: H.D. and the Spirit of the Gift." *Contemporary Literature* 27 (Winter 1986): 411–36.

——— "Science and the Mythopoeic Mind: The Case of H.D." In *Chaos and Order: Complex Dynamics in Literature and Science,* edited by N. Katharine Hayles. Chicago: University of Chicago Press, in press.

——— "Trans-Actions: Body and Soul in H.D.'s Poetry." Paper delivered at Modern Language Association, December 1985.

Mulvey, Laura. "Visual Pleasure and Narrative Cinema." *Screen* 16 (Autumn 1975):6–18.

Murry, John Middleton. *Son of Woman.* London: Jonathan Cape, (1932) 1936.

Nardi, Marcia.   Review of *Heliodora*. *New Republic* 41 (28 January 1925): 266.
New Larousse Encyclopedia of Mythology. New York: Prometheus, 1968.
Olney, James, ed.   *Autobiography: Essays Theoretical and Critical*. Princeton: Princeton University Press, 1980.
    Metaphors of Self: The Meaning of Autobiography. Princeton: Princeton University Press, 1972.
Orr, D. W.   "Transference and Countertransference: A Historical Survey." *Journal of American Psychoanalysis* 2 (1954): 621–70.
Ostriker, Alicia.   "No Rule of Procedure: The Open Poetics of H.D." *Agenda* 25 (Autumn–Winter 1987–8): 145–54.
    "Response to Homans's 'Her Very Own Howl.' " *Signs* 10 (Spring 1985): 597–600.
    Stealing the Language: The Emergence of Women's Poetry in America. Boston: Beacon, 1986.
    "The Thieves of Language: Women Poets and Revisionist Mythmaking." In *The New Feminist Criticism*, by Showalter, pp. 314–38.
    "What Do Women (Poets) Want?: H.D. and Marianne Moore as Poetic Ancestresses." *Contemporary Literature* 27 (Winter 1986): 475–92.
    Writing Like a Woman. Ann Arbor: University of Michigan Press, 1983.
Pascal, Roy.   *Design and Truth in Autobiography*. London: Routledge and Kegan Paul, 1960.
Patmore, Brigit.   *My Friends When Young*. London: Heinemann, 1968.
    No More Tomorrow. London: Century, 1929.
Pearson, Norman Holmes.   Foreword to *Hermetic Definition*, by H.D., pp. *v–viii*.
    Letters to H.D. H.D. Papers. Beinecke Library, Yale University, New Haven, CT.
    Ms. Notes for H.D. Biography. H.D. Papers. Beinecke Library, Yale University New Haven, CT.
Peck, John.   "Passio Perpetuse H.D." *Parnassus* 3 (Spring–Summer 1975): 42–74.
Plato.   *The Symposium*. Translator, Benjamin Jowett. New York: Liberal Arts Press, 1948.
Poe, Edgar Allan.   *Selected Writings*, Edward H. Davidson, editor. Boston: Houghton Mifflin, 1956.
Pondrom, Cyrena N.   "H.D. and the Origins of Modernism." *Sagetrieb* 4 (Spring 1985):73–100.
    "Marianne Moore and H.D.: Female Community and Poetic Achievement." In *Marianne Moore: Woman and Poet*, edited by Patricia Willis, pp. 1–32. Orono, ME: National Poetry Foundation, 1990.
    ed. "Selected Letters from H.D. to F. S. Flint: A Commentary on the Imagist Period." *Contemporary Literature* 10 (Autumn 1969): 557–86.
Porter, Charles A.   Foreword to special issue, *Men/Women of Letters*. *Yale French Studies* 71 (1986):1–14.
Pound, Ezra.   *A Lume Spento and Other Early Poems*. London: Faber and Faber, 1965.
    Hilda's Book. In *End to Torment*, by H.D., pp. 67–84.

"James Joyce: At Last the Novel Appears." *The Egoist* 4 (February 1917): 21–2.

Lustra. In *Personae* 81–126.

Personae: Collected Shorter Poems. New York: New Directions, (1926) 1971.

Selected Letters, 1907–1941. D. D. Paige, editor. 1950. New York: New Directions, 1971.

Selected Prose – 1909–1965, William Cookson, editor. New York: New Directions, 1973.

"Vortex." *Blast* 1 (20 June 1914): 153–4.

"Vorticism." *Fortnightly Review* (September 1914): 461–71.

Pound, Omar and Robert Spoo, eds. *Ezra Pound and Margaret Cravens: A Tragic Friendship, 1910–1912.* Durham, NC: Duke University Press, 1988.

Quinn, Vincent. "H.D.'s 'Hermetic Definition': The Poet as Archetypal Mother." *Contemporary Literature* 18 (Winter 1977): 51–61.

Quinones, Ricardo J. *Mapping Literary Modernism: Time and Development.* Princeton, NJ: Princteon University Press, 1985.

Renza, Louis A. "The Veto of the Imagination: A Theory of Autobiography." In *Autobiography,* edited by Olney, pp. 268–95.

Rich, Adrienne. "Compulsory Heterosexuality and Lesbian Existence." *Signs* 5 (Autumn 1980): 631–0.

The Dream of a Common Language: Poems 1974–1977. New York: Norton, 1978.

Richetti, John J. *Popular Fiction before Richardson: Narrative Patterns, 1700–1739.* London: Oxford University Press, 1961.

Ricoeur, Paul. "Narrative Time." In *On Narrative,* edited by W. J. T. Mitchell, pp. 165–86. Chicago: University of Chicago Press, 1981.

Riddel, Joseph N. "H.D. and the Poetics of 'Spiritual Realism.' " *Contemporary Literature* 10 (Autumn 1969): 435–46.

"H.D.'s Scene of Writing – Poetry as (AND) Analysis." *Studies in the Literary Imagination* 12 (Spring 1979): 41–59.

Rieff, Philip. *Freud: The Mind of the Moralist.* New York: Doubleday, 1961.

Riffaterre, Michael. "The Intertextual Unconscious." *Critical Inquiry* 13 (Winter 1987): 371–85.

Roazen, Paul. *Freud and His Followers.* New York: New American Library, 1971.

Robinson, Janice S. *H.D.: The Life and Work of an American Poet.* Boston: Houghton Mifflin, 1982.

Romm, Sharon. *The Unwelcome Intruder: Freud's Struggle with Cancer.* New York: Praeger, 1983.

Romig, Evelyn M. "An Achievement of H.D. and Theodore Roethke: Psychoanalysis and the Poetics of Teaching." *Literature and Psychology* 28 (1978): 105–11.

Rosenberg, Samuel. *Why Freud Fainted.* New York: Bobbs Merrill, 1978.

Roth, Michael S. *Psycho-Analysis as History: Negation and Freedom in Freud.* Ithaca, NY: Cornell University Press, 1987.

Roustang, Francois. *Dire Mastery: Discipleship from Freud to Lacan.* Translator, N. Lukacher. Baltimore, MD: The Johns Hopkins University Press, 1982.

Rowbotham, Sheila. *Women's Consciousness, Man's World*. Baltimore, MD: Penguin, 1974.

Ruitenbeek, H. M., ed. *Freud as We Knew Him*. Detroit, MI: Wayne State University Press, 1973.

Ryan, Michael. "Self-De(con)struction." *Diacritics* 6 (Spring 1976): 41–3.

Satterthwaite, Alfred. "John Cournos and 'H.D.' " *Twentieth-Century Literature* 22 (December 1976): 394–410.

Schaffner, Perdita. "The Egyptian Cat." In *Hedylus*, by H.D., pp. 142–6.

Introduction to *The Hedgehog*, by H.D., p. *vii–xiii*.

Introduction to *Nights*, by H.D., pp. *ix–xvi*.

"Pandora's Box." In *HERmione*, by H.D., pp. *vii–xi*.

"A Profound Animal." In *Bid Me to Live (A Madrigal)*, by H.D., pp. 185–94.

"Running." *The Iowa Review* 16 (Fall 1986): 7–13.

"Unless a Bomb Falls...," In *The Gift*, by H.D., pp. *ix–xv*.

Schenck, Celeste M. "Exiled by Genre: Modernism, Community and the Politics of Exile." In *Women's Writing in Exile*, edited by Mary Lynn Broe and Angela Ingram, pp. 225–50. Chapel Hill, NC: University of North Carolina Press, 1989.

"Songs (from) the Bride: Feminism, Psychoanalysis, Genre." *Literature and Psychology* 33 (1987): 109–19.

Scholes, Robert and Robert Kellogg. *The Nature of Narrative*. New York: Oxford University Press, 1966.

Schwartz, Sanford. *The Matrix of Modernism: Pound, Eliot, and Early Twentieth-Century Thought*. Princeton, NJ: Princeton University Press, 1985.

Schweik, Susan. *A Gulf So Deeply Cut: American Women Poets and the Second World War*. Madison: University of Wisconsin Press, in press.

Scott, Bonnie Kime. *The Gender of Modernism*. Bloomington: Indiana University Press, 1990.

Joyce and Feminism. Bloomington: Indiana University Press, 1984.

Shakespeare, William. *The Winter's Tale*. New York: Signet, 1963.

Shange, Ntozake. *Nappy Edges*. New York: Bantam, 1980.

Shanks, Edward. "Snootness." *Saturday Review* 142 (21 August 1926): 204.

Shelley, Percy Bysshe. *The Complete Poetical Works*, Thomas Hutchinson, editor. London: Oxford University Press, 1960.

Showalter, Elaine. "Feminist Criticism in the Wilderness." In *The New Feminist Criticism*, Showalter, pp. 243–70.

ed. *The New Feminist Criticism: Essays on Women, Literature, and Theory*. New York: Pantheon, 1985.

Serres, Michel. *Hermes: Literature, Science, Philosophy*, Josué V. Herari and David F. Bell, editors. Baltimore, MD: The Johns Hopkins University Press, 1982.

Silverstein, Louis. *H.D.: A Chronological Account*, in progress.

Sinclair, May. "Two Notes." *The Egoist* 2 (1 June 1915): 88–9.

"The Poems of H.D." *Fortnightly Review* 71 (1 March 1927): 329–45.

Sitwell, Edith.   Letters to H.D.   H.D.   Papers. Beinecke Library, Yale University, New Haven, CT.

Smith, Paul.   *Discerning the Subject.* Minneapolis: University of Minnesota Press, 1988.

"H.D.'s Identity." *Women's Studies* 10 (1984): 321–38.

Pound Revised. London: Croom Helm, 1983.

Smith, Penny.   "Hilda Doolittle and Frances Gregg."   *The Powys Review* 6 (1988): 46–51.

Smith, Sidonie.   *A Poetics of Women's Autobiography: Marginality and the Fictions of Self-Representation.* Bloomington: Indiana University Press, 1987.

Smith-Rosenberg, Carroll.   "The Female World of Love and Ritual: Relations between Women in Nineteenth-Century America." *Signs* 1 (1975): 1–29.

Spacks, Patricia Meyer.   *Imagining a Self: Autobiography and Novel in Eighteenth-Century England.* Cambridge: Harvard University Press, 1976.

"Selves in Hiding." In *Women's Autobiography,* edited by Jelinek, pp. 112–32.

Spencer, Jane.   *The Rise of the Woman Novelist: From Aphra Behn to Jane Austen.* Oxford: Basil Blackwell, 1986.

Spengemann, William C.   *The Forms of Autobiography: Episodes in the History of a Literary Genre.* New Haven: Yale University Press, 1980.

Stanton, Domna C., ed. "Autogynography: Is the Subject Different?" In *The Female Autograph,* edited by Stanton, pp. 3–20.

The Female Autograph: Theory and Practice of Autobiography from the Tenth to the Twentieth Century. Chicago: University of Chicago Press, 1987.

Stewart, Grace.   *A New Mythos: The Novel of the Artist as Heroine, 1877–1977.* Montreal: Eden Press, 1981.

Stimpson, Catharine R.   "Zero Degree Deviancy: The Lesbian Novel in English." *Critical Inquiry* 8 (Winter 1981): 363–79.

Stone, Albert.   *Autobiographical Occasions and Original Acts: Versions of American Identity from Henry Adams to Nate Shaw.* Philadelphia: University of Pennsylvania Press, 1982.

Storm, Marion.   "H.D.'s 'Palimpsest,' Limited to 700 Copies, Is Decipherable Only by a Very Few Clairvoyant Readers." *New York Evening Post Literary World* (27 November 1926): 3.

Sullivan, J. W. N.   "A Sketch of Einstein's Theory." *The Adelphi* 2 (December 1924): 597–605.

Swann, Thomas Burnett.   *The Classical World of H.D.* Lincoln: University of Nebraska Press, 1962.

Swinburne, Algernon Charles.   "Atalanta in Calydon." *The Poems of Swinburne,* IV. London: Chatto and Windus, 1909, pp. 235–334.

Poems and Ballads, First Series. London: William Heinemann, (1866) 1927.

Poems and Ballads, Second Series. 3rd. edition. London: Chatto and Windus, 1882.

Taylor, Gordon O.   "Voices from the Veil: Black American Autobiography." *The Georgia Review* 35 (Summer 1981): 341–61.

Trilling, Lionel.   "Freud and Literature." *The Liberal Imagination: Essays on Society and Literature.* New York: Anchor, (1950) 1953.

Troy, William.   "White Lightning."   *The New Republic* 52 (24 August 1927): 24–5.

Ulmer, Gregory.   "The Discourse of the Imaginary." *Diacritics* 10 (March 1980): 61–75.

Untermeyer, Louis.   *American Poetry Since 1900*. New York: Henry Holt, 1923, pp. 309–16.

"Fire and Ice." *The New Republic* 27 (28 December 1921): 133–4.

"The Perfect Imagist." *Saturday Review of Literature* 1 (8 November 1924): 260.

Van Doren, Mark.   "First Glance." *Nation* 123 (22 December 1926): 668.

Wagner-Martin, Linda W.   "H.D.'s Fiction: Convolutions to Clarity." In *Breaking the Sequence: Women's Experimental Fiction*, edited by Ellen G. Friedman and Miriam Fuchs, pp. 148–60.

Walker, Alice.   "In Search of Our Mothers' Gardens." In *In Search of Our Mothers' Gardens: Womanist Prose*, pp. 231–43. New York: Harcourt Brace Jovanovich, 1983.

Wallace, Emily.   "Afterword: The House of the Father's Science and the Mother's Art." *William Carlos Williams Newsletter* 2 (1976): 4–5.

"Athene's Owl." *Poesis* 6 (1985): 98–123.

Walsh, John.   Afterword to *Hedylus*, by H.D., pp. 147–56.

Watt, Ian.   *The Rise of the Novel*. Berkeley: University of California Press, 1964.

Wayne, June.   "The Male Artist as a Stereotypical Female." In *Feminist Collage: Educating Women in the Visual Arts*, edited by Judy Loeb, pp. 28–37. New York: Teacher's College Press, 1979.

Waugh, Patricia.   *Metafiction: The Theory and Practice of Self-Conscious Fiction*. London: Methuen, 1985.

White, Eric Walter.   *Images of H.D. / From The Mystery*. London: Enitharmon Press, 1976.

White, Hayden.   *Tropics of Discourse: Essays in Cultural Criticism*. Baltimore, MD: The Johns Hopkins University Press, 1978.

Whitall, James.   *English Years*. New York: Harcourt, Brace and World, 1935.

Weigle, Maria.   *Spiders and Spinsters: Women and Mythology*. Albuquerque: University of New Mexico Press, 1982.

Wilde, Oscar.   *The Poems of Oscar Wilde*. London: Methuen, (1908) 1969.

Wilkinson, Louis.   *The Buffoon*. New York: Knopf, 1916.

Williams, William Carlos.   *Kora in Hell: Improvisations*. In *Imaginations*, edited by Webster Scott, pp. 3–84. New York: New Directions, (1920) 1970.

Willis, Susan.   "Black Women Writers." In *Making a Difference: Feminist Literary Criticism*, edited by Gayle Greene and Copelia Kahn, pp. 211–37. London: Methuen, 1985.

Wolle, Francis.   *A Moravian Heritage*. Boulder, CO: Empire Reproduction and Printing Co., 1972.

Woolf, Virginia.   *The Common Reader, First Series*. New York: Harcourt Brace Jovanovich, (1925) 1953.

Mrs. Dalloway. New York: Harcourt Brace Jovanovich, (1925) 1953.

Granite and Rainbow. New York: Harcourt Brace Jovanovich, 1958.

"Modern Fiction." In *Common Reader*, pp. 150–8.

Moments of Being, Jeanne Schulkind, editor. Second edition. New York: Harcourt Brace Jovanovich, (1976) 1985.

"Mr. Bennett and Mrs. Brown." In *The Captain's Death Bed and Other Essays.* New York: Harcourt Brace Jovanovich, 1950.

"Professions for Women." In *The Death of the Moth and Other Essays.* New York: Harcourt Brace Jovanovich, (1942) 1970.

A Room of One's Own. New York: Harcourt Brace Jovanovich, (1929) 1957.

Three Guineas. New York: Harcourt, Brace and World, (1938) 1963.

To the Lighthouse. New York: Harcourt, Brace and World, (1927) 1955.

The Waves. New York: Harcourt Brace Jovanovich, (1931) 1959.

Wortis, Joseph. *Fragments of an Analysis with Freud.* New York: Simon and Schuster, 1954.

Wright, George. "The Lyric Moment: Simple Present Verbs in English Poems." *PMLA* 89 (May 1974): 563–79.

Yaeger, Patricia. *Honey-Mad Women: Emancipatory Strategies in Women's Writing.* New York: Columbia University Press, 1988.

Zilboorg, Caroline, ed. Letters from Aldington to H.D., in progress.

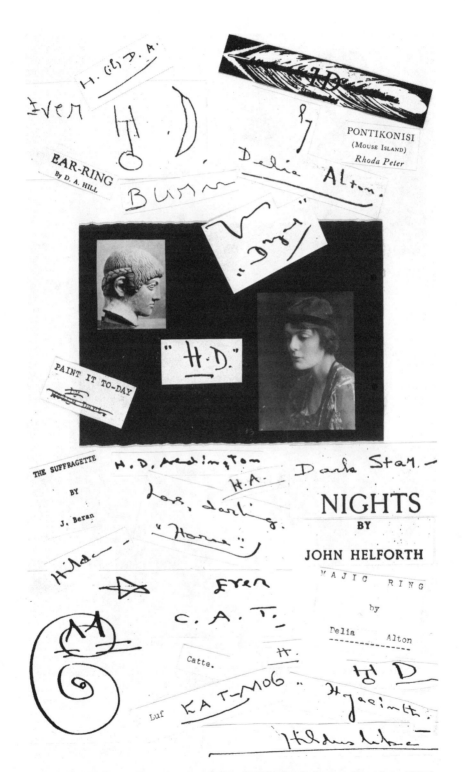

1. Signs, Signets, and Signatures – Masks of Hilda Doolittle on a Page from H.D.'s Scrapbook

2. Between Scientist/Father and Artist/Mother – Hilda, Professor Charles Leander Doolittle at the Flower Observatory, Helen Eugenia Wolle in Art Class

3. Out of the Chrysalis – Hilda, Her Father, Aunt Laura, Mother, Aunt Agnes, and Ezra Pound

4. Love and Poetry – Hilda, Ezra Pound, and Frances Josepha Gregg

5. Love and War – Richard Aldington, H.D., the Battlefield, and the War at Home

6. Wartime Companions – Dorothy Yorke, John Cournos, Richard Aldington, D. H. Lawrence, and Brigit Patmore

7. Images of H.D. – The 1920s

8. Faces of Bryher – The 1910s through the 1930s

9. Artemisia – Collages of H.D. and Bryher from H.D.'s Scrapbook

We must have some fun—some great adventures — I am torn between a desire for a quite place with Perdita & fairy-books & Noahs arks and dolls, and a wild adventure. Perhaps, in time, I will have both.

Dear Ezra ... I knew all about Richard. He can get a divorce
any time if he will do it in the right way. I don't know what I do mean.
I mean he could have had it ten years ago if it hadn't been for Perdita.
I was quite unprepaired for the experience, I mean the terror of feeling
that that wadge of bird-feathers and ~~entire scented~~ petticoats HAD
to be protested. The freedom of my spirit ... went. I was no
longer free. Now almost for the first time in ten years ... I am FREE .

10. Mothers/Daughters – H.D., Helen, and Frances Perdita Aldington Macpherson

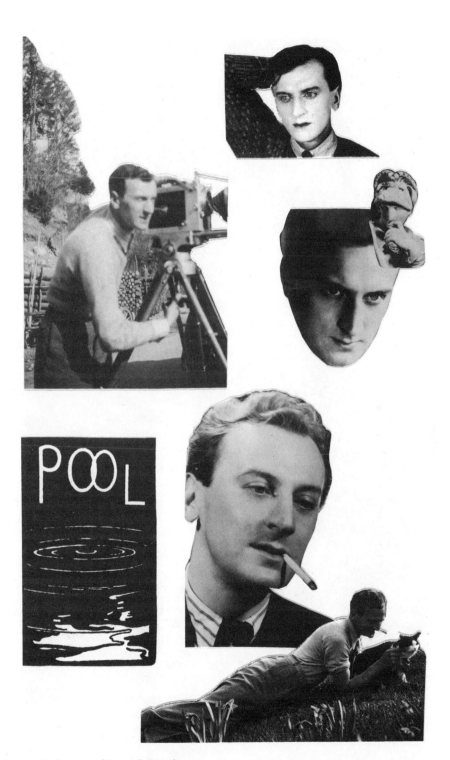

11. Reflections of Kenneth Macpherson

12. Séances in Vienna – H.D. and Sigmund Freud

13. Psyche Reborn in the *City of Ruin* – H.D., the Battle of Britain, and the Moravian Church of Bethlehem, Pennsylvania

blue ~~coloured~~ shantung, fine nice shoulder beneath the thin
shirting. Hermione slipped a long hand into the open space
of the wide flung wide collar, felt a smooth surface of polished
clear smooth marble. Long dynamic hand ran across the smooth
narrow surface, felt thud-thud, heavy thud-thud of rather too
heavy bursting heart-beat. Thud-thud, heaving like the heavy
foot that had trod heavy on the fine moss. The thud-thud was
heavy, did not go with the sursurring of his voice when he wasn't
being funny, did not go with the green of (now they were right)
grey-green forest eyes. The eyes when he said Hermione that way
were green and grey. ~~Your eyes are green, Georgio. Your eyes~~
are grey-green". "Your eyes are grey, Hermione, your eyes are
green-grey." "You repeat yourself Georgio. You repeat me. Is
this Echo and Narcisse?", George ~~drawn away~~ The face of ~~his~~ but, his narrow thighs
rest~~ing~~ed against her wide-flung rumpled dress-stuff. Against
the thin-etched bone, etched thin under the rumpled dress stuff,
she felt heavier bone crushing down, pressing down. "If I put
a nut," she thought irreverently, "between those two stone hip
joints, it would be cracked utterly." She heard a voice ring
high and high and high. Her thought could only just follow the
voice that was flung winged silver, (her laughter?) silver wing,
winged voice high and high into the (now she saw them) down
dropping seven-branched larch boughs. "A nut, a nut would be
cracked between our hip-bones utterly." High and high, words
~~went with the laughter meaning nothing, meaning everything.~~

1. Censoring Erotic Violation – Typescript Page from *HER*

(Hermione didn't know what she was saying, didn't
care. Eugenia wouldn't listen anyway. She went on :)

unscrewed,

~~she was would totter forward, would fall over like a scare-crow~~
~~when you hurl a pumpkin at it. If I hurl a pumpkin at Eugenia~~
~~Her head will roll off and they will hold me responsible for~~
~~matricide.~~

"But you can't go on this way." Eugenia would say that
again and she would say it again ~~and she would say it again.~~ I
will give her, Hermione said, seven times to say it. She has
said it seven times. Now she can say it another seven times.
If she says it another seven times ~~————————————————~~
~~only to hurl a pumpkin at her but there were no pumpkins.~~

"Well, what are you thinking, darling?" "I don't know)
Eugenia - " "I've been hurt you know Hermione by the way you
call me ~~by that name~~ Eugenia ." "Shall I call you Gart then simply?
It's rather confusing calling everybody Gart. You're Gart and
Minnie is Gart and papa is Gart and Bertrand is Gart. I am Gart too, I suppose. If I say
Gart everybody will run including Jook and Mandy for I suppose
Jook is rightful Gart and Mandy. ~~right to have Gart hurt across~~
~~————————— prairie pays —————————~~ "Mandy
belongs to us. Mandy belongs to me. Mandy is mine. This
business of the United States, United States of America doing
away with states being separate with separate states and each
state with its own laws is what is responsible for all this
mob-rule". (Get her off, hare and hounds, you can't go on this
way.) "You get no sort of cohesion out of a thing so immense.
You can't expect every one of us equally to sympathise with

2. Suppression of Matricidal Desire – Typescript Page from *HER*

3. Erasure of Freud's Symbolic Gesture – The Gift of *Leonardo da Vinci* and Manuscript Pages from *Tribute to Freud*

Notes for Frontis, Collages, and Figures

Frontispiece: Dramatis Personae: H.D. probably supplied this *dramatis personae* and scratched out Helga Doorn in the late 1940s or early 1950s when she reviewed her unpublished manuscripts and made some corrections before she sent them to Norman Holmes Pearson for her "shelf" at Yale. Notations of "Vaumawr" allude to the name of Hermione's college, which New Directions changed to Bryn Mawr in the published text.

Collages: These collages were inspired by H.D.'s Scrapbook, a forty-page photo album to which H.D. and her immediate family added from the 1920s until the mid-1930s. The Scrapbook includes pages of snapshots arranged in conventional block patterns as well as pages with elaborately constructed collages made up of cut photos superimposed on each other. Someone (perhaps Norman Holmes Pearson) has penciled in on page 21 "made by Kenneth 1921," next to the collage of H.D. lying in the grass between two temple ruins. Diana Collecott, in "Images of H.D.," has concluded from that notation that Macpherson probably constructed all the collages, perhaps even the entire Scrapbook. She may be correct, but I am not entirely convinced; if he had done so, I believe the penciled notation would have been made at the front of the Scrapbook. H.D., Bryher, and possibly also Perdita probably arranged some of the pages. A number of the images are artfully constructed, especially those that superimpose classical antiquities onto contemporary photos, while other pages look more like a conventional photo album. Pages were still being made in the mid-1930s when Macpherson had basically left the ménage.

I have cut and rearranged many images from H.D.'s Scrapbook for my collages. Most of the photos are part of the Collection of American Literature, Beinecke Rare Book and Manuscript Library, Yale University. I am indebted to Beinecke for permission to reproduce these photos, as well as to the generosity of Perdita Schaffner and the Estate of Hilda Doolittle. Information about the photos follows, beginning with the upper left hand corner of each collage and proceeding clockwise.

Collage 1: Signs, Signets, and Signatures: I have superimposed various signatures from letters, manuscripts, typescripts, and published works on a page from H.D.'s Scrapbook, a collage that juxtaposes a photo of a bronze antiquity with one of H.D., taken probably in 1919 or 1920. 1. *Ever H.D.*: Astrological Signature in a letter to Silvia Dobson, Saturday [1934?] that plays on the favorable alignment of Uranus and the Moon in H.D.'s chart. 2. *H.(il)D.A.*: Signature in a letter to Viola Jordan, 20 November 1936[?] that alludes to D. A. Hill, the pen name for "Ear-Ring" and (originally) *The Hedgehog*. 3. *Ear-Ring by D.A. Hill*: Title and name of published story. 4. *BURN*: Penciled across an undated letter to an unknown person, probably a lawyer, regarding her marriage [1937?]; the account is one of the many versions H.D. wrote about the events of 1913–19. 5. *H.D. by Delia Alton*: Title page for the typescript; H.D. used her logo designed by George Plank, crossed out the address, and added her nom de plume in pencil. 6. *Pontikonisi (Mouse Island) Rhoda Peter*: Printed title caption, 1932. 7. *Yours "Dryad"*: Letter to Pound, 24 March 1933; Pound's name for H.D. was "Dryad," and H.D. regularly signed her letters to him with this name. 8. *"H.D."*: Signature used by Amy Lowell under photo of H.D. in *Tendencies in Modern American Poetry*; H.D. sometimes used quotation marks around her pen name in the 1910s and early 1920s, but eliminated the marks around "H.D." in her letters by the mid-1920s. 9. *Dark Star-Nights by John Helforth*: Printed title page with H.D.'s handwritten addition, c. 1935. 10. *Majic Ring by Delia Alton*: Typescript for the unpublished novel, written in 1943–1944; Delia Alton is the name for both the persona and writer of *Majic Ring* and *The Sword Went Out to Sea*. 11. *H.D.*: Another astrological signature that uses the symbol for Uranus for the "H.," in a letter to Silvia Dobson, Thursday [1935]. 12. *"Hyacinth"*: Letter to Havelock Ellis, 19 March 1929; H.D. regularly signed her letters to Ellis with the name Hyacinth or "H.," for short. 13. *Hildushka*: Letter to John Cournos, Friday [8 September? 1919]; H.D. used this name with Cournos, an American of Russian-Jewish heritage. 14. *H*: Letter to Viola Jordan, 4 March [1920?]. 15. *KAT-MOG*: Letter to Bryher and Macpherson, 12 May 1933; KAT (sometimes CAT) was H.D.'s predominant pet name in her intimate circle from the late 1920s well into the 1930s; Mog was Macpherson's particular pet name for H.D. 16. *Catte*: Letter to Bryher, Sunday [1935]; H.D. wrote that Catte was Perdita's spelling in her letters to her mother. 18. *Ever C.A.T.* [with star and cat sketch]: Letter to Silvia Dobson, Sunday [1935]; during the 1930s (especially 1934–5), H.D. often used this type of cat sketch as signature in letters to intimate friends and family members; the star, which alludes multiply to astrology, astronomy, and cinema, appeared mainly in letters to Dobson. 17. *Love, darling, "Horse"*: Letter to Bryher, 15 June 1923; "Horse" was H.D.'s pet name with Bryher in the early 1920s, alternatingly occasionally with "Unicorn" and "Giraffe." 18. *H.A.*: Letter to Bryher, 19 April 1919; H.D.'s letters to Bryher in 1919 are regularly signed "H.A." 19. *H.D. Aldington*: A signature that appears above H.D.'s bookplate in a book she owned. 20. *The Suffragette by J. Beran*: Title page, typescript, c. 1913. 21. *Paint It To-Day by Helga Dart*: Title page for typescript of unpublished novel, c. 1921; H.D. probably crossed out "Helga Dart" in the late 1940s and 1950s when she sent the typescript to Pearson. See Chapter 1 for a discussion of the significance of H.D.'s multiple names and signatures.

Collage 2: *Between Scientist/Father and Artist/Mother*: 1. Helen Eugenia Wolle Doolittle in art class, c. 1871. 2. Zeus and Flower Observatory, Upper Darby, Pennsylvania; collage from H.D.'s Scrapbook. 3. Professor Charles Leander Doolittle, Director of the Flower Observatory, c. 1900. 4. Hilda, c. 1900. See Chapters 2, 4, and 5 for discussions of H.D.'s representations of herself in relation to her parents.

Collage 3: *Out of the Chrysalis*: 1. Professor Doolittle and Hilda, c. 1907. 2. Helen Wolle Doolittle (middle) with her sister Laura Wolle Jenkins (left), her half-sister Agnes Seidel Howard, and Hilda, c. 1905–7. 3. Hilda, c. 1905; Pound also kept a print of this photo. 4. Ezra Pound, c. early 1900s. See Chapters 2, 4, and 5 for discussions of H.D.'s autobiographical constructions of her family and engagement to Pound.

Collage 4: *Love and Poetry*: 1. Frances Josepha Gregg, c. early 1900s. 2. Ezra Pound, by Alvin Langdon Coburn, 1913, used in *Lustra*. 3. Hilda, Friends Central Yearbook, 1905; Gregg pasted this photo into her copy of *Sea Garden*, alongside a poem she wrote for H.D. (See Guest, *Herself Defined*, illustrations). 4. Frances Josepha Gregg Wilkinson, c. 1912 [?]; original photo also includes Frances' mother and another woman. See Chapter 2 for a discussion of H.D.'s narrative of the triadic erotic and poetic relation among the three who loved each other.

Collage 5: *Love and War*: 1. Richard Aldington, c. 1911. H.D., c. mid-1910s (?); photo taken in London and made into a postcard, with one print inscribed for Marianne Moore. 2. King George and Queen Mary viewing the damage after air raid in Warrington Crescent, London, in March 1918. 3. Aldington in officer's uniform, c. 1918; Aldington enlisted as a private in May, 1916 under threat of conscription, was promoted and left for France in December of 1916, returned for officer training in 1917, received his commission as 2nd lieutenant in November of 1917, and returned to France in 1918, where he spent most of the year (see Silverstein, *H.D.: A Chronological Account*). 4. H.D., Mecklenburgh Square, 1917; Amy Lowell used a similar photo from the same series for her *Tendencies in American Poetry*. 5. After the Battle of the Somme, 1916. See Chapters 3 and 4 for discussions of the fiction H.D. wrote based on her prewar love for Aldington and the dissolution of her marriage during the war.

Collage 6: Wartime Companions: 1. Dorothy Yorke, painted by D. H. Lawrence, at Beinecke. 2. John Cournos, c. late 1910s, from H.D.'s Scrapbook. 3. Richard Aldington, c. 1917–18, from H.D.'s Scrapbook. 4. Brigit Patmore, c. 1910s, from H.D.'s Scrapbook. 5. D. H. Lawrence, by Edward Weston, c. 1925; news clipping in H.D.'s Scrapbook (on page with several images of Aldington) and probably the print H.D. kept on her desk in Vienna in the spring of 1933. Aldington's affair with Yorke began in 1917, and after the war, he lived with her until 1928, when he left her to live with Patmore for about ten years, thereby returning to the woman he had been with when Patmore introduced him to H.D. Cournos was in love with Yorke, whom he left in H.D.'s care at Mecklenburgh Square when he went to Russia in 1917. This collage should include an image of Cecil Gray, Perdita's father, but H.D. did not keep a photo of him in her Scrapbook or her collection of photos, and I have not been able to locate a photo of Gray from this period. See Chapters 3 and 4 for discussions of H.D.'s reconstitutions of this network.

Collage 7: Images of H.D. – The 1920s: 1. H.D., c. 1919–20. 2. H.D., c. late 1920s [?]. 3. H.D., by Man Ray, 1922; another photo from this series was in H.D.'s Scrapbook. 4. H.D., Film cut from *Wing Beat*, 1927, also printed in *Close Up*.

Collage 8: Faces of Bryher – The 1920s through the 1930s: 1. Winifred Bryher, c. late 1910s (?), in H.D.'s Scrapbook. 2. Bryher, c. 1922, in H.D.'s Scrapbook. 3. Collage in H.D.'s Scrapbook composed of double image of Bryher by Man Ray, c. 1922 and a cut-out of a baby, presumably Bryher. 4. Bryher, by Carl Van Vechten, c. mid-1930s. 5. Bryher, Passport Photo, c. 1920–2.

Collage 9: Artemisia: Collages of H.D. and Bryher: The four collages are from H.D.'s Scrapbook, made perhaps by Macpherson with photos taken by Bryher and H.D., in Cornwall or Carmel Highlands, California, c. 1919–21 (see Collecot, "Images of H.D."). 1. H.D. in a bas relief of Hygeia. 2. H.D. under the wings of *Niké* (Victory). 3. H.D. and Bryher in the tidepools of Cornwall or California. 4. H.D. in the woods; photo may be the one of "your snap-shots in the woods" to which Marianne Moore referred approvingly in her letter to H.D., 27 March 1921. 5. H.D. in pants. See Chapter 3 for a discussion of H.D.'s Artemisian landscapes and discourses in her fiction.

Collage 10: Mothers/Daughters: 1. From a letter to Bryher written by H.D. from the Hotel du Littoral in London in April of 1919, when H.D. spent a few days with Aldington in an attempted reunion; it reads: "We must have some fun – some great adventures – I am torn between a desire for any little place with Perdita & fairy-books and Noah's arks and dolls, and a wild adventure. Perhaps, in time, I will have both." 2. Francis Perdita Aldington and Helen Woole Doolittle, c. 1924. 3. Perdita Macpherson and one of the Kenwin dogs, c. mid-1930s. 4. H.D., Letter to Ezra Pound, 20 February [1929], written when Pound was acting, briefly, as a go-between; after leaving Dorothy Yorke in 1928, Aldington inquired about a divorce so that he could marry Brigit Patmore, but he gave up the plan when Brigit's huband refused; H.D. alluded to how Perdita's 1928 adoption by the Macphersons left her feeling "free" for the first time from the terror she felt from the threat of sending her to jail that Aldington had made at the Hotel du Littoral to prevent her from registering Perdita with his name. 5. Perdita Macpherson and one of the Kenwin apes, c. early 1930s, in H.D.'s Scrapbook. 6. H.D. and Frances Perdita Aldington, 1919. See Chapters 3 and 4 for discussions of H.D.'s experience and representations of mothers and daughters.

Collage 11: Reflections of Kenneth Macpherson: 1. Macpherson and his movie camera, c. 1927–30. 2. Macpherson, film cut from *Wing Beat*, 1927, also printed in *Close Up* and pasted in H.D.'s Scrapbook. 3. Macpherson and Athena, Collage from H.D.'s Scrapbook, c. late 1920s. 4. Macpherson, by Ker-Seymour, 1934. 5. Macpherson and probably Perdita's cat, at Kenwin, c. 1933 [?]; when in Vienna, H.D. asked for photos of Kenwin for herself and to show Freud; this may have been one of the ones Bryher sent. 6. Logo for POOL Productions, the film company founded by Bryher and Macpherson that produced *Wing Beat*, *Foothills*, and *Borderline* and published *Close Up*. See Chapters 1, 2, and 4 for discussions of H.D.'s representations of Macpherson.

Collage 12: Séances in Vienna: 1. Civil War in Vienna, 1934. 2. One of Freud's favorite antiquities, a statue of Athena, about which H.D. wrote in *Tribute to Freud*. Freud handed her the statue one day, announced that it was his favorite, and said "She is perfect . . . *only she has lost her spear*" (69), a comment that became the occasion for her poem "The Master," which she suppressed. In 1938, when Freud believed that he would not be able to take his collection with him in his flight to London, he selected this statue as the only antiquity he would take. In fact, he was able to take the entire collection of over 2,000 pieces. 3. Etching of Freud, by Ferdinand Schmutzer, 1926; H.D. purchased a copy of this etching in 1933 during her first analysis with Freud and considered it a favorite image of him. The original hung in Freud's dining room at Bergasse IX. 4. A portion of Freud's bookshelf, with books on Egypt by Willis Budge and Breasted that H.D. knew well. 5. H.D., c. early to mid-1930s. See Chapter 5 for a discussion of H.D.'s writings about her analysis with Freud.

Collage 13: Psyche Reborn in the City of Ruin: 1. A London street after a bombing raid during the Battle of Britain, 1941, about which H.D. wrote in *The Gift* and *Trilogy*. 2. The Moravian Church in Bethlehem, Pennsylvania, where her mother's family had settled in the mid-eighteenth century and where H.D. lived until 1895; this church reappears in the "spacious, bare meeting-house" of the poet's dream vision in *The Walls Do Not Fall* (*Trilogy* 523–4) and in *The Gift*, written during the Battle of Britain. 3. H.D., c. late 1930s or early 1940s [?]. See Chapter 5 for a discussion of H.D.'s autobiographical narrative about World War II and the significance of her Moravian heritage.

Illustrations from H.D.'s Typescripts and Manuscripts

Figure 1: Censoring Erotic Violation – Typescript Page from HER: Probably in the late 1940s or early 1950s, H.D. deleted portions of an erotic scene between George and Hermione from the typescript of *HER*. Her's sense of violation is even more direct here than the images of suffocation left in the text.

Figure 2: Suppression of Matricidal Desire – Typescript Page from HER: Probably in the late 1940s or early 1950s, H.D. deleted here and elsewhere in the typescript of *HER* violent fantasies directed by Hermione at the novel's mother figure, Eugenia Gart. Deleted material on this page includes: "I will kill her. I have only to hurl a pumpkin at her."

Figure 3: Erasures of Freud's Symbolic Gesture – The Gift of Leonardo da Vinci and Manuscript Pages from Tribute to Freud: H.D. deleted the following paragraph from the manuscript before she published "Writing on the Wall" in serial form in *Life and Letters Today*, the text that became *Tribute to Freud* in 1956:

> The dead were living as examples, inspirational or otherwise. The one book of his he ~~gave~~ inscribed for me, was a recent ~~translation~~ publication of his brochure on Leonado da Vinci, translated from German into Italian. Was it "by chance

or intention" that he linked me in his creative, vivid discrimination, with translation, with art, with ~~that gre~~the accredited greatest of living renaissance innovators, thinkers & artists?

The deleted passage, which speculates on whether Freud meant to link her with da Vinci, would have appeared at the end of section eight in *Tribute to Freud* (14). See *Borderline* for her association of da Vinci with Renaissance modernism and with Macpherson's genius, which I have argued was a screen behind which she hid her own poetics.

Index

Achilles, 183, 204, 228, 242, 296, 305, 342, 386n5
Ackroyd, Peter, 375n20
"Acon," 51, 381n5
Adelphi, The, 371n34, 398n28
Adorno, Theodor, 55
Advent, epigraph, xi, 9, 27, 56, 72, 86–7, 221, 228, 232, 237, 283, 294, 295, 297, 299–301, 308, 312, 315–19, 322, 323, 325, 327, 336, 342, 360, 368n12, 369n19, 372n43, 374n15, 389n25, 390n36, 397n20, 399n42, 399n44, 402n18 403n34, 404n41
Aeschylus, 404n41
Aiken, Conrad, 26, 28, 30–1, 32, 283, 292, 372n45, 376n30
Alcott, Louisa May, 349
Aldington, Richard, 141, 148, 157, 193, 213, 222, 229, 232, 292, 294, 295, 319, 320–1, 374n12, 376n38, 381n9, 390n30, 393n62, 396n17, 397n21; affairs of, 42, 63, 64, 154, 178, 292, 384n36, 387n11, 387–8n16, 396n17, 399n41; H.D.'s letters to, 168, 370n31, 374n17, 386n6, 389n25; H.D.'s representation of, 64–5, 69–70, 139, 144–55, 166–70, 174–5, 176–84, 198, 199, 200–1, 213, 228, 238, 241–3, 246, 255, 338–9; H.D.'s work and, 370n29, 370n31, 371n34, 371n36, 374n8, 374n9, 375–6n29; letters to H.D., 376n38, 377n44, 381n9, 387n11, 387n12, 388n17, 389n22, 389n25; Per-

dita and, 63, 154, 227, 388n17, 396n17; representation of H.D., 85, 136–7, 320–1, 393n64, 398n33; travels with H.D. in Italy, 143, 148, 179, 206; World War I and, 61, 63, 136–9, 167, 182–3, 387n10; "Amalfi," 182, 390n34; "Captive," 386n5, 387n10; "Compensation," 167; *Death of a Hero*, 150; "Epilogue," 167; "Greek Epigram," 402n24; *Images of War*, 138; *Images*, 49, 138–9; "Lesbia," 393n59; *Life for Life's Sake*, 374n8; "Madrigal," 136, 137; "Modern Poetry," 375–6n29; "Reflections," 206, 386n5; *Reverie*, 137–8, 139; "Synthetic Sonnets," 386n5; "The Poplar," 49; "The Faun Captive," 387n10; *War and Love*, 138. *See also* H.D.
Alton, Delia, 43–6, 80, 144, 212, 214, 357, 361, 374n17, 392n49
"Amaranth," 64–5, 356, 371n38
America, United States of, 7, 13, 33, 38, 58, 133, 157, 171, 194, 200, 206, 218–19, 221, 222, 223, 224, 231, 240, 241, 261, 287, 290, 322, 349, 350, 367n2, 387n15, 391n47, 391n48, 392n57, 394n10. *See also* H.D.
Anderson, Margaret, 8, 21
Anderson, Hans Christian, 114
androcentrism, *see* patriarchy
androgyny, 151, 161–2, 164, 165, 183, 217, 253, 264, 268, 310–11, 329, 375n25, 392n55

This index does not include items in the Chronology: Dating H.D.'s Writing, the notes for the collages and figures, and the Works Cited.

CAMBRIDGE STUDIES IN AMERICAN LITERATURE AND
CULTURE

Editor

Albert Gelpi, Stanford University

*Now available in hardcover and paperback

ACE7985

5/14/91